'As CFA UK continues to support the i[...]
sustainability challenges, we are delig[...]
publication.'

'What really impressed me about the b[...] .....y and invaluable overview of fixed income and responsible investment. This enables readers to understand the relevance of sustainability to fixed income, with real life examples and contributions from practitioners and organisations. Considerable work has gone into outlining the outcomes that have been achieved and to reflect on the lessons learned. The approach taken is, commendably, one that impresses upon readers the dynamic nature of the sustainable finance movement and its relationship with fixed income, always keen to offer practical suggestions on how progress might be encouraged and developed.'

Fraser Lundie, Board member, CFA UK, and Head of
Fixed Income, Federated Hermes

'How can we ensure that fixed income investments contribute to the goals of sustainable development? What role do standards and green taxonomies play in encouraging investment in socially and environmentally sustainable activities? How can we encourage greater investment in emerging markets? This book analyses the theory and the practice of responsible investment in fixed income markets. It is an invaluable guide to policymakers looking to design and implement policies and frameworks to drive sustainable finance.'

Helena Viñes Fiestas, Commissioner of the Spanish Financial
Markets Authority and Rapporteur of the EU Platform on
Sustainable Finance

'This book fills a critical gap in the responsible investment literature. It provides academics and researchers with rich practical insights into the realities of how investors take account of environmental, social and governance (ESG) issues in their investment practices and processes, and into the costs and benefits of doing so. It also identifies those areas – impact assessment, the influence of regulations, standards and taxonomies, the relationship between sustainability and financial performance – where academics and practitioners should work together in coming years.'

Simon Dietz, Professor of Environmental Policy, London
School of Economics

'This is a timely publication providing much needed, practical advice from experts with hands-on experience. Fixed income markets have always lagged their equity peers when it comes to ESG integration, analysis and innovation. Making the leap to corporate debt is one step, but investors, issuers and regulators alike have struggled with how to bridge the gap to other types of issuers and assets. The book is a welcome complement to the work the World Bank has been doing on sovereign ESG analysis and will be particularly useful for local investors in our client countries which have major allocations to public issuers and real asset classes.'

Fiona Stewart, Lead Financial Sector Specialist, World Bank

'Despite being the world's largest investment asset class, little is known about how fixed income investors might support and enable the transition to a low-carbon economy. This timely book comprehensively addresses that gap. It describes exactly how investors integrate social and environmental factors into their investment research and decision-making and into their engagement. And, critically, it explains how investors and other stakeholders can work together to ensure that the fixed income markets respond effectively and at the scale needed to the threats, challenges, risks, opportunities and needs presented by climate change and sustainable development.'

Adam Matthews, Chief Responsible Investment Officer (CRIO),
Church of England Pensions Board and Chair, Transition
Pathway Initiative (TPI)

'We've seen so much traction in capital markets around commitments to sustainable finance and development. The challenge now is how to put those commitments into practice, particularly in the world of fixed income. This book offers clear insights and a practical roadmap to help investors, companies, governments and NGOs turn their pledges into results.'

Peter T. Grauer, Chairman, Bloomberg LP

Responsible Investment in Fixed Income Markets

This book provides the world's first comprehensive account of responsible investment for fixed income investors. It enables readers to understand the key characteristics of fixed income investments and the relevance of sustainability-related issues to fixed income markets.

The expert contributors to this volume explain how sustainability-related issues can be taken into account in fixed income research and decision-making, in portfolio construction, and in active ownership (engagement). They provide a series of detailed case-studies from different parts of the fixed income market (corporate investment grade and high yield, emerging markets, sovereign and municipal debt), from a range of organisations with a variety of investment approaches. The contributors also provide in–depth critical analysis of key issues such as the role and influence of credit rating agencies, green bonds, data and public policy in shaping investment practice.

For investors, this book provides practical guidance on how to improve the financial and the sustainability performance of their fixed income investments. For stakeholders such as companies, civil society organisations, and governments it allows them to understand the role that fixed income might play in delivering the Sustainable Development Goals (SDGs), and to understand how they might encourage fixed income investors to pay greater attention to sustainability-related issues in their investment practices and processes.

Joshua Kendall is Head of Sustainable Fixed Income at Bloomberg, and was previously Head of Responsible Investment Research and Stewardship at Insight Investment. He is an experienced responsible investment practitioner, whose experience extends across investment management, ESG research and stewardship.

Dr Rory Sullivan is CEO of Chronos Sustainability and Visiting Professor in Practice at the Grantham Research Institute on Climate Change and the Environment at the London School of Economics. He is an internationally recognised expert on climate change and investment.

Responsible Investment
Series Editor: Dr Rory Sullivan

The ground-breaking **Responsible Investment** series provides a forum for outstanding empirical and theoretical work on all aspects of responsible investment, allowing the tensions and practical realities of responsible investment to be addressed in a readable, robust, and conceptually and empirically rigorous format.

The subject areas covered include:

- The financial, environmental, social, and governance outcomes from responsible investment
- Responsible investment in different asset classes
- Responsible investment in different geographies
- The implementation of responsible investment by different actors (e.g. pension funds, asset managers, sovereign wealth funds, private equity funds, insurance companies), and in different geographic regions
- The role that has been played by collaborative initiatives such as the UN Principles for Responsible Investment, UNEPFI and the investor networks on climate change
- Public policy and responsible investment

Valuing Corporate Responsibility
How Do Investors Really Use Corporate Responsibility Information?
Rory Sullivan

Responsible Investment
Edited by Rory Sullivan and Craig Mackenzie

Climate Change and the Governance of Corporations
Lessons from the Retail Sector
Edited by Rory Sullivan and Andy Gouldson

Responsible Investment in Fixed Income Markets
Edited by Joshua Kendall and Rory Sullivan

Responsible Investment in Fixed Income Markets

Edited by
Joshua Kendall and Rory Sullivan

LONDON AND NEW YORK

Cover image: © Getty Images / Overearth. Cover design: Amanda Williams.

First published 2023
by Routledge
4 Park Square, Milton Park, Abingdon, Oxon OX14 4RN

and by Routledge
605 Third Avenue, New York, NY 10158

Routledge is an imprint of the Taylor & Francis Group, an informa business

British Library Cataloguing-in-Publication Data
A catalogue record for this book is available from the British Library

Library of Congress Cataloging-in-Publication Data
Names: Kendall, Joshua, 1985- editor. | Sullivan, Rory, 1968- editor.
Title: Responsible investment in fixed income markets / edited by Joshua Kendall and Rory Sullivan.
Description: New York, NY: Routledge, 2023. | Series: The responsible investment series | Includes bibliographical references and index. |
Identifiers: LCCN 2022015711 (print) | LCCN 2022015712 (ebook) | ISBN 9780367518325 (hardback) | ISBN 9781032350103 (paperback) | ISBN 9781003055341 (ebook)
Subjects: LCSH: Investments—Moral and ethical aspects. | Fixed-income securities. | Corporations—Investor relations.
Classification: LCC HG4515.13 R47 2023 (print) | LCC HG4515.13 (ebook) |
DDC 332.6—dc23/eng/20220512
LC record available at https://lccn.loc.gov/2022015711
LC ebook record available at https://lccn.loc.gov/2022015712

ISBN: 9780367518325 (hbk)
ISBN: 9781032350103 (pbk)
ISBN: 9781003055341 (ebk)

DOI: 10.4324/9781003055341

Typeset in Bembo
by codeMantra

To my wife and the future we build together.

Joshua Kendall

To my wife Melinda and our daughters Claire and Laura.

Rory Sullivan

Contents

Acronyms   xiii
List of contributors   xvii

1 **Introduction**   1
   RORY SULLIVAN AND JOSHUA KENDALL

PART 1
Fundamentals   7

2 **Essential Concepts in Fixed Income Investing I:**
   Function and Analysis   9
   DAVID OAKES

3 **Essential Concepts in Fixed Income Investing II:**
   Participants and Portfolios   38
   DAVID OAKES

4 **The Landscape of Responsible Investment and**
   Fixed Income   68
   CARMEN NUZZO AND SIXTINE DUBOST

PART 2
Sovereign Investing   93

5 **ESG Factors in Sovereign Debt Investing**   95
   JAMES LOCKHART SMITH, MARIANA MAGALDI DE SOUSA,
   MY-LINH NGO, JANA VELEBOVA AND DAVID WILLE

 6 **ESG Considerations in Sovereign and Public Finance
    Credit Analysis**   116
    JOAN FELDBAUM-VIDRA, EMILIE NADLER AND
    ANDREA TORRES VILLANUEVA

 7 **Sovereign ESG Risk Analysis and Engagement**   133
    SCOTT MATHER AND LUPIN RAHMAN

PART 3
Corporate Investing   155

 8 **The Stewardship Mechanisms of Corporate
    Bond Investors**   157
    ARABELLA TURNER

 9 **Connecting ESG Factors with Credit Ratings**   177
    ANDREW STEEL AND JUSTIN SLOGGETT

10 **The Role of ESG Risk Factors in Corporate
    Credit Analysis**   197
    JOSHUA KENDALL AND TUDOR THOMAS

11 **Responsible Investment Strategies in Corporate
    Fixed Income**   218
    ALEX EVERETT AND KEITH LOGAN

12 **ESG Research in Different Fixed
    Income Sectors**   233
    ROBERT FERNANDEZ

PART 4
Impact Investing   251

13 **Impact Investing in Fixed Income Markets**   253
    JOHANNA KÖB

14 **The Impact Bond Market**   275
    MANUEL ADAMINI AND KRISTA TUKIAINEN

15 Using Bond Markets to Achieve Issuer Sustainability Outcomes   298

PETER MUNRO

16 Impact Bonds: Issuers and Investors   316

RADEK JÁN, THOMAS GIRARD AND THIBAUT CUILLIÈRE

PART 5
Market Influencers   341

17 The Role of Sustainable Treasury Teams   343

ARTHUR KREBBERS AND JASPREET SINGH

18 ESG Data, Ratings, and Indexes   363

KEVIN KWOK

19 Assessing the Responsible Investment Performance of Fixed Income Fund Managers   384

TOMI NUMMELA AND SARIKA GOEL

20 Delivering Sustainable Investment Objectives through the Capital Markets   400

DORIS KRAMER AND CAROLINE HORBRÜGGER

PART 6
Investment Products   415

21 Investment Product Design and Development   417

MICHAEL RIDLEY

22 Understanding Trends and Drivers in Fixed Income Investment Products   427

HORTENSE BIOY AND BENJAMIN JOSEPH

PART 7
Looking Forward   447

23 Regulation, Policy, and Fixed Income   449

WILL MARTINDALE

24 Measuring the Impacts of Climate Change   465
JAMES EDWARDS, TAMARA STRAUS AND
NATALIE AMBROSIO PREUDHOMME

**25 Fixed Income Markets and Responsible Investment:
The Past, the Present and the Future**   486
RORY SULLIVAN AND JOSHUA KENDALL

Index   495

Acronyms

ABS	asset-backed security
ADB	Asian Development Bank
AfDB	African Development Bank
ALM	asset-liability management
APAC	Asia-Pacific
ASEAN	Association of Southeast Asian Nations
AUD	Australian dollar
AUM	assets under management
bp	basis point (one hundredth of one percent, 0.01%)
bps	basis points
BPV	basis point value
BRL	Brazilian real
CAB	Climate Awareness Bond (EIB)
CAD	Canadian dollar
CAPM	Capital Asset Pricing Model
CBI	Climate Bonds Initiative
CDO	collateralised debt obligation
CDP	(previously) Carbon Disclosure Project
CDS	credit default swap
CDSB	Climate Disclosure Standards Board
CEO	chief executive officer
CFO	chief financial officer
CHF	Swiss franc
CHP	combined heat and power
CNY	Chinese yuan
CO_2	carbon dioxide
CO_2e	carbon dioxide (equivalent)
CPR	Conditional Prepayment Rate
CRA	credit rating agency
CSR	corporate social responsibility
DEI	diversity, equity, and inclusion
DKK	Danish krone
DNO	(electricity) distribution network operator

DTS	duration times spread
EBIT	earnings before interest and taxes
EBITDA	earnings before interest, taxes, depreciation and amortisation
EBRD	European Bank for Reconstruction and Development
EIB	European Investment Bank
EM	emerging market
ESG	environmental, social, and governance
ESMA	European Securities and Market Authority
EU	European Union
EUR	Euro
EV	electric vehicle
FSB	Financial Stability Board
FSCO	Financial Services Commission of Ontario
GBP	Green Bond Principles
GBS	Green Bond Standard
GCAM	General Change Asssessment Model
gCO_2/kWh	grammes of carbon dioxide per kilowatt hour
GDP	gross domestic product
GHG	greenhouse gas
GICS	Global Industry Classification Standard
GIIN	Global Impact Investing Network
GPFG	Government Pension Fund Global (Norway)
GRI	Global Reporting Initiative
GSE	government sponsored entity
GSIA	Global Sustainable Investment Alliance
GWh-e/y	gigawatt-hours (electrical) per year
GWh-th/y	gigawatt-hours (thermal) per year
GWh/y	gigawatt-hours per year
HCM	human capital management
HKD	Hong Kong dollar
HY	high yield
IAM	integrated assessment models
IBRD	International Bank for Reconstruction and Development
ICMA	International Capital Market Association
IDB	Inter-American Development Bank
IEA	International Energy Agency
IFC	International Finance Corporation
IFI	international financial institution
IG	investment grade
IIRC	International Integrated Reporting Council
IMF	International Monetary Fund
INR	Indian rupee
IPCC	Intergovernmental Panel on Climate Change
IPSS	National Institute of Population and Social Security Research (Japan)

IPT	initial pricing talk
JPY	Japanese yen
KBRA	Kroll Bond Rating Agency
km	kilometres
KPI	key performance indicator
ktCO₂e	kilotonnes of carbon dioxide (equivalent)
LA	Los Angeles (US)
LCS	liquidity cost scores
LDI	liability driven investment
LGC	Local Government Commission (North Carolina, US)
LMA	Loan Market Association
MBS	mortgage-backed security
MDB	multilateral development bank
MLI	multilateral lending institution
MW-e	megawatt (electrical)
MW-th	megawatt (thermal)
MXN	Mexican peso
NASA	National Aeronautics and Space Administration (US)
NC	North Carolina (US)
NDC	Nationally Determined Contribution
NGFS	Network for Greening the Financial System
NGO	non-governmental organisation
NIB	Nordic Investment Bank
NIP	new issuance premium
NOK	Norwegian krone
NPCC	New York City Panel on Climate Change
NRCD	National Development and Reform Commission (China)
NRSO	Nationally Recognized Statistical Rating Organization
NYC	New York City (US)
OAS	option-adjusted spread
OECD	Organisation for Economic Cooperation and Development
OHCHR	(UN) Office of the High Commissioner for Human Rights
OPIM	Operating Principles for Impact Management
PD	probability of default
PGE	Pacific Gas and Electric
PLN	Polish zloty
PRI	Principles for Responsible Investment
Q&A	question and answer
R&D	research and development
RCF	revolving credit facility
REIT	real estate investment trust
RFP	request for proposal
RFQ	request for quote
RMAP	Responsible Minerals Assurance Process
S&P	Standard and Poor's

SASB	Sustainability Accounting Standards Board
SBP	Social Bond Principles
SDG	Sustainable Development Goal
SEK	Swedish krona
SIFMA	Securities Industry and Financial Markets Association
SLBP	Sustainability-linked Bond Principles
SLLP	Sustainability-Linked Loan Principles
SME	small and medium-sized enterprise
SOFR	Secured Overnight Financing Rate
SPO	Second Party Opinion
SPV	special purpose vehicle
SRI	socially responsible investment
SSA	Sovereign, supranational and agency
SSP	Shared Socioeconomic Pathway
SST	Stakeholder Salience Theory
TCFD	Task Force on Climate-related Financial-Related Disclosures
TEG	Technical Expert Group
TIPS	Treasury Inflation Protected Securities
TRY	Turkish lira
UK	United Kingdom
UN	United Nations
UNCTAD	United Nations Conference on Trade and Development
UNDP	United Nations Development Programme
UNGC	UN Global Compact
UoP	use-of-proceeds
US	United States
USD	US dollar
WBS	whole business securitisation
ZAR	South African rand

Contributors

Editors

Joshua Kendall is Head of Sustainable Fixed Income at Bloomberg, developing ESG solutions for fixed income investors globally. Joshua was previously Head of Responsible Investment Research and Stewardship at Insight Investment, a UK-headquartered investment manager and one of the world's foremost fixed income investment managers. In this role Joshua applied responsible investment themes into fixed income investing, stewardship activities and portfolio management, and led the development of various innovative and industry leading ESG processes, covering climate change, impact investing, corporate debt, structured finance, and sovereign debt. Joshua has more than twelve years' responsible investment experience, having previously held roles at MSCI, GMI Ratings and the Principles for Responsible Investment. He has written extensively on responsible investment and ESG issues, is a contributor to many industry initiatives, and is regularly interviewed by the trade and business press on sustainable investment issues. He holds an MSc from the University of London, a BA (Hons) from the University of Manchester and is currently completing an EMBA programme at Henley Business School. He also holds the Investment Management Certificate from the CFA Society of the UK, and helped to develop its ESG Certificate.

Rory Sullivan is CEO of Chronos Sustainability – a specialist advisory firm which delivers transformative, systemic change in the social and environmental performance of key industry sectors – and a Visiting Professor in Practice at the Grantham Research Institute on Climate Change and the Environment at the London School of Economics and Political Science (LSE). Rory is an internationally recognised expert on responsible investment, and has worked extensively with a range of organisations – including UNEP FI, the World Economic Forum, the Principles for Responsible Investment, the Transition Pathway Initiative, the Institutional Investors Group on Climate Change, the World Bank and Climate Action 100+ (CA100+) – to develop and implement global programmes on responsible investment. He has also supported many of the world's leading asset owners and asset managers to develop and implement their responsible investment strategies. He is the author/editor of nine books, over 40 peer-reviewed journal articles, and over 50 book chapters on responsible investment and sustainability-related investment issues. Rory holds a PhD from the University of London, an MEL from the University of Sydney, an MSc from the University of Manchester, and a BE from University College Cork.

Contributors

Manuel Adamini is Director, Responsible Investment Strategist with Columbia Threadneedle Investments. His responsibilities are to embed responsible investment-related risk and return considerations into the fiduciary investment process and into the strategic investment advice offered to clients, and to position the firm as a thought leader. Manuel was previously Head of Investor Engagement and Senior Advisor at the Climate Bonds Initiative, Head of Responsible Investing at Dutch asset manager ACTIAM and served as a member of the Extractive Industries Transparency Initiative's (EITI) International Board. He is a frequent speaker and moderator at international conferences, and a regular writer and commentator on responsible investment and climate finance. Manuel holds an MSc in Economics and International Management from Maastricht University, and has also studied at Université de Montréal in Canada and at Aachen University in Germany. He is fluent in Dutch, German, French and English.

Natalie Ambrosio Preudhomme is Director of Communications at Four Twenty Seven, part of Moody's ESG Solutions, where she manages publications, thought leadership and outreach. She leverages her background in climate adaptation, communications, and environmental sciences to translate technical information into actionable insights for resilience-building across sectors. Her publications include *Community Resilience and Adaptive Capacity: A Meaningful Investment Across Assets*, published by the Federal Reserve Bank of San Francisco, and the chapter 'Asset Level Physical Climate Risk Disclosure' in the book *Values at Work: Sustainable Investing and ESG Reporting*. Natalie hold a bachelor's degree in environmental science and journalism, ethics, and democracy from the University of Notre Dame.

Hortense Bioy is Global Director of Sustainability Research at Morningstar. Hortense leads Morningstar's ESG fund research efforts globally, with the objective of educating investors and providing them with the research and tools they need to evaluate funds through an ESG lens. Prior to assuming this role in early 2021, she was responsible for Morningstar's European sustainability research for three years and European passive fund research for seven years. Hortense joined Morningstar in 2010 from Bloomberg where she was a financial journalist. She began her career as an M&A analyst at Société Générale in Hong Kong. Hortense holds a master's degree in finance from Paris Dauphine University, a postgraduate degree in finance from Paris Sorbonne University, and is a CFA Charterholder.

Thibaut Cuillière has more than 20 years' experience in financial analysis and market strategy. He has worked at Natixis (and its predecessor company, Natexis, since 2005), primarily in the areas of credit strategy and credit research. Since 2018, Thibaut has led the Natixis Real Asset and Green research team, and has also been responsible for the publication of a range of market indicators that measure the appetite for green and sustainable bonds in both primary and secondary markets. Thibaut is a graduate from the French School of Engineering ENSAE (Ecole Nationale de la Statistique et de l'Administration Economique), specialising in economy, statistics and finance, and also holds a master's degree in econometrics from Paris-La Sorbonne University.

Sixtine Dubost is a Senior Associate, Investment Practices at the Principles for Responsible Investment (PRI). She is part of the fixed income team, working on the ESG in credit risk and ratings initiative, which aims to enhance the transparent and systematic integration of ESG factors in credit risk analysis. Prior to joining the PRI in 2020, Sixtine was a consultant for Aurexia, a management consulting firm operating within the financial services industry. Sixtine holds a master's degree in asset management from the Paris-Dauphine University, where she also obtained her bachelor's qualification in management.

James Edwards is a Director of Research and Modelling at Moody's Analytics (MA). He is leading the initiative to model climate risk within MA's credit and financial risk metrics for corporates, financials, SMEs, and sovereigns. He also works in the development of MA's structural public-firm risk models, provisioning tools, and fixed-income valuation products. He is based in New York City and holds a PhD in Economics from the University of Chicago.

Alex Everett, CFA was an Investment Manager at Cameron Hume where he supported investment decision-making, ESG and macroeconomic analysis across actively-managed client portfolios. He contributed significantly towards the integration of ESG into investment research at the firm. Alex frequently produces thought-leadership articles and reports and his writing has been featured in the *Australian Financial Review*. He holds an MA in economics from the University of Edinburgh and is a CFA Charterholder.

Joan Feldbaum-Vidra is the Managing Director of the Sovereigns Group at KBRA, with nearly 25 years of experience working in country risk.

Prior to joining KBRA, Joan was head of Sovereigns at ARC Ratings, based in Europe. She previously worked for several years as a consultant to institutional investors with a special focus on emerging markets and frontier economies. Joan began her career as a sovereign analyst at Moody's Investors Service. She is active in a variety of global debt and emerging market investment associations, including as a member of the Bretton Woods Committee. Joan holds a BS from Cornell University and an MA from the Johns Hopkins School of Advanced International Studies.

Robert Fernandez is Director, ESG Research at Breckinridge Capital Advisors. He is also a member of the firm's Sustainability Committee. In his role, Rob leads Breckinridge's ongoing ESG integration and engagement efforts. He has been with the firm since 2010 and has over 23 years' of research experience. Prior to Breckinridge, Rob was a senior research analyst at Opus Investment Management. Rob is a member of the Board of Directors for the United Way of Massachusetts Bay and Merrimack Valley. He holds a BS from Boston College and an MBA from the Boston University School of Management. He is a CFA Charterholder and an FSA Credential holder.

Thomas Girard is Global Head of Green & Sustainable (G&S) Syndicate at Natixis, and has over 20 years' experience in wealth management advisory, responsible investment, and green and sustainable finance. he joined Natixis GSH in 2018 as product specialist responsible for the business development towards non-banking financial institutions and created the G&S Syndicate Team in July 2020 to optimize the syndication and distribution of green and sustainable assets at global scale. He was previously a Senior ESG Analyst is Natixis's sell-side team, and also worked at MSCI ESG Research and at ORSE. Thomas holds master's degrees in business law from the University of Strathclyde and in finance and control from the Université Jean-Moulin Lyon III, and an MBA in operational management and sustainable performance from ISC Paris.

Sarika Goel is a Principal in Mercer's Wealth Business. She leads the global Responsible Investment Manager Research, where she focuses on building and expanding research coverage of responsible investment strategies. She is a member of the Strategic Research Group and responsible for intellectual capital focusing on implementable solutions in sustainability themes. Prior to joining Mercer in 2010, Sarika spent three years at RBC Wealth Management in London within the Advisory and Discretionary business groups. Previously, she spent two years as an equity research associate at Scotia Capital in Toronto, Canada, covering the Canadian Banks and Diversified Financials sectors. Sarika holds an MBA from the Rotman School of Management, University of Toronto, and is a CFA Charterholder.

Caroline Horbrügger is Senior Manager Sustainable Investment in KfW's asset management division. Having a focus on green bonds, she monitors market developments and is responsible for the continuous development of the approach for KfW's green bond portfolio. She also conducts detailed assessments of green bonds prior to investment. Actively engaged in the Green Bond Principles, she has especially contributed to the work of the Impact Reporting working group and has been involved in the development of the Handbook Harmonized Framework for Impact Reporting. She holds a Master of Finance from Frankfurt School of Finance and Management.

Radek Ján was, until June 2022, a thematic analyst at Natixis, where he held dual positions at CIB Research and at the Green & Sustainable Hub, focusing on sustainability, infrastructure, and energy transition. His work included the creation of thematic content for financing solutions and advisory services as well as analysis of trends in green bond markets. He co-wrote thematic studies about desalination and water and wrote studies about waste management and rail transport. Radek graduated from Sciences Po Paris (MSc Finance and Strategy) and the London School of Economics (MSc Environmental Economics and Climate Change).

Benjamin Joseph is a Senior Investment Strategist at Franklin Templeton Investments. Prior to assuming this role in August 2021, he was Senior Manager Research Analyst at Morningstar, where he focused on fixed income investment strategies for over for years. Before joining Morningstar, Benjamin spent five years in the start-up ecosystem including two years managing a global commodities research company in Paris. Prior to that, he spent six years in the hedge fund industry as an analyst and a fund of hedge funds portfolio manager in Paris and New York. Benjamin holds a bachelor's degree in international business from Regent's Business School London, a master's degree in business administration from Université Paris-Dauphine, a specialist postgraduate degree in financial techniques from ESSEC Business School, and is a Chartered Alternative Investment Analyst.

Johanna Köb is Head of Responsible Investment at Zurich Insurance Company, where she oversees the implementation of the Swiss insurer's responsible investment strategy for the USD 200bn portfolio of group assets. She joined the company in 2012 and has been instrumental in building the company's multiaward-winning approach to ESG integration and impact investing. She has helped pioneer several sustainable asset classes, notably green bonds (she co-chaired the steering committee for the Green and Social Bond Principles for four years) and has a keen interest in mainstreaming impact investment with integrity. She holds a BA and an MA from the Universität St. Gallen, and an MA from Tufts University.

Doris Kramer is Head of Sustainable Investment in KfW's asset management division. She oversees the sustainable investment approach for KfW's liquidity portfolio and the setup of a dedicated green bond portfolio under a special mandate of the German Ministry for the Environment. Doris has been a member of the Executive Committee of the Green and Social Bond Principles since 2015. As part of the Technical Expert Group, set up by the EU Commission, Doris contributed to the recommendations for an EU Green Bond Standard. Doris has worked at KfW for over two decades and in various departments including export and project financing as well as treasury and asset management. She holds a diploma in Business Administration from the Georg-August-University of Göttingen.

Arthur Krebbers is Head of Corporate Climate and ESG Capital Markets at NatWest. He has been supporting corporate and investor clients with their ESG strategies since 2014 and has over 12 years of international capital markets experience. His areas of expertise include debt structuring and marketing, ESG rating management as well as responsible investment portfolio construction. Arthur publishes the *Issue Your Greens* newsletter, covering pertinent developments within the asset class. His research on sustainable finance has been featured in a range of media outlets. Arthur has a PhD in Finance and is a Visiting Lecturer at Strathclyde University Business School.

Kevin Kwok is Head of ESG Solutions Americas, Capital Financing & Investment Banking at HSBC. Previously Kevin developed Fixed Income ESG Research at MSCI, chairing the Fixed Income Methodology Committee and sitting on the Bloomberg Barclays MSCI Global Green Bond Index selection committee. Prior to joining MSCI, Kevin was an Associate Director in S&P Global Ratings' Energy, Materials, and Commodities practice and a member of its Sustainable Finance team. In private equity, he advised and raised capital in the energy sector. He also managed CDO portfolios at BNY Mellon. Kevin received an Earth Institute Fellowship to complete an MS in Sustainability Management at Columbia University. He holds a BA in Economics from UT Austin and an MBA from University of Houston. Kevin previously served in the US Peace Corps in Mali, West Africa.

James Lockhart Smith is VP, Markets at Verisk Maplecroft. He has led Verisk Maplecroft's work with the financial sector since 2015, researching the ESG, climate and political risk impacts, and dependencies of market actors and delivering actionable data analytics and insights for clients. James previously led the company's Latin America research team for four years. Before that, he worked at the International Institute for Strategic Studies (IISS), where he focused on Latin American defence and security policy challenges, and as a political risk analyst. He is the principal author of a book on Andean insurgency, speaks and writes Spanish at a professional level, and has a master's degree in Latin American Politics from the University of London.

Keith Logan was previously Client Relationship Manager at Cameron Hume where he helped manage and develop relationships with potential clients, consultants, and other market participants. Previously, Keith was a managing director in the Global Markets division at State Street Bank, supporting multi-asset investment research and trading activities for a wide range of clients. Keith has further experience working within the Treasury function with Lloyds TSB and Union Discount.

Mariana Magaldi de Sousa is an affiliated professor at the Center for Research and Teaching in Economics (CIDE) in Mexico City. She specialises in development economics, financial regulation, and international political economy. Her articles have appeared in books published by Harvard and Stanford University Presses as well as in academic journals such as the *Journal of Banking Regulation* and the *Journal of Business Ethics.* Dr. Magaldi has won a series of research grants and awards including a Fulbright scholarship. She has worked as principal analyst at Verisk Maplecroft, and as a consultant for the Inter-American Development Bank (IDB), the Center for Global Development (CGD), and the Ministries of Economy and Social Development in Mexico. Dr. Magaldi holds a master's degree in Economics and a doctoral degree in Political Science from the University of Notre Dame.

Will Martindale is Group Head of Sustainability at Cardano, where he provides specialist input on all aspects of Cardano's sustainability activities. He was previously Director of Policy and Research at PRI, the United Nations-supported Principles for Responsible Investment, where he led PRI's global regulatory affairs and public policy activities. Will has a background in banking, joining JPMorgan's graduate programme in June 2004. In September 2010, Will joined French bank, BNP Paribas, as a business manager for their credit trading desk. Will holds a MSc in Comparative Politics from the London School of Economics and a BSc in Maths from King's College London.

Scott Mather is PIMCO's CIO US Core Strategies, a managing director in PIMCO's Newport Beach office, a member of the PIMCO Investment Committee and a generalist portfolio manager. Mr. Mather also oversees the firm's global ESG portfolio integration and sustainable investment activities. Previously, he was head of global portfolio management. He also served as a managing director of Allianz Global Investors KAG. Prior to these roles, Mr. Mather co-headed PIMCO's mortgage- and asset-backed securities team. Before joining PIMCO in 1998, he was a fixed income trader specialising in mortgage-backed securities at Goldman Sachs in New York. He has 26 years of investment experience and holds a master's degree in engineering, as well as undergraduate degrees, from the University of Pennsylvania.

Peter Munro is Head of Division, Capital Markets Department at the European Investment Bank (EIB). He re-joined EIB in 2019 to lead and advise on ESG finance, investor, and credit ratings. He created and leads a new Advisory Programme for Sustainable Debt Issuance, and co-leads for EIB at the EU Platform on Sustainable Finance, the Green & Social Bond Principles Executive Committee, and Network on Greening the Financial System. Between 2016 and 2019 Peter was seconded to act as Director at the International Capital Markets Association, focusing on market and product development for the Green Bond Principles. His previous experience includes a decade of marketing green bonds at EIB, and working in investor relations, marketing, and economic analysis at firms including Citigate Dewe Rogerson and the German Treuhandanstalt privatisation agency. Peter has a degree in Philosophy, Politics & Economics from Oxford University, and has also studies at INSEAD and at London Business School.

Emilie Nadler is an ESG Associate in the Credit Policy Group at KBRA, where she works to better integrate environmental, social, and governance considerations into KBRA analyses. Emilie began her professional career at KBRA, where she has worked since completing her graduate studies. Emilie holds a BA in government and English from Skidmore College, and received an MPP from Georgetown University's McCourt School of Public Policy.

My-Linh Ngo is Head of ESG Investment at BlueBay Asset Management. She has spent over two decades in the field of sustainable and responsible/ESG investing, working across equity and fixed income asset classes, on ESG focussed strategies and integrating ESG analysis into conventional portfolios. She currently heads up the incorporation of ESG factors and risks at BlueBay Asset Management, a specialist fixed income asset manager, overseeing the firm's strategy, policies, and practices in this area. My-Linh represents BlueBay externally in a range of committees and working groups focussed on driving best practice on ESG investing, particularly those focussed on the fixed income asset class. Her previous roles have been at Schroders Investment Management where she was an ESG Analyst, and at Henderson Global Investors where she was an Associate Director – SRI Research. She holds a master's in Leadership for Sustainable Development from Middlesex University/Forum for the Future, a master's in Environmental Management Systems & Auditing, and a degree in Environmental Sciences, both from the University of East Anglia.

Tomi Nummela is Director, Sustainable Investing at Blackrock. He was, until November 2021, Principal, Responsible Investment Consultant at Mercer Investments where he advised asset owner clients on the integration of ESG and sustainability issues into investment decision-making. He has authored reports on asset owner investment strategies and policies, manager selection and investment practices across asset classes. Before joining Mercer, Tomi headed the Principles for Responsible Investment's (PRI) investment practice development and worked at the University of Cambridge delivering a Responsible Investment thought-leadership program.

Before this, he worked for over a decade in investment banking in senior debt and equity capital market origination roles at Société Générale, ABN AMRO Rothschild and ABN AMRO. Tomi holds a master's degree in Finance from the University of Turku from his native Finland, and an MBA in Corporate Social Responsibility from the University of Nottingham. He is a Chartered Alternative Investment Analyst (CAIA).

Carmen Nuzzo is Head of Fixed Income at the Principles for Responsible Investment (PRI). At PRI, she is responsible for the PRI fixed income flagship programme, which includes the ESG in credit risk and ratings initiative, sovereign, sub-sovereign, securitised products, and private debt workstreams. Carmen works with investors, credit rating agencies, issuers, information providers, and other stakeholders to improve the understanding of how environmental, social, and governance factors impact debt instrument pricing. Prior to joining the PRI in 2017, she was an Executive Director at Morgan Stanley, and started her career as a macroeconomist in 1993 at Salomon Brothers, subsequently working for Citigroup, with stints in the not-for-profit sector. Carmen holds a PhD in corporate finance and capital markets from the Università degli Studi di Bergamo, and a degree in Political Science (Economics Major) from the Università La Sapienza in Rome.

David Oakes is CEO of Dauphin Financial Training Inc. and is the course author and principal trainer for the International Capital Market Association (ICMA) Fixed Income Certificate, a leading qualification for finance professionals. He designs and delivers training programmes for financial institutions, securities exchanges, central banks, regulatory agencies, and technology companies worldwide, with a special emphasis on fixed income markets and derivatives. David was previously Director of Academic and Professional Education at the ICMA Centre at the University of Reading and Lecturer in Finance at Warwick Business School and the University of Exeter. He has an MSc in Economics from the London School of Economics and Political Science.

Lupin Rahman is an Executive Vice President and Portfolio Manager in PIMCO's London office. She is PIMCO's global head of sovereign credit on the emerging markets portfolio management team and responsible for ESG integration across PIMCO's investment strategies. Prior to joining PIMCO in 2008, she spent five years at the International Monetary Fund as an emerging markets macroeconomist. Before joining the IMF, she worked for the World Bank, the Centre for Economic Performance, and STICERD (the Suntory and Toyota International Centres for Economics and Related Disciplines). She has 23 years of investment experience and holds a PhD in economics from the London School of Economics.

Michael Ridley is a Director and Senior Responsible Investment Specialist at HSBC Global Asset Management (GAM) where he leads on green bonds, sustainable infrastructure, and biodiversity. Prior to joining HSBC

GAM, Michael was Global Head of ESG Fixed Income Research at HSBC where he led research on green bonds and ESG integration. Michael was twice voted No. 2 green bond analyst in the Euromoney global fixed income research poll. Michael has previously held senior credit research roles for Citigroup and for Mizuho International. He has also worked as a consultant to the UK's Carbon Trust and to the German government development agency GiZ. Michael holds a PhD in Environmental Economics from University College London and master's degrees from Yale University and the London School of Economics.

Jaspreet Singh is a founding member of the ESG Advisory team at NatWest and is currently a Vice-President in the US Sustainable Finance Capital Markets team, supporting US corporate customers to align their sustainability strategy with their treasury policy. His areas of expertise include structuring and executing financing transactions linked to ESG factors, developing investor materials to support corporates with their ESG messaging and providing best in class advice on the latest sustainable finance regulation. Jaspreet has a BSc in Accounting and Economics from Lancaster University and holds a Certificate in ESG Investing from the CFA Institute.

Justin Sloggett is a Director and Head of ESG Integration and Reporting within the Sustainable Finance Group at Fitch Ratings. Before starting at Fitch Ratings, Justin was Head of ESG Investment Research and Head of Public Markets at the Principles for Responsible Investment, where he ran the Listed Equity and Fixed Income work streams. Justin previously worked for the Co-operative Asset Management as a Responsible Investment Analyst, and for F&C Asset Management PLC (now BMO Global Asset Management) as an Investment Support Analyst within the Alternative Assets teams. Justin graduated from the University of Nottingham with a master's degree in mechanical engineering and is also a CFA Charterholder.

Andrew Steel is Global Group Head of Sustainable Finance at Fitch, and created their ESG analysis framework. He has held several senior positions in Fitch including leading its Asia Pacific Corporate Ratings, EMEA Corporate Ratings and the EMEA energy, utilities, project finance and transportation analytical groups. Prior to Fitch Andrew ran ABN Amro's project finance, power, and utilities group. He has a background in private equity, energy, mezzanine financing, leveraged buy-outs, and M&A lending and advisory. Whilst at Fitch, Andrew was an independent expert for the UN ECE on risk and sustainable energy development, and is currently an advisory committee member of the PRI credit ratings initiative. Andrew graduated in Psychology from Bristol University, and has a postgraduate diploma from INSEAD business school.

Tamara Straus is an Assistant Director of Research at Moody's Analytics, focused on ESG and climate risk. Previously, she served as Director of Communications for the UC Berkeley Blum Center for Developing Economies and as Senior Editor of the Stanford Social Innovation Review. She holds bachelor's and master's degrees from Colombia University.

Tudor Thomas is a Quantitative Researcher with Insight Investment. He joined Insight in April 2019, and his team leads the development of the Insight's quantitative ESG data products. Prior to Insight, Tudor was a Data Scientist at Tails.com. He has also worked with the London Fire Brigade as a Data Scientist Fellow, modelling fire risk and creating a measure of fire station preparedness. Tudor graduated from the University of Melbourne with a BSc in Mathematics and Physics. He also holds MASt and PhD degrees in Physics, both from the University of Cambridge.

Andrea Torres Villanueva is an ESG Associate in the Credit Policy Group at KBRA. Before joining KBRA in 2020, Andrea worked in the Financing for Sustainable Development Office at the United Nations after completing her graduate studies. Prior to graduate school, Andrea served as a senior analyst in Evercore's Public Finance Division in Mexico City. She holds a BA in economics from Instituto Tecnológico Autónomo de México (ITAM), and an MPP from Georgetown University's McCourt School of Public Policy.

Krista Tukiainen is Head of Market Intelligence at Climate Bonds Initiative (CBI). She manages CBI's market data products and solutions on green and sustainable fixed income, which are aimed at protecting the market against greenwashing and facilitating the flow of capital to Paris-aligned assets, projects, activities, and issuers. She also oversees a global research programme focused on identifying the barriers and enablers of growth in green and sustainable debt finance, including issues such as impact, additionality, and the green transition. Prior to joining CBI, Krista worked as a Consultant at the University of Cambridge's Centre for Sustainable Development, and as a Sustainability Consultant role at London-based boutique firm, Longevity Partners. Krista holds a bachelor's degree in economics, and a MSc in Environmental Policy and Regulation from the London School of Economics

Arabella Turner was previously a Senior ESG Specialist at Pictet Asset Management where she was responsible for leading the firmwide ESG engagement programme and contributing to active ownership initiatives at the Pictet Group level. Arabella joined Pictet Asset Management's UK sales team in 2012 before moving to the ESG team in 2017. Prior to Pictet, she worked at Goldman Sachs within the asset management division. Arabella holds a master's degree in Sustainability Leadership from the University of Cambridge, a bachelor's degree in Classics from the University of Pennsylvania, and the Investment Management Certificate.

Jana Velebova is a Senior Portfolio Manager within the Emerging Markets Team at BlueBay Asset Management. Prior to joining BlueBay in December 2014, Jana was a Partner and Portfolio Manager at Rogge, where she co-led the emerging market team in London and Singapore and managed emerging market assets across a range of active global fixed income and currency portfolios. Following experience in banking, she started her investment management career at Threadneedle in 2006, where she became a deputy fund manager in the Emerging market fixed income team. She holds a BSc in International Economics from the University of Economics in Prague, an LLM in Finance from J.W. Goethe University in Frankfurt and a Postgraduate Certificate in Complex System Modelling from King's College, London. Jana is a CFA Charterholder and holds the Certificate in ESG Investing.

David Wille is a principal analyst with Verisk Maplecroft's Markets team investigating the interaction between economics and political, ESG, and climate risks for multinational organizations and financial institutions. Prior to Verisk Maplecroft, David spent three years as an analyst in the financial services practice for the business research and advisory firm CEB (now Gartner) and was also a researcher at an economics think tank in the Washington, DC area. David has a master's degree in economics from George Mason University and bachelor's degree from Northwestern University.

1 Introduction

Rory Sullivan and Joshua Kendall

The Fixed Income Market

For over 400 years, fixed income securities have been an essential source of capital for companies and for governments. Fixed income markets – colloquially referred to as debt or credit markets – are now a critical part of the financial system and play a central role in modern economies. Behind almost every mortgage, large business transaction, and public service investment, a fixed income investor is allocating capital in the expectation of receiving a return on that investment at an agreed future time, where the return is commensurate with the risk associated with the investment.

Depending on how it is measured, fixed income is the world's largest investment asset class. At the end of 2020, the size of global fixed income markets – measured in terms of the notional outstanding debt – was approximately 195 trillion US dollars. This fixed income market is made up of several sub-asset classes; the two largest are sovereign bonds (47%) and corporate bonds (30%), with other significant sub-asset classes including municipal bonds (2%), asset-backed securities (17%), and corporate loans at (4%).

Fixed income markets are growing strongly. In the period 2010–2020, the annual compound growth increase in new debt issuance was over 40% for corporate bonds and over 25% for sovereign bonds. As a consequence of the COVID-19 pandemic, bond issuance has accelerated further as debt capital markets have become a vital source of funding for corporates and sovereigns dealing with the economic fallout from the pandemic.

The Sustainability Imperative

We are writing this book at a point when the importance of investors paying attention to sustainability-related issues has never been clearer. For example, a recent report from the World Economic Forum estimates that around half the world's total gross domestic product (GDP) is moderately or highly dependent on nature and its services (WEF, 2020). At the same time, the Climate Policy Initiative estimates that the annual amounts invested in the low-carbon transition are approximately one third of what is needed (Climate Policy Initiative, 2020).

DOI: 10.4324/9781003055341-1

Investors, across all asset classes, have responded to the risks and the opportunities presented by these sustainability-related issues. They have made commitments to responsible investment, to taking explicit account of environmental, social and governance (commonly referred to as ESG) issues in their investment processes, to encouraging the companies and other entities in which they invest to have high standards of social and environmental performance, and to supporting public policy action on issues such as climate change.

In listed equities and in property, these efforts have been extensively discussed and described in both the academic and in the practitioner literature. However, despite its importance, fixed income has received nothing like the same level of attention. Apart from discussions around green, transition, social, and other impact bonds, there is little discussion of the role that fixed income investment can or could play in enabling climate action or sustainable development more generally. There is even less discussion of the roles and responsibilities of investment system actors – investment managers, asset owners, insurance companies, investment consultants, credit rating agencies, development banks, and policymakers, to name but a few – might play in directing fixed income investment to more sustainable ends. Many stakeholders have simply assumed that bondholders could not or would not take account of ESG issues into their investment processes. They have also assumed, or at least asserted, that bondholders have limited ability to exert influence over the entities in which they invest, and that bondholders have limited financial interest in taking action.

When we look at investment practice, we see that these assumptions do not hold true. Many bond investors now routinely analyse sustainability-related issues in their investment processes and look to encourage better standards of corporate governance and corporate responsibility in the entities in which they invest. Many large investors have extended their commitments to responsible investment from listed equities to their wider portfolios, including fixed income. An increasing number integrate ESG issues into their investment research and decision-making and look to engage with fixed income issuers (in particular with corporate issuers). Fixed income investors are also collaborating with their industry peers and working with initiatives such as the Principles for Responsible Investment to drive awareness and action on sustainability and fixed income. Green bonds have brought bondholders, underwriters, and issuers together to develop standard frameworks that are now commonly used by bond issuers, and that have played a key role in driving the growth in this part of the investment market.

These changes are not confined to investors. For example, the major credit rating agencies all explicitly consider ESG issues in their credit ratings; the main investment consultants advise their asset owner clients on how well investments managers are performing on ESG issues; many data providers provide ESG-related data and information relating to corporates and other debt issuers; and regulators are focusing much more attention on financial system stability and the risks presented by issues such as climate change.

About This Book

Despite these changes, there has been relatively little systematic analysis of whether the efforts that have been made have led to better social or environmental outcomes or whether the costs of analysing and acting on social and environmental issues outweigh the benefits. These are hugely important issues, given the potential contribution of fixed income markets to sustainability goals and outcomes.

This book therefore has three main objectives. The first is to provide an introduction to fixed income and to fixed income and responsible investment, so that readers – be they policymakers, ESG professionals, investment analysts seeking to understand the relevance of ESG to fixed income, investors and issuers affected by ESG issues – have a basic understanding of fixed income and its relevance to sustainability. The second objective is to present the work of some of the leading practitioners and organisations – institutional investors, credit rating agencies, data providers, and investment consultants – to show the range of practices, to demonstrate the outcomes that have been achieved and to reflect on the lessons learned. The third is to explain why fixed income investment is so important to global discussions around sustainable development and responsible investing, and to offer practical suggestions on how this might be encouraged and developed.

The book is divided into seven sections. The first section – Fundamentals – comprises Chapters 2–4, and focuses on the general characteristics of the fixed income asset class. Chapters 2 and 3, both written by David Oakes, cover core fixed income topics such as the investment characteristics of fixed income securities, the methods commonly used by investors to measure risk, and the roles played by different market participants, including credit rating agencies, credit analysts, securitisation structurers, portfolio managers, and institutional and private investors. In Chapter 4, Carmen Nuzzo and Sixtine Dubost from the Principles for Responsible Investment explain why fixed income investors are paying attention to ESG issues, and how this attention is shaping investment practices and performance.

The next three sections – Sovereign Investing, Corporate Investing, and Impact Investing – focus on the practicalities of fixed income investment, with practitioners presenting their analysis of the case for responsible investment in fixed income investing and offering their reflections on the challenges they have encountered and the lessons they have learned.

The Sovereign Investing section includes three chapters. Chapter 5 (written by James Lockhart Smith, Mariana Magaldi de Sousa, My-Linh Ngo, Jana Velebova, and David Wille) focuses on how BlueBay Asset Management has worked with Verisk Maplecroft to integrate ESG factors into its investment process. Chapter 7 by Scott Mather and Lupin Rahman describes how PIMCO assesses the financial relevance of ESG issues for sovereign issuers and incorporates this information into its investment decisions at the issuer and at the portfolio level. These chapters bookend Chapter 6 by

Joan Feldbaum-Vidra, Emilie Nadler, and Andrea Torres Villanueva, which describes how KBRA, a credit rating agency, assesses sovereigns, with a particular focus on how ESG factors influence sovereign and municipal ratings.

The next section, Corporate Investing, begins with Chapter 8 from Arabella Turner of Pictet Asset Management examining how corporate bondholders might enhance the efficacy and impact of their ESG-related engagement. This is followed by Chapter 9 by Andrew Steel and Justin Sloggett of Fitch Ratings who explain how credit rating agencies take account of ESG issues when analysing corporate issuers. Chapters 10–12 are practitioner case studies from Joshua Kendall and Tudor Thomas of Insight Investment, Alex Everett and Keith Logan of Cameron Hume, and Robert Fernandez of Breckinridge, respectively. These authors describe how they analyse and assess the financial significance of ESG issues for corporates, and how this information informs their investment research and decision-making.

The Impact Investing section – Chapters 13–16 – examines the social, environmental, and governance outcomes (or impacts) that can be achieved through an explicit focus on outcomes and impacts in the investment process. In Chapter 13, Johanna Köb of Zurich Insurance Group describes Zurich's experience as a major institutional investor with impact investing, and the potential for impact investing to allocate large volumes of capital to environmental and social issues. Manuel Adamini and Krista Tukiainen from the Climate Bonds Initiative then look at the impact bond market (green bonds, transition bonds, social impact bonds), analysing the size of the market, the impacts that can be delivered, and the key challenges facing issuers and investors. The Impact Investing section concludes with two quite different perspectives on impact investing. First, Peter Munro from the European Investment Bank describes the role that promotional or development banks can play in supporting the impact investing market through their own direct investments and lending activities, and through their wider role in growing and catalysing action through, for example, issuing green bonds and promoting standards and encouraging effective policy action. Second, in Chapter 16 Radek Ján, Thomas Girard, and Thibaut Cuillière from Natixis describe the impact bond lifecycle, discussing both the financial characteristics of these bonds and the social and environmental impact that these bonds might have.

The fifth section of the book – Market Influencers – looks beyond investors and credit rating agencies to examine how other actors might shape the fixed income market from a social and environmental perspective. Arthur Krebbers and Jaspreet Singh of NatWest Markets (Chapter 17) discuss the role of corporate treasury teams; Kevin Kwok of MSCI (Chapter 18) explores the role of ESG data providers in fixed income; Tomi Nummela and Sarika Goel from Mercer Investments (Chapter 19) discuss the role that investment consultants play in responsible investment; and finally Doris Kramer and Caroline Horbrügger from KfW (Chapter 20) discuss the role that development banks can play in growing and developing sustainable investment.

Most investors invest through funds. The sixth section – Investment Products – therefore focuses on investment funds and products. In Chapter 21, Michael Ridley of HSBC Global Asset Management describes the process for developing an ESG or sustainability bond product, highlighting the options that are available and the trade-offs that are made when designing a sustainability-oriented fixed income product. Hortense Bioy and Benjamin Joseph of Morningstar then provide an overview of the market for fixed income and ESG or responsible investment products. They describe the range of products that are available, the various labels and categories of products, and the trends in demand for these products.

The final section of the book – Looking Forward – considers how changing external conditions will shape investment practice, in particular the attention investors pay to ESG issues and to responsible investment. In Chapter 23, Will Martindale (of Cardano, but writing in his previous role as Head of Policy at the Principles for Responsible Investment) describes the changing landscape of responsible investment policy and regulation. This is followed by Chapter 24 by James Edwards, Tamara Straus, and Natalie Ambrosio Preudhomme (from Moody's Analytics and Moody's ESG Solutions) who describe how climate change-related risks and opportunities can be integrated into credit research and decision-making. The final chapter, Chapter 25, by Rory Sullivan and Joshua Kendall brings the key themes and insights from the book together. They describe the current state of play, both those areas where good progress has been made and those where much more is needed. They conclude by examining the actions and interventions needed to ensure that the fixed income markets respond effectively – in a timely manner and at the scale needed – to the threats, challenges, risks, opportunities, and needs presented by climate change and sustainable development.

References

Climate Policy Initiative (2020), *Updated View on the Global Landscape of Climate Finance 2019*. [online]. Available from: https://www.climatepolicyinitiative.org/wp-content/uploads/2020/12/Updated-View-on-the-2019-Global-Landscape-of-Climate-Finance-1.pdf (Accessed 25 June 2021).

World Economic Forum (2020), *Nature Risk Rising: Why the Crisis Engulfing Nature Matters for Business and the Economy* (World Economic Forum, Geneva). [online]. Available from: http://www3.weforum.org/docs/WEF_New_Nature_Economy_Report_2020.pdf (Accessed 25 June 2021).

Part 1
Fundamentals

2 Essential Concepts in Fixed Income Investing I

Function and Analysis

David Oakes

Introduction

Fixed income securities are a core component of how capital markets enable societies to transform savings into productive investment that will generate future wealth. This chapter describes the structure and function of fixed income markets, the key characteristics of fixed income securities, and the methods commonly used to measure risk and relative value in fixed income securities and portfolios. This provides context for the issues that arise in later chapters of this book, such as the motivations of fixed income investment managers and the importance of controlling for key risk characteristics when assessing the impact of ESG criteria on portfolio performance.

The first section introduces the function of fixed income capital markets. The second, the central role of bond prices and yield. The third, the influence of interest rates. The fourth, credit risk and credit spreads. The fifth, the credit default swap market. The sixth, bond covenants and issuer default. And lastly, bond security and seniority.

Fixed Income Markets and Fixed Income Securities

In this section we define and describe bond cash flows, primary market issuance (public issues and private placements), secondary market trading (market structure and trading protocols), and bond market participants.

Fixed income markets are substantial in size and scope. They include both fixed income securities (i.e. bonds) and bank lending. This chapter focuses almost exclusively on bonds.

Bonds

A bond is a lending agreement between a borrower (the issuer) and a group of lenders (the investors or bondholders). The issuer receives the principal

DOI: 10.4324/9781003055341-3

amount when the bond is issued and promises to repay it at the maturity date. Usually, the issuer will also make regularly scheduled cash interest payments at an agreed rate during the life of the bond; these are known as coupon payments (see Figure 2.1).

Consider a specific example. Figure 2.2 shows data relating to an Apple Inc. 2.90% coupon bond maturing on 12 September 2027. The bond is denominated in US dollars, and the total nominal amount outstanding is $2 billion; this is the amount that must be repaid by Apple Inc. to investors when the bond matures on 12 September 2027. During the life of the bond, Apple Inc. must also pay investors coupon interest semi-annually (i.e. twice each year) at a fixed annual rate of 2.90%. These payments are made on semi-annual anniversaries of the maturity date. The bond was issued in September 2017 and has been assigned a credit rating of AA+ by S&P and Aa1 by Moody's Investor Services (more information on credit ratings is given in Chapter 3).

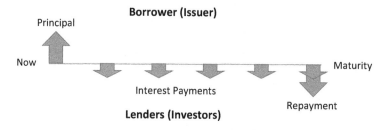

Figure 2.1 Borrower and Lender Cash Payments Illustration.

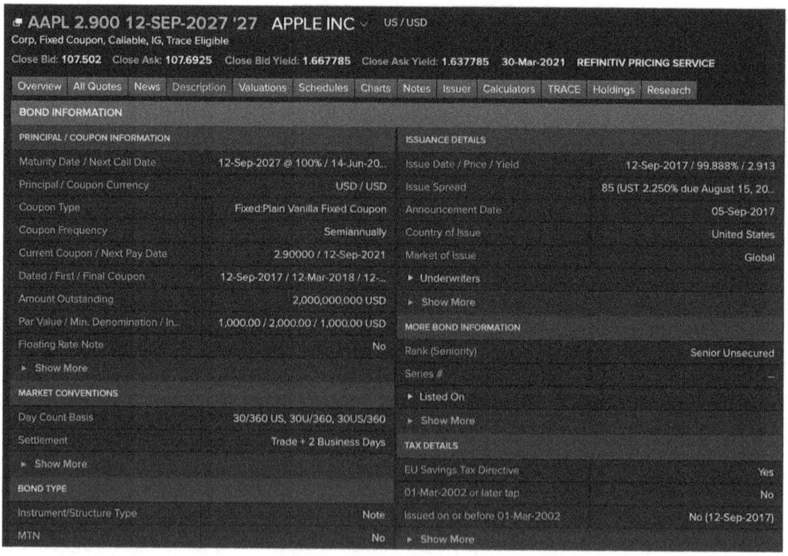

Figure 2.2 Bond Data Example for Apple Inc. 2027 Bond.
Source: Refinitiv Eikon.

Bonds are issued and first sold to investors in the primary market. Most bonds are offered in a public sale of securities to many investors, but they may also be offered through a private placement to a select group of investors. In a public offering, the issuer will usually be required to disclose financial and other relevant information to investors in a prospectus that describes the bond issue. Private placements are subject to less stringent disclosure requirements.

Once a bond has been issued, it is freely transferable between investors. Trading between investors takes place in the secondary market. Traditionally, most of this trading has been conducted on an over-the-counter basis in markets in which liquidity is provided by dealers who act as principals, quoting bid and offer prices at which they are willing to buy and sell securities. Dealers who provide these services are known as market makers. This is quite different from equity markets, where much of the trading takes place on organised exchanges through a central limit order book (i.e. a centralised database that allows buyers to be matched with sellers). There are several reasons for this difference.

First, bond markets are much more fragmented than equity markets. There are about 44,000 listed companies in the world, but the number of outstanding bond issues is much larger (World Federation of Exchanges Database, 2020). Many companies have dozens of bond issues, and a large financial institution may have hundreds. To provide just one example, the 500 companies that comprise the S&P 500 stock index have about 12,000 distinct bonds outstanding (Theisen, 2018).

Second, bond trades are of much larger average size than equity trades. The average equity trade size on the London Stock Exchange is about £5,000 (London Stock Exchange, 2020). But the average trade size for corporate bonds is about €1 million (Hill and Callsen, 2020), while the average trade size for liquid government bonds is on the order of €5 million (Baker et al., 2018).

Third, most bonds trade very infrequently. The top 50 S&P 500 stocks by volume trade about 60,000 times per day, but the 50 most liquid investment-grade bonds trade only about 20 times per day, and the most liquid high yield bonds trade even less frequently (Theisen, 2018). Many corporate bonds trade, at most, several times a year.

Fragmented markets, large average trade size, and infrequent trading mean that there is less natural liquidity. Instead, liquidity is provided by dealers (often investment banks) who warehouse risk. In recent years, secondary market trading in bonds has become increasingly electronic. Much of this electronic market operates on a request for quote (RFQ) basis, in which dealers continue to be the main providers of liquidity, with true all-to-all trading based on anonymous RFQ or a central limit order book limited to the most liquid markets for bonds of the highest credit quality.

Regulatory reforms since the financial crisis, including tightened regulatory capital and liquidity requirements, have led some investment banks to withdraw from acting as dealers in fixed income securities and others to narrow the range of securities in which they make markets or limit the market conditions in which they offer liquidity. This can lead to inadequate liquidity and high volatility in prices and spreads during periods of market stress, when the order flow is unbalanced (Hill and Callsen, 2020). As we explain below, liquidity is an important risk factor that affects returns on bonds.

Fixed income securities are issued and traded with a wide variety of structures, including:

- Fixed coupon bonds
- Floating coupon bonds (often known as floating rate notes)
- Zero-coupon bonds
- Inflation-linked bonds
- Securitisations (e.g. mortgage-backed securities and other asset-backed securities)
- Covered bonds
- Convertible bonds (i.e. bonds that may be exchanged for equity of the issuer)
- Bonds with other types of embedded optionality (e.g. callable and puttable bonds)

Each of these structures creates its own profile of exposure to interest rates and other risk factors that affect return. When combined with wide variation in credit quality across issuers as disparate as sovereign governments and sub-investment grade companies, they create a market that is rich in opportunity but also in complexity.

Market Participants

Fixed income markets involve a wide variety of participants, as illustrated in Figure 2.3.

Borrowers include sovereign governments, state and provincial governments, local authorities and public sector institutions, government agencies, supranational organisations, and many different financial and non-financial corporate entities. These borrowers have different objectives and different resources from which to repay their debt, creating different risk exposures for investors.

Globally, about 68% of the total nominal amount outstanding consists of bonds issued by sovereign, supra-national and agency borrowers, with the remaining 32% issued by corporate entities. About 53% of outstanding corporate bonds are issued by financial institutions (International Capital Market Association, 2020).

Lenders and investors include banks and other financial institutions; institutional investors such as endowments, pension funds, insurance companies,

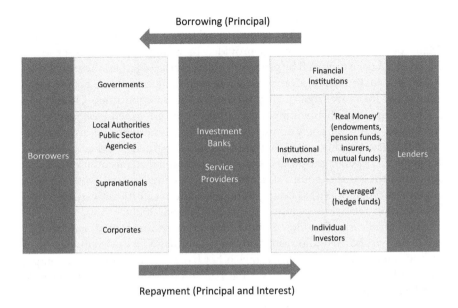

Borrowing (Principal)

Repayment (Principal and Interest)

Figure 2.3 Key Fixed Income Market Participants.

mutual funds, and private funds; and individual investors. These investors have different horizons and different risk appetites, and hence follow investment strategies with different objectives. As in other markets, we sometimes distinguish between 'real money' investors, who hold predominantly long-only positions in securities and make limited use of leverage, and 'leveraged' investors such as hedge funds that may make greater use of short positions, external borrowing, and derivatives. As the next chapter explains, 'real money' investors are typically judged against a benchmark that represents the universe of securities from which they are selecting, whereas 'leveraged' investors focus on objectives such as absolute returns or enhanced downside protection.

Financial institutions such as investment banks are also active participants in fixed income markets, helping borrowers raise money by issuing securities in the primary market and providing liquidity by acting as dealers in the secondary market. They also help issuers and institutional investors to manage risk (e.g. with derivatives) and provide credit analysis, valuation, and trade execution services. Many other institutions provide services that are essential to the operation of fixed income markets. Custodians and clearing and payment systems provide the institutional framework that supports trading, legal and accountancy firms provide essential professional services, and credit rating agencies offer independent assessments of credit risk. In the world of responsible investing, these are supplemented by institutions that provide environmental, social, and governance (ESG) ratings and verify or certify the alignment of borrowing programmes with environmental and social objectives. The role of rating agencies is detailed in Chapter 3.

Bank lending is an important source of financing for many companies. Many of these loans are a credit provided by a single lender. Larger loans, however, may be provided by group of lenders acting together; these are called syndicated loans. Syndication allows lenders to share risk. Some borrowers in syndicated loans are high quality investment grade companies. Other loans for lower quality sub-investment grade borrowers are called leveraged loans. Leveraged loans are a key source of financing in mergers and acquisitions, including leveraged buyouts; they are also used to refinance existing debt and for general corporate purposes. Globally, syndicated loans account on average for about the same amount of corporate net borrowing (i.e. gross borrowing minus redemptions) as bonds, although there is significant variation over time in their relative importance (Goel and Serena, 2020).

Once syndication has closed and a loan has been distributed, lenders may sell all or part of their allocation to other investors, who are themselves then free to trade in the loan. This allows other banks, specialist finance companies, and institutional investors such as pension funds, insurance companies, and hedge funds to participate in the market. Liquidity is limited, however, with much of the trading concentrated in leveraged loans (Loan Market Association, 2018).

In the remaining sections of this chapter, we provide the analytical tools necessary to navigate the complexity of bond markets and show how they are used to assess relative value in fixed income securities.

Bond Price and Yield

In this section we define and describe nominal amount, clean price, accrued interest, dirty price, zero-coupon yield, yield to maturity, coupon effect, and convexity.

Bond Prices

Bond prices are quoted as a percentage of the nominal amount of securities to be delivered from the seller to the buyer. The nominal amount is measured by the redemption amount to be repaid by the issuer at maturity. For example, the Government of Canada 0.5% coupon bond maturing on 1 December 2030 (Figure 2.4) was quoted at a price of 90.97 for settlement on 6 April 2021. An investor who buys the bond at this price will pay CAD 90.97 for every CAD 100 to be repaid by the Government of Canada at maturity.

The quoted price is typically a clean price: it does not include coupon interest that has accrued since the coupon was last paid but has not yet been distributed to investors. The full market value of the bond per 100 nominal, including this accrued interest, is its dirty price; this is the amount on which

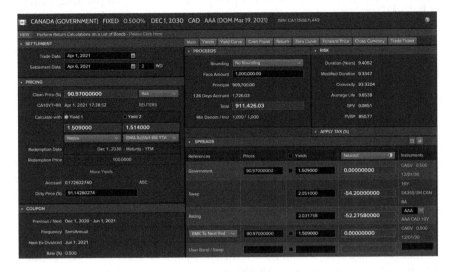

Figure 2.4 Government of Canada 0.5% Coupon Bond.
Source: Refinitiv Eikon.

settlement is based. In Figure 2.4, the interest that has accrued in the 126 days since the coupon was last paid is 0.172602740 per 100 nominal, giving a dirty price of 91.14260274. An investor who buys CAD 1 million nominal of the bond will therefore be required to pay CAD 911,426.03 to the seller, of which CAD 1,726.03 is accrued interest.

Different markets use different rules (known as day count conventions) for calculating accrued interest, which results in small differences for bonds with otherwise similar terms and dates. Quoting clean prices rather than dirty prices makes it easier for market participants to recognise changes in price that reflect genuine changes in market conditions.

The price at which a bond trades should reflect the present value that investors assign to each of its promised future cash flows. A present value is simply the amount that investors are willing to pay today to receive a given cash flow on some future date. For example, an investor who invests $100 for one year at an interest rate of 10% per year expects to receive a payment of $110 one year from today. Equivalently, we could say that the present value of $110 to be received one year from today is $100. By the same reasoning, the present value of $100 to be received one year from today is $90.91, since investing $90.91 today to receive $100 one year from now will result in a return of 10% per year. Interest rates are prices that relate present and future values.

Bond Yield

Investors may discount future cash flows from the same issuer to be received at different future dates (e.g. one year from now and five years from now) at different rates. We call these term-specific interest rates zero-coupon yields.

For example, the one-year zero-coupon yield for bonds of a particular issuer might be 1%, while the five-year zero-coupon yield is 3%. For consistency, we would expect an investor to use the same set of zero-coupon yields to value different bonds of the same issuer that carry the same credit risk. Section "Credit Risk and Credit Spreads" shows how zero-coupon yield curves for sovereign issuers and swaps are used to measure credit spreads.

In practice, investors often compare bonds in terms of their yield to maturity. The yield to maturity is the single interest rate which, when used to discount all a bond's promised future cash flows, gives a present value equal to a bond's dirty price. This is also the internal rate of return on the bond. The yield to maturity has the advantage that it can be calculated by looking at a single bond in isolation, without the need to look at all bonds of the same type as when estimating a zero-coupon yield curve.

A bond's yield to maturity may be quite different than the zero-coupon yield for the period corresponding to its life. For example, if the one-year zero-coupon yield is 1% and the five-year zero-coupon yield of 3%, the yield to maturity on a five-year bond will be less than 3%, since investors will discount coupon payments made earlier in the bond's life at lower rates.

Investors are interested in yields because, in a very approximate sense, the yield represents the return that they are offered for investing in a bond. A bond that is trading at a higher yield will, other things remaining equal, be trading at a lower price relative to the future cash flows that it promises to pay investors. For equivalent levels of risk, investors can be expected to prefer investing in bonds (and bond portfolios) that offer higher returns.

Comparisons between bonds based on their yields can be misleading. The return investors earn on a bond will only be equal to its yield to maturity if any coupon interest that is received can be reinvested at a rate equal to the bond's yield; since interest rates change over time, this will not generally be the case. In addition, bonds with different coupon rates may trade at different yields to maturity even when investors are discounting the promised future cash flows from both bonds at the same set of zero-coupon yields, because the size of the coupon affects the timing of cash flows received by investors. This coupon effect can cause bonds with higher coupon rates to trade at relatively lower yields when the zero-coupon yield curve is positively sloped (i.e. when long-term rates are higher than short-term rates).

The Government of Canada bond in Figure 2.4 is trading at a yield of 1.509%. There is a one-to-one relationship between a bond's price and its yield, so that knowing a bond's price is equivalent to knowing its yield. Both contain the same information, presented in different ways. If the bond were to trade at a higher price, it would have a lower calculated yield, and vice versa. This makes sense since a higher price would mean that investors were discounting the bond's promised cash flows at lower rates. For a fixed coupon bond, each small increase in yield corresponds to a slightly smaller reduction in price than the last, so that the relationship between price and yield is convex, as illustrated in Figure 2.5.

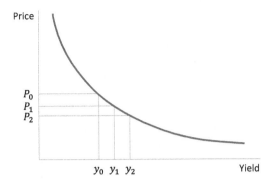

Figure 2.5 Relationship between Bond Price and Bond Yield.

This convexity in the relationship between price and yield, which reflects convexity in the relationship between the price and the relevant zero-coupon yields, can be important in managing interest rate risk, particularly in positions that will be held for a significant period or may be subject to large changes in interest rates. Since the sensitivity of a bond's price to a small change in rates changes as interest rates change, the risk characteristics of bond trades and portfolios will change over time. Positions that were initially hedged will become unhedged and will need to be rebalanced, and the impact of yield curve movements on the market value of bond trades or portfolios will change. Considering the impact of convexity can be particularly important in periods of high interest rate volatility. Other things remaining equal, convexity is an increasing function of a bond's time to maturity, so convexity may also be more important for longer-dated bonds.

Interest Rates

In this section we define and describe real interest rates, inflation-linked bonds, breakeven inflation rates, traditional monetary policy, asset purchase programmes, negative policy rates, basis point value, DV01, Macaulay duration, and modified duration.

Influencing Factors

Many factors contribute to changes in the level of interest rates and the shape of the yield curve. For example, real interest rates (i.e. the returns earned by investors after allowing for price inflation) depend on the economy's potential growth rate. The potential growth rate in turn depends on growth in productivity and the development and diffusion of technology. Sectoral and structural changes in the economy also affect real interest rates since productivity growth may be weaker in some sectors than in others. A final contributing factor is demography: an aging population may imply a lower demand for capital, slower productivity growth, and an increased saving rate, resulting in lower real interest rates (Lane, 2019).

Most financial contracts, of course, specify payments in nominal (i.e. money) terms. Since inflation erodes the purchasing power of money, investors will demand higher nominal returns to offset expected inflation. They may also demand an inflation risk premium to compensate for uncertainty about future inflation rates. Inflation compensation and inflation risk can be particularly significant factors driving changes in long-term interest rates.

Many governments (and some corporations) issue inflation-linked bonds that are designed to protect investors from inflation risk. These bonds pay a real coupon, and their price and yield are quoted in real terms. The coupon payments made to investors are calculated by applying the real coupon rate to the principal amount multiplied by an index ratio that reflects realised inflation between when the bond was issued and the payment date. Thus, for example, if prices have increased by 10% since the bond was issued, the index ratio would be 1.1, and an inflation-linked bond with an annual real coupon rate of 1% would pay coupon interest of 1.1%. At maturity, the bond repays the inflation-adjusted principal, based on realised inflation between the issue date and the maturity date. Whenever the bond is bought or sold, the clean price and accrued interest in real terms are applied to the inflation-adjusted principal for the value date. Adjusting the principal amount on each date ensures that the cash flows paid to investors include compensation for any inflation experienced during the life of the bond, which protects them from inflation risk.

Globally, the market value of outstanding inflation-linked bonds is about $3.1 trillion. The US market is the largest component, with about $1.4 trillion in market value. Inflation-linked bonds issued by the US Treasury are called Treasury Inflation Protected Securities (TIPS). There are also important inflation-linked bond markets in the UK, France, Italy, and several other developed markets. Brazil is by some distance the largest emerging market issuer.

The difference between the nominal yield on an ordinary bond and the real yield on an inflation-linked bond of the same maturity is called the breakeven inflation rate for that maturity. For example, if the nominal yield on an ordinary ten-year bond is 3% and the real yield on a ten-year inflation-linked bond is 1%, then the ten-year breakeven inflation rate is 2% per year. Inflation at the breakeven inflation rate would make investors indifferent between holding the nominal and inflation-linked bonds, since the realised total nominal yield would be the same on both bonds. This makes breakeven inflation rates an important market-based reference for inflation expectations, and they are closely monitored by market participants.

The fiscal stance of the government is another important factor affecting interest rates. A budget deficit will increase the amount the government has to borrow to finance its spending, resulting in increased issuance of government debt securities. Other things remaining equal, this is likely to increase interest rates, since investors will demand higher returns in exchange for holding the increased amount of debt. A budget surplus will reduce the amount the government has to borrow, resulting in reduced issuance of government debt and lower rates. In practice, of course, the actual impact of fiscal policy on interest rates will be complicated by additional factors, including how near the economy is to full employment, how it affects the exchange rate and the trade balance, and how it interacts with monetary policy decisions made by the central bank. In general, however, the fiscal stance is likely to have a significant influence on rates.

The final major factor driving interest rates and the shape of the yield curve is monetary policy. Central banks adjust official interest rates and intervene in markets in other ways that change the marginal cost of liquidity in the financial system; this in turn affects market interest rates and aggregate demand (i.e. the total demand for goods and services in the economy). For most central banks, the primary objective of monetary policy is price stability, often defined in terms of a target for the rate of change in consumer prices (e.g. a year-on-year increase of less than 2% in the consumer price index). In pursuit of this objective, the bank adjusts policy to maintain aggregate demand near the level of aggregate supply that is consistent with the economy's potential output at full employment. Monetary policy may also be adjusted in pursuit of secondary objectives such as full employment and balanced economic growth. In some countries, monetary policy may be used to manage the exchange rate.

Traditionally, monetary policy has focused mainly on the central bank's ability to control short-term interest rates. This may be done directly by setting an official rate at which the central bank provides short-term liquidity to financial institutions in exchange for eligible collateral (as in the case of the main refinancing operations rate of the European Central Bank or bank rate at the Bank of England) or indirectly by using open-market operations (i.e. purchases or sales of securities with other market participants) to adjust the total quantity of reserve assets so as to change the marginal cost at which one bank can obtain additional liquidity from another (as in the case of the US Federal Reserve's target rate for Federal Funds). In either case, the immediate impact is on short-term interest rates. Since a change in policy changes expectations about future levels of interest rates, however, longer-term interest rates are also affected. Over time, changes in market interest rates will affect the decisions that households and businesses make about saving, spending, and investing, and therefore aggregate demand.

One consequence of traditional monetary policy influencing short-term interest rates is that, historically, short-term interest rates have been more volatile than long-term interest rates. Changes in monetary policy produce immediate and significant changes in short-term rates. The response of long-term rates, however, is moderated by the process of expectation formation. Long-term interest rates are also anchored to some extent by the long-term potential growth rate. As a result, changes in the level of interest rates that result from changes in monetary policy have often been accompanied by changes in the slope and shape of the yield curve. Tighter monetary policy (in which the central bank increases short-term interest rates to reduce aggregate demand) has often resulted in a flattening of the yield curve (i.e. an increase in short-term rates relative to long-term rates), while looser monetary policy has often resulted in steepening of the yield curve. These changes in the slope of the yield curve may also be accompanied by changes in its shape (Figure 2.6).

A deeper understanding of these dynamics can help market participants design more effective trades that express views about yield curve movements and more effective hedges for bond portfolios or other positions exposed to interest rate risk.

Since the financial crisis of 2007–2008, central banks have increasingly adopted non-traditional monetary policy measures, including asset purchase programmes commonly known as quantitative easing. These are large-scale purchases of public sector (and, in some cases, private sector) fixed income securities by the central bank. The central bank holds the purchased securities on its balance sheet and pays for them by creating new reserve deposits at the central bank. This increases liquidity in the banking system, just as when the central bank conducts open market operations in traditional monetary policy. But asset purchases by central banks since the financial crisis have been on a much larger scale than traditional open market operations, and they have for the most part involved longer-term debt securities.

Asset purchase programmes offer central banks a way to reduce long-term rates directly to stimulate aggregate demand even when the short-term policy

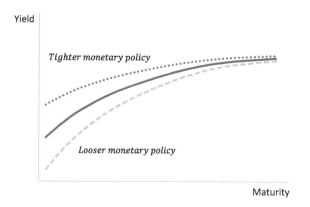

Figure 2.6 Monetary Policy Impacts on Bond Yield Curves.

or target rate has been reduced to zero. This creates an alternative channel through which monetary policy can operate but can alter the dynamics of the yield curve. Asset purchases change long-term interest rates, while short-term rates remain anchored by the central bank's policy or target rate being held near zero. The combined effect is to reduce the relative volatility of short-term rates and perhaps also the responsiveness of rates of all maturities to economic news (Swanson and Williams, 2014). In this environment, the traditional view of how monetary policy affects the slope and shape of the yield curve may be of limited relevance.

In some markets, such as Japan and the Eurozone, central banks have also experimented with negative policy rates that penalise banks for holding excess reserves, as an additional measure to encourage lending and stimulate aggregate demand. This has resulted in negative yields on government bonds in those markets even at medium and long maturities.

The European Central Bank stopped making net asset purchases in 2019, and the US Federal Reserve reduced the quantity of assets held on its balance sheet during the same period. Both institutions, however, quickly reversed this change and initiated new large-scale asset purchase programmes in 2020 in response to the financial and economic consequences of the COVID-19 pandemic. Central banks in other markets responded to the crisis in a similar way, flooding the market with liquidity and reducing interest rates to historically low levels. In 2022, central banks reversed course again, responding to increased price inflation linked to the impact of the war in Ukraine on food and energy prices and other factors by increasing policy rates and ending or reversing net purchases under asset purchase programmes.

Interest Rate Risk

Holding any fixed income security is subject to fluctuations in value due to changes in underlying interest rates. Identifying and controlling this interest rate risk is a key element of fixed income analysis and fixed income portfolio management.

There are many ways in which interest rate risk can be measured. The simple measures that investors use consider the price-yield relationship as a proxy for the relationship between a bond's price and changes in the underlying zero-coupon yield curve.

In a fixed income trading context, the most used risk measure of this type is basis point value (BPV). The BPV is the change in the bond's price that would result from a one-basis-point change in its yield (one basis point is 1/100th of a percentage point). This can be calculated simply by 'bumping' the yield by one basis point and recalculating the bond's price.

For the Government of Canada bond in Figure 2.4, the BPV is shown as 0.0851. Investors therefore estimate that a one-basis-point upward shift in the relevant yield curve would cause the price of the bond to fall by approximately

0.0851 per 100 nominal. A downward shift in the yield curve would result in a similar increase in price.

The BPV can be used to calculate the approximate change in mark-to-market value of a position of given nominal size for a one-basis-point shift in the yield curve. This is usually called the DV01 of the position. In our example, the DV01 of a position of CAD 1 million nominal in the bond is reported as CAD 850.77. Investors would expect to lose approximately this amount on a long position of CAD 1 million nominal in the bond if the yield curve were to shift upward by one basis point. In Figure 2.4, this is labeled PVBP, or price value of a basis point. There is some inconsistency in the labels applied to risk measures by different market participants.

The DV01 of a trading position or portfolio that contains multiple bonds is simply the sum of the DV01s of the individual positions. This makes DV01 especially useful in situations in which we are exposed to interest rate risk on multiple positions or in which we are using one financial instrument to hedge the interest rate risk on another.

In a fixed income portfolio management context, it is more common to describe interest rate risk in terms of duration. Two duration measures are reported for our example: Macaulay duration (9.4052) and modified duration (9.3347). As their size suggests, each of these duration measures is closely related to the bond's BPV.

The Macaulay duration is the bond's present-value-weighted time to re-payment, measured in years. For a coupon-paying bond, the Macaulay dura-tion will be less than the bond's maturity, because some of the cash flows will be received before the final redemption date. For a zero-coupon bond, the Macaulay duration will be equal to the maturity. These same properties hold even in a negative-yield environment (Barber and Dandapani, 2017).

Other things remaining equal, a shorter maturity, a higher coupon, or a higher yield will each result in a Macaulay duration that is a smaller number of years. Since these characteristics are also empirically associated with lower sensitivity to interest rate changes, duration is a good proxy for interest rate risk.

The modified duration is the Macaulay duration divided by one plus the bond's yield per coupon period. It is also measured in years but is often in-terpreted as the approximate percentage change in the bond's value for a one percentage point change in rates.

Durations do not 'add up' across positions in the simple way that DV01s do, but it is a simple matter to calculate the weighted average duration of a portfolio that contains multiple bonds.

BPV, DV01 and duration are 'local' measures of interest rate risk, in the sense that they only give accurate estimates of changes in value for small changes in the level of interest rates. As rates change, so will a bond's sensi-tivity to interest rates. The rate at which this occurs is indicated by the bond's convexity. In general terms, the higher the convexity, the more rapidly the bond's BPV, DV01 or duration will change as rates change. Like duration, a bond's convexity is affected by its coupon, its maturity, and its yield. For the bond in Figure 2.4, the convexity is reported as 93.3204. This is of the same magnitude as the square of the bond's duration (9.4052 years). Indeed, for a zero-coupon bond, the convexity is equal to the square of the number of years to maturity.

Credit Risk and Credit Spreads

> In this section we define and describe credit risk, exposure at default, default probability, loss given default, recovery rate, counterparty risk, credit spread, Z-spread, option-adjusted spread (OAS), and asset swap margin.

Credit Risk

All bonds are subject to credit risk: even the most highly rated sovereign may, in extreme circumstances, fail to repay its debt in a timely manner. For corporate bonds, however, as well as for some sovereigns, credit risk is a key driver of relative value.

Credit risk is the risk that a promised future payment will not be made. In lending agreements like bonds, credit risk is the risk that the borrower will not make interest and principal payments in full as they fall due. This depends on three factors:

- Exposure at default (i.e. the amount that investors are owed when the borrower defaults)
- Default probability (i.e. the probability that the borrower will default over a given horizon)
- Loss given default (i.e. the fraction of the total exposure at default that investors are ultimately unable to recover following default). We can also express this in terms of the recovery rate, which is just one minus the loss given default.

In principle, these three factors may all be unknown quantities to be estimated, and they may be inter-related. This can make credit risk very difficult to analyse. This is especially true in derivatives markets, where investors are exposed to the credit risk of their counterparties.

Consider, for example, a five-year fixed-for-floating interest rate swap in which Investor A is the fixed-rate payer and Investor B is the floating-rate payer. This means that Investor A has committed to pay Investor B a fixed annual interest rate on a specified notional amount over the next five years. Like the coupon payments in a bond, these fixed payments will be made at a specified frequency (e.g. annually) and calculated using an agreed day count convention. In exchange, Investor B has committed to pay Investor A interest on the same notional amount over the same period, but their payments will be calculated by applying a specified market reference interest rate that may increase or decrease over time as market conditions change. For example, they may make payments based on the USD Secured Overnight Financing Rate (SOFR) compounded daily over each annual settlement period. Since the USD SOFR rate will change over time, Investor B's payments to Investor A will be variable or floating.[1]

By convention, investors agree a fixed rate such that the present value of the fixed payments over the life of the swap is equal to the present value of the projected floating payments. The initial mark-to-market value of the swap is therefore zero. Over time, however, interest rates may change. This will change both the projected future SOFR rates and the interest rates at which the fixed and floating cash flows are discounted, which will change the mark-to-market value of the swap. In general, a fixed-rate payer will make a mark-to-market profit if rates go up (since this will increase the projected future floating payments and decrease the present value of the fixed payments) and a mark-to-market loss if rates go down. For the floating-rate payer, the situation is reversed: they will make a mark-to-market loss if rates go up and a mark-to-market profit if rates go down.

If a counterparty defaults (e.g. because they become insolvent), an investor will need to enter into a replacement swap with another counterparty. Since we cannot know how interest rates may change over the life of the swap, investors cannot be certain in advance how much they might lose if their counterparty were to default on some future date. Investors call this risk counterparty risk. It is a type of credit risk, but it also involves market risk, because the size of the exposure at default will depend on what happens to the level of interest rates. The joint evolution of these two sources of risk over the life of the swap may be quite complex, which makes counterparty risk difficult to analyse. In practice, counterparty risk in derivatives is managed through a combination of close-out netting (where two counterparties agree to offset the mark-to-market values of derivatives within a specified netting set in the event that either counterparty defaults) and collateralisation (where the counterparty with a positive mark-to-market value in the netted positions takes cash or other assets from the other counterparty that can be liquidated in the event of default). Counterparties also frequently make price or valuation adjustments to derivatives to account for counterparty risk that is not fully collateralised; collectively, these valuation adjustments are known as XVA.

For bonds and loans, things are a bit simpler, because investors can usually take their exposure at default to be equal to the promised redemption amount or balance outstanding. This allows investors to concentrate on analysing default probabilities and recovery rates when measuring credit risk.

Even with this simplifying assumption, however, measuring credit risk remains complicated. Companies operate in a wide variety of markets, sectors, and industries, creating exposure to a broad range of systematic and idiosyncratic risks. Sovereign borrowers are also subject to many different risks. Each entity (whether corporate or sovereign) that issues a bond will have its own default probability for each future horizon, and these probabilities will change over time as the credit quality of the entity deteriorates or improves in response to changing economic conditions.

There may also be default dependence among entities (i.e. they may have a greater or lesser tendency to default at or near the same time). This is particularly important when investors have joint exposure to several entities, as in a bond portfolio or through the collateral pool in a securitisation, since it may have a significant impact on the shape of the loss distribution and the level of unexpected loss due to default.

Finally, the various debt obligations issued by an entity may differ in seniority and security. As we discuss further below, these factors affect the expected recovery rate on an obligation in the event of default and are therefore an important consideration in measuring credit risk.

Credit Spreads

Investors are compensated for bearing credit risk. In bond markets, this takes the form of a credit spread: an enhanced return that compensates for expected default losses. We measure the credit spread at which each bond is trading relative to a specific benchmark; the benchmark is typically either government

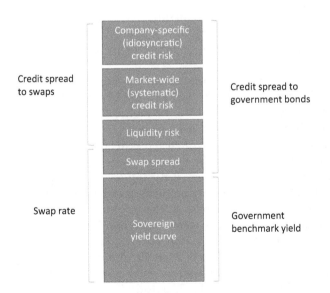

Figure 2.7 Relationship between Credit Spreads and Benchmark Returns.

bonds (i.e. the sovereign yield curve) or interest rate swaps. Figure 2.7 illustrates the relationship between credit spreads and benchmark returns.

The credit spread at which a bond trades relative to either benchmark will be driven by both company-specific and market-wide risk factors. When performing credit analysis, investors often focus on company-specific risks, but it is important to remember that credit spreads tend to widen or tighten together as the economic outlook changes. Credit spreads typically tighten during periods of economic expansion and widen during periods of economic contraction, and a widening of credit spreads may predict a future economic downturn (Gilchrist and Zakrajšek, 2012).

Liquidity (i.e. the ability to buy or sell an asset quickly without suffering a large adverse movement in price) is another important factor affecting bond returns. Investors value liquidity, and they demand compensation for holding illiquid assets. Liquidity in corporate bonds varies widely across issuers and issues, and part of the spread at which an illiquid bond trades relative to the benchmark will in fact be compensation for liquidity risk rather than credit risk. It is important to control for this when making comparisons between bonds.

The swap spread is the difference between the swap rate for a given tenor and the government bond yield for the corresponding maturity; it reflects differences in credit risk, liquidity, and other factors between the swap market and the government bond market. In some markets, it is not uncommon for swap rates to be lower than government bond yields, especially at longer maturities. In this case, the swap spread will be negative, and credit spreads measured relative to the swap benchmark will be larger than credit spreads measured relative to government bonds.

Credit spreads can be measured in different ways. Figure 2.8 shows some of these measures for the Apple Inc. 2.90% coupon bond maturing in September 2027. The bond was trading at a price of 107.777 to yield 1.624495% for settlement on 1 April 2021.

The simplest credit spread measure is the nominal spread, which is just the difference between the bond's yield and the benchmark government bond yield or swap rate for the same maturity. Figure 2.8 shows that the Apple Inc. 2.90% bond is trading at a nominal spread to government bonds of approximately 25.0 basis points. This is calculated as the difference between the yield on the Apple Inc. bond and the yield on a US Treasury bond of a similar maturity (the 1.25% US Treasury maturing on 31 March 2028). Similarly, the Apple Inc. bond is trading at a nominal spread of approximately 38.4 basis points to swaps (the comparison is to the six-year USD swap rate). In some financial market information systems, these nominal spreads are referred to as the G-spread and the I-spread, respectively.

Investors can obtain more robust credit spread measures by considering the shape of the relevant zero-coupon yield curve. One way in which this can be done is by calculating the Z-spread. The Z-spread is the number of basis points that must be added to each point on the benchmark zero-coupon

Figure 2.8 Credit Spread Measures for Apple Inc. 2027 Bond.
Source: Refinitiv Eikon.

yield curve to obtain a set of interest rates which, when applied to the bond's promised cash flows, give them a present value equal to the bond's market value. The Apple Inc. bond is trading at a Z-spread of approximately 34.2 basis points to swaps. Investors are therefore discounting the bond's cash flows at rates about 34.2 basis points higher than apply in the swap market for each future date as compensation for the additional credit risk associated with investing in the Apple Inc. bond.

Like the Z-spread, the option-adjusted spread (OAS) considers the shape of the benchmark zero-coupon yield curve. In addition, it adjusts for the value of any optionality in the bond that might affect the future cash flows received by investors. This can be an important consideration for callable bonds and for mortgage-backed securities that are subject to prepayment risk. For the Apple Inc. bond, the OAS is about 32.4 basis points, which is similar to the Z-spread.

Finally, the asset swap margin is the spread to the floating reference rate in the swap market that can be earned by combining a long position in the bond with a pay-fixed position in an interest rate swap. This asset swap structure hedges the interest rate risk in the bond but leaves the investor with exposure to the credit risk. The asset swap margin is therefore another measure of the credit spread that investors can earn as compensation for the credit risk in the bond.

The Z-spread, OAS, and asset swap margin show that investors are currently being offered a credit spread on the order of 32 to 34 basis points per year relative to swaps for taking on the credit risk associated with the Apple Inc. bond. By comparing this with the credit spreads at which other bonds are trading and the results of their own credit analysis, investors can determine which bonds look rich or cheap in terms of the compensation they offer for credit risk. Credit spreads are therefore a critical input to credit fixed income investment decisions.

Credit Default Swaps

In this section we define and describe credit default swaps (CDSs), credit events, CDS premium and credit event payments, protection buyer and protection seller, CDS par spread, fixed coupon rates and upfront payments, and CDS indices.

Credit spreads measure the compensation offered to investors for taking the credit risk of corporate or sovereign entities in the bond market. For some entities, it may also be possible for investors to take long or short exposure to credit risk through credit derivatives such as a credit default swap (CDS). The CDS market is an alternative venue for trading credit risk, and CDS premiums are a kind of credit spread.

A CDS is a derivative security in which one party makes a payoff to the other when a specified reference entity suffers a credit event. The reference entity may be a corporate or sovereign entity (in the case of single-name CDS) or a credit index based on a portfolio of corporate or sovereign entities (in the case of index CDS). For corporate entities, typical credit events include bankruptcy, failure to pay, and (in some markets) restructuring. For sovereign entities, typical credit events include failure to pay, repudiation, and moratorium.

The CDS market is a market for protection from credit events. The protection buyer makes periodic payments (called the CDS premium) to the protection seller over the life of the CDS contract or until a credit event occurs. If a credit event occurs during the life of the CDS contract, the protection seller makes a credit event payment to the protection buyer. This payment is structured as compensation for credit losses that would be suffered by debtholders following a credit event and is based on the recovery rate of a specified reference obligation of the reference entity. The CDS premium is the price that the protection buyer pays for protection from credit events that might affect the reference entity, and it is the price that the protection seller charges for taking the risk that they will have to make a credit event payment (and therefore suffer a loss) if a credit event occurs.

The full annualised market value of this protection is called the CDS par spread. It is measured in basis points per year and is applied to the notional amount traded in the CDS. If the reference entity is more likely to suffer a credit event, the protection seller will demand a larger par spread because they are exposed to greater risk. The protection buyer will be willing to pay a larger par spread because they are more likely to receive the credit event payment. Similarly, if the reference entity is less likely to suffer a credit event, the CDS par spread will be smaller.

In this sense, the CDS par spread is another measure of the credit spread for the reference entity. Investors expect to observe larger par spreads for entities that are weaker credits, and the par spread of a given entity to increase if its credit quality deteriorates.

Figure 2.9 shows the position of a protection buyer in a five-year CDS with Apple Inc. as the reference entity. The notional amount is USD 1 million, and the par spread (which is labelled 'Trade Level' in the screen image) is 28.3054 basis points per year.

If the credit quality of Apple Inc. were to deteriorate, the par spread would increase; if it were to improve, the par spread would decrease. These changes would result in a mark-to-market profit or loss, respectively, to the protection buyer in the CDS.

In practice, CDSs trade under market conventions that include standard coupon and maturity dates, a full first coupon, fixed coupon rates, and upfront payments. These conventions simplify cash flows and risk management in CDS and facilitate central clearing. Under these conventions, investors pay a fixed coupon of 100 basis points per year (labelled 'Running Coupon' in Figure 2.9) for five-year protection on Apple Inc. Since the market value of the protection (as measured by the par spread) is about 28 basis points per year, the fixed coupon is overpayment for protection. As compensation for this overpayment, the protection buyer will receive an upfront payment from the protection seller. Figure 2.9 shows that this upfront payment will be approximately 3.6860% of the notional amount. On a notional USD 1 million, this will be $36,860. A further adjustment is required for the accrued CDS coupon on the trade date.

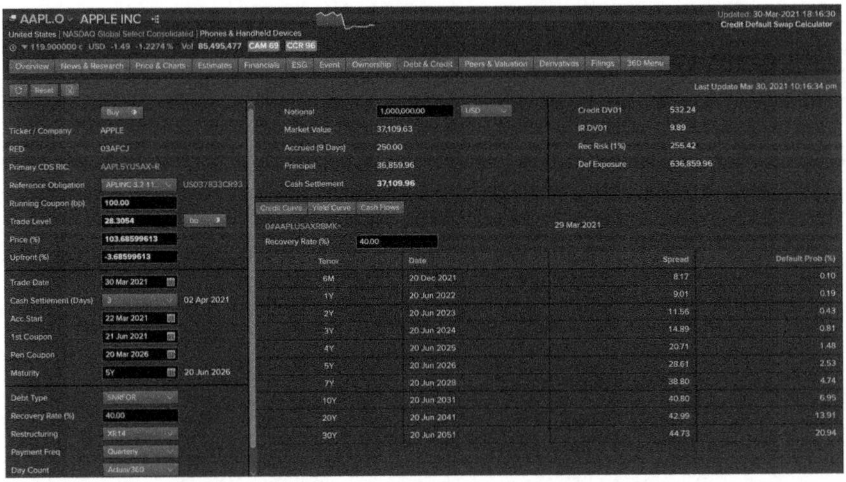

Figure 2.9 CDS Data for Apple Inc.
Source: Refinitiv Eikon.

The CDS par spread for Apple, Inc. in Figure 2.9 is slightly lower than the credit spreads reported for the Apple, Inc. bond in Figure 2.8. One reason for this difference is the time horizon: the bond has over six years remaining to maturity, whereas the CDS is for protection over a five-year period. It is quite common for investors to demand a larger spread for taking exposure to the credit risk of a particular entity over a longer period. The two instruments may also differ in liquidity and in their exposure to specific credit events that might affect Apple Inc.

Market participants can use CDSs to trade outright and relative value views on credit risk as an alternative to trading in credit risky bonds. For example, an investor who thinks that the credit quality of Apple Inc. is likely to deteriorate might choose to buy five-year protection on Apple when it is trading at a par spread of 28 basis points per year. If the investor is right, the credit quality will deteriorate and the par spread will increase (say, to 40 basis points per year). The investor can close out their position by selling protection at the wider spread, realising a profit. Similarly, an investor who thinks that the credit quality of Apple, Inc. is likely to deteriorate relative to the credit quality of Samsung Electronics Co., Ltd. might choose to buy five-year protection on Apple and sell five-year protection on Samsung. If they are right, the par spread on Apple will increase relative to the par spread on Samsung, and they will make a profit when closing their position, selling protection on Apple, and buying protection on Samsung. CDSs can also be used to hedge credit risk.

We have focused in this section on single-name CDS on corporate reference entities. Single-name CDSs on sovereign reference entities can be used to hedge credit risk, but their use in trading strategies is constrained by the European Short Selling Regulation, which includes a prohibition on entering into uncovered sovereign CDS (Howell, 2016).

The most liquid CDSs reference credit indices rather than individual reference entities. A credit index is constructed from a portfolio of reference entities. Buying or selling protection in index CDS creates exposure to a representative set of names from a part of the credit market. Trading index CDSs can be an efficient and effective way to express broad views on credit risk and to hedge credit exposure on portfolios.

Among the most widely traded CDSs are those that reference the CDX North America Investment Grade index (an equally weighted portfolio of 125 North American investment grade entities) and the iTraxx Europe Investment Grade index (an equally weighted portfolio of 125 European investment grade entities). There are also liquid markets in CDS that reference high yield and emerging market indices.

Covenants and Default

In this section we define and describe affirmative covenants, negative covenants (including negative pledge), maintenance and incurrence financial covenants, events of default, and cross-default and cross-acceleration clauses.

Covenants are restrictions on what the borrower can or cannot do during the life of a lending agreement. They are intended to protect investors and play a critical role in determining what constitutes an event of default. Because covenant packages vary widely across different types of bonds and loans, assessing covenant protection is a key element of credit analysis.

There are three main types of covenant:

- Affirmative
- Negative
- Financial

Affirmative covenants state what a borrower must do to be in compliance with the lending agreement (e.g. paying taxes and maintaining the condition of assets). They are, for the most part, legally important but uninteresting 'boilerplate' undertakings expected of any borrower.

Negative covenants limit what the borrower can do during the life of the lending agreement (e.g. limits on issuing debt or disposing of assets). Typically, they are intended to protect cash and assets on which investors will rely for recovery in the event of default. Negative covenants can be highly structured and specific to an individual issue. In some cases, they may have carve-outs that specify exceptions to the restrictions that they impose or baskets that allow deviation from the covenant up to a specified amount.

A negative pledge is a promise by the borrower not to create a security interest against assets without creating an equal and rateable lien to secure existing lenders covered by the pledge. This is the one negative covenant that is included in almost all lending agreements, including even unsecured investment grade bonds. It offers at least some protection to lenders who cannot obtain security through pledged collateral. It is, however, only enforceable against the grantor of the pledge and not against third parties who purchase the assets or obtain a security interest in violation of the pledge. This can limit its effectiveness (Bjerre, 1999).

Financial covenants require the borrower to meet certain financial performance measures during the life of the lending agreement (e.g. leverage ratio tests or coverage ratio tests). They may be maintenance or incurrence in type. Maintenance covenants are tested throughout the life of the agreement, typically at each financial reporting date. Failure to meet the specified test is a breach of the covenant. Incurrence covenants are tested only if the issuer takes a specific action, such as issuing new debt or an acquisition.

There can be significant differences in the covenant protection offered to lenders in bonds and loans. For example, lenders in leveraged loans (i.e. syndicated loans to sub-investment-grade borrowers) have traditionally been protected by both maintenance and incurrence covenants, whereas high yield bonds (i.e. bonds issued by sub-investment grade borrowers) usually include only incurrence covenants. Investors in high yield bonds are therefore less well protected, since maintenance covenants can act as an early warning system for increased credit risk. In recent years, however, leveraged loan issuance has been predominantly in the form of 'covenant-lite' loans which do not include maintenance covenants, blurring this distinction. Investment grade bonds usually offer investors little covenant protection, often limited to negative pledge and cross-default clauses.

Covenants are a governance issue as well as a credit issue since they affect the relationships among different stakeholders. Framed in this way, increased focus on ESG ratings may pressure issuers to strengthen covenant protection on high-yield debt (Walsh, 2020). In principle, environmental and sustainability goals can also be directly expressed as covenants in lending agreements. While this is rare, market practice continues to evolve. For example, Enel, an Italian utility company, issued a bond in September 2019 containing a covenant that would increase the coupon paid to investors by 25 basis points if the company did not meet a specified target for installed renewable generation capacity by the end of 2021 (Taylor, 2020).

Defaults are events or circumstances lenders and courts agree are sufficiently serious to justify the lender terminating the financing. These may relate to non-performance of the lending agreement (e.g. breach of obligations) or to credit events affecting the borrower (e.g. insolvency proceedings). An event of default will usually result in suspension of the borrower's right to draw down a loan and the acceleration of repayment of amounts due.

Cross-default or cross-acceleration clauses ensure that default on one obligation triggers default on other obligations of the same entity so that borrowers cannot selectively default on individual obligations. Not all lending agreements include cross-default or cross-acceleration clauses, but they are sufficiently common that, when analysing credit risk, we can usually think of default probabilities as attaching to entities rather than to obligations. The expected recovery rate in the event of default, however, can only be understood in the context of individual obligations.

Defaults due to the issuer violating the terms of the agreement that are not a failure to pay (e.g. by breaching a maintenance covenant) are called technical defaults. Although these may result in acceleration, they can instead lead to a compensating amendment to the lending agreement. This is less relevant for bonds than loans since bonds typically do not contain maintenance covenants. Payment defaults are more serious. If the failure to pay is not made good within a specified cure period, the investors may accelerate repayment. The issuer is likely to seek to restructure its debt under the protection of the relevant bankruptcy laws.

Security and Seniority

In this section we define and describe secured and unsecured bonds, fixed and floating charges, seniority, contractual subordination, structural subordination, and lien subordination.

Security and seniority are key factors affecting the recovery rate on individual obligations in the event of default and therefore a further important element in assessing credit risk.

A company may issue both secured and unsecured bonds. Secured bonds are backed by specific assets of the issuer. This security may be in the form of either a fixed charge (i.e. a charge over a fixed asset which the borrower is not permitted to sell, transfer, or dispose of during the life of the agreement) or a floating charge (i.e. a charge over assets that vary in quantity and value over time, such as inventory, and which only crystallises into a fixed charge in the event of default). Unsecured bonds are not backed by specific assets; they represent a general claim on the issuer.

Security in the form of pledged collateral enhances the credit quality of a bond or loan by granting secured lenders a prior claim over the assets in the event of default. This places them ahead of unsecured creditors and increases their expected recovery rate.

Seniority also affects the order of repayment of an issuer's obligations in the event of default. Senior claims must be repaid before claims that are subordinated to them. This gives senior claims a higher expected recovery rate, and therefore lower credit risk, than subordinated claims. Claims that have the same seniority or ranking in the event of default are described as being *pari passu*.

Security and seniority interact in ways that complicate the ranking of claims since secured claims have a prior claim on specific assets. This means that a secured claim may benefit from a higher recovery rate than a nominally senior but unsecured claim of the same entity. Any part of a secured claim that is not recovered from the assets on which it is secured becomes an unsecured claim and ranks *pari passu* with other unsecured claims of the same seniority.

Companies typically rely on various funding sources, including bank loans, bonds of differing degrees of seniority, and equity (Figure 2.10). Some of a company's debt obligations may be secured, while others are unsecured. Complex corporate structures, subsidiary guarantees, and other factors add further complexity. In practice, ranking claims can be difficult and requires careful analysis.

There are three different forms of subordination:

* Contractual subordination
* Structural subordination
* Lien subordination

Contractual subordination arises when debt is expressly subordinated by its own contractual terms. For example, a company may issue subordinated bonds that, in the event of default, will not be repaid until the company's senior debt has been repaid in full.

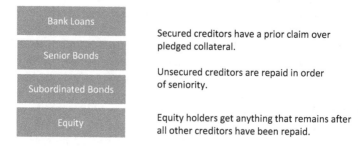

Figure 2.10 Corporate Capital Structure Ranking Hierarchy.

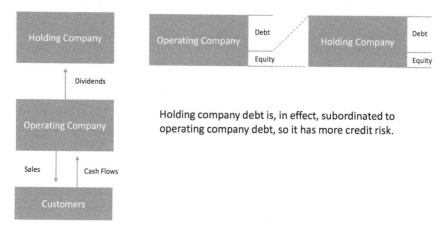

Figure 2.11 Relationship between Holding and Operating Companies.

Structural subordination arises when debt is effectively subordinated because of the issuer's place in a larger corporate structure (see Figure 2.11 for an illustration of different relationships). A common example is when a holding company that owns an operating company issues debt. In the event of default, investors in the holding company debt will rank behind all the creditors of the operating company and its subsidiaries, including unsecured and subordinated creditors, since their only claim is through the equity of the operating company held by the holding company. This makes the debt of the holding company structurally subordinated to the debt of the operating company, whatever its apparent contractual seniority. In some cases, however, the operating company may guarantee the debt of its holding company parent. This so-called upstream guarantee may overcome the structural subordination so that the claims of holding company creditors rank *pari passu* with those of operating company creditors. Many issuers are part of complex corporate structures that may create structural subordination.

The final type of subordination is another example of how security and seniority may interact. Leveraged loans are typically senior debt secured by a first lien (i.e. a priority legal claim) on assets of the issuer. High yield bonds

Debt type	Emergence Year			Default Year		
	2020	2019	1987-2020	2020	2019	1987-2020
Revolvers*	78.6%	89.6%	86.3%	81.8%	79.9%	86.3%
Term Loans**	48.5%	58.1%	72.6%	50.1%	52.7%	72.6%
Senior Secured Bonds	34.8%	45.9%	61.5%	34.8%	44.6%	61.4%
Senior Unsecured Bonds	8.6%	31.3%	46.9%	8.6%	40.5%	46.9%
Subordinated Bonds	0.9%	24.7%	27.9%	0.9%	24.7%	27.9%

The Moody's Ultimate Recovery Database primarily covers default resolutions of US nonfinancial companies. * Revolvers include cash revolvers and borrowing base facilities. ** Term loans refer to all types of term loans: first, second-lien, unsecured; for example in 2020 default cohort, there were 33 term loans, where only five were second-lien, the rest were first-lien term loans.

Figure 2.12 Ultimate Recovery Rates for US Non-Financial Companies.
Source: Moody's Investors Service, 2021.

may be secured or unsecured. If they are first-lien secured, then they rank *pari passu* with bank loans secured by a first lien on the same assets. In some cases, however, they may be secured by a second lien. This means that, in the event of default, they will receive proceeds from the collateral only after the first-lien debt has been repaid in full. This reduces their expected recovery rate, giving rise to lien subordination.

Security and seniority have a marked impact on recovery rates in the event of default (Figure 2.12). Average recovery rates on bank loans (most of which are senior debt secured by a first lien on assets) are significantly higher than recovery rates on other types of debt. Average recovery rates on senior secured bonds are greater than those on senior unsecured bonds, reflecting the value of security, and average recovery rates on subordinated bonds are lower than those on senior bonds.

Conclusions

Fixed income securities are an important part of the capital markets, providing stable long-term financing to companies and governments and wide-ranging combinations of risk and return to investors. Assessing these opportunities requires a clear understanding of interest rate risk and credit risk.

With respect to interest rate risk, maturity and coupon rate are key factors to be considered when selecting bonds and constructing fixed income portfolios. Many factors contribute to changes in the level of interest rates and the shape of the yield curve, including both traditional and non-traditional monetary policy actions by the central bank.

With respect to credit risk, investors must consider both the probability that an issuer will default over a given horizon and the expected recovery rate on specific obligations of the issuer in the event of default. Recovery rates depend on seniority, security, and other factors that may interact in complex ways.

The next chapter looks in more detail at how the ideas and tools described in this chapter are used by a variety of market participants, including credit rating agencies, credit analysts, securitisation structurers, portfolio managers, and institutional and private investors.

Note

1 SOFR is the reference rate for floating payments in the USD swap market, For swaps denominated in other currencies, other reference rates are used (e.g. SONIA in the sterling market). Prior to the end of 2021, interest rate swaps referenced forward-looking term LIBOR rates, but these rates have been discontinued.

References

Baker, L., McPhail, L. and Tuckman, B. (2018), *The Liquidity Hierarchy in the US Treasury Market: Summary Statistics from CBOT Futures and TRACE Bond Data. CFTC Research Paper.* [online]. Available at https://www.cftc.gov/sites/default/files/2018-11/Liquidity%20Hierarchy%20in%20Tsy%20Mkt%20v4_ada.pdf (Accessed 10 April 2021).

Barber, J. R. and Dandapani, K. (2017), 'Interest Rate Risk in a Negative Yielding World', *Frontiers in Finance and Economics*, 14(2), pp. 1–19.

Bjerre, C. (1999), 'Secured Transactions Inside Out: Negative Pledge Covenants Property and Perfection', *Cornell Law Review,* 84(2), pp. 305–393.

Gilchrist, S. and Zakrajšek, E. (2012), 'Credit Spreads and Business Cycle Fluctuations', *American Economic Review*, 102(4), pp. 1692–1720.

Goel, T. and Serena, J. M. (2020), 'Bonds and Syndicated Loans during the Covid-19 Crisis: Decoupled again?' *BIS Bulletin*, 29. [online]. Available at https://www.bis.org/publ/bisbull29.pdf (Accessed 20 December 2020).

Hill, A. and Callsen, G. (2020), *Time to Act: ICMA's 3rd Study into the State and Evolution of the European Investment Grade Corporate Bond Market* (International Capital Market Association). [online]. Available at https://www.icmagroup.org/assets/documents/Regulatory/Secondary-markets/Time-to-act-ICMAs-3rd-study-into-the-state-and-evolution-of-the-European-investment-grade-corporate-bond-secondary-market-040320.pdf (Accessed 10 April 2021).

Howell, E. (2016), 'Regulatory Intervention in the European Sovereign Credit Default Swap Market', *European Business Organization Law Review*, 17, pp. 319–353.

International Capital Market Association. (2020), *Bond Market Size.* [online]. Available at https://www.icmagroup.org/Regulatory-Policy-and-Market-Practice/Secondary-Markets/bond-market-size/ (Accessed 10 December 2020).

Lane, P. (2019), 'Determinants of the Real Interest Rate. Remarks at the National Treasury Management Agency'. [online]. Available at https://www.ecb.europa.eu/press/key/date/2019/html/ecb.sp191128_1~de8e7283e6.en.html, (Accessed 10 December 2020).

Loan Market Association (2018), *A Guide to Secondary Loan Market Transactions.* [online]. Available at https://www.lma.eu.com/application/files/2315/5653/5076/LMA-Guide-to-the-Secondary-Loan-Market-Transactions.pdf (Accessed 2 April 2020).

London Stock Exchange (2020), *Secondary Markets Factsheet.* [online]. Available at https://docs.londonstockexchange.com/sites/default/files/reports/Secondary%20Markets%20factsheet%20November%202020.pdf (Accessed 20 December 2020).

Moody's Investors Service (2021), *Annual Default Study: Following a Sharp Rise in 2020, Corporate Defaults will Drop in 2021.* Available at https://www.moodys.com/researchdocumentcontentpage.aspx?docid=PBC_1258722 (Accessed 2 April 2020).

Swanson, E. T. and Williams, J. C. (2014), 'Measuring the Effect of the Zero Lower Bound and Medium- and Longer-Term Interest Rates', *American Economic Review*, 104(10), pp. 3154–3185.

Taylor, B. (2020), 'Send Bond Covenants into Battle Against Climate Change', *Financial Times*, 17 August 2020. [online]. Available at https://www.ft.com/content/0472f192-00e3-4119-a8a7-c5b1a379fbce (Accessed 31 August 2020).

Theisen, A. (2018), *Developments in Credit Market Liquidity. Citi Global Credit and Securitized Markets Presentation.* [online]. Available at https://www.sec.gov/spotlight/fixed-income-advisory-committee/citi-developments-in-credit-market-liquidity-fimsa-011118.pdf (Accessed 1 September 2020).

Walsh, T. (2020), 'ESG Reframes Weak Covenants as Governance Issue', *International Financing Review*, 2322. [online]. Available at https://www.ifre.com/story/2266019/esg-reframes-weak-covenants-as-governance-issue-l5n2as4rf (Accessed 10 April 2020)

World Federation of Exchanges Database (2020), *2019 Annual Statistics Guide.* [online]. Available at https://www.world-exchanges.org/our-work/articles/2019-annual-statistics-guide (Accessed 20 December 2020).

3 Essential Concepts in Fixed Income Investing II

Participants and Portfolios

David Oakes

Chapter 2 (Fixed Income Investments) introduced ideas and analytical tools that measure risk and relative value in fixed income markets. This chapter shows how these ideas are applied by market participants. The extensive ways institutions and individuals contribute to the market functioning mean the chapter cannot possibly cover all its features. But the analysis is designed to illustrate the salient areas that investors and issuers focus on.

The first section reviews the central role and methodologies of credit rating agencies. The second, the responsibilities and priorities of credit analysts. The third, the purpose behind securitisation structures. The fourth, how portfolio managers use the tools described in the opening sections to make investment decisions. And lastly, a focus on performance measurement and attribution.

Credit Ratings

> In this section we define and describe credit rating, credit rating agency, credit rating methodology, cumulative default rate, and credit rating performance.

Most debt securities issued by companies have a credit rating assigned by one or more independent credit rating agency (CRA), and credit ratings are a practical requirement for access to public debt markets. Issuers pay CRAs to assign ratings to their debt and to monitor and update those ratings over time. Once a rating has been assigned, investors can usually access it free of charge. Many investors in corporate bonds rely on ratings when constructing investment portfolios and on credit analysis generated by CRAs when assessing credit quality.

Credit Rating Methodologies

Credit ratings are opinions about credit risk. They are forward-looking assessments of the borrower's ability and willingness to meet its obligations to lenders in full and on time. These opinions are relative: they rank an issuer or an obligation relative to other issuers or obligations, rather than express an

DOI: 10.4324/9781003055341-4

		Standard & Poor's (S&P)	Fitch Ratings	Moody's	Description
Investment Grade	Highest Quality	AAA	AAA	Aaa	Highest quality, subject to lowest level of credit risk. Extremely strong capacity to meet financial commitments.
Investment Grade	High Quality	AA+ AA AA-	AA+ AA AA-	Aa1 Aa2 Aa3	High quality, subject to very low credit risk. Very strong capacity to meet financial commitments.
Investment Grade	Medium Quality	A+ A A-	A+ A A-	A1 A2 A3	Upper-medium quality, subject to low credit risk. Strong capacity to meet financial commitments, but somewhat susceptible to adverse economic conditions.
Investment Grade		BBB+ BBB BBB-	BBB+ BBB BBB-	Baa1 Baa2 Baa3	Medium quality, subject to moderate credit risk. Adequate capacity to meet financial commitments, but more subject to adverse economic conditions.
Speculative (High Yield)	Speculative	BB+ BB BB-	BB+ BB BB-	Ba1 Ba2 Ba3	Speculative, subject to substantial credit risk. Less vulnerable in near term but faces major ongoing uncertainties with respect to adverse conditions.
Speculative (High Yield)		B+ B B-	B+ B B-	B1 B2 B3	Speculative, subject to high credit risk. More vulnerable to adverse conditions but currently has the capacity to meet financial commitments.
Speculative (High Yield)		CCC+ CCC CCC-	CCC	Caa2 Caa2 Caa3	Speculative, of poor standing, and subject to very high credit risk. Currently vulnerable and dependent on favourable conditions to meet financial commitments.
Speculative (High Yield)		CC C	CC C	Ca	Highly speculative. Default has not occurred but is a virtual certainty, with low expected recovery.
	Default	D	D	C	In default

Figure 3.1 Summary of the Credit Rating Scales of Three Major Credit Rating Agencies.

absolute view about the probability of loss due to a company defaulting on its obligations.

As seen in Figure 3.1, the highest quality rating (AAA or Aaa) is reserved for entities of excellent credit quality that are subject to the lowest level of credit risk. These entities are judged to have an extremely strong capacity to meet their financial commitments. As we move down the table, lower ratings (AA or Aa2, A or A2, BBB or Baa2, and so on) reflect increasing credit risk and greater exposure to possible default losses triggered by adverse economic or business conditions.

Issuers and obligations are commonly grouped into two broad categories: investment grade and speculative. Investment grade credits are of high to medium credit quality, corresponding to credit ratings from AAA (Aaa) to BBB- (Baa3). Speculative credits are of weaker credit quality, corresponding to ratings of BB+ (Ba1) or lower. These weaker credits are much more likely to default, and investors will demand larger credit spreads for holding them in portfolios. Issuers and obligations in this category are therefore also referred to as high yield.

This distinction between investment grade and speculative ratings is of practical importance because mutual funds and other institutional investors often operate under strict limits on the proportion of their holdings that can be allocated to speculative grade debt. This limits the market for this debt and makes it important for issuers who want to maintain access to debt financing to retain their investment grade rating. An issuer that loses its investment grade rating may find it difficult to raise debt financing or may only be able to do so at increased cost.

Many factors may contribute to a company losing its investment grade status. In February 2020, for example, Kraft Heinz, the global food and beverage company, was downgraded to BB+ over concerns that it was maintaining an aggressive financial policy (including high leverage and unchanged dividend payments to shareholders) in the face of a continued decline in earnings (Fitch Ratings, 2020a). In March and April 2020, Marks & Spencer, the UK-based retailer, was also downgraded to BB+, largely in response to concern about the adverse impact on the company's clothing and home division of the partial lockdown imposed in response to the COVID-19 pandemic (Fitch Ratings, 2020b).

Each rated entity is assigned an issuer rating. Ratings for corporate issuers are based on a broad range of financial and non-financial factors, including the competitive position of the company, its management and governance, and key financial indicators. Ratings for sovereign issuers are similarly based on a range of factors correlated with ability to pay.

Ratings are also assigned to individual obligations. In addition to the credit quality of the issuer, an obligation rating considers other factors that may affect credit quality, such as security and seniority. As we saw in the last chapter, these can have a significant impact on recovery rates. In some cases, the agency may also issue a separate recovery rating.

The rating assigned to an entity or obligation may change over time. If the agency anticipates that a rating may change over the next one to two years, it may issue a ratings outlook. The outlook will indicate that the possible change is positive, negative, stable, or developing (i.e. that it is uncertain whether the rating will be revised upward or downward). If a change in rating is anticipated in the near term (e.g. within 90 days), the agency may place the rating on credit watch. Ratings may also change without first being placed on ratings outlook or credit watch.

Rating agencies try to apply a consistent methodology when assigning ratings to issuers in the same sector and to similar obligations. For issuer ratings, this often involves identifying key business and financial risk factors and assigning scores for each factor. These scores are combined to arrive at a preliminary rating. This preliminary rating may then be modified in light of factors not explicitly considered when assigning factor scores. Ratings for individual obligations are then derived from issuer ratings by considering additional factors that affect recovery rates, such as security and seniority.

The methodologies that agencies use to assign ratings in specific sectors and industries are complex and allow considerable scope for expert judgement. The factors and weightings considered when assigning a company rating in the retail industry, for example, will be different than those considered for a company in aerospace and defence. To illustrate the process by which ratings are assigned, consider again the Apple Inc. 2.90% coupon bond maturing on 12 September 2027 described in the previous chapter. This senior

Broad Rating Factor	Factor Weighting	Rating Sub-Factor	Sub-Factor Weighting
Scale	20%	Revenue	10%
		EBIT	10%
Business Profile	15%	Business Profile	15%
Profitability & Efficiency	20%	EBITDA Margin	10%
		Operating Income ROA (Net of Cash[5])	10%
Leverage and Coverage	30%	Debt / EBITDA	10%
		EBIT / Interest Expense	10%
		FCF / Debt	10%
Financial Policy	15%	Financial Policy	15%
Total	100%	Total	100%

Figure 3.2 Methodology Scorecard for Diversified Technology Sector.
Source: Moody's Investor Services, 2018.

unsecured bond had an S&P rating of AA+ and a Moody's rating of Aa1. Moody's rating will have been based primarily on its Diversified Technology rating methodology (Figure 3.2).

Each sub-factor is assigned a score, typically based on historical data over the preceding 12 months, although the rating committee may also choose to consider expected future performance. The scores for each sub-factor are mapped to a broad Moody's rating category and these are converted to a numerical value. For example, Aaa = 1; Aa = 3; A = 6; Baa = 9; Ba = 12, and so on.

Finally, the sub-factor scores are combined to give factor scores and the weighted average factor score (based on the weightings described in the methodology) is mapped back to an alphanumeric rating based on the ranges described in Figure 3.3.

Before assigning a rating, however, the rating committee will also consider factors not explicitly referenced by the scorecard. For example, there may be a reason to believe that the future performance of the company will differ from that indicated by the largely historical data used in the scoring process. Other factors such as the quality of management, corporate governance, and the quality and reliability of financial data may also be considered. Excess cash holdings, liquidity management, and event risk are additional factors that are usually assessed on a qualitative basis rather than through the scorecard. Once all of these factors have been considered, a final rating is assigned. Obligation ratings for subordinated bonds are likely to be reduced relative to the issuer or senior unsecured rating (a process known as 'notching') to reflect the lower expected recovery rate on subordinated debt.

Moody's identified several key rating considerations in a periodic review of its Apple Inc. ratings in September 2020, including the company's 'exceptional liquidity, solid profitability, growing business diversification, and ... expectations for about $50 billion in free cash flow in fiscal year 2021'

Scorecard-Indicated Outcome	Aggregate Weighted Total Factor Score
Aaa	x < 1.5
Aa1	1.5 ≤ x < 2.5
Aa2	2.5 ≤ x < 3.5
Aa3	3.5 ≤ x < 4.5
A1	4.5 ≤ x < 5.5
A2	5.5 ≤ x < 6.5
A3	6.5 ≤ x < 7.5
Baa1	7.5 ≤ x < 8.5
Baa2	8.5 ≤ x < 9.5
Baa3	9.5 ≤ x < 10.5
Ba1	10.5 ≤ x < 11.5
Ba2	11.5 ≤ x < 12.5
Ba3	12.5 ≤ x < 13.5
B1	13.5 ≤ x < 14.5
B2	14.5 ≤ x < 15.5
B3	15.5 ≤ x < 16.5
Caa1	16.5 ≤ x < 17.5
Caa2	17.5 ≤ x < 18.5
Caa3	18.5 ≤ x < 19.5
Ca	x ≥ 19.5

Figure 3.3 Scorecard Credit Rating Outcome.
Source: Moody's Investor Services, 2018.

(Moody's Investors Service, 2020b). These factors were still relevant in early 2021 and are likely to have contributed to the solid investment grade rating and stable outlook for the Apple Inc. 2.90% coupon bond at that time.

Credit Rating Performance

Credit ratings are only useful to investors if they contain timely information about how likely an issuer is to default and (in the case of obligation or re-covery ratings) the likely recovery rate in the event of default. Evidence on this point is mixed.

Lower credit ratings do correspond to higher default rates over both short and long time spans in every region of the world. In this sense, credit ratings contain information that helps predict defaults. Investment grade issuers seldom default, and issuers frequently experience a series of ratings downgrades as they move towards default (Figure 3.4).

The frequency at which AAA-rated issuers defaulted one year after issuance is 0.00%. Even over a ten-year horizon, this frequency remains small (0.70%). As we move down the table into lower rating classes default frequencies increase, exactly as we might expect if ratings successfully distinguish between weaker and stronger credits. Note also that the cumulative default frequency increases with the horizon for all rating classes.

Default frequencies for sovereign issuers show a similar pattern to those for corporate issuers across rating classes and over time, with default rates on foreign-currency-denominated debt in general higher than those on local-currency denominated debt (S&P Global Ratings, 2020b) (Figure 3.5).

The relative, rather than absolute, performance of ratings can be measured by comparing the proportion of issuers within each rating class to the proportion of issuers who default over a specific horizon. Figure 3.6 shows this relationship for global corporate defaults over a one-year horizon. The horizontal axis measures the cumulative proportion of issuers, ordered by rating from lowest to highest. The vertical axis measures the cumulative proportion of defaulters, also ordered by rating. If ratings perfectly ordered issuers according to default risk, all of the defaults would come from the issuers that had the lowest ratings. This would give a relationship like the kinked line labelled 'Ideal Curve' in the diagram. If instead ratings were entirely random and contained no information, ordering issuers according to their rating would make no difference to the cumulative proportion of defaults. This

Rating	(%) Time Horizon Years														
	1	2	3	4	5	6	7	8	9	10	11	12	13	14	15
AAA	0.0	0.0	0.1	0.2	0.3	0.5	0.5	0.6	0.6	0.7	0.7	0.8	0.8	0.8	0.9
AA	0.0	0.1	0.1	0.2	0.3	0.4	0.5	0.6	0.6	0.7	0.8	0.8	0.9	0.9	1.0
A	0.1	0.1	0.2	0.3	0.5	0.6	0.8	0.9	1.1	1.2	1.3	1.5	1.6	1.7	1.8
BBB	0.2	0.4	0.8	1.1	1.5	1.9	2.3	2.6	2.9	3.2	3.6	3.8	4.0	4.3	4.5
BB	0.6	1.9	3.5	5.0	6.4	7.8	8.9	9.9	10.8	11.6	12.3	13.0	13.6	14.1	14.7
B	3.3	7.8	11.8	14.9	17.4	19.4	21.0	22.3	23.5	24.6	25.6	26.3	27.0	27.6	28.2
CCC/CC	28.3	38.3	43.4	46.4	48.6	49.6	50.8	51.5	52.2	52.8	53.2	53.7	54.2	54.7	54.8
Investment Grade	0.1	0.2	0.4	0.6	0.9	1.1	1.3	1.5	1.7	1.9	2.1	2.2	2.4	2.5	2.7
Speculative Grade	3.7	7.2	10.2	12.6	14.6	16.3	17.7	18.8	19.9	20.8	21.6	22.3	22.9	23.5	24.0
All	1.5	3.0	4.3	5.4	6.3	7.0	7.6	8.2	8.7	9.1	9.5	9.8	10.1	10.4	10.7

Figure 3.4 Percentage Global Corporate Average Cumulative Default Rates (1981–2020).

Rating	(%) Time Horizon Years														
	1	2	3	4	5	6	7	8	9	10	11	12	13	14	15
AAA	0.0	0.0	0.0	0.0	0.0	0.0	0.0	0.0	0.0	0.0	0.0	0.0	0.0	0.0	0.0
AA	0.0	0.0	0.0	0.0	0.0	0.0	0.0	0.0	0.0	0.0	0.0	0.0	0.0	0.0	0.0
A	0.0	0.0	0.3	0.8	1.4	2.0	2.6	3.2	3.9	4.7	5.5	6.3	7.2	7.8	8.9
BBB	0.0	0.5	1.2	1.8	2.3	2.9	3.6	4.0	4.4	4.8	5.3	5.8	6.3	7.4	8.1
BB	0.4	1.5	2.1	2.8	4.1	5.4	6.7	8.5	9.8	10.8	11.6	12.4	13.3	14.3	14.9
B	2.3	5.6	8.6	11.5	14.0	16.1	18.3	20.4	21.8	22.9	24.6	26.1	26.7	27.3	28.1
CCC/CC	38.6	45.7	53.9	56.6	59.5	65.3	68.2	68.2	68.2	68.2	68.2	68.2	68.2	68.2	68.2
Investment Grade	0.0	0.1	0.3	0.6	0.8	1.1	1.4	1.6	1.8	2.1	2.3	2.6	2.9	3.2	3.5
Speculative Grade	2.9	5.4	7.5	9.3	11.3	13.1	15.0	16.8	18.1	19.1	20.3	21.3	22.0	22.8	23.4
All	1.1	2.1	3.0	3.8	4.7	5.5	6.3	7.1	7.6	8.1	8.6	9.2	9.6	10.0	10.4

Figure 3.5 Sovereign Local Currency Cumulative Average Default Rates (1981–2019).
Sources: S&P Global Ratings Research and S&P Global Market Intelligence's CreditPro®. S&P Global Ratings, 2020b.

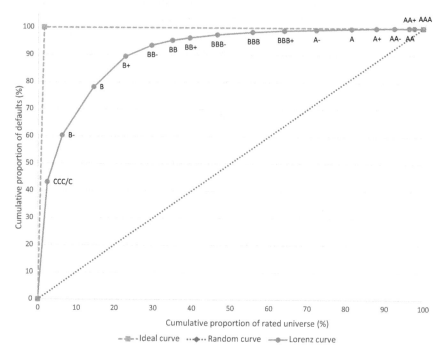

Figure 3.6 Global One-Year Relative Corporate Ratings Performance (1981–2019). Source: S&P Global Ratings, 2020a.

would give a relationship like the diagonal line labelled 'Random Curve' in the diagram, along which the cumulative proportion of defaults is the same as the cumulative proportion of issuers considered. The actual performance of ratings is shown in the diagram by the curve that passes through points labelled with rating classes, which is called a Lorenz curve. It shows, for example, that approximately 80% of defaults came from issuers rated B or lower, which made up less than 15% of all issuers (S&P Global Ratings, 2020a).

Over this short horizon, the relative performance of ratings is quite good: most of the defaults come from the lowest rating classes, and almost all the defaulting entities had speculative-grade ratings one year prior to default. Over longer horizons, as we might expect, the relationship is less ideal, since entities often experience multiple successive downgrades on their way to default. Figure 3.7 shows the relative performance of corporate ratings over a 5-year horizon.

A larger proportion of defaults come from the higher rating classes, including a significant number from entities that had investment grade ratings five years prior to default. Similar patterns are observed in the relative performance of sovereign credit ratings.

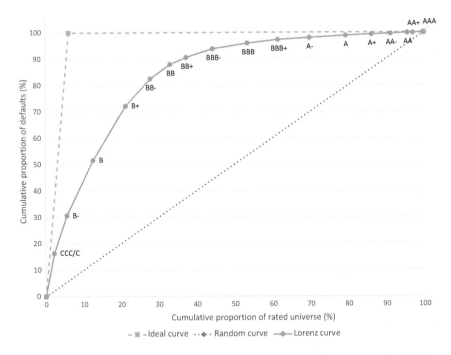

Figure 3.7 Global Five-Year Relative Corporate Ratings Performance (1981–2019).
Source: S&P Global Ratings, 2020a.

Rating agencies must strike a difficult balance in assigning ratings that are accurate at a point in time and sufficiently forward-looking to apply through the economic cycle. There is evidence that ratings vary more over time than would be consistent with the long-term, through-the-cycle horizon that the agencies themselves claim to adopt (Lobo et al., 2017).

Credit ratings do not have the same meaning when assigned to different asset classes or instrument types. Default rates by initial rating, accuracy ratios (a measure of the extent to which bonds default from lower rating categories), and migration metrics all vary significantly across broad asset classes (e.g. corporate versus sovereign debt) and can be very different for structured finance products than for ordinary bonds (Cornaggia et al., 2017). This is an important factor for investors to consider when using ratings to assess credit quality.

Finally, there is the question of whether rating upgrades and downgrades lead or lag changes in market perception of credit risk as reflected in credit spreads. Earlier studies suggest that rating announcements (including rating reviews) contain information that affects credit spreads. In this sense, ratings are useful to investors and not redundant (Micu et al., 2006). More recent studies suggest that, for issuers on which credit default swaps (CDS) are traded, the information content of rating changes and reviews is reflected in CDS spreads before the change in rating is announced. The monitoring role of rating agencies may therefore be less important to investors when the CDS market offers an alternative venue for trading credit risk (Kiesel et al., 2018). There is, however, limited liquidity in single-name CDS on most individual entities.

The Rise of ESG

Environmental, social, and governance (ESG) factors can have an important impact on credit ratings. Governance issues are, of course, central to any assessment of a company's ability to carry out its strategy and control risk. But environmental and climate issues may also create risks that reduce credit quality or opportunities that improve business prospects for certain companies; this is particularly true in the energy sector (S&P Global Ratings, 2017). Social factors also have an increasingly important impact on ratings (S&P Global Ratings, 2018). Overall, Moody's estimates that ESG risks were material in one-third of its private sector ratings actions in 2019 (Moody's Investors Service, 2020a).

Methods like those used in credit ratings can be used to create independent ESG ratings. Many different companies offer ESG ratings or scores, including MSCI, Sustainalytics, Bloomberg, and Refinitiv. The major credit rating agencies have also moved into this space by acquiring existing ESG rating companies. Typically, ESG ratings are assigned through rules-based methodologies that combine scores for various environmental, social, and governance factors, much as we saw earlier is the case for credit ratings. As with credit ratings, ESG ratings must strike a balance between point-in-time accuracy and forward-looking stability. They must also apply a consistent methodology across issuers and over time.

Credit Analysis

> In this section we define and describe corporate credit analysis, earnings and cash flow measures, financial ratios, and sovereign credit analysis and ratings.

Credit ratings contain valuable information about the credit quality of issuers and obligations, and many market participants rely on that information when making investment decisions. As we have seen, however, ratings are imperfect. Institutional investors such as pension funds, insurance companies, investment companies, and hedge funds employ credit analysts to generate independent credit research that can help them construct more effective credit portfolios, and investment banks offer credit research to their clients.

Corporate Issuers

There are multiple ways to conduct credit analysis. For corporate entities and obligations, one possibility is to start from the 'top-down' by assessing risk at the level of the global economy. This includes analysis of the current and forecasted macroeconomic environment and its likely impact on individual industries and sectors. The competitive situation, management, and financial health of entities then follows. At a final stage, we might identify character-istics of individual obligations, such as security or seniority, that affect their value.

Macroeconomic factors are external sources of systematic risk that contrib-ute to credit spreads, including general macroeconomic conditions (e.g. the unemployment rate and the inflation rate), the direction of the economy (e.g. real GDP growth), and financial market conditions (e.g. interest rates and stock market conditions). In empirical studies, however, the significance level and even the signs of coefficients for these variables can depend on which variables are included, which makes it difficult to draw clear conclusions about how to incorporate macroeconomic analysis when measuring credit risk (Figlewski et al., 2012).

Credit spreads are also subject to external and internal non-financial risks that are specific to each entity. These may be related to the competitive po-sition of the company within its industry, its ability to maintain or improve that position over time, or its ability to organise itself to take maximum advantage of competitive opportunities. We can think of these as sources of idiosyncratic or entity-specific risk.

One popular framework for analysing competition is Porter's Five Forces. This emphasizes the importance of customers, suppliers, potential entrants, and substitute products in shaping competition among rival companies and determining profitability and potential growth (Porter, 1979). A company's ability to organise effectively to solve problems can also be a critical factor determining its success. Entity level analysis of credit risk may therefore also benefit from a consistent approach to assessing organisation effectiveness. One way is through the McKinsey 7-S framework, which emphasises that structure is not organisation (Waterman et al., 1980).

Credit risk and credit spreads also depend on financial risk factors that affect the entity's ability to generate the cash flows needed to service its debt. Credit analysts can assess the financial health of the company by per-forming financial analysis. The quality of this analysis may be constrained by the quality of the information available and the frequency with which it is updated.

Since companies must generate cash to make coupon and redemption pay-ments, analysis of company-specific credit risk often focuses on financial risk factors related to earnings and cash flow. For public companies, historical values can be calculated from the figures reported in financial statements. For private companies, these must be estimated. Professional analysts also issue forecasts of earnings that can be used to assess the near-term financial health of the company. Earnings measures include:

- EBIT (Earnings Before Interest and Taxes)
- EBITDA (Earnings Before Interest, Taxes, Depreciation, and Amortisation)

EBITDA is essentially net income with interest, taxes, depreciation, and amortisation added back in. It is often used to compare profitability between companies and industries, because it eliminates from reported earnings the effect of financing and accounting decisions related to operating capital. EBITDA does not, however, measure cash flows available to make payments to investors, since funding working capital and replacing worn-out capital are essential to the continued health of the company. EBIT also does not measure cash flows available to investors, since reported depreciation and amortisation are accounting numbers that may, in some cases, show little relation to required investment in new and replacement capital. Wherever possible, therefore, financial analysis of the company should focus on measures directly related to cash flows. Two such measures are usually constructed:

- Operating cash flow (EBITDA minus cash interest and taxes paid, adjusted for changes in working capital and other non-cash items in the income statement)
- Free cash flow (operating cash flow minus capital expenditures)

Ultimately, free cash flow represents cash available for distribution to investors, including the company's bondholders. It is important that these measures be forward-looking, since investors are interested in the company's ability to meet future debt payment obligations.

Analysts also construct and analyse other fundamental measures related to company performance, including profitability and earnings quality (the proportion of earnings that is cash rather than accrued earnings).

Beyond these measures of current and forecast performance, analysis of company-specific credit risk focuses on actual and forecast values for key financial ratios related to the ability of the company to meet debt service payments and its general financial health. These include:

- Leverage (Debt/Equity or Debt/Assets)
- Debt to EBITDA (Debt/EBITDA)
- Current ratio (Current Assets/Current Liabilities)
- Quick ratio (Liquid Assets/Current Liabilities)
- Interest coverage (EBIT/Interest or EBITDA/Interest)

Leverage matters because a company with more debt on its balance sheet may be at greater risk of financial distress in an economic downturn as it struggles to meet payment obligations to its creditors. Coverage ratios assess the ability to service debt from forecast earnings.

These factors are also key inputs in credit ratings. This makes sense, since a credit rating is a forward-looking assessment of credit risk. There are also similarities between the use of forecast earnings, cash flows, and financial ratios in credit analysis and their use in equity analysis. In equity analysis, however, the objective is usually to value a company's operations so as to estimate the fair value of the shareholders' residual claim on the company's assets. Credit analysis focuses much more directly on the company's ability to generate the free cash flows it will need to meet its obligations to creditors in full and on time.

Once this entity-level credit analysis is complete, further adjustment may be needed to consider the impact of security, seniority, and covenant protection on specific obligations.

Sovereign Issuers

For sovereign entities, a different approach is required. Sovereign governments differ from other issuers in several ways: they have the ability to reduce expenditures or increase taxes to service debt; there is no higher authority to compel debt resolution in the event of default; and there is a high probability that they will survive even in the event of default. Sovereign credit analysis therefore focuses on factors related to the strength of the economy, the quality of institutions and governance, and the government's fiscal position. It also typically includes an assessment of the sovereign's exposure to events that might adversely affect its ability to meet its obligations to creditors, such as political upheaval, loss of access to funding needed to refinance maturing debt, or a banking crisis.

These same factors inform sovereign credit ratings. As with ratings for corporate entities, the process often begins with a scorecard that indicates key factors and sub-factors and the weights assigned to them (Figure 3.8).

The combined factor scores are used to determine a three-notch range on Moody's alphanumeric scale for the preliminary issuer rating. This preliminary rating may then be subject to modification based on other considerations, such as partial guarantees from other entities (e.g. multilateral development banks) and event risk and ESG factors not captured in the scorecard. Central bank debt may also require special consideration (Moody's Investors Service, 2019).

Issuer ratings for sovereigns typically apply to senior unsecured debt. As with corporate entities, ratings for debt that is not senior unsecured may be 'notched' upward or downward to reflect differences in security and seniority. For the most part, sovereign credit ratings do not distinguish between foreign currency and local currency obligations. Where a government faces constraints on access to external liquidity, however, its foreign currency debt may be assigned a lower rating.

Credit risk is a key factor influencing returns on fixed income securities, making reliable credit analysis critical to constructing and managing fixed income portfolios. Credit analysis can also provide valuable insights for issuers and their investment banking advisors.

Factor	Sub-factor	Sub-factor Weighting	Metric/Sub-sub-factor	Metric / Sub-sub-Factor Weighting
Factor: Economic Strength	Growth Dynamics	35%	Average Real GDP Growth $_{t-4\ to\ t+5}$	25%
			Volatility in Real GDP Growth $_{t-9\ to\ t}$	10%
	Scale of the Economy	30%	Nominal GDP (US$ bn) $_t$	30%
	National Income	35%	GDP per Capita (PPP, Int. USD) $_t$	35%
	Adjustment to Factor Score	0 - 9 notches	Other	
Factor: Institutions and Governance Strength	Quality of Institutions	40%	Quality of Legislative and Executive Institutions	20%
			Strength of Civil Society and the Judiciary	20%
	Policy Effectiveness	60%	Fiscal Policy Effectiveness	30%
			Monetary and Macroeconomic Policy Effectiveness	30%
	Adjustment to Factor Score	0 - 3 notches	Government Default History and Track Record of Arrears	
		0 - 3 notches	Other	
Factor: Fiscal Strength	Debt Burden	50%[1]	General Government Debt / GDP $_t$	25%
			General Government Debt / Revenue $_t$	25%
	Debt Affordability	50%[1]	General Government Interest Payments / Revenue $_t$	25%
			General Government Interest Payments / GDP $_t$	25%
	Adjustments to Factor Score	0 - 6 notches	Debt Trend $_{t-4\ to\ t+1}$	
			General Government Foreign Currency Debt / General Government Debt $_t$	
			Other Non-Financial Public Sector Debt / GDP $_t$	
			Public Sector Financial Assets and Sovereign Wealth Funds / General Government Debt $_t$	
		0 - 3 notches	Other	
Factor: Susceptibility to Event Risk	Political Risk	Minimum Function[2]	Domestic Political and Geopolitical Risk	
	Government Liquidity Risk	Minimum Function[2]	Ease of Access to Funding	
	Banking Sector Risk	Minimum Function[2]	0 - 2 scoring categories	Adjustment to Sub-factor Score High Refinancing Risk
			Risk of Banking Sector Credit Event (BSCE)	
			Total Domestic Bank Assets / GDP $_t$	
			0 - 2 scoring categories	Adjustment to Sub-factor Score
	External Vulnerability Risk	Minimum Function[2]	External Vulnerability Risk	
			0 - 2 scoring categories	Adjustment to Sub-factor Score
	Adjustment to Factor Score	0-2 scores		

[1] For more details about how these weights may vary, please refer to our discussion on the Treatment of Reserve Currency Countries and HIPC/IDA Countries within the Fiscal Strength section of the methodology.

[2] The aggregation of Political Risk, Government Liquidity Risk, Banking Sector Risk and External Vulnerability Risk follows a minimum function, i.e. as soon as one area of risk warrants an assessment of elevated risk, the country's overall Susceptibility to Event Risk is scored at that specific, elevated level.

Figure 3.8 Sovereign Bond Ratings Scorecard.
Source: Moody's Investor Service, 2019.

Securitisation and Covered Bonds

In this section we define and describe securitisation, collateral pool, special purpose vehicle (SPV), mortgage-backed securities (MBS), asset-backed securities (ABS), credit enhancement, collateralised debt obligations (CDO), and covered bonds.

Fixed income instruments expose investors to various risks. In this sense, every bond or loan has certain inherent risk characteristics that may make it appealing to different investors.

By combining bonds or loans and making use of specially designed legal entities and security structures, however, it is possible to create new financial instruments with quite different cash flows and risk profiles than those of the ordinary bonds or loans from which they are constructed. These new instruments, some of which may be quite complex, can be marketed to investors with specific risk appetites and offer alternative sources of financing for corporate borrowers and financial institutions. We call the process by which these new instruments are created structured finance. A core element of structured finance is securitisation.

Securitisation

Securitisation is a structured finance technique in which assets or receivables that generate cash flows are purchased by a Special Purpose Vehicle (SPV) that simultaneously issues securities that are sold to investors. The purchase price paid by the investors for the securities funds the purchase of the assets, and the cash flows generated by the assets or receivables are used to pay interest and principal on the securities.

The securitised assets or receivables are sometimes referred to as the collateral pool. The purpose of securitisation is to convert these illiquid assets into securities that can be sold to investors.

Many different types of collateral may be securitised. Common examples include:

- Mortgage-backed securities (MBS) based on residential or commercial mortgage loans
- Asset-backed securities (ABS) based on consumer loans (e.g. credit card receivables or automobile leases)
- Whole business securitisations (WBS) based on receivables of a whole operating business (e.g. sports franchise ticket revenue)

In the simplest securitisations, the SPV issues a single class of securities. Since payments to these securities must be financed by payments made by the collateral, they share the risk and return characteristics of the collateral pool. These are known as pass-through securities.

In more complex securitisations, the SPV may issue several classes of securities, each with a different priority claim on the collateral assets and on the cash flows that they generate. In effect, the SPV creates a capital structure of debt obligations backed by the collateral, each with its own risk and return characteristics. These more complex securitisations are known as collateralised debt obligations (CDOs) and each security class is called a tranche of the CDO.

There are several steps to create a simple securitisation. First, the originator of the loans or receivables to be securitised segregates them from other business receipts and creates the SPV. Next, the originator transfers the rights to the receivables to the SPV in exchange for the purchase price. Finally, the SPV issues ABS instruments to investors, using the receipts from the sale of the ABS to finance the acquisition of the collateral from the originator and using the cash flows generated by the collateral to make interest and principal payments to investors.

Two important motives for securitisation are cheaper funding and credit arbitrage. The securitised assets may have lower credit risk than the originator or they may be a statistically more reliable source of credit risk. By segregating the collateral assets and securitising them, the originator may reduce its funding costs. Because securitisation is, in part, about repackaging illiquid assets as securities that can be sold to investors, the originator or manager of a securitisation can demand a premium from investors for granting them access to a pool of risk to which they would not normally have exposure (e.g. residential mortgages, credit card loans, or student loans). More generally, securitisation is an alternative funding source for originators. Banks, for example, can use securitisation to finance mortgage loans rather than relying solely on deposits from their customers.

There are two other motives for securitisation that, while once important drivers of the market, have become less significant in recent years. The first of these is balance sheet benefits: removing receivables from the balance sheet may improve return on capital. Achieving this off-balance-sheet treatment, however, is increasingly difficult under current accounting and regulatory practices. The second motive is reducing regulatory capital. This has also become more difficult to achieve since regulatory reforms tightened rules regarding the quantity and quality of capital that must be held by banks.

The SPV is designed to ensure that it is bankruptcy remote (i.e. that it is unlikely to be the subject of insolvency proceedings) and that it will be treated separately from the originator in the event of insolvency. To this end, securitisation often involves a true sale of the underlying receivables to the SPV. These become the SPV's only asset, and it does not engage in any other type of business. It is also typically prohibited from incurring debt or other obligations, which reduces the risk that it will become insolvent through its own activities. These steps protect investors in the securitisation from claims made by creditors of the originator and ensure that their only exposure is to the risk in the collateral pool.

Securitisations use various techniques to enhance the credit quality of the securities they sell to investors. These include over-collateralisation (in which the total value of the collateral assets held by the SPV is greater than the nominal amount of securities that it issues) and excess spread (in which the income the SPV receives on the collateral is greater than the income it promises to pay to investors). This provides a cushion that can be used to protect investors from default losses or payment delays on the collateral.

Collateralised debt obligations (CDOs) are also a form of credit enhancement. In a CDO, each tranche is protected from default by the tranches that are subordinated to it since default losses on the collateral pool are absorbed from the bottom of the structure upward. This makes it possible to create senior tranches that have little credit risk and can obtain a AAA rating, even when the average credit quality of the collateral pool is much lower. In effect,

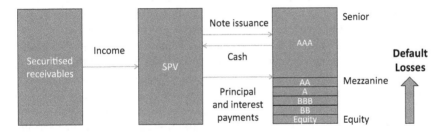

Figure 3.9 Illustration of CDO Structure.

the credit quality of the senior tranches is enhanced through the process of subordination (Figure 3.9).

The degree of protection enjoyed by the senior tranches depends critically on default dependence in the collateral pool. Higher default dependence changes the shape of the loss distribution since it increases the probability that many different credits will default together. This increases the unexpected loss on the portfolio (i.e. the level of loss that we would not expect to be exceeded over a given horizon at a specified high level of probability).

A large unexpected loss will eat deeper into the structure of the CDO and may result in losses even to the senior tranche, despite the apparent protection provided by the subordinated tranches. But default is a relatively rare event and may occur at different future horizons, which has significant practical consequences for modelling. Failure to adequately capture the level of default correlation and its potential impact on senior tranches, particularly in structures based on mortgage loans, appears to have been a major factor in the enormous losses suffered by some investors during the financial crisis. By one estimate, over 13,250 AAA-rated tranches with a nominal value of $1.26 trillion issued between 2000 and 2007 defaulted between 2008 and 2014, and the credit risk on these tranches may have been understated by 26% (Nickerson and Griffin, 2017).

Covered Bonds

Covered bonds are debt instruments issued (or in some cases sponsored) by a financial institution and secured by a priority claim on a specified pool of high-quality collateral (typically mortgage or public sector loans). In many parts of the world, covered bonds are more common than securitisations and serve a similar purpose of diversifying funding for illiquid assets.

Covered bonds are an important part of the European fixed income market, originating in the German Pfandbrief system created in 18th-century Prussia. During this long history, there have been many changes in the covered bond structure and in the regulations that govern the market, most recently a common legislative framework for covered bonds in the European Union, introduced in 2019.

Investors in a covered bond have dual recourse in the event of insolvency, against the issuer and against the collateral pool that covers the bonds. This is a significant contrast to investors in a securitisation, who only have recourse to the collateral. The assets in the cover pool remain on the issuer's balance sheet rather than being transferred in a true sale to an SPV, and the principal and interest on the bonds are typically paid from the issuer's general business receipts rather than from the cash flows generated by the cover pool.

Covered bonds offer a stable source of long-term financing to banks that is arguably less exposed to the problem of moral hazard than securitisation. An originator that can move assets off its balance sheet through securitisation may have a reduced incentive to pay close attention to the credit and other risks associated with those assets.

Fixed Income Portfolio Management

In this section we define and describe fund objectives, benchmarks, active and passive investing, tracking error, beta, alpha, liability driven investment (LDI), contributions to duration, spread duration, duration times spread (DTS), liquidity cost scores (LCS), and empirical duration.

Most fixed income investment occurs through institutional investors. The investment objectives and constraints of institutional investors vary widely, and this affects the instruments they hold and how their portfolios are managed. A pension fund, for example, will have long-term horizons; this may lead it to invest in bonds with longer maturities or durations and instruments that manage inflation risk. Private funds and endowments may face less pressure than mutual funds to provide immediate liquidity to investors and meet short-term performance goals, and so can hold less-liquid securities for longer. A hedge fund following a fixed income arbitrage strategy, on the other hand, may place several trades designed to exploit relative value opportunities that it rebalances frequently.

Setting Objectives

Portfolio managers will be responsible for deciding how to construct a portfolio to meet specified objectives. This means making decisions about how much exposure to take to interest rate risk at different points on the yield curve; how much credit risk to take and in which sectors or industries to take it; which specific issuers offer the best value for taking interest rate and credit risk at a particular point in time; and, increasingly, what weight to give to ESG criteria in choosing investments. Ultimately, these choices will determine the returns earned by investors and the risks to which they are exposed.

Fixed income funds vary widely in legal structure as well as investment strategy. Some are public, and others are private. Some are open-ended with unlimited lives, and others are closed-ended with fixed lives. Some follow strategies designed to generate absolute returns by exploiting relative value opportunities among different fixed income instruments (e.g. fixed income arbitrage or convertible arbitrage hedge funds), while others specialise in strategies that may result in concentrated holdings of illiquid investments (e.g. distressed debt and private debt funds). In many cases, however, a fund is likely to consist of predominantly long positions in ordinary government and corporate bonds, and its managers will be judged by how their performance compares to a specified benchmark.

A benchmark is a standard of comparison for performance measurement and risk analysis. In portfolio management, benchmarks are often indices constructed from the returns on traded assets. In fixed income markets, different indices track returns on bonds of different types (e.g. short-maturity and long-maturity government debt, securitisations, and investment grade and high yield corporate bonds) in various regions.

A fund's benchmark indicates its policy or style and acts as a control on risk. Defining and choosing a suitable benchmark is therefore a key element of fixed income portfolio management. Investors may choose portfolios containing bonds from issuers that meet certain ESG criteria. Since this reduces the universe of securities from which they select portfolios, it might be expected to affect performance. This in turn affects the choice of benchmark relative to which performance should be measured. In most cases, it will be appropriate to choose a benchmark that reflects the ESG 'tilt' of the portfolio.

Fund management may be either passive or active. Passive funds attempt to match the benchmark by selecting a portfolio of bonds with similar composition and risk factor exposure to the benchmark. They target low tracking error relative to the benchmark and offer investors a convenient, low-cost method of gaining exposure to a particular asset class. Active funds attempt to outperform the benchmark by choosing portfolios with different security, sector, asset class, or risk factor weights from within the investment universe defined by the benchmark. They try to maximise active return relative to the benchmark (i.e. alpha), subject to a constraint on tracking error (definitions of key terms are given in Box 1 below).

Since passive investors earn the market return (before costs), active investors as a group must also earn the market return (before costs). To generate value after considering costs, an active investor must therefore outperform not just passive investors but also other active investors. This requires exceptional sources of alpha that can be applied across the portfolio and over time, while controlling risk (Sharpe, 1991). In fixed income markets, this means that successful active managers must consistently identify ways of taking exposure to interest rate risk and credit risk that generate returns superior to those on the benchmark without taking significantly greater risk. Many factors may contribute to such success, including a better understanding of

BOX 3.1 Key Investment Terms and Terminology

Portfolio managers use specialised vocabulary to describe key measures and concepts. Some of the more important terms are defined here.

Active return is portfolio return relative to the benchmark. It is the result of deviations of the weights allocated to holdings in the portfolio from the weights in which those holdings appear in the benchmark. These active allocations are sometimes called active bets. In fixed income portfolios, these bets typically relate to interest rate risk or credit risk.

Tracking error is the annualised standard deviation of the active return. It measures risk exposure relative to the benchmark. Low tracking error is a key objective of passive investing. For active investing, tracking error measures **active risk**. Active managers have more opportunity to add value when their expected active return is high relative to their active risk.

Residual return is portfolio return that is uncorrelated with the benchmark. It can be measured through a time-series regression of portfolio returns on benchmark returns. This finds the straight line that best describes the relationship between portfolio returns and benchmark returns. Regression separates return into two parts: systematic return, which is perfectly correlated with the benchmark, and residual return, which is uncorrelated with the benchmark.

Beta is the sensitivity of the portfolio to the benchmark. It can be estimated by the coefficient (i.e. parameter estimate) corresponding to the slope of the fitted line in the time series regression described above. The estimated beta is proportional to the covariance between portfolio return and benchmark return. In this sense, it measures the amount of 'benchmark risk' in the portfolio; benchmark risk is also called systematic risk. Portfolios with beta greater than one have more systematic risk than the benchmark, and those with beta smaller than one have less.

Alpha is expected residual return. It can be estimated by the constant term in the time-series regression described above and measures the expected return that is not explained by the return on the benchmark. Looking backward, the realised alpha of a portfolio is the average of realised residual returns. Looking forward, forecast alpha is the forecast residual return for the portfolio. The objective of active investing is to generate positive alpha, since positive alpha is positive expected return that is not explained by passive exposure to the benchmark.

For an active manager who chooses a portfolio each period with beta equal to one with respect to the benchmark, active risk and return will equal residual risk and return, so alpha will also be equal to expected active return. In practice, this is the way in which we usually express alpha.

the nature and timing of yield curve movements, superior credit analysis, and more effective control of trading costs. Greater skill in assessing ESG risks and opportunities may also contribute to alpha.

Comparing a portfolio's performance to a benchmark is a reasonable way of measuring success in many fund management contexts. When performance is measured relative to a benchmark, the benchmark acts as a control on risk. Active investors hope to outperform the benchmark by earning positive alpha, but only so long as this does not come at the expense of high tracking error, since high tracking error might indicate that the return was earned by deviating significantly from the investment policy implied by the benchmark. Some institutional investors, however, create portfolios expressly for the purpose of funding specific future liabilities. In this case, it may make more sense to construct a portfolio designed to minimise the risk of failing to meet that objective and to measure success in those terms. We call this approach liability driven investment (LDI).

Consider, for example, a pension fund. The fund receives investable contributions from its members while they are working and promises to pay benefits to members when they retire. These benefits are the fund's liabilities. A key factor determining the present value of the fund's liabilities is interest rates: higher rates will reduce the present value of the liabilities and lower rates will increase it. Since pension fund liabilities are long-dated, they are particularly sensitive to interest rates. Another key factor is inflation, particularly in defined benefit schemes (i.e. schemes in which benefits are linked to an employee's earning history rather than depending on investment returns), since these benefits are often indexed to inflation. Higher expected inflation will increase the present value of the fund's liabilities and lower expected inflation will decrease it. A pension fund therefore faces significant exposure to interest rate risk and inflation risk, and it makes sense for the fund to choose an investment portfolio that hedges its exposures to these risks.

One way to do this is by allocating to fixed income securities. As we have seen, bond prices are in general inversely related to interest rates. Investing in bonds means that the present value of pension fund's assets will increase or decrease in value as interest rates go down or go up, matching the change in the present value of its liabilities. Ordinary bonds, however, cannot offer the fund protection against an increase in expected inflation. To hedge this risk, an investor may allocate to inflation-linked bonds. As we saw in the last chapter, the present value of these bonds will increase or decrease with expected inflation, matching the impact of inflation on the fund's liabilities. In practice, an investor may choose to hedge some of its interest rate and inflation risk using derivatives such as interest rate swaps and inflation swaps rather than bonds. This allows the fund to hedge risks related to its liabilities without sacrificing the higher returns it might earn through allocation to other asset classes. It can also help overcome problems related to the relatively limited supply of long-maturity bonds and illiquidity in the bond market.

Funds following LDI strategies are likely to measure success in terms of their ability to hedge risk by matching assets to liabilities rather than in terms of their performance relative to a benchmark.

Duration and Credit Spreads

Asset allocation in a portfolio or benchmark is normally described in terms of portfolio weights (i.e. the percentage of the market value of the portfolio devoted to each asset). This works well for equity portfolios, where differences in risk and return are largely the result of decisions to invest in particular sectors, industries, or companies. For fixed income portfolios, however, this is not sufficient because differences in duration can result in portfolios with the same allocation in terms of market weights having different exposures to interest rate changes. Asset allocations for fixed income portfolios are therefore often expressed in terms of contributions to duration. These are calculated as the product of the percentage of portfolio market value represented by each cell (i.e. each set of securities with similar characteristics) and the average duration of the securities in that cell. A cell's contribution to duration is the sensitivity of the portfolio to a parallel shift in the yields of all the securities in the cell.

For credit portfolios, the corresponding duration measure is spread duration (i.e. sensitivity to a parallel shift in credit spreads). Investors express asset allocation in terms of contributions to spread duration, which are measured as the product of the percentage of portfolio market value represented by each cell and the average spread duration of the securities in that cell. Spread durations are usually calculated with respect to changes in the OAS or Z-spread.

The concept of active allocation can be extended to this framework. For example, the active spread duration bet for a cell is the product of the active allocation to that cell in terms of portfolio weight and its spread duration. An overweight of 3% to a cell with spread duration of five years is an active spread duration bet of 0.15 years on that cell (calculated as 3% of five years).

Empirically, however, credit spreads do not move in parallel. A systematic widening of credit spreads has a larger effect on credits that are already trading at higher spreads than it does on those with similar characteristics and spread duration that are trading at lower spreads. In effect, bad news has a proportionately larger impact on weaker credits. This suggests that spread duration may not adequately capture the dynamics of credit portfolio risk. Many market participants instead measure the sensitivity of portfolios to credit spread changes by duration times spread (DTS). A bond's DTS, as the name suggests, is calculated as its spread duration multiplied by the spread at which it is currently trading. It measures sensitivity to relative rather than absolute changes in credit spread (Dor et al., 2012).

In this framework, contributions to DTS take the place of contributions to spread duration. They are calculated as the product of the percentage of portfolio market value represented by each cell, the average spread duration of the securities in that cell, and their average spread. Cells or portfolios with different spreads and spread durations but similar DTS should exhibit the same degree of excess return volatility arising from credit risk. For example, an overweight of 5% to a cell that is implemented by purchasing bonds with an average spread of 80 basis points and spread duration of three years will be equivalent to an overweight of 3% based on bonds with an average spread of 50 basis points and spread duration of eight years (Dor et al., 2012).

One advantage of using DTS is that a wider spread is interpreted immediately as indicating higher spread volatility, without the delay associated with conventional spread volatility measures based on historical data. This can help investors make more timely adjustments to their portfolios in periods in which credit risk is changing rapidly.

As we saw in the last chapter, liquidity is important to investors, and bonds that are less liquid will trade at spreads that include a liquidity risk premium. For managers of fixed income portfolios, illiquidity increases expected future trading costs associated with managing the portfolio, which reduces returns. Many managers use liquidity cost scores (LCS) to track and manage liquidity risk in their portfolios. For bonds that are quoted in terms of spreads, the LCS is the difference between the bid and ask spreads multiplied by the bond's spread duration. For bonds that are quoted in terms of price, the LCS is the difference between the bid and ask prices divide by the bid price. In either case, the LCS is the round-trip cost of an institutional-size transaction in the bond. Bonds with higher LCS are less liquid, and those with lower LCS more liquid (Dor et al., 2012).

Fixed income investment managers can use LCS as a filter to select bonds, to identify liquidity costs embedded in credit spreads, and to construct liquidity-optimal execution strategies (e.g., by selling illiquid bonds first in a credit crisis).

It may also be necessary to adjust duration measures when analysing credit-risky bonds. Credit spreads are typically negatively correlated with changes in benchmark interest rates, dampening the impact of a change in rates. The empirical duration of a bond (i.e. its actual sensitivity to a change in rates) may therefore be significantly less than its analytical duration calculated using the methods described in the last chapter; this effect is particularly pronounced for high yield bonds. Empirical durations for these bonds can be based on regression estimates.

Default dependence and concentration also affect fixed income portfolio risk. Higher default dependence changes the shape of the loss distribution since it increases the probability that many different credits will default together. This increases the unexpected loss on the portfolio. Higher concentration of exposures has a similar effect. In a well-diversified portfolio, the exposure to any one credit is limited. In a concentrated portfolio, however, default by a credit to which we have a large exposure can produce a large loss relative to the portfolio. This will increase unexpected loss in much the same way as default dependence. Concentration risk is typically managed by imposing limits on exposure to individual issuers or sectors. In an actively managed portfolio, this can constrain the search for alpha. Some managers therefore prefer to implement caps on contributions to DTS rather than portfolio weights since this allows larger concentrations in low-spread issuers while imposing stricter limits on high-spread issuers (Dor et al., 2012).

Interaction with ESG Criteria

In addition to screens or tilts based on ESG criteria, active ESG strategies may include intentional or unintentional active bets on duration and credit spreads. These will contribute to the risk and return on the portfolio and should be properly accounted for in terms of contributions to duration and contributions to DTS. If the liquidity of bonds selected using ESG criteria differs from that of other bonds, this may also affect returns. Finally, screening on ESG criteria may result in more concentrated portfolios. If this is the case, investors should be aware that this may increase the level of unexpected loss on the portfolio.

Performance Measurement and Attribution

> In this section we define and describe carry, roll down, sale and re-purchase agreement (repo), forward yield, Sharpe ratio, volatility, and Jensen's alpha.

Investors and fund sponsors require accurate measures of fund performance and suitable methods for attributing that performance to choices made in constructing and managing a portfolio.

Return

The total return earned by holding a bond over a period has two sources: income earned from coupon interest and the change in the bond's price between the start and end of the period. These two sources of return are closely related to two measures that are often used in analysing returns: carry and roll down.

Carry is defined as the net income associated with holding a position over time. For example, if investors buy a bond and hold it for a period of one month, they will earn one month of accrued coupon interest on the bond, but they must also pay one month of interest on the money borrowed. Bond purchases are often financed through sale and repurchase agreements (known as repo agreements) in which the bond is used as collateral to borrow money on a secured basis from a repo dealer. The cost of funding the bond will depend on the interest rate in this transaction, which is called the repo rate. Since the coupon rate on the bond may be higher or lower than the repo rate, the carry may be positive or negative. Carry is a predictable element of return that determines a target level for the trade. If the carry is negative, then the bond must increase in price over the holding period by more than the negative carry if investors are to make money. If the carry is positive, then investors will make money so long as the bond does not fall in price by more than the carry over the holding period.

Since most bonds have a finite life, however, their remaining time to maturity will be shorter at the end of the holding period than it was at the beginning. At the end of a one-month holding period, for example, a five-year bond will have a remaining life of fours year and 11 months. Its promised cash flows will fall on nearer dates, and they will be discounted at interest rates that correspond to those nearer dates. As a result, it will trade at a different price at the end of the holding period than it did at the beginning, even if the yield curve has not changed. Investors call this effect roll down. The reason for this name becomes clear if we think about what happens when the yield curve is positively sloped (i.e. long-term rates are higher than short-term rates). The bond will increase in price over the holding period because its cash flows will be discounted at lower rates at the end of the period, so investors benefit from 'rolling down' the yield curve (Figure 3.10).

Roll down is a less predictable element of return than carry because we cannot be certain what will happen to interest rates over the holding period. If rates were to increase, for example, this might more than offset any impact that the shortening of maturity has on the bond's price.

In fixed income trading, projected roll down is often reported on the assumption that the yield curve will remain unchanged, but other scenarios may be just as likely. One scenario of particular interest is if rates move over time to the levels implied by forward yields (i.e. the yields at which bonds are trading at the start of the holding period for delivery at the end of the holding period rather than immediately). If this occurs, then any effect due to roll down will be exactly offset by carry and investors will make neither a profit nor a loss on the trade. To make a profit on a trade, the sum of the carry and

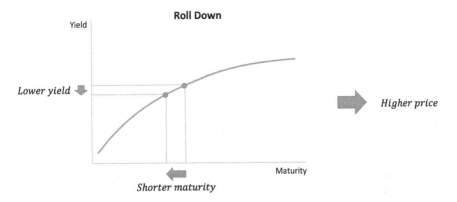

Figure 3.10 Roll Down Illustration.

the actual roll down (i.e. the repricing of the bond based on what actually happens to the yield curve) must be positive.

Carry and roll down are obviously important in determining returns on bond portfolios as well as individual bonds. In portfolio management contexts, however, the meaning of these terms can be somewhat more ambiguous than in fixed income trading. Part of the reason for this is that a fund may hold a bond for a long period of time. This complicates the calculation of income on the position, since it will be necessary to consider income earned from reinvesting coupon payments. Carry calculations are also less likely to take into account funding costs, since the money used to purchase bonds is provided by the fund's investors. Carry is therefore usually taken to be the income earned by receiving and reinvesting coupon payments. Some portfolio managers, however, define carry to include the element of return that we have called roll down (Bacon, 2019). Usually, but not always, these calculations assume that the yield curve is unchanged over the holding period (Kojien et al., 2018). Regardless of the precise definitions used, projected carry and roll down are clearly key factors to be considered by investors and fund managers, and the actual carry and roll down experienced by a fund will to a considerable extent determine its performance over time.

For credit portfolios, changes in credit spreads are another key factor affecting performance. Investors will want to understand what credit bets were made by the portfolio manager and how they contributed to the fund's performance.

Risk

Fixed income investors are also, of course, concerned about risk. They will want to construct measures of portfolio risk as well as return and may assess portfolio performance in terms of risk-adjusted returns.

One widely used measure of risk-adjusted return is the Sharpe ratio. This is the ratio of the excess return on the portfolio (i.e. its return in excess of the risk-free rate) to the standard deviation of the excess return. The standard deviation measures the dispersion in the excess return and is calculated as the square root of its variance; in financial markets, the standard deviation of return is often called volatility. The Sharpe ratio therefore measures the excess return on the portfolio per unit of risk, as measured by volatility. If the Sharpe ratio for a fund is higher than the Sharpe ratio for its benchmark, then the fund has outperformed the benchmark. More generally, investors may compare the performance of different funds in terms of their Sharpe ratios and portfolio managers may assess possible investment strategies in terms of their projected Sharpe ratios (Sharpe, 1966). Such comparisons should be treated with caution, however, since applying a Sharpe ratio to an individual fund in isolation ignores the correlation that the fund may have with other components of investor's total portfolio.

Risk-adjusted return can also be measured by comparing the return on the portfolio to its expected return based on a specific asset pricing model, such as the Capital Asset Pricing Model (CAPM). The CAPM suggests that the expected excess return on a portfolio should be proportional to its sensitivity to the excess return on a broadly diversified 'market' portfolio. This sensitivity is measured by the fund's beta with respect to the market portfolio, where beta is defined in much the same way as we defined the beta of a fund with respect to its benchmark in the previous section (Sharpe, 1964). The risk-adjusted return on the portfolio can be measured by its return relative to its expected return as predicted by the CAPM. This measure of risk-adjusted return is called Jensen's alpha (Jensen, 1968). Operationally, this is equivalent to the way the alpha of a portfolio is measured with respect to its benchmark in the last section.

Many fixed income investment managers rely primarily on judgement when selecting bonds and constructing portfolios, informed to a greater or lesser extent by quantitative analysis of credit risk and interest rate risk. Some managers, however, take a more explicitly quantitative approach. This can include the use of optimisation in asset allocation.

An optimiser is a mathematical tool or algorithm for identifying efficient portfolios based on estimated or forecast expected returns and covariances. The covariances are functions of the standard deviations of return and correlations between assets. All these inputs will be measured with error, so optimisation will tend to over-allocate to assets or asset classes whose returns are overestimated or whose standard deviations of return and correlations with other assets are under-estimated. In this sense, optimisation can be a tool for maximising estimation errors (Michaud, 1989). Various techniques can reduce the impact of estimation error, including bootstrapping and Monte Carlo methods for resampling (Michaud and Michaud, 2008). Alternatively, some investment managers prefer to avoid optimisation altogether and construct equal-weighted portfolios from securities selected on the basis of judgement or quantitative analysis.

Regardless of how a portfolio is constructed, portfolio managers, sponsors, and investors will require answers to basic questions about its performance. These include: was the portfolio consistent with the stated investment policy? Did it expose investors to acceptable levels of risk? How did the active allocation decisions made by managers contribute to its risk and return? What risk factors had the largest impact on performance? These questions are the subject of performance attribution analysis.

This requires constructing a suitable factor model for fixed income risk. Many such models exist and differ significantly in content and emphasis (Figure 3.11). These models can be used to explain performance in terms of exposure to identifiable risk factors. For example, investors may have made significant active bets related to the shape of the yield curve or the credit spread on high yield debt, which affected investor performance relative to

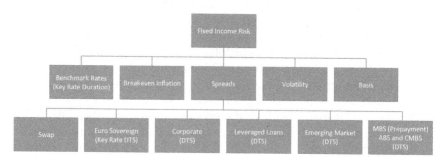

Figure 3.11 MSCI Fixed Income Factor Model.
Source: Shepard and Zhou, 2020.

the benchmark. Understanding this relationship is critical to controlling risk and generating alpha.

Exposure to benchmark interest rates (e.g. government bonds and swaps) is captured by key rate durations. These measure the sensitivity of a security or portfolio to a shift in the benchmark yield for a specific maturity, providing a more granular assessment of interest rate risk than ordinary duration. This helps capture the portfolio's sensitivity to twists or other changes in the shape of the yield curve as well as to changes in the level of interest rates. DTS models capture exposure to changes in credit spreads on corporate bonds, leveraged loans, ABS, and other credit-risky instruments. Key rate DTS models are used for credit spreads on Euro sovereign debt relative to Germany to capture differences in spread risk forecasts across maturities. Jointly, these DTS models capture the portfolio's exposure to credit risk. The risk model also includes key rate breakeven inflation factors for inflation–linked bonds, implied volatility factors for bonds with embedded optionality (e.g. callable bonds or MBS), and basis factors that model spreads between closely related instruments (e.g. on-the-run and off-the-run government bonds) that may change over time. Currency risk and issuer-specific risk (which can be important for concentrated portfolios) are also modelled. Together, the factors in the model are designed to capture all the key drivers of fixed income risk and return.

Risk models can also be used to reduce tracking error in passive investment strategies and to improve the efficiency of portfolio optimisation by allowing covariances to be estimated from a relatively small number of risk factors.

Conclusion

This chapter provided a common framework for interpreting the practices and recommendations of fixed income investors and portfolio managers. This influenced our decision to focus mainly on applications related to credit analysis (including credit ratings) and fixed income portfolio management, since integrating ESG factors into those processes is a critical step towards wider acceptance of the principle of responsible investing by both issuers and investors.

Choices based on ESG factors may affect the interest rate and credit risk structure of a portfolio, and investors should control for this when measuring and attributing performance. They should also consider the impact of ESG factors on credit ratings and credit analysis. When read in conjunction with the other contributions to this volume, this chapter and the previous chapter will provide investors with the tools they need to make more effective decisions as they expand their responsible investing universe to include fixed income markets.

References

Bacon, C. (2019), *Performance Attribution: History and Progress.* [online]. Available at https://www.cfainstitute.org/-/media/documents/book/rf-lit-review/2019/rflr-performance-attribution.ashx (Accessed 10 April 2021).

Cornaggia, J. N., Cornaggia, K. J. and Hund, J. E. (2017), 'Credit Ratings across Asset Classes: A Long-Term Perspective', *Review of Finance*, 21(2), pp. 465–509.

Dor, A. B., Dynkin, L., Hyman, J. and Phelps, B. (2012), *Quantitative Credit Portfolio Management: Practical Innovations for Measuring and Controlling Liquidity, Spread, and Issuer Concentration Risk* (Wiley, Hoboken).

Figlewski, S., Frydman, H. and Liang, W. (2012), 'Modeling the Effect of Macroeconomic Factors on Corporate Default and Credit Rating Transitions', *International Review of Economics and Finance*, 21(1), pp. 87–105.

Fitch Ratings. (2020a), *Fitch Downgrades Kraft Heinz IDR to 'BB+'; Outlook Stable.* [online]. Available at https://www.fitchratings.com/research/corporate-finance/fitch-downgrades-kraft-heinz-idr-to-bb-outlook-stable-14-02-2020 (Accessed 15 December 2020).

Fitch Ratings. (2020b), *Fitch Downgrades M&S to 'BB+'; Outlook Stable.* [online]. Available at https://www.fitchratings.com/research/corporate-finance/fitch-downgrades-m-s-to-bb-outlook-stable-09-04-2020 (Accessed 15 December 2020).

Jensen, M. C. (1968). 'The Performance of Mutual Funds in the Period 1945–1964', *Journal of Finance*, 23(2), pp. 389–416.

Kiesel, F., Kolaric, S., Norden, L. and Schiereck, D. (2018), *Does CDS Trading Impact the Information Content of the Rating Review Process?* [online]. Available at https://www.efmaefm.org/0efmameetings/EFMA%20ANNUAL%20MEETINGS/2018-Milan/papers/EFMA2018_0223_fullpaper.pdf (Accessed 12 April 2021).

Kojien, R. S. J., Moskowitz, T. J., Pederson, L. H. and Vrugt, E. B. (2018), 'Carry', *Journal of Financial Economics*, 127(2), pp. 197–225.

Lobo, G. J., Paugam, L., Stolowy, H. and Astolfi, P. (2017), 'The Effects of Business and Financial Market Cycles on Credit Ratings: Evidence from the Last Two Decades', *Abacus*, 52(1), pp. 59–93.

Michaud, R. (1989), 'The Markowitz Optimization Enigma: Is "Optimized" Optimal?', *Financial Analysts Journal*, 45(1), pp. 31–42.

Michaud, R. and Michaud, R. (2008), 'Estimation Error and Portfolio Optimization: A Resampling Solution', *Journal of Investment Management*, 6(1), pp. 8–28.

Micu, M., Remolona, E. and Wooldridge, P. (2006), *The Price Impact of Rating Announcements: Which Announcements Matter? Bank for International Settlements Working Paper No. 207.* [online]. Available at https://www.bis.org/publ/work207.pdf (Accessed 12 April 2021).

Moody's Investors Service (2018), *Diversified Technology Rating Methodology.* [online]. Available at http://www.moodys.com/researchdocumentcontentpage.aspx?docid=PBC_1130737 (Accessed 12 April 2021).

Moody's Investors Service (2019), *Sovereign Ratings Methodology.* [online]. Available at https://www.moodys.com/viewresearchdoc.aspx?docid=PBC_1158631&WT.mc_id=RateSov (Accessed 12 April 2021).

Moody's Investors Service (2020a), *ESG Risks Material in 33% of Moody's 2019 Private-sector Issuer Rating Actions.* [online]. Available at https://www.moodys.com/research/Moodys-ESG-risks-material-in-33-of-Moodys-2019-private-PBC_1218114 (Accessed 12 April 2021).

Moody's Investors Service (2020b), *Moody's Announces Completion of a Periodic Review of Ratings of Apple Inc.* [online]. Available at https://www.moodys.com/research/Moodys-announces-completion-of-a-periodic-review-of-ratings-of--PR_432432 (Accessed 12 April 2021).

Nickerson J. and Griffin, J. M. (2017), 'Debt Correlations in the Wake of the Financial Crisis: What are Appropriate Default Correlations for Structured Products?', *Journal of Financial Economics*, 125(3), pp. 454–474.

Porter, M. E. (1979), 'How Competitive Forces Shape Strategy', *Harvard Business Review*, 57(2), pp. 137–145.

S&P Global Ratings (2017), *How Environmental and Climate Risks and Opportunities Factor into Credit Ratings – An Update.* [online]. Available at https://www.spratings.com/documents/20184/1634005/How+Environmental+And+Climate+Risks+And+Opportunities+Factor+Into+Global+Corporate+Ratings+-+An+Update/5119c3fa-7901-4da2-bc90-9ad6e1836801 (Accessed 12 April 2021).

S&P Global Ratings (2018), *How Social Risks and Opportunities Factor Into Global Corporate Ratings.* [online]. Available at https://www.spglobal.com/en/research-insights/articles/how-social-risks-and-opportunities-factor-into-global-corporate-rating (Accessed 12 April 2021).

S&P Global Ratings (2020a), *2019 Annual Global Corporate Default and Rating Transition Study.* [online]. Available at https://www.spglobal.com/ratings/en/research/articles/200429-default-transition-and-recovery-2019-annual-global-corporate-default-and-rating-transition-study-11444862 (Accessed 12 April 2021).

S&P Global Ratings (2020b), *2019 Annual Sovereign Default and Rating Transition Study.* [online]. Available at https://www.standardandpoors.com/en_US/delegate/getPDF;jsessionid=5BE1C9E0C5BEBE81DDB776059E32A4B1?articleId=2487381&type=COMMENTS&subType=REGULATORY (Accessed 12 April 2021).

S&P Global Ratings (2021), *2020 Annual Global Corporate Default and Rating Transition Study.* [online]. Available at https://www.spglobal.com/ratings/en/research/articles/200429-default-transition-and-recovery-2019-annual-global-corporate-default-and-rating-transition-study-11444862 (Accessed 12 April 2021).

Sharpe, W. F. (1964), 'Capital Asset Prices: A Theory of Market Equilibrium Under Conditions of Risk', *Journal of Finance*, 19(3), pp. 425–442.

Sharpe, W. F. (1966), 'Mutual Fund Performance', *Journal of Business*, 39(1), pp. 119–138.

Sharpe, W. F. (1991), 'The Arithmetic of Active Management', *Financial Analysts Journal*, 7(1), pp. 7–9.

Shepard, P. and Zhou, C. (2020). *MSCI Fixed Income Factor Model.* [online]. Available at https://www.msci.com/documents/10199/81a99b08-6659-421f-ae4f-5c775b6b439b (Accessed 12 April 2021).

Waterman, R. K. Jr., Peters, T. J. and Phillips, J. R. (1980), 'Structure Is Not Organization', *Business Horizons*, 23(3), pp. 14–26.

4 The Landscape of Responsible Investment and Fixed Income

Carmen Nuzzo and Sixtine Dubost

Introduction

Global debt reached US$226 trillion at the end of 2020 – equivalent to more than 256% of global GDP – with more than three quarters of this from public and non-financial corporate entities[1]. This staggering number, partly exacerbated by the COVID-19 pandemic, implies that debt capital markets are becoming an increasingly important segment of the responsible investment agenda. More and more, investors are appreciating that the risk assessment of fixed income instruments needs to be more holistic than in the past, and that they need to build frameworks that allow for a more systematic consideration of environment, social, and governance (ESG) factors, beyond traditional financial metrics. In addition, there is growing realisation that long-term returns are dependent on stable, functioning, and well-governed production and economic systems.

As funding providers, fixed income investors play a unique role in promoting sustainable investing practices. Their capital allocation decisions affect the environment and society. By embedding ESG considerations into these decisions, they can impact the cost of capital for debt-issuing entities and can channel funds towards those that are contributing to more sustainable business and growth models (through delivering positive real-world outcomes and/or through reducing negative impacts).

Admittedly, until recently, low central bank policy rates and quantitative monetary policy easing have created a distortion in risk pricing that is not conducive to this investor mindset. Nevertheless, the responsible investment movement continues to grow, as attested by the rising number of signatories of the Principles for Responsible Investment (PRI), the growth in the number of countries that have committing to net zero carbon emissions over the next 30–40 years, and the rapid growth in responsible investment-related regulation (see Chapter 23).

This chapter explores why the focus of responsible investment has expanded to fixed markets and how this interest is shaping the practices and performance of issuers and of investors. It focuses on the following nine themes:

DOI: 10.4324/9781003055341-5

1   The PRI
2   Responsible investment in fixed income: drivers and barriers
3   Market size and characteristics
4   Approaches and strategies for incorporating ESG into investment decision-making
5   PRI signatory practices
6   The PRI's ESG in Credit Risk and Ratings Initiative
7   Different types of issuers
8   Bondholder engagement: goals and challenges
9   Data availability, ESG information providers, and fixed income

The PRI

The PRI is a global investor association that promotes responsible investment, defined as a strategy and practice to incorporate ESG factors in investment decisions and active ownership. This approach complements traditional financial analysis.

The PRI works with its international network of signatories to put the six Principles for Responsible Investment (see Box 4.1) into practice, with the goal of guiding and supporting them in understanding the investment implications of ESG issues, integrating them into investment decisions, and promoting active ownership. Investors publicly commit to adopt and implement them where consistent with their fiduciary responsibilities.

BOX 4.1 WHAT ARE THE SIX PRINCIPLES FOR RESPONSIBLE INVESTMENT?[2]

The six Principles for Responsible Investment are a voluntary and aspirational set of investment principles that offer a menu of possible actions for incorporating ESG issues into investment practices.

Principle 1: We will incorporate ESG issues into investment analysis and decision-making processes.

Principle 2: We will be active owners and incorporate ESG issues into our ownership policies and practices.

Principle 3: We will seek appropriate disclosure on ESG issues by the entities in which we invest.

Principle 4: We will promote acceptance and implementation of the Principles within the investment industry.

Principle 5: We will work together to enhance our effectiveness in implementing the Principles.

Principle 6: We will each report on our activities and progress towards implementing the Principles.

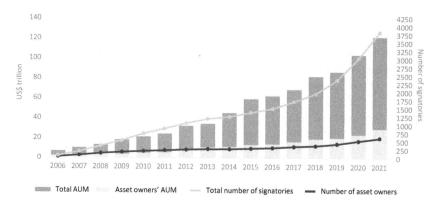

Figure 4.1 PRI's Signatory Base.
Source: PRI.
⋆Total AUM include reported AUM and AUM of new signatories provided in sign-up sheet that signed up by end of March of that year.

The original investor group was convened by the (UN) Secretary-General Kofi Annan in 2005 and the PRI was officially launched in April 2006. Since then, the number of signatories has grown from 100 to over 3,000 (see Figure 4.1). The majority are asset managers, with asset owners (pension, insurance, and sovereign funds as well as family offices) representing about 20%.

Responsible Investment in Fixed Income: Drivers and Barriers

Fixed income investors have embraced the concept of responsible investment later than shareholders due to a combination of factors. These include the complexity of fixed income instruments, the lack of formal voting rights associated with these instruments (which has acted as a deterrent to engagement with issuers), and limited academic and market research on the links between ESG consideration and bond performance. The incorporation of ESG factors in fixed income products has also been held back by the limited understanding of the financial materiality of ESG topics, and by the difficulty in applying the responsible investment approaches developed for listed equities to fixed income (see Chapter 8).

Despite these challenges, fixed income investor appetite for responsible investment has grown rapidly in recent years, particularly since the adoption of the UN 2030 Agenda for Sustainable Development[3] by UN member states in 2015 and the signing of the 2015 Paris Agreement on Climate Change.[4] Other factors have also played an important role in increasing investor interest:

- Responsible investment is increasingly seen as a risk management tool, driven both by the number of examples demonstrating that ESG factors may affect investment valuations and by the increased availability of data to measure these factors.
- Demand from retail and institutional investors for responsible investment products.
- Growing acceptance that the concept of fiduciary duty is evolving and that it should be interpreted in a more holistic way, beyond mere financial returns.
- The growth of sustainable finance-related regulation, in particular in the European Union.
- The rapid growth in the thematic bonds market where proceeds are ring-fenced to specific projects or funds are raised to deliver strategic outcomes with environmental or societal benefits (Figure 4.2).

Fixed income investors also increasingly recognise that many ESG factors contribute to inflation dynamics (oil and soft commodity prices, demographic trends that influence consumption, and savings patterns or carbon taxes, to name a few); and inflation together with fiscal and monetary policy, has long been the main areas of focus for bondholders. Moreover, many ESG factors contribute to GDP growth (which, in turn is important for inflation, fiscal and debt sustainability as well as currency stability) and can affect the credit risk (i.e. the probability that a debt issuer may not honour its repayment promise on time and in full) of sovereign and sub-sovereign issuers.

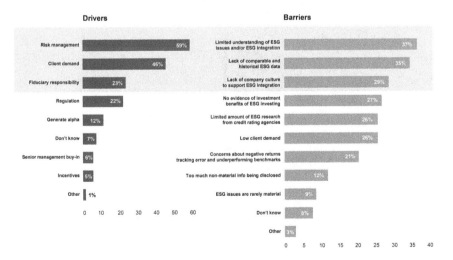

Figure 4.2 ESG Integration in Fixed Income: Drivers and Barriers.
Sources: CFA Institute and PRI, 2018.

Market Size and Characteristics

The 2019 PRI signatory survey provides a snapshot of ESG practices in fixed income assets. For the 1,706 PRI signatories that responded, debt instruments accounted for US$42.8 trillion or 46% of the total signatory AUM (see Figure 4.3).

Within the debt instruments category, sovereign, supra-national, and agency bonds represented nearly 45% of invested AUM, followed by non-financial corporate bonds at 23%, and smaller shares in financial corporate bonds, securitised products and other debt instruments (Figure 4.4).

Approaches and Strategies for Incorporating ESG into Investment Decision-Making

Compared to shareholders (or listed equity investors), fixed income investors are more concerned about downside risks. Material ESG factors are therefore assessed by fixed income investors primarily from a downside risk perspective when making an investment decision. Having said that, ESG analysis is increasingly used by fixed income investors to enhance returns or for relative value investment strategies. Another important point of difference is that bond duration is an important consideration, and fixed income investors need

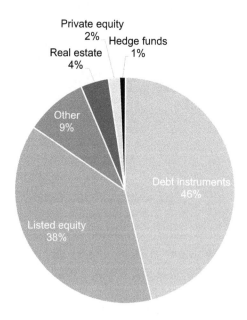

Figure 4.3 Breakdown of Reported AUM Invested in all Asset Classes, 2019. Source: PRI.

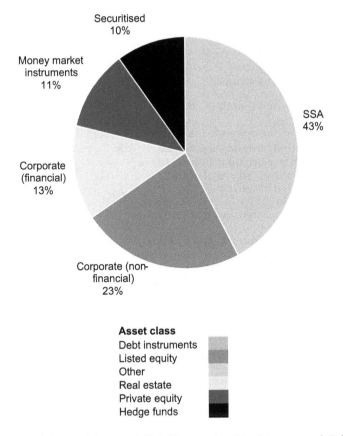

Figure 4.4 Breakdown of Reported AUM Invested in Fixed Income and Other Debt Instruments, 2019.

Source: PRI.

to consider whether a particular issue will become material during or after the lifetime of the bond.

ESG Investment Approaches

Broadly speaking, ESG factors can be incorporated into fixed income investment strategies using three approaches: integration, screening, and thematic. Investors select between, or combine, these approaches based on their investment objectives. These range from integrating ESG factors in the analysis to enhance the investment risk-return profile, to using specific norms for screening (i.e. avoiding specific sectors or only including selected ones) to investing with a theme (i.e. driving capital towards particular environmental and/or social goals). Table 4.1 presents a broad overview of some of the differences between the different approaches.

Table 4.1 Comparing Key Characteristics of ESG Incorporation Approaches in Fixed Income.

	Integration	Screening	Thematic
Gives a more complete picture of the risks and opportunities faced by an issuer	•		
Is applicable to investors that have no interest in considerations outside of their risk return profile	•		
Largely about managing downside risk	•		
Can fit within existing investment processes	•	•	•
Restricts investment in certain industrial sectors, geographic regions, or individual issuers, typically for ethical reasons		•	•
Non-financially material ESG factors or ethical considerations are incorporated into investment decisions		•	•
Directs capital towards issuers or securities that contribute to environmental or social outcomes			•
Largely about identifying opportunities			•

This tables gives a broad overview of some of the differences between the major types of ESG incorporation. It is not a detailed or exhaustive classification.

Integration – Adding ESG Factors to Financial Analysis

Integration involves identifying and assessing material EGS factors alongside traditional financial factors when making an investment decision about a specific issuer or security, or the overall portfolio structure. Integration typically encompasses three steps:

1 Investment research: Identifying material ESG factors (at the issuer level, as well as for individual securities) that may impact downside risk (or provide topics for engagement).
2 Security valuation: Integrating the material ESG factors into financial analysis and valuation (e.g. through internal credit assessments, forecasted financials and ratios, relative ranking, relative value/spread analysis, and security sensitivity/scenario analysis).
3 Portfolio management: Including the ESG analysis in decisions about risk management and portfolio construction (e.g. through sector weightings).

The integration approach varies according to the issuer type, depending on whether the debt instrument is issued on the private or public market, and whether the issuer is a corporate, a sovereign, a sub-sovereign, or a supranational entity. Each issuer type presents investors with different data disclosure and engagement challenges.

Many ESG factors have traditionally featured in debt instrument valuations, but have not been labelled as such. For example, the composition and the independence of a corporate board, as well as internal controls and risk management protocols, are typically part of the assessment of governance. This remains the predominant factor in the ESG integration process, as it affects more directly one of the primary risks for bondholders, credit risk. However, there are also new other governance aspects that are now becoming relevant. Examples include board diversity, pay structures, and inclusiveness. Furthermore, social and environmental factors are becoming increasingly relevant: for example, labour standards in the supply chain, employee health, and safety as well as climate change – both physical risks and risks related to the transition to a low-carbon economy.

Screening – Filtering the Investable Universe

Screening uses a set of filters to determine which issuers, sectors, or activities are eligible to be included in a portfolio based on investor preferences, values, or ethics. Filters are typically based on including or excluding particular products, services, or practices. For example, a screen might be used to exclude the highest carbon emitters from a portfolio, or to target only the lowest emitters. ESG scores for screening can be obtained from specialist ESG service providers, or by creating a proprietary scoring methodology.

Screening can be performed in three different ways:

- Negative screening (i.e. avoiding the worst performers). This involves excluding certain sectors, issuers, or securities for poor ESG performance relative to industry peers, or based on specific ESG criteria (e.g. avoiding particular products/services, regions, or business practices).
- Norm-based screening (i.e. screening issuers against minimum standards of business practice based on international norms). Commonly used frameworks include UN treaties, UN Security Council sanctions, the UN Global Compact, the Universal Declaration on Human Rights Declaration, and the Organisation for Economic Cooperation and Development Guidelines for Multinational Enterprises.
- Positive screening (i.e. investing in sectors, issuers, or projects because they have better ESG performance than their industry peers).

Thematic – Allocating Capital Towards Environmental or Social Outcomes

Thematic investing identifies and allocates capital to themes or assets related to certain environmental or social outcomes, such as clean energy, energy efficiency, or sustainable agriculture.

Green bonds fall into this category. These are a rapidly growing segment of fixed income products that are specifically earmarked to fund climate and environmental projects. In 2019, global green bond and loan issuance set a new record, exceeding US$ 257 billion, an increase of 51% compared to 2018. (Climate Bond Initiative, 2020a, b). These bonds are generally issued in accordance with various international standards and frameworks; examples include the Green Bond Principles, the Green Loan Principles, the Climate Bonds Standard, and local standards such as Japan's green bond guidelines and taxonomy. Green bonds have been issued by corporates, sovereigns, supra-nationals, agencies, and sub-nationals. Other types of thematic bonds include social bonds, sustainability bonds, and Islamic bonds (sukuk).

PRI Signatory Practices

A combination of screening and thematic approaches is the most popular ESG fixed income incorporation approach among PRI signatories (see Figure 4.5). In 2019, more than 35% of PRI's signatories adopted this mix in 2019, up from 31% in 2017 (no data are available for 2018). The second most common option was integration alone (around 25% in both 2017 and 2019), with 19% of signatories opting for screening only (compared to 22% in 2017).

Screening

The screening for ESG issues when constructing a portfolio has a long history within responsible investment (Sparkes, 2002). It is mostly implemented through exclusion rules (negative screening). Figure 4.6 shows that negative screening was adopted by more than 90% of PRI signatories investing in fixed income assets in 2019, with approximately half using positive/best-in-class screening.

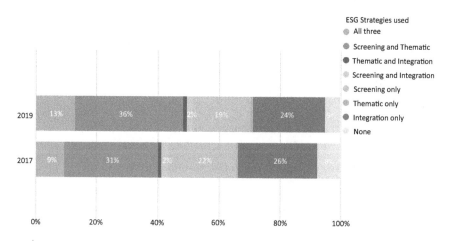

Figure 4.5 ESG Methodology Breakdown for Fixed Income Assets.
Source: PRI.

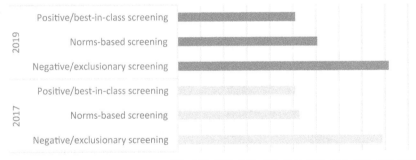

Figure 4.6 Screening Methods (percentage of PRI signatories, 2019).
Source: PRI.

As screening can be both positive and negative, choosing the right criteria is one of the biggest investor challenges. These criteria, or filters, are
usually based on data received from third-party vendors, which feed into
internal systems. Screening can also introduce biases, by underweighting or
overweighting certain industries or issuers. Many investors now use a mix
of both approaches, screening out companies which do not respect certain
requirements, and proactively choosing the best issuers which are making a
difference in each sector.

Thematic

Bonds linked to environmental goals are highly popular amongst investors
(69% of signatories had invested in such bonds in 2019), compared to bonds
linked to social goals (33%) or bonds linked to both environmental and social
goals (39%) (see Figure 4.7).

To ensure enforcement of ESG promises in their thematic investments,
66% of signatories require that themed bond proceeds are only allocated
to environmentally or socially beneficial projects, and 62% of signatories
require the issuer to demonstrate a process determining the eligibility
of projects to which themed bond proceeds are allocated. There is also a
small but growing segment of the market, albeit expanding rapidly amidst
rising demand for such products, that contribute to environmental and
societal outcomes.

The main challenges lie around greenwashing and the lack of a standardised definition. A universal definition of green, social, or sustainable bonds
does not exist yet – although some standards are becoming a wider-used reference, notably the International Capital Market Association (ICMA) Green

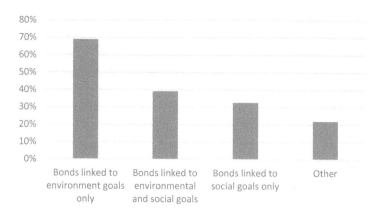

Figure 4.7 Thematic Investments Breakdown (percentage of PRI signatories, 2019). Source: PRI.

Bonds Principles[5] and the Climate Bonds Initiative (CBI) Green Bond Principles and Climate Bond Standard.[6]

Increased transparency and accountability are crucial to the integrity of the market. Issuers' compliance with the green bond principles or social bond guidelines is currently voluntary. Whilst thematic bonds are often accompanied by certifications and third-party verifications, creditors have limited options should the proceeds not be allocated according to the initial objectives. Therefore careful due diligence by investors is required prior to the purchase of these bonds as well as ongoing monitoring and tracking.

More recently, a new class of thematic bonds has emerged, the so-called sustainability-linked bonds (SLB), with variable coupon payments depending on the achievement of selected key performance indicators or targets (such as increasing the use of recycled materials or a reducing greenhouse gas emissions). The effectiveness of these products in driving sustainable goals lies with the credibility of the targets which need to be ambitious, but also realistic at the same time.

Integration

Among the various ESG integration methods available to investors, integrating ESG analysis into fundamental analysis is, by far, the most popular, followed almost equally by: ranking an issuer based on its ESG 'profile' relative to a chosen peer group, adjusting issuers' internal credit assessments, and integrating ESG analysis into portfolio weighting decisions. More advanced practices (e.g. sensitivity analysis and scenario analysis) are less frequent (Figure 4.8).

A CFA-PRI survey (CFA and PRI, 2019) of 1,100 financial professionals globally showed that practitioners all around the world believed that ESG issues impact corporate bond an sovereign debt prices, to an extent. The survey also

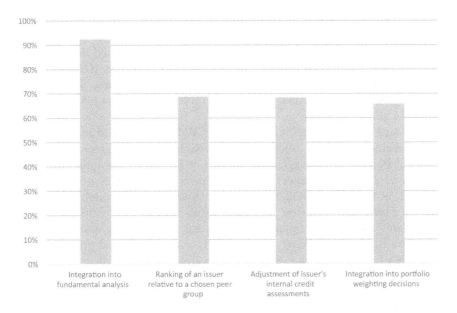

Figure 4.8 ESG Integration Methods (percentage of PRI signatories, 2019).
Source: PRI.

found that there are still noticeable regional differences on how investment managers and asset owners integrate ESG factors in their practices, with the common perception being that Western Europe is more advanced and that Asia and the Americas are lagging.

The PRI's ESG in Credit Risk and Ratings Initiative

Although ESG factors are not new to credit risk analysis, the extent to which these factors are *explicitly* and *systematically* considered by fixed income investors is. As investors start building more formal processes and frameworks in their fixed income valuations, credit risk is the area in which consideration of ESG factors is easier to conceptualise, as many ESG factors can impair an issuer's willingness and ability to repay its debt promises.

ESG factors may also affect bond valuations through other channels, such as their impact on inflation and on economic growth. However, these links have not attracted market participants' attention, although it is noteworthy that a rapidly expanding group of central banks and supervisors, the Network for Greening the Financial System,[7] is now convening regularly on a voluntary basis to share best practice, to contribute to the development of environmental and climate risk management in the financial sector, and to mobilise mainstream finance to support the transition towards a sustainable economy.

The PRI has focused on credit risk as a central element of its fixed income workstream. Its flagship programme, the ESG in Credit Risk and Ratings Initiative,[8] aims to enhance the transparent and systematic incorporation of ESG factors in credit risk analysis. This project was launched in 2016 with a Statement[9] signed by investors and credit rating agencies (CRAs), committing to work collaboratively towards the Initiative's goals. To date, the Statement has been signed by close to 180 investors with over US$40 trillion of AUM and 27 CRAs.

The range of signatories, investors, and CRAs is very broad and is diversified globally. Big players – such as Goldman Sachs Asset Management, Legal & General Investment Management, Allianz or PIMCO – are supporting this Initiative, alongside smaller investment managers and asset owners – the Church of Sweden, CCOO, and Vancity Investment Management for instance. Fixed income assets represent nearly two thirds of the Statement signatories' AUM. The uptake by CRAs has been equally quite remarkable. The Initiative is actively supported by the three largest global players (Moody's Investors Service, S&P Global Ratings and Fitch Ratings) as well as more regional and specialised ones (e.g. Liberum Ratings in Brazil, China Chengxin International Credit Rating in China, Nordic Credit Rating in the Nordic countries). These agencies are not all at the same stage of development, and have different resources and expertise, but they are all working towards the same goals.

Effectively, the PRI is facilitating a dialogue between investors and CRAs to cultivate a common language and discuss and understand the materiality of ESG risks to creditworthiness. The initiative's seminal work recognised that many ESG factors had traditionally been considered withing credit risk analysis, especially governance. At the same time, it highlighted that a large number of ESG factors were new and their financial implications needed to be better researched and understood. Both sides concurred that they were in the early phase of formalising a systematic approach to considering environmental and social factors and making ESG factors more explicit. Furthermore, they recognised that assessing where these are relevant and how they can impact balance sheets and cash flow projections needed more work.

At the start of the initiative, there were some disconnects between investors and CRAs. These disconnects informed the subsequent work that the PRI conducted by organising over 20 forums in 15 countries for credit practitioners to discuss them. Some were misconceptions, others real challenges. We provide a brief description of the main four issues below.

1   Materiality of ESG Factors

One initial disconnect was on the relevance of ESG factors for credit risk, as not all ESG factors alter the probability of default of an issuer or of a single issue – which is what CRAs assess. However, ESG factors may negatively affect the trading performance of a bond – which is what investors focus on – or may become material beyond typical credit rating horizons. For example, a company may easily meet the costs of an environmental accident, but if the frequency of accidents and their magnitude starts to increase (all else being equal), its financial strength may deteriorate.

Forum discussions considered the value of using ESG factors as early indicators that can expose inadequate management oversight and potentially anticipate deteriorating credit conditions – even before traditional financial metrics worsen. These discussions also helped to clarify that the materiality of ESG issues from a credit risk perspective depends on many factors, such as the financial profile of an entity, its sector and geographical location, as well as the type and characteristics of a bond. Moreover, on the environmental front, the importance of differentiating between physical and transition risks (including policy developments) was highlighted.

2   Time Horizons

The most contentious disconnect proved the issue of time horizons, with CRAs typically looking three to five years ahead in their corporate analysis, whilst investors were demanding that CRAs take a more forward-looking in addressing long-term trends, risk trajectories, and their potential triggers. Participants agreed that there is no silver bullet to identify the right time horizon over which to assess ESG factors in credit risk analysis. However, they concurred on the benefits of gathering insight about future environmental and social factors to better evaluate the quality of governance, as well as the sustainability of business models.

Due to the multi-dimensional nature of ESG factors, difficulties in modelling non-financial factors and capturing data interdependencies were cited among the biggest obstacles to ESG consideration in credit risk analysis. Specifically, the interplay between the following was flagged: (1) the long-term structural trends that tend to influence ESG risks; (2) the probability that ESG-related incidents will materialise and the timing of when these issues will materialise; (3) the risk of these incidents reoccurring; and (4) their impact on an issuer's credit fundamentals and issuer's ability to adjust its business model by buying or selling companies and introducing or reacting to disruptive technology.

3   Organisational Approaches to ESG

Expertise and resources have been improving among both investors and CRAs, particularly where there is senior management buy-in. The level of CRA participation is a testament to this. However, building a formal framework to ensure that credit analysts systematically consider ESG factors is still a work in progress. Different approaches that could be taken were considered, including developing skills in-house, insourcing external expertise, or outsourcing on an ad-hoc basis.

Overcoming internal inertia is another obstacle. While some investors and CRAs are making headway, for other market players breaking down barriers, addressing siloed work practices, and securing internal buy-in is challenging. Another hurdle is how to incentivise and reward analysts that are the best at unlocking ESG value because it can take decades for corporate strategies to produce tangible results, or for blow-up events to materialise. Finally, the benefits and drawbacks of a built-in approach, which is integrated but more challenging to demonstrate, were considered versus an add-on approach (with a separate ESG score that may obfuscate the credit-focussed analysis).

4   Communication and Transparency

Communication and transparency specifically on ESG topics were limited at the start of the initiative, partly due to a lack of meaningful outreach or engagement, but are now improving. Gaps exist at different levels of the investment chain – not only between investors and CRAs but between asset owners and asset managers and, ultimately, bond issuers. Few participants were aware that some CRAs were making ESG factors more transparent in their methodologies and research, and of the rating changes which had occurred as a result.

Several options on how to improve CRA communication were discussed, including how they present ratings and signal long-term risks. Ideas ranged from a separate ESG section within credit opinions to sectoral and scenario analysis.

Importantly, since the initiative started, there has been notable regulatory changes amid growing realisation that ESG issues, such as climate change, can represent systemic risks to financial markets. For example, as of March 2020, among other information, CRAs in Europe need to disclose in their press releases or reports whether the key drivers behind the change of rating and/or outlook correspond to identified ESG factors (ESMA, 2019).

The PRI work is still ongoing but the transformation it has seen, especially at the CRAs' organisational level, has been remarkable. As a result of the interaction with the PRI signatories and increased regulatory scrutiny, the largest CRAs now have dedicated ESG web pages with sectoral and thematic research, they have appointed analysts and clear senior leaders who are responsible for ensuring ESG factors are fully integrated in credit opinions and discussed at rating committees, and many have improved their analytical tools, partly also through acquisitions of ESG providers of data and services. More importantly, the number of credit rating actions (whether upgrades, downgrades, or affirmation of opinions) that have ESG factors explicitly mentioned among their key drivers has been rising (Figure 4.9).[10]

Despite the progress, more work lies ahead. The forum discussions revealed that some of the initial perceived investor-CRA disconnects are shared challenges that credit practitioners face as they build a more systematic framework to consider ESG factors, and that more efforts are needed to (a) assess ESG factors' materiality and, in the case of investors, performance attribution; (b) monitor the ESG triggers that may

		ANALYSIS			ORGANISATION			TRANSPARENCY AND COMMUNICATION	
Research	**Examples of credit rating changes**	**Organisational changes**	**Analyst training**	**ESG (non-credit rating) products**	**Methodology clarification**	**Dedicated web pages**	**Compilations**	**Events**	
Sector or thematic articles enhancing the appreciation of credit-relevant ESG factors	Instances where ESG factors have contributed to a change in rating opinion or outlook	Dedicated analysts/working groups and clear senior leadership	Regular ESG educational programmes/ modules and seminars	ESG/ sustainability/ green bond or other thematic bond evaluations	ESG indicators are implicit in the methodology but have been clarified through notes	Web pages that facilitate dissemination	Research highlights on the credit implications of ESG trends and factors	ESG-specific conferences or sessions as part of mainstream events	

Figure 4.9 CRA Progress on ESG Integration.
Source: PRI, 2018.

CRAS	INVESTORS AND CRAs	INVESTORS
▪ Map ESG credit-relevant factors and flag triggers that could alter medium to long-term assessments ▪ Improve ESG factor signposting and be more explicit in commentaries ▪ Increase outreach on ESG topics	▪ Categorise ESG factors by type, relevance and urgency ▪ Conduct regular retrospective analysis and assess the evolution of ESG consideration ▪ Recognise credit-relevant time horizons ▪ Provide analysts with ongoing training ▪ Engage with issuers on ESG topics ▪ Improve disclosure and transparency	▪ Set up internal frameworks to make ESG consideration more systematic ▪ Do not confuse the purpose of credit ratings and ESG assessment services ▪ Be more proactive with issuers, service providers and in public consultations

Figure 4.10 Identified Action Areas for Investors and CRAs.
Source: PRI, 2018.

alter credit risk assessments and threaten the sustainability of business models over the long term; and (c) reach a minimum level of ESG standardisation. Against this backdrop, the PRI compiled a list of action areas, which are aimed at improving the process and output of ESG consideration in credit risk analysis (see Figure 4.10). Some areas target both CRAs and investors, and others are more tailored to either stakeholder.

Through the forums that were held in Mainland China, Latin America, and South Africa, the initiative also highlighted how ESG factors evaluation and relevance vary by countries and that, although awareness of the need for augmented risk assessments in emerging markets is also improving, more tailored regional work is needed in these countries.

The initiative is still ongoing and has embarked in a second phase of the project, to broaden the investor-CRA dialogue to other key stakeholders, primarily corporate borrowers, to improve data disclosure and engagement.[11] The outreach has also started to extend to ESG information providers and investment consultants.

Different Types of Issuers

The way ESG factors are considered into debt instrument valuations varies depending on the issuing entity. For example, ESG data disclosure may differ with the size of a company or if the debt instrument is private or public. The materiality of ESG factors and their weights in the analysis changes depend on whether the issuer is a corporate, a sovereign, a sub-sovereign entity, or a supranational.

In addition to its broader work on ESG in credit risk, PRI is also conducting dedicated work on how to consider ESG factors in sovereign debt analysis[12] and has started investigating ESG considerations in sub-sovereign debt instruments and structured products. Whilst the work in these two latter areas is still evolving, the work that the PRI has been conducting on ESG integration for sovereign bonds has revealed some important points:

- Sovereign bond investors already integrate some ESG metrics into research, valuations, and asset selection, while some financial and macroeconomic indicators have an ESG component. However, *systematic* ESG incorporation is rarely applied to sovereign debt, due to a lack of consistency in defining and measuring material ESG factors, and overall less developed tools and techniques (PRI, 2019).
- The spectrum of ESG data that is comparable across countries is broader than that available for corporate issuers and released at regular intervals. Many are available free of charge from national statistics and reputable international institutions, such as the World Bank, which now has a dedicated ESG portal,[13] the International Monetary Fund (IMF), and the World Economic Forum.
- Governance has traditionally been regarded as the most material ESG factor and has been extensively incorporated into credit rating models and valuations, in a similar manner to corporate bond analysis. In contrast to corporate bonds, however, social factors (such as demographic changes, education, human capital, living standards, and income inequality) appear to have relatively more weight than environmental factors in sovereign bond evaluations, although the impact of environmental issues is expected to increase over time.
- Engagement with sovereigns has a different purpose to engagement with corporate issuers; it can be more challenging but remains very important for fact finding. For example, it may provide a better understanding of topics or in geographies where standard economic data is difficult to collate. Furthermore, it is an important channel to convey investors' expectations, and for sovereigns to understand how their borrowing costs may vary depending on their ESG performance. The following section on bondholder engagement elaborates on some of these points more in-depth.

Bondholder Engagement: Goals and Challenges

Issuer engagement is key to responsible investment in any asset class, and debt instruments are no exception (PRI, 2018).

Historically, engagement in an ESG context has been viewed as a more prominent domain for equity investors, who have embraced ESG integration and used annual general meetings, quarterly analyst calls, and voting rights to engage, support, or challenge corporate management and strategies, either individually or collaboratively.

However, attention to the importance of ESG engagement has shifted to other asset classes more recently, including fixed income, where engagement is conducted with different goals and through different channels, compared to those available to shareholders. Indeed, in 2019, almost a third of PRI signatories were engaging on more than half of their AUM, compared to only 14% in 2017 (see Figure 4.11). At the same time, the number of signatories not engaging at all shrank significantly, from 43% in 2017 to 7% in 2019.

Unlike shareholders, bondholders cannot appoint directors to run corporate operations. However, in their capacity as a source of corporate external financing, bondholders' expectations are an important signal for corporate management and public issuing entities.

Through the engagement process – known also as active ownership – fixed income investors can not only improve their due diligence and research ahead of investment decisions, but also encourage issuers to increase ESG data disclosure, better manage material ESG risks, and help issuers improve

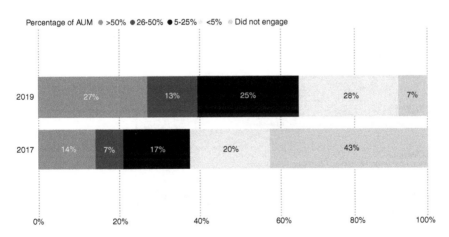

Figure 4.11 Share of Fixed Income Assets under Management on which PRI Signatories Engage.

Source: PRI.

ESG practices. To this end, good engagement requires identifying relevant ESG factors, choosing issuers to engage with, setting objectives, tracking results, and feeding those results back into investment decision making (see Figure 4.12). Persistence, consistency, and listening are key.

Bondholders can decide to engage with issuers for a variety of reasons (e.g. as part of their due diligence for risk assessment) to respond to requests from clients, or for regulatory requirements. Based on their annual reporting activity, it appears that most PRI signatories engage to gain an understanding of an issuer's ESG strategy and/or management, to encourage improved and increased ESG disclosure, and to influence issuer practice on ESG issues.

Bondholder ESG engagement can be prioritised based on size, credit quality, duration of holdings, and degree of existing transparency. Its effectiveness can be maximised depending on the timing of engagement across the bond issuance lifecycle (for example pre-, at or post-issuance), whether the debt is publicly issued or privately placed, or whether the issuer expects to return to the market. For example, engagement could take place during investor roadshows, at debt origination and reissuance, within private or public meetings. Finally, investors can engage individually or in collaboration with other investors (including across asset classes).

Whilst bondholders have a less established culture of engagement than listed equity investors, a dialogue with issuing entities is a better proposition than divesting. This step is relatively more effective if it is part of an escalation process and if it is done at scale.

One of the main challenges for bondholder engagement is establishing who is the right counterpart to engage with:

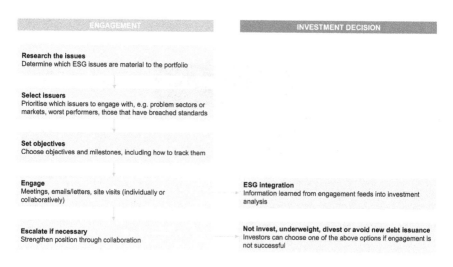

Figure 4.12 Key Steps in the Engagement Process.
Source: PRI.

- For corporate bond investors, this would ideally be the chief financial officer (CFO) or treasury department official. However, this is not always easy, as meetings with CFOs or treasurers are often narrowly focused on technical, debt-related matters and do not provide the space or opportunity to cover the broader strategic considerations that can be important to ESG discussions.
- For sovereign debt investors, the engagement process includes a variety of stakeholders, beyond government officials, including opposition parties, trade unions, employers' associations, media representatives, and supranational entities such as the IMF, the World Bank or the OECD that conduct regular country research. Importantly, when engaging directly with governmental institutions, sovereign bondholders do not approach sovereign issuers for lobbying, advocacy, or for targeting regulatory or legislative changes; rather to enhance credit-relevant ESG disclosure and better assess the ESG factors that can affect fiscal sustainability (PRI, 2020b).

There are also other engagement challenges, such as foreign currency portfolio constraints, which limit the investable universe (especially for pension and insurance funds); the size of bond holdings (which may be too small or too big); the issuer location (in emerging or advanced economies); and the lack of an 'engagement mindset', depending on the purpose of the bond investment (e.g. if it is done for liquidity purposes only) and on the fixed income instrument maturity.

For all these reasons, the degree of engagement varies but, in general, engagement with sovereigns on ESG topics is perceived to be more difficult than with corporates and therefore relatively less common – partly also because of fears that voicing concerns about ESG issues affecting growth and public accounts may be misinterpreted as political criticism.

Indeed, according to the 2019 reporting data, a third of PRI signatories engaged with corporate issuers on more than half of their assets under management, compared to 21% for SSA issuers. Moreover, less than 2% of signatories did not engage at all on their corporate bond holdings, compared to 20% for SSA bonds.

Still, framing engagement around ESG disclosure and progress towards existing policy commitment is important. For example, investors can ask for better disclosure about alignment with the Sustainable Development Goals (SDGs)[14] and government plans to achieve them, or track progress against the Paris Agreement commitments. Disclosure frameworks such as the Task Force on Climate-related Financial Disclosures (TCFD) and targeted initiatives such as Climate Action 100+ (CA100+) currently do not exist for sovereigns.

In the case of engagement with both corporate and sovereign issuers, for now, examples of collaborative initiatives are limited (notably there is an ongoing one on deforestation). However, as PRI signatories continue to grow, so will opportunities for collaborative action[15]. It is worth noting that

Principle 5 of the six Principles for Responsible Investment encourages collaboration by investors to enhance the effectiveness of their responsible investment approach.

Moreover, by discussing the reasons behind the increasing appetite for thematic bonds, investors can help issuers understand that, by growing the bond supply in this market segment, they would send an important signal about their commitment to sustainability policies. They would also provide strategic direction, create domestic green markets, and attract capital towards goals that can make their business model (in the case of corporates) or their country's growth model (in the case of sovereigns) more sustainable. At the same time, they would provide investors with an opportunity to allocate capital thematically as well as to measure the environmental or societal outcome of their investments beyond financial returns.

Data Availability, ESG Information Providers, and Fixed Income

In implementing ESG incorporation techniques, investors increasingly utilise a range of data and information to make investment decisions, beyond traditional financial metrics. They may access data directly from issuers (often with challenges related to the public or private status of a company, in the case of corporate bond issuers, or to its size) and other stakeholders such as industry associations or regulators.

Many also subscribe to ESG information providers (i.e. third-party vendors of ESG data, services, opinions and/or ratings). Some focus on issuers (corporate, sovereign or sub-sovereign); some are sectoral or issue focused; and some provide tools that facilitate ESG portfolio analytics (e.g. carbon footprint, impact investing). Their products and services can be utilised by different stakeholders and the methodologies, nature and scope of the data inputs may vary. However, they all share the same ESG or sustainability focus.

Given that responsible investment approaches originally developed in equity investing, it is not surprising that, for commercial reasons, much of the available ESG data is more useful for equity investors. Similarly, ESG information providers have prioritised issuer coverage and tools which suit equity investors. With the adoption of responsible investment expanding to other asset classes, such providers are also being utilised by fixed income investors.

Some third-party providers assemble multiple available ESG metrics and produce synthetic indicators, which are now commonly known in the market as 'ESG ratings'. These are not credit products and, to avoid any confusion, we prefer to refer to them as 'ESG evaluations'. ESG evaluations profile (equity or debt) issuers based on their ESG credentials. They are non-regulated products, unlike credit ratings.

ESG evaluations and credit ratings are distinct but complementary products. However, the work that the PRI has conducted so far has revealed that there is confusion amongst market participants about what these indicators measure and how they should be interpreted, often because some of the issues that they capture overlap. Moreover, this confusion has increased further since the recent flurry of M&A activity, with some CRAs buying ESG information providers (and now offering both credit ratings and ESG evaluations) and vice versa.

A PRI survey revealed that more than three-quarters of respondents use third-party ESG resources as an input into their in-house proprietary ESG toolkits, as opposed to using them as primary ESG data without conducting internal analysis (PRI, 2020a). This suggests that fixed income investors are beginning to be more sophisticated, building their own in-house ESG research and analytical systems. At the same time, however, credit ratings cannot be completely ignored: they play an important role in investment decisions, as most of the asset managers who participated in the survey manage strategies and mandates that are limited by credit ratings. This implies that the way ESG factors contribute to forming credit rating opinions, when they are material to credit risk, needs to be well communicated, as the difference between investment grade (IG) and high-yield (HY) instruments has implications for the investable universe.

The PRI survey also contained questions to gauge the extent to which fixed income investors are satisfied with the products and/or services they subscribe to and why. At the issuer or portfolio level, most respondents stated they are satisfied with the coverage for IG corporate issuers, financials, and developed markets, but have identified major gaps for all other types of issuers. These include HY and emerging market (EM) corporates, leveraged loans, private debt issuers, US municipal bonds, and structured products. This bias is not surprising, given that many IG corporates have equity listings. ESG information providers have received this feedback from their clients and have been working on expanding their coverage for HY and EM in the past years. They are aware of the remaining gaps, especially on private companies and non-corporate issuers.

Ultimately, though, it is the investor's responsibility to choose and interpret the relevant ESG information and integrate it in investment decisions. This task is not easy, in the absence of data standardisation and with multiple issuer reporting frameworks – such as CDP, the Global Reporting Initiative, the Sustainability Accounting Standards Board or the TCFD. However, the sector is dynamic and evolving. It suffices to think how ESG information providers have proliferated and how many more data and analysis they produce now compared to a few years ago. Furthermore, regulatory pressures are mounting. The EU Non-Financial Reporting Directive came into force in 2018 and has been adapted to national law in all 28 EU member states. And the UK is the first G20 country to enshrine into law mandatory TCFD reporting guidelines for large companies and financial institutions.[16]

Conclusions

The unprecedented rise in private and public debt witnessed during the past decade means that fixed income is an area where responsible investors can make a real contribution to making markets more sustainable. Given issuers' current large funding and refinancing needs, which have been boosted by a protracted period of low interest rates and, more recently, also the COVID-19 fallout, incorporating systematically ESG criteria in investment analysis can enhance risk assessments, allow investors the opportunity to allocate capital on a thematic basis, and enable investor to measure and report on the environmental and societal outcomes of their investments.

Here, rapidly growing market segments such as those of green, social and, more recently, SDG bonds, can help meet investors' increasing ESG product appetite. Aside from the challenges related to the assurance of the use of proceeds of these bonds and the marketing spin attached to these products to boost their attractiveness, such new instruments can channel capital to specific products with measurable ESG key performance indicators (KPIs) and trackable progress. Indeed, some corporates have already started issuing instruments whose coupon payments are adjusted depending on attainment of sustainability objectives. As just one example, in September 2019, ENEL issued an SLB whose coupon can vary according to the firm's progress towards the SDGs.[17]

The ESG fixed income market is dynamic and gradually evolving from niche to mainstream. Despite its complexity, it is a unique market segment that can satisfy investors' increasing ESG appetite as well as funding the sectors and the issuers which are actively transitioning to more sustainable business and growth models or to a low-carbon economy. This could be achieved either by supporting borrowers that contribute to positive real-world outcomes or less negative ones. If future funding (whether through thematic or traditional bonds) is more contingent on the achievement by issuers of sustainability KPIs and targets, for example via the inclusion of covenants in bond prospectuses or offering memoranda, this could be a powerful tool to achieve these goals.

Furthermore, the variety of fixed income instruments offers different levers to responsible investors to make a difference. For example, beyond corporate and sovereign bonds, how to apply ESG consideration in private debt, sub-sovereign, and securitised products investing are the new areas that investors are beginning to focus on. The latter, in particular, is very complex. However, it might play an important role in the funding of the post-COVID recovery given that bank lending is increasingly limited.

Ultimately, though, what is important is that investors appreciate that their investment decisions and capital allocation have real-world consequences. At the same time, issuers need to understand that their cost of capital is becoming more dependent on their ESG profile and performance because investors will increasingly reward/penalise issuers with positive/negative ESG credentials.

Notes

1 International Monetary Fund Global Debt Database. https://www.imf.org/external/datamapper/datasets/GDD.
2 https://www.unpri.org/pri/about-the-pri.
3 https://sdgs.un.org/2030agenda.
4 https://unfccc.int/process-and-meetings/the-paris-agreement/the-paris-agreement.
5 https://www.icmagroup.org/assets/documents/Regulatory/Green-Bonds/Green-Bonds-Principles-June-2018-270520.pdf.
6 https://www.climatebonds.net/market/best-practice-guidelines.
7 https://www.ngfs.net/en.
8 http://www.unpri.org/credit-ratings.
9 For a full list of the Statement's investor and CRA signatories, see https://www.unpri.org/credit-risk-and-ratings/statement-on-esg-in-credit-risk-and-ratings-available-in-different-languages/77.article
10 See, for example, the fixed income case-studies and quarterly reports produced by the PRI at https://www.unpri.org/investment-tools/fixed-income
11 For further information on the workshops for investors, CRAs and corporate issuers, see https://www.unpri.org/credit-risk-and-ratings/bringing-credit-analysts-and-issuers-together-workshop-series/5596.article.
12 http://www.unpri.org/sovereign-debt.
13 https://datatopics.worldbank.org/esg/.
14 https://sdgs.un.org/2030agenda.
15 https://www.environmental-finance.com/content/analysis/green-bond-comment-december-its-time-for-a-ca100-for-sovereigns.html?utm_source=041219na&utm_medium=email&utm_campaign=alert.
16 https://www.gov.uk/government/news/uk-to-enshrine-mandatory-climate-disclosures-for-largest-companies-in-law.
17 https://www.enel.com/investors/investing/sdg-bond.

References

CFA Institute and PRI (2018), *Guidance and Case Studies for ESG Integration – Equities and Fixed Income* (CFA Institute, London; PRI, London).

CFA Institute and PRI (2019), *ESG Integration in Europe, the Middle East and Africa: Markets, Practices and Data* (CFA Institute, London; PRI, London).

Climate Bond Initiative (2020a), *2019 Green Bond Market Summary* (Climate Bond Initiative, London).

Climate Bond Initiative (2020b), *Sovereign Green Bonds Briefing* (Climate Bond Initiative, London)

European Securities and Market Authority (ESMA) (2019), Final Report: Guidelines on Disclosure Requirements Applicable to Credit Ratings. [online]. Available at: https://www.esma.europa.eu/sites/default/files/library/esma33-9-320_final_report_guidelines_on_disclosure_requirements_applicable_to_credit_rating_agencies.pdf.

PRI (2018), *ESG Engagement for Fixed Income Investors* (PRI, London).

PRI (2017–2019), *Shifting Perceptions: ESG, Credit Risk and Ratings – Part 1-3* (PRI, London).

PRI (2019), *A Practical Guide to ESG Integration in Sovereign Debt* (PRI, London).

PRI (2020a), *Broadening the Outreach to ESG Information Providers* (PRI, London).

PRI (2020b), *ESG Engagement for Sovereign Debt Investors* (PRI, London).

Sparkes, R. (2002), *Socially Responsible Investment: A Global Revolution* (John Wiley & Sons, Chichester).

Part 2
Sovereign Investing

5   ESG Factors in Sovereign Debt Investing[1]

James Lockhart Smith, Mariana Magaldi de Sousa, My-Linh Ngo, Jana Velebova and David Wille

As environmental, social, and governance (ESG) factors have moved up the agenda for sovereign debt investors, many have been drawn to the experience and techniques developed for and by equity investors. However, the sovereign debt asset class brings distinct challenges and opportunities for investors, necessitating the development of new approaches for integrating ESG factors into investment decision-making.

The research summarised in this chapter shows how debt markets price in ESG factors, using an innovative approach to measuring country ESG risk that better accounts for its complexity and multi-dimensional character. The results are compelling: ESG considerations should be central to investment decision-making. We find support for the widespread belief among practitioners that, all else being equal, better ESG performance is associated with lower spreads. We also find some counter-intuitive and troubling exceptions and striking inefficiencies. Our findings indicate how investors can take ESG factors into account more effectively in portfolio management, even while working within the structural constraints imposed on them by the asset class.

The chapter begins with an overview of the key challenges facing sovereign investors, with a focus on structural constraints and data. We then review the research methodology developed by Verisk Maplecroft and Blue-Bay Asset Management to measure sovereign risks in portfolios, followed by a review the market pricing of ESG factors using an internal methodology. Finally, we present the investment implications from our research and show how ESG factors can be incorporated into portfolio analysis.

About Verisk Maplecroft and Bluebay Asset Management

Verisk Maplecroft helps organisations identify, map, and manage the full spectrum of risks affecting their global operations, supply chains, and investments. From emerging ESG trends and political risks to climate change and labour rights, the company combines unique data assets with expert analysis and specialist advisory services to provide the actionable intelligence its clients need to make more strategic decisions in an increasingly volatile world.

DOI: 10.4324/9781003055341-7

BlueBay Asset Management – a wholly owned subsidiary of Royal Bank of Canada – is an active specialist fixed income manager, with over US$75 billion in assets under management (as of 31 December 2020). It invests globally for clients across corporate and sovereign debt, rates, and FX, fully integrating ESG into the investment process. BlueBay has been taking account of ESG factors in its sovereign debt investing strategies since it began to manage such strategies in 2002. Having taken a more strategic approach to ESG investment management since 2013, in 2018 BlueBay enhanced its approach by rolling out a framework to systematically evaluate material ESG factors in fundamental credit research across sovereigns and corporates.

The Challenges of ESG Integration in Sovereign Bond Investing

ESG or responsible investment – the intentional incorporation of ESG factors into the investment process – has surged in recent years as asset owners and managers have sought to demonstrate a more holistic, long-term, and responsible approach to their investment practices, in line with their commitments to the UN-backed Principles for Responsible Investment (PRI), and driven by the needs and demands of their clients and other stakeholders. Investors initially approached sovereign debt markets looking to implement the ESG strategies developed for listed equities, the first asset class where ESG incorporation was implemented more widely; these were initially negative or positive screening or tilting, and more recently ESG integration, thematic investing, impact investing and engagement. In 2020, COVID-19's economic impacts have shown their potential to drive some of these themes forward, for instance, by encouraging investors to formalise their integration efforts (PRI, 2020, p. 20) or prompting some sovereigns or supranationals to consider bond issuances that specifically target pandemic responses or recoveries (Bahceli, 2020). In general, however, lessons learned in the stock market have not been readily transferable. Sovereign ESG investing has emerged as a separate discipline, and in some ways a more challenging one.

Structural and Technical Constraints

The difficulty of incorporating ESG factors in sovereign debt is partly due to structural and technical factors. Most obviously, there are less than 200 sovereign issuers – and in practice, many fewer are available to most investors because of their segmentation into either developed or emerging market strategies and because of technical barriers to being investable. Any form of screening in a sovereign context – for example, conduct-based negative screening on human rights performance – has, therefore, proportionately greater impacts on the investment universe, tracking error, and ultimately portfolio diversification.

Furthermore, as with all fixed income, the return upside is capped (Ngo, 2016). This not only has the potential to limit ESG investors' focus to downside risk management – but means that positive screening or tilting can, under some circumstances, damage returns. Unless countries default, weaker ESG performers may generate more returns given the higher yields they offer as compensation for the greater risk.

Finally, despite recent advances, sovereign thematic investing and engagement remain challenging in relative terms. Sovereign issuers may be increasingly open to taking on debt with use-of-proceeds restrictions, especially in relation to the low carbon transition, but do not present the same level of opportunity as corporates. Creditors, in general, have much less leverage than shareholders, and those holding sovereign debt have the least leverage of all: governments are primarily focused on satisfying their electorates or other stakeholders (Hohmann, 2012) while investors have to be careful not to be seen unduly interfering in issues of sovereignty.

Sourcing and Making Sense of Data

Beyond structural factors, early sovereign ESG pioneers were also held back by a lack of data – partly because many governments have been slower in providing consistent data than companies. The situation has improved in recent years. Some intergovernmental organisations now aggregate basic open-source data, and some data analytics firms have created comprehensive country ESG datasets.

While, as ever, more remains to be done on this front, the industry's key challenge is arguably no longer sourcing data, but using it effectively. Given the constraints discussed above, ESG integration plays a key role for most practitioners. In that context, effective integration means – or aspires to mean – understanding which ESG factors will impact the credit risk of a sovereign issuer, by how much, and when.

Macroeconomic research has shown how some individual ESG factors, particularly corruption, are relevant to economic outcomes or sovereign credit risk (Ciocchini et al., 2003; Depken et al., 2006; Paserman, 2017; International Monetary Fund, 2019). In efficient markets, material ESG impacts should be priced into sovereign debt spreads, which constantly signal investors' views on countries' ability to pay their debts. However, effective ESG integration in sovereigns is significantly more difficult than ESG integration incorporates. In terms of scale, countries are considerably larger than companies: credit risk is driven by the combined interactions of national economies, political systems, and ecosystems with each other and the global economy (Schlüter et al., 2019). In addition, mechanisms obliging governments to pay directly for the ESG costs they incur are weaker than for corporates, despite the growing use of environmental or social conditionalities by trade partners, notably the EU (Zamfir, 2018). The multidimensionality of ESG – a basket of factors that might affect each other but are fundamentally different from each other – exacerbates the challenges here, especially when making sense of aggregate ESG scores, as does a relative lack of academic and industry research on the materiality of sovereign ESG factors for market pricing. It is precisely because of these difficulties that the investment opportunity is significant for those who can do this well.

Both Verisk Maplecroft and BlueBay believe understanding a country's sustainability matters not only for achieving better risk-adjusted returns but as an increasingly urgent ethical and societal challenge. Evidence is mounting of rapid climate change (Lenton et al., 2016). Good governance and human rights, already on the back foot in multiple emerging and developed markets, faced new threats in 2020 due to the COVID-19 pandemic (OHCHR, 2020). While global poverty was decreasing until recently, the pandemic is likely to have stalled or reversed this trend – in some regions to a devastating degree (Sumner et al., 2020).

In this context, fixed income investors have the potential to substantially influence issuers' behaviour. Direct engagement allows investors to push for improvement in key areas, including through sharing their own perspectives with policymakers on the links between strong ESG performance and financial resilience. Meanwhile, investors' collective preferences affect countries' funding costs. In the domain of responsible investing, this can translate into meaningful financial and reputational incentives for governments. Where irreversible and systemic climate and biodiversity impacts are concerned, moreover, investors can aspire to contribute to preventing the worst-case outcomes – for markets as well as the environment. As both engagement and ESG integration become more common, investors are likely to start fulfilling this role in practice, not just in theory.

Measuring Sovereign ESG Risks

Methodology

The first stage of our research involved finding a way to measure sovereign ESG performance that would better reflect its inherent complexity and multidimensionality than traditional methods, and its materiality in debt markets. Instead of simple or weighted averages of dozens of underlying factors, we use a conceptual framework assigning over 80 ESG factors (see Table 5.1) from Verisk Maplecroft's country dataset to three different categories or dimensions for each environmental, social, and governance pillar, as shown in Table 5.2.

We then used cluster analysis on 198 countries to place countries into one of three clusters (low, medium, and high performance) in each of the nine dimensions each year over six years between 2013 and 2018.[2] Using three clusters across the nine dimensions of the typology means each country was thus assigned one type out of almost 20,000 (3^9) possible permutations.

Table 5.1 Factors Included in our Conceptual Framework for Measuring Sovereign ESG.

	Environment ('E')	Social ('S')	Governance ('G')
Current	• Hydro-meteorological natural hazards • Geophysical natural hazards • Food security • Deforestation • Water quality • Water stress trend • Air quality • CO_2 emissions • GHG emissions reduction: progress towards targets • Renewable electricity output • Carbon intensity: trend	• Economic complexity • Poverty • Inequality • Healthcare capacity • Life expectancy at birth • Digital inclusion • Tax burden • Labour costs • Physical connectivity • Transport infrastructure • Financial development • Logistics • Migrant workers • Trafficking in persons • Modern slavery • Decent working time • Decent wages • Occupational health and safety • Sexual minorities • Discrimination in the workplace • Criminality • Torture • Extrajudicial or unlawful killings • Arbitrary arrest and detention • Security forces and human rights • Land, property and housing rights	• Mechanisms for channelling discontent • Marginalised groups • Government effectiveness • Government stability • Freedom of assembly • Freedom of opinion and expression • Corruption • Contract enforcement process • Ethical behaviour of firms • Regulatory framework • Trade sanctions • Resource nationalism
Future	• Water stress • Biodiversity and protected areas (marine) • Biodiversity and protected areas (terrestrial) • Carbon intensity • Climate change exposure • Climate change exposure (offshore)	• Working-age population trends • Young workers • Child labour • Education • Human capital	• Civil unrest: frequency and impact • State instability • Democratic governance • Corruption trend • Strength of auditing and reporting standards • Respect for property rights

(Continued)

	Environment ('E')	Social ('S')	Governance ('G')
Resilience	• Food import security • Water security • Environmental regulatory framework • Climate change adaptive capacity • Renewable energy potential • Carbon policy • Waste management • Natural hazard vulnerability	• Financial resilience • Judicial effectiveness • Freedom of association and collective bargaining	• Separation of powers • Judicial independence • Efficacy of corporate boards • Investor protection • Efficacy of the regulatory system

Table 5.2 ESG Conceptual Framework and Number of Assigned Factors.

	Environment ('E')	Social ('S')	Governance ('G')
Current	11	26	12
Future	6	5	6
Resilience	8	3	5

Cluster analysis addresses the challenge that ESG factors have so many loosely connected dimensions by letting us group all of the variables into a smaller number of dimensions – in this case, nine – and analyse them on that basis. The specific method we used is known as two-step clustering.[3] We analysed the country data across all of the variables in each dimension of the typology to place countries into one of three clusters for that dimension. For example, Figure 5.1 shows the cluster affiliations of all countries in 2017 in one dimension – social resilience – and their risk categories for the three variables included in that dimension.

Cluster analysis generates cluster affiliations which are not scores, but categories that should not necessarily be interpreted as being worse or better than each other. However, in the case of our country ESG dataset, the correlations between the numerous variables in each dimension mean that in almost all cases, the resulting cluster affiliations can indeed be interpreted in this way. This is with the important exception of the future environmental dimension, where the data unambiguously indicated that those countries with the highest stocks of terrestrial biodiversity (a positive attribute) also had the highest exposure to physical climate change risks (a negative attribute). In our typology, this was identified as the low ESG performance cluster for this dimension.

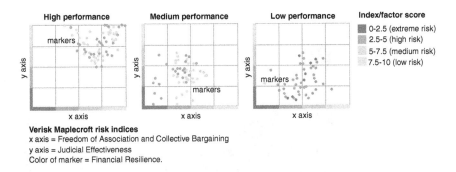

Figure 5.1 Social Resilience Clusters in 2017.

Which ESG Factors Matter the Most?

The results suggest our country ESG performance typology effectively identifies investment-relevant differences between countries and structural changes in the ESG profile of a single country. Figure 5.2, for example, shows the overall performance of all countries in 2018,[4] picking out two clusters of countries sharing the same nine-dimensional ESG types as examples. Differences between countries and changes over time are likely to be material because they represent major differences or changes in underlying ESG fundamentals.

Such changes may be material because of the way ESG performance is distributed in each dimension. The way countries typically group together reflects the complexity of global political, economic, and environmental systems. Distributions of countries on many individual ESG factors are not 'normal' bell curves but instead multimodal (i.e. they have multiple and potentially many peaks). Some countries group together in clusters around points of temporary equilibrium but can also be subject to positive/negative feedback loops that take hold when they cross tipping points. Albeit with some simplification, our cluster analysis captures this in each dimension across all the factors. Furthermore, as shown in Figure 5.2, the distribution of country types across all nine dimensions shows similar clustering.

We expect these dynamics to inform market-risk pricing such that differences in cluster affiliations and hence ESG type between countries, or movements between ESG types by a country, will be much more material than differences or movements that do not translate into any such change. ESG dynamics will be secondary to investors' decision-making, except when they imply a departure from equilibrium, thus becoming a primary concern. It is also possible that changes in a country's nine-dimensional type could also be investment-relevant in terms of perception – not just ESG fundamentals – insofar as investors working in low-information contexts use similarity between countries as a shortcut for pricing risk.

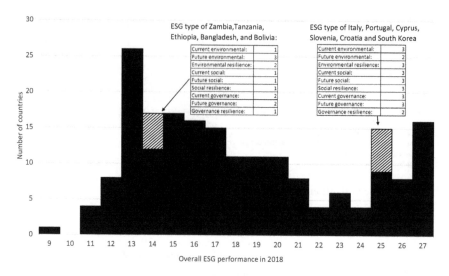

Figure 5.2 Global ESG Types and Overall Performance in 2018.

Analysis of the relationship between ESG performance changes and spread changes strongly suggests our typology captures investment-material momentum. For example, Figure 5.3, which compares countries' ESG performance between 2013 and 2018, confirms most countries with improving ESG parameters also saw their spreads narrow, although the relationship with negative ESG momentum was less clear (perhaps because of overall market dynamics and macroeconomic factors during the sample period).

The same tendency can be seen in Figure 5.4, which shows average spread behaviour over the 12-months following a change in ESG performance. The apparently more ambivalent relationship between deteriorating ESG performance and spreads is particularly interesting in highlighting inefficiencies that could, in theory, be exploited for generating investment outperformance. Markets react, but with a substantial time lag, and may even initially interpret negative ESG momentum as positive.

In Figure 5.5, we look specifically at Brazil to show the prominent role ESG dynamics can play in markets. The corruption investigations associated with the 'Lava Jato' scandal had immediate political consequences, aggravating an economic recession by paralysing policymaking and damaging business confidence, and eventually resulting in the impeachment of President Dilma Rousseff in 2016.

Our model shows Brazil traded expensively relative to its economic and ESG fundamentals and its peers in 2013, with poor ESG performance driving a sizeable proportion of the country spread, and a steady deterioration in

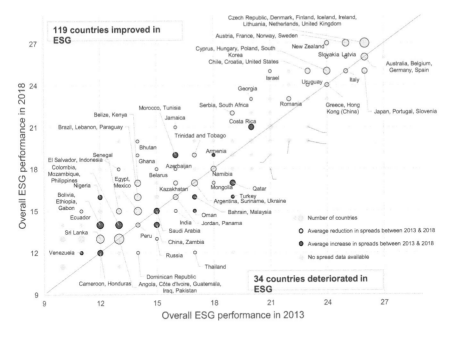

Figure 5.3 Changes in ESG Profile and Spreads 2013–2018.

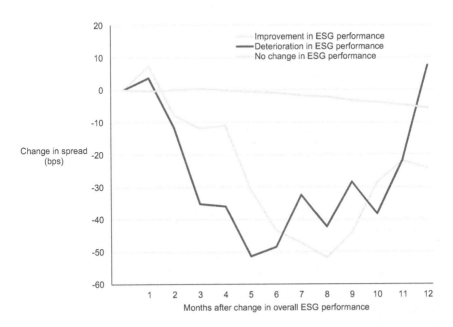

Figure 5.4 Markets May Price in Positive ESG Changes More Quickly Than Negative ESG Changes.

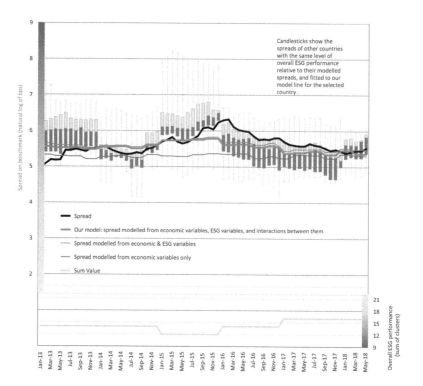

Figure 5.5 Brazil.

ESG performance through to 2015 presaging an increase in spreads. It also indicates that the turning point came in the second half of 2015 when lagging market concerns peaked and credit rating agencies S&P Global Ratings and Fitch Ratings downgraded Brazil into high-yield territory, citing the effects of the Lava Jato investigations on political dynamics as a rationale for their downgrade. In early 2016, the ESG momentum changed direction, and the debt entered cheap territory. Through to 2018, it slowly moved back towards valuations in line with the country's economic and ESG fundamentals.

Understanding How Sovereign Debt Markets Price in ESG Risks

This section assesses the direct and indirect influence of ESG factors in risk premia once all other country-level and global-macro effects have been considered.

Methodology

We carried out panel regressions with fixed effects on a dataset of 97 countries for the period between January 2013 and May 2018 including the main developed, emerging, and frontier markets. We included different aspects of ESG performance defined by the ESG classifications established in our typology as independent variables and controlled for relevant country-level economic and global-macro factors. This method allowed us to account for unobserved differences between countries. It also helped distinguish the differences between and within countries in terms of the explanatory power of our models. To provide some basic insights into how levels of economic performance affect the pricing of ESG factors, we also segment countries into strong, medium, and weak performers. Lastly, to better understand how ESG factors help to explain how investors price macroeconomic variables, we add interaction terms to our panel regressions with ESG factors as intervening variables, again using our ESG classifications and the various macroeconomic factors as independent variables.[5]

Results

Key Conclusion 1: ESG Factors Matter for Sovereign Debt Markets, with Better ESG Performance Associated with Lower Risk Premia

ESG characteristics appear to significantly influence market pricing of sovereign debt, presumably because of their perceived impact on economic outcomes and ultimately credit risk, and thus should not be disregarded in conventional sovereign analysis. Figure 5.6 summarises the simplest of our regression results – a test of the independent explanatory power of the sum of the clusters in a given ESG type, which increases in line with the overall level of ESG performance.[6]

Figure 5.6 shows that a one-unit increase in ESG performance relates to a 6.95% reduction in spread levels – which across the full range of ESG

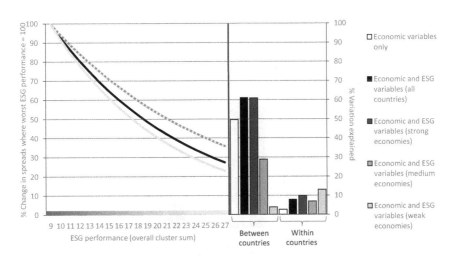

Figure 5.6 Analysis of Overall ESG Performance Shows That All Else Being Equal, Better ESG Performance Means Lower Spreads.

performance, indicates the spreads of the best ESG performers are 70% lower than those of the worst. Relative to economic variables alone, including ESG performance in the model adds 11.5% more explanatory power to differences in spread levels between countries – a meaningful boost. However, when we segment countries by economic performance, this version of the model becomes progressively weaker for medium and weak economies. This suggests that ESG factors stop being as directly relevant for investors once credit risk breaches a given threshold as countries fall below a certain level of economic performance. This version of the model also does not explain variation within countries effectively, likely because within the constrained time horizon of our study, changing macroeconomic factors are overwhelmingly the dominant driver of short-term spread changes.

Key Conclusion 2: Governance and Social Factors Are the Most Material for Investors

Our analysis also provides valuable insights into the investment materiality of different ESG factors. Figure 5.7 shows how spreads respond to overall performance in each of the environmental, social and governance categories separately.[7] ESG performance directly explains more of the differences between countries than within countries over time and appears to be much less relevant for weak economies: the explanatory power of the model for these is much lower.

Furthermore, both social and governance factors behave as expected, with better performance being associated with lower spreads. Governance performance is particularly important, with a one-unit improvement being associated with a 12.72% reduction in spreads. In contrast, environmental factors seem to be disregarded by markets, with a lack of any clear relationship between environmental risk factors and spread performance.

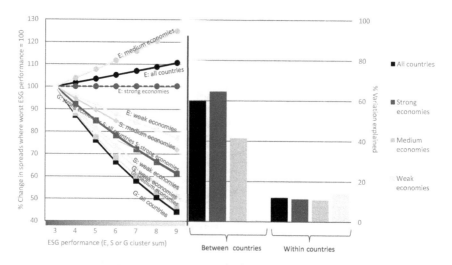

Figure 5.7 Differences in the Impact of ESG Factors on Spreads.

Key Conclusion 3: Markets May Not Yet Be Pricing in Environmental Risks Adequately

Our results point to what looks like a key blind spot – environmental risk. Figure 5.8 suggests that, at a high level, investors essentially ignore countries' environmental performance – or even actively penalise better performance.

Analysing the three environmental dimensions in our typology separately, as shown in Figure 5.8, which compares the difference in spreads associated with a country being a low or medium performer rather than a high performer in each dimension, provides more clarity. Disaggregating ESG factors in this way – and hence differentiating between current and future risk – is particularly important in relation to the environment because of the likely mismatch between the time horizons of most investors and the timeframe in which environmental risk might materialise.

This mismatch of time horizons is implied in the way that markets ignore current environmental performance, encompassing factors such as water quality and air quality. However, our results also show that investors actively penalise better performance in the future environmental dimension with higher spreads.

As for what could be driving these surprising results, the future environmental performance groupings are largely driven by two factors with particularly strong fits to the cluster assignations – exposure to physical climate change risk, and levels of terrestrial biodiversity. Those countries with the most exposure to physical climate change risk – categorised as low performers here – also have the highest levels of biodiversity. Single factor regression analysis on climate change exposure and biodiversity shows investors do price the debt of more climate change-exposed countries more cheaply; and that when countries have similar climate change exposure, investors prefer those with higher biodiversity.

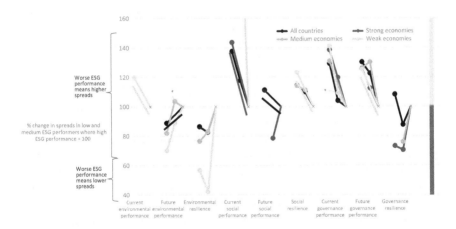

Figure 5.8 Analysis of the Nine ESG Dimensions Highlights Key Market Blind Spots.
Note: All results have P values ≤0.001, except when: labelled with ★★, denoting a P value ≤0.01, or ★, denoting a P value ≤0.05. Results with P values >0.05 are not shown. The lower the value, the lower the probability that the result is random and ESG is actually irrelevant to spreads. P ≤ 0.001 means no more than 0.1% probability that the result is random.

In this context, the results in Figure 5.8 suggest that biodiversity weighs much more in the balance for markets than climate change exposure. Investors are unlikely to be focused on biodiversity in literal terms, but as a broad proxy for a country still having significant natural resources available for exploitation.

Figure 5.8 also appears to suggest that markets penalise better performance in the environmental resilience dimension, which includes environmental regulation and carbon policy, in all except the strongest economies. Investors still prefer countries that have ineffective environmental regulations, water and waste management, and are not making an effort to decarbonise. The exceptions are economies that are robust enough to absorb the cost of high performance in these areas, which is expensive and only designed to pay off in the long term outside market time horizons.

This suggests that the growing strategic focus on environmental and climate risk has not yet translated into meaningful changes in market behaviour. We acknowledge that our research only represents a snapshot of a few years, and the situation may already be changing gradually. However, it is also plausible that investors will eventually face an abrupt repricing of some environmental risks, especially those related to climate change, when either the risks themselves or market perceptions of their materiality cross a tipping point.

Key Conclusion 4: ESG Risk Factors Are Non-linear in Their Credit Risk Impacts

Examining the nine ESG dimensions individually also shows us that good governance is not always associated with lower spreads. In particular, the way markets price performance in the governance resilience dimension – which includes the separation of powers, judicial independence, the efficacy of the regulatory system, and levels of investor protection – is non-linear. In general, markets prefer medium governance performance in this area of ESG to low performance – but they also appear to prefer medium to high performance.

When countries have no institutions capable of checking the power of the head of state, policymaking may be arbitrary and political uncertainty high, potentially affecting credit risk. In this context, the introduction of basic institutions represents an improvement, rewarded by markets with lower spreads. At the other extreme, however, countries with more developed political institutions that are independent of and can control the executive face another risk: political gridlock preventing the government from being able to pass reforms to meet changing macroeconomic circumstances (Cox and McCubbins, 2000). Even if authoritarian countries are in the long term arguably more prone to disorderly political change, investors may judge that such change is relatively unlikely to occur within an investment-relevant time horizon.

Key Conclusion 5: ESG Performance Changes How Markets Price Global Macro Factors

By adding interaction terms to our model, we find that ESG performance also appears to be relevant indirectly: it helps to explain differences in how debt markets price other factors. We identify interesting relationships with some country-level macroeconomic variables: for example, inflation is in general not a significant driver of spread behaviour but becomes one in certain types of economies that are laggards in specific areas of environmental or social performance.

However, the most notable interactions appear to occur with the two global macro factors in our model. As shown in Figure 5.9, which captures how differences in ESG performance affect the impact on spreads of a given global macro change, these are US monetary policy as a proxy for global credit conditions, and the CBOE Volatility Index (VIX) as a proxy for global risk sentiment.[8]

Figure 5.9 Differences in ESG Performance May Affect How Markets Respond to Global Macro Factors. Dark circles show increase in spreads and light circles show decrease in spreads.

Without accounting for ESG, higher US Federal Reserve effective federal funds rates mean higher spreads, as expected. However, countries that underperform on governance see their spreads widen less or even narrow slightly. While this requires further investigation, it likely represents the same ambivalence towards the political risks associated with democracies. Far from being more reliable borrowers, when debt servicing becomes more expensive, democracies may be seen by markets as less reliable. This could be, for example, because political leaders are more beholden to demands for alternative policies that conflict with debt repayment obligations (Henrik et al., 2011).

Counterintuitively, increases in the VIX index imply lower spreads in general, suggesting the VIX – at least under recent market conditions – is less a traditional barometer of global risk sentiment than a red flag for US equities prompting investors to look for uncorrelated assets elsewhere. However, our model highlights an important exception to this rule – countries exhibiting ESG underperformance (especially in relation to governance) and weaker economies (where concerns over credit quality prevail).

Investment Implications

We believe our research into the role of ESG factors in sovereign debt investing can inform fundamental credit analysis, investment decision-making, portfolio construction, and product development.

BlueBay rolled out its proprietary ESG integration framework for sovereign issuers in 2018. This framework manages some unique challenges faced by fixed income investors: the need for multi-layered investment analysis (tenor, structure, and currency of instruments), fragmented ESG data sources, and the difficulties of engaging with governments on these issues. The sovereign ESG evaluation model is used to derive a Fundamental ESG (Risk) Rating, which draws on ESG metrics and insights derived from Verisk Maplecroft – and is complemented by BlueBay's own insights. Portfolio managers and sovereign analysts also assign an Investment ESG Score to every individual security, based on BlueBay's assessment of how that issuer's fundamental ESG risks are likely to impact investment performance (Table 5.3).

This approach produces two ESG metrics for every investment decision (one at the issuer level, the Fundamental ESG Risk Rating to capture the sustainability materiality; and the other at the issue level, the Investment ESG Score, which signals the investment materiality), allowing BlueBay to more effectively reflect the multidimensional materiality of ESG factors when investing in the fixed income asset class. The logic and interplay of the two ESG metrics are similar to how credit ratings work where a fundamental credit rating is assigned for an issuer but where the rating for specific bonds from that issuer can deviate from the credit rating depending on the specific security characteristics. The ESG evaluation is an input in the fundamental driver for every investment idea (the others encompass valuation and technical drivers), aggregated to generate a conviction score. The extent to which

Table 5.3 BlueBay Sovereign Issuer ESG Output Metrics

Fundamental ESG (Risk) Rating [Issuer Level]	*Investment ESG Score [Issue/Security Level]*	
Very high ESG risks	−3	Very high ESG investment-related risks
High ESG risks	−2	High ESG investment-related risks
Medium ESG risks	−1	Some ESG investment-related risks
Low ESG risks	0	ESG considerations are unlikely to have an impact
Very low ESG risks	1	Some investment opportunities as a result of ESG considerations
	2	High investment opportunities as a result of ESG considerations
	3	Very high investment opportunities as a result of ESG considerations

ESG is investment relevant or material to the trade depends on the extent to which the fundamentals are the key drivers, or whether it is more down to technical or valuations. In this way, the framework allows BlueBay to appropriately reflect ESG trajectories in the direction and sizing of every trade.

Differentiating between countries using ESG characteristics can help investors prioritise their time and effort for maximal benefit. While ESG factors are multi-dimensional in their interactions and impacts, it is both possible and helpful to generalise and group countries for the purposes of fundamental credit analysis. Given that the sensitivity of risk premia to ESG is non-linear, analysts and portfolio managers can also use similar frameworks to prioritise what issues and developments to monitor as potentially most investment-material.

Taking account of ESG factors translates into potential investment opportunities; ESG integration is not just about risk management. It is noteworthy just how inefficient markets still are in relation to ESG factors. In general, when the ESG characteristics of a country change, spreads are usually slow to adjust and may even move counterintuitively, with country credit risks often persistently overpriced or undervalued for many months afterwards. Persistent mispricing of environmental performance is particularly important to note for active investors, as it indicates a potential long-term alpha opportunity.

Active management can add value to ESG sovereign debt investing. While applying quantitative techniques and models can provide insights, both individual countries and the global economy are complex systems that defy easy prediction. As such, modelled solutions are unlikely to ever fully suffice. We see an enduring role for analyst and portfolio manager judgement to respond to inevitable and unpredictable events and focus on their impacts. Even if a rules-based quantitative application can generate some investment outperformance under certain market conditions, there will always be a role for active management.

The findings are also relevant as policymakers and stakeholders worldwide confront environmental challenges of unprecedented scale and urgency, as well as the persistence of some social risks and resurgence of others. That sovereign debt markets have in the recent past ignored climate change-related and environmental risks underscores the wider mismatch between financial incentives and what is needed to avoid irreversible harms. The research can inform investors looking to achieve positive real-world outcomes by constructing investment portfolios linked to the United Nations Sustainable Development Goals (UN SDGs) or sovereign ESG-labelled bonds.

There is one caveat. The research summarised in this chapter focuses entirely on how ESG factors are priced under normal circumstances. That does not translate into findings on how ESG factors should be priced and will be priced in the future; we expect to rerun and improve our approach as data availability and quality improve. As more investors look to construct their own strategies, they will benefit from seeking protection against abrupt repricing as a result of rare or unforeseen events, cascading risks, or shifts in sentiment. The COVID-19 pandemic has served as a powerful reminder of such risks. Sovereign debt investors now consider the role of ESG investing not just as an incremental enhancement to best practice in the good times, but an essential support in times of market turmoil.

Conclusions

This joint research by BlueBay and Verisk Maplecroft identified important investment results. First, that market pricing of ESG risk factors in sovereign credit spreads is highly imperfect – most obviously for environmental factors, which represent a key blind spot – but also in the social and governance dimensions. As part of this, we showed that markets are slow to react to shifts in all three of environmental, social, and governance categories, underscoring the impact on the investment performance of timely assessment of deteriorating or improving ESG dynamics.

Second, ESG risk factors are highly non-linear, making markets prone to the risk of abrupt repricing when factors reach tipping points. These clearly point towards alpha opportunities for fund managers who successfully integrate ESG into their investment processes.

ESG integration can be a tool to enhance investment risk management, particularly given the non-linear impact of ESG on risk premia. The empirical evidence clearly supports the argument that sovereign debt analysis, which includes ESG considerations alongside standard macroeconomic variables, is more robust than analysis based on those macroeconomic variables alone. Good ESG performance by sovereigns is generally rewarded by lower credit risk, as measured by spreads. The results reaffirm the importance of governance and social factors for credit risks, as well as revealing some interesting insights into contrarian market preferences in some dimensions (e.g. governance) as well as potential blind spots in the pricing of ESG risks (e.g. environment). They also show that ESG is an implicit consideration for markets – even if only as a litmus test for various aspects of credit quality – when it comes to pricing in other factors such as rate rises by the US Federal Reserve.

These outcomes have shaped our thinking around the factors that have been most prominent in driving market price action. However, while the approach and models we used in this research were extremely helpful in explaining historical price action, how markets price ESG factors into sovereign spreads in the future is a different matter. We believe these relationships will remain highly dynamic and change over time, making qualitative assessment just as important as quantitative analysis. This requires investment teams to focus on changes in the materiality of individual ESG factors to benefit from transitions to new ESG investment regimes.

Notes

1 The views expressed in this chapter are those of the authors and are not necessarily the views of Verisk Maplecroft or BlueBay Asset Management.
2 Cluster analysis involves the use of an algorithm to segment countries into groups of entities that are similar. It can be carried out across two or more variables simultaneously.
3 Two-step clustering enables the creation of groups using categorical or continuous variables alike, and can find the best natural fit to select the number of clusters – though in this instance the clustering yielded either two or three clusters in all dimensions, and so we decided to use three clusters for the sake of consistency. We were also able to rank the individual variables in each dimension based on their strength of fit as an indicator of their importance as predictors for the eventual cluster assignations.
4 Here, we define the overall performance as a sum of all the cluster numbers across the nine dimensions of the country typology, where 'low' performance = 1, 'medium' performance = 2, and 'high' performance = 3.
5 We modelled and controlled for the effect of eight country-level economic variables: real GDP (% change), GDP per capita, consumer price inflation, dollar exchange rate (% change), current account balance (% of GDP), total foreign reserves (% of GDP), fiscal balance (% of GDP) and external debt (% of GDP). We also modelled and controlled for two global economic variables: the CBOE Volatility Index (VIX) as a simple proxy for global risk appetite, and the US Federal Reserve effective federal funds rate as a simple proxy for global credit conditions. Sources for the ten macroeconomic variables are Factset, the International Monetary Fund, the World Bank, and the St. Louis Federal Reserve.

   For the dependent variable, we worked with monthly spread data, using the natural logarithm of spreads because the relationship between spreads and ESG performance is exponential. For countries for which yield data were consistently available, we used spreads of yields on the relevant safe asset (German bunds for European markets, and US Treasuries for all other markets). For practical purposes, in the case of emerging and frontier markets, we measured these using J.P. Morgan EMBI Global (EMBIG) Index country-level spreads and hence disregarded slight differences in duration and changes over time in the selection of the instruments underlying the index. For other countries, we used credit default swap spreads on the same safe assets. In pursuit of maximum coverage, we used 5-year credit default swaps, which is typically the most liquid tenor, despite the longer duration of most EMBIG instruments. For practical purposes, the advantages of the increased sample size weighed more in the balance than the resulting differences in duration and instrument type.

6 The cluster sums here used the same approach as in Figure 5.3: 'low' performance equals 1, 'medium' performance equals 2, 'high' performance equals 3, and the nine cluster values were added together.

7 Here, we also use the sum of cluster values in each category, though in this case possible outcomes range between 3 and 9, because environmental, social and governance have three dimensions each.

8 The CBOE Volatility Index (VIX) is a financial benchmark that 'estimates expected volatility by aggregating the weighted prices of S&P 500 Index (SPX^{SM}) puts and calls over a wide range of strike prices. Specifically, the prices used to calculate VIX Index values are midpoints of real-time SPX option bid/ask price quotations' (Cboe Global Markets Inc., 2020).

References

Bahceli, Y. (2020), 'EU Makes Bond Market History with Record $275 bln Demand for SURE Issue – Bankers'. [online]. Available from https://uk.reuters.com/article/uk-eu-recovery-bond-issuance-idUKKBN2751Q9 (Accessed 13 November 2020).

Cboe Global Markets Inc. (2020), *How Is the VIX Index Calculated?* [online]. Available from https://markets.cboe.com/tradable_products/vix/ (Accessed 15 November 2020).

Ciocchini, F., Durbin, E. and Tat-chee Ng, D. (2003), *Does Corruption Increase Emerging Market Bond Spreads? Working Paper 2003-03.* [online]. Available from http://ageconsearch.umn.edu/record/127179/files/Cornell_Dyson_wp0303.pdf (Accessed 15 November 2020).

Cox, G.W. and McCubbins, M.D. (2000), *The Institutional Determinants of Economic Policy Outcomes.* [online]. Available from https://wcfia.harvard.edu/publications/institutional-determinants-economic-policy-outcomes (Accessed 13 November 2020).

Depken, C.A., LaFountain, C. and Butters, R. (2006), *Corruption and Creditworthiness: Evidence from Sovereign Credit Ratings.* University of Texas Working Paper. [online]. Available from https://ideas.repec.org/p/txa/wpaper/0601.html (Accessed 1 June 2022).

Henrik, E., Müller, L. and Trebesch, C. (2011), *Democracies Default Differently: Regime Type and Sovereign Debt Crisis Resolution.* [online]. Available from https://www.sfb-governance.de/teilprojekte/projekte_phase_1/projektbereich_d/d4/DDD_Enderlein_et_al.pdf (Accessed 13 November 2020).

Hohmann, S. (2012) *The Political Economy of Sovereign Default: Theory and Empirics.* [online]. Available from http://books.openedition.org/iheid/520 (Accessed 13 November 2020).

International Monetary Fund. (2019), 'Curbing Corruption', *Fiscal Monitor,* 39(60). [online]. Available from https://www.imf.org/~/media/Files/Publications/fiscal-monitor/2019/April/English/text.ashx?la=en (Accessed 6 September 2020).

Lenton, T.M., Rockström, J., Gaffney, O., Rahmstorf, S., Richardson, K., Steffen, W. and Ngo, M.-L. (2016), 'The Differences Between Incorporating ESG into Fixed Income and Equities', *Environmental Finance*. [online]. Available from https://www.environmental-finance.com/content/analysis/the-differences-between-incorporating-esg-into-fixed-income-and-equities.html (Accessed 13 November 2020).

Office of the High Commissioner for Human Rights (OHCHR) (2020), *Covid-19 Guidance*. [online]. Available from https://www.ohchr.org/Documents/Events/COVID-19_Guidance.pdf (Accessed 13 November 2020).

Paserman, M. (2017), 'Comovement or Safe Haven? The Effect of Corruption on the Market Risk of Sovereign Bonds of Emerging Economies During Financial Crises', *Journal of International Money and Finance*, 76, pp. 106–132.

Principles for Responsible Investment (2020), *ESG Engagement for Sovereign Debt Investors*. [online]. Available from https://www.unpri.org/download?ac=12018 (Accessed 13 November 2020).

Schlüter, M., Haider, J., Lade, S.J., Lindkvist, E., Martin, R., Orach, K., Wijermans, N. and Folke, C. (2019), Capturing emergent phenomena in social-ecological systems: an analytical framework. *Ecology and Society* 24(3), p. 11. Available from: https://doi.org/10.5751/ES-11012-240311 (accessed 13 November 2020).

Zamfir, I. (2018), Human Rights in EU Trade Policy, European Parliamentary Research Service. Available from: https://www.europarl.europa.eu/RegData/etudes/BRIE/2018/621905/EPRS_BRI(2018)621905_EN.pdf (accessed 13 November 2020).

6 ESG Considerations in Sovereign and Public Finance Credit Analysis

Joan Feldbaum-Vidra, Emilie Nadler and Andrea Torres Villanueva

KBRA

Credit rating agencies (CRAs) play a significant role in identifying ESG factors that have a meaningful impact on credit quality. At Kroll Bond Rating Agency (KBRA) (see Box 6.1), all our rated sectors, including sovereign and public finance, incorporate ESG considerations when they are relevant to credit analysis; our analysis also includes an evaluation of risk mitigation efforts, where appropriate. Factors that influence credit risk are not static and require ongoing surveillance, which is an important part of the credit process. Another key feature of credit analysis is understanding changes in consumer, investor, and other constituent's behaviour, as these changes can have a meaningful impact on issuer financial strength by altering revenues or affecting the access to and cost of capital. Consumer and investor preferences are increasingly shifting towards well-governed entities that create a positive social and environmental impact. As such, should these trends be sustained, the growing preference for ESG investments may feature more prominently in credit risk analysis going forward.

BOX 6.1 About KBRA

KBRA is a full-service global credit rating agency (CRA) whose mission is to set a standard of excellence by providing financial markets with transparent, responsive, and timely credit analysis. Established in 2010 as a challenger brand, KBRA offers market participants an alternative solution to incumbent CRAs by delivering in-depth research across various sectors, primarily in the US and European markets. Since the company was founded, KBRA has published over 39,000 ratings. KBRA's US entity is registered with the US Securities and Exchange Commission as a Nationally Recognized Statistical Rating Organization (NRSRO) and its affiliate, KBRA Europe, is registered as a CRA with the European Securities and Markets Authority (ESMA).

DOI: 10.4324/9781003055341-8

KBRA is a signatory of the Principles for Responsible Investment (PRI), a UN-sponsored organisation of financial sector participants, including investors, asset managers, and service providers, dedicated to promoting ESG considerations in investment decisions. KBRA has also signed PRI's Statement on ESG in Credit Ratings and supports greater clarity and transparency around ESG risks and opportunities in credit analysis. By signing the PRI, KBRA emphasises the importance of ESG issues in credit ratings and highlights its commitment to assessing ESG considerations transparently in credit research and analysis.

KBRA's priority is to evaluate the different credit-related factors that may meaningfully influence credit analysis, some of which may be ESG factors. This chapter aims to provide insight into how ESG considerations are incorporated into our credit analysis. The chapter is divided into five sections. The first section gives a general description of credit risk and the process of analysing public finance and sovereign ratings. In the second section, the relocation of Indonesia's capital city and the cities in the US that demonstrate climate leadership are used to highlight credit-relevant environmental considerations. The third section analyses credit-relevant social considerations and discusses the impact they can have on credit analysis, using the examples of Japan's ageing demographics and the influence of trade unions on policy in France. The fourth section highlights credit-relevant governance considerations and discusses them in the context of Norway's proactive management of its finances and the importance of governance indicators in United States (US) public finance ratings. The last section includes reflections from the case-studies and concluding thoughts on ESG considerations in sovereign and public finance credit analysis.

Understanding Credit Risk

KBRA's approach to credit analysis is holistic and incorporates all relevant factors that will have a meaningful impact on credit, including quantitative and qualitative factors. In sovereign and public finance ratings, the analysis is based on a forward-looking evaluation of an issuer's ability and willingness to repay its debt obligations and the strength of the management of government activities, which critically impact key rating determinants.

The ESG factors that influence our credit analysis vary widely depending on location and the credit characteristics of individual issuers or issuances. For instance, some areas of the world are more vulnerable to severe weather events or sea level rise. In addition, ESG considerations can differ in advanced versus emerging economies. With respect to environmental factors, wealthier and more institutionally developed economies may be better positioned to take precautionary steps that mitigate risks, although no country is entirely immune to natural disasters. Concerning social factors, many institutionally advanced economies are more effective at enriching their populations and reducing social disruption. Although levels of income inequality may be generally higher in emerging markets, many advanced economies face these challenges as well. Regarding governance, advanced economies generally have stronger governance profiles, although this is not always the case.

ESG considerations can be important to credit but many ESG factors are not likely to be financially material; only a subset of ESG factors influence the risk of default and are considered relevant in the credit evaluation of an issuer. Some ESG factors, especially related to environmental and social considerations, can be challenging to capture in credit risk analysis because the timeframe of risk is longer-term, and its course can be unpredictable. This is especially true for environmental factors, where – taking global warming as an example – much is dependent on the trajectory of global regulations aimed to mitigate the effects of climate change.

Given these complexities and challenges, KBRA uses a two-step process to identify credit-relevant ESG considerations. First, we identify those ESG factors that have a direct impact on the given transaction. We define direct impact as those factors that have a clear, tangible impact on credit, are typically quantifiable, and the assessment of which is generally rooted in existing methodologies. Where relevant, these are considered as key credit considerations in our analysis and are detailed in our rating reports.

The second step is to analyse an issuer's management of ESG risks and opportunities by evaluating its strategy for identifying, preparing for, and mitigating them. KBRA also reviews the affordability of an issuer's management plan to address ESG risks and opportunities and whether it is achievable at the given rating level. Assessing management performance and capability has long held an outsize role in many of our rating methodologies. Hence, it is a natural extension to integrate certain ESG issues into the analysis of management teams. Our management review also typically includes an evaluation of an issuer's exposure to changes in stakeholder preferences and how that may influence creditworthiness. For sovereigns and public entities, stakeholders refer to multi-national or international lenders, regulators, citizens, and voters, among other groups. A key consideration in our credit process is evaluating how management responds and plans for (often competing) stakeholder interests and policy goals that present ESG risks and opportunities.

ESG factors increasingly pose challenges and opportunities for management. Some may be near-term, some may be longer-term, but how an entity prepares and strategises for anticipated ESG risks and opportunities informs our evaluation of management effectiveness. Thus, our assessment of management is the guiding compass for how we understand ESG impact on credit risk analysis.

The following sections highlight case studies of how ESG factors are incorporated into credit rating analysis and their influence on an issuer's credit profile. However, the illustrations are not intended to provide a comprehensive credit evaluation of any issuer. In a credit opinion, all credit-relevant factors, including ESG and non-ESG considerations, are assessed to provide a view on creditworthiness.

Environmental Considerations

Environmental factors may be directly relevant to an issuer's credit profile but are also important considerations in our review of management. In KBRA's view, many governments have become more focused on climate change and have increased the level of management awareness and constituent engagement. Some of the key environmental factors that influence the credit analysis of sovereigns and public entities include climate change, natural disasters and other extreme weather events, environmental hazards, and natural resource allocation, among others.

Risk management related to environmental factors is central to credit analysis. While multiple solutions may be needed, and sovereign and sub-sovereign efforts vary, proactive risk mitigation efforts may be beneficial to an issuer's credit profile and reflect positively on the issuer's management team. Government administrations that address needed adaptive infrastructure or land-use planning with climate change in mind can preserve, and potentially enhance, the long-term economic health of a country or sub-sovereign jurisdiction.

In our analysis of environmental risks, KBRA often relies on publicly available information, but may also examine data provided by third-party sources such as project feasibility or engineering studies. When the focus is on macro and fiscal results, the credit analysis is data driven and relies on forecasts and trend analysis.

Environmental Case-Study 1: Relocating Indonesia's Capital City

In August 2019, the Indonesian government revealed plans to relocate the country's capital from Jakarta to the island of Borneo. The administration indicated that ESG risks, including overcrowding, pollution, sea level rise, and subsidence, prompted the relocation decision. This decision has credit implications and may affect Indonesia's creditworthiness and access to capital. The relocation can stem downward credit pressure on the rating and may also help enhance the sovereign's credit profile if it increases private investment and improves dynamism.

The city of Jakarta is sinking at a rapid rate; depending on location, it is sinking between 1 and 15 centimetres per year (Abidin et al., 2011). Some areas of North Jakarta are sinking even more rapidly, and projections estimate that most of the area could be flooded by mid-century. Subsidence in Jakarta is primarily due to uncontrolled groundwater extraction. Since authorities cannot meet the demand for water, businesses and private homes are forced to carry out their own groundwater extractions, a largely unregulated activity. Currently, about 40% of Jakarta lies below sea level and the city is increasingly at risk from flooding (World Bank, 2011). In January 2020, heavy storms in the capital city left approximately 400,000 people displaced because of flooding and climate change, which will likely continue to accelerate the rate and strength of severe weather. These events have the potential to impair economic activity and reduce economic efficiency in the country. If not adequately mitigated, these risks could result in lost government revenues and declining incomes, important considerations evaluating macroeconomic performance and government financial strength.

Social factors also are a motivation to move the capital. Jakarta is one of the most populated cities in the world, which has led to overcrowding. Jakarta is ranked tenth in the list of global cities with the highest levels of traffic congestion (TomTom, 2019). The traffic congestion, a by-product of outdated infrastructure and overcrowding, stymies investment and lowers overall productivity, which generally are viewed as negative factors for creditworthiness. Indonesian wealth also is largely concentrated in Jakarta and its surrounding areas. Jakarta accounts for 17.6% of Indonesia's GDP and Java, the island on which Jakarta is located, accounts for almost 60% (BPS-Statistics Indonesia, 2020). The relocation of the capital to Borneo is expected to result in greater rebalancing and redistribution of wealth. This redistribution may lead to lower inequality levels and socio-political risk, which may in turn positively influence credit as these risks can affect the assessment of structural robustness.

Though the relocation may mitigate some environmental and social risks, it may also give rise to new ones. Forced population relocation can be socially disruptive and the move will also likely involve, at least to some extent, some environmental destruction in Borneo. Mindful of the adverse consequences and the environmental and social concerns associated with the relocation, the government will prioritise more sustainable technologies to create a new capital 'smart city'. Such plans could serve as a blueprint for other smart cities, thereby creating positive multiplier effects. Relocating Indonesia's capital will also have a positive social impact. The move is likely to create a new centre of economic activity, creating new jobs and opportunities for Borneo residents while also potentially attracting increased private investment into Indonesia, which has beneficial implications for creditworthiness.

This case-study shows how some important ESG factors may influence sovereign credit metrics. It also highlights the complexity of decision-making around ESG factors and the need to balance key stakeholder preferences of the country's citizens and multinational investors. As often is the case in policymaking, there are opportunity costs that deserve consideration. Indonesia's sensitivity to mounting environmental and social risk and its proactive policy stance on these issues are potentially helpful to its credit profile if it brings about greater investment and enhances the economy without causing too much disruption to social harmony in the country. These dynamics could boost the country's growth and macroeconomic performance while positively influencing government finances through potentially increased revenues. However, from a credit perspective, the capital move is probably most impactful for stemming the credit deterioration that could result from mounting sea level rise and subsidence, and the concentration of economic and political activity in Jakarta.

In conclusion, the implications of the relocation are difficult to isolate and their direct impact on credit is not entirely quantifiable. Continued management of ESG risks and opportunities arising with the relocation will need to be monitored to understand the impact on the sovereign's creditworthiness. On balance, it appears the ESG-driven relocation will prove to be a positive, and it is, therefore, viewed as a strength in KBRA's evaluation of ESG risk management that could also moderate downward credit pressure on the sovereign.

Environmental Case-Study 2: Local Climate Leadership in the US

Climate change is a top policy priority globally, as its impacts are likely to affect long-term capital needs, suppress government revenues, disrupt economies, impact public health, and displace populations. As the effects of climate change grow more extreme, governments are increasingly looking to environmental policies to mitigate these risks. This is especially true in the European Union with the European Green Deal, focusing on renewable energy expansion and energy efficiency projects to achieve carbon neutrality by 2050. The impetus for US Federal climate mitigation policies, however, is notably absent, which is pushing some states and cities to pursue their own environmental agenda. From a credit perspective, states and municipalities actively working to address and mitigate environmental risks are likely to have a stronger management profile and better governance practices in place, which may lead to higher credit ratings and better access to capital.

Environmental risks, such as sea level rises and changes in weather patterns vary by location but are becoming a pressing issue for many US states and municipalities. Some public finance issuers in the US have become increasingly focused on climate change and have raised management awareness and community participation. The impact of climate change on credit risk is measured in several ways, including on demographic trends such as population, changes in taxable values of property, and mitigation costs. In some ratings, for instance, credit analysts may evaluate trends in the number of oppressive heat days to understand the potential impact on migration patterns or on the operation of municipal facilities such as airports. In some coastal communities, analysts may request projections of property values at risk under various sea level-rising scenarios. While there is no source of climate data that perfectly correlates to credit risk, there is a long-standing relationship between good governance, effective planning, and stronger municipal finances.

Therefore, good credit risk analysis will focus on management teams' ability to identify, plan, and affordably mitigate environmental risks.

The two most populated cities in the US, New York City (NYC) and Los Angeles (LA), provide an example of proactive climate change leadership and positive ESG risk management. These two cities have robust plans to combat the impact of climate change. LA has the LA Green New Deal Sustainable City pLAn, which aims to curb the effects of climate change on its communities. NYC's OneNYC 2050 details projects to address both social inequality in the city and environmental risks, and identifies coastal flooding and extreme heat as significant threats. The cities have partnered with national and global organisations and are committed to policies consistent with the 2015 Paris Agreement on Climate Change. Both are leaders in promoting sustainability and aggressively pursue renewable energy projects to achieve carbon neutrality by 2050.

While climate risks differ between the nation's largest cities, temperature rise is a commonality. According to the National Weather Service (2020), heat is the number one weather-related killer in the US and extreme heat days are expected to increase as climate change continues. Between 1971 and 2000, NYC experienced, on average, two extreme heat days per year, while LA experienced one day per year. Without bold global climate action, NYC is expected to have an average of 42 extreme heat days per year by the late 21st century (between 2070 and 2099), while LA is projected to have 32 (Dahl et al., 2019).[1] The New York City Panel on Climate Change (NPCC) projects that the city's mean annual temperature will increase by 5.7°F by 2050 (NPCC, 2015). Consequently, both cities are taking proactive measures against becoming heat islands. For example, LA is using cool roofs and pavement, and urban greening, while NYC is focusing on planting trees and using reflective paint to coat roofs.

The Southwest is the hottest and driest region in the US. Although drought conditions have been better in Southern California compared to the rest of the region, droughts and heatwaves in the Southwest are projected to become more severe over the coming decades (NASA, 2020). In response to historical droughts, LA is committed to water conservation with a goal of recycling 100% of all wastewater for beneficial reuse by 2035 (City of Los Angeles, 2019). The city administration believes that through management, expanded recycling and conservation programs, updated infrastructure, and the development of other local resources, it will have an adequate water supply for the foreseeable future.

As sea levels rise in US coastal areas, the amount of property and infrastructure in NYC that is susceptible to coastal flooding is increasing. Sea level rise in NYC exceeds the global average (NPCC, 2015). The Lower Manhattan Climate Resilience Study found that by 2100, daily tidal flows are expected to impact 20% of the streets in Lower Manhattan and over 10% of properties in the area (City of New York and NYCEDC, 2019). In response, NYC continues to invest in flood-risk-reduction projects to protect

Manhattan and other city boroughs from flooding. The city's strategic plan includes numerous flood-risk-reduction projects, such as extending Manhattan's shoreline and integrating a sea protective barrier.

The measures that NYC and LA are taking to guard against current and future environmental risks are credit positives in our evaluation of management. In addition, they can meaningfully impact other credit factors: the actions are expected to drive job creation and economic growth; LA alone plans to create 300,000 green jobs by 2035 and 400,000 by 2050 (City of Los Angeles, 2019). All things being equal, communities like NYC and LA will be better positioned to respond to climate change and may also have stronger overall credit profiles. These communities are also likely to have improved market access to capital and additional resources and will be able to fund planning and adaptation projects that address their own climate risks.

Local governments in the US are increasingly incorporating environmental risks into their management processes. Environmental factors pose risks that need to be actively mitigated, and certain improvements are necessary to ensure that governments can successfully continue to provide services and maintain financial stability. The timing of expected impact varies considerably among public finance issuers, with some low-lying coastal cities and states already investing heavily in climate mitigation and aggressively addressing inland flooding due to increased storm events. States and municipalities that are not taking preventative measures to reduce climate change impacts are more likely to see their credit profiles deteriorate and revenue sources tighten in years to come, which has negative implications for creditworthiness.

Social Considerations

Social factors are integral to sovereign and public finance credit analysis as they can reflect the strength of an issuer's tax base and ensure the smooth functioning of government activity. Socio-political risk is commonly a guiding compass for macroeconomic policy formation. High levels of socio-political risk can constrain structural reform and limit fiscal policy flexibility. Likewise, a high degree of political instability and security risk can deter private investment and raise the cost of capital, thereby impairing an issuer's credit profile through dulling economic growth and amplifying the government debt burden. Social credit considerations may include political stability, social harmony, human capital development, health and welfare, employment, and labour market conditions, as well as per capita income. The availability of public goods, including access to education, clean water and sanitation, and affordable housing, may also be important social credit considerations.

Social factors can often directly inform credit analysis, as the strength of a sovereign or sub-sovereign's resource base strongly correlates with economic and fiscal conditions. Evaluating demographic and population trends is another integral part of sovereign and public finance credit analysis as these factors impact the macroeconomic profile of a jurisdiction. Understanding the underlying reasons for current demographic trends may include an analysis of national and regional economic shifts and the ageing of a given population, among other considerations. KBRA also evaluates the strength of the government's management of social issues. For example, if population trends are negative and continued decline is expected, an assessment of the government's response to these negative trends may be considered.

Social Case-Study 1: Ageing Population Dynamics

In Japan, population dynamics and projections create a direct credit issue for the country's future economic vibrancy and could potentially impair government financial stability and flexibility, core considerations for sovereign credit analysis. Japan's adverse demographics are well-diagnosed and studied.

Japan's population has the highest share of people aged 65 or older in the world, standing at 28% of its population in 2019 (World Bank, 2019a). This number is expected to rise such that 30% of people in Japan will be 65 or older by 2030 and, by 2065, the number will increase to 38.4% (National Institute of Population and Social Security Research (IPSS), 2019). Japan's average life expectancy is 84 years, the second-highest average in the world after Hong Kong (World Bank, 2019b). Meanwhile, Japan's fertility rate has been on a declining trend, averaging 1.42 births per woman in 2018 (World Bank, 2019c). The estimated number of babies born in 2019 hit a record low in the country at 864,000 births (Kajimoto, 2019). As a result, Japan's population is expected to decrease from 124 million in 2018 to around 88 million by 2065 (IPSS, 2019). These demographic trends are critical in the assessment of Japan's sovereign creditworthiness because of their fiscal and macroeconomic implications. These implications include a large fiscal debt, deflation risks, and weak economic growth.

The increasing share of elderly citizens in Japan translates to a rising social security burden. In addition, these circumstances threaten to dampen tax mobilisation, as a low fertility rate implies there will be fewer young workers to enter the labour market, thereby reducing productivity and tightening revenue sources. Reductions in the labour force will probably mean that some of Japan's largest industries, such as motor vehicles and electronics, will face labour shortages, although these potential shortages could be addressed by offshoring production.

The management of Japan's demographic profile also factors into its sovereign creditworthiness. Japan has introduced policies to mitigate these demographic challenges. The government has prioritised increasing the number of women in Japan's workforce. The "Womenomics" initiative incentivises businesses to hire and promote female employees and evidence suggests that it is working. The percentage of Japan's female population in the workforce in their prime working years has increased from 73.6% in 2013 to 80% in 2019 (OECD, 2020a).[2] The government has also expanded childcare access in the country by creating free preschool education, making it easier for mothers to join the labour market. Japan has also prioritised increasing the share of foreign workers by loosening the country's migrant labour laws and allowing up to 350,000 foreign workers to enter the country over a five-year period (Milly, 2020). However, to date, immigration has been short of what is needed to solve bottlenecks.

While potentially helping to stem demographic risks, these policies also reflect competing stakeholder preferences within Japanese society. On the one hand, the government wants to prioritise Japanese citizens entering the workforce to retain homogeneity in its population and increase productivity. On the other hand, however, the continued need for workers is pushing the government to loosen immigration laws, potentially disrupting social harmony in the population.

Due to these stakeholder constraints, Japan's current ESG risk management is not considered sufficiently robust to offset the expected effect of deteriorating demographics on the country's fiscal health. Demographic issues are likely to continue to negatively affect productivity and economic growth, and to directly influence the sovereign's credit profile. The fiscal expense associated with rising social security costs and the shortage of labour may negatively impact Japan's long-term debt sustainability and, therefore, its credit profile. Should deterioration worsen beyond expectations, or other credit risks become more pronounced, there could be a further negative impact on the country's sovereign creditworthiness beyond what is already incorporated.

Social Case-Study 2: Social Harmony and Labour

France's political scene is lively and represented by parties from across the political spectrum. Public protests and demonstrations occur regularly but, from a credit perspective, do not meaningfully impact the smooth functioning of political institutions even if they may dilute policy formation. For example, in 2018, the outbreak of the 'gilets jaunes' protests against planned fuel hikes escalated into a wider protest against government policy, the country's high tax burden, and perceptions of widening inequality. This in turn prompted the government to cancel the fuel price hike and did not meaningfully impact creditworthiness.

Similarly, government attempts at labour reform often encounter opposition from pressure groups, such as the trade union movement. Though only 10.3% of employees are unionised in France, legislation passed in 2007 highlights the importance of trade unions in France to national political bargaining; when developing legislation regarding labour relations, employment, and training, the French government must consult with trade unions (Dares, 2021).

The French government is committed to a wide-ranging reform agenda that aims to create a fairer society, unleash the French economy's full potential, address climate change, and transform public finances. Tax and benefit reforms include making low-wage jobs more attractive by reducing employer social security contribution, capping the compensation level in unfair dismissals, and decreasing the risks associated with hiring employees on a permanent contract (Carcillo et al., 2019). France's labour law overhaul lays the groundwork for stronger potential growth and could be rating positive for France, although there has been backsliding due to opposition, causing some dilution of the reform initiative. Nevertheless, the labour market reforms could result in more investment, which could be beneficial to France's credit profile.

Currently, pension reform is top of the government's agenda, but the changes proposed in late 2019 have faced opposition by trade unions, leading recently to the longest strike since 1968. French workers retire earlier and with more benefits than workers in any other OECD country, although the effective retirement age is on the rise due to past reforms. Additionally, France's spending on pensions is among the highest in OECD countries, equivalent to almost 14% of GDP (OECD, 2020b). The proposal to increase the retirement age by two years to 64 could save billions. However, strikes in early 2020 pushed the government to make concessions to garner enough support.

The government's management of the labour market and of pension reform incorporates policies that consider constituent preferences. The administration's challenge is balancing trade unions' demands with other important stakeholders' preferences, like sovereign debt investors, who tend to prioritise stronger performance metrics that would likely come from enhanced labour and pension market reform. For the most part, France's government has been able to manage stakeholder priorities in a way that allows for social harmony. However, this has resulted in reform dilution, which moderates the potential positive impact of the full reform agenda on France's creditworthiness.

Governance Considerations

Historically, governance considerations have been an important part of credit risk analysis and are critical to understanding an issuer's financial strength. Credit-relevant governance factors are often correlated with an issuer's willingness and ability to pay its debt obligations. In sovereign and public finance analysis, governance factors are more likely to have a direct credit impact and refer, fundamentally, to the effectiveness of policymaking institutions and the legal framework. The main broad categories of governance considerations that can directly influence sovereign and public finance ratings include the policy environment, the quality of political institutions, corruption, and transparency and accountability.

A wide range of governance factors that reflect a government's financial strength are often analysed, including bureaucratic experience and track record. An assessment of the government's financial management processes, policies, and procedures, as well as its management of economic resources, is also critical to credit analysis. Financial stability, fiscal flexibility, and access to liquidity are important determinants of debt repayment prospects. Another relevant governance factor is budgetary management, which includes an analysis of the government's ability to predict revenue and expenditures accurately.

In addition, the business environment and the rule of law are often integral to investment decisions and, therefore, the availability and cost of capital for a government. Cybersecurity is another credit-relevant governance factor, as the security systems that a government has in place can reflect its preparedness for an attack and the strength of its risk management profile. Where meaningful cybersecurity risks are evident, or vulnerability is high, these could be a rating driver to the extent it would affect macroeconomic and fiscal performance.

Governance Case-Study 1: Norway's Sovereign Wealth Fund Limits Energy Concentration Risk while Encouraging an ESG Sensitive Transformation

The Government Pension Fund Global (GPFG), Norway's sovereign wealth fund, is a financial management tool used by the Norwegian government to manage surplus oil revenues and mitigate the effects of external shocks that could potentially affect oil prices. Created in 1990, the fund helps Norway avoid Dutch disease, which often plagues natural resource-rich countries, by helping sterilise the income from oil so as not to dampen the competitiveness of other industries. The GPFG is an important credit consideration as it creates a source of liquidity for the country and is a financial reserve that can supply vital funding for future generations. This supply of liquidity and the responsible management of the GPFG underpins the country's creditworthiness.

The GPFG represents a constructive sovereign financial management strategy and was designed for long-term investing. Although the GPFG's management's responsibility has been delegated to Norges Bank (Norway's central bank), Norway's Ministry of Finance monitors the fund's operational management and determines the long-term strategy. Under the fiscal rule, the government can only spend the expected real return on the fund, which keeps the fund from depleting and limits annual withdrawals to about 3% (NBIM, 2019). Withdrawals from the GPFG are also permitted to stabilise economic fluctuations.

Contributions from the fund account for approximately 20% of the country's budget. Although oil revenues have been transferred to the fund since 1996, more than half of its value today has been earned by its investments. The fund reached a market value of $1.15 trillion at the end of 2019 (NBIM, 2020a). Between 1998 and 2019, the fund generated a 6.1% annual return (NBIM, 2020b).

The fund's overall goal is to achieve the highest possible returns, but the Council on Ethics, along with a set of ethical guidelines for the fund, were created in 2004 to ensure that investments are also ethically aligned. Based on the Council's recommendation, Norges Bank makes the investment decision in accordance with certain ethical criteria delineated in the guideline, excluding non-compliant entities from the fund's portfolio. The fund cannot invest in companies that produce or sell weapons, produce tobacco, or if there is an 'unacceptable risk that the company contributes to or is responsible for' (Government of Norway, 2019, p. 3). According to the guidelines, examples of unacceptable risks are human rights violations, high levels of greenhouse gas emissions, severe environmental damage, and violations of fundamental ethic norms. GPFG's actions are closely followed by investors worldwide since the fund holds 1.5% of all the companies listed globally (NBIM, 2019).

The GPFG's diversified investment strategy, not only in terms of geographical composition but also in its mix of investments in equities, fixed income, and real estate assets, reduces the fund's exposure to financial risks and highlights Norway's responsible approach to managing its resources. This prudent management of the GPFG, the liquidity that it provides, and the role it plays in fostering macroeconomic and financial stability, represent a positive sovereign governance strategy and contribute favourably to the sovereign's creditworthiness.

Governance Case-Study 2: Governance Indicators in US Public Finance Analysis

In most US local government public finance ratings, governance issues are central to the credit analysis as the effects of managerial decisions can have long-lasting credit implications, both positive and negative. The US has more than 50,000 state and local issuers, and laws and governance practices vary significantly from state to state. Each state has a unique statutory framework, as well as its own level of state oversight and involvement in local government affairs. Each municipal credit rating reflects the strengths and weaknesses of that specific issuer. For example, the factors used to assess the risk of bonds issued by a municipal airport are very different to those used to analyse a city's transit authority. In almost all public finance asset classes such as public hospitals, toll roads, transit systems, states, or cities, the assessment of management is typically among the most important considerations.

Evaluating the strengths and weaknesses of a state's management is crucial given that it not only impacts the state but also the state's local jurisdictions, such as counties, cities, and its public agencies. Many factors reviewed in assessing a state's financial management structure are highly qualitative. These factors may include the actions taken by the state to maintain fiscal stability, the depth and experience of the financial management team, the flexibility of the statutory framework for state decision-making, state management's philosophy regarding funding and financial reserves, the quality and frequency of the state's fiscal monitoring, and its process for revenue forecasting.

There is a significant variation amongst states in the level of oversight and support or intervention provided to municipalities under fiscal stress. A high level of state oversight and involvement in assisting fiscally distressed local governments often has positive credit implications since it shows commitment to long-term fiscal stability and commitment to provide public services.

In the Great Depression, issuers in the State of North Carolina (NC) led the nation in the number of local government bond defaults. The state subsequently adopted revised statutes, giving the state government substantial oversight powers carried out by the state's Local Government Commission (LGC), enabling it to intervene in managing local finances if their financial situation deteriorates. For instance, in 2019, the LGC assumed control of the town of Eureka, NC, due to its mismanagement of sewer system funds (North Carolina Department of State Treasurer, 2019). The LGC must approve all local government debt issuance and provides guidance and financial oversight. Furthermore, state law mandates that all local elected officials obtain government ethics training, which is satisfied through attending a class at the University of North Carolina's School of Government. Local debt issuers in NC now lead the nation for the percentage of highly-rated issuers, reflecting the credit strengths conferred by their favourable governance profile and prudent fiscal management.

In New York State, the State Comptroller established an early warning system to identify local governments' and school districts' fiscal problems. Utilising disclosure from local governments and school districts, the Fiscal Stress Monitoring System measures financial health based on a set of financial indicators (including cash levels, reserves, and short-term borrowing) as well as economic and demographic indicators. These indicators inform the strength of a government's local resource base and reflect the local government's financial strength and ability to generate revenue and repay its debt. When deemed a fiscal crisis that cannot be resolved without assistance, a Fiscal Stability Authority is created by the state. The Authority is required to review the county's budget and four-year financial plan, monthly budget monitoring reports, sales tax revenue trends, annual and quarterly financial statements, and cash flows.

For example, the Erie County Fiscal Stability Authority was created in 2005 following a financial crisis that surfaced from poor financial management (New York State Senate, 2020). The authority switched from an advisory to control capacity in 2006 upon determining an imminent fiscal crisis. Under a control period, an Authority has significantly greater powers, including final approval of contracts, the terms of borrowing and county financial plans; the establishment of maximum spending levels; and imposing a wage or hiring freeze. After the Erie County budget was balanced, the board switched back to an advisory role in 2009. The Erie Authority will be in effect until no later than the end of December 2039 (New York State Senate, 2020). It can switch anytime to a control capacity if, for instance, the county operates on a deficit of more than 1% or loses its ability to borrow money.

In most states, local governments maintain autonomy in developing their financial management systems, but the state government can play a vital role in encouraging good practices, which often has a positive effect on municipal credit profiles. While a statutory framework and state intervention help foster strong governance and, therefore, can strengthen an issuer's credit profile, the ability and experience of a local government's management team is also a critical credit consideration. Our review of management typically includes an analysis of the policies a jurisdiction has in place, the procedures for monitoring operations, its track record of financial controls, and the effectiveness of planning and forecasting, among other considerations. The ability and willingness of municipal management teams to plan for and maintain financial stability are key credit strengths. KBRA also considers how a local government approaches the long-term planning needs related to ESG risks in our assessment of management.

Conclusions

The case studies in this chapter show the importance of ESG considerations to sovereign and public finance credit rating analysis. They also show that the relevance of these considerations can vary considerably depending on the context and the issuer. A transparent and constructive policy agenda and coherent management strategy are often significant drivers for reducing credit risk for public issuers. In addition, risk mitigation efforts and an evaluation of an issuer's vulnerability to changes in consumer and investor behaviour, ESG-related or otherwise, are also essential parts of credit risk evaluations.

A frequent challenge is that ESG factors are broad, diverse, and have no precise definitions or common standards. The factors, metrics, and data used in assessing ESG can vary widely. ESG considerations, and their relevance to credit, are continually evolving and tend to be longer-term in nature and interdependent. These dynamics highlight the need for surveillance reviews, a crucial part of credit analysis, where credit considerations are continuously reassessed. Another essential part of the credit process is topical research on factors that are currently credit risks, or likely to become credit risks. This is especially important with regards to ESG topics, as much depends on global policy responses and enhanced data availability.

KBRA seeks to provide transparency around all relevant credit factors in our ratings, which appraise ESG factors alongside all other credit-relevant factors. Our credit analysis focuses on an issuer's awareness, planning, and its ability to mitigate (and utilise) its unique ESG risks (and opportunities) it faces. As ESG considerations continue to emerge as credit risks, evaluating an issuer's management of ESG factors will become increasingly important in credit rating analysis. In some ratings, ESG considerations can be crucial, but one factor alone does not usually drive a credit rating. Instead, a sovereign or public finance rating incorporates a wide variety of qualitative and quantitative credit factors and is a holistic analysis of the willingness and ability of a government to repay its debt obligations.

Notes

1 The Union of Concerned Scientists analyses extreme heat days under four scenarios where the heat index or "feels like" temperature is above 90 degrees Fahrenheit, 100 degrees Fahrenheit, 105 degrees Fahrenheit, and "off the charts," which is a heat index above 127 degrees Fahrenheit. The data presented here use the above 100°F scenario.
2 The OECD defines prime working age as between 25 and 54 years old.

References

Abidin, H., Andreas, H., Gumilar, I. and Deguchi, T. (2011), 'Land Subsidence of Jakarta (Indonesia) and Its Relation with Urban Development', *Natural Hazards*, 59(3), pp. 1753–1771.

BPS-Statistics Indonesia (2020), *Trends of the Selected Socio-Economic Indicators of Indonesia (May 2020)* (Badan Pusat Statistik, Jakarta).

Carcillo, S., Goujard, A., Hijzen, A. and Thewissen, S. (2019), *Assessing Recent Reforms and Policy Directions in France: Implementing the OECD Jobs Strategy. OECD Social, Employment and Migration Working Papers* (OECD, Paris).

City of Los Angeles (2019), *L.A.'s Green New Deal - Sustainable City Plan 2019.* [online]. Available at: https://plan.lamayor.org/sites/default/files/pLAn_2019_final.pdf (Accessed 06 August 2020).

City of New York (2019), *OneNYC 2050: A Livable Climate.* [online]. Available at: https://onenyc.cityofnewyork.us/strategies/a-livable-climate/ (Accessed 06 August 2020).

City of New York and NYCEDC (2019), *Lower Manhattan Climate Resilience Study.* [online]. Available at: https://edc.nyc/sites/default/files/filemanager/Projects/LMCR/Final_Image/Lower_Manhattan_Climate_Resilience_March_2019.pdf (Accessed 6 August 2020).

Dahl, K. et al. (2019). *Killer Heat in the United States: Climate Choices and the Future of Dangerously Hot Days.* [online]. Available at: https://www.ucsusa.org/resources/killer-heat-united-states-0 (Accessed 07 August 2020).

Dares (2021), *La Syndicalisation.* [online]. Available at: https://dares.travail-emploi.gouv.fr/donnees/la-syndicalisation https://dares.travail-emploi.gouv.fr/dares-etudes-et-statistiques/statistiques-de-a-a-z/article/la-syndicalisation (Accessed 21 December 2021).

Government of Norway (2019), *Guidelines for Observation and Exclusion from the Government Pension Fund Global.* [online]. Available at: https://www.regjeringen.no/contentassets/9d68c55c272c41e99f0bf45d24397d8c/guidelines-for-observation-and-exclusion-from-the-gpfg---01.09.2019.pdf (Accessed 06 August 2020).

Kajimoto, T. (2019), 'Fewer than 900,000 New Japanese Babies this Year for First Time on Record'. [online]. Available at: https://www.reuters.com/article/us-japan-population-births/fewer-than-900000-new-japanese-babies-this-year-for-first-time-on-record-idUSKBN1YS0FX (Accessed 06 August 2020).

Milly, D. (2020), *Japan's Labor Migration Reforms: Breaking with the Past?.* [online]. Available at: https://www.migrationpolicy.org/article/japan-labor-migration-reforms-breaking-past (Accessed 06 August 2020).

NASA (2020), 'The Effects of Climate Change'. [online]. Available at: https://climate.nasa.gov/effects/ (Accessed 06 August 2020).

National Institute of Population and Social Security Research (IPSS) (2019), *Population and Social Security in Japan (2019 Edition)*. [online]. Available at: http://www.ipss.go.jp/s-info/e/pssj/pssj2019.pdf (Accessed 06 August 2020).

National Weather Service (2020), *Heat Safety Tips and Resources*. [online]. Available at: https://www.weather.gov/safety/heat (Accessed 07 August 2020).

NBIM (2019), 'The Fund: About the Fund'. [online]. Available at: https://www.nbim.no/en/the-fund/about-the-fund/ (Accessed 06 August 2020).

NBIM (2020a), 'The Fund: Market Value'. [online]. Available at: https://www.nbim.no/en/the-fund/market-value/ (Accessed 06 August 2020).

NBIM (2020b), 'The Fund: Returns'. [online]. Available at: https://www.nbim.no/en/the-fund/returns/ (Accessed 06 August 2020).

New York State Senate (2020), *Article 10-D Title 3. Sections (§§) 3950–3973*. [online]. Available at: https://www.nysenate.gov/legislation/laws/PBA/A10-DT3 (Accessed 06 August 2020).

North Carolina Department of State Treasurer (2019), 'Town of Eureka Community Meeting Presentation'. [online]. Available at: https://files.nc.gov/nctreasurer/documents/files/SLGFD/LGC/Eureka/july-29-2019-information-session-presentation-.pdf (Accessed 06 August 2020).

NPCC (2015), 'New York City Panel on Climate Change 2015 Report Executive Summary', *Annals of the New York Academy of Sciences*, 1336, pp. 9–17.

Organisation for Economic Cooperation and Development (OECD) (2020a), 'Labour Force Statistics by Sex and Age (Indicators)'. [online]. Available at: https://stats.oecd.org/restsdmx/sdmx.ashx/GetDataStructure/LFS_SEXAGE_I_R (Accessed 07 August 2020).

Organisation for Economic Cooperation and Development (OECD) (2020b), 'Pension Spending (Indicator)'. [online]. Available at: https://data.oecd.org/socialexp/pension-spending.htm#indicator-chart (Accessed 06 August 2020).

TomTom (2019), 'TomTom Traffic Index'. [online]. Available at: https://www.tom-tom.com/en_gb/traffic-index/ranking/ (Accessed 27 August 2020).

World Bank (2011), *Jakarta: Urban Challenges in a Changing Climate*. [online]. Available at: http://documents.worldbank.org/curated/en/132781468039870805/Jakarta-Urban-challenges-in-a-changing-climate (Accessed 06 August 2020).

World Bank (2019a), 'Population Ages 65 and Above (% of Total Population) – Japan'. [online]. Available at: https://data.worldbank.org/indicator/SP.POP.65UP.TO.ZS?locations=JP (Accessed 06 August 2020).

World Bank (2019b), 'Life Expectancy at Birth, Total (Years) – Japan'. [online]. Available at: https://data.worldbank.org/indicator/SP.DYN.LE00.IN?locations=-JP&most_recent_value_desc=true (Accessed 06 August 2020).

World Bank (2019c), 'Fertility Rate, Total (Births Per Woman) – Japan'. [online]. Available at: https://data.worldbank.org/indicator/SP.DYN.TFRT.IN?locations=JP (Accessed 06 August 2020).

World Bank (2020), 'GDP (Current US$) – Indonesia'. [online]. Available at: https://data.worldbank.org/indicator/NY.GDP.MKTP.CD?locations=ID (Accessed 18 August 2020).

7 Sovereign ESG Risk Analysis and Engagement[1]

Scott Mather and Lupin Rahman

PIMCO

There is a growing recognition that environmental, social and governance (ESG)[2] factors are important in fostering long-term sustainable growth and sovereign credit improvements. Many mainstream sovereign credit risk assessments are consequently systematically factoring in these ESG or sustainability variables. At the same time, many asset owners and asset managers are realising that the breadth and depth of sovereign bond markets and the recurring nature of financing make fixed income investors a meaningful force in influencing sovereign issuers on responsible investment themes.

With $2 trillion of client assets under management, PIMCO is one of the world's largest fixed income investment managers. Our size and long-lasting relationships with issuers put us in a prime position to engage with governments around the world. As a leading investor, we can help steer those public offices toward a more sustainable model.

This chapter describes how PIMCO integrates ESG and sustainability themes into its sovereign fixed income investment process. We start by reviewing how ESG and sustainability factors are incorporated into our sovereign credit risk analysis and how ESG factors are considered in investment portfolios. We then expand on how engagement with issuers can achieve change and the process PIMCO undertakes. We follow this by presenting in-house research capturing how ESG factors relate historically to sovereign credit returns, and we conclude by discussing emerging themes in ESG and sovereign investing and areas for future work.

PIMCO'S ESG Approach

Our responsible investment approach focuses on ESG integration and sustainability-centred solutions.

The basis of our first pillar, ESG integration, is to factor ESG considerations into our broad issuer risk assessments and into the investment process, as aligned with portfolio objectives, risk tolerance, and sustainability focus. ESG and sustainability considerations are an increasingly important input

DOI: 10.4324/9781003055341-9

when evaluating economies, markets, and corporate business models, and when evaluating long-term investment opportunities and risks for all asset classes. In addition to standard credit metrics like balance sheet indicators, we believe that incorporating information on ESG factors in our issuer assessments makes for better overall credit analysis and is consistent with our goal of targeting attractive risk-adjusted returns.

ESG Risk Assessment in *Macroeconomic Outlooks*

PIMCO's ESG integration process begins by identifying key ESG risk factors when formulating our top-down macroeconomic outlook. We believe that such analysis is fundamental to making sound investment decisions in line with long-term sustainability.

The process emphasises rigorous analysis of broad secular trends, which are at the core of both global sustainability and long-term asset return potential. The first and most important step is to identify the major long-term themes that may affect the global economy and financial markets; examples include long-term demographics, the impact of technological disruptions, and geopolitical trends. Our annual Secular Forum event, which gathers a global team of investment professionals, is devoted to identifying and analysing these trends that have the potential to significantly disrupt the global economy, financial markets, and investors' portfolios over the long term. The analysis of ESG-related issues fits directly into that process. In past forums, the potential for social unrest, political transitions, and green technology, to name but a few, have been identified as key themes (see, for example, PIMCO 2019).

ESG-related factors in particular have been a focus of discussion since the global financial crisis in 2008, which drove a seismic shift in societal preferences, income distribution, political choices, and the growth of China. More recently, in our 2020 Secular Forum, PIMCO recognised climate change vulnerability and the human impact of climate-related issues as a key secular theme of focus. These issues have become more apparent and acute given high-profile physical risk events such as wildfires in Australia and California and global record-setting temperatures. In addition, transition risks related to the move to a greener economy have become an area of increasing focus for policymakers, corporate and sovereign issuers, consumers, and asset owners. The consequence is that investors must continue to factor in additional government responses to climate and other environmental risks from regulation and public policy. The 2020 forum identified China's rise, populism, and technology as macroeconomic disrupters likely to become even more pronounced over the next three to five years.

We consider these trends as likely to affect government policy, consumer preferences, capital flows, and asset prices over the secular horizon, and we look to assess their impact in our macro analysis of the global economy and across asset classes. Looking specifically at the secular theme of climate change, we assess physical and transition risks across the fixed income asset class, identifying and ranking sectors and issuers on their vulnerability. For sovereign issuers this includes assessing the impact of climate risk on a country's long-term growth path, the impact of carbon tax policies on budget balances, the transition path and cost for the energy and utility sectors, and the overall impact on the sovereign's debt ratios and credit risk. Our assessment includes scenario analysis of various future states of the world depending on how far along societies are on tackling climate change at the global level (e.g. whether we are in a 'hot-house' [as described by the Network for Greening the Financial System 2020 for example] world, business as usual, or aligned with the Paris agreement). We then assess how these developments may affect how markets function (e.g. with the birth of carbon trading), how firms may organise themselves (e.g. decreasing travel or implementing carbon offsetting programmes), how regulators and international bodies may operate, and how asset allocators may change their preferences.

Evaluating ESG Risk Factors in Credit Research

We combine the thematic guidance from our Secular Forum with detailed bottom-up analysis across sectors and issuers. This is carried out by our global credit research team who evaluate ESG-related issues as part of their credit analysis. Using a proprietary framework covering a wide range of ESG parameters, analysts review issuers' ESG performance based on public information (such as published data), recent news and controversies, and through regular interaction with C-suite officials and senior leadership, including government ministries or heads of government-related entities.

We assign issuers a proprietary numerical ESG score, derived from a quantitative framework covering a large number of indicators measuring different environmental, social and governance sub-pillars. This composite score is converted into ranks and quintiles from 1 to 5 with 5 being the 'best' ESG score. This grouping allows us to assess how issuers fare versus one another based on measurable indicators, and thus helps analysts to identify issuers on the ESG spectrum. We distinguish between 'Leading Practice' issuers, 'Better than Peers' issuers, 'In Line with Peers' issuers, 'Weaker than Peers' issuers, and those that raise 'Significant Concerns'.

This ESG score is supplemented by bottom-up country assessments to provide greater granularity and information on qualitative aspects of ESG such as policy orientation, interference with elections, and press freedom. This analysis, together with observed trends in the numerical score, enables analysts to come to a forward-looking ESG trend assessment, which assigns an issuer's ESG performance into one of three categories: improving, stable, or deteriorating. To complete the exercise, analysts examine whether there are any key red flags or controversies which may not be captured by the data. Together, these four elements – the composite score, the bottom-up assessment, the forward-looking ESG trend assessment, and red flag capture – constitute

PIMCO's assessment of how an issuer currently performs relative to its peers with regard to ESG factors. Together with market valuation considerations and other credit research and analysis, ESG evaluation informs the analyst's overall assessment of whether a specific bond is appropriate for portfolios.

PIMCO's portfolio managers and analyst teams evaluate and weigh a variety of financial and nonfinancial factors, which can include ESG considerations, when making investment decisions. PIMCO relies primarily on internal research by our credit analyst team for issuer selection and investment decision-making. PIMCO also draws from third-party ESG data providers including Bloomberg, MSCI, Reuters, Standard and Poor's (S&P), Sustainalytics, Maplecroft, and others. Research and analysis provided by external sources helps PIMCO understand and anticipate the views of market participants, and thereby gauge market sentiment and trends.

Our internal frameworks are regularly assessed and evolve as data availability in the ESG space improves over time and as more actors in the fixed income landscape focus on ESG considerations. Moreover, as assessment of ESG factors becomes more widespread, we are able to supplement and cross-check our own in-house analysis (e.g. as credit rating agencies explicitly start to incorporate ESG into their risk frameworks), providing a more robust assessment of the issuers in our scope.

We see challenges and areas for development. These include problems with the visibility of ESG risks, which play out over various timeframes, but are often reactively considered. This points to problems with a lack of reliable and consistent ESG data, an often-discussed concern, although the data are still broad enough to capture many themes investors consider salient. Many ESG factors are also difficult or inconsistently quantified, such as social issues, and are therefore more difficult to accurately evaluate and price. Other key challenges include assessing ESG risks that can be latent for a long time but pose significant downside risks if triggered, as well as accounting for the more indirect impacts of ESG issues on sovereign risk. Incorporating all these considerations is an ongoing task resulting in continual updating and evolution of our ESG tools and frameworks and our sovereign assessments.

Application: Evaluating ESG Risks in Sovereign Issuers

Traditional sovereign credit analysis focuses on financial and macroeconomic variables that materially affect a country's probability of default and the expected loss if default occurs. Today, it is increasingly apparent that a government's ability and willingness to meet its financial obligations is also influenced by politics, governance, social considerations, natural disasters, and the longer-term impact of environmental factors.

Integrating ESG factors into sovereign risk analysis adds a holistic and long-term perspective that is aligned with investing in sovereign fixed income. In addition to their long maturity, sovereign bonds have fewer available enforcement mechanisms compared with other types of bonds, and sovereign governments have broader objectives than profit maximisation or narrow economic goals. As a result, frameworks with longer horizons that consider a multitude of risks may offer a prudent approach to assessing sovereign risks and creditworthiness. Add to this the increasing body of research demonstrating that ESG variables are significant in driving macro outcomes (see, for example, Berg et al. 2016; Capelle-Blancard et al. 2016) and, in turn, medium–term sovereign credit trajectories, means we believe incorporating ESG into sovereign analysis is critical to bondholders. We explore the question of whether ESG matters for the market pricing of sovereign credit risk in a later section of this chapter.

ESG criteria have been an integral part of PIMCO's sovereign ratings analysis since 2011. Our in-house sovereign credit rating framework explicitly incorporates ESG variables with a substantial weight in the overall ratings. The ESG factors we take into account include measures of physical and transition climate risk, income inequality, quality of human capital, life expectancy and infant mortality, governance effectiveness, voice and accountability, and control of corruption. These variables are selected based on those which are quantifiable and are material in driving fundamental sovereign credit risk over long periods.

To supplement the PIMCO sovereign ratings we have developed a standalone ESG scoring framework[3] that covers a wide range of sustainability indicators across the E, S, and G pillars. Each pillar comprises sub-pillars (see Table 7.1), which in turn comprise a broad set of variables ranging from the quality of the judicial system, biodiversity indicators, protection of minority rights, measures of the informal sector, sexual rights, minimum labour standards, and quality of governance. These variables are normalised with a score of 1–100 and then aggregated across each sub-pillar and then each ESG pillar with equal weights. The composite numerical score is then converted to quintiles categorised from 1 to 5 with 3 categorised as 'In Line with Peers', 1 as 'Significant Concerns', and 5 as 'Leading Practice'.

Table 7.1 Selected Sovereign ESG *Factors* in the PIMCO ESG Scoring Framework.

Environment Sub-Pillars	Social Sub-Pillars	Governance Sub-Pillars
Physical risks	Civil & political rights	Contracts & rule of law
Transition risks	Health, education, & well-being	Democracy & institutions
Biodiversity	Labour rights & workforce	Quality of government
Environment policy		Regulatory framework
		Risk of instability
		Regulatory quality

Source: PIMCO.

We believe this extensive range of ESG parameters provides an important indicator of sustainable and inclusive growth and results in a more holistic assessment of a country's development path and ability to withstand shocks. Each factor may not have a direct causal link to sovereign risk and instead may work through more diffuse and latent channels versus traditional drivers of economic growth such as physical investment or domestic consumption. Nonetheless, we include them in our overall sovereign risk assessments; by analysing ESG factors alongside traditional financial factors, we believe we have a more complete picture of the risk and return opportunities for sovereigns. We see this comprehensive approach and systematic framework for identifying and assessing risk factors as helping us to better assess sovereign issuers on their credit and ESG credentials and thereby seek positive risk-adjusted investment outcomes.

The PIMCO ESG scores are supplemented with in-depth ESG country assessments, which cover both qualitative and quantitative variables that may impact the ESG trajectory of a sovereign. Quantitative factors include the components of our ESG score, which are supplemented with real-time information. Qualitative factors may include policy platforms or social themes gaining ground at the grassroots levels (e.g. anti-immigrant political movements, or consumers focusing on green issues). These bottom-up country ESG assessments are coupled with our sovereign ESG trend forecasts (positive, stable, negative) and our red flag/controversy markers to provide valuable input into our sovereign credit risk assessments (see Figure 7.1).

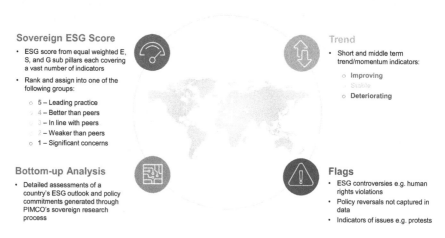

Figure 7.1 PIMCO Sovereign ESG Framework.

Case-Study: Country A (A Small Latin American Open Economy)[4]

Sovereign ESG Score:
Composite Score: In Line with Peers
Environment Pillar: Weaker than Peers
Social Pillar: In Line with Peers
Governance Pillar: In Line with Peers

Bottom-Up Analysis (Summary):

Country A ranks in line with its peers for governance driven by very low risk of instability, civil unrest, conflict intensity, or terrorism risk. However, it falls short relative to peers on the strength of its institutions, which is predominantly driven by high levels of corruption. The nature of corruption is systemic, extends across both the public and private sectors, and affects the effectiveness of institutions. Civil and political rights in Country A are protected by law but the country struggles with a lack of enforcement due to a corrupt police and judicial system. The country has a long history of mistreating vulnerable groups such as migrants as well as the LGBTQ+ community. It ranks in line with emerging market (EM) peers across most social sub-pillars with the main shortfall being a weak social system caused by insufficient funds. Country A has weak environmental institutions and the government prioritises economic growth over environmental concerns. Whilst a climate and environmental legislation framework exists, enforcement rates are low. The country is highly dependent on international funding to achieve environmental targets. Its Weaker than Peers score for environmental factors is driven by weak scores for carbon policy, quality of biodiversity, trends in deforestation, and water pollution. It has ratified the Paris Agreement and pledges to reduce emissions by 25% by 2030, from 2010 levels.

Trend Assessment:

Country A is improving marginally on overall ESG factors driven by improvements on social pillars over the past three years. This has followed a change in government, which has seen greater protections for minorities and a broader social safety net focusing on poverty reduction and targeted health services.

Red Flags/Controversies:

Discrimination against Migrants, Corruption Scandals in Government Procurement, High Criminality Risks Due to Narcotics Transit.

In Focus: Environmental Scoring for Sovereigns

From a macro perspective, climate-related risks to the global economy are real and alarming. Despite progress in some areas, broad global trends remain deeply concerning as the concentration of carbon dioxide (CO_2) in the atmosphere continues to rise, and at the current pace is projected to lead to a temperature rise exceeding 3°C by 2100. By some estimates, climate change could result in multitrillions of dollars of economic losses and a large negative impact on global GDP, in addition to the profound impact on communities and ecosystems (Intergovernmental Panel on Climate Change, 2018).

Given the rising importance of climate change in assessing sovereign credit risk, we augment our sovereign ESG analysis with broader coverage of environmental factors. To ensure we have a robust long-term, top-down perspective on climate risk, PIMCO designed and developed its Climate Macro Tracker. This proprietary tool monitors the broad momentum in climate change across

Theme	Metric	Data	Trend	1.5°C–2°C Alignment	Gap
Macro climate					
Carbon emissions	Carbon dioxide (CO_2) in parts per million (ppm)	411 ppm	Negative	No	Large
Temperature	Human-caused global warming vs. pre-industrial time	1.0°C	Negative	No	Large
Temperature	Forecast temperature rise by 2100 vs. pre-industrial time based on current pledges	>3.0°C	Negative	No	Large
Temperature	Four hottest years on record	2018, 2017, 2016, 2015	Negative	No	Large
Physical risks	Losses from natural catastrophes	160 billion USD	Negative	No	Large
Physical risks	Sea level rise	3.4 mm/year	Negative	No	Large
People	People displaced in 2018 due to disasters linked to weather and climate events (as share of total number of displaced persons)	2.3 million (13%)	Negative	No	Large
Nature	Number of species threatened with extinction (share of total)	1 million (25%)	Negative	No	Large
Energy supply and storage					
Renewables	Modern renewables share of global total final energy consumption (excluding traditional biomass)	10.6%	Mixed	Mixed	Medium
Storage	Deployed energy storage	620MWh	Positive	Yes	None
Coal	Coal share of energy generation	27%	Negative	No	Large
Energy demand					
Industry	Industry CO_2 emissions growth	1.1%	Positive	No	Small
Transport	Electric vehicles (EVs) share of global light vehicle sales	1%	Positive	Nearly	Small
Transport	Annual average fuel efficiency improvements in aviation	3.7%	Positive	No	Medium
Transport	Fuel efficiency improvement per vehicle-km in international shipping	1%	Positive	No	Large
Buildings	High-efficiency buildings share of construction (building stocks)	5% (1%)	Positive	No	Large
Carbon pricing and investment					
Carbon price	Carbon price range in major regions based on existing policies and announcements (2018-2050E)	USD 5–40t/CO_2e	Positive	No	Large
Low-carbon energy investment	Annual average investment in low-carbon energy (supply and demand) and grids	Approx. 900 billion USD	Negative	No	Large

Figure 7.2 PIMCO Climate Macro Tracker Sample Data (July 2019).

Source: PIMCO supplemented by data from sources including, BP, International Energy Agency (IEA), Bloomberg, Climate Action Tracker, Munich Re, NASA, United Nations as of July 2019. The data on energy are predominantly from the IEA, which produces reference scenarios based on global warming pathways and potential policy responses, resulting in different levels of energy demand and fuel mixes. As of July 2019.

key themes and scenarios, and measures the gap between real-world metrics and global climate goals. Along with the challenges and risks, we monitor climate-related macro trends (regulations, energy, and technology, for example) likely to create business and investment opportunities. Figure 7.2 presents a sample of the information contained in the Tracker (using data as at July 2019).

PIMCO produces sovereign climate risk scores that examine both physical and transition risks. The scores comprise a host of metrics that capture each country's exposure and readiness to cope with climate change, connecting environmental with economic variables. Energy-intensive and fossil-fuel-dependent economies are much more likely to be affected by the transition to cleaner energy, but the pace will be key to each sovereign's ability to manage the transition risks, as well as the country's savings buffer and reforms to shore up growth from other sectors. Conversely, rising temperatures and physical climate risks are likely to disproportionally affect the credit risk of developing and smaller countries. We expect this analysis will become more relevant over time as we anticipate physical risk from climate change affecting the cost of capital for governments in vulnerable countries.

We also analyse green bonds as part of our sovereign environmental risk assessment process given the rise in sovereign issuance of this structure of instrument. Our PIMCO green bond scoring system allows for differentiation among green bond issuers as well assessing the use of proceeds for the specific green project in question. Scores are based on assessments both prior to and after issuance, mapping them across a spectrum based on strategic fit, potential positive environmental impact, red flags, and reporting, resulting in PIMCO's impact score for green bonds. A similar framework is applied to other ESG instruments, such as social bonds and bonds linked to the Sustainable Development Goals (SDGs).

Together, these indicators enable us to take a more granular look at the environmental risks and opportunities faced by individual sovereigns depending on their specific starting points.

Engaging with Sovereigns

Engagement is a critical component of PIMCO's sovereign analysis; it enhances our understanding of underlying credit risks and opportunities and also enables a constructive dialogue with issuers on their sustainability journey.

We view engagement as a voluntary understanding to attain an identified objective that benefits all parties involved. Historically, investor interaction with sovereigns typically focused on improving financial and balance sheet metrics like the budget balance, external vulnerability, or macroeconomic policy coordination. The objective in these cases was to improve understanding of credit trends and to ameliorate negative outcomes like corruption in public procurement or inefficiencies in government spending. With the growing focus on sustainability, the concept of sovereign engagement has broadened to include discussions on ESG practices and outcomes. These range across various thematic issues, such as climate policy, labour conditions, SDG targets and frameworks, and the financing plans to achieve them.

PIMCO's engagement with sovereign issuers looks to lower credit risk and improve long-term sustainability by encouraging behaviour to improve fundamental credit metrics, ESG outcomes, and ESG policy oversight. Default and spread widening are dominant risks in fixed income investing, and so taking an active approach to avoiding potential losers and identifying potential winners is one of the most significant factors in portfolio management. PIMCO's ESG engagement with issuers is intended to enhance this analysis.

We have found that, as significant lenders of capital with scale and with scope, we can often exert meaningful influence over issuers' ESG risk management and disclosure. In this regard, we have observed many issuers are becoming more attuned to their creditors' interests. By investing in sovereigns willing to improve their ESG practices, we believe we can help drive greater change than through investing solely in those that achieve the best ESG scores or by excluding those that achieve the worst ESG scores. Engagement also enables a deeper assessment of broader credit and ESG risks, especially in countries that are lagging on sustainability or implementing negative shifts in policy. This we believe reduces credit risk, unlocks value not yet priced by the market, and influences positive change.

We take a multi-pronged approach to engagement. Our engagement with sovereign issuers includes one-to-one meetings and in-depth country visits, peer-group roundtables, industry group discussions, and coordination with international financial institutions. As one of the largest bond investors in the world with a long history in sovereign bond markets, we have several touchpoints for interacting with issuers. We often meet directly with individual senior government officials via video and phone calls, and during primary issuance roadshows and non-deal roadshows. During our in-country visits, we generally meet with government ministry officials, central bank staff, local business leaders, banks, consultants, trade unions, journalists, non-governmental organisations, local IFI (international financial institution) offices, and members of civil society.

Beyond PIMCO one-to-one interactions with country-specific officials and stakeholders, we often coordinate with our peers on the buy and sell sides on critical ESG themes pertinent to sovereign risk, and we participate in industry organisation roundtables (e.g. via the Principles for Responsible Investment's (PRI's) Sovereign Working Group or the Emerging Markets Investor Alliance). In addition, we collaborate with international organisations such as the International Monetary Fund (IMF), the World Bank, and the United Nations (UN) to identify solutions for the ESG engagement themes on which we are focused for each sovereign. This enables us to have a coordinated approach across many prominent actors.

PIMCO's engagement is guided by the following principles:

- Think like a treasurer: We seek to identify issuers with the capacity to change and then develop a set of core engagement objectives.
- Engage like a partner: We believe that successful engagement is based on collaboration, a productive dialogue, and mutual agreement on objectives.
- Hold to account as a lender: We measure progress against pre-defined objectives or outcomes, and agree on planned remedies if underperformance is material.

Sovereigns are uniquely complex given their need to balance multiple objectives beyond profit maximisation, and to address the preferences of their citizens. Given this, our sovereign engagement themes generally cover a broad range of topics that we believe are aligned with balanced and sustainable development, such as credit and macroeconomic topics as well as questions pertinent to evolving ESG variables and risks. The latter can include topics like the management of elections, government effectiveness, management of social and labour protests, government welfare spending, and environmental policies.

Our overarching engagement themes cover climate risk policies, meeting the Sustainable Development Goals (SDGs), and safeguarding low-income earners and workers' welfare during the COVID-19 pandemic. Beyond these, engagement themes and objectives differ from country to country depending on the criticality of the issue and the ability to implement change. For example, in countries facing high physical risk from climate change, the objective could be to shore up savings and safeguard local incomes from these shocks; in countries where transition risk is the key environmental issue, the objectives may focus on adjusting the energy mix or carbon pricing policies. Discussions with countries where minority groups are facing discrimination from official institutions may focus on corrective policies, or on improved monitoring where corruption in procurement is an issue.

The outcome of our interaction with sovereigns could range from better evaluation of ESG and credit risks to shifts in policies and, eventually, outcomes. While an ESG scoring profile is based on historical behaviour, engagement enables us to evaluate how the issuer is likely to address ESG risk factors going forward, as well as their trajectory and aspirations. This dialogue is a critical input into our forward-looking ESG trend assessment. The outcome of this engagement is included in PIMCO's ESG score, often pushing the overall score higher or lower. Our discussions with sovereigns can also lead to shifts in outcomes or policies, such as increasing a focus on green projects within the budget or increasing investments in renewable energy to improve the country's energy mix. We believe we have played a role in encouraging sovereigns to build out their green and social frameworks to issue in the green and social bond markets and to set up the infrastructure to achieve the SDG targets and issue SDG-linked instruments.

Case-Study: South American Sovereign Nation

As we expect climate action to become more important for sovereign investing, it is the job of active managers to identify the issuers with innovative approaches to sustainability. By actively engaging with each sovereign issuer on climate change mitigation and readiness, we can evaluate these considerations and integrate them into our ESG and investment assessments.

Country B scored below peers in PIMCO's ESG score, but its future trend is rated positively. The nation has a long history of political tension between the government and rebel forces, and while significant social tensions persist, the government has been making progress on achieving a resolution with the rebels as well as implementing a set of ambitious environmental commitments.

In our dialogues with the government, we encouraged them to focus on environmental sustainability. We have shared our view that, as foreign investors, we believe it is important to see progress on their stated sustainability goals and for them to thoughtfully balance the trade-offs between conservation policy and concurrent pushes for greater economic development that relies on extractive industries, a government priority.

While there is opportunity for improvement on several ESG issues, we were encouraged by the meaningful outcomes of their environmental sustainability agenda, which includes emissions reduction and zero deforestation goals by 2030. Further, a carbon tax has been in place since 2017, driving innovation in carbon pricing and underscoring the government's commitment.

ESG in Sovereign Investing

We have so far laid out how we assess ESG risks and how we engage with sovereigns. How does investing with ESG considerations work in practice?

Every portfolio is managed according to its specific investment objectives, which may include ESG considerations among other factors. PIMCO portfolio managers can access a variety of ESG information, depending on the degree of granularity required in order to inform their capital allocation and portfolio construction decisions. For some, the ESG score may be all they desire as a summary of the issuer's overall management of ESG risks. For others, a deeper understanding can be gathered by reviewing a breakdown of the ESG score and its drivers.

Our credit analysts highlight ESG assessments in their credit research notes, alongside our internal credit ratings and recommendations for portfolio managers to consider when they are evaluating investments for all PIMCO portfolios, including non-ESG-dedicated accounts. Analysts' ESG views include narrative assessments and rationales for material factors that have the potential to affect investment performance. These assessments can be relevant in shaping investments in our portfolios.

At the portfolio level, a PIMCO portfolio manager managing a sovereign credit bond portfolio may align exposures taking not only standard risk factors such as duration, market value at risk, volatility, and curve, but also credit and ESG risks. The portfolio manager may look to optimise ESG risks for each credit rating exposure in the portfolio if faced with a choice between two sovereigns with similar fundamental risk profiles trading at comparable spread levels but with different ESG scores. The manager may also choose to hold a higher percentage of ESG/green/social/SDG-linked instruments in a portfolio while still targeting similar duration and curve positions. Or the manager may seek to underweight issuers or sectors that appear misaligned with long-term sustainability trends and vulnerable to climate change transition risks, such as fossil fuel producers/exporters.

At the bond level, PIMCO's analysts and traders assess each issuer's bonds to determine fair pricing and whether its credit and ESG risks are being appropriately compensated for in the current market price. This assessment is in addition to traditional valuation metrics such as historical pricing, peer-to-peer comparisons, and compensation for the bond's maturity or amortisation schedule.

From an ESG investment perspective, the overall decision to invest in the bond or not can be laid out in a simple framework incorporating ESG scores/ risks and the bond's current market valuation. The illustration in Figure 7.3 separates potential investments into four quadrants:

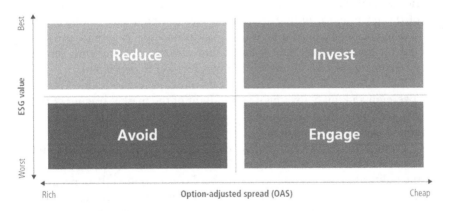

Figure 7.3 ESG Relative Valuation.

Source: PIMCO. For illustrative purposes only.

Note: The terms 'cheap' and 'rich' as used herein generally refer to a security or asset class that is deemed to be substantially under- or overpriced compared to both its historical average as well as to the investment manager's future expectations. There is no guarantee of future results or that a security's valuation will ensure a profit or protect against a loss.

1   Invest in issuers trading at attractive valuations and with strong or improving ESG profiles;
2   Engage with issuers trading cheaply, but which have weaker ESG profiles;
3   Reduce exposures to issuers trading at unattractive valuations despite strong ESG profiles; and
4   Avoid/sell issuers with unattractive valuations and weak or worsening ESG profiles.

In practice, the investment landscape is a continuum, not discrete quadrants, but this delineation helps illustrate factors informing investment decisions when looking at any type of sovereign risk, including ESG risks.

Case-Study: South Africa

In July 2015, corruption allegations emerged about former South African President Jacob Zuma. A power struggle within the African National Congress followed, resulting in a deteriorating institutional framework, with frequent changes of finance ministers, fiscal slippage, and political turbulence.

When the allegations first surfaced, we initiated a reassessment of South Africa's political and governance risks, and a senior PIMCO team made a due diligence trip to the country. The objective was to understand the economic and institutional impact as well as the social consequences of the diversion of fiscal resources away from health and education.

Following in-depth discussions with government officials and a detailed analysis, we downgraded our internal credit rating for South Africa several quarters ahead of the major rating agencies. The weight of the governance indicators within our sovereign ESG ratings, our assessment of the impact of weaker institutions on economic growth and on the country's debt burden, and our engagement with senior government officials all influenced our decision to downgrade.

This downgrade led us to re-evaluate our exposure to South African sovereign and quasi-sovereign risk in light of the market pricing of the risk and, ultimately, to reduce exposure across PIMCO's dedicated and non-dedicated ESG accounts.

From 2015 to 2017, we remained engaged with the government and key stakeholders in South Africa. This helped us to better understand the political dynamics and relay investors' concerns directly to decision makers. Today, under new leadership, South Africa is advancing reforms to improve governance and transparency, and to reduce corruption – promising signs that the country is on the long road to recovery.

Case-Study: Municipalities

Municipal bonds are debt securities issued by a US state or local government or territory, or one of their agencies. The proceeds raised are directed towards either general funding for the municipality or a specific project or purpose, such as construction of roads or schools. ESG analysis of municipal bonds includes tools and insights that are often relevant to sovereign ESG risk assessment.

From an ESG perspective, while most tax-exempt municipal bonds[5] earn their tax-exempt status due to some degree of social or public purpose (infrastructure, education, healthcare, etc.), not all municipal bonds have the same degree of sustainability characteristics. We consider issuer-level ESG factors across more than 50,000 muni bond issuers to better understand the risks, opportunities, and social impact of these bonds.

We assess the sustainability of municipal bonds across a range of factors, resulting in a PIMCO muni ESG score; these are calculated in a similar manner to the ESG scores discussed above for credits. We exclude sectors, such as 'sin-tax' bonds, that do not meet our sustainability standards. For sectors that are eligible for consideration, we rank each issuer relative to peers within that muni sector or industry across a range of variables, aligned to the SDGs, within the ESG pillars (See Table 7.2).

We determine ESG scores within each of the three categories using the same ESG framework outlined above. These scores, along with public data, are weighted to create an overall ESG score for each individual issue; different bonds from the same issuer may have different ESG scores depending on the specific bond's use of proceeds.

While we believe municipalities (issuers) should be recognised for promoting positive ESG standards, adequate consideration should also be given to the specific issues and their projects (use of proceeds), along with the issue's and issuer's overall outlook across the three ESG pillars. We strive to maintain a dialogue with these issuers to promote sustainable projects and use these discussions as a qualitative assessment of the issuer's sustainability characteristics while seeking an attractive risk/reward profile for our investors.

To create consistency across our research process, we follow a similar engagement and credit research process for municipalities as for sovereigns. This approach ensures that we embed a cultural acceptance of sustainability issues across our firm.

Table 7.2 SDG Factors in the PIMCO Municipality ESG Score.

Environment	Social	Governance
Waste Disposal	*Wealth Distribution/Poverty*	*Accreditation Issues*
• SDG 6: Clean water and sanitation • SDG 12: Responsible Consumption and Production, SDG 14: Life Below Water	• SDG 1: No poverty • SDG 2: Zero hunger	• SDG 4: Quality education
Drinking Water Treatment and Recycling	*Graduation Rates*	*Management Diversity*
• SDG 6: Clean water and sanitation • SDG 14: Life below water	• SDG 4: Quality education	• SDG 5: Gender equality • SDG 10: Reduced inequalities
Energy Efficiency and Carbon Emissions	*Employment Profile*	*Accounting/Reporting Philosophy and Pension Funding Discipline*
• SDG 7: Affordable and clean energy • SDG 14: Life below water	• SDG 8: Decent work and economic growth	• SDG 16: Peace, justice, strong institutions • SDG 17: Partnership for the goals
Regulatory Efforts and Response	*Affordable Housing*	*Accounting/Reporting Philosophy and Pension Funding Discipline*
• SDG 13: Climate action	• SDG 11: Sustainable cities and communities	• SDG 16: Peace, justice, strong institutions • SDG 17: Partnership for the goals

ESG and Sovereign Debt Performance

In 2020 PIMCO tested the relationship of our ESG signals to conventional financial risk indicators for sovereign bonds. We analysed 100 developed and emerging market sovereigns over 2006–2018 with variables including credit spreads and prices, country-specific macroeconomic and credit indicators, and global financial market indicator factors.

Our research showed that the PIMCO ESG scores generally aligned with sovereign credit spreads over that time frame. Debt issued by countries with high social and governance scores tended to have tighter credit spreads. By testing a sustainability-focused investment strategy, we were able to test whether sustainability tilts would detract from investment returns. We found no evidence over our historical time frame that an ESG-focused investment strategy resulted in any investment disadvantage. This is discussed in more detail below, and additional information on the methodology and results is presented in PIMCO (2020).

Result One

Our first finding was that ESG matters for the pricing of sovereign risk. We found that sovereign ESG scores are significant determinants of the level of sovereign spreads over and above the effect of macroeconomic, credit, regional, and global market variables. In other words, ESG factors have a direct, independent effect on sovereign spreads and don't necessarily only have an effect via their impact on financial variables. Specifically, on average, countries in the top quintile are expected to have spreads 87% tighter than those in the bottom quintile, all else equal (Figure 7.4).

Moreover, we found that changes in ESG scores are also significant in determining changes in sovereign spreads. So, if a given country improves its ESG score from the bottom quintile to the top quintile in one year, it should expect to see its sovereign credit spreads tighten. These results imply that not only does ESG matter in driving long-term sovereign spreads, but it is also a likely driver of short-term spread dynamics. Previously, the prevalent belief was that, as ESG variables tend to be slow-moving, their effects would have market implications only over time via changes in other 'real' financial variables. The short-term effect of ESG is likely to be influenced by several factors, including the increasing spotlight on ESG variables as determinants of credit risk and opportunity; the greater incidence of changes in ESG factors

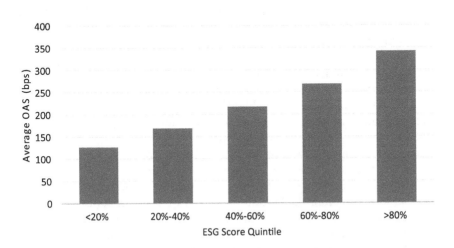

Figure 7.4 Model-Projected OAS of Five-Year Sovereign Credit by Quintiles of ESG Scores, 2018.
Source: PIMCO 2020.

like climate change, social risks, and politics affecting sovereign credit risk; and the role of asset owners and regulators incorporating ESG factors.

Result Two

Countries with more stable governments and higher human capital generally have better growth trajectories and lower risks of profligate or inefficient spending, leading to better credit ratios over time. Moreover, our robustness checks – including varying lag structures (where lagged social and governance variables are still significant) – implied that the causality runs from the sub-pillars to credit spreads and not the other way around. In other words, higher social and governance scores lead to tighter spreads, and not vice versa. Importantly, we observed these effects not only over long-time horizons, but also over the near term.

Looking at the environmental sub-pillar, the regression results indicated that a better (lower) environmental score was associated, all things being equal, with wider credit spreads. These are plausible results, for fossil fuel consumption is closely linked with the financial development of an economy in that it indicates industrial scale and activity, with developed countries generally consuming more natural materials.

Result Three

We found that, all things being equal, developed market sovereign spreads were tighter, on average, than those of emerging markets. This implies that if we consider two sovereigns – one developed and one emerging – with identical ESG ratings, identical financials, and similar geographic attributes, we would expect the developed market spread to be tighter than that of the emerging market. This finding is consistent with the view that emerging market spreads reflect other factors beyond quantitative macroeconomic, credit, and ESG factors, such as greater uncertainty of outcomes and lower market liquidity.

ESG-related variables also showed evidence of long-term relationships with sovereign credit spreads. Interestingly, while the magnitude of the governance and environmental variables was similar across both emerging and developed markets, the social coefficient was much higher for developed markets than for emerging markets (even though both are significant). We interpret this to mean that changes in social indicators tend to affect developed market spreads more than emerging market spreads.

For emerging markets, our research suggested that a country that improves its social indicator from the bottom to the top quintile should expect to see spreads tighten by 64% (350 bps using 2018 data), all else being equal. If it improved its governance score by a similar magnitude, its spreads should tighten by 85% (440 bps using 2018 data). We also found that developed market spreads showed no significant relationship to changes in any environmental, social or governance factor.

Result Four

With respect to investment performance, we found no evidence of any significant additional cost (or reward) associated with sustainability-focused investing. Our analysis found positive performance for sustainability-oriented long/short trading strategies, and this held whether the strategy was based on levels of ESG scores or on changes in ESG scores. We are cautious in interpreting this as meaning that ESG investing strategies outperform non-ESG-aware strategies, as the estimated Sharpe ratios were not significant at the 95% level. We also recognise that as sustainable investing is a new phenomenon, it is possible that as prices reach their equilibrium with respect to differences in ESG score, early effects that might result in positive returns for better scores in the near term may fizzle out in the future.

Result Five

Our research suggested that return strategy performance deteriorates as the lag in information increases, as demonstrated by a falling Sharpe ratio. This was particularly the case with strategies based on improving/deteriorating ESG scores. This finding argues for the use of forward-looking, real-time analysis that anticipates published ESG metrics. It also implies a need for deep ESG analysis incorporating both quantitative and qualitative factors when assessing sovereign credit risk.

We believe that taken together, these findings emphasise the importance of active management in ESG-focused portfolios and sovereign credit analysis that incorporates ESG factors on an ongoing basis.

Conclusion

The increasing focus on ESG issues in sovereign investing presents significant opportunities, in our view. We believe there are analytical methods comparable to corporate sustainability investing that enable a comprehensive valuation of ESG issues and their application into sovereign bond analysis and portfolio construction. Indeed, we see an increasing urgency to build methods that can appraise environment-related issues specifically and price these risks as climate concerns rise up the agenda for clients and regulators.

We find that ESG considerations matter for sovereign bond investors: ESG scores exhibit correlation with spread levels and dynamics and show high levels of explanatory power and significance with respect to spreads, even when other relevant variables are taken out of the picture. In the context of a backtested trading strategy, we find no evidence that a higher weighting in sustainability-compliant sovereigns results in any investment disadvantage. In fact, our results suggest that a timely anticipation of ESG scores may improve potential investment performance, and supports the case for active management in the ESG space (PIMCO 2020).

Notes

1 PIMCO is not affiliated with, nor does it endorse the views of the author or any contributors to this book. The information provided in this chapter is for illustrative purposes only and should not be considered as investment advice or a recommendation by PIMCO of any particular security, strategy, or investment product.

2 PIMCO is committed to the integration of Environmental, Social and Governance ("ESG") factors into our broad research process and engaging with issuers on sustainability factors and our climate change investment analysis. At PIMCO, we define ESG integration as the consistent consideration of material ESG factors into our investment research process, which may include, but are not limited to, climate change risks, diversity, inclusion and social equality, regulatory risks, human capital management, and others. Further information is available in PIMCO's Environmental, Social and Governance (ESG) Investment Policy Statement.

3 Refer to *Evaluating ESG risk factors in credit research* for additional information on the PIMCO ESG composite score.

4 This chapter contains examples of the PIMCO's ESG research capability and ESG engagement capability and is not intended to represent any specific portfolio's performance or how a portfolio will be invested or allocated at any particular time. PIMCO's ESG processes may yield different results than other investment managers and a company's ESG rankings and factors may change over time. The data contained within examples may be stale and should not be relied upon as investment advice or a recommendation of any particular security, strategy or investment product. In selecting case studies, PIMCO considers investment performance in addition to other factors, including, but not limited to, whether the example illustrates the particular investment strategy being featured and processes applied by PIMCO to making investment decisions. Information contained herein has been obtained from sources believed to be reliable, but not guaranteed.

5 Income from municipal bonds for US domiciled investors is exempt from federal income tax and may be subject to state and local taxes and at times the alternative minimum tax.

References

Berg, F., Margaretic, P. and Pouget, S. (2016), Sovereign Bond Spreads and Extra-Financial Performance: An Empirical Analysis of Emerging Markets. Working Papers Central Bank of Chile 789. [online]. Available at https://si2.bcentral.cl/public/pdf/documentos-trabajo/pdf/dtbc789.pdf (Accessed 6 May 2021).

Capelle-Blancard, G., Crifo, P., Diaye, M., Scholtens, B. and Oueghlissi, R. (2016), Environmental, Social and Governance (ESG) Performance and Sovereign Bond Spreads: An Empirical Analysis of OECD Countries. [online]. Available at https://ssrn.com/abstract=2874262 (Accessed 6 May 2021).

Intergovernmental Panel on Climate Change (2018), Global Warming of 1.5°C. An IPCC Special Report on the impacts of global warming of 1.5°C above pre-industrial levels and related global greenhouse gas emission pathways, in the context of strengthening the global response to the threat of climate change, sustainable development, and efforts to eradicate poverty. [online]. Available at https://www.ipcc.ch/site/assets/uploads/sites/2/2019/06/SR15_Full_Report_Low_Res.pdf (Accessed 6 May 2021).

Network for Greening the Financial System (NGFS) (2020), *NGFS Climate Scenarios for Central Banks and Supervisors*. June 2020 [online]. Available at https://www.ngfs.net/sites/default/files/medias/documents/820184_ngfs_scenarios_final_version_v6.pdf (Accessed 6 May 2021).

PIMCO (2019), *Dealing with Disruption*. [online]. Available at https://global.pimco.com/en-gbl/insights/economic-and-market-commentary/secular-outlook/2019/economic-outlook-2019 (Accessed 20 December 2020).

PIMCO (2020), *Does ESG Matter for Sovereign Debt Investing?* [online]. Available at https://global.pimco.com/en-gbl/insights/viewpoints/in-depth/does-esg-matter-for-sovereign-debt-investing (Accessed 20 December 2020).

Part 3
Corporate Investing

8 The Stewardship Mechanisms of Corporate Bond Investors

Arabella Turner

Introduction

The rise of the Principles for Responsible Investment (PRI), the growth in the number of national stewardship codes, and new regulation such as the European Shareholder Rights Directive have catalysed a significant increase in the level of investor participation in corporate environmental, social, and governance (ESG) issues-related engagement. There is now an extensive literature on corporate engagement in relation to listed equities covering topics, such as the drivers and value of engagement, trends in engagement participation, and the engagement process itself. However, despite the dominance of the bond market as a source of corporate financing (Schwarcz, 2017) and its susceptibility to the negative impact of ESG risks, much less has been written about or is known about corporate bond engagement.

This chapter focuses specifically on ESG engagement and corporate fixed income, to examine how corporate bondholders might enhance the efficacy and impact of their ESG-related engagement. It also provides insights into the reasons why corporate bondholders do, and do not, engage with investee companies, and the lessons that bondholders can learn from the experiences of listed equity engagers.

Stakeholder Salience Theory

Mitchell, Agle and Wood (1997) were the first to propose a theoretical model for the discussion of the effectiveness of corporate engagement by stakeholders (Majoch et al., 2014). Their Stakeholder Salience Theory (SST) was developed to help identify 'to whom (or what) do managers pay attention?' (p. 853). This theory posits that stakeholders must have one or more of power (normative, coercive, utilitarian), legitimacy (individual, organisational, societal), or urgency (time-sensitivity, criticality to stakeholder) in order to appear 'salient' in the eyes of corporate management. Mitchell et al. (1997) recognised that these attributes are 'socially constructed, not objective, reality' (p. 868) and are subject to constant change.

Gifford (2010) applied SST to shareholders and found the theory to be highly relevant. He added pragmatic legitimacy to the existing theory while

DOI: 10.4324/9781003055341-11

also suggesting that assessments of salience needed to account for, what he referred to as, 'moderating factors'; these included coalition-building, the size of the investor (in terms of assets under management), the degree of alignment of investor and management values, and timing. Through case-study research into the engagement carried out by Calvert Investment Management, Majoch et al. (2014, p. 109) confirmed both the 'relevance of Mitchell et al.'s framework for successful shareholder engagements and the additions made to it by Gifford'.

Further enhancements have since been made by other commentators, notably Gond and Piani (2012), who highlighted the importance of distinguishing between the salience of the investor and their ESG claim(s). Gond and Piani (2012) also emphasised the significance of the societal criticality of the claim.

Table 8.1 summarises the 16 SST factors (and their definitions) that underpin the research upon which this chapter is based. Unless otherwise stated, these definitions are based on Gifford (2010), but have been modified to be relevant for corporate bond investors as well as for equity investors.

Table 8.1 Stakeholder Salience Theory Terms.

Category	SST Term	Definition/Meaning
Legitimacy	Individual legitimacy	• Credibility, expertise, experience and status of the individuals engaging with the company
	Organisational legitimacy	• Legitimacy of the claim on the company • Alignment between investors' interests and those of the company • Perception that the organisation is a credible and respected member of the investment community • Consistency of message from different parts of the organisation
	Pragmatic legitimacy	• The investor has a strong argument for why the proposed action is in the interests of the company • The investor provides new information to the company
	Societal legitimacy: investor	• The investor/claim embodies or reflects a position widely accepted in society
	Societal legitimacy: claim (Gond and Piani, 2012)	• Existence of norms or codes of conduct • Supportive political and policy environment
Power	Normative power	• Public or private statements • Shareholder resolutions or other activities that affect the company's or individual managers' reputation
	Coercive power	• Use of formal investor rights including legal proceedings
	Utilitarian power	• Provision or withdrawal of capital or other resources from companies (investment, divestment)

Category	SST Term	Definition/Meaning
Urgency	Urgency: time-sensitivity	• Benchmarks with deadlines for response • Use of any form of deadline to create time pressure
	Urgency: criticality to investor	• Assertiveness of tone • Persistence • Willingness to apply resources
	Urgency: societal criticality (claim) (Gond and Piani, 2012)	• Level of criticality imposed by broader societal trends and public policy
Moderating factors	Timing	• Attributes are not drawn upon at the same time but applied sequentially as the engagement escalates
	Management values: investor	• Values of the target company managers
	Management values: claim	
	Coalition building	• Building coalitions with other investors and stakeholders
	Relative size of investor	• Size of the stake, the investor, and the company

---

BOX 8.1 About the Research

This chapter is based on research conducted as part of a Degree of Master of Studies in Sustainability Leadership at the University of Cambridge (Turner, 2016). The research involved two main elements. The first element comprised 21 semi-structured interviews with asset managers and engagement service providers, most of whom were based in Europe. Of these, 12 were with equity engagers (including those that combine equity and corporate bond engagement but lead the process with their equity holdings) and nine with corporate bond engagers. The second element comprised an extensive review of the academic literature; publicly available engagement-related reports from a broad range of European institutional investors and case-studies published by a leading global engagement service provider.

The interview questions were designed to gather high-level contextual information surrounding engagement processes, approaches, and trends as well as to probe the 16 factors linked to enhanced stakeholder salience (see Table 8.1). Interviewees were asked to discuss and describe one or more successful engagement examples (i.e. where the engagement led to improvements in the company's ESG performance) in which they had either personally participated or closely witnessed. The findings from the pool of engagement examples provided were numerically coded and mapped onto one of the SST factors (see Table 8.1) to identify which engagement strategies had the greatest influence on issuers.

In order to effectively code the engagement examples provided during the interviews, each SST factor was scored between 0 and 3 depending on its relative degree of importance to the successful outcome of the engagement. A score of 3 was awarded if the SST factor proved critical to the successful engagement outcome; conversely, if a factor was non-existent in the engagement process, it scored 0 (for further details, see Turner, 2016). A framework for the distribution of interviewee responses was used to standardise the coding process and minimise the researcher's own interpretative biases.

In addition, recognising that engagement strategies and approaches may differ depending on the engager's degree of ambition, a more subjective 'ambition' score of between 1 and 3 was assigned to each engagement example provided. The score took a number of factors into account, such as, the nature of the ESG issue, the company's domicile, and the investor's holding size and was designed to enable fair comparative analysis across the examples provided.

While this chapter is primarily based on research conducted in 2016, it has been updated to reflect more recent developments and analysis of corporate bondholder engagement (in particular, recent publications from PRI, 2018a; ShareAction, 2019).

An Overview of the Literature on Engagement

This section reviews the existing literature surrounding corporate ESG engagement practices, in particular, the literature on the efficacy of different engagement mechanisms. While this literature is predominantly focussed on shareholder engagement, there has been recent growth in the attention paid to corporate bond engagement practices. The corporate bond engagement literature has, to date, primarily focused on the barriers to corporate bond engagement (see, for example, Inderst and Stewart, 2018; PRI, 2018a; ShareAction, 2019), largely using case studies to explore the business case for engagement by corporate bondholders and to provide guidance to engagement practitioners.

What is Engagement and Why is it Important?

'ESG engagement' refers to any communication between an investor and investee company that seeks to influence the direction or behaviour of the company on ESG practices or to increase disclosure (Eurosif, 2013; Goldstein, 2014; Majoch et al., 2014; PRI, 2018a). Corporate ESG engagement has grown and continues to grow quickly (Eurosif, 2018; GSIA, 2018), with the Global Sustainable Investment Alliance (GSIA) reporting a 17% growth in ESG engagement globally between 2016 and 2018.

According to the PRI (2018b), active ownership is 'one of the most effective mechanisms to reduce risks, maximise returns and have a positive impact on society and the environment' (p. 8). Not only does this help to explain the growth in investor-led ESG engagement in recent years, it also points to the multitude of benefits both financial (Dimson et al., 2015, 2017; Hoepner and Nilsson, 2017) and non-financial (Ceres et al., 2019; Majoch et al., 2014; PRI, 2018c) available to investors who pursue an ESG engagement strategy.

Means of Engagement and their Effectiveness

In order to enhance the salience and, in turn, the impact of engagement, investors have a host of engagement mechanisms to choose from (Eurosif, 2013; Goldstein, 2014; The Conference Board, 2014). There is considerable debate surrounding whether private dialogue (e.g. letter writing, emails, one-to-one meetings etc.) or public engagement is a more effective strategy with which to influence corporate policies and practices (Goodman et al., 2014). Logsdon and Van Buren (2008) recognise the different skills required for successful engagement in the public and private spheres, although they contend that private dialogue is ultimately more effective. This sentiment is echoed by Wolff et al. (2017), who find that personal interaction is 'consistently associated with a higher probability of engagement success' (p. 4). Conversely, Clark et al. (2008), De Bakker et al. (2008) and Eesley et al. (2006) herald the superior impact of public engagement, which can be played out in the full glare of the media.

Ferraro and Beunza (2014) identify the strengths of both public and private engagement and suggest that both could be 'complimentary in driving a movement's agenda' (p. 8). Indeed, in practice, shareholder resolutions combined with private dialogue form a common and influential approach to shareholder engagement (Barber, 2007; Ceres et al., 2019; Lee and Lounsbury, 2011; Majoch et al., 2014; Waygood, 2004).

PRI (2018a) use case studies to provide practical guidance on enhancing the efficacy of private dialogue for corporate bond engagers. This guidance highlights unique considerations for prioritising candidates for bond engagement including, for example, the size and duration of holdings and credit quality. It also describes additional determinants of effective engagement including; the benefits of issuer access and influence associated with privately placed debt; and the dependence of issuers on regular refinancing (and, therefore, sensitivity to interest rate risk and investor demand).

Ceres et al. (2019) emphasise the powerful role that investor collaboration can play in materially impacting corporate ESG performance. Collective engagement is described by Eurosif (2013) as 'significant because it reduces costs and increases the probability of a successful outcome' (p. 49). Further, the PRI (2018b) argue that collective engagement may 'give more traction to ESG issues within corporations, given the total amount of assets under management usually involved in such processes' (p. 39).

While numerous challenges surrounding collaborative engagement are also highlighted in the literature, in particular, as the practice relates to corporate bond engagement (ShareAction, 2019; PRI, 2018a), the argument that collaborative engagement benefits equity and corporate bond engagers is widely supported (Ceres et al., 2019; Dimson et al., 2017; Goodman et al., 2013; Inderst and Stewart, 2018; Majoch et al., 2014; PRI, 2018a, 2018b).

Finally, whether individual or collective, private dialogue is not always a successful strategy for engagers to pursue and commands significant expertise (Ferraro and Beunza, 2014). Indeed, the mechanisms that explain effective dialogue on ESG factors are extremely hard to monitor (given that it is normally conducted privately behind 'closed doors') and, as such, it is 'unclear how and when dialogue can lead to changes in corporate policies' (p. 4). Ceres et al. (2019) herald the efficacy of private dialogue by investors and assert that its success 'seems to lie in the subtleties of how to engage, when to engage and who to engage with' (p. 24).

Voice Versus Exit

Engagement strategies can be 'an effective and valuable way of bringing ESG concerns to the attention of companies' (Majoch et al., 2014, p. 110). However, not all investors are able to successfully exercise their 'voice' (Hirschman, 1970) in a manner that leads to a change of behaviour or practice within the investee company (Ceres et al., 2019; Gifford, 2010). In these instances, investors have the choice to hold their existing exposure (while accepting the ESG weakness), reduce exposure, or divest (Eurosif, 2013).

While the literature debates the superiority of 'voice' versus 'exit' (Ferraro and Beunza, 2013; Hirschman, 1970) as a strategy for influencing companies on ESG issues, there is strong evidence to suggest that the former is more effective (Hermes EOS, 2015; PRI, 2018b). While divestment can be a useful tool to negatively impact a company's reputation (thereby potentially increasing their cost of capital) and to raise an issue up the political agenda, 'divestment alone leaves investors with no voice and no potential to help drive responsible corporate practices' (PRI, 2018b, p. 8). Further 'only engagement can help tackle [the ESG weakness] whilst reducing investment risks and improving financial returns' (Hermes EOS, 2015, p. 3).

Concluding Comments

In order to mitigate the need to 'exit' and, instead, benefit from the financial and non-financial benefits of successful ESG engagement, it follows that investors need to identify and understand how to maximise their 'stakeholder salience' in the eyes of corporate management (Ceres et al., 2019; Gifford, 2010; Majoch et al., 2014; Mitchell et al., 1997). Indeed, determining the success factors for ESG engagers is particularly pressing for corporate bondholders given that the movement is in its infancy and is poorly understood to date (PRI, 2018a; Richardson, 2013; ShareAction, 2019).

BOX 8.2 How Does Corporate Bondholder Engagement Differ from Shareholder Engagement?

As owners of a company, shareholders are represented by a board of directors and may attend Annual General Meetings (AGMs), vote, and file shareholder resolutions.

In contrast, bondholders, as lenders of capital, are not 'owners' of a company's economic interest and, therefore, have no legal right to vote or file shareholder resolutions at AGMs. While 'bondholders generally have fewer obvious opportunities to engage with companies' (Inderst and Stewart, 2018, p. 11) bondholders may attend bond roadshows and they do command power through their right to negotiate ESG terms within bond covenants and through their ability to invest in corporate debt issuance (Richardson, 2013; ShareAction, 2019).

Indeed, Inderst and Stewart (2018) describe how a new debt issuance can be an appropriate juncture at which to engage bond issuers that repeatedly come to the market. Further, companies refinancing regularly are more likely to be sensitive to investor demand, and therefore, engagement by investors (PRI, 2018a). Hoepner (2015) and ShareAction (2019) both highlight the unique power that corporate bond investors (in particular, high yield investors) have to directly increase the cost of capital for highly leveraged issuers through divestment or refusal to refinance debt. Finally, PRI (2018a) asserts that, given the increased significance of today's bond market, 'fixed income investors have a strong argument for public companies to pay attention to their concerns' (p. 27).

Analysis of Successful Engagement Initiatives

In the interviews conducted for this research (see Box 8.1), interviewees were asked to present examples of successful engagement initiatives that were then assessed against the 16 SST factors (see Table 8.1). In total, 21 interviewees presented 16 examples of successful equity engagements and 9 examples of successful fixed income engagements.

Analysis of Equity Engagement Initiatives

Of the 16 examples of successful equity engagements, five were provided by engagement service providers, ten by asset managers, and one by ShareAction, a charity whose mission is, in part, to provide investors with guidance on ESG engagement. Nine of the examples relate to engagement on equity holdings only, while seven examples combine equity and corporate bond holdings, albeit to varying degrees.

In many cases, the issuer engagement examples encompass multiple ESG issues. In total, eight governance, eight social, and six environmental claims were addressed through the examples provided. The issuers represented are predominantly domiciled in Europe and ten out of 16 are 'large-cap' companies (i.e. with a market capitalisation of greater than USD5 billion).

The results of the assessment of these examples against the SST factors are presented in Table 8.2. Table 8.2 also provides contextual information on each engagement, specifically whether the lead engager was an asset manager (AM), a charity, or an engagement service provider (ESP); whether the subject of the engagement was an environmental (E), social (S), and/or governance (G) issue; where the company is headquartered or listed; the size of the company and the degree of ambition associated with the engagement (see Box 8.1 above).

These examples suggest that the societal legitimacy of the claim is the single, most important factor leading to greatest stakeholder salience for equity investors. Other factors that were consistently emphasised as being instrumental to the positive outcome of the engagement include: organisational legitimacy; urgency (criticality to investor); urgency (societal criticality of the claim); the alignment of management values in relation to the claim; and the size of assets the investor represented.

The SST factor that appears to contribute least to the positive outcome of the equity engagement process is utilitarian power, which refers to an investor's ability to reward or punish issuers through investment or divestment respectively. Other factors that were considered less influential in procuring a positive engagement outcome include individual legitimacy, normative power (relating to activities that affect the company's or management's reputation) and urgency (time sensitivity).

A review of the responses as they relate to the overarching SST categories (power, legitimacy, urgency, and Gifford's moderating factors) provides further insight. The results suggest that successful equity engagement outcomes are most commonly linked to urgency, due to interviewee consensus on the need for urgency (criticality to investor) and the societal criticality of the claim. Likewise, legitimacy appears to play a vital role in the engagement process, resulting from interviewee emphasis on organisational legitimacy

Table 8.2 Analysis of Equity Engagement Initiatives.

Interviewee & Company	Engager Type	ESG Issue	Company HQ	Company Size	Engagement Ambition	Individual Legitimacy	Organisational Legitimacy	Pragmatic Legitimacy	Societal Legitimacy of Investor	Societal Legitimacy of Claim	Power – Normative	Power – Coercive	Power – Utilitarian	Urgency – Time Sensitivity	Urgency – Criticality to Investor	Urgency – Criticality of Claim (political and societal)	Timing	Management Values (Investor)	Management Values (Claims)	Coalition Building	Size of Investor/s
Allianz Global Investors – ESG Analyst	AM	E	Germany	Mid Cap	1	2	2	3	2	3	1	1	2	2	2	2	1	2	3	0	2
Hemes EOS – Head of Engagement	ESP	G	Germany	Large Cap	2	2	1	3	1	3	3	2	2	2	3	3	3	2	2	0	1
Hemes EOS – Head of Engagement	ESP	S & G	Taiwan	Large Cap	3	2	1	1	1	3	2	3	1	2	3	2	3	1	2	3	3
Swiss ESP – Head of Responsible Investment	ESP	E,S & G	Switzerland	Large Cap	2	3	3	2	3	3	2	3	1	1	2	3	3	2	2	1	3
Alliance Trust – Portfolio Manager	AM	S	UK	Large Cap	3	2	1	3	2	3	1	1	2	1	3	3	2	3	3	3	2
ShareAction – Engagement Manager	Charity	E&S	UK	Large Cap	2–3	2	1	2	2	2	3	3	1	2	2	3	2	0	0	3	3
ISS Ethix – Head of SRI	ESP	S	Nordic	Large Cap	1	1	2	3	3	3	2	1	2	1	2	3	2	3	3	3	2
Allianz Global Investors – ESG Analyst	AM	G	European	Mid Cap	2	2	2	1	2	1	1	3	1	3	2	1	3	2	3	0	3

(Continued)

Stakeholder Salience Theory

Interviewee & Company	Engager Type	ESG Issue	Company HQ	Company Size	Engagement Ambition	Individual Legitimacy	Organisational Legitimacy	Pragmatic Legitimacy	Societal Legitimacy of Investor	Societal Legitimacy of Claim	Power – Normative	Power – Coercive	Power – Utilitarian	Urgency – Time Sensitivity	Urgency – Criticality to Investor	Urgency – Criticality of Claim (political and societal)	Timing	Management Values (Investor)	Management Values (Claims)	Coalition Building	Size of Investor/s
							Legitimacy					*Power*			*Urgency*			*Gifford's Moderating Factors*			
Allianz Global Investors – ESG Analyst	AM	G	South Korean	Large Cap	2	2	3	2	3	2	3	2	1	2	3	2	2	2	1	3	3
Pictet Asset Management – Portfolio Manager	AM	G	Swiss	Mid Cap	1-2	2	3	2	2	1	2	3	1	3	3	1	1	2	2	3	3
Pictet Asset Management – Portfolio Manager	AM	G	Swiss	Small Cap	1-2	2	3	3	2	1	1	2	1	2	2	1	1	3	3	0	3
Schroders – Head of Responsible Investment	AM	E	UK & Aus'lia	Large Cap	2-3	1	2	3	1	3	1	1	1	1	2	3	1	2	2	2	2
CCLA – Head of Responsible Investment	AM	E	UK	All Cap	2-3	1	2	2	3	3	1	2	1	2	2	3	1	2	2	2	1
CCLA – Head of Responsible Investment	AM	S	UK	Large Cap	2	3	2	1	3	3	2	2	2	2	3	3	2	3	3	2	1
UNPRI – Head of Environmental Issues	ESP	E, S	Singapore	Mid Cap	3	1	2	2	3	3	1	1	1	1	3	3	2	2	2	3	2
Swiss AM – Head of Stewardship	AM	G	Chile	Large Cap	3	2	3	1	1	3	1	3	1	2	2	3	2	3	3	3	3
TOTAL (no.)					30	35	34	34	40	27	33	21	29	39	39	31	34	37	37	31	37
TOTAL (%)					5.6%	6.6%	6.4%	6.4%	7.5%	5.1%	6.2%	4.0%	5.5%	7.3%	7.3%	5.8%	6.4%	7.0%	7.0%	5.8%	7.0%

and societal legitimacy of the claim. There is also considerable consensus surrounding the importance of Gifford's moderating factors, in particular, alignment of management values (claim) and the size of assets that the engager represents. Finally, the examples suggest that power has a weaker association with successful equity engagement. Within this, normative and utilitarian power were considered to have little influence on the engagement process, while coercive power (referring to the implementation of investor rights) was believed to be more influential.

An interesting anomaly in the findings concerns the role of coalition-building. While the data in Table 8.2 suggest that coalition-building is not critical to the success of equity engagement, a different picture emerges when we exclude those cases where organisations engaged on their own and did not seek to build coalitions. In cases where coalition-building was used, it tended to achieve a high score relating to its degree of importance within the engagement process. Further, when the results are analysed by scale of ambition, coalition-building emerges as one of the factors leading to greatest stakeholder salience across the more ambitious equity engagement initiatives.

Analysis of Corporate Bond Engagement Initiatives

In total, interviewees presented 11 examples of fixed income engagements, 9 of which were considered successful and two were considered unsuccessful (or did not meet the engagers' desired objectives). All examples focused on engagement as it relates to corporate bond holdings except for 2 cases, where the engagement was directed at industry bodies (a ratings agency and a stock exchange respectively).

As with the equity engagement examples, in many cases, multiple ESG issues were captured within a single company engagement initiative. In total, seven governance, seven social, and seven environmental claims were addressed in the examples provided.

The majority of examples relate to large-cap issuers, although examples were also provided for medium- and small-cap companies (in addition to one private company). Where a credit rating is applicable, there is a 50:50 split roughly across investment grade and high yield issuers. Similar to the equity examples, the majority of the investee companies are domiciled in Europe, although two emerging markets (Turkey and Guatemala) are also represented by the examples.

The results of the assessment of these examples against the SST factors are presented in Table 8.3 along with contextual information for each.

The ambition scores associated with all 11 examples are consistently at the higher end of the spectrum (most receiving a 2 or 3). Given that corporate bond engagement was a relatively new endeavour at the time the interviews were conducted, companies and investors had little experience of what constitutes effective engagement. As such, corporate bond engagements were

Table 8.3 Analysis of Corporate Bond Engagement Initiatives.

Interviewee & Company	Engager Type	ESG Issue	Company HQ	Company size	Credit Rating	Stakeholder Salience Theory													Gifford's Moderating Factors				
						Engagement Ambition	Legitimacy					Power			Urgency			Timing	Management Values (Investor)	Management Values (Claims)	Coalition Building	Size of Investor/s	
							Individual Legitimacy	Organisational Legitimacy	Pragmatic Legitimacy	Societal Legitimacy of Investor	Societal Legitimacy of Claim	Power – Normative	Power – Coercive	Power – Utilitarian	Urgency – Time Sensitivity	Urgency – Criticality to Investor	Urgency – Criticality of Claim (political and societal)					
Successful Examples																						
Global Fixed Income Manager – ESG Analyst; Example 1	AM	ESG	Global	Multi	N/A	3	1	3	2	3	2	3	1	1	2	2	2	1	2	1	3	2
Global Fixed Income Manager – ESG Analyst; Example 2	AM	S/ESG	Guatemala	Unknown	BB	2	3	2	3	2	1	1	1	1	2	3	1	1	2	2	0	1
Aviva Investors – Head of Engagement	AM	S	UK	Large Cap	BBB+	3	3	3	2	2	3	1	1	1	1	2	3	2	2	3	0	3
Mirova – Portfolio Manager	AM	E, S	France	Large Cap	A	2	1	2	1	2	2	1	2	1	2	3	2	1	3	3	1	1

Insight Investment Management – Head of Credit	AM	G	Swiss	Mid Cap	High Yield	3	3	3	1	2	1	1	1	2	3	2	1	3	3	3
UK AM – ESG Analyst	AM	E	UK & Aus'lia	Large Cap	A	2	3	3	2	1	1	1	2	2	3	2	2	2	3	3
Global Fixed Income AM – Portfolio Manager	AM	S,G	UK	Large Cap	BBB-	2	3	3	2	1	1	2	1	1	3	2	3	3	0	3
German Development Bank (DB) – Senior Manager	DB	ESG	Europe	Large Cap	Inv. Grade	2	2	2	1	1	1	3	1	1	1	3	2	1	0	1
Swiss AM – Head of Responsible Investment	AM	ESG	Multi	Multi	N/A	2	2	2	1	1	1	3	2	2	1	2	2	2	0	1
Total (no.)						**21**	**23**	**19**	**22**	**19**	**11**	**10**	**15**	**15**	**18**	**18**	**14**	**21**	**20**	**10**	**18**
Total (%)						7.7%	8.4%	6.9%	8.0%	6.9%	4.0%	3.6%	5.5%	5.5%	6.6%	6.6%	5.1%	7.7%	7.3%	3.6%	6.6%
Unsuccessful Examples																				
Aviva Investors AM – Head of Engagement	AM	E	UK	Private	N/A	3	2	2	3	2	1	1	3	3	2	3	2	3	2	0	1
Insight Investment Management – Head of Credit	AM	G	Turkey	Small Cap	BBB-	3	2	1	2	1	1	1	3	2	2	1	1	1	1	0	1
Total (no.)						**4**	**3**	**5**	**3**	**4**	**2**	**2**	**6**	**5**	**4**	**4**	**3**	**4**	**3**	**0**	**2**
Total (%)						7.4%	5.6%	9.3%	5.6%	7.4%	3.7%	3.7%	11.1%	9.3%	7.4%	7.4%	5.6%	7.4%	5.6%	0.0%	3.7%

inherently considered to have a greater element of ambition regardless of other contributing factors.

The coded results from the nine successful engagement examples reveal that legitimacy relating to the individual and the organisation (including the organisation's societal legitimacy) as well as the alignment of management values to the investor and their claims are the most influential SST factors in the corporate bond engagement process. One interviewee described the situation as one in which investors need to 'develop consent to agree a common goal [with the issuer]' in order to empower companies that are 'able and willing' to improve their ESG performance. Conversely, power-related factors appear to be least influential.

While it is difficult to draw any firm conclusions from the two unsuccessful engagement examples, it is notable that, contrary to the positive examples, organisational legitimacy, societal legitimacy (investor), and alignment of management values (claim) are all poorly represented.

Similar to the equity findings, relatively few of the examples incorporate coalition-building. However, in the few instances in which collaboration was used within the engagement process, it was viewed as integral to the success of the engagement. Interviewees highlighted how the fragmented nature of the bond market coupled with a lack of transparency (particularly within the secondary market) makes it hard to identify fellow bondholders of the same company (see also Gowland, 2015; PRI, 2018a). Consequently, it can be extremely challenging for corporate bondholders to build investor coalitions.

From a high-level perspective, the results reveal that legitimacy – in particular, individual and organisational legitimacy (including societal legitimacy of the investor) – is key to successful corporate bond engagement. This is followed in roughly equal measure by Gifford's moderating factors (in particular, the alignment of management values in relation to the investor and their claim) and urgency. However, similar to the equity engagement findings, power seems to have a relatively limited association with successful corporate bond engagement. This was confirmed by some of the interviewees who, in their general comments, pointed to the perceived lack of stakeholder power linked to this asset class. For example, a head of engagement commented that, since bondholders are not company owners, there are 'less swords hanging over the meeting' and 'you need to establish yourself as a consulting friend'. Another interviewee remarked that 'once the bond is issued, there is not much you can do to change it', noting that '[as an engager] you are unable to perpetually threaten divestment in the way that you can with equities'.

Timeliness is also an important consideration. While bond engagers are able to attend roadshows ahead of a new bond issuance and to negotiate covenants with companies, the window to negotiate covenants tends to be extremely short. A number of interviewees commented that, if you are to succeed at integrating ESG factors into the terms, it is likely that numerous investors will be required to make the same request. One portfolio manager summarised the covenant negotiating process as a case of 'take it or leave it' for bond investors. These comments may help to explain why timing was not identified as a critical factor for enhancing stakeholder salience in the examples presented by the interviewees. While acknowledging these issues, PRI (2018a) note that bondholders have ongoing influence and interactions with companies post-issuance particularly in instances where the company is 'seeking to renegotiate contractual obligations [or] refinance' (p. 28).

There were conflicting views among interviewees (and in the literature) around whether it is easier to engage with high yield or investment grade issuers. Some interviewees suggested that bond engagers can generate more impact with high yield companies given that they are typically smaller in size, have reduced access to funding sources, and have a greater dependence on leverage. Indeed, denying future debt to highly leveraged companies (and, thereby, enhancing the engager's degree of utilitarian power) is seen as an effective escalation tool in the literature by sources, such as, Hoepner (2015). One interviewee commented that high yield companies tend to grant investors greater access to senior management than investment grade companies making them easier to engage. However, other interviewees noted that larger investment grade companies are often more experienced in dealing with ESG queries from investors, making them potentially easier to engage with. PRI (2018a) observe that while 'in principle, high yield issuers are more likely to be receptive to engagement by bondholders…engagement in high yield can actually be more challenging' (p. 40).

Enhancing the Efficacy of Corporate Fixed Income Engagement

The case for engagement with corporate fixed income issuers is clear, and it is likely that the level of engagement with fixed income issuers will continue to grow as bond investors become increasingly aware of the links between ESG risks and investment returns (PRI, 2018a). Acknowledging that the formal rights and privileges associated with corporate bondholders differ from shareholders, the question this chapter has sought to answer is: how can corporate fixed income engagers maximise their impact and influence on issuers? Five insights emerge from the research presented here.

The first is that legitimacy is key. Mitchell et al. (1997) refer to legitimacy as 'a generalised perception or assumption that the actions of an entity are desirable, proper or appropriate within some socially constructed system of norms, values, beliefs and definitions' (p. 866). The research results suggest that, in order for corporate bond engagers to enhance their influence over investee companies on ESG issues, they need to establish strong individual, organisational and societal legitimacy (at an investor level). An important element of this is the credibility of the individuals involved in the engagement. A widely held view, across both the equity and fixed income interviewees was that, in order to enhance the legitimacy of an engagement, communication with the company should either include or be solely executed by the investment manager (or portfolio manager) and/or the financial analyst. Many commented that ESG engagement individuals (or teams) alone are not able to generate a sufficient degree of credibility to influence companies on ESG issues (see also PRI, 2018a).

Interviewees across both asset classes confirmed that organisational legitimacy was paramount to the overall impact of the engagement. Three interviews specifically highlighted the importance of local 'on the ground' presence and knowledge in countries and regions where gaining traction through engagement is more complex, such as the emerging markets (see also Wolff et al., 2017).

Another element to maximising overall legitimacy in the corporate bond engagement process concerns pragmatic legitimacy, specifically the need to articulate a clear and concise business case to companies. This is not just about the financial business case or understanding the business model ('to avoid companies running rings around you', as noted by one participant) but also about presenting the competitive business case for achieving recognised leadership on material ESG factors, which was described by a number of interviewees as a strong motivator for corporate action. This sentiment is supported by PRI (2018a) who highlight the need to demonstrate the benefit of the ESG claim to issuers and to share best practices across companies within a peer group.

Second, urgency and Gifford's moderating factors (in particular, the alignment of management values with both the investor and their claim) were identified as important to the corporate bond engagement process by a majority of interviewees, albeit to a lesser degree than legitimacy. It is, however, relevant to note that urgency as an overarching attribute appears to be significantly less important in the corporate fixed income engagement process than in the listed equities engagement process (where urgency is considered to be the most influential overarching SST factor in the engagement process). While Celik et al. (2015) suggest this may be attributable to the fact that corporate bondholders have fewer formal opportunities to impose time-sensitive deadlines on companies, this appears at best a partial explanation. Given that societal urgency and legitimacy of the ESG claim both receive strong support in the equity examples, it follows that bondholders may benefit from selecting ESG issues for engagement that complement these findings.

Third, perhaps surprisingly, all facets of power are consistently underrepresented in the positive examples, possibly suggesting that this is not a factor necessary for successful corporate bond engagement. However, some caution must be applied to this finding since there exists a difference between explicit power (which could be captured through the interview responses) and implicit power, which by its very nature, is latent and harder to detect. Interestingly, almost all interviewees for this research considered the explicit use of power as an inferior strategy for effective engagement. While power was perceived to play a more influential role in the equity engagement process, most interviewees across asset classes stressed the importance of building legitimacy and trust, and finding common ground and interests, through private dialogue, such as 1-1 meetings, letters, emails, and phone conversations. Another interesting perspective presented by some interviewees was that bondholders may find it advantageous to boost their utilitarian power by preferentially engaging with companies that have a greater dependence on debt refinancing. Some interviewees further noted that bond engagers have the ability to exercise coercive power through the negotiation of bond covenants.

Fourth, coalition-building is a potentially powerful form of leverage across corporate bond and listed equity engagement practices (see, for example, Inderst and Stewart (2018) and ShareAction (2019)). However, building coalitions in the bond space alone is uniquely challenging given the lack of transparency on underlying bond investors. This is not insurmountable. Investor collaborations and networks – for example the PRI's Investor Collaboration Platform – allow investors to propose engagement initiatives and to identify other bondholders and shareholders who may be willing to support a particular collaborative engagement.

Finally, for those investors that have exposure to an issuer's equity as well as bonds, combining engagement is an effective way of leveraging influence (see, for example, PRI, 2018a; ShareAction, 2019). In practice, this may mean, for example lobbying at bond roadshows in addition to AGM's; ensuring that representatives from both the bond and equity investment teams are present at company meetings; and engaging with investor relations representatives in addition to senior management and board members in order to maximise internal awareness and debate across the issuer. According to one asset manager interviewed for this research, leveraging both equity and bond rights where possible could enable the investor to build awareness around ESG issues at various access points within the company and ultimately enhance the overall power, legitimacy and urgency associated with the engagement.

References

Barber, B. (2007), 'Monitoring the Monitor: Evaluating CalPERS' Activism', *The Journal of Investing*, 16(4), pp. 66–80.

Çelik, S., Demirtas, G. and Isaksson, M. (2015), *Corporate Bonds, Bondholders and Corporate Governance. OECD Corporate Governance Working Papers, No. 16* (OECD Publishing, Paris).

Ceres, Environmental Defense Fund, and KKS Advisors (2019), *The Role of Investors in Supporting Better Corporate ESG Performance: Influence Strategies for Sustainable and Long-term Value Creation* (Meridian Institute, Washington, DC). [online]. Available at: www.ceres.org (Accessed: 15 October 2020).

Clark, G.L., Salo, J. and Hebb, T. (2008), 'Social and Environmental Shareholder Activism in the Public Spotlight: US Corporate Annual Meetings, Campaign Strategies, and Environmental Performance, 2001–04', *Environment and Planning A*, 40(6), pp. 1370–1390.

De Bakker, F. and Den Hond, F. (2008), 'Introducing the Politics of Stakeholder Influence - A Review Essay', *Business & Society*, 47(1), pp. 8–20.

Dimson, E., Karakaş, O. and Li, X. (2015), 'Active Ownership', *Review of Financial Studies*, 28(12), pp. 3225–3268.

Dimson, E., Karakas, O. and Li, X. (2017), 'Local Leads Backed by Global Scale: The Drivers of Successful Engagement', *PRI Academic Network: RI Quarterly*. [online]. Available at: https://www.unpri.org/download?ac=5545 (Accessed: 13 October 2020).

Eesley, C. and Lenox, M. (2006), 'Secondary Stakeholder Actions and the Selection of Firm Targets', *Academy of Management Proceedings*, 2006(1), pp. B1–B6.

Eurosif (2013), *Shareholder Stewardship: European ESG Engagement Practices 2013* (Eurosif, Brussels).

Eurosif (2018), *European SRI Study 2018* (Eurosif, Brussels). [online]. Available at: http://www.eurosif.org/wp-content/uploads/2018/11/European-SRI-2018-Study.pdf (Accessed: 15 October 2020).

Ferraro, F. and Beunza, D. (2013), *Understanding Voice: Mechanisms of Influence in Shareholder Engagement* [online]. Available at: http://www.hbs.edu/faculty/conferences/2013-paulrlawrence/Documents/Ferraro.Beunza.Understanding-Voice.pdf (Accessed: 23 August 2015).

Ferraro, F. and Beunza, D. (2014), 'Why Talk? A Process Model of Dialogue in Shareholder Engagement', *SSRN Electronic Journal*. [online]. Available at: http://www.ssrn.com/abstract=2419571 (Accessed: 15 June 2016).

Gifford, J. (2010), 'Effective Shareholder Engagement: The Factors that Contribute to Shareholder Salience', *Journal of Business Ethics*, 92, pp. 79–97.

Global Sustainable Investment Alliance [GSIA] (2018), *2018 Global Sustainable Investment Review* [online]. Available at: http://www.gsi-alliance.org/wp-content/uploads/2019/03/GSIR_Review2018.3.28.pdf (Accessed: 15 October 2020).

Goldstein, M. (2014), *Defining Engagement: An Update on the Evolving Relationship Between Shareholders, Directors and Executives* [online]. Available at: https://www2.deloitte.com/content/dam/Deloitte/se/Documents/corporate-governance/engagement-between-corporations-and-investors-at-all-time-high._IRRC_May 2014.pdf (Accessed: 16 October 2020).

Gond, J.-P. and Piani, V. (2012), 'Enabling Institutional Investors' Collective Action: The Role of the Principles for Responsible Investment Initiative', *Business & Society*, 52(1), pp. 64–104.

Goodman, J., Hebb, T. and Hoepner, A. (2014), 'Shareholder Dialogue Behind the Scenes: Addressing the Bulk of the Iceberg', *Academy of Management Proceedings*, 2014(1), pp. 17084–17084.

Goodman, J., Louche, C., Van Cranenburgh, K. and Arenas, D. (2013), 'Social Shareholder Engagement: The Dynamics of Voice and Exit', *Journal of Business Ethics*, 125(2), pp. 193–210.

Gowland, P. (2015), *Bondholder Engagement is Already Happening. Like It or Not!* (Morrow Sodali, London) [online]. Available at: https://morrowsodali.com/uploads/insights/attachments/1449253250-A.0169.pdf (Accessed: 15 October 2020).

Hermes EOS (2015), *Why Engagement Trumps Divestment in the Battle against Climate Change* (Hermes EOS, London) [online]. Available at: http://blog.hermeseos.com/why-engagement-trumps-divestment-in-the-battle-against-climate-change/ (Accessed: 5 July 2015).

Hirschman, A.O. (1970), *Exit, Voice, and Loyalty: Responses to Decline in Firms, Organizations, and States* (Harvard University Press, Harvard, MA).

Hoepner, A. (2015), *How to Impact Climate Justice: Engage in Equities, Deny Debt* [online]. Available at: https://www.linkedin.com/pulse/all-fossil-fuel-divestment-campaigners-engage-equities-hoepner

Hoepner, A. and Nilsson, M. (2017), 'Expertise Among SRI Fixed Income Funds and their Management Companies', *SSRN Electronic Journal.* [online]. https://papers.ssrn.com/sol3/papers.cfm?abstract_id=2517057 (Accessed: 2 April 2021).

Inderst, G. and Stewart, F. (2018), *Incorporating Environmental, Social and Governance (ESG) Factors into Fixed Income Investment* (The World Bank Group, Washington, DC). [online]. Available at: http://documents1.worldbank.org/curated/en/913961524150628959/pdf/125442-REPL-PUBLIC-Incorporating-ESG-Factors-into-Fixed-Income-Investment-Final-April26-LowRes.pdf (Accessed: 15 October 2020).

Lee, M. and Lounsbury, M. (2011), 'Domesticating Radical Rant and Rage: An Exploration of the Consequences of Environmental Shareholder Resolutions on Corporate Environmental Performance', *Business & Society*, 50(1), pp. 155–188.

Logsdon, J. and Van Buren, H. (2008), 'Beyond the Proxy Vote: Dialogues Between Shareholder Activists and Corporations', *Journal of Business Ethics*, 87(S1), pp. 353–365.

Majoch, A., Gifford, E. and Hoepner, A. (2014), 'Active Ownership and ESG Performance', *SSRN Electronic Journal* [online]. Available at: http://papers.ssrn.com/abstract=2496903 (Accessed: 22 August 2015).

Mitchell, R., Agle, B. and Wood, D. (1997), 'Toward a Theory of Stakeholder Identification and Salience: Defining the Principle of Who and What Really Counts', *Academy of Management Review*, 22(4), pp. 853–886.

Principles for Responsible Investment [PRI] (2018a), *ESG Engagement for Fixed Income Investors* (PRI, London). [online]. Available at: https://www.unpri.org/download?ac=4449 (Accessed: 13 October 2020)

Principles for Responsible Investment [PRI] (2018b), *A Practical Guide to Active Ownership in Listed Equity* (PRI, London) [online]. Available at: https://www.unpri.org/download?ac=4151 (Accessed: 13 October 2020).

Principles for Responsible Investment [PRI] (2018c), *How ESG Engagement Creates Value for Investors and Companies* (PRI, London) [online]. Available at: https://www.unpri.org/download?ac=4637 (Accessed: 13 October 2020).

Richardson, B. (2013), *Fiduciary Law and Responsible Investing: In Nature's Trust.* (Routledge, London).

Schwarcz, S. (2017), 'Rethinking Corporate Governance for a Bondholder Financed, Systemically Risky World', *William & Mary Law Review*, 58. [online]. Available at: https://scholarship.law.duke.edu/faculty_scholarship/3582 (Accessed: 15 October 2020).

ShareAction (2019), *Sleeping Giants: Are Bond Investors Ready to Act on Climate Change?* (ShareAction, London). [online]. Available at: https://shareaction.org/wp-content/uploads/2019/01/Sleeping-Giants.pdf (Accessed: 13 October 2020).

The Conference Board (2014), *Guidelines for Engagement|The Conference Board.* [online]. Available at: https://www.conference-board.org/topics/publicationdetail.cfm?publicationid=2708 (Accessed: 11 October 2015).

Turner, A. (2016), *How Can Investors Enhance the Efficacy of Corporate Environmental, Social & Governance (ESG) Engagement?* (Master of Studies dissertation, University of Cambridge).

Waygood, S. (2004), *NGOs and Equity Investment: A Critical Assessment of the Practices of UK NGOs in Using the Capital Market as a Campaign Device* (Doctoral dissertation, University of Surrey). [online] Available at: http://libsta28.lib.cam.ac.uk:2220/docview/301669634?pq-origsite=summon (Accessed: 11 October 2015).

Wolff, M., Jacobey, L. and Coskun, H. (2017), *Talk Is Not Cheap: The Role of Interpersonal Communication as a Success Factor of Engagements on ESG Matters* [online]. Available at: https://www.management.uni-goettingen.de (Accessed: 15 October 2020).

9 Connecting ESG Factors with Credit Ratings

Andrew Steel and Justin Sloggett

In fixed income the assessment of creditworthiness requires a detailed understanding of business risks, financial risks, and structural risks. Investors increasingly pay attention to how ESG issues can affect credit quality, and the risk adjusted return of their portfolios. This enables investors to form a view on the level of downside risk exposure an investment contains, including from environmental, social, and governance (ESG) factors, and whether the risk/reward equation is sufficient for inclusion within their portfolio.

As a credit rating agency Fitch Ratings (Fitch) has been a key facilitator for capital markets since 1914. Founded as The Fitch Publishing Company it initially published financial statistics on stocks and bonds. In 1924, it expanded its activities with a bond ratings business and in the same year, Fitch created the AAA to D credit rating scale that was subsequently licenced to other ratings agencies. Traditionally, credit analysts have approached credit risk assessment by balancing qualitative and quantitative risk factors to derive an overall view on susceptibility to default risk, without the need to consider ESG risks as a separate sub-category. To assess and report on ESG risks as a separate sub-category within credit, the need arises to identify and extract sustainability risk factors contained within traditional qualitative and quantitative analysis methodologies, so that they can be transparently evaluated.

Credit rating agencies are one source of third-party ESG information and opinions. In response to investor demand, they have been increasing their ESG offerings significantly in recent years; some have acquired non-ratings ESG capability whereas others, including Fitch, have adapted and integrated ESG into their ratings research. The non-rating products acquired offer dedicated ESG data, research and tools but with no inherent link to credit ratings.

Fitch has integrated ESG credit issues within analytical products and its core ratings business and developed credit-relevant ESG scores and tailored ESG reporting to further promote and improve the transparency of ESG considerations in the ratings process, credit ratings, and analysis. Implementing this framework has helped Fitch build up practical experience in how to integrate ESG factors into financial analysis, and how these factors can impact an issuer's credit rating.

DOI: 10.4324/9781003055341-12

This chapter starts by providing an overview of how Fitch integrates ESG issues into credit analysis, both theoretically and in practice. It then analyses how and why ESG issues affect credit, and concludes with a discussion of the emerging trends and challenges affecting fixed income investors and rating agencies.

Integrating ESG Credit Risks

Credit Process

ESG integration has been interpreted differently by financial market participants across the investment value chain, although most consider it to be the systematic and explicit inclusion of ESG factors into investment analysis and processes. In line with this interpretation, material ESG credit issues are structurally embedded into Fitch's analytical processes across all major asset classes. The issue for ratings agencies then becomes how to systematically extract and display the elements of sector-specific ESG credit risks that impact the credit profiles of rated entities and transactions.

Investors are increasingly focusing on how to develop a holistic picture of non-ESG and ESG credit risks that impact their holdings and portfolios. Investors have called on the credit ratings agencies to better clarify the relevance and materiality of ESG issues to the entities and transactions that they rate, not only at a systemic and sector level, but also for individual entities and transactions. Their goal is to understand the key rating drivers and qualitative and quantitative assumptions used to arrive at a rating opinion. Fitch has sought to address these requirements by developing an integrated framework for its ratings research that transparently displays the impact of individual ESG risks to each and every rating it produces across all asset classes.

The credit rating analysis conducted by Fitch analysts involves a three-pronged approach. First, reference to publicly available criteria that describes Fitch's key rating drivers for a particular sector. Second, forward-looking qualitative and quantitative assessments of an issuer's financial and business profiles, based on confidential and non-confidential information. Third, stress-testing of the issuer's creditworthiness. Within the sector-specific criteria, credit models, and proprietary forecasting models, there are numerous indicators linked to credit drivers. For example, patent protection profile is a credit driver specific to the pharmaceuticals sector, whereas contract risk management and order book and revenue visibility are specific to the engineering and construction sector. These indicators have been back-tested for evidence of materiality (e.g. against past defaults and credit rating transitions) and stress-tested through Fitch's own proprietary forecasting models to produce base-case and stress-case scenarios for rated entities (stress tests can vary by sector and region across; e.g., a sharp economic downturn).

If material to a rating, ESG indicators are identified using a framework that is integrated with set criteria and that enables risks to be tracked in credit models, forecasted financials, and credit metrics (see Table 9.1). For

Table 9.1 Fitch's ESG General Issue Risk Categories – ESG Relevance Score Framework.

Environmental	Social	Governance
GHG emissions & air quality	Human rights, community relations, access & affordability	**Management strategy**
Energy management	Customer welfare – fair messaging, privacy & data security	**Governance structure**
Water & wastewater management	Labour relations & practices (+international public finance: government-related entities; US public finance: tax only)	**Group structure**
Waste and hazardous materials management; ecological impacts	Employee wellbeing	**Financial transparency**
Exposure to environmental impacts	Exposure to social impacts	**Political stability and rights**
Water resources and management	**Human rights and political freedoms**	**Rule of law, institutional & regulatory quality, control of corruption**
Biodiversity and natural resource management	**Human development, health and education**	**International relations and trade**
Natural disasters and climate change	**Employment and income equality (sovereigns only)**	**Creditor rights**
	Public safety and security	**Data quality and transparency**
	Population demographics (sovereigns only)	Rule of law, institutional & regulatory quality
	Demographic trends (international public finance: government-related entities; US public finance: tax only)	Transaction & collateral structure
		Transaction parties & operational risk
		Data Quality & privacy

Key:
Applies to all analytical groups
Applies to corporates, financial institutions, IPF: GREs, USPF: revenue, infrastructure, structured finance
Applies to corporates, financial institutions, IPF: GREs, USPF: revenue, infrastructure

example, regulation of emissions and pollutants from vehicles sold in the auto manufacturers sector is already incorporated into our assessment on brand positioning, profitability, and financial structure of issuers. However, when ESG indicators are not currently material to a rating, it is difficult for investors to see how they are monitored for relevance and materiality. But Fitch's framework has been designed to indicate levels of 'relevance' for factors that have potential to cause credit impact in a sector but are not yet material. We turn to materiality in the next section.

Fitch has developed an integrated ESG analysis framework, known as the ESG Relevance Score Framework, with its analysts, which identifies the credit relevance of ESG risk factors at a sector specific level (based on over 100 industry-based templates), and enables analysts to indicate the credit impact of these ESG risks to ratings of individual entities or transactions. In the rating recommendation, analysts determine if any Environment, Social, or Governance factor in the overall analysis contributed to a change in the issuer's creditworthiness. Where they are determined to have influenced a rating decision, an elevated Relevance Score is assigned in the appropriate category. Analysts do not assess ESG indicators based on ethical, moral, or political considerations as credit ratings are opinions on pure credit risk.

Identifying Material ESG Issues

Materiality is an abstract concept and there can be differing views on which ESG issues are material. Material ESG issues for most fixed income portfolio managers and analysts will encompass the following three criteria: (1) relevance to the business model and strategy of a sector and its constituents; (2) materiality to the entity's financial performance; and (3) materiality to the entity's security price. Fitch analysts consider ESG systemic sector risks to determine relevance and, if relevant, how they then affect the financial performance of an entity or transaction under a rating base case forecast.

Fitch developed its ESG Relevance Score Framework to capture all relevant and material ESG credit issues for all the asset classes that it rates (Table 9.1). All analysts refer to and complete standardised, sector-specific scoring templates when allocating ESG Relevance Scores across 14 or 15 ESG issues, concurrent with the assignment of credit ratings and opinions. The analyst's scoring process is stylised in the decision tree in Figure 9.1.

Whether an ESG factor is material to an entity can depend on a variety of factors, including the region it operates in and the entity's business model. For example, a coal power generator's highly carbon intensive business model may be material if it operates in Europe, where tight carbon pricing regulations impose a cost to the business. This may be different if it operates in Asia, where regulation does not impact its credit profile to the same extent. The impact from regulation will also depend on industry structure and the pricing power. In Europe, even the impact of the European emissions trading scheme was moderated for those issuers that could pass on higher carbon costs to end customers.

This transparent, systematic, and explicit approach to ESG integration ensures that all Fitch analysts consider relevant and/or material ESG credit issues. The advantage of Fitch's approach is that our ESG analysis is completely integrated into our credit analysis, and fully transparent to issuers and investors.

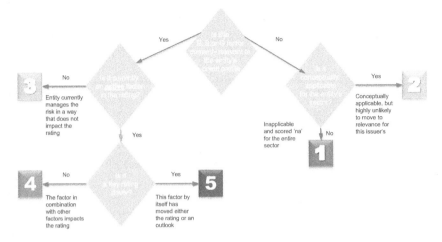

Figure 9.1 ESG Relevance Score Decision Tree.

BOX 9.1 More Transparency Demanded of Credit Rating Agencies

Fitch's response to investor calls for greater transparency and granularity around ESG, and its impact on individual credit ratings of issuers and transactions, has been to display the impact of these factors within its credit research. Fitch achieved this by working with sector analysts globally to extract the elements of ESG risk contained within its rating criteria and to develop a consistent scoring framework that indicates the level of impact from ESG issues on every rating decision.

ESG Relevance Scores clearly illustrate the link between rating drivers contained in ratings criteria and broader ESG risks. They do this by identifying ESG risk factors that are credit relevant at a sector level, and then by the analysts assessing the level of materiality for each risk for individual issuers and transactions.

When rating analysts assign an ESG Relevance Score, it articulates the level of influence an identified environmental, social, or governance risk has had on a credit rating decision. Each entity or transaction receives 14 or 15 ESG Relevance Scores based on five environmental, five social and four or five governance general risk categories. Scores range from 1 to 5 where an ESG Relevance Score of 1 indicates no credit relevance at either a sector or entity level whereas an ESG Relevance Score of 5 indicates a single identified environmental, social, or governance risk that is unambiguously causing a change to the current rating level (Figure 9.2).

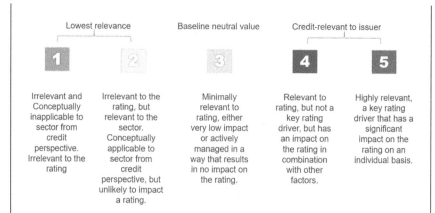

Figure 9.2 Definitions for the 1 to 5 Scale of ESG Relevance Scores.
Source: Fitch Ratings

Integration in Practice – Case Studies

Case-Study 1: ESG Credit Drivers Placing Kemble on Rating Watch

Kemble Water Finance Limited (Kemble) was put on Rating Watch Negative on 5 December 2019 due to several ESG factors. The company suffered a significant reduction in its financial headroom as a result of fines imposed by the regulator on its main subsidiary, Thames Water, for missing water leakage abatement targets. This was sufficient to trigger a negative rating watch for Kemble's rating as there was a significant probability of Kemble's financial profile weakening to a level no longer commensurate with a 'BB-' rating with new price controls being imposed by the regulator. Fitch's analyst for Kemble noted this key rating driver and several other ESG-influenced rating drivers:

1   Water & wastewater management, a key rating driver, received an ESG Relevance Score of 5 as the company had received a large regulatory fine amounting to GBP120 million (in 17/18 prices) for missing its leakage performance targets. As a result of this penalty, its Issuer Debt Rating and senior secured rating were placed on Rating Watch Negative.

2   Kemble had an ESG Relevance Score of 4 for Exposure to Environmental Impacts due to rapid freeze/thaw conditions in winter and extreme heat in summer during 2018, which caused higher

leakage and number of main bursts, which eventually resulted in additional costs. This had a negative impact on the credit profile.

3   Kemble had an ESG Relevance Score of 4 for Customer Welfare, Product Safety, Data Security due to the large penalties (GBP103 million in 2019/2020) prices received for poor customer service performance. These penalties put further pressure on future cash flows.

4   Kemble had an ESG Relevance Score of 4 for Group Structure as its debt was structurally and contractually subordinated to TWUL's debt.

On 9 April 2020, Kemble was downgraded to B+. The downgrade reflected pressure from the above risk factors on Kemble's and Thames Water Utilities Limited's financial profiles as a result of the UK water industry regulator's (Ofwat) challenging final price determinations for a new regulatory regime.

Case-Study 2: Physical Risks of Climate Change: Assessing Geography of Exposure in US Residential Mortgage-backed Securities (MBSs)

Two contrasting transaction examples of risk exposure and credit relevance of physical climate risks to US retail mortgage-backed securities are BRAVO Residential Funding Trust 2019–2022 and Sequoia Mortgage Trust 2020–2023. These transactions highlight the key role of asset location and geographical concentration, together with underlying fundamentals as key drivers of credit risk.

BRAVO Residential Funding Trust 2019–2022 (ESG Relevance Score of 5)

This rated transaction consisted of 7,026 prime quality seasoned residential mortgage loans with a total balance of $425.9 million as of the cutoff date. The pool had an unusually low average loan-to-value ratio of 49.6%, with 94% of fixed-rate mortgages under 30 years duration, and 90% of payments made on time in the past two years. Despite this, there were several negative factors driving the overall elevated ESG Relevance Score of 5, indicating a direct impact on the ratings driven by Exposure to Environmental Impacts (see Figure 9.3).

Due to the large concentration of assets in the Gulf Coast region, there was a far greater natural disaster and catastrophe risk in this pool compared to most transactions. Approximately 43% of the pool was concentrated

General Issues	Score	Sector-Specific Issues	Reference	Overall E Score
GHG Emissions & Air Quality	1	n/a	n/a	5
Energy Management	1	n/a	n/a	4
Water & Wastewater Management	1	n/a	n/a	3
Waste & Hazardous Materials Management; Ecological Impacts	2	Environmental site risk and associated remediation/liability costs; sustainable building practices including Green building certificate credentials	Asset Quality; Financial Structure; Surveillance	2
Exposure to Environmental Impacts	5	Asset, operations and/or cash flow exposure to extreme weather events and other catastrophe risk, including but not limited to flooding, hurricanes, tornadoes, and earthquakes	Asset Quality; Financial Structure; Surveillance	1

Figure 9.3 Extract from Published ESG Navigator for Transaction BRAVO Residential Funding Trust 2019–2020 Explaining ESG Relevance Score of 5.

in Louisiana and an additional 33% in Texas. This resulted in a 1.16x probability of default (PD) adjustment for the geographic concentration, and increased Fitch's expected loss by 104 bps. This is one of the largest adjustments Fitch has made for geographic concentration.

Nearly a quarter of the pool was located in an area recently listed by federal agencies as a natural disaster area as a result of Hurricane Barry in 2019. Fitch haircut property values for homes located in these areas by 10% to reflect the potential risk of property damage. Multiple studies of US Federal Emergency Management Agency natural disaster areas find a significant detrimental effect on local property values, accounting for other factors, driven by higher insurance premiums and anticipation of future damage.

To account for potential future risk of natural disaster, the catastrophe risk adjustment added 28bps to expected loss levels; however, given the highly concentrated profile of the pool, Fitch doubled the catastrophe risk adjustment to 56bps.

Sequoia Mortgage Trust 2020–2023 (ESG Relevance Score of 3)

This mortgage pool consists of very high-quality 30-year and 25-year, fixed-rate, fully amortising loans to borrowers with strong credit profiles, relatively low leverage, and large liquid reserves. The pool has a combined loan-to-value ratio of 68%. Approximately 44% of the pool is concentrated in California with relatively low municipal concentration.

The largest municipal concentration is Los Angeles (20.4%) followed by Miami (11.7%) and New York (7.2%). These account for nearly 40% of the pool. As a result, Fitch applied a 1.03x probability of default (PD) adjustment for geographic concentration.

An ESG Relevance Score of 3 for Exposure to Environmental Impacts reflects the fact that this transaction has cash flow exposure to extreme weather events such as flooding, hurricanes, tornados, and earthquakes, although these exposures have minimal impact on the rating given the characteristics outlined above. There is some evidence of insurers withdrawing from high wildfire risk areas such as parts of California, but in most cases these properties would be covered by standard insurance policies.

Sequoia Mortgage Trust 2020–2023 demonstrates that rated transactions with high geographical concentration but strong underlying credit profiles and shorter average loan maturities will be better placed to manage these risks. This underlines the importance of integrating ESG factors in credit ratings research in a consistent and transparent way, whilst providing reasonable forward-looking assessments of these risks.

How ESG Issues Affect Credit

ESG issues can affect credit profiles both on an entity-specific and sectoral level and can be considered in credit analysis either as potential risks, or as impacts that are already taking place. ESG credit issues can be one-off (such as fines or penalties for a particular incident or event), or ongoing (such as demand shifts or strategic changes driven by secular trends). They impact the credit worthiness of issuers within a sector to varying degrees dependent on the business and financial profile of an entity or transaction. ESG considerations in lending and investment decisions are starting to affect some issuers' ability to raise finance, and there is growing evidence that material ESG issues do impact the credit quality of issuers across all asset classes and sectors.

Transmission Channels

When assessing the credit relevance of ESG issues for ratings, Fitch analysts focus on cashflow impact, primarily changes to liquidity and leverage metrics resulting from existing or forecast ESG risks. Fitch's analysis and monitoring of ESG credit risks for over 10,000 entities and transactions clearly demonstrates that the business and financial profiles of issuers/transactions vary in their ability to absorb or mitigate the negative cashflow impact of ESG risks materialising, both within and across sectors (Table 9.2). The ability of an entity or transaction to absorb and mitigate short-term cashflow impacts from ESG risks, under the analyst's base case ratings forecasts, ultimately

Table 9.2 Environmental and Social Risks in Credit: Transmission Mechanisms.

Financial Impacts	Example	ESG Risk
Demand shifts (regulatory)	Chilean utilities with coal exposure.	Government regulations leading to reduced use of coal.
Demand shifts (social)	Tobacco	Continued decline in consumption and regulatory risk connected with the widespread well-publicised health effects of tobacco products.
Penalties and fines, legal risks	Australian banks	Remediation programmes underway following Royal Commission investigation into misconduct.
Operational costs	San Francisco Bay Area Rapid Transit District	Recent strikes with resulting contracts more favourable to unions than to the issuer, limiting expenditure flexibility.
Operational disruptions	Cenovus Energy Inc (Canadian corporate)	High exposure to pipeline and logistics takeaway capacity, which has been delayed multiple times due to social resistance to pipelines in Canada. This has widened the Canadian oil price differential to record levels and negatively impacts producers like Cenovus.
Financing constraints	Corecivic Inc (US Prison REIT)	Pullback of financing from US and international banks.
Strategic shifts	Global auto manufacturers	Tightening global emissions legislation remains a pivotal issue for the industry. Adoption rate of electric vehicles (EV) is still uncertain and depends on factors outside of car makers' control, such as the development of charging infrastructure. In addition, EVs are less profitable, so an increasing share of EVs will initially burden manufacturers' earnings.
Asset values	FLNG Liquefaction (2&3) LLC (infrastructure project)	Exposure to Hurricane Harvey caused delays and cost overruns, which remain an issue.
External support	Structured agency notes	Programme focused on customer welfare and fair messaging while driving strong performance contributing to reduced expected losses, which has a positive impact on the credit profile, and is relevant to the ratings in conjunction with other factors.

determines the level of credit exposure within the rating profile. This focus on cashflow and downside protection, within a defined forecast period, contrasts significantly with equities where aspects such as growth potential and news flow also play a significant role in share prices.

Individual ESG risk factors, if they materialise, can often affect several different aspects of qualitative and quantitative risk analysis and the impact can vary dependent on the individual business and financial profile of an entity. It is therefore important to consider whether an ESG issue materialises as a credit driver or is transmitted through one or more existing credit drivers. While governance risks are typically assessed directly in credit analysis, they can also affect other areas such as profitability and financing flexibility. As governance risks are often credit drivers, they are the most material across all asset classes and sectors. The distribution of Fitch's ESG Relevance Scores for 1,039 issuers in the financial institution asset class, for example, shows governance risks as the most relevant for rating decisions as of 2 September 2020 (15% of financial institution issuers scored '4' or more in at least one governance category, compared to 2% for social risks and 1% for environmental risks).

In contrast, environmental and social risks are generally assessed in reference to other credit drivers. When they are credit drivers, ESG issues tend to have a clearer influence on credit profiles compared to when they compete with other risk sub-factors. The materiality of environmental and social issues varies much more than governance factors depending on sector and sub-sector. Based on credit ratings as of 30 June 2020, we can see that all rated corporate issuers in the Alcoholic Beverage, Non-alcoholic Beverage and Protein sectors received an ESG Relevance Score of 3 for Water & Wastewater Management, which indicates water issues are relevant to the sector and either have very low impact or are being actively managed by entities to ensure they do not impact the credit profile. On the other hand, all rated issuers in the Airlines sector received an ESG Relevance Score of 1, which indicates water issues are irrelevant to the sector and entities from a credit perspective.

Regional and country-specific factors also affect the materiality of environmental and social issues. In Brazil, 11.3% and 7.6% of rated corporate issuers received ESG relevance scores of either 4 or 5 for social issues and environmental issues respectively. This compares to Spain, where 0% and 4% of rated corporate issuers received ESG relevance scores of either 4 or 5 for social issues and environmental issues, respectively.

Governance elements are overall the most dynamic risk factor from a credit perspective. This is likely to continue, in part due to higher credit relevance overall compared to environmental and social factors, and also greater susceptibility to score changes driven by unforeseen events such as operational errors, regulatory investigations, or abrupt changes to management and board composition.

Credit Structural Shifts

Integrated ESG credit analysis can identify patterns and trends related to ESG risk issues, identify mispriced issuers with governance deficits and/or environmental and social mismanagement, and provide indicators that could help avoid future losses and/or bankruptcies. For example, a study by Bank of America Merrill Lynch[1] shows that an investor who only held companies within the S&P 500 with above-average ESG scores on environmental and social subsectors would have avoided 15 out of 17 (90%) bankruptcies between 2008 and 2015 (Subramanian et al., 2016).

The impact of ESG risk issues on credit has often been difficult for market participants to identify, given the complexity of the interaction between individual ESG risks and multiple credit factors. While this theoretically creates outperformance opportunities, it also means that many investors cannot identify and mitigate downside risks related to these sub-categories or are yet to have gathered enough historic performance data to clearly identify potential return impacts from implementing an ESG-tilted strategy. This is likely to change as data become available to verify that there are ESG credit trends that can cause structural disruption to economies, governments, businesses, and people. Fitch's ESG Relevance Scores are a significant step forward in consistently and transparently providing an independent and objective view of the impact of ESG on credit, and as more participants follow this integrated approach comparable data sets should become more consistent and comprehensive.

Our research shows that material ESG issues can influence the credit quality, and thereby probability of default, for individual issuers over a short to medium investment horizon. ESG credit trends, often long-term and secular in nature, can affect individual issuers, or all issuers within a sector, and can prove fatal to issuers with poorly-aligned business models and operations that don't adapt over time. Fitch's ESG Relevance Scores show that these structural shifts can influence the credit ratings for multiple issuers across a sector.

For example, health-related shifts in consumption and regulation have influenced ratings in the Food, Tobacco and Beverages sector, while social and political pressures to contain healthcare costs has affected the Healthcare and Pharmaceutical industries by limiting pricing power. Pressures on healthcare costs have also extended to related companies in other sectors, such as real estate investment trusts (REITs) operating healthcare real estate. The tightening of global emissions remains a pivotal risk factor for the automobile industry, particularly as many manufacturers are increasing investment to facilitate a business shift towards electric vehicles.

Access to Capital

Asset flows into ESG-mandated funds and the mainstreaming of ESG-integrated investment processes of asset owners and asset managers has inevitably led to more consideration of ESG issues in lending and investment decisions. The number of funds with an explicit ESG mandate has increased to 1,931 at September 2019, up from 913 in 2010 (IMF, 2019). Global banks are also increasingly embedding ESG factors into their risk-management frameworks. More than half the 182 banks that took part in Fitch's ESG Bank survey said they incorporated ESG considerations "always" or "most of the time" into most of their risk-management processes (Fitch, 2019). Collectively, this is increasing the influence of ESG issues in lending and investment decisions, in some cases reducing access to capital for issuers. Fitch is increasingly monitoring the ESG practices of financial institutions, as changes could affect the financing flexibility for certain entities and sectors.

There are already examples where credit ratings have been affected because financing vulnerabilities were exacerbated by financial institution ESG policies. For example, the ratings of CoreCivic were downgraded as a result of US and international banks announcing plans to stop providing financial services to private prison operators, thereby constraining access to capital. Global concerns about coal usage have extended to the supply chain, affecting financing for Australian coal export terminals. In both these examples, financing vulnerabilities already existed. Prison real estate generally lacks secured property mortgage access, a key contingent liquidity source for equity REITS. Australian coal export terminals have bullet maturities that result in the need for periodic refinancing.

Why Does ESG Matter?

ESG issues influence credit quality and ratings, as shown by Fitch's ESG Relevance Scores (Table 9.3). While there is variation in influence across asset classes, and both between and within industry sectors, overall around 17% of Fitch's credit ratings base case forecasts see an influence from ESG (as of end-2020). The specific ESG issues that are relevant and material to different asset classes vary. For example, rule of law and quality of political institutions would be relevant to sovereign credit ratings, whereas governance issues for structured finance transactions are more related to the transaction structure or counterparties.

Occasionally ESG influences can be positive. For example, Latin American pulp and paper companies that benefit from being able to sell excess energy to the grid from cogeneration based upon a renewable resource.

Table 9.3 ESG Relevance Scores Coverage and Impact by Asset Class.

Asset Class	ESG Templates	# of Issuers/ Transactions Scored	# of Data Points	% Impacted from ESG Factors
Corporates	52	1,547	21,336	23%
Financial institutions	4	1,380	14,546	16%
Sovereigns and supranationals	2	146	2170	100%
Public finance & infrastructure	25	2,656	38,248	5%
Structured finance	20	4,588	64,232	19%
Total	102	10,317	145,633	17%

Ultimately, however, the majority of ESG factors represent downside risks for fixed income investors. With a rising number of portfolio managers and credit analysts integrating ESG research in their credit analysis, and with more societal and regulatory pressure on banks and investors to include ESG considerations in their lending and investment decisions, the credit relevance of ESG issues is rising and ESG credit trends will cause structural shifts to sectors and economies.

Integrated ESG credit analysis at an individual entity and transaction level provides crucial insights on the credit relevance and materiality of ESG issues and trends. As ESG risks can materialise in a variety of ways an investment process and analytical tools that captures both non-ESG and ESG risks will assist with identifying material credit issues and how they are likely to affect credit profiles and/or bond valuations. This fundamental analysis also provides investors and analysts with a competitive edge over those who do not assess ESG considerations, especially as assets continue to flow into ESG-mandated funds and away from issuers with high ESG risk levels.

Emerging Trends and Challenges

The ESG landscape is evolving rapidly driven by, for example, the ongoing introduction of new policies targeting ESG issues, increases in the quality and availability of ESG data, and the emergence of new ESG risks. An understanding of these developments, the implications they could have on credit risk, and the challenges that can arise in trying to respond to these developments are crucial to Fitch's credit analysis.

Regulatory Pressure

The influence of ESG risks on financing decisions will grow over time as regulatory pressures push more banks and investors to consider ESG issues. Regulation has become an ESG credit trend that is driving awareness and uptake of ESG investing, adding momentum to asset owners' desires to demonstrate that they 'do good' as well as 'do well'. At the same time, these pressures can also influence credit profiles, and hence our credit analysis.

Policies aimed at tackling climate change are increasing significantly across the world, encouraging banks to place more emphasis on ESG issues, particularly in areas such as climate risk. Most of the largest global systemically important banks are carrying out forward-looking climate scenario analysis, using reporting initiatives like the Task Force on Climate-related Financial Disclosures (TCFD) to guide their disclosure and response. Investors are also feeling pressure to integrate climate data and tools into their investment process and PRI signatories are experiencing mandatory climate reporting.

Climate policies to date have only had a limited impact on the credit profiles in Fitch's rated universe. The exceptions are select sectors and jurisdictions – examples include automobile manufacturers or the more carbon-intensive utilities in Europe – where policy pressures are greater. This reflects the fact that many policies have not yet become financially demanding for issuers over a short to medium-term or are currently very limited in scope. Mitigation and transition measures have also been widespread in countries for certain 'key' industries, with measures such as free carbon certificate allocations. These factors help to explain why present climate regulations are proving insufficient to create enough momentum for countries to meet their Paris Agreement commitments. The gap between policies and pledges appears to be increasing, creating potential for a sudden, rapid, and sustained tightening of climate policies (a scenario referred to by the UN Principles of Responsible Investment as the "Inevitable Policy Response"[1]), particularly as there is increasing political emphasis on climate change in many countries.

Reflecting investor demand for a long-term view on the relative vulnerability of sectors and entities to longer term ESG-related changes, Fitch introduced ESG Vulnerability Scores for different sectors. These scores started with the utilities sector in October 2020 to provide analysis on how vulnerabilities would evolve up to 2050 in a global transition scenario where climate change is limited to a 2°C rise. A second report with ESG Vulnerability Scores for the Oil & Gas and Chemicals sectors was released in January 2021. Fitch intends to provide these long-term vulnerability scores for all major industry sectors, offering a time series long-term credit risk profile for sectors, sub-sectors, and geographies globally. Vulnerability scores enable a long-term relative credit risk exposure comparison between geographies, sectors, and sub-sectors. Risk levels vary from scores that represent an 'existential threat' to those that reflect credit supportive conditions.

The European Union is widely viewed as the global leader in ESG regulation having implemented several crucial initiatives, and ESG-related regulations – the Non-Financial Reporting Directive and the Low Carbon Markets Regulation. These initiatives have created the foundation for further improvements in ESG data, research, and standards globally. The Chinese government, along with its associations and security exchanges, have also promoted ESG investing through their Guidelines for Establishing a Green Financial System and through the mandatory disclosure requirements of environmental information by listed companies. However, there are regulatory headwinds in other countries, such as in the US, as well as a trend towards nationalism which potentially could have a significant negative impact on credit profiles, particularly if future policy adjustments are abrupt.

An area of great interest for many countries has been the EU taxonomy for sustainable activities developed by the European Commission. The taxonomy proposal forms the basis for setting clear standards of what can be classified as green or sustainable in relation to financial products. While the development of the EU taxonomy is not expected to have broad credit risk implications in the near-term, progress towards more universally accepted definitions and standards may pave the way for policy and market innovations that may lead to financing advantages for sustainable activities, such as the deployment of public capital or direct subsidies.

Credit Relevance of Social Issues

Where Fitch considers social factors to be potentially material they are included within the ESG Relevance Score framework. While sovereign credit analysis has always included social structure and stability, for other issuers these factors have rarely been considered systematically. For non-public sector entities, Fitch has identified five main social risk categories: (1) Human Rights and Community Relations; (2) Customer Welfare; (3) Labour Relations and Practices; (4) Employee Wellbeing; and (5) Exposure to Social Impacts. Each of these risks is further defined depending on the issuer's sector. For example, for a corporate issuer in the hotel/lodging industry, Customer Welfare in relation to data security and guest health and safety are sector-specific key risks for analysts to pay particular attention to in determining credit materiality. In contrast, an infrastructure credit for a large-scale transportation project would be more likely to face social risks from public resistance in the construction phase leading to delays and/or cost overruns – identified as a sector-specific risk under Exposure to Social Impacts.

Another ESG credit trend gaining significant momentum is the perception around income inequality and broader economic unfairness, relevant to sovereign and public finance issuers. Social discontent from this perception could lead to unrest with political consequences, as well as policy responses that may have both macro and sector-specific implications. Recent social unrest in Chile prompted the president to introduce legislation to overturn a recent increase in utility rates, guarantee a minimum assured income, raise pensions, and introduce medical insurance for catastrophic illness. In this case, the combination of fiscal and economic policy response to the unrest will erode the strength of the sovereign balance sheet under Fitch's base case rating forecasts (albeit from a relatively strong position compared to peers). These actions highlight the potential for sudden and rapid shifts in both the economic and regulatory landscape, which are not necessarily consistent with long-term environmental goals and objectives. Social concerns can also affect companies directly through labour strikes or disruption of projects by local communities, and the direction of climate-related policy for countries will need to consider this broader social and political backdrop. Social disapproval related to perceived excess corporate profitability or irresponsible behaviour has resulted in policy and regulatory actions, particularly in developed economies. For example, there has been widespread cross-party agreement in the US to control drug prices. This has resulted in regulatory scrutiny over drug pricing, in turn, becoming a material risk to credit ratings for many pharmaceutical issuers.

Ageing populations are likely to result in healthcare costs remaining contentious in many countries. Demographic trends have the potential to exacerbate and widen socioeconomic divides. Unstable demographic profiles such as rapid youth population growth can foment unstable social and political environments, with adverse implications for sovereign ratings. If large numbers of young people are unable to find jobs and see little prospect of having a family or status in society, then anger, frustration, and social unrest may follow. This is more likely if there is high unemployment and poor governance. In the case of Saudi Arabia, an ESG Relevance Score of 3 was attributed to general risk category "Employment and Income Equality" due to its young, rapidly growing, and underemployed population contributing to political stability risks and creating upward pressure on government spending and debt.

Overcoming Challenges to ESG Integration

Significant interest in integrating ESG risk issues into credit decision processes from some asset owners and asset managers began to accelerate in the early 2010s. Despite the slow start compared to equities, ESG-integrated processes such as due diligence frameworks and the use of proprietary or third-party ESG scores are now commonplace among fixed income investors. Both asset owners and asset managers have expanded their ESG expertise and coverage to fixed income and benefited from the lessons learnt by equity practitioners. Service providers have emerged to innovate and develop data and tools for fixed income practitioners. However, ESG integration in credit risk analysis is still not a mainstream practice, and many portfolio managers and analysts struggle to understand how to interpret and incorporate ESG research into their due diligence and security valuations.

Incomplete and non-comparable datasets are a significant problem for credit risk analysis, for both Fitch as a credit rating agency as well as other market participants. Historical ESG information is limited, often selective, and inconsistent; one year it is reported, the next year it is not, and there is usually a time lag between the publication of the data point and when it was measured. The level of ESG reporting varies by region, sector and entity, and numerous sustainability reporting frameworks contribute to the non-standardisation of data across regions and immaterial data reporting. This challenge requires time to be resolved as ESG data collection becomes more consistent and mainstream. Service providers and investors are keen for further alignment of ESG reporting frameworks – these include Global Reporting Initiative (GRI), the International Integrated Reporting Council (IIRC), the Sustainability Accounting Standards Board (SASB), Task Force on Climate-related Financial Related Disclosures (TCFD), CDP – with the goal of increasing structured ESG data and reporting. However, there is limited consensus on what metrics to use, which adds to the difficulties with identifying ESG credit risks and performing peer comparisons. The availability of data can be particularly challenging where ESG risks are predominantly along the value chain where reporting is more limited, for example deforestation and modern slavery. However, Fitch often has the opportunity to engage with issuers directly as part of the credit rating process to understand material ESG risks, and these can be reflected within its' Relevance Score and Vulnerability Score frameworks.

The different characteristics of fixed income instruments bring specific challenges to integrating ESG issues into credit risk assessment. The fixed income market is relatively opaque due to lower news coverage and less liquidity compared to equities. It is also harder to navigate due to the variety of issuing entities and transactions, instrument types, fixed maturities, and structures. The lack of transparency and multitude of variables inherent to the fixed income market brings additional dimensions and layers of complexity to analysing and identifying ESG factors.

As a credit rating agency, Fitch's function has always been to evaluate both internal and external factors affecting issuers to determine their material financial impact. The firm faced its own challenges in deciding how best to incorporate ESG risks into an established and well-respected analytical framework. We found that governance issues are priced more efficiently compared to environmental and social factors within fixed income, as governance quality has traditionally been included as an indication of creditworthiness. However, regulation, client demand, and public pressure are casting the spotlight on social and environmental issues as they have a broader societal impact than corporate governance concerns. As such, Fitch has ensured that its approach to sustainable finance places equal value on environmental, social, and governance risks.

Conclusion

The growth in interest around sustainability issues from investors has led to widespread integration of ESG factors into investment processes and strategies. As investors become more sophisticated in their investment approaches, there is clear evidence that ESG integration can be approached from various perspectives (e.g. as a method to achieve sustainability impact objectives through investments, finding investment opportunities, managing downside risks). Investors are also modifying their approaches to better cater to specific asset classes. This has drawn attention to how ESG factors should be integrated into credit risk analysis. Against this backdrop, investors continue to call on the credit ratings agencies to better clarify the relevance and materiality of ESG issues.

Fitch has developed credit-relevant ESG scores and tailored ESG reporting to further promote and improve the transparency of ESG considerations into credit ratings and analysis. Implementing a consistent cross-asset framework has helped Fitch build up practical experience in how to integrate ESG factors into financial and credit analysis, and has provided Fitch with a more systematic approach to monitor how ESG trends are influencing credit across asset classes, sectors and regions. The influence of ESG credit risks in practice can vary considerably depending on these characteristics, as well as for the specific ESG issue. How, for example, physical climate risks affects the credit profile of a European water utility will vastly differ from how it affects US residential MBS. This highlights the nuanced and sector focused approach required to understand the impact of ESG factors on credit ratings.

Governance risks are the most material across asset classes, and are typically assessed directly in credit analysis, although they can also affect other areas such as profitability and financial flexibility. In contrast, environmental and social risks are generally assessed as part of other credit drivers with the potential to impact multiple different aspects of traditional quantitative and qualitative areas of analysis. Understanding these issues requires detailed examination of the transmission mechanisms through which these risks affect a credit profile. Both environmental and social risks can broadly affect issuers across a sector (e.g. through sector-wide regulation, or individual entities involved in an incident that results in a loss, fine, or other penalty). The increasing consideration of ESG factors by financial institutions in their lending and investment decisions is also affecting financing conditions for selected entities and sectors. Understanding these transmissions mechanisms and how they evolve is key to incorporating ESG into credit analysis.

Whilst the future is hard to predict, the growing societal and political focus on sustainability issues means that the influence of ESG factors on credit profiles will grow, as regulations tighten and ESG considerations drive customers and issuing entities. This will increase the importance for investors and other market participants of incorporating ESG factors into credit analysis. The quality and availability of data remains a challenge in fully understanding the impact of ESG factors on credit risks, but both are improving as ESG data standards gradually harmonise and reporting of ESG data becomes more consistent and comparable. We expect to see an increase in data disclosure, net zero commitments, and science-based targets to enable those commitments to be monitored and measured.

There is a long journey ahead to achieve decarbonization and climate stability, and Fitch remains committed and focused on integrating ESG factors into its analytical processes, to better inform investors and issuers on the relevance and materiality of ESG to their investment and funding decisions.

Note

1 https://www.unpri.org/sustainability-issues/climate-change/inevitable-policy-response.

References

Fitch Ratings (2019), Banks' Risk Management Embraces ESG. [online]. Available at: https://www.fitchratings.com/research/banks/banks-risk-management-embraces-esg-04-12-2019 (Accessed 12 May 2021).

International Monetary Fund (IMF) (2019), *Global Financial Stability Report: Lower for Longer* (IMF, Washington, DC). [online]. Available at: https://www.imf.org/en/Publications/GFSR/Issues/2019/10/01/global-financial-stability-report-october-2019 (Accessed 12 May 2021).

Subramanian, S., Suzuki, D., Makedon, J., Hall, J., Pouey, M. and Bonilla, J. (2016), *Equity Strategy Focus Point: ESG: Good Companies Can Make Good Stocks* (Bank of America Merrill Lynch). Available at: https://www.iccr.org/sites/default/files/page_attachments/equitystrategyfocuspoint_esg.pdf (Accessed 12 May 2021).

10 The Role of ESG Risk Factors in Corporate Credit Analysis[1]

Joshua Kendall and Tudor Thomas

Introduction

Insight Investment (Insight) is one of Europe's top-five largest investment managers for pension funds, insurers, sovereign wealth funds, and financial institutions (IPE, 2021). More than $200 billion of these assets are in corporate fixed income.

In 2002 Insight began developing responsible investing principles into its corporate debt investment processes, defining these principles as the appraisal, management, and control of credit risks and opportunities stemming from sustainability themes. Insight believes that investment outcomes are more achievable and resilient if they combine sustainability and financial inputs. Sustainability-related regulations can impact entire sectors and cause structural shifts that influence short-term and long-term business decisions. And frequent corporate failings show how inadequate governance and an ineffective management response to the challenges posed by social, ethical, and environmental issues may impair a company's creditworthiness.

This chapter describes Insight's approach to incorporating sustainability risk factors into corporate investment grade, high yield, and emerging market debt asset classes. It begins by describing the history and evolution of Insight's process. It then discusses the qualitative methods and quantitative techniques that underpin the research and stewardship process today. Two investment grade case-studies – one a bottom-up credit review and one a review of performance data from the COVID-19 bear market – are used to illustrate the role that ESG factors could play in managing credit portfolios.

Responsible Investment Foundations

Insight's responsible investment programme started with a policy in 2002 that explained 'investment returns can be enhanced if the companies Insight invest in maintain high standards of corporate governance and corporate responsibility'. The policy acknowledged that Insight had a critical market role, noting that

DOI: 10.4324/9781003055341-13

> Investors have become a powerful force for corporate accountability with regard to questions of corporate governance, but they have for the most part, been silent on the question of corporate responsibility. Investors have a responsibility, an interest and a substantial opportunity to play a powerful role in encouraging more responsible business practice.
>
> (Insight Investment, 2002)

Insight's early responsible investment efforts focused on engagement with companies and policymakers (see Mackenzie (2006), Sullivan and Mackenzie (2006, 2008), and Waygood (2006)). For example, Insight led working groups at the Extractive Industries Transparency Initiative to introduce industry reporting standards. Insight also played a leading role in investor collaborations on thematic issues such as climate change through the Institutional Investor Group on Climate Change (Sullivan, Robins, et al., 2005). In 2005 and 2006, Insight was a member of the expert group that developed the UN-supported Principles for Responsible Investment (PRI) initiative, becoming a founding signatory in 2006. In 2007, Insight was the first asset manager in the world to publish an annual responsible investment report (*Putting Principles into Practice* (Insight Investment, 2007)) explaining how it had implemented the PRI's six principles.

Insight started to focus on sustainability-related investment research in 2004 and 2005, driven by high-profile frauds in 2001 and 2002 – Enron and Worldcom, respectively – and by the introduction of the EU Emissions Trading Scheme, which had potentially significant financial implications for European electricity utilities (ten Kate and Evans, 2006; Sullivan, 2011).

Insight began to address ESG issues within investment decisions as part of a corporate risk initiative, which began in 2005. This early work faced practical challenges: the limited availability of sustainability information from third-party sources, the absence of common frameworks to incorporate non-financial information into credit decisions, and a lack of consensus on what constituted materiality.

To enable further progress, several internal working groups were established to focus on specific issues, and were charged with developing risk indicators, identifying data sources, and creating analytical tools that could be routinely used by credit analysts in their company assessments (Insight, 2007). A corporate governance working group, for example, developed and scored 10 risk indicators to assess companies' governance. The responsible investment team then researched companies in more detail and wrote a short note on each laggard company to capture an overall view. The scores and notes were made available to all credit analysts and fund managers through Insight's central research database.

Around the same time specialist research firms started to provide more structure and consistency to ESG information and ratings. These data were introduced into a new risk framework to capture ESG and traditional credit risk factors (Insight's Landmine Checklist). This Checklist identified the six factors considered to pose the most acute downside risks that may result in sudden or unanticipated changes in a company's creditworthiness (Table 10.1). Analysts considered each factor within their credit analysis, according to its relevance and materiality to the issuer. The process was therefore tailored to the issuer, and the attention to each landmine varied by company size, sector, and ownership.

Analysts' ability to understand the interaction and influence of these landmines created a better assessment of the expected performance of corporate bonds so that portfolios could benefit from market inefficiencies and changes (ten Kate and Evans, 2006). The framework was also updated regularly. While litigation was a consistent concern for around ten years, it was dropped as the number of litigation events fell and companies' ability to manage these events made it less material. This was replaced by leveraged buy-out or activism risk assessments, a relevant credit risk factor facing bondholders from corporate actions. Another evolution related to governance. The Checklist started with a governance assessment because this was most likely to get credit analyst and portfolio manager support, as there was general agreement that governance risks were more material and that governance-related information was generally much better (e.g. standardisation of governance metrics and best practice codes). As ESG information has matured, Insight has moved towards proprietary ESG rating signals that align with an in-house view on sustainability risk factors (see Table 10.1).

Regulatory and ESG risks often overlapped for key sectors. For example, analysts assigned European utilities a weak (in Insight's case a 4 or 5) score in 2005 because of the emerging European Union Emission Trading Scheme but not a low ESG score, which, at that time, was driven mostly by governance concerns. But as the relevance of ESG issues evolved, Insight needed a broader understanding of sustainability risks. This meant that the ESG risk

Table 10.1 The Evolution of the Insight Landmine Checklist.

2006 Landmine Checklist	2011 Landmine Checklist	2015 Landmine Checklist	2021 Landmine Checklist
Liquidity	Liquidity	Liquidity	Liquidity
Contingent liabilities	Contingent liabilities	Contingent liabilities	Climate
Regulatory	Regulatory	Regulatory	Regulatory
Litigation	Litigation	ESG (MSCI ESG ratings)	ESG (insight)
Governance & accounting (governance metrics international)	Governance & corporate behaviour (GMI ratings)	Event	Event
Event	Event	Leveraged buy-out /activist	Leveraged buy-out /activist

indicators moved from being predominantly governance-focused in 2006 to taking a broader view of sustainability risks by 2012. In 2021, the growing urgency of climate action and improved availability of climate data meant that a distinct climate risk rating was required to capture these issues; by that time, contingent liability risks were considered less relevant for most issuers in Insight's universe.

Monitoring

Using ESG ratings that were structured around an internal 1–5 rating framework across sectors allowed investment teams to review issuers' ESG performance and set certain thresholds for routine investigation. Originally a manual exercise with data in spreadsheets, Insight prioritised the bottom 5% of issuers on a monitoring list, and positive exposure to such issuers across portfolios required sign-off by the Head of Credit Analysis, and in many cases engagement with the issuer (Insight, 2012). For each company on the ESG Risk Review watchlist analysts compiled a brief description of the risks and assessed their significance, with this exercise repeated every quarter.

Monitoring moved gradually from predominantly focusing on governance to all low-scoring signals, including controversial business activities, climate risk, and sustainability. The degree of stringency has also grown, with approximately 10% of issuers routinely monitored for their ESG performance (Insight, 2020a). This threshold aligns with Insight's internal rating system, which assigns the bottom decile to issuers with the lowest ratings, and reflects the growing sensitivity of asset owners to holding issuers with inadequate sustainability performance. Today, a quarterly evaluation of ESG sustainability ratings takes place, with investment teams actively discussing emerging or ongoing ESG issues, rating changes, engagement priorities, and the results from internal or external research (Insight, 2020a).

Stewardship

Insight has been engaging with companies since 2002. The original rationale was to protect and enhance companies' returns and to deliver on Insight's wider responsibility to ensure that investee companies were managed to high ethical, social and environmental standards (Insight, 2008).

Three principal factors originally guided Insight's selection of engagement topics: The materiality or business relevance of a particular theme or issue to companies or sectors; the likelihood that analyst intervention would significantly affect a company's conduct or contribute constructively to an evolving debate; and the seriousness of the ESG issues in question (Insight, 2007).

Unusually for a fixed income manager, in 2010 Insight signed up to the (heavily equity focused) UK Stewardship Code (Insight, 2011). This was despite arguments that the lack of formal ownership rights removed obligations or responsibilities from bondholders, or that issuers were not interested in the opinions of creditors. Insight has never believed fixed income investors cannot hold companies accountable. For example, in 2006 Insight noted:

> If issues of concern arise once a bond has been issued, bond-holders can indicate to management that they would look upon new issues... less favourably in the future if the issues are not addressed, for instance, signalling that a higher return would be required.
>
> (ten Kate and Evans, 2006)

In 2010, Insight updated its responsible investment policy to acknowledge 'Engagement with companies [is] the most appropriate way available to better understand matters that materially impact the long-term performance of the business' (Insight, 2012). During the 2018 consultation update to the UK Stewardship Code, Insight argued that a broader definition of stewardship should include the responsibilities and rights of bondholders (Insight, 2018).

Insight's Qualitative and Quantitative Process Methods

This section explains how Insight assesses ESG issues, engages with companies and how ESG analysis and engagement is embedded within the overall credit process.

How Insight Assesses ESG Factors

After an initial screening to select bonds that meet Insight's credit prerequuisites (e.g. in relation to liquidity), a full investment analysis that combines ESG risk screening and financial analysis is conducted.

Credit analysts appraise ESG information to determine the materiality of the issue. While a financial appraisal is desirable, not all ESG risks can be quantified within cash-flow models precisely. This is principally due to time horizons: long-term sustainability risks are difficult to determine precisely as the issuer, technology, or regulatory changes all influence credit outcomes (Sullivan 2011). Sustainability issues become financially material credit issues over time as certainty rises and as policymakers respond. For example, European utilities have seen a changing credit outlook in face of gradually stricter regulatory conditions that have promoted renewables over fossil fuel power generation.

Insight's analysts interrogate the financial impact of ESG risks such as declining revenues, higher expenses, product demand and weaker margins, higher capital expenditure or fines, penalties, and sanctions. This analysis begins with a review of the Insight ESG dashboard, an interactive data tool built with a Tableau technology interface that houses Insight's proprietary ESG data warehousing and ratings. This enables analysts to probe the quantitative Insight ESG ratings to understand the precise metrics and factors influencing an issuer's near-term performance.

Insight's ESG Ratings

In 2019 Insight created a proprietary rating that it believes more accurately reflects the risks faced by issuers by introducing analysts' qualitative judgement into the rating process (Insight, 2020b). The entire process was overseen by Insight's ESG team with inputs from investment teams to ensure the ratings reflect material risks that different industries and corporates face.

Sourcing and Warehousing Data

The methodology incorporates ESG data from four independent sources. The providers are selected for their data depth and coverage. Preliminary quality control on the datasets highlight any obvious problems, such as new or incomplete fields. Bespoke software helps to assign global company identifiers to the data provided. This remedies cases where the ultimate parent of the issuer is a sovereign (or a sovereign agency, central bank, etc.), where the issuer's credit is not underwritten in any meaningful way by the sovereign entity. The 'mapped' raw data is added to a database, giving Insight a structure to house and create ESG ratings more accurately.

Framework Development

As a first step input data from third parties is weighted according to Insight's assessment of their relevance and quality. Insight's responsible investment team identifies the strengths and weaknesses of different providers' methodologies, selecting, aggregating, and weighting the data to ensure the model reflects the most relevant and high-quality information. Second, Insight's analysts review key ESG factors for each sector to ensure material risks are reflected with a larger weight within the model. For example, pollution is a risk factor for mining companies but not advertising companies. Over time, the relevance of these issues may change, while for others – such as corporate governance issues – they remain a key concern regardless of the sector.

Ratings Production

Key issue scores are grouped and then aggregated to generate thematic scores, followed by separate environmental, social, and governance pillar ratings (see example in Table 10.2). The overall ESG rating indicates an issuer's performance relative to its peers, meaning there will be a similar proportion of highly rated companies within each sector (e.g. the banking and energy sectors), even though these sectors face very different ESG risks.

Table 10.2 Environment Pillar Score and Environment Theme Scores.

Theme	Key Issue	Score	Weight
Climate change	Carbon emissions	6.6	14%
Climate change	Carbon financing and exposure	7.9	5%
Climate change	Product footprint	6.7	8%
Natural capital	Biodiversity and land use	1.5	19%
Natural capital	Raw material sourcing	5.3	7%
Natural capital	Water management	2.2	19%
Pollution	Pollution and Waste	1.2	17%
Environmental controversy	Environmental controversy	0.0	11%
Environment pillar	**Overall**	**3.1**	**100%**

Source: Insight Investment, 2020b.

Output

As Insight's objectives – to minimise credit risk – interact with asset owner's objectives to embed sustainability issues into portfolio construction, raw scores are renormalised within each GICS industry group to identify issuers that are best-in-class for their industry group (the top 10% receive a 1 rating and the bottom 10% a 5 rating; 30% of issuers receive a 3 rating). In addition, to support more asset classes, secondary renormalised scores specifically for emerging market and high yield issuers were created. By introducing separate scores, Insight could avoid situations where the ESG ratings are skewed in favour of specific asset classes or geographies (Insight, 2020b).

A further enhancement maps ESG ratings across the entire credit hierarchy for an issuer. Through a comprehensive mapping strategy, the 2,300 parent entities in corporate bond benchmarks with ESG ratings are mapped to approximately 700,000 holding companies. On a case-by-case basis, parent-child hierarchies are broken where risk is not meaningfully inherited in either direction, such as Berkshire Hathaway Energy Co. (BRKHEC; Utilities), which is disconnected from Berkshire Hathaway Inc. (BRK; Financials). ESG ratings are captured within a central infrastructure and database, which feeds downstream portfolio and credit analysis systems.

Update Cycle

As ESG information proliferates amongst credit rating agencies and sell-side research firms, better visibility and consistent (quarterly) updates of underlying ESG risk drivers in Insight's assessment improves analysts' efficiency during the due diligence process. Analysts could more accurately focus on material risk areas using specially designed ESG research tools, which Insight anticipates will be more relevant as the volume of sustainability data rises with regulation. However, quantitative data is no replacement for analyst knowledge: if an analyst believes that a rating is too high or too low as a result of incorrect data, and that this warrants adjustment, there is a formal process by which they may apply to an independent internal group for a rating change. Members exclude portfolio managers or analysts with potential conflicts of interest. All ESG rating changes are documented and reviewed.

How Insight Engages with Issuers

As a matter of policy, where appropriate analysts meet with issuers. Analysts draw on their sector expertise and the ESG dashboard to identify the engagement issues relevant for each issuer. The engagement programme, which is supported by cross-sector specialist ESG analysts, seeks to achieve one or more of the following objectives:

1   **To assess the materiality of ESG issues**. Materiality-focused ESG assessments aim to make a judgement call on management's understanding and performance of sustainability risks. The ESG research phase often reveals issues that analysts consider creditworthy, especially new, disruptive, and strategic risks. This is the most common analyst engagement. Analysts will go into meetings with the goal of pinpointing management responses to these risks, alongside reviewing finance and business issues. While most engagements are designed to be proactive, they could also be reactive. This was the case for the Brumadinho dam tailings disaster in 2019, where Insight organised engagements with debt-issuing mining companies to learn more about how they managed tailing dam-related risks.

2   **To improve sustainability transparency**. For many private companies, in particular those where ESG ratings are not available, Insight's analysts send the company a detailed questionnaire to harvest specific data points. Customised for specific sectors, the questionnaires are used by different corporate debt investment teams. Typical questions include 'Do you have a workplace safety policy' and 'What percentage of employees are female'. Credit analysts work with the ESG team to produce the surveys. More than 400 responses have been received since 2016. Where analysts require ratings at a short notice, for example for a new issue, a shortened survey using information from their own previous interaction with the issuer is completed. Common questions include 'How strong is their dialogue with investors?', 'Is there an independent audit committee?' and 'Have there been more than 5 executive changes in the last 2 years?' The responses for all survey types are weighted to produce ESG scores and red flags. Analysts then consider their materiality and credit relevance, just like for conventional quantitative ESG ratings.

3   To collaborate with other investors on specific themes. Insight works with other investors to encourage a change or improvement in company behaviour through network groups including Climate Action 100+, CDP and the PRI. ESG specialists lead these engagements because they

are frequently resource-intensive and long-term, requiring a different set of skills and industry knowledge. While investor groups may have a shareholder focus (and may focus on the use of shareholder resolutions as an influencing strategy), many thematic issues like climate change benefit from bondholders and shareholders working together. Insight does not believe any investor alone can reorient issuers towards sustainability behaviours; but collective and regular communication as an investor group could achieve greater access and influence the largest bond issuers.

4   **To have a greater positive impact**. Impact engagement involves two activities. First, direct interaction with issuers on behavioural characteristics that require improvement. These often focus on transparency, such as working with issuers on preparing their sustainability reports, climate strategy, or developing ESG KPIs. The second, and the more common engagement for Insight, is on green or social bond programmes. Insight analyses impact bonds using a proprietary framework, and Insight frequently identifies misalignments between what analysts expect an impact bond to achieve, and what an issuer claims to achieve, creating potential integrity issues. Since 2016, Insight has assessed more than 300 impact bond issuers, with approximately 20% receiving the lowest Insight rating, meaning they cannot be added to clients' sustainability-focused portfolios (Insight, 2020a). Insight analysts provide feedback direct to issuers or syndicate banks, as Insight believes that providing such feedback will help raise bond quality across the market.

Analysts approach each meeting with a list of questions or themes to discuss with management, using inputs from the research process. Insight requires analysts assign one of four entries for each ESG engagement:

i   **Satisfied,** i.e. the issuer provided a reasonable response to questions and no further concerns identified
ii   **Monitor,** i.e. the issuer provided reasonable responses but ongoing monitoring will be required
iii **Follow-up**, i.e. the issuer provided some reasonable responses to questions, but outstanding questions remain and additional engagement with the issuer is required
iv   **Escalate**, i.e. unsatisfactory responses and immediate evaluation of issues required internally or with the company

Stewardship activity is now an integral part of Insight's credit analyst performance objectives. This has been supported by issuers' willingness to engage on ESG factors: sustainability discussions have become more frequent, with issuers incorporating ESG content within their presentations and even hosting dedicated sustainability strategy conversations and updates. All engagement information with issuers is entered into engagement notes which are stored centrally and include drop-down fields and note boxes for tracking and reporting. In 2020, more than 80% of Insight's direct interactions with debt issuers in 2021 included some form of dialogue on one or more ESG topics. These engagements covered companies from than 60 countries, including around half from emerging markets. Thirty-three percent of meetings were one–on–one, and 61% of meetings included a board or senior management official (Insight, 2021).

How the Process Joins Together

An investment decision is rarely the result of any single factor. ESG factors may tip the scales when the research process integrates ESG factors, or they may have no influence at all. The research process is not looking to achieve specific outcomes, such as identifying companies with the best sustainability strategy. If elevated ESG risks are identified, analysts often expect a commensurate financial compensation, such as a higher coupon, coupon steps, or covenant protections, depending on the asset class. This means the ultimate decision to recommend a bond is made in the best interest of all investors by focusing on the likelihood of a deterioration in credit quality, balanced against appropriate mitigants, to determine bond fair value.

While a materiality assessment has consistently featured within Insight's process, what analysts consider material is changing. Analysts are now expected to consider ESG risks over both the short-term and the long-term. Short-term risks are often more practical to assess given a reasonable level of visibility on business activities. Long-term risks, such as climate change, are often harder to quantify but that does not mean they are any less material. In certain portfolios, for example, analysts have recommended selling several long-dated oil and gas bonds from some long-term investment portfolios because of their incompatibility with a low-carbon economy. Recommendations are captured within credit notes, which contain both structured and unstructured ESG indicators, and are available to the investment team when published (Figure 10.1).

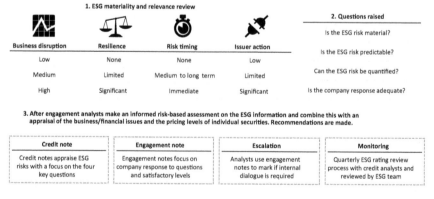

Figure 10.1 Process Diagram for Insight's Decision-Making Process.

An internal group brings investment teams together as part of a regular review of stewardship and ESG investment activity. The group reviews quarterly ESG rating changes and recommends engagement action. 'Laggard' companies are also monitored against their ESG ratings performance, and issuers with a '5' rating may be prioritised for engagement.

Issuers are increasingly removed from portfolios, even if there is an ESG premium. ESG factors are increasingly formalised in investment guidelines with a higher degree of specificity, and corporate pledges have been made which set a general direction for investment managers and asset owners. These commitments complement investment mandate guidelines from asset owners demanding more ESG outcomes and this frequently involves screening issues or raising the ESG quality hurdle for inclusion in portfolios, leading to active ESG restrictions. This points to an evolving use of ESG information. It is no longer just about assessing materiality, but building an investment portfolio that aligns with a client's values – and these are increasingly sustainability focused. The implication is that the ESG research cycle, which has historically been an entirely qualitative process involving review, monitoring, and engagement, now routinely applies ESG rating overlays that filter out companies to direct portfolio construction.

Case–Study: ESG Factors in Portfolio Decisions

'Buy and maintain' portfolios aim deliver a targeted yield with minimal portfolio turnover and transaction costs. Bonds are typically bought at new issue and will remain in portfolios until their maturity. A popular long-term investment style for many institutional investors such as pension schemes and insurance companies, buy and maintain portfolios allocate towards long-tenured bonds to match liabilities. This case study examines how bonds issued by a global automobile manufacturer were sold from Insight's buy and maintain portfolios. A key factor was decreasing confidence from the investment team in the company's ability to manage key ESG risks.

Assessment

There was low industry consensus on the bond issuer's ESG profile. Comparing Insight's ESG ratings with three other providers (which are normalised for comparability) shows the lack of agreement (See Table 10.3). Insight's quantitative methodology placed the company in the lowest ESG rating bucket, driven by low performance for product quality/safety, product environmental footprint, controversial events, and ownership concerns. Examining the Insight ESG dashboard the credit analyst was alerted to four specific risks.

1 **Regulation.** Vehicle efficiency standards are rising. In Europe, for example, carbon dioxide (CO_2) efficiency is an important near-term regulatory risk, with manufacturers effectively facing a choice between

Table 10.3 ESG Ratings by Provider.

Ratings Source	ESG Rating
Insight	5
Provider 1	4
Provider 2	3
Provider 3	2

substantial fines or selling electric vehicles (EVs) at low margins to bring down their fleet average CO_2 emissions. Home to more than 25% of global sales, Europe's stricter vehicle emissions standards are expensive for the company, which has made substantial investments in research and development, amounting to 5% of total revenue, to meet emission targets. Conversely, less stringent emission regulation in the US, another major market for the company, will likely cause a slower technological consumer shift, meaning the development payback is much longer. Regulation may have a positive impact for the environment, but the pace of change (and a company's response) can have downsides. Transitioning from old to new technologies is expensive for auto manufacturers, with significant cost outlays and uncertain returns, even though EVs initially did command higher consumer prices. For investors, understanding the scale and type of technological investment, as well as any project partners, are relevant risk measurements. Issuers are vulnerable to investing too much and too early in uncertain technologies or developments.

2   **Demand**. While still a relatively small share of auto sales, EV demand is forecast to rise substantially, with meaningful growth beginning around the mid-2020s as technology, consumer taste, and government action converge to increase green technology adoption. EV sales are expected to rise to 10% of auto sales by 2025, 25% by 2030, and 50% by 2038 (BNEF, 2020). Rising EV production will be a significant cash flow headwind. In a market of changing consumer demands the company has become too dependent on 'gas guzzlers', responsible for some 50% of all models sold in the US, which while more profitable than conventional models, are also subject to tougher emission rules. This affords protection given a slower pace of regulation on emission standards, but it also makes it more expensive to make a return on EV investment.

3   **Product safety**. Auto manufacturers have a long history of bad publicity negatively impacting on sales. By some distance Insight's ESG ratings model flagged product safety as an area of concern. Insight's analysis suggested that warranty payments, a reasonable yardstick for product safety, were increasing versus earnings; in fact, the company's payments were materially higher than the industry medium as a percentage of revenue and percentage of EBIT. Warranty expenses point to other potential problems with the manufacturing process, which may mean underinvestment and further costs ahead.

4   **Management**. The company has experienced executive instability. Insight sees high executive turnover as a strategic and governance concern, in particular given the structural challenges facing the autos sector where navigating the uncertainty ahead requires leadership and the ability to execute the company's strategy, not behaviours driven by concerns about their short-term security.

Engagement

A dedicated ESG-focused call was coordinated with senior management. The investor relations, treasury, and sustainability teams present on the call discussed questions the Insight analyst had identified during the research process. The company showed that it had a high-level understanding of the risks, but there was a lack of depth and explanation on the key issues of safety, product quality, and warranties. Several enhancements had been made, including a centralisation of core engineering responsibilities rather than separate quality teams. Despite these improvements, the company did not provide information on its targets for recalls or for warranty payments.

The company acknowledged that quality issues were affecting auto sales. While its own engineering and safety processes were identifying problems, the lack of detail regarding timings for new vehicle production and sales targets meant the company could not provide a clear account of how quickly product improvements could be made. Further, the information provided on the steps being taken to improve product quality was not convincing.

Adding to concerns were the company's financial and operating disclosures. The company stated that it would be moving to quarterly rather than monthly reporting of volume sales numbers, arguing that monthly sales are 'too volatile'. While Insight was aware of the implications of overly focusing on short-term numbers, the investment team was not reassured by these proposals as they signalled governance weaknesses at a time when greater transparency was needed to reassure investors about the company's performance.

Investment Conclusions

Applying the information gained from the credit research and issuer engagement, it became clear the headwinds facing the company and the limited financial levers available to protect its balance sheet, improve cash flow and increase product margins. Dialogue further supported the analyst's appraisal of the relevant issues flagged by the Insight ESG ratings and isolate the unmanaged risks. The analyst recommended selling the company's bonds from buy and maintain portfolios, with the principal reasons being the worst-in-class ESG performance, inadequate disclosures on financial and non-financial factors, and uncertainty over future strategy, especially with the EV transition.

In a subsequent sector review the company came bottom in a fundamental rank of industry peers (Table 10.4). Compared with its peers, the landmine checklist performance was consistently amongst the worst. Following a wider investment team discussion, other portfolios were positioned to avoid, hold an underweight position or, in the case of sustainability-focused accounts, to sell bonds.

In 2020 the company's credit ratings were downgraded from investment grade to non-investment grade classification. Commenting on reasons for the downgrade Moody's, a credit rating agency, explained that vehicle sales would be influenced by shifts in market sentiment but the firm's ability to achieve customer acceptance and earn an economic return are uncertain. The avoidable risk highlighted by the Insight ESG ratings and engagement helped to navigate the sustainability complexities of a large debt issuer and influence portfolio outcomes.

Case-Study: The Covid-19 Bear Market and ESG Ratings

The gradual shift towards sustainability-oriented portfolios marks a change from traditional responsible investment approaches. Sustainability portfolios are structurally designed to avoid the worst ESG-rated issuers and to preferentially invest in better ESG-rated issuers. This section tests the implications of this strategy by evaluating the performance of investment grade Euro credit benchmark bonds during the COVID-19 market sell-off and recovery.

The Initial Bond Sell-off

The Z-spreads[2] of issuers with strong Insight ESG ratings were more resilient during the market sell-off (which Insight defines as two-months from 09 March 2020). Table 10.5 considers the distribution of median Z-spread moves and credit quality (as at before the sell-off). While all Z-spreads widened, those with good credit ratings and the best Insight ESG ratings widened the least.

Table 10.4 Insight Credit Analyst Sector Ranking.

Rank	Liquidity	Climate Risk	Regulatory	Event Risk	LBO Risk	Environment	Social	Governance	ESG Overall
1	1	2	5	1	1	4	4	5	5
2	1	3	4	2	2	2	2	4	3
3	1	3	3	1	1	2	3	4	3
4	1	2	4	3	4	4	3	4	4
5	1	3	4	2	1	1	4	3	3
6	1	3	4	3	3	3	1	2	1
7	3	3	2	1	1	1	2	3	3
8	1	3	4	3	3	4	5	3	4
9	1	N/A	3	1	1	1	3	3	4
10	2	3	4	3	3	5	3	3	4
11	1	3	4	3	3	3	1	4	3
Company	1	4	4	3	3	4	4	4	5

Table 10.5 Spread Widening of European Corporates in the COVID-19 Sell-Off.

		Insight ESG Rating				
		1	2	3	4	5
AAA, AA and A (high quality)	Z-spread move (bps)	38	42	53	53	53
BBB (low quality)		64	73	81	88	69

Source: Insight Investment.

Within the universe of high-quality credits, the median spread-widening increased from 38 to 53 bps between issuers with best and worst ESG ratings respectively. However, for high-quality credit, Insight did not see a material correlation between spread widening and the ESG rating for issuers in the bottom 30% by ESG performance. In fact, these issuers exhibited the same performance distribution irrespective of ESG rating. This suggests the demand for best-in-class ESG issuance within this low-risk asset class remained comparatively strong, but that the median difference in fair value was in the region of +53 bps and more closely related to the credit rating.

In contrast, the performance of BBB bonds exhibited a stronger relationship with the Insight ESG ratings. For the top 90% of issuers in this credit category, the median spread-widening increased from 64 to 88 bps between the best and second-to-worst ESG category. The comparatively better performance of the worst ESG rating category is explained by the fact the category contained a major benchmark constituent, a German automaker with large benchmark weight, whose bonds outperformed the peer group over the period due to resilient financial results and due to the European Central Bank's bond-buying programme, which was extended and broadened over this period.

To investigate this result further, Insight looked to identify the most predictive components from Insight's set of 32 underlying ESG indicators, such as pay, labour management, and climate change. Using a supervised machine learning procedure, Insight determined the average spread move of 400 constituent issuers and split them into quartiles; the first quartile (Q1) represented best-performing companies whose bond spreads widened least, and the fourth quartile (Q4) contained worst-performing companies whose bond spreads had widened most. Insight then trained a classifier model to predict the spread move quartile based on the underlying ESG credentials, with the results summarised in Table 10.6.[3]

Overall, the predictive power of the raw thematic indicators was weak, and the model was less accurate than randomly guessing (25% is the common benchmark for such a routine). However, the model accurately predicted the bottom-quartile of issuers by spread performance. This suggests that ESG information alone could have been used to accurately forecast which issuers

Table 10.6 Predictions of Quartiles versus Actual.

| | | Predicted | | | |
		Q1	Q2	Q3	Q4
	Q1	29%	18%	24%	29%
	Q2	44%	11%	22%	22%
Actual	Q3	33%	17%	33%	17%
	Q4	9%	0%	27%	64%

Table 10.7 Most Predictive Features, in Q4 2019 (Top) and the First Four Months of 2020 (Bottom).

Feature	Credit Rating (Benchmark)	Pay	Human Capital	Health and Safety	Ownership	Board
Oct.–Dec., 2019	3.4%	1.2%	1.0%	0.9%	0.6%	0.6%

Feature	Credit Rating (Benchmark)	Privacy & Data Security	Pollution & Waste	Pay	Financial Security	Environmental Controversy
Jan.–Apr., 2020	5.5%	1.4%	0.8%	0.5%	0.3%	0.3%

Source: Insight Investment.

would have the worst spread performance during the bond sell-off, but that ESG indicators were unable to predict which issuers would fare best, or even have an average spread performance.

Predicting Performance

To determine which ESG factors contained the information that was most predictive of bond spread moves, Insight calculated the feature importance[4] using the same classifier described above. To measure relative importance, credit ratings were included as a data field to benchmark the ESG factors. Of the 32 key issue scores that make up the Insight ESG rating, the top five key issues are summarised in Table 10.7, alongside the credit rating (benchmark).

For the final quarter of 2019, the most important ESG attribute predicting spread performance was 'pay', with its feature importance, as measured in this way, being roughly a third that of credit ratings. Specifically, for companies that perform well on this metric, remuneration is appropriately disclosed, in line with peers, and with performance links. This is an interesting result: bondholders have little influence over remuneration packages, and yet those with high performance on this metric structurally outperform in credit markets.

Three of the top five most important features pertain to corporate governance. Other rating signals for 'board' and 'ownership' were of comparable (but lesser) importance, and between one quarter to one third of the importance of credit ratings, and with the same directional correlation, meaning performance on these metrics suggests strong financial performance. Companies with strong board and ownership scores had appropriately qualified board members that are independent from management, and an absence of controlling shareholders, respectively. Of the EUR-denominated corporate universe, issuers whose spreads tightened had broadly stronger corporate governance.

For the first four months of 2020, the predictive power of any individual ESG metric in this period was more subdued compared to credit ratings. Credit ratings are considered by most investors to be strongly indicative of credit risk, and hence issuers with inferior credit ratings sold off widely as investors sought to reduce risk. Intriguingly, 'privacy and data security' was the strongest ESG signal, although this was principally detecting an existing industry skew in metric: banks (which sold off extensively) typically underperform on this metric, whereas pharmaceuticals, materials, and industrials (which sold off to a lesser extent) whose core business is unrelated to sensitive personal information, typically perform well. It was a similar story for waste pollution; the worst performers are principally in the transportation (particularly airlines) industry, which, unrelated to pollution and waste, sold-off extensively, and better performers are consumer discretionary/staples, again unrelated to pollution and waste, sold-off less.

ESG features demonstrate some correlation to financial performance, but it is unclear whether there is causation. ESG factor information is not timely or frequent enough to expect a positive relationship. However, Insight observes growing evidence that the market applies some ESG risk premia: better ESG rated issuers overall yield a meaningful correlation with spread performance (relative to the universe) and the weakest ESG performers more likely to experience higher credit spreads.

Lessons for Investors

This analysis points to three general implications for investors that use ESG ratings.

First, ESG ratings have the potential to isolate issuers with weaker anticipated financial performance. This suggests that investors are more likely to consider ESG downside risks and that avoiding issuers perceived to be laggards may be supportive to performance. However, there are exceptions and the results from Insight's research may be exaggerated by the presence of European investors paying more attention to ESG factors than investors in other markets. Therefore, applying rules to automatically avoid the worst rated issuers may have uncertain portfolio outcomes for different asset classes. Instead, prioritising ESG integration, with an objective to assess salient risk factors, should remain the primary use of ESG ratings. For Insight this means a process to closely monitor and review companies within the lowest ESG rating buckets and action taken to avoid negative performance.

Second, predictive alpha-generating signals from ESG ratings are not a reliable replacement for analyst oversight. ESG rating tilts towards better rated companies may appear to offer an incremental performance gain (or loss reduction), but this is not consistent across all sectors or issuers and may not be over time. A tandem quantitative-qualitative approach, where ESG ratings can be appropriately scrutinised, allows a fair cross-sector comparison to be interrogated against the known merits and shortcomings of relying on ESG ratings alone. This is important because the most predictive signals are partitioned across several key issues, particularly those pertaining to governance; therefore, bondholders seeking to avoid short-term ESG risk need to closely appraise specific issues. For investors this means observing not just ESG rating moves but the inputs into the ratings as well.

Third, optimising processes, particularly around corporate stewardship, could address the incomplete information that can exist from ESG ratings. Analysts need to exercise due caution before attributing too much importance to any individual ESG metric. This aligns with Insight's general view that a materiality assessment should be applied to ESG ratings, as not every issue is of equal importance or has an impact for bondholders. For active and for buy and maintain strategies this means directly discussing issues with companies to determine if ESG information is, for example, out of date, not yet broadly disclosed or priced-in by investors. Wider use of ESG ratings by investors to guide stewardship behaviours presents challenges: engagement duplication is likely commonplace as investors focus on similar themes, and better rated issuers face lower investor scrutiny. To maximise their benefits, ESG ratings should therefore be part of the general toolkit available in the responsible investment process.

Conclusion

Insight's focus on integration, monitoring and stewardship continues to be relevant even as Insight's understanding has shifted through changing asset owner and industry pressures. With bonds more likely to be influenced by sustainability factors, processes that focus on defining and measuring them are central. While the research methods today include a sophisticated matrix of data, tools, infrastructure, and resourcing, they work best if embedded within the overall investment process and with support from investment teams.

Insight finds that applying greater use of ESG ratings may help investors to identify issuers that are more likely to experience credit rating downgrades and widening credit spreads. This tells Insight that markets may start to price more ESG factors over time and failing to consider them may be negative for investment portfolios. This is best shown by the COVID-19 pandemic with

ESG leaders experiencing less volatility. In a world facing greater uncertainty and risks, the ability to identify both leaders and laggards will be more relevant, and ESG information can show bondholders key insights financial information alone cannot.

Stewardship is a tool available to bondholders that can enhance decisions and guide company behaviour. Without discussing ESG issues with companies, risks may not be appropriately considered. Many issuers now focus on sustainability and are sensitive to protecting their reputation, giving investors opportunities to discuss ESG factors routinely. Efficiency from stewardship activity will become more relevant as scrutiny grows and ESG rating signals become more sophisticated in highlighting the salient risk factors to prioritise.

Looking ahead, efforts to improve data so that it is transparent, forward-looking, and timely will be more important. Patchy data limits investment analysis in high yield and emerging markets compared with investment grade issuers, even though ESG factors can be impactful to bondholders. Methods to absorb key information direct from issuers helps to partly fill this gap, but consistency, quality, and disclosure issues remain a challenge for investors.

Notes

1 This chapter should not be relied upon as an accurate representation of Insight's responsible investment process at any specific point in time and is based on the author's understanding of the Insight process. Joshua Kendall co-authored the chapter in his former position at Insight and is no longer an employee at Insight.

2 The z-spread, also known as the zero-volatility spread, is the amount of yield investors receive from a non-Treasury bond above the yield for the same-maturity Treasury bond. Because the Z-spread measures the spread that an investor expects to receive over the entirety of the Treasury yield curve, it gives a more realistic valuation of a security instead of a single-point metric, such as a bond's maturity date. The Z-spread will be lower for stronger credit quality companies and a high or increasing Z-spread implies increasing credit risk. Investors pay close attention to Z-spread performance.

3 Insight trained a random forest classifier to predict the change in Z-spread over the first four months of 2020. For a quantitative description on random forest classifiers, see Breiman (2001). The training set was curated to minimise sources of noise (such as the differences due to currency denomination and hedging) and known covariances such as ESG performance by geography. As such, the dataset used is smaller (compared to the variance in the target). Therefore, while care was taken to preserve the quality of analysis (such as separating training, validation, and test sets, scaling the systems), the conclusions presented above should be interpreted with some caution.

4 By removing each data field sequentially, retraining the model, and evaluating the difference in negative log loss (a proxy for accuracy), Insight discovers how important each field is to the (modest) accuracy of the final model. Insight repeated this procedure 50 times and report the median negative log loss here. For the reader that is unfamiliar with this approach, a value of zero suggests that removing the data field made no difference to the accuracy of the model.

References

BNEF (2020), *Electric Vehicle Outlook 2020.* [online]. Available from https://about.bnef.com/electric-vehicle-outlook/ (Accessed 4 November 2020).

Breiman, L. (2001), 'Random Forests', *Machine Learning*, Vol. 45, pp. 5–32.

Insight Investment (2002), *Responsible Investment Policy* (Insight Investment, London).

Insight Investment (2007), *Putting Principles into Practice: 2006* (Insight Investment, London).

Insight Investment (2008), *Putting Principles into Practice: 2008* (Insight Investment, London).

Insight Investment (2011), *Putting Principles into Practice: 2011* (Insight Investment, London).

Insight Investment (2012), *Putting Principles into Practice: 2012* (Insight Investment, London).

Insight Investment (2018), *Consultation Response to Proposed Revisions to the UK Corporate Governance Code.* [online]. Available from https://www.insightinvestment.com/globalassets/documents/responsible-investment/policy-responses/february-2018-consultation-response-to-proposed-revisions-to-the-uk-corporate-governance-code.pdf (Accessed 4 November 2020).

Insight Investment (2020a), *Responsible Horizons* [online]. Available from https://www.insightinvestment.com/globalassets/documents/responsible-investment/responsible-investment-reports/uk-responsible-horizons-report-2020.pdf (Accessed 12 December 2020).

Insight Investment (2020b), *Insight ESG Fixed Income Ratings.* [online]. Available from https://www.insightinvestment.com/globalassets/documents/recent-thinking/uk-insight-esg-ratings-methodology.pdf (Accessed 4 November 2020).

Insight Investment (2021), *Putting Principles into Practice: 2021* (Insight Investment, London).

IPE (2021), *Top 120 European Institutional Managers 2021.* [online]. Available from https://www.ipe.com/reports/top-120-european-institutional-managers-2021/10053127.article.

Mackenzie, C. and Sullivan, R. (2006), 'Insight's Approach to Activism on Corporate Responsibility Issues'. In Sullivan, R. and Mackenzie, C. (eds.) *Responsible Investment* (Greenleaf Publishing, Sheffield), pp. 184–195.

Sullivan, R. (2011), *Valuing Corporate Responsibility: How Do Investors Really Use Corporate Responsibility Information?* (Greenleaf Publishing, Sheffield).

Sullivan, R. and Mackenzie, C. (2006), 'The Practice of Responsible Investment'. In Sullivan, R. and Mackenzie, C. (eds.) *Responsible Investment* (Greenleaf Publishing, Sheffield), pp. 332–346.

Sullivan, R. and Mackenzie, C. (2008), 'Can Investor Activism Play a Meaningful Role in Addressing Market Failures?', *Journal of Corporate Citizenship*, Issue 31 (Autumn 2008), pp. 77–88.

Sullivan, R., Robins, N., Russell, D. and Barnes, H. (2005), 'Investor Collaboration on Climate Change: The Work of the IIGCC'. In Tang, K. (ed.) *The Finance of Climate Change: A Guide for Governments, Corporations and Investors* (Risk Books, London), pp. 197–210.

ten Kate, K. and Evans, A. (2006), 'Integrating Governance, Social, Ethical and Environmental Issues into the Corporate Bond Investment Process'. In Sullivan, R. and Mackenzie, C. (eds.) *Responsible Investment* (Greenleaf Publishing, Sheffield).

Waygood, S., Sullivan, R. and Morley, A. (2006), 'Harnessing Investors to Implement Health and Safety Public Policy'. In Sullivan, R. and Mackenzie, C. (eds.) *Responsible Investment* (Greenleaf Publishing, Sheffield), pp. 322–330.

11 Responsible Investment Strategies in Corporate Fixed Income

Alex Everett and Keith Logan

Introduction

Understanding risk is central to the functioning of the markets in which we operate. Mark Carney, the former Governor of the Bank of England, noted in 2018 that 'when risks are unknown or ill-defined, the market cannot allocate resources in an efficient and profitable manner' (Carney, 2018). ESG factors are a necessary feature of any risk analysis of an issuer and its borrowing costs. Without integrating ESG issues, we would be neither able to weigh investment risks accurately nor able to pursue sustainable risk-adjusted returns on behalf of our clients.

In successfully developing our ESG process as a smaller asset manager,[1] our intention is to ensure that every investment decision benefits from the integrated management of ESG issues, as defined by the World Bank (Inderst and Stewart, 2018). We combine ESG insights with investment information to support our work in three areas: investment research, client activity, and issuer engagement. These three themes are the chapter's focus.

The first section in this chapter introduces our investment process and in-house analytical tools. The second section explains how clients' investment goals and our ESG processes are aligned. The third section examines how we engage with issuers on ESG matters, and includes our reflections on the challenges faced by a smaller asset manager. We then present three case studies that illustrate how ESG factors influenced our investment decisions and the response of the wider market.

Integration of ESG Factors

Our investment team compares bonds to peers, considering relative pricing and the impact of ESG scores before analysing each issuer in further detail. To arrive at a final investment decision, we weigh the underlying ESG risks alongside the corporate health of the issuer and market factors. This provides us with a broad-based integrated view of an issuer's ability and willingness to pay bondholders.

An integrated ESG research process features prominently in our investigation of issuer-specific risks. We consider the likelihood of downside credit

DOI: 10.4324/9781003055341-14

events, because our research shows that credit spreads often do not reflect ESG factors until after a negative event occurs (see the case studies below). Measuring how an issuer controls its exposure to a range of ESG factors helps us to better understand future costs and whether these may affect credit quality. We have developed credit reports that contain a dedicated section in which our analysts and portfolio managers consider information on material ESG factors for each issuer.

Risks and opportunities arising from ESG factors vary in their magnitude and significance. As such, we must consider an ESG factor's relevance to an issuer's operations. We weigh materiality using MSCI ESG Research's ESG ratings data (see Chapter 18) as a starting point, and complement this with our own analysis. For example, at a high level, issues of community relations are likely to strongly impact a mining company that engages in exploration and resource extraction. However, the cultural or environmental sensitivity of the areas a mining company explores, and the quality of the overriding governance process, are both important determinants of the risk posed by the activity. An illustration of what we see as a failure of corporate governance is Rio Tinto's destruction of sacred rock shelters in the Juukan Gorge in May 2020 (Everett, 2020). The issues identified by third parties can alert us to emergent risks, which may lead us to place more weight on certain ESG factors during our credit evaluation.

Our in-house analytical tool, *CaTo*, allows us to carry out our integrated ESG investment process at scale. This is best demonstrated with an example. In Figure 11.1 we show a representative group of issuers, all of which are USD-denominated AA-credit-rated issuers in the Banking sector. We plot *CaTo*'s calculation of each bond's spread to the local swap curve by tenor. The central curve indicates the sector's average spread. We differentiate between

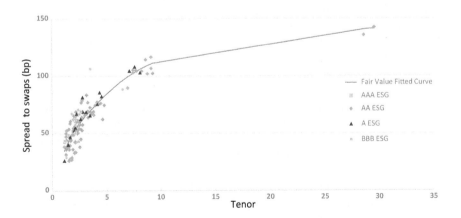

Figure 11.1 USD Banking AA- Bonds Spread with Corresponding ESG Rating.
Sources: Cameron Hume – CaTo, MSCI, Bloomberg Barclays. December 2018.

the bonds using their ESG rating, as shown in Figure 11.1. This analysis allows our investment team to focus on issuers with strong ESG credentials and on bonds that are attractively priced, while immediately dismissing those who manage ESG risks poorly but lack a compensating higher yield.

Clearly, a single, summary ESG score cannot capture all ESG risks. There is a growing body of research that has highlighted the divergence between top-level ESG ratings, owing to mismatched measurement, scope, or weights (see, for example, Berg, Kölbel and Rigobon, 2020). Such divergence creates two opportunities. First, the existence of a range of views is precisely why ESG integration is so important; 'if there were one unambiguously correct ESG rating, it would be priced into the market' (Edmans, 2020). Second, the value of additional information is increased. To this end, our analysis extends significantly beyond ESG ratings. Using *CaTo* and a range of other research tools, we consider the broader ESG data available to us, alongside a multitude of quantitative and qualitative economic, fundamental and issuer-specific factors within our credit process. We conduct our own real-time analysis alongside ESG information, thereby reducing the risk of out-of-date ESG information undermining our analysis (Inderst and Stewart, 2018).

In summary, our investment team assess the extent bond prices reflect the ability and willingness of an issuer to meet its contracted payments. We compare spreads within and between issuers, considering ESG risks alongside other issuer-specific risks when making an investment decision.

Integrating Client Motives

Client Policies and Expectations

There are four main reasons why clients pursue an ESG approach: a wish to protect against ESG tail risk; benefit from ESG opportunity upside; influence change; and reflect their values and policies. These aims do not need to be mutually exclusive. ESG integration brings these disparate motives together by allowing us to work with our clients to build ESG objectives into policy frameworks and governance procedures.

In our experience, clients have traditionally expressed their ESG policies in terms of an ethical code. These clients would identify as 'values-driven' ESG investors and their policy would be expressed using red lines, such as cigarette manufacturing, coal mining or other extractive industries. Increasingly, we find ourselves working with clients who would be better described as 'returns-driven' ESG investors. The portfolios of returns-driven ESG investors comprise issuers with strong ESG risk management as well as more 'traditional' macro investment strategies: seeking sustainable returns from a global opportunity set while mitigating a range of ESG risks. The development of such an ESG policy may influence product design, but typically focuses on verifying that the portfolio is aligned with each client's ESG policy and providing confirmatory reporting.

This more modern approach can incorporate policies that focus on an ESG issue that is specifically important to the client or their end investors. One such example is human capital management, which concerns issues such as employee welfare, pay equality, and union relationships, and is frequently discussed in relation to the giant American retailer, Walmart. Many clients have chosen to exclude Walmart from their portfolios. Our sense, though, is that the decision to exclude Walmart is indicative of a broader concern. Namely, clients do not take issue specifically with Walmart, but rather with all corporates who manage their workforce poorly. This has the makings of a modern ESG policy, one that is complementary to the engagement-based approaches of equity investors and plays to the nature of the bond market.

A policy approach creates investment rules that operate at an aggregate ESG level or thematic level. For example, a modern ESG policy may exclude all issuers whose relative management of key ESG risks falls in the bottom quartile, rather than only one or two totemic issuers, such as Walmart. Informing issuers that you will withhold lending until they exit the bottom quartile provides them with a measurable objective that can be clearly communicated.

This approach seems to have two advantages over a list of excluded names: expressed in these terms the criteria for exclusion are clear, making our clients' policies more transparent and robust to scrutiny. Further, by setting a relative criterion – the bottom quartile – it may incentivise all issuers to improve, giving rise to a net societal benefit.

A concern that arises with such a policy is that it may reduce portfolio diversification and cause negative portfolio outcomes. Within bond portfolios, this concern can be swiftly laid to rest. The observation that bonds have down-side but no up-side is flippant, but it does capture a feature of the bond market: the security specific element of returns is small and frequently negligible. The return of an investment grade bond portfolio is dominated by traditional factors such as currency, tenor and credit quality. The performance of two portfolios that have these characteristics in common, but which are composed of different securities, will typically be near identical. In other words, a policy that influences which securities are selected, but which does not otherwise affect the characteristics of the portfolio will not adversely influence returns.

This has important implications for the integration of ESG in fixed income portfolios. First, it is a feature that distinguishes fixed income from equity investment and which allows the modern policy-based approach we advocate. Second, our research shows that ESG factors influence spreads significantly only in the case of a material bad event. If ESG factors have no significant impact upon spreads, then fixed income investors are not compensated for poor ESG practices, nor do they suffer lower spreads for investing in those issuers with good ESG practices. Consequently, investors can comfortably exclude a proportion of issuers in a given sector for poor ESG practices without fear of consequential negative implications on their portfolio.

Developing the Walmart example, we demonstrate the negligible duration effect of excluding a large tranche of corporate issuers based upon human capital management. In Figure 11.2 we plot the impact upon a sample credit portfolio's weighted duration at varying levels of a single policy-based exclusion. The data covers around 15,000 credit holdings in the Bloomberg Barclays Global Aggregate, with exclusion criteria defined using the MSCI score for human capital management. Excluding the bottom quartile of issuers by this measure leads to a maximum of a 0.1 year change in net weighted duration. Even excluding *all* issuers with non-zero exposure to human capital management risks leads to a maximum 0.14 per year divergence from the weighted duration of the full credit universe. In any case, this represents a negligible and easily replaceable difference in a broader credit portfolio, highlighting the power of using fixed income to enforce a policy-based exclusions approach.

Transparency

An important feature of our approach is the transparency of our actions. We believe that holding ourselves to client scrutiny makes us better investors and gives our clients confidence in the integrity of our process. It allows clients to understand the exposures taken and to engage both with us and, if necessary, the issuers to which they are exposed.

The ESG integration process outlined above means that we can demonstrate to clients that we are implementing their policy to, for example, select issuers that exceed their minimum standards, or to overweight relative to a certain ESG key issue and flag for their attention any potential concerns.

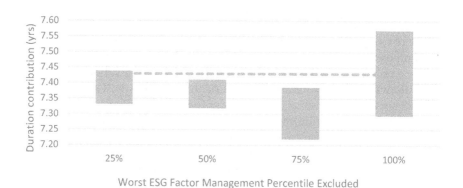

Figure 11.2 Minimum and Maximum Weighted Duration Contribution of Credit, Within Varying Quartiles of Exclusions.
Sources: Cameron Hume – CaTo, MSCI, Bloomberg Barclays[2].

Further, we can help our clients to monitor progress against ESG measures. This is expected to grow in importance over time. In particular, awareness of climate issues considerably increases demand for progress monitoring and reporting (Fulton, 2020).

How we report depends upon the policy of the portfolio in question. We have a fund for which the ESG policy is intentionally simple: to invest in corporates and sovereigns that manage their ESG exposures better than their peers. To verify our adherence to this policy, we report at least quarterly on ESG rating exposures in the fund and its benchmark, using data from MSCI alongside portfolio and benchmark data.

More specific policy requirements in an investment management agreement allow us to go further still: we report upon thematic scores and weights, along with the risks and opportunities presented by individual holdings or sub-sectors. We work with these clients to ensure the specific measures of a stated policy requirement have been met and use the full range of tools available to us through *CaTo* to report on our activities.

Transparency of this nature is not only a guiding principle from the PRI, but also furthers our ability to engage with our clients – a crucial component of a successful ESG-integrated responsible investment process. Of course, we also report on our investment approach to the PRI. This reporting process is an important exercise, which compels us to consider our approach per sub-asset class in detail, and to articulate this clearly.

Corporate Engagement

We do not believe being a fixed income investor precludes ESG engagement. Indeed, the CFA Institute Research Foundation has suggested that ESG engagement from the perspective of debt markets may be more impactful upon corporates' actions than through public equities (Matos, 2020).

From the earliest days of bond issuance in the late 1600s, bonds have been an important, stable, and cost-effective source of finance for companies, sovereigns, and supranational borrowers, and thus for economic growth. Bondholders are significant providers of capital and can directly influence the business practices of borrowers. Rather than pressuring boards for changes in management practices, linking ESG-related issues to the cost of debt is a form of engagement that is felt directly on a business' income statement.

A key avenue to engagement is via the syndicate desks who liaise with the institutional investment community in placing new issues. Syndicate desks establish lending appetite and 'build a book' of interested parties at spreads which indicate the market's perception of the risks incurred in lending. A little over 7,000 bonds (worth around \$2.9 trillion) were issued in the US corporate market during 2020, despite the Covid-19 induced turbulence and spread-widening seen in March. This indicates the considerable engagement opportunity presented by the book-building process.

The cost of debt can provide an explicit signal to management of the need to engage with bondholders. As mentioned previously, our analysis suggests that clients generally receive little marginal compensation from investment in an issuer that manages its ESG risks poorly relative to a comparable issuer that manages them well. Hence, if a bond is offered at a spread that does not adequately reflect the investment risks, we decline to participate and discuss this rationale with the syndicate desk, which is then fed back to the issuer. Vice versa, where ESG risks are priced appropriately or an issuer demonstrates appropriate management of key issues, we inform the syndicate desks that this has motivated our participation.

For example, Citi came to market with a 15-year bond in January 2020, priced to yield 95bp over mid-swaps. This not only placed this issue at an indicative price premium relative to its peer group, but it also failed to account for Citi's then BB ESG rating, largely attributable to concerns around internal controls and other Social controversies, as flagged by MSCI. A similar story could be found with the 4-year Volkswagen issue offered at mid-swaps +105 bp in February 2020 – Volkswagen's ESG travails relative to emissions are well documented. Neither bond was considered a suitable holding owing to the inappropriate pricing of ESG risks. In each case we directly engaged with syndicate desks to pass on this feedback to the issuer.

Positive examples abound, too: we participated in new issues from both John Deere and Apple in 2020, because in our view the potential returns due in part to strong ESG management were under-priced in both cases. On entry, both John Deere and Apple were priced more cheaply than peers at +70 and +110 bp over mid-swaps, respectively, despite their ESG risk management credentials.

New issues are our primary avenue for engagement, but there is also some scope to engage within the active secondary market. We frequently express our views on participation in the context of ESG factors, in addition to traditional price indicators. Counterparties such as investment banks actively manage their bond inventories, setting bid-ask spreads in order to attract buyers and sellers as needed. As per our approach with new issues, where spreads do not reflect ESG risks appropriately, we discuss this with the counterparties. Anecdotally, the counterparties we liaise with at Cameron Hume are increasingly highlighting ESG practices within their sales communications.

Challenges Faced as a Smaller Manager

We recognise that as a smaller asset manager, our scope to influence change may be relatively small, if we act in isolation. Candidly, influence tends to grow with size. However, it is our belief that by working with our clients we can greatly amplify the effect of our engagement for the benefit of all stakeholders.

Our clients may, by virtue of their equity holdings or their reputation, be able to effect change more readily than we can on their behalf. This further vindicates the reporting element of our ESG integration. As discussed previously, we inform our clients on the full extent of their ESG exposures, from top-level ESG ratings to specific exposures to key issues such as labour management. All this is possible with relative ease, owing to the deep integration of ESG within our investment process using *CaTo*.

This sums up the implications of our size relative to larger managers across the spectrum of ESG integration. We have invested significantly in our infrastructure in order to achieve analytical scale and a competency beyond our peer group in issues of governance and strategy. The benefits to our clients may be seen in the breadth and depth of service we can provide and in the effectiveness of the ESG engagement we can facilitate.

Case Studies

Case-Study 1: Pacific Gas & Electric

Arid Northern California is doubtless a challenging environment in which to safely operate a power supplier. Rainfall is scarce, vegetation is surprisingly abundant, and energy must travel significant distances to reach consumers. The population is dispersed across the state in both densely populated cities and scattered rural communities. A network of power lines, gas mains, and routing stations crisscrosses the landscape, providing hundreds of miles of infrastructure and potential risks.

Wildfires have become an expectation for those living in the 70,000 square miles between the Pacific Ocean and the Sierra Nevada (PGE, 2020b). The volume of energy transmitted might suggest that wildfire risk is an unavoidable statistical likelihood. However, energy suppliers must bear some of the burden of risk mitigation. Pacific Gas and Electric (PGE), incorporated in 1905, is the single supplier in this region providing natural gas and electricity to approximately 16 million people, and enjoying a state-approved monopoly.

In recent decades, observers have drawn attention to PGE's under-investment in risk mitigation, including its failure to carry out urgent replacement of steel towers that were later known to have contributed to wildfires (Gold, 2019). As a result of proven culpability for the 2015 Butte Fire, a 2018 Camp Fire and others, PGE have faced – and honoured – litigation claims amounting to $25 billion as of June 2020. This, of course, is only partial compensation for the unquantifiable loss of human life for which PGE was found responsible (PGE, 2020a). ESG factors have consequences in the real and financial worlds.

Capital market participants appear not to have shared this view until it was 'too late'. Figure 11.3 shows a time series of both the company's share price and the spread of its 20-year debt (an indicator of

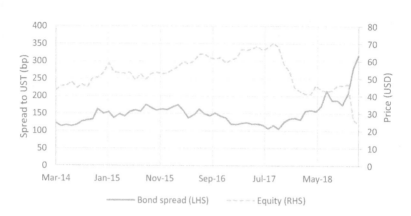

Figure 11.3 PGE Spread and Equity Price History (plotted until default in January 2019).

Source: Cameron Hume – CaTo, Bloomberg. Bond: USD PCG 4.75% 2044-02-15. Equity: PCG-US.

the premium demanded by the market as compensation for the risk of lending). Neither indicator offers any clear warning sign until late 2017, at which point the share price began to fall, though it was not until August 2018 that spreads began to rise substantially.

We exited our position in the PGE's long-dated 2044 bonds before the precipitous spread widening seen in Q4 2018. The company had encountered a credit event and it was clear to our investment team that the spread was not adequately compensating investors given the rise in ESG issues with the company.

Case-Study 2: Swedbank

In 2019 Swedish and Estonian watchdogs opened a joint probe into allegations of money-laundering through a Danske-bank related branch of Swedbank in Estonia. This sent shockwaves through Swedbank's creditors, and spreads widened considerably: in 2018 its March 2022 bond was trading 3bp inside its peer group, but by late March 2019- after news broke in February 2019- Swedbank's 2022 bond spread was almost 70bp wide versus its peer group.

Prior to the scandal, Swedbank was rated AA ESG, an ESG 'leader' in MSCI's nomenclature (reinforced by a commensurate rating from Sustainalytics, another ESG ratings provider). The analysis from MSCI noted a highly effective governance structure. Sure enough, within

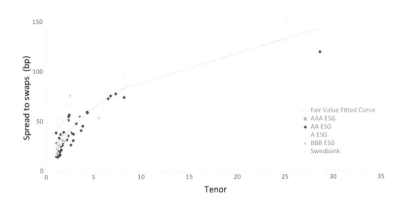

Figure 11.4 USD Banking AA- Bonds Universe and Swedbank March 2022
        Bonds.
Source: Cameron Hume – CaTo, Barclays, October 2019.

weeks, Swedbank had replaced its CEO, set up a dedicated unit to
investigate and deter future control failures, and the non-executive
chair had voluntarily passed on the role to a full-time replacement for
more focused oversight. In short, the company had acted decisively
and effectively to limit the fallout of an ultimately isolated negative
event. By Q4 2019 Swedbank's spreads had tightened considerably,
trading at +28bp to the peer group (see Figure 11.4). That said, it is
notable that in May 2019, MSCI downgraded Swedbank to A ESG
rating, principally as a result of a 'controversy deduction' (score penalty) relating to the aforementioned money-laundering. No controversy exists in a vacuum.

The Swedbank example demonstrates how at Cameron Hume we
apply ESG factors at a top level before investigating individual issuers and associated market pricing, then opening or closing positions as
appropriate. In this case, we were comfortable that on a broad basis,
strong governance would facilitate a robust response to the material
negative event described above. This enabled us to take advantage: we
bought the March 2022 bonds in April 2019, subsequently profiting
from the 40bp spread tightening described above.

This example underlines the importance of considering multiple factors when making an investment decision. Damaging headlines – and
associated uncertainty – might create an abrupt blowout in spreads, and
when considered in isolation would be a cause for concern. However,
when considered in the context of the business' overall ESG performance and as part of a broader credit process, a more complete picture
is revealed and investment opportunities identified.

Case-Study 3: Equifax

Cyber security issues are relevant for both the governance and social performance of a firm. These risks can introduce a very real impact upon financial, reputational and sustainability outcomes. Our analysis suggests that cyber issues are only priced after a negative event has occurred, and investors will then demand a significant risk premium. This was made abundantly clear with respect to Equifax and its data breach in 2017.

Equifax reported a data breach in September 2017 that exposed sensitive information, including the names, dates of birth, social security numbers, driving license numbers, and addresses of almost 150 million customers. In another governance controversy, the company then failed to notify its customers until six weeks later, while three senior company executives sold shares worth almost $1.8 million in the days following the discovery of the breach (Bloomberg, 2017).

Equifax built its global business and reputation as a leader in managing and protecting sensitive customer data. Nevertheless, its management of cyber-security risks was sub-standard. In March 2017, the US Department for Homeland Security alerted the company over cyber-security vulnerabilities, but the company decided not to act on the information (Federal Trade Commission, 2019). ESG rating agencies had carried out their own research, and also concluded that data security and privacy measures were insufficient.

A US class action settlement announced in 2020 relating to the company's failure to protect key personal information led to fines and compensation claims from individuals whose data were made public. Costs are still to be determined, but are estimated to be as high as $800 m (equifaxbreachsettlement.com, 2020). This settlement also requires the company to spend $1 billion over five years to improve its data security, on top of a similar amount it has already spent since the breach. In addition, the company must obtain third-party assessments of its data security processes every two years.

We examine the relationship between credit and ESG ratings and the impact on credit spreads following the data breach.

Equifax Bond Spreads Movement

There was little indication from credit spreads that bond markets were unduly concerned by the company's cyber-security risks. Figure 11.5 illustrates the spread decomposition for Equifax 3.3% 2022 bonds. The estimated spread shows where a bond with similar characteristics would be expected to trade, and we can see that from 2013 to 2015 Equifax bonds closely tracked this

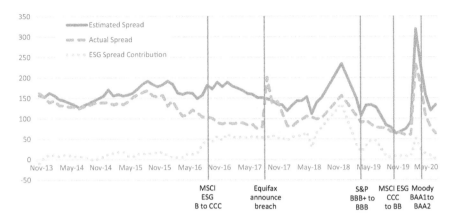

Figure 11.5 Equifax 3.3% 2022 Bond Spread Decomposition.
Source: Cameron Hume – CaTo, Bloomberg.

line. At this point Equifax had a B ESG rating from MSCI, and investors were typically paid only around 10 bp to compensate for exposure to poorly managed ESG risks. This is indicated by the dotted line for ESG Spread Contribution: our estimate of the spread component explained by ESG factors.

Our assessment illustrates a potential conflict between an issuer's prioritisation of ESG rating or credit rating, which can have implications for the future cost of financing. Prior to the breach we concluded ESG risk factors were not adequately priced in terms of spread and that reliance on credit ratings alone would not have been enough to compensate for potential cyber-security risks inherent within the company. Rating agencies and credit spreads did not reflect this ESG risk. Following the breach, the company was compelled to invest heavily to improve its data security measures. Although this investment led to an improved ESG rating of BB, the company's credit rating was downgraded one notch to BAA2 owing to associated remedial costs of almost $3.4 billion.

Given the choice, would investors have preferred Equifax to have addressed their cyber-security vulnerabilities to improve their ESG rating at the expense of their credit rating? This question goes to the heart of the interaction between credit and ESG ratings. Equifax could have invested to mitigate IT vulnerabilities at the expense of shareholder returns or a credit downgrade. Instead they left themselves open to the risk of a significant ESG event.

Our credit modelling using *CaTo* helps us to establish the less costly approach. We compare Equifax against two synthetic 'alter egos'. The first, a 'risk-on' Equifax, has a credit rating of BAA1 and ESG rating of CCC (the dotted line in Figure 11.6). The second, a 'prudent' Equifax, has chosen to improve data security prior to the breach, leading to a poorer credit rating of

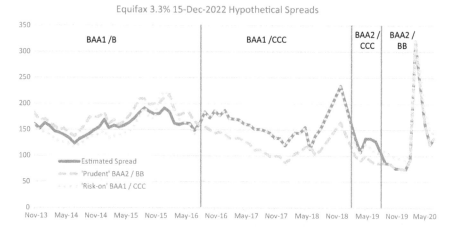

Figure 11.6 Equifax 3.3% 2022 Hypothetical Spreads.
Source: Cameron Hume – CaTo.

BAA2 but better ESG rating of BB (the dashed line in Figure 11.6). We also show the estimate for the actual Equifax bonds that had an ESG and credit rating that varied over this period (the solid line in Figure 11.6).

Prior to 2016, we estimate that the bonds of a prudent Equifax management approach would have a higher spread than the risk-loving version. Investors paid more attention to credit quality than to the ESG rating. This situation reversed mid-2016 when the bonds of the prudent Equifax traded tighter. At this point it would have lowered a company's financing cost (to the benefit of credit investors) to target a higher ESG rating at the expense of credit rating.

This analysis is based on a very large universe of bonds and clearly there will be bonds and issuers that differ from this average trend. We can see in the earlier Figure 11.5 (produced using the same model) that Equifax investors did not mark the bonds down despite the CCC ESG rating, as they did for other issuers. This highlights the importance of ESG integration. Had investors paid more attention to the poor ESG rating, it would have made financial sense for Equifax to react prior to the breach, avoiding unnecessary market volatility, fines, and reputational damage for a data security improvement they were obliged to implement anyway.

Despite such improvements, Equifax remains an industry laggard. Investors are now offered a slim additional spread – under 5 bp – to accept the remaining ESG risks. The relatively low overall ESG rating of BB is offset by the upward momentum in the rating. Given the slim premium on the bonds and the remaining ESG risks, we do not hold Equifax bonds in our clients' portfolios, believing there to be more attractive alternatives with stronger ESG credentials.

Conclusion

We began to more explicitly integrate ESG considerations into our investment process in 2015 after becoming signatories to the PRI. Our decision to integrate ESG factors in the investment process has helped our investors to control and mitigate risk in our clients' portfolios, and to add value to our credit selection process.

Managing global bond portfolios through an ESG lens can reveal responses to long-term systemic risks, such as climate change, corporate governance structures, or poor environmental or social credentials, all of which complement our fundamental research approach. Integrating ESG signals within our analytical suite has been invaluable, enabling our analysts and portfolio managers to evaluate ESG risks at the start of their credit investigations, rather than as an afterthought.

The practical insights we have gained have helped our investment team avoid events that have led to the decline in the credit quality of bonds or a widening of an issuer's credit spread by uncovering under-priced risks. We expect that ESG datasets will become richer, through regulation and widespread adoption, and that more reliable and consistent information will be collected that will help guide our approach over time.

Clients will be the primary beneficiaries of this change. Many asset owners are demanding greater reporting of the influence of ESG considerations on their portfolios, and ultimately all will seek greater disclosure on new and emerging ESG topics. For example, in our analysis of the pricing of climate risk, we see little evidence of suitable spread compensation from issuers with high carbon emissions exposure and poor transition plans. Surely, where this is the case clients should expect investment action.

It is abundantly clear that a proverbial corner has been turned. Whether for return or values-driven ends – or the combination – many institutional asset owners today show a clear desire not just to integrate but to prioritise responsible and sustainable investment practices. Our investor-led approach complements traditional fixed income processes while helping investors meet their ESG objectives.

Notes

1 Cameron Hume ceased trading as an investment manager in 2022.
2 The exclusions are based upon non-zero weighted MSCI Human Capital Theme Scores within a sample of c.15,000 corporate bonds.

References

Berg, F., Kölbel, J. and Rigobon, R. (2020), 'Aggregate Confusion: The Divergence of ESG Ratings', *SSRN Electronic Journal*. [online]. Available at SSRN: https://ssrn.com/abstract=3438533 (Accessed: 2 April 2021).

Bloomberg (2017), *Three Equifax Managers Sold Stock Before Cyber Hack Revealed.* [online]. Available at: https://www.bloomberg.com/news/articles/2017-09-07/three-equifax-executives-sold-stock-before-revealing-cyber-hack (Accessed: 13 August 2020).

Carney, M. (2018), *A Transition in Thinking and Action.* [online]. Available at: https://www.bankofengland.co.uk/-/media/boe/files/speech/2018/a-transition-in-thinking-and-action-speech-by-mark-carney.pdf (Accessed: 26 October 2020).

Edmans, A. (2020), *The Inconsistency of ESG Ratings: Implications for Investors.* [online]. Available at: https://www.growthepie.net/the-inconsistency-of-esg-ratings/ (Accessed: 27 May 2020).

Equifaxbreachsettlement.com (2020), *Equifax Data Breach Settlement.* [online]. Available at: https://www.equifaxbreachsettlement.com (Accessed: 13 August 2020).

Everett, A. (2020), *Rio Tinto's Juukan Gorge Fail Is Bond Market Opportunity.* [online]. Available at: https://www.afr.com/companies/mining/rio-tinto-s-juukan-gorge-fail-is-bond-market-opportunity-20201013-p564pa (Accessed: 13 October 2020).

Federal Trade Commission (2019), *$575 Million Equifax Settlement Illustrates Security Basics for Your Business.* [online]. Available at: https://www.ftc.gov/news-events/blogs/business-blog/2019/07/575-million-equifax-settlement-illustrates-security-basics (Accessed: 26 October 2020).

Fulton, M. (2020), *Pathways to Net Zero: Scenario Architecture for Strategic Resilience Testing and Planning* (Energy Transition Advisers and PRI, London).

Gold, K. (2019), *PG&E Knew for Years Its Lines Could Spark Wildfires, and Didn't Fix Them.* [online]. Available at: https://www.wsj.com/articles/pg-e-knew-for-years-its-lines-could-spark-wildfires-and-didnt-fix-them-11562768885 (Accessed: 26 October 2020).

Inderst, G. and Stewart, F. (2018), *Incorporating Environmental, Social and Governance Factors into Fixed Income Investment* (The World Bank Group, Washington, DC).

Matos, P. (2020), *ESG and Responsible Institutional Investing around the World, a Critical Review* (CFA Institute Research Foundation, Charlottesville, VA).

Pacific Gas and Electric (PGE) (2020a), *PG&E Achieves Bankruptcy Court Confirmation of Its Plan of Reorganization.* [online]. Available at: https://www.pge.com/en/about/newsroom/newsdetails/index.page?title=20200620_pge_achieves_bankruptcy_court_confirmation_of_its_plan_of_reorganization (Accessed: 14 August 2020).

Pacific Gas and Electric (PGE) (2020b), *PGE: Company Profile.* [online]. Available at: https://www.pge.com/en_US/about-pge/company-information/profile/profile.page (Accessed: 4 June 2020).

12 ESG Research in Different Fixed Income Sectors

Robert Fernandez

Breckinridge Capital Advisors

Breckinridge Capital Advisors (Breckinridge) is a US-based investment grade bond manager that has systematically integrated environmental, social, and governance (ESG) considerations into its credit research process since 2011. Our mission is to provide the highest calibre of investment grade fixed income management and thereby direct capital from long-term investors to responsible debt issuers. As an investment grade fixed income investor, Breckinridge prioritises long-term value creation over short-term market gains and believes that ESG considerations align with this perspective. We serve institutional as well as individual clients by offering taxable and tax-efficient US dollar-denominated bond strategies. Our primary objectives are to preserve capital while building a reliable source of income, and to take advantage of opportunities to improve total return.

ESG analysis plays a key role in delivering these investment objectives. Breckinridge considers ESG issues as a part of its investment process that can help identify and assess long-term and idiosyncratic risks. We believe ESG integration enables our investment team to gain deeper insight into the underlying risk and value of an investment. Breckinridge's founder and President Peter Coffin explained his views on ESG in fixed income security analysis: 'We believe that future costs associated with unsustainable practices have to be recognised and reflected in the price of the bond' (Fischer, 2013). As at 31 March 2021, Breckinridge managed over $45 billion in assets in separately managed accounts. In addition to ESG-integrated offerings, the firm offers clients a range of specifically designated sustainable strategies that emphasise specific ESG objectives.

This chapter describes Breckinridge's approach to incorporating ESG considerations into fixed income investments. More specifically, it explains our philosophy and processes for including ESG into the investment evaluation of issuers or securities for three important fixed income sectors: (1) corporations; (2) US state and local governments, and (3) securitised products including mortgaged-backed securities (MBS) and asset backed securities (ABS). Overall, these three sectors represent approximately 89% of the US debt market, excluding US Treasuries (SIFMA, 2021).

DOI: 10.4324/9781003055341-15

Corporate Bonds

Research Approach

When assessing a corporate bond for investment, Breckinridge's corporate research analysts are responsible for performing both fundamental credit research and ESG analysis for the issuer. Our analysts evaluate an issuer's business profile, market position, and competitive strengths and weaknesses alongside traditional credit measures (such as margins, leverage, and cash flow). The analyst then evaluates management of sector-specific material ESG indicators, such as carbon emissions, workplace injury rates and board of directors' composition. Our ESG integration methodology combines a review of qualitative ESG considerations with the quantitative assessment of ESG data and a formal engagement programme (see Figure 12.1).

Our qualitative research includes evaluating corporate sustainability reports and issuer performance on material ESG issues relative to peers. Sector-based materiality in ESG analysis is an important input. We are informed by the corporate sustainability reporting guidelines prepared for 77 industries by the Sustainability Accounting Standards Board (SASB). A non-profit, sustainability standard setter based in the US, SASB defines sustainability materiality 'as issues that are reasonably likely to impact the financial condition or operating performance of a company and therefore are most important to investors' (SASB, 2021). Breckinridge's view of materiality aligns with SASB's definition, agreeing that ESG analysis should emphasise a company's exposure to, and management of, financial risks that are most likely to be credit consequential.

The pharmaceutical sector provides a relevant example of how Breckinridge is informed by SASB's standards. The material ESG issues for the industry include access and affordability, product quality and safety, and business

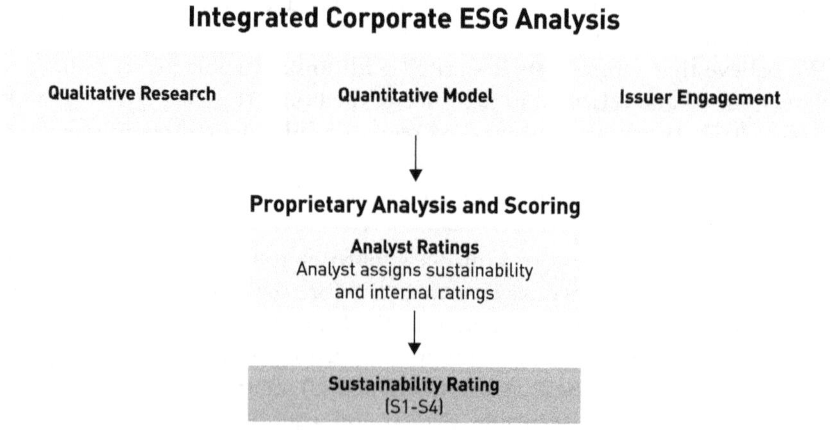

Integrated Corporate ESG Analysis

Figure 12.1 Corporate ESG Research Approach.

ethics. The sector is heavily regulated and requires long lead times for developing new drugs. As a result, to be successful these companies need to pursue long-term management strategies that carefully invest in research and development (R&D). Considering management's performance on material ESG issues such as access and affordability can assist investors in identifying pharmaceutical companies willing to make long-term R&D investments, compared with companies prioritising mergers and acquisitions to boost stock prices or supplement a poorly developed R&D programme. SASB standards for pharmaceutical companies include metrics for drug safety and ethical marketing which, if disclosed and monitored by the research analyst, can be used as an input into forecasting long-term risks and financial performance.

Breckinridge's quantitative assessment consists of two elements: (1) Sector-specific proprietary models that incorporate third-party ESG scores as well as company-reported ESG data, and (2) sector-based comparable factsheets that provide additional insight into company ESG performance on material ESG issues.

In 2012, Breckinridge created its own quantitative ESG scoring tool, with the goal of developing a comprehensive view of a company's ESG profile. We obtain data points from two sources: ESG research providers and company-reported ESG data. Since the methodologies from ESG research providers can vary, our aggregated model seeks to counter rating subjectivity.

The ESG ratings model was constructed for 14 sectors of the corporate fixed income market including banks, communications, and utilities. It consists of various data inputs, with materiality weightings assigned by the research team to reflect their views on the specific sectors. The data used include company-reported information such as Scope 1 and 2 greenhouse gas emissions, measures for workforce health and safety, and the existence of governance-related policies. The model generates a score ranging from 0, which is indicative of poor ESG performance, to 100, representative of a strong ESG profile. The ratings model resides on Breckinridge's proprietary information system platform and can be accessed by the entire investment team.

Our sector-based ESG factsheets supplement the model by presenting a selection of material ESG data deemed particularly relevant for a corporate sector. These datasets were created by the research team, informed by SASB, and offer ESG metric comparisons across several sectors. Data are obtained from various public sources, as well as key issue scores from ESG research providers.

Analysts use the results of the ESG model and factsheets to draw conclusions on a company's ESG profile. In addition, the ESG scores can be used to assess the ESG performance of a company versus its peer group or a broader set of issuers.

Engagement

Finally, Breckinridge believes in active ownership by directly engaging with company management. Through engagement, Breckinridge seeks to:

- Gain a better understanding of the ESG profile of the issuer, industry, or sector, by identifying issues, opportunities, and risks.
- Provide an investment idea generation platform for our analysts.
- Encourage the transparent reporting of material ESG issues, as improved disclosure enhances our ESG analysis to the benefit of the marketplace and our clients.

The corporate research team collaborates with the director of ESG research to identify companies for engagement and prepare questions for discussion. Both the sector analyst and the ESG research director participate in these engagements. Reports summarising the key findings from the company discussions are recorded and made available to the investment team.

Analysts incorporate important takeaways from the engagement discussions with an issuing company into their ESG analysis. Our engagement discussions also cover ESG issues pertinent to the sector. Engagement provides us with the opportunity to hear an issuer's perspective, to interact with management teams, and to ask questions that address material credit and ESG factors.

Breckinridge measures the effectiveness of an engagement through a simple evaluation scheme. The analyst and the director of ESG research rate two elements of corporate disclosure: (1) the value of the information conveyed by the company representatives during the conversation, and (2) the quality of the company's ESG reporting. The two indicators are mapped into a matrix as shown in Figure 12.2, for calendar years 2018 and 2020.

Bond issuers are more attentive today than in the past to their reporting about ESG issues and to their progress in addressing them. Improved

Percentages for 2018 and 2020 add to 100% to reflect breakdown of calls into the four categories.

Figure 12.2 Evaluation of Corporate Engagement Discussions.
Source: Breckinridge Capital Advisors, as of December 31, 2020.
Note: Information is based on all corporate engagement calls completed in 2018 and 2020. Chart reflects our analysts' views at the time of engagement.

articulation of a sustainability strategy reflects improved sustainability reporting. Our own experience echoes analysis by the Governance and Accountability Institute, which found that 90% of S&P 500 companies published a corporate sustainability report in 2019, up from 20% in 2011 (Governance & Accountability Institute, 2020).

Improved sustainability reporting can enhance how a company's sustainability strategy is articulated externally and can help drive progress across the organisation. As we heard from a major pharmaceutical company during a recent engagement discussion, its efforts to become a leader in the quality of its ESG reporting is central to its sustainability approach. In this engagement, company representatives noted how reporting helps 'to identify key material ESG trends, opens the door to conversations internally, and assists management in navigating through such challenges as the pandemic'.

Our analysts have noted a meaningful increase in the percentage of calls during which a 'well-articulated' sustainability strategy was discussed, meaning that we believe there is a clear sustainability strategy in place. The percentage of calls revealing what we consider to be, an 'inadequate' or 'underdeveloped' strategy has declined from 2018 to 2020. Only a minor increase in the number of companies that have sound reporting but had an uninformative call was noted during the same period.

Breckinridge seeks to have impact through its engagement activities in two ways. First, by actively communicating our commitment to ESG analysis, we demonstrate to companies that ESG analysis is useful to us and valuable in our research. Notably, we have been informed by investor relations representatives on several occasions that we are among a minority of bondholders to pose ESG-related questions. The conversations are not always one-sided, with us solely making inquiries about a company's practices. On several occasions, we have been asked by company representatives to share our perspective as an ESG-integrated investor. For example, we have been asked to describe our ESG research approach, what ESG research providers we subscribe to and why, and what aspects of the company's ESG disclosure we found most useful. In our opinion, these inquiries have led to meaningful exchanges of information and practices from both an issuer and investor's perspective.

Second, we seek to encourage progress on company sustainability efforts by participating in collaborative engagements. Breckinridge has partnered with other stakeholders to engage with companies about ESG issues. One example is our work with Ceres, the sustainability non-profit based in Boston, MA, which provides consulting services to help companies advance their sustainability performance. Ceres facilitates discussions with companies and their stakeholders to help guide and inform the management team on ESG issues. Through these discussions, with participants that have included non-governmental organisations and other investors, Breckinridge has offered its perspective to company management teams about their plans for sustainability reporting and their approaches to developing a materiality matrix, a tool frequently used to define a corporate sustainability strategy. Since 2019,

Breckinridge has participated in five Ceres-led engagements with companies in the food and beverage, asset management and technology sectors. Another example is our involvement in the Climate Action 100+, an investor-led initiative calling on the world's largest greenhouse gas emitting companies to act on climate risks. Breckinridge is a lead engagement investor with three companies and, as part of the Climate Action 100+ Initiative, we are working with other investors to encourage three US-based companies to achieve progress on the initiative's goals, which include ensuring that there is explicit board of director oversight of climate risks.

Ratings

Credit and ESG information gathered through engagement is captured in Breckinridge's credit analysts' recommendations. These recommendations include an internal rating, a sustainability rating, and an investment opinion. The internal rating conveys the analyst's credit view on a corporate issuer, including default characteristics, and trading valuation considerations used by traders and portfolio managers for portfolio construction and risk management. The sustainability rating is used to express the analyst's view on the company's oversight and management of ESG risks. The sustainability rating may influence the analyst's fundamental credit opinion and internal rating on the issuer. The investment recommendation, which includes the internal and sustainability ratings, is distributed to the investment team, and helps to drive security selection and portfolio positioning.

Analysts assign sustainability performance according to the following four-category scale:

- S1: minimal ESG risks
- S2: higher yet modest ESG risks
- S3: moderate ESG risks and is generally performing weaker than its peers
- S4: elevated or high ESG risks

The sustainability rating is also used to determine eligibility for Breckinridge's sustainable portfolios. These portfolios are offered to clients who seek to align their values or mission with their investments. In these portfolios, we invest in corporate and municipal securities with S1 and S2 sustainability ratings, as assigned by our analysts. These companies are considered to have best-in-class, in the case of S1s, or better-than-peers, ESG performance. In general, companies with S1 or S2 ratings are characterised as having robust management of material ESG risks and are leaders in sustainability reporting. Companies assigned S3 or S4 sustainability ratings typically trail their peers in terms of ESG risk management, may have a history of ESG-related controversies, may have set inadequate ESG targets such as greenhouse gas emissions reductions, and may demonstrate poor commitment to ESG disclosure and transparency.

Case-Study: Corporate ESG Spotlight: Diversity, Equity & Inclusion

Due to demographic changes and a heightened societal focus, diversity, equity, and inclusion (DEI), an element of human capital management (HCM), is becoming an increasingly material ESG issue for US companies. DEI issues are evolving and have slightly differing definitions offered by companies and non-profits. SASB states that diversity and inclusion is a company's ability to ensure that its culture and hiring and promotion practices embrace building a diverse and inclusive workforce that reflects the composition of the local talent pools and its customer base (Wilson, 2020).

When a company effectively implements a DEI strategy, it can create a culture of belonging. This fosters an environment that recognises, rewards, and utilises the full potential of the individual employee. Its culture is likely to be characterised by innovation and open collaboration. It is an ideal state that can be difficult to achieve, but many companies are embarking on this journey to remain competitive and be an employer of choice for job seekers.

Breckinridge integrates DEI considerations into the research process in varying ways, depending on the sector and the availability of DEI related metrics, to assess materiality. The following summary provides a high-level overview of some DEI considerations during our investment process.

DEI issues are considered particularly material for companies with large workforces or where intellectual capital represents a key competitive advantage. For sectors where Breckinridge has deemed DEI to be a key consideration from credit and ESG perspectives, analysts review the related corporate disclosure, and engage with companies on these issues to review disclosures and performance.

Human capital is an important corporate asset for the Financials sector, for example. Managing DEI factors effectively allows banks to expand their candidate pool and provide for enhanced diversity of background, perspective, and experience. Our ESG analysis for banks includes quantitative metrics related to DEI such as representation of women and minorities among executives, managers, and employees as well as on the board of directors; in addition to the presence of female executives and/or CEOs.

An example of assessing DEI considerations in our ESG research and engagement activity is found in the analysis of a large, regional US bank. Breckinridge held an engagement call with management representatives from the bank to discuss its performance on material ESG topics, such as customer data privacy and security and talent retention and recruitment strategies. Breckinridge was interested in gaining a better understanding of the bank's attention to these ESG risks. Going into the discussion, Breckinridge rated the bank S3, viewing its ESG risk management as weaker than peers. Engagement attendees from the bank included the director of corporate responsibility, the head of sustainability, and the director of investor relations.

On the call, we learned that management was focused on improving the bank's ESG performance and disclosure to enhance its reputation and brand. In addition, we determined that the bank's commitment to DEI was being seen internally as a differentiator. We viewed it as a genuine effort to improve its DEI practices, and this was supported by data, as representation of women in senior roles had surpassed peers and was trending towards continued improvement.

As a demonstration of its commitment to advancing its ESG performance, Breckinridge was invited by the bank to participate remotely in a subsequent meeting with its Corporate Sustainability Council, comprised of multiple executives from across the organisation. During the meeting, we commented on the evolution of sustainable investing, described the mission and progress being made on reporting standards by the SASB, and discussed ways the bank could benefit by enhancing its reporting on material ESG issues. Bank representatives expressed appreciation for our input and noted that it would help advance the bank's sustainability efforts.

Based on the bank's progress identified during the engagement discussions and its improved disclosure and stronger performance on key ESG issues, Breckinridge's analyst decided to upgrade the bank's sustainability rating. The upgrade made the bank's bonds eligible for Breckinridge's sustainable portfolios. We have since built a position in the bonds.

US State and Local Governments

Research Approach

Breckinridge's approach to ESG analysis for US state and local government issuers consists of quantitative and qualitative research, and a formal issuer engagement programme.

To guide our municipal ESG analysis, we employ ten separate frameworks to assess ESG risks for issuers in the largest municipal sectors, including water utilities and hospital systems (Figure 12.3). The frameworks reside on our internal technology platform, where they are accessed by the municipal bond analysts and are used to produce a sustainability score. The ESG factors assessed in the frameworks reflect our analysts' views of the key ESG drivers that could affect the credit quality of the issuer being evaluated for investment. The frameworks use data that we obtain from a variety of public sources that include the US Census Bureau. Examples of metrics used in our frameworks include access and affordability indicators for colleges and universities; high school graduation rates for states; and renewable energy generation mix statistics for municipal electric utilities.

Figure 12.3 Municipal Bond Research Approach.

Each framework incorporates at least ten metrics, which were selected to assess the issuer's performance for each related ESG issue. The metrics are weighted on a 100-point scale and are scored individually to reflect the nature of the data. The scoring reflects the issuer's performance on the metric relative to its sector or similarly sized peers. Like for corporate bonds, the municipal bond ESG frameworks generate a score ranging from 0, which is indicative of poor ESG performance, to the maximum of 100, which is representative of a strong ESG profile.

As an example, we created a model to assess ESG issues for local government bond issuers, such as cities and counties. The model features 19 indicators that evaluate a community for its exposure to a variety of ESG risks such as physical climate risks, including heat stress and exposure to coastal flooding; social issues including income inequality and housing affordability; and governance measures such as the quality of financial and sustainability disclosure. This framework along with the models we created for states and school districts was influenced by the work of the Social Progress Imperative[1]. This organisation produces a globally recognized methodology called the Social Progress Index that gauges a community's social performance across three categories: (A) Basic Human Needs, (B) Foundations of Well Being, and (C) Opportunity. Integration of the Social Progress Index into three of our municipal ESG frameworks reflects Breckinridge's belief that a community that is inclusive may be likely to create and support a vibrant economy and attract talented and diverse residents. These attributes may be positive from a credit perspective, possibly lowering the risk of investing in the communities over the long term.

An indicator used in the methodology to assess ESG risks for water and sewer issuers is offered as an additional illustration of our ESG approach. The purpose of a municipal water system is to provide a reliable supply of water to its retail and commercial customers. However, a drought can negatively impact that supply. Our ESG framework for the sector incorporates a freely available drought monitor measure. Points are allocated based on the severity of the drought being experienced by the issuer; the more intense the drought, the fewer the points assigned in the framework.

Qualitative ESG research for municipal bonds includes assessing a US state and local government issuer's sustainability and/or climate action strategy, risk preparedness, and commitment. In the case of the water system example described above, the analyst will review its drought resiliency plan to determine if the management team has an effective water supply strategy in place.

Finally, Breckinridge's municipal bond ESG research involves direct engagement discussions with issuers. Importantly, engagement with municipalities differs from our corporate ESG discussions, due primarily to the size of the US municipal bond market: there are an estimated 50,000 issuers, compared to 698 investment grade corporate issuers in the Bloomberg Barclays US Aggregate Bond Index (Municipal Securities Rule Making Board, 2018). As a result, engagements with company management teams are more likely to yield useful takeaways about an individual company under review for investment, given our broad research coverage of the market. Due to the significantly larger size of the municipal market, our engagement findings often offer additional insights on sector themes or ESG issues that may prove material to our analysis.

Our analysts consider the sustainability score, the ESG qualitative research, and relevant takeaways from engagement discussions when determining the sustainability rating for the issuer. The sustainability rating for municipals follows the same four-category scale as described above for corporates. Our analysts are informed by the sustainability rating when assigning the issuer's overall credit rating. Like corporate bonds, the sustainability rating is also used to determine eligibility for Breckinridge's sustainable portfolios.

Municipalities with S1 or S2 ratings are generally less exposed to ESG risks as measured by our ESG frameworks and/or have demonstrated strong management of the risks. Additionally, the issuers will likely demonstrate good sustainability disclosure practices. S3 and S4 ratings are assigned to issuers that may have an elevated exposure to ESG risks, have recently experienced an ESG-related controversy and/or are considered to have inadequate ESG planning and reporting.

US State and Local Government ESG Issue Spotlight: Climate Risks

Breckinridge believes municipalities that are conscious of and effective in managing ESG issues are likely to carry less credit risk over the long term. A key focus area is how an issuer considers climate risks. In our opinion, climate change is the most worrisome and threatening of all the ESG issues assessed by Breckinridge's research team.

Climate change poses both risks and opportunities for municipal issuers, depending on geography, the built environment, and the local economy. We assess an issuer's exposure to hurricanes, flooding, and wildfires using metrics produced by a third-party data vendor. These data help us gauge the magnitude of an issuer's physical climate risk relative to implementation of proactive solutions like forward-looking land use planning or more stringent building codes. Breckinridge's municipal analysts also consider climate transition risks and opportunities, such as job-market exposure to carbon-intensive industries or emerging clean technologies. Although the following sequence of events remains an infrequent occurrence, the management of climate risks may lead to an uptick in issuer downgrades by credit rating agencies, financial distress, and a devaluation of our investments.

We view climate risk as a threat multiplier: current climate events can magnify existing credit weaknesses of a municipal bond issuer. For example, pensions are a growing cost for many cities. Layering on climate change challenges and the potentially large associated costs of adaptation or mitigation potentially could create a competing fiscal demand that might complicate a city's efforts to control pension costs.

Another example is the vulnerability faced by cities that are underinvesting in their infrastructure. Many cities, towns and utilities across the country are grappling with deferred maintenance backlogs. This underinvestment can be exacerbated by climate change as illustrated in the following examples. In early 2020 in a city situated in south-eastern US, more than 200 million gallons of sewage spilled into the city's waterways due to sewer pipe breaches. Our analysis of the city's financial statements concluded the city had been underinvesting in its sewer system. The age-of-plant had increased meaningfully, and aggregate five-year capital spending lagged depreciation. News reports cited rising sea levels due to a changing climate and saltwater intrusion as factors accelerating the deteriorating sewage pipes and were contributing factors in the spills (Brasileiro and Harris, 2020). The snowstorm that ravaged Texas in early 2021 is another example of where poor upkeep of infrastructure was exacerbated by a lack of investment in climate change preparedness, leading to widespread power cuts. A similar situation unfolded in California during the state's 2019 wildfires, which led to billions of dollars in damage, fines, and settlements for both municipalities and PG&E, the electric utility.

Knowing an issuer's exposure to risks, such as rising sea levels or wildfires, is critical to developing a forward-looking credit profile. For example, according to the Union of Concerned Scientists, the frequency of extreme heat days will rise in the coming years (Dahl et al., 2019). This risk places stress on utility grids and community services, and disproportionately affects more vulnerable populations, including the elderly and low-income. It also has a detrimental effect on the agricultural sector, creating additional stress in communities dependent on farming-related jobs and economic activity (Newburger, 2019). Affected communities will face pressure to diversify their economies and could become more dependent on federal or state governments to compensate their losses. A sample of US municipal issuers and the related climate change impacts is provided in Table 12.1.

Municipal climate adaptation and resiliency projects require commitment of time and money to develop and apply. Therefore, issuers will continue to be exposed in the near-term to the effects of these long-term risks. Understanding the challenges confronting issuers, the potential long-term cost of managing, mitigating, or adapting to its effects, and the potential comparative

Table 12.1 US Municipalities and Potential Climate Impacts.

US Municipal Bond Issuer	Potential Climate Change Impacts
Atlantic Coastal Communities	An increase in extreme rainfall events and sea level rise threaten housing, coastal energy, and roads.
Cities in the Southeast	Rising temperatures pose risks to human health from disease-carrying insects and heat stress.
Electric Utilities in the Northwest	Change in the amount and timing of rainfall threatens future dependability of hydropower.
Infrastructure in the Northeast	Ageing highways and bridges will encounter a warmer and wetter climate, marked by heavier rains and storm surges.

Source: US Global Change Research Program, 2018.

benefits to a municipality that undertakes an effective response is essential to a comprehensive and forward-looking credit analysis. Breckinridge periodically engages directly with certain issuers to raise their awareness of relevant climate issues. Engaging directly with issuers allows us to discuss mitigation and adaptation strategies as well as making these issuers aware that investors are monitoring performance.

Climate risks are generally perceived to pose challenges over a longer time, but we are now seeing near-term, financially material effects for some municipalities. Looking ahead, events often attributed to the risks associated with climate change will likely occur more frequently and their effects will be felt more widely.

Unmanaged climate risks can influence our credit opinion on a municipal issuer. The output from the framework for a county issuer in a state situated on the US Gulf Coast underscored its exposure to physical climate risk, including hurricanes, flooding, and heat stress. Breckinridge's municipal analyst who covers the state found that county officials had no plans to combat these challenges. The analyst downgraded the issuer's sustainability rating based on insufficient progress towards addressing these climate risks. The analyst then incorporated these sustainability considerations into our decision to keep the internal credit rating at its current level, despite the issuer's improving finances and low debt burden. Absent the ESG risk, the analyst would likely have upgraded the internal credit rating. Expressed another way, the bond prices were not commensurate with the risks we had identified, and we therefore avoided investing in this issuer.

Securitised Products

Mortgage-Backed Securities

MBS are bundles of home loans bought from originating entities and wrapped into a security offering. MBS investors receive periodic payments of both principal and interest that is passed through from the borrowers of the underlying mortgages to the bondholder. We believe that the quality and performance of an MBS needs to be assessed based on the underlying mortgage loans or assets in the pool.

Given that, our process incorporates analysis of how natural disasters such as flooding, water stress, heat stress, and hurricanes accelerate mortgage prepayment rates, which can improve our insight into MBS risks. A natural disaster can accelerate the principal prepayment of mortgages in the affected area, as victims qualify for mortgage relief. Therefore, natural disasters impact broad prepayment trends, altering the cash flows and therefore impacting investor returns.

Unlike other municipal and corporate bonds, agency MBS have low credit risk thanks to explicit or implicit guarantees from government-sponsored entities (GSEs) such as the Government National Mortgage Association (Ginnie Mae), Federal National Mortgage Association (Fannie Mae), and Federal Home Loan Mortgage Corporation (Freddie Mac). Prepayment risk is a key risk for agency MBS because it can affect the timing of cash flows, which drives realised returns from the underlying pool of mortgages.

To better understand prepayment risk in MBS, members of our investment team analysed the buyout policies of GSEs as they relate to environmental disasters, such as the hurricanes that hit the states of Florida and Texas in 2017. The team also researched the experiential effect that these events historically had on mortgage prepayment speeds. Breckinridge compared prepayment speeds 6–12 months after the occurrence of a natural disaster in various geographic regions against the national average of prepayment speeds over the same time period. Our research isolated the occurrence and effect of natural disaster-related buyouts on prepayment speeds.

Using this data, we developed a methodology in 2019 to adjust the annualised percentage of a mortgage pool expected to be prepaid above and beyond scheduled amortisation in a year, also known as the Conditional Prepayment Rates (CPR). The adjustment is based on the exposure to climate-related risk factors based on the geographic composition of the underlying loans. We leveraged our municipal ESG analysis and data purchased from a climate research consultant to create the climate risk score at a US state level.

We assess and assign a climate risk score based on the geographic composition of the underlying mortgages to generate an overall climate-risk score at the security level. The climate risk score is used to adjust the CPR for each security that we evaluate. By integrating the climate risk score, we change the relative value assessment for all MBS considered for investment through an increase of the projected CPR. To illustrate this process, we have provided a hypothetical example in Figure 12.4. The methodology described here and summarised in Figure 12.4 also applies to our purchase of agency commercial mortgage-backed securities.

The process does not produce a sustainability rating, as our ESG evaluation for MBS emphasises climate risk, its impact on prepayment speeds, and therefore relative value. Sustainability ratings are used for corporations and

Hypothetical MBS Comprised of Loans from U.S. Five States

MBS BY STATE	CLIMATE RISK SCORE BY STATE	X	% OF STATE TO TOTAL MBS	OVERALL CLIMATE RISK SCORE (WEIGHTED)	UNADJUSTED CPR	CPR ADJUSTED FOR CLIMATE RISKS
State A	State Score 1		20%			
State B	State Score 2		20%			
State C	State Score 3		20%	XYZ + X% = X%		
State D	State Score 4		20%			
State E	State Score 5		20%			

Figure 12.4 Hypothetical Example of MBS Climate Risk Analysis.

municipals as comprehensive measures of ESG risks and, by extension, credit risks.

The biggest challenge when attempting to assess climate risks for MBS is the lack of disclosure. For privacy reasons, the GSEs made the decision to stop disclosing any information about the location of the homes that back the mortgages within the pool, with the exception of information on the state in which the homes are located. As result, an investor is unable to determine if a home for an underlying mortgage is located on the coast, where it may be subject to flooding, or in an inland region exposed to other climate change effects.

Breckinridge raised this concern during a discussion with a GSE in late 2020. We learned during the engagement that the GSE was in the early stages of considering climate risks in its underwriting process and across the organisation. To kickstart the effort, the GSE had established an interdepartmental sustainability committee. We were encouraged to be told that the GSE is open to collaborating with investors to better understand and address climate change and other ESG risks.

Finally, we created a model for considering social issues when determining the eligibility of MBS for sustainable portfolios. As sustainably-oriented clients have an interest in directing their capital to impactful purposes, we invest in an MBS for a sustainable portfolio if it meets our internal social impact criteria. We measure housing affordability, poverty levels, and homeownership levels for US states. The states are ranked according to an aggregated score for the three social measures. Based on the ranking, an MBS with underlying mortgages from a state with more elevated poverty, with more expensive housing, and lower homeownership rate would be eligible for investment in sustainable portfolios.

Asset-Backed Securities

ABS are fixed income investments backed by pools of auto, credit card, small business, and student loans, among other types of securities. The loans are originated by a bank or other financial institution. To create the security, the loans are transferred from the institution's balance sheet to a special purpose entity, which will hold the loans, act as trustee, and often service the loans. Breckinridge assesses the creditworthiness of the loan pool before investing in the ABS security. We analyse traditional credit measures that include but are not limited to debt-to-income and loan-to-value ratios and default and delinquency data.

From an ESG analysis perspective, evaluating an ABS security follows our corporate ESG approach. Specifically, we assess the ESG profile of the originating bank or financial institution for the ABS security under consideration for investment given the linkage to the parent. Our assessment consists of the three-pronged approach: our quantitative ESG model, our in-depth qualitative ESG research, and an active issuer engagement programme. The sustainability profile and relevant sustainability rating may influence the analyst's fundamental credit opinion and internal rating on the issuer of the ABS. In addition, the sustainability rating is used to determine eligibility for Breckinridge's sustainable portfolios.

We continue to look for ways to incorporate additional ESG considerations at the security level. However, data availability remains an issue. ESG information that would be helpful for analysing the loan pool includes the location of the asset underlying a specific loan and the credit score of the borrower. However, this information is unavailable due in part to privacy concerns, which is an understandable concern of regulators. Due to the lack of ESG -specific information on the security level, our ESG approach for ABS is, therefore, focused on the issuer.

Conclusion

Examining non-traditional financial factors in US fixed income has been a hallmark of Breckinridge's research process for more than a decade. We believe that looking beyond traditional data with ESG integration techniques and analysis is a critical part of robust research, enabling us to gain deeper insight into the underlying risk and value of an investment. As investment grade fixed income investors, we prioritise long-term value creation over short-term market gains, and ESG considerations align with this perspective. Simply put, ESG research is more than simply a product option; it is intrinsic to our investment philosophy.

Breckinridge's approach to ESG integration is customised to the unique challenges of each asset class. For corporates, there is currently inadequate, but improving, availability of standardised ESG disclosure by companies. Third-party providers play an important role in organising ESG information and appraising ESG performance. In addition, we engage with up to one-third of our covered companies annually. It is resource-intensive work, but it is a worthwhile endeavour given the insights gained from the discussions.

Our municipal bond ESG approach utilises data that are publicly available and can be applied to a large universe of issuers. Standardised ESG information is obtained from third-party sources, such as the Environmental Protection Agency, but we would welcome additional reporting, especially around climate risks, directly from issuers. Engagements with issuers complement the risk process with findings more applicable to sectors and understanding of ESG themes.

Finally, for securitised products, ESG evaluation of individual securities is understandably limited due to privacy concerns. Our approach is differentiated based on information that can be accessed, analysed, and measured. The lack of available information at the security level requires our focus on the originating bank or financial institution. Climate risks do not cover all potential physical risks that assets are exposed to, which creates further requirements for transparency by issuers.

Over many years we have advanced our efforts on ESG research, engagement, and partnerships. Our ESG tools and capabilities developed to date enhance our insights into the ESG exposure of issuers and into how they are managing the risks. In the coming years, we hope to augment our process and confront data challenges by further exploring the use of alternative methods for examining ESG risks, such as through artificial intelligence and satellite remote sensing. Breckinridge intends to stay focused on innovation and excellence in ESG integration across fixed income asset classes.

Note

1 See https://www.socialprogress.org/.

References

Brasileiro, A. and Harris, A. (2020), 'Sea Rise Is Making Fort Lauderdale's Sewage Leaks Worse'. [online]. Available at: https://wusfnews.wusf.usf.edu/2020-01-09/sea-rise-is-making-fort-lauderdales-sewage-leaks-worse (Accessed 20 May 2021).

Dahl, K., Licker, R., Abatzoglou, J. and Declet-Barreto, J. (2019), 'Increased Frequency of and Population Exposure to Extreme Heat Index Days in the United States during the 21st Century', *Environmental Research Communications*, 1(7). Available at: https://iopscience.iop.org/article/10.1088/2515-7620/ab27cf/pdf (Accessed 20 May 2021).

Fischer, M. (2013), 'An SRI Bond Filter', *Private Wealth*. [online]. Available at: https://www.fa-mag.com/news/an-sri-bond-filter-13566.html?issue=206 (Accessed 20 May 2021).

Governance & Accountability Institute (2020), *Flash Report S&P500: Trends on the Sustainability Reporting Practices of S&P 500 Index Companies*. [online]. Available at: https://www.ga-institute.com/research-reports/flash-reports/2020-sp-500-flash-report.html (Accessed 20 May 2021).

Municipal Securities Rulemaking Board (2018), *Self-Regulation and the Municipal Securities Market*. [online]. Available at: http://www.msrb.org/MarketTopics/~/media/8059A52FBF15407FA8A8568E3F4A10CD.ashx (Accessed 20 May 2021).

Newburger, E. (2019), 'It Never Stops: US Farmers Now Face Extreme Heat Wave after Floods and Trade War'. [online]. Available at: https://www.cnbc.com/2019/07/19/extreme-heat-wave-hits-us-farmers-already-suffering-from-flooding.html (Accessed 20 May 2021).

Securities Industry and Financial Markets Association (SIFMA) (2021), 'Fixed Income Outstanding'. [online]. Available at: https://www.sifma.org/resources/research/fixed-income-chart/ (Accessed 20 May 2021).

Sustainability Accounting Standards Board (SASB) (2021), 'Materiality Map'. [online]. Available at: https://www.sasb.org/standards-overview/materiality-map/ (Accessed 20 May 2021).

US Global Change Research Program (2018), *Fourth National Climate Assessment. Volume II: Impacts, Risks, and Adaptation in the United States* (US Government Publishing Office, Washington, DC). [online]. Available at: https://nca2018.globalchange.gov/downloads/NCA4_2018_FullReport.pdf (Accessed 20 May 2021).

Wilson, K. (2020), 'Exploring Diversity & Inclusion in the SASB Standards' [online]. Available at: https://www.sasb.org/blog/exploring-diversity-inclusion-in-the-sasb-standards/ (Accessed 20 May 2021).

Part 4

Impact Investing

13 Impact Investing in Fixed Income Markets

Johanna Köb

After many years as a niche approach impact investing is receiving increasing attention from mainstream investors. As the strategy matures, the investment opportunities are robust and demand is growing despite differences in investors' approaches and definitions.

At Zurich Insurance Group (Zurich) we believe impact investing is not only an opportunity to intentionally target a specific social or environmental objective, but also to generate financial returns commensurate with our risk-return expectations. By extension, introducing an impact investing approach also has the potential to drive positive internal changes through clearer processes and guidelines. Initiatives like the Operating Principles for Impact Management (The Principles, 2019) provide an end-to-end reference point for investors to embed impact in a comparable way to the Principles for Responsible Investment (PRI) for investors to integrate environmental, social, and governance (ESG) risk.

While impact investing has its roots in private markets, fixed income as an asset class has matured as impact markets and can offer a starting point for institutional investors wishing to build an impact investing approach. This chapter takes a broad look at impact investing and how it applies to fixed income markets.

We begin by providing an overview of the landscape of definitions and frameworks governing the impact investing market. We demonstrate how impact investing can fulfil its purpose – allocating capital to solve environmental and social issues – by embracing a broad spectrum of investors and suggest solutions to some of the industry's debates. We then discuss how fixed income markets can be seen through an impact lens. Finally, we use Zurich Insurance Group's (Zurich) impact investing journey as a case study. Within this we describe Zurich's principal investment approach to managing fixed income assets and the impact investing framework and philosophy underpinning our work, the practical ways we apply an impact approach, how we evaluate use-of-proceed bonds, how we distinguish impact investing from footprinting, and how we measure impact, with a particular focus on measuring our climate impact.

DOI: 10.4324/9781003055341-17

About Impact Investing

Definitions

Impact investing is an investment style that has become one of the strategic tools found in the responsible investment toolbox. The term was originally coined by the Global Impact Investing Network (GIIN), and is defined as: 'Investments made with the intention to generate positive, measurable social and environmental impact alongside a financial return' (GIIN, 2021a).

These investments can be made in both developed and developing markets, by a host of different investors, in different asset classes and with varying return objectives – from concessionary to market-rate-return seeking. However, intentionality, measurability, and profitability are the core defining elements of the approach. What sets impact investments apart, is that positive impact is not a mere side-effect of an investment or business strategy – it becomes an explicit part of the investment objective, can be formulated in an *ex ante* hypothesis, and can be measured with reasonable effort *ex post*. The link of money invested and impact created is a relatively direct one, driven by the investor's intention to improve social and environmental outcomes. The underlying theory of change of impact investment is to use the allocation power of capital markets to directly address some of the world's most pressing social and environmental issues.

In 2019 the GIIN, after a thorough consultation with leading impact investors, provided further clarity on how to approach impact investing by publishing the core characteristics of impact investing. These are presented in Box 13.1.

BOX 13.1 The Core Characteristics of Impact Investing (GIIN, 2021b)

1 **Intentionality**:

- Impact investing is marked by an intentional desire to contribute to measurable social or environmental benefit. Impact investors aim to solve problems and address opportunities. This is at the heart of what differentiates impact investing from other investment approaches that may incorporate impact considerations.

2 **Use Evidence and Impact Data in Investment Design**:

- Investments cannot be designed on hunches, and impact investing needs to use evidence and data where available to drive intelligent investment design that will be useful in contributing to social and environmental benefits.

3   **Manage Impact Performance**:

- Impact investing comes with a specific intention and necessitates that investments be managed towards that intention. This includes having feedback loops in place and communicating performance information to support others in the investment chain to manage towards impact.

4   **Contribute to Growth of Industry**:

- Investors with credible impact investing practices use shared industry terms, conventions, and indicators for describing their impact strategies, goals, and performance. They also share learnings where possible to enable others to learn from their experience as to what actually contributes to social and environmental benefit.

These characteristics were further developed into the Operating Principles for Impact Management (The Principles) (2019). The IFC-led initiative brought leading impact investors together to establish a framework that provides an end-to-end reference point for investors to embed impact in a comparable way to what the Principles for Responsible Investment (PRI) did for investors' focus on ESG risk and active ownership. The Principles were published and welcomed their founding signatories in April 2019 (Figure 13.1).

Impact measurement is often considered the most challenging part of impact investing: both at the level of the individual project or investee and at the portfolio (or aggregate) level. A variety of organizations are working on providing guidance on which metrics to use in order to measure not only positive impact but also important negative outcomes, and how to harmonize the underlying methodologies and assumptions in order to increase comparability. Examples include the GIIN's IRIS metrics,[1] the HIPSO framework established by development finance institutions[2] and the Green and Social Bond Principle's proposed impact metrics for green and social bonds[3] (Green Bond Principles and ICMA, 2020; ICMA and the Social Bonds Principles, 2020).

Harnessing the Power of Capital Markets to Do Good

The aim of impact investing is that of problem solving, or intentionally doing measurable good for people and the planet while simultaneously doing financially well. While some pressing sustainability issues can be tackled by private actors and market mechanisms, many require a collaborative approach with non-profit, governmental, and non-governmental actors to address public good elements of an environmental or social solution. As a result, the impact

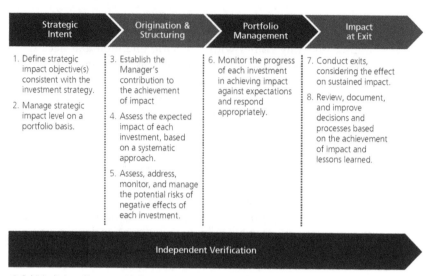

Figure 13.1 OPIM 9 Principles and Framework.
Source: Zurich Insurance Group (2020), adapted from OPIM (2019).

investing market is organised in a loose ecosystem in which concessionary capital and individual investors can target higher risks or prove concepts – while institutional investors will likely have to rely on lower risk, market-rate returns and plain vanilla structures, but can bring scale and long-term investment horizons to the table.

In either case, impact investing is distinguishable from philanthropy, where money is given away to achieve a positive impact (i.e. incurring a 100% loss). The varying size, structure, and profitability of the projects underlying impact investments and the diverse ecosystems of impact investors – spanning foundations and endowments, (mostly) high net-worth investors, asset managers and large institutional investors – are both important features of the impact investing ecosystem. As the market matures, the connection points between various segments of the ecosystem will need to become more institutionally joined up in order to more effectively span the entire process from proof-of-concept and blended finance to scalable and institutionalised capital allocation.

Impact investment is still a comparatively small market opportunity. In 2020, the Global Impact Investing Network (GIIN) estimated its size at US\$715bn, up from US\$502 in 2019 and US\$228 in 2018. This methodology uses self-reported information. It only comprises parts of the use-of-proceed bond market (defined as green, social, and sustainability bonds), which is larger (GIIN, 2020).

Core Debates

As impact investing moves closer to the mainstream, the industry is going through a healthy debate on definitions, standards, metrics, and vocabulary. This becomes apparent to new participants. Some of it is simply semantics, in other cases it is important to distinguish between the various concepts and philosophical issues. In this section we will examine two of the most important: distinguishing the 'impact of investing' from 'impact investing', and the question of additionality as a qualifying factor for impact investing.

Intentionality and Measurability

The question that most often lies at the heart of the impact investing definition debate is: Does every investment have an impact – and should therefore be called impact investing? Every investment, regardless of asset class, has an impact on communities, people's lives, and the environment. Companies or assets such as buildings and infrastructure are built and operated, and in the process, jobs are created or lost; products are introduced, sold, and consumed, or services delivered; natural resources harvested and processed; energy produced and consumed; waste and emissions created or mitigated. Accordingly, every investment has a footprint, both positive and negative, that affects the real economy, our environment, and our communities. In a portfolio view, such positive and negative footprints automatically come with every investment opportunity, but are often neither measured nor intentionally managed.

However, intentionality and measurability lie at the core of the impact investment definition. Conceptually it is easiest to think of 'impact investing' as a strategic approach, where capital is allocated with the intention to create a positive environmental or social outcome, which can be assumed *ex ante* and measured *ex post*. In contrast, we suggest using the term 'footprinting' for quantifying the sum of the negative and positive outcomes, which simply come with the nature of investing – or in other words: the impact of investing. We have developed thinking around the terminology at Zurich, which we discuss in more detail in the case-study section below.

Additionality

The second important point of debate concerns additionality. Additionality is a term of high relevance and debate. Some investors only count investments as impact investments if they fulfil the criterion of additionality in its original definition. Others, like Zurich, consider impact on a spectrum from light to deep impact, creating some flexibility around the meaning and how impact opportunities can apply to existing investment portfolios.

The term additionality stems from the field of development aid, ensuring that projects carried out with Western tax money in developing countries were truly additional, in the sense that they only financed programs that could not have be undertaken by the local government or local private markets. Additionality, with that same understanding, was also used in the Clean Development Mechanism of the 1997 Kyoto Protocol to make sure that carbon credits could only be produced through, for example, additional carbon sinks such as a newly planted mangrove forest, as opposed to one that existed before but was not declared as carbon credit producing.

When translating this concept to impact investing with its original meaning of 'something is enabled through finance that would not otherwise have happened' we quickly run into a trade-off with profitability. As discussed above, impact investments are not philanthropy – they always create a form of return, across a broad spectrum from concessionary to market-rate returns, hosting a range of investors with differing impact/risk/return expectations. Most institutional investors will, like Zurich, need to focus on opportunities that deliver positive impact on top of risk-adjusted market rate returns due to their fiduciary duty. In order to generate market rate returns, a functioning market for those impact assets is a necessary condition. Institutional investors also prefer liquid markets, which requires a minimum size and depth of the market, regular turnover, larger ticket sizes and standardised investment structures. The presence of such a deep and liquid market makes it harder to argue that the impact would never have happened (i.e. that the impact project would have never been financed) without the involvement of a specific investor, as in a functioning market other investors could and would have taken the specific investor's place.

Following the additionality logic, only projects that break new market ground or are in proof-of-concept stages could claim to be truly additional. As fundamentally important as these parts of the market are, they are often not scalable enough to deploy the capital needed to solve broader social and environmental issues without public capital. The entire spectrum of the impact investing ecosystem is needed if we are to channel capital at the scale needed towards better social and environmental outcomes.

Our view is that this debate can be resolved by acknowledging that the strict understanding of additionality in terms of 'not having happened otherwise' should only be applied to certain parts of the impact investing market and should not form a qualifying criterion for impact investing overall. Instead, we frame additionality in terms of 'value added', a concept that can be applied to all impact investments. There are three ways to measure an investor's contribution to creating that added value:

- Adding on: Determine whether new capital is provided and where it is deployed. For example, is capital allocated in the primary or secondary market? Is it financing new projects/assets or refinancing existing ones and under which conditions? Are volumes of impact investments deployed growing over time or steadily redeployed to new projects?
- Depth of impact: A good impact measurement system includes combining impact metrics and their qualifying contextual factors, and will

support investors to assess the total amount, intensity (measured in terms of the impact achieved per dollar invested) and quality of impact created.
- Market development: Breaking new ground, pioneering efforts, generating broader learning effects for a single investor or the overall market that lead to higher quality or volume of impact in the mid-term are value adding elements for the overall impact investing market.

Impact Investing in Fixed Income Markets

While impact investing has its roots in private markets, today impact opportunities can be found in any asset class where a good link between an intentional up-front impact hypothesis and ex-post measurement of the impact created can be established.

Fixed income markets are an especially interesting asset class to examine through an impact lens as:

- They come in a broad variety of investment instruments.
- They bring together a large number of investors, in particular institutional investors who typically have a substantial asset allocation to fixed income markets.
- They tend to be well understood by investors, which lowers barriers to entry.
- They move vast amounts of capital.

Examples of the investment instruments that can fulfil impact investing conditions include green or social infrastructure debt, natural capital debt, microfinance debt funds, private debt funds targeting specific environmental or social impacts, and green, social, and sustainability bonds. In the next section, we will examine some of these instruments, and how they can be part of the impact investing leg of a broader responsible investment strategy with the example of Zurich.

Impact Investing at Zurich Insurance Group

Our Core Investment Approach

Being a responsible company is at the foundation of our business. It influences our daily decisions and long-term planning. We believe creating long-term, sustainable value is not only possible, but necessary to generate superior risk-adjusted returns for our customers and shareholders. Our responsible investment strategy is built around three core pillars – ESG integration, impact investing and advancing together – and covers the entirety of our proprietary assets, where we match a variety of responsible investment tools[4] with the asset classes where they have most practical influence. Since Zurich manages approximately US$200 billion of own assets, we can achieve outcomes that benefit both people and the planet.

ESG factors influence investment risks and opportunities. Therefore, we proactively include ESG factors in the investment process across asset classes and alongside traditional financial metrics and risk management practices. The starting point in insurance investment management is asset-liability management (ALM), an integrated process that matches the duration of Zurich's insurance liabilities with a portfolio of minimum risk assets, usually government bonds. This starting point in combination with regulatory requirements and allocated capital is used to define the strategic asset allocation. This allocation is the result of a disciplined process that distils all investable asset classes into a small set of understandable and transparent systematic market risk factors that cannot be diversified, and looks for the optimal mix of risk factors that will result in the highest risk-adjusted market returns for a certain level of allocated capital. We have found no evidence that ESG issues are associated with a systematic market-risk factor and premium that could be reflected in the ALM and strategic asset allocation processes. Based on this, we believe that ESG issues are best reflected when selecting individual securities or assets.

Zurich's assets are managed by over 40 internal and external asset managers according to clearly defined investment management agreements, objectives, and guidelines. We rely on the skill of these asset managers to build portfolios that achieve our investment and sustainability goals (Figure 13.2). We monitor and emphasise a robust process and commitment around four key areas:

1   Training. ESG factors can affect risk and return. The channels through which they affect risk and return are sometimes complex and vary from sector to sector. It is important that portfolio managers receive adequate and regular training to help them understand the economic importance

	2019	2018	Change	2017	2016	2015
External asset managers who are signatories to PRI (%)[1]	**81.3%**	74.2%	7.1 pts	71.0%	74.1%	70.4%
Group assets managed by PRI signatories (%)[2]	**97.5%**	97.2%	0.3 pts	97.2%	97.7%	98.1%
Total amount of impact investments (USD millions)[3]	**4,555**	3,790	20.2%	2,830	1,704	1,031
Investment portfolio (USD millions)[4]	**204,803**	195,472	4.8%	207,261	195,852	191,238

[1] The United-Nations supported Principles for Responsible Investment (PRI).

[2] Including assets managed by Zurich.

[3] Impact investments in 2019 consisted of: green bonds (USD 3.1 billion), social and sustainability bonds (USD 539 million), investments committed to private equity funds (USD 163 million, thereof 36 percent drawn down) and impact infrastructure private debt (USD 747 million).

[4] Investment portfolio is calculated on a market basis, and is different from the total Group investments reported in the Consolidated Financial Statements, which is calculated on an accounting basis and doesn't include cash and cash equivalents.

Figure 13.2 Zurich's Responsible Investment KPIs as of 2020.

of ESG issues, especially as ESG has only recently – and partially – been included in finance and business school curriculums.

2   Access to information. To reflect ESG issues in investment decisions, portfolio managers need access to relevant information in the form of ESG analysis, ratings, and data. This can be supplied by specialised external providers, dedicated in-house teams, or broker research.

3   Investment process. A clear understanding is needed around the process to consider ESG factors in decisions to buy/sell, or overweight/underweight a security or asset. This process should be documented and consistently applied.

4   Active ownership. Asset managers are required to integrate relevant ESG issues in discussions with investee companies, either as part of regular company meetings, or through separate channels, as well as in their proxy voting policy and practice.

It is not our objective to systematically exclude companies or assets from the investment universe. Just as we do not determine exclusion criteria based on traditional financial metrics, such as maximum price/earnings ratios or minimum interest coverage ratios, we also do not specify exclusion criteria such as minimum ESG scores or ratings. We prefer to work closely with our managers to make sure that the requirements for integrating ESG factors are reflected in their investment processes.

Having said this, out company-wide process assesses specific ethical concerns or market failures. It can result in us making selective exclusions implemented consistently across insurance underwriting and investment activities. We use independent research and ESG information to guide this process.

Due to the long-term liabilities we hold as an insurance company, close to 80% of our portfolio is allocated to fixed income, spanning a variety of asset classes from private debt to sovereign debt and corporate credit. Accordingly, our impact investing strategy focuses predominantly on this asset class.

Our Impact Investing Framework

We have a history of developing and innovating our impact investing approach. Impact investing was adopted formally within our first responsible investment strategy in 2012. We started by allocating to green bonds, then adding impact private equity, social, and sustainability bonds, and finally green and social infrastructure debt.

Externally communicated impact targets are an important driver for our investing strategy. We started our target-setting journey by pledging to invest US$1 billion into green bonds in 2013 – at a time where the entire market had a size of around US$13bn – and quickly raised this to US$2 billion. Having met these targets, in 2017 we became the first private sector investor to add impact targets to allocation targets: we set targets of investing US$ 5bn in impact investments, of helping to avoid 5 million tonnes of carbon dioxide (equivalent) (CO_2e) and of benefiting 5 million people per year. Setting these targets required us to develop procedures to scrutinise the impact numbers reported by our investee companies and third-party managers as well as a methodology that would allow for aggregating impact numbers across a variety of portfolios, instruments, and asset classes. When in September 2020 we exceeded our original allocation target of US$ 5 billion, we decided to again lead the market by dropping the practice of setting allocation targets, and instead become the first large institutional investor to steer an impact portfolio through impact targets only.

As of Q4 2021, Zurich held an impact investing portfolio of US$ 7.0 billion across various asset classes (including green, social, and sustainability bonds, infrastructure debt and private equity), which helped to avoid 4.6 million tonnes of CO_2e and to improve the lives of 3.6 million people, all on an annual basis. Getting to this point involved setting a strategy to ensure senior stakeholders and investment staff were informed and committed to these goals.

Zurich is directly exposed to challenges such as climate change, resource depletion, and water risk through its investment and insurance activities. As an insurer we have a direct interest in sustainable global economic growth and supporting communities to become more resilient confronting environmental and social challenges. Impact investments can help address these issues in a targeted way and offer a financial return commensurate with the risks.

Our initial priority was to focus on the asset classes and/or topics with most relevance and importance. This involved reviewing our existing asset allocation and investment approach through an impact investing lens and identifying opportunities where our allocation, expertise, and the impact investing market converged. We were clear that impact investing would only be sustainable as an investment style if it could be integrated into the overall investment management process. We recognised that opportunistic investments can supplement the portfolio occasionally, but to be effective impact investing should be integral to the portfolio. This meant developing dedicated strategies for impact within asset classes that formed part of the wider investment strategy.

In 2013 Zurich joined the GIIN's Investor council and in 2019 Zurich became a founding signatory to the IFC-led The Principles initiative, which provides a holistic framework for investors to develop and organise their entire impact management process. The 9 Principles (see Figure 13.1) ensure impact is applied across the investment lifecycle while enabling comparability and reducing concerns over impact-washing. Being part of these industry networks helped develop our thinking when setting up our initial impact investing strategy, and subsequently provided useful fora to share our experience and to engage with other like-minded investors, further driving tools and methodologies.

Within the impact investing ecosystem discussed above, as an institutional investor Zurich focuses only on opportunities that deliver positive impact at risk-adjusted market rate returns. High-quality impact investment opportunities are only available for certain pockets of our investment portfolio, but with enough scale to apply across our overall approach. This enables us to develop market-rate investment opportunities that fit the structured and regulated approach and return expectations of an insurance investor, and at the same time achieve a measurable contribution through our impact investments. We do this in two main ways. First, we mitigate environmental risks by supporting a climate neutral economy and encouraging environmentally friendly technologies. Zurich will consider impact investments that help increase energy efficiency, generate renewable energy, or mitigate climate change and/or protect the environment in other ways. Second, we increase community resilience by helping to build 'community capital', and address the needs of populations that lack traditional means to achieve such goals (the 'under-served populations').

While the market is not deep enough to support this objective fully, it is also one of our explicit objectives to support the impact investing mainstreaming through collaborative engagement and investments. To support market development and achieve scale and portfolio diversification, we may target impact topics beyond those already mentioned.

Our Impact Investing Approach

When identifying potential impact opportunities, we assess whether the investment:

- Meets our definition of impact investing (intentionality, measurability, and profitability).
- Supports our impact objectives with enough quality (mitigating environmental risks and increasing community resilience).
- Contributes to our impact targets (avoid the emission of 5 million tons of CO_2e per year and make a positive contribution to the lives of 5 million people).
- Contributes to further development of the impact investing market.

From a financial perspective, we also consider:

- Whether the risk/return profile is in line with Zurich's requirements for a specific asset class.
- Whether the universe of assets for a given type of impact investment is large enough to define a meaningful allocation, build a diversified portfolio, and re-invest capital over time.
- Whether Zurich, or an institutional-quality external asset manager, has the capability and expertise to manage the asset.
- The ESG risks associated with the underlying asset as part of a holistic asset selection process.
- The regulatory and other constrains that apply to Zurich as an insurance company.

Table 13.1 Comparing Footprinting and Impact Investing.

Footprinting	Impact Investing	
	Impact	Deep Impact
Positive and negative impact	Positive impact	Positive impact
Measurability	Intentionality	Intentionality
Profitability	Measurability	Measurability
	Profitability	Profitability
		Additionality

We habitually combine impact investing with the other elements of our responsible investment strategy: for every impact decision we consider ESG risks and opportunities for valuation purposes. We decline investments if we consider these risks are disproportional or if they reduce the impact hypothesis. Active ownership tools are used to understand the impact intended and engage with issuers on topics ranging from their measurement framework to project implementation and market development.

At Zurich we clearly distinguish impact investing from what we refer to as 'footprinting' (Table 13.1).

Footprinting

As discussed above, we believe that every investment portfolio or investment fund has a footprint that shows the positive and negative effects of various environmental and social dimensions that happen intentionally or unintentionally by owning or lending towards an asset. Tools are increasingly available to measure these effects. For example, carbon emission footprints, or the share of 'green' and 'brown' revenues generated by companies.

In a way, footprinting can be interpreted as the outcomes-focused sibling of ESG integration. While ESG integration focuses on identifying, pricing, and optimizing risks and opportunities, footprinting takes a holistic look at all positive and negative outcomes an investment leaves in the world – to the degree it can currently be captured through reporting. One might argue that most positive footprints, especially if they are increasing over time can be translated into ESG opportunities, while negative footprints can translate into ESG risks. At this point in time, the translation logic is imperfect, but increasingly joined together by responsible investors. As a responsible investment style, the insights created from footprinting and the theory of change behind proactively managing footprints is similar to that of ESG integration: the first priority is to create transparency through ESG reporting. Investors might then start to optimize for an increased positive footprint, aim to decrease negative footprints, or price the difference. Influence is exerted through changes in capital allocation and valuation which over time translates into a change in cost of capital for both more and less sustainable companies.

The objective behind footprinting focuses on transparency. We aim to understand the entities we have exposure to and the overall contribution to sustainability themes that are both important drivers of risk and part of our overarching objective.

Impact Investing

In contrast, impact investing is centered around positive impacts. At Zurich, we follow the GIIN definition of impact investing described above: investment opportunities that intentionally target a specific positive social or environmental impact, which is measured. These investments are profitable, meaning that they generate a market-rate financial return commensurate with their risk. Accordingly, creating positive impact is not a mere side effect of an investment. Instead it becomes part of the investment objective, and can be assessed with both an ex-ante hypothesis and measured ex post (see Figure 13.3).

Based on our experience as impact investor we also distinguish between different impact opportunities ranging from lighter to deeper impact. We measure the depth of impact in two ways: (1) through the impact intensity of a project (impact created/US$million invested) within its qualitative context, and (2) through the catalysing effect investments had in changing how we invest, or in contributing to overall market growth. For example, by allocating to a new asset class, geography, or structure, or supporting projects, and asset classes that influence their broader market environment.

Footprinting	Impact investing	
	Impact	**Deep Impact**
• Ex-post: measurement	• Ex-ante: dedicated allocation or systematic tilt in portfolio • Limited complexity • Ex-post: measurement • Examples: green and social bonds; overweight in renewable energy assets; health care private equity fund	• Ex-ante: dedicated allocation or systematic tilt in portfolio • More complexity: new and less familiar risks; non-traditional structures; smaller transaction size; increased due diligence effort • Ex-post: measurement • Examples: backing first-time environmental technologies fund; emerging and frontier market private equity or debt; pay-for-performance structures

Figure 13.3 Setting Impact Approaches.

Use-of-proceed Bonds

Within the fixed income asset classes offering impact investing opportunities, Zurich allocates to infrastructure private debt as well as use-of-proceed bonds, defined as green, social, and sustainability bonds that provide impact measurement.

Use-of-proceeds (UoP) bonds governed by the Green and Social Bond Principles, as well as the Sustainability Bond Guidelines all have to target environmental objectives, social objectives, for a specific target population or a combination of both in the case of sustainability bonds, and create a significant benefit in these areas. Reporting on the allocation of proceeds is mandatory, while impact reporting is encouraged as best practice. Indeed, a large amount of issuers report on the impact created through their use-of-proceeds bonds – which are those that we consider as 'impact assets' and target as part of our impact investing strategy at Zurich. For the purpose of this case-study, we will focus on those instruments.

Investing in green, social, and sustainability bonds is the principal way we execute our impact strategy by allocation. In 2021, from our overall US$ 7.0 billion allocation to impact instruments, US$ 5.8 billion had been allocated to green, social, and sustainability bonds. To capture the breadth of credit instruments and issuers represented in the use-of-proceed bond market, Zurich has defined two separate but complementary approaches for investing in them.

First, we have established a dedicated green bond mandate for supranational green bonds issued in US dollars. Assets with minimum credit risk, such as those issued (or explicitly guaranteed) by national governments or supranational institutions, form a very significant part of Zurich's asset allocation. In line with our established approach to define portfolios along credit sector and currency lines, Zurich has carved out a dedicated green bond mandate to invest in US dollar-denominated green bonds by supranational issuers on its North American balance sheet. This mandate is managed by an external asset manager with up to US$1 billion.

Second, we have integrated green, social, and sustainability bonds in existing fixed income portfolios. Zurich captures other credit sectors, issuers, and currencies through a complementary approach. Rather than creating multiple green bond portfolios reflecting different credit sectors and currencies, or cross currency, cross-credit-sector portfolios that would not fit Zurich's established approach to credit investing, an internal green bond expert was appointed to coordinate and facilitate use-of-proceed bond investments across Zurich's many existing balance sheets, portfolios, and asset managers. In this way, Zurich has allocated over US$4 billion to use-of-proceed bonds and is expecting to maintain and further grow this approach.

Our Bond Evaluation Process for Impact Assets

Zurich supports the Green Bond Principles, Social Bond Principles and Guidelines for Sustainability Bonds. Our qualitative process applies several criteria, described below, and through this analysis bonds are subsequently added to portfolios if financial prerequisites are met.

Bond Quality

When analysing use-of-proceeds bonds and assessing if they qualify as impact instruments, Zurich focuses primarily on the financed projects and their *ex ante* potential for positive impact. If the *ex ante* potential of the projects to contribute to environmental or social improvements is promising, the proposed projects or selection framework will be evaluated in the context of the issuing entity. Analysts gauge the issuer's sincerity of intent, and assess if the projects are anchored in the issuer's overall environmental, social, or sustainability strategy.

Even initial steps, if rooted in a sound strategy and critical to progress, will be preferred over opportunistic approaches that are divorced from the issuing entity's business model or sustainability strategy. Zurich also carefully analyses the potential ESG risks that might be associated with green or social projects, as well as the issuer's track record in implementing projects that do pose such ESG risks.

ESG factors provide valuable insights into the potential risks and expected returns across asset classes. Accordingly, Zurich uses the issuer's ESG rating as a second step after a use-of-proceeds bond has been identified as an impact instrument to evaluate risks and opportunities associated with specific ESG factors and determine a bond's fair value. ESG factors may well affect the cost of capital and issuing a green bond may signal lower risks to investors related to its overall ESG profile. Zurich expects these characteristics to reduce the cost of capital for all securities of the same issuer, not just that of issuer's use-of-proceeds bonds.

Incremental Benefits

Not all activities with environmental benefits are considered equally 'green'. An example could be investing in electric vehicle manufacturers when use of public transport has a better (lower) overall environmental impact. In general, it is preferable to consider incremental environmental benefits than no progress, and green bonds are a good instrument to engage issuers with less-than-perfect environmental credentials, if the trajectory of their actions is clear.

There are sectors that have a challenging role addressing the six key environmental objectives considered by the Green Bond Principles (i.e. climate change mitigation, climate change adaptation, natural resource conservation, biodiversity conservation, and pollution prevention and control). When incremental green benefits are targeted within an inherently 'brown' activity, Zurich will pay specific attention to the level of ambition displayed in the proposed improvements to classify such a bond 'green' rather than just 'conventional.' Especially with regards to climate transition, we expect ambitious transition targets and clear pathways in place for carbon intensive or hard to abate sectors, but will consider financing such transitions within the boundaries of credible strategic frameworks as part of our own journey to a fully climate neutral balance sheet by 2050.

Over time, impact measurement is the right instrument to assess the relative environmental as well as social benefits of underlying activities. As the use-of-proceed bond market grows and develops, investors will learn more about the environmental and social benefits of different activities through greater transparency and better, comparable, and well-contextualized impact reporting.

Transparency

The issuer must have a clear and transparent framework to allocate funds from a use-of-proceeds bond to underlying projects. Categories of eligible projects must be clearly defined. The proceeds from use-of-proceeds bonds should be held in a separate account or otherwise tracked to ensure robust governance over bond allocations and accurate reporting.

So-called 'second opinions' on the processes provided by third parties are welcome and encouraged but are not an absolute requirement. Similarly, independent third-party verification of impact metrics is encouraged but not required. Of greater overall value is if the issuer publicly provides complete and transparent information. While Zurich may invest in bonds issued by companies whose whole portfolio of activities could be considered green or social (often referred to as pure plays) in the absence of a clear use-of-proceeds provision and impact reporting, we will not classify such bonds as impact instruments.

A complete list of projects receiving funding from use-of-proceeds bonds must be made available to investors once proceeds are disbursed. Where confidentiality requirements limit the details that can be made public, generic descriptions are acceptable. Issuers must be committed to make good-faith efforts over time to report on the positive environmental and social impact of the projects. Zurich is fully aware of the challenges and limitations of impact reporting and understands that quantitative performance measures may not always be readily available. Still, Zurich expects issuers to report at least one relevant metric per category of projects funded, even if the metric cannot be established for the complete portfolio of projects. Green, social, and sustainability bonds that do not report impact on at least a set of core metrics after a reasonable amount of time, which may be needed to set up first-generation impact reporting frameworks, will not be counted as impact instruments.

Our Approach to Impact Measurement

Measurement helps investors make better investment decisions and communicate to our own stakeholders. It also demonstrates that financial returns can be balanced with environmental and social returns. As the first private-sector investor to commit to specific impact targets, we chose to develop a methodology that allows us to measure impact at a portfolio level – across asset classes and underlying investment instruments and share it back with the market as part of our 'advancing together' strategy.

Metrics

Zurich developed a measurement framework to measure the impact across its impact portfolio for two defined impact metrics: 'CO2-equivalent emissions avoided' and 'number of people who benefited'.

Data on emissions of greenhouse gases (generally quoted in tonnes of CO2-equivalent emissions) is a commonly used indicator to assess the climate impact of an asset. 'Avoided' CO_2e emissions are calculated against a baseline scenario that reflects the most likely project outcomes or level of service achieved in the higher-carbon status quo of the economy (also referred to as 'net' or 'relative' emissions; subtracting the baseline emissions from the absolute, or gross emissions, equals the emissions 'reduced/avoided').

To measure our social objective to 'increase community resilience,' we count the number of people who have benefited from services in education, health, housing or financial inclusion, and other measures aimed at improving lives, improvements that are directly related to Zurich's investments. There is no common market definition for 'people benefited'. While the metric is commonly reported, looking into the reported details is important, and it is necessary to set one's own standard. In our measure we only count those individuals who are part of a specific targeted audience previously unable to access those services, as opposed to the potential audience.

Comparability

Using self-reported numbers and measuring impact through two broadly defined metrics means summing up a heterogeneous field of numbers. By applying a strict definition of what an impact investment is and looking into the wider set of impact metrics for specific investments, we can be sure that the quality of our impact investments is upheld.

Zurich aims to match an investment's impact to a portfolio's invested amount over a series of years. We thus seek to provide impact numbers on an annualised basis, rather than calculating the impact over the entire life of the project, or over the financing period. It is in our own best interest to report only the impact of what we effectively finance. While we acknowledge that the marginal impact of an underlying asset might change as the asset matures (e.g. decreasing impact with changing baseline numbers), the average annualised impact data over an asset lifecycle will provide a balance of the ramp-up and the full operation period.

To make sure we count only the impact an impact investor is financing, impact investors are encouraged to report pro-rata shares. If an impact investor claims the full positive impact of every project, the impact investor would overstate their achievement. For use-of-proceed bonds the pro-rata share is calculated as the impact based on the share of the total project cost that is eligible for the specific use-of-proceed bond.

Measurement

There are two principal steps involved in calculating our overall impact. Step one presumes all data has been captured for projects, including the annualised amount of carbon avoided, along with holdings data. The calculations presented in Figure 13.4 are based on the following equation:

Sum of pro-rata impact of issuer = Total project impact × % Share of total project financing × % Eligibility for use-of-proceed bonds

Step two requires aggregating data on a portfolio level (as shown in Figure 13.5). Matured bonds are excluded and only bonds up to the date the impact report refers to are included in the calculations (therefore excluding 2015 and 2016 maturing bonds, and 2020 bonds). This way of accounting allows us to implicitly extrapolate an issuer's impact that was reported by the amount of additional bonds we bought.

Presuming Zurich holds as of December 2018 green bonds of this issuer of US$295,307,464, the allocation to a portfolio of projects will be as follows:

Impact pro-rata for Zurich's share = Full impact of the project pool × (Zurich outstanding issuance toward specific issuer/full outstanding currency as of time impact report refers to

On that basis, the pro-rate impact for Zurich's share would be 8,472,231 × (295,307,464/3,052,133,600) = 819,709 tonnes CO_2e. That is, Zurich helped to avoid 819,709 tonnes of CO_2e through the financing of green bonds from this specific issuer.

Project	Annual project tCO2e avoided	Loan approved (USDm)	Full project cost (USDm)	% of loan of full project costs	Eligibility for Green Bond (USDm)	% of loan eligible for green bond	Annual pro-rata share tCO2e avoided
1	330,000	50.00	120	42%	16.70	33%	45,925
2	1,000,000	66.08	153	43%	60.06	91%	393,733
3	35,000	40.90	71.6	57%	37.90	93%	18,527
4							...
Total							8,472,231

Figure 13.4 Impact Reported for Sample Green Bond in FY 2017.

ISIN	Issue date	Maturity	Curr	Amount outstanding (CCY)	Amount outstanding (USD)
XS	21.05.2012	19.05.2016	AUD	Matured	
XS	21.05.2012	21.05.2015	TRY	Matured	
XS	26.08.2014	27.08.2019	NZD	3,000,000	2,133,600
XS	19.03.2015	19.03.2025	USD	500,000,000	500,000,000
XS	16.08.2016	16.08.2019	USD	800,000,000	800,000,000
XS	16.08.2016	14.08.2026	USD	500,000,000	500,000,000
XS	10.08.2017	10.08.2022	USD	750,000,000	750,000,000
XS	10.08.2017	10.08.2027	USD	500,000,000	500,000,000
XS	22.03.2018	22.03.2020	HKD	100,000,000	783,480,000
XS	03.04.2018	03.04.2020	HKD	400,000,000	3,133,520,000
Outstanding issuance					**3,052,133,600**

Figure 13.5 Summarised Outstanding Currency.

The same logic holds true for calculating and aggregating the number of people benefited.

While we believe the proposed methodology is a reasonable indication of impact, there are limitations. Given we report using self-reported data by issuers, we disregard different baselines and methodologies when reporting on aggregated CO_2e emissions avoided or people benefited. There is also a discrepancy in the timing of impact reported versus the underlying exposure to the investment. The impact data of the most recent issues is not included when Zurich calculates its latest level of investments. An extrapolation exercise aims to take this into account.

Impact numbers can vary over time for a number of reasons:

- The larger an impact portfolio becomes, the more individual assets, bonds, or issuers will be part of it. The overall effects and dynamics will become more 'alive' with new investments entering the portfolio and other maturing or being sold on a more frequent basis.
- Depending on the type of underlying project, some impacts may only happen once – others will generate annual impact over a variety of years, which might or might not be aligned with the maturity structure of the instrument (an investee might stop reporting with final allocation and before bond maturity; or impact will be generated long into the future but reporting will stop with the instrument maturing).
- Bonds that refinance impact projects will be able to report earlier on the impact created, while bonds that allocate capital to a new set of projects will be subject to a sometimes substantial time lag between capital allocation and impact reporting but might add more value.
- The time lag effect in combination with our volume formula creates a J-curve effect: an issuer that has a good track record of deploying projects to impact and therefore collects fresh capital, will – by dividing impact

reported by the full amount of use-of-proceed bonds outstanding – reduce the impact/US$ for the outstanding portfolio until the new projects are up, running and measured.

- Some impact categories might show diminishing marginal effects. One of these examples is CO_2e avoided: Adding green energy to a relatively green local grid will yield less CO_2e avoided per US$ invested than the first renewable energy plant in a purely fossil powered grid. While this effect might decrease impact numbers over time – contextual interpretation will show that this effect is a good sign for environmental progress in some geographies.

- Better reporting might decrease numbers: Experience shows that first generation reporting frameworks work with assumptions, which sometimes turn out to be too generous. More accurate reporting and experience often decreases impact numbers and increases contextual quality. Counterintuitively – this is a good sign for the progress of the industry.

It is exactly these lessons that lie at the core of impact investment: once impact is habitually measured across projects and time, the resulting numbers in combination with every project's unique context will teach the investor valuable lessons on where deployed capital can create the highest contextualized impact. A higher impact intensity is not better under every circumstance, but the investor's intentionality around impact investing will greatly benefit from these lessons.

Conclusions

Impact investing is a valuable addition to responsible investment. Rather than be treated as a mutually exclusive investment approach, it should be seen as part of the emerging toolbox available to investors committed to responsible investing. This means it can be combined with other methods, such as ESG integration techniques and active ownership, to effectively appraise issuers, value fixed income instruments, and strategically allocate portfolios towards increased positive environmental or social impacts.

However, there are challenges. Lacking a clear impact definition can create confusion and invites criticism from new entrants, regulators, and investors alike for either being too complex, too opaque, or too strict. Alarm over greenwashing and impact-washing is evidence that the impact market faces similar nascent challenges to ESG integration, in that it is still poorly understood. Impact investing is a story still being written, but we are convinced its application will solidify over time and with practice. In the meantime, we have proposed a pragmatic way forward to resolve two of the core debates. When distinguishing between impact investing as an investment strategy and the broader discussion of the impacts of investing, we propose to clearly distinguish the concept of impact investing (positive impact/measurability/intentionality) from footprinting (negative and positive impacts/measurable/

intentional and unintentional). In the debate on whether additionality has to form a qualifying aspect of impact investing, we suggest framing the concept more broadly as 'value added', which can be provided by an impact investor through added capital, depth of impact, or a contribution to the development of the impact investing market.

Despite these ongoing debates, the impact investing market is not bifurcated but firmly accepts the need for a pragmatic approach that incorporates the needs of large institutional investors with wide capital pools. Although still comparatively small relative to overall capital markets, the impact investing market is now large and mature enough for more investors to join. Starting by viewing fixed income markets through an impact lens can be a good entry point, especially for institutional investors.

The use-of-proceeds market shows the clearest evidence that impact investing can be accelerated and that wide opportunities exist. It is necessary to find a balanced approach unique to the context, and which is necessary to understand the improvement, changes, and impact created by each bond. This leads directly to building a measurement framework and the necessary infrastructure. Impact investing requires more resources, processes, and top-down support. The impact investing market is accessible to new entrants, while further work on scaling markets, solidifying instruments, as well as harmonising and improving the quality of data, metrics, processes, and transparency is best tackled through ongoing collaboration.

More work is required across the industry, especially around creating dedicated impact mandates or tilting for impact within existing mandates or adding additional asset classes and topics over time to designing and improving a measurement system. More work is also required to better join up the various pockets within the impact investing ecosystem that lead from proof-of-concept and blended finance vehicles breaking new impact ground to standardized instruments that can be scaled by institutional investors in order to more effectively move capital to fund solutions to some of our most pressing social and environmental issues.

Notes

1 https://iris.thegiin.org/
2 https://indicators.ifipartnership.org/
3 See, generally, https://www.icmagroup.org/green-social-and-sustainability-bonds/resource-centre/
4 ESG integration, active ownership, impact investing, selective exclusion screens and a net-zero by 2050 decarbonisation target.

References

Global Impact Investing Network (GIIN) (2020), *2020 Annual Impact Investor Survey.* [online]. Available at: https://thegiin.org/assets/GIIN%20Annual%20Impact%20Investor%20Survey%202020.pdf (Accessed 2 April 2021).

Global Impact Investing Network (GIIN) (2021a), 'What You Need to Know About Impact Investing'. [online]. Available at: https://thegiin.org/impact-investing/need-to-know/ (Accessed 2 April 2021).

Global Impact Investing Network (GIIN) (2021b), 'Core Characteristics of Impact Investing'. [online]. Available at: https://thegiin.org/characteristics (Accessed 2 April 2021).

Green Bond Principles and ICMA (2020), *Handbook – Harmonized Framework for Impact Reporting*. [online]. Available at: https://www.icmagroup.org/assets/documents/Regulatory/Green-Bonds/Handbook-Harmonized-Framework-for-Impact-Reporting-December-2020-151220.pdf (Accessed 11 January 2021).

International Capital Market Association (ICMA) and the Social Bonds Principles (2020), *Working Towards a Harmonized Framework for Impact Reporting for Social Bonds*. [online]. Available at: https://www.icmagroup.org/assets/documents/Regulatory/Green-Bonds/June-2020/Harmonized-Framework-for-Impact-Reporting-for-Social-BondsJune-2020-090620.pdf (Accessed 2 April 2021).

Operating Principles for Impact Management (OPIM) (2019), *Investing for Impact: Operating Principles for Impact Management*. [online]. Available at: https://www.impactprinciples.org/sites/default/files/2019-06/Impact%20Investing_Principles_FINAL_4-25-19_footnote%20change_web.pdf (Accessed 2 April 2021).

Zurich Insurance Group (2020), *Operating Principles for Impact Management*. [online]. Available at: https://www.zurich.com/-/media/project/zurich/dotcom/sustainability/docs/operating-principles-for-impact-management_disclosure-statement.pdf (Accessed 2 April 2021).

14 The Impact Bond Market[1]

Manuel Adamini and Krista Tukiainen

Global surface temperatures in 2019 were the second warmest since modern recordkeeping began in 1880 (NASA, 2020). This warming puts global ecosystems, already under massive pressure from an ever-growing human population, under further strain. Meaningfully addressing climate change through mitigation and adaptation measures requires transformations spanning all sectors of the economy. That commands huge amounts of investments. Deep and liquid pools of capital must be unlocked through innovative financial solutions. One such innovation is sustainable debt, with green bonds being its most important segment. As of the end of 2020, the green bond market had grown to US$1 trillion issued, with thousands of issues from about 65 countries (Climate Bonds Initiative, 2021). Add to that more than US$370 billion in social and sustainability bonds, many of which also dedicate proceeds to climate mitigation or resilience, and the impact bond market is an asset class in its own right and expected to grow considerably.

This chapter looks at the impact bond market in depth. First, we present a market overview. Second, we explore the characteristics of bonds and impact bonds, with a particular focus on green bonds as the largest component of the market. Third, we analyse the impact bond market from a regional and a technical perspective. We conclude by offering some reflections on the key challenges facing issuers and investors.

Market Overview

Green Bond Basics

Green bonds are structured like regular bonds: debt instruments through which corporates, governments, and other entities can source funding from investors in debt capital markets. Typically, bonds are organised as fixed-term debt contracts, often with a set interest rate or coupon. The key difference between green and conventional (or vanilla) bonds is that the funding raised from green bonds is earmarked to a set of predetermined assets and projects contributing to climate change mitigation, adaptation, and/or resilience, along with other environmental objectives.

DOI: 10.4324/9781003055341-18

The process and definitions for green bond issuance have been shaped by market actors. The most widely adopted framework is the International Capital Markets Association's (ICMA) Green Bond Principles (GBP) (GBP and ICMA, 2018). Initially drafted by a group of banks in 2014 and updated regularly since, the GBP were intended to denote market-wide best practice with a focus on the green bond issuance process by setting out green project categories and guidelines around allocating, managing, and reporting on green bond funding. They comprise four core aspects: (1) use of proceeds; (2) processes for project evaluation and selection; (3) management of proceeds; and (4) reporting. Sister guidelines for loan lenders and borrowers – the Loan Market Association's (LMA) Green Loan Principles (LMA, 2018) – outline a similar framework for green-labelled loans. Both have been widely adopted as a global reference point by issuers and investors and lenders and borrowers alike.

Issuing a Green Bond

Bringing green bonds to market requires debt issuers to pay special attention to the types of assets and projects that will make up the pool of investments eligible for the green bond. These project categories – and in some cases standalone project details – are usually outlined in a document known as the issuer's green bond framework. This lists the criteria that eligible projects must meet, as well as any exclusion criteria, such as fossil fuel-related investments.

Green bond issuers frequently commit to report on how proceeds are used. The intent to report is typically communicated before the bond issuance date in the bond framework, with the actual reporting made available later. Post-issuance reporting is a basic tenet of green bonds. The disclosure of what is financed under a green bond (issuance programme) provides the transparency needed to build investor confidence, market credibility and integrity, and thereby reduces opportunities for 'greenwashing'. Increasingly, there is also an element of reporting on the impact of green bond funding, such as reductions in greenhouse gas emissions.

External Reviews

It is common for issuers to solicit help with drafting the framework and setting up the necessary reporting mechanisms, data collection, and management systems. In addition, market best practice dictates that the framework, which outlines the issuer's overall approach to green bonds, should be assessed for robustness by an outside entity conducting an external review. This involves an independent expert perspective on the issuer's processes and definitions for selecting eligible projects and allocating funding to them, as well as any commitments to transparency via periodic reporting.

The most common green bond external review is a Second Party Opinion (SPO), pioneered by CICERO with their Shades of Green assessment. Its approach dates to one of the world's first green bonds issued by the World Bank in 2008, for which CICERO provided advice and commentary. Market advice has been refined and revised as other players, such as Sustainalytics, ISS ESG, and V.E. have entered the market.

An SPO provides an indication of the expected impacts – positive and negative – of each green bond framework's financing categories. Commentary around compliance with the GBP or other frameworks, such as the EU green taxonomy, may also be included. The SPO model benefits from a relatively high degree of standardisation, aided in part by guidance for providers formulated by ICMA, as well as the European Commission's proposed Green Bond Standard. SPOs offer investors and other parties an opportunity to draw relevant comparisons between green issuance frameworks from different issuers. The Climate Bonds Initiative (2021) finds that 60% of global green bond volume benefits from a valid SPO; in Europe, the number is closer to 100%.

Some issuers opt for green bond ratings issued by credit rating agencies (CRAs). Distinct from traditional credit ratings and akin to other external reviews, green bond ratings focus on the environmental credentials of the bond's use of proceeds as opposed to the issuer's creditworthiness. Green bond rating documents tend to cover similar aspects to those outlined in SPOs, including judgements on compliance with international guidelines and green definitions, and possible risks or controversies. However, these documents are less standardised between different providers than their SPO counterparts. The share of green bonds covered by green bond ratings reflects this trend, standing at only 5%. Regional variations remain: green bond ratings are popular in Japan where R&I and Japan Credit Rating Agency have assessed approximately 44% of local green issuance (Figure 14.1).

Green bond issuers may also opt for assurance reporting provided by an auditing firm. This process considers if the proceeds in a green framework align with global green definitions, assured using a global accounting standard such as the ISAE3000. Assurance is the most robust form of external review but is limited to cases where assets and projects have already been identified, as opposed to outlining eligible categories. It is thus more common to see assurance reports at the post-issuance stage, verifying the disbursement of proceeds to eligible projects. Approximately 11% of green bonds receive assurance.

About 17% of green bonds include certification under the Climate Bonds Standard – a labelling scheme for bonds, loans, and other debt instruments made up of process rules and sector-specific, climate science-aligned performance criteria for green investments. For the certification process issuers must appoint an Approved Verifier to conduct continuous assurance at both the pre- and post-issuance stage to demonstrate compliance with the relevant sector criteria. Certification is broadly comparable to assurance in terms of process robustness but also offers prescriptive definitions on climate-alignment.

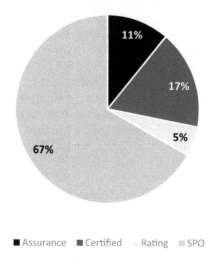

Figure 14.1 Share of Green Bond External Reviews.
Source: Based on Cumulative Issuance by Number.

Bond Labelling

Labelling combined with clear process guidelines for selecting, managing, and communicating allocations of eligible investments can help investors avoid greenwashing. Bond labelling can provide a reliability signal to investors attempting to navigate and scrutinise sustainable debt. Current market practice predominantly relies on issuers to self-label their bonds. This adds to the importance of independent external reviews to scrutinise how the green bond fits the issuer's broader strategy around climate change and other sustainability issues.

Added transparency and earmarked proceeds are not unique to green-labelled debt, with social and sustainability-labelled debt exhibiting identical features. The latter involves a combination of green and social project categories, often characterised by contributions mapped to the UN Sustainable Development Goals (SDGs). Recently, COVID 19-response bonds (pandemic bonds) have been introduced as a subcategory to the social bond universe, though their use ofproceeds is often only very loosely defined. Together, these combined segments are referred to as the green, social, and sustainability or GSS impact bond universe (Figure 14.2).

To guide good practice around social bonds, ICMA released the Social Bond Principles (SBP) in June 2018, building on an initial Social Bond

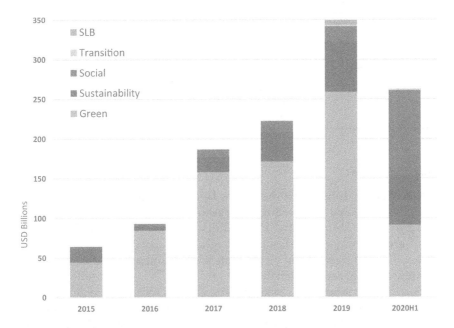

Figure 14.2 Impact Bond Categorisation.
Source: CBI, 2021.

Guidance document from 2016. Updated in June 2020 to further elaborate on social projects funded via labelled bonds, the principles outline processes around transparency and disclosure to maximise positive impacts and communicate this to investors in a consistent manner (ICMA, 2020). ICMA published the Sustainability Bond Guidelines in 2018 to extend the good practice recommendations around transparency and subsequent market integrity within a hybrid theme, drawing upon both GBPs and SBPs.

ICMA continues to contribute to the discourse and development of best practice guidance by running several influential working groups on market innovation. Examples include those on impact reporting, sustainability-linked bonds and, most recently, climate transition finance. The LMA has similarly continued formulating guidance in the loans space, publishing the Sustainability-Linked Loan Principles in 2019.

CBI's analysis finds that bonds issued under the three umbrella themes – green, social, and sustainability – feature a total of at least 60 different labels (Table 14.1). In particular, sustainability-themed labels are growing in popularity, with 40% of treasurers commenting they would consider 'sustainability' over other labels. Several large corporates, including Alphabet Inc with the largest issued labelled bond, have introduced sustainability-themed debt to meet their funding needs (Porat, 2020).

Table 14.1 Selection of Impact Bond Labels.

Green	Social	Sustainability
Green	Social	Sustainability
Green rewards	Social housing	Sustainable development
Climate awareness	Vaccine	Sustainable
Solar	SDG housing	SDG
Environmental	Social inclusion	SRI
Water	Education, youth, and employment	ESG

Source: CBI, 2020a.

Transition Bonds

A widely debated and controversial new label entrant is the 'transition bond'. These bonds extend the labelling and earmarking of proceeds to sectors that find it harder to abate negative externalities or do not fall within the existing set of green definitions and must undergo a low-carbon transition to meet global climate targets. Examples include steel, aluminum, and cement production, mining, and industrials.

This segment is poised for rapid growth as issuers will likely come under increasing stakeholder and regulatory pressure to transition away from assets and activities at risk of becoming stranded. Concerns exist around the relevance, reliability, and availability of transition pathways – and thus the appropriate uses of transition bond proceeds. Several developments aimed at addressing these concerns include the ICMA Climate Transition Finance Handbook (Climate Transition Finance and ICMA, 2020) and the CBI whitepaper on Financing Credible Transitions (CBI, 2020b). While consensus-building is progressing, investors will need to place this nascent market segment under additional scrutiny to ensure no 'transition-washing' occurs.

A further development includes KPI-linked debt instruments, also known as Sustainability-Linked Bonds (SLBs) and Sustainability-Linked Loans (SLLs). These bonds and loans are tied to the issuer meeting one or more predefined, time-bound key performance indicators (KPIs) related to wider sustainability performance targets. In principle, there are few restrictions on how the issuer spends proceeds; so long as the performance improvements are verifiably achieved. An example includes Italian energy utility Enel. To avoid a step-up of the bond's coupon by 25 basis points, the company in September 2019 committed to increase its installed renewable energy generation capacity to 55% by the end of 2021.

Some market participants have concerns related to SLBs and transition bonds. Specifically, questions remain around appropriate sector and/or issuer pathways to decarbonise and implement other sustainability-related improvements. It is frequently unclear what constitutes a sufficient ambition for the KPIs (Nordea, 2020a). Many have, however, welcomed the entity-level target mechanism to encourage more issuance from entities that have greater need to improve their operational environmental footprint (Franklin et al.,

2020) and may struggle to identify a large enough pool of eligible assets or projects for a use of proceeds labelled bond. Signs that this may hold true are already visible with, for example, UAE airline Etihad, fashion house Chanel, and British retailer Tesco all issuing SLBs.

Green Beyond Bonds

The green label can be applied not only to bonds but to virtually any debt format, including loans, private placements, asset-backed securities (ABS), covered bonds, Schuldscheine, and Sukuk (Figure 14.3).

ABS are currently the largest of these segments with roughly $126.5 billion of green-labelled volume issued since the first deals in 2012 from US government-backed mortgage lending institution Fannie Mae. A pioneer in green ABS, Fannie Mae's Green Rewards programme is securitised on mortgage payments and finances energy and water efficiency improvements to multi-family dwellings across the US. As at the end of 2020, the agency's total green ABS issuance amounted to $87.6 billion, or roughly 70% of global green ABS.

Issuances of green-labelled Sukuk – a bond-like financial certificate representing an ownership share of an eligible asset portfolio – has also seen growth with issuance from the Middle East and Southeast Asia. This includes the Islamic Development Bank, the Indonesian Government, and Saudi Electricity. Further growth is expected as local green debt capital markets develop in these regions and beyond.

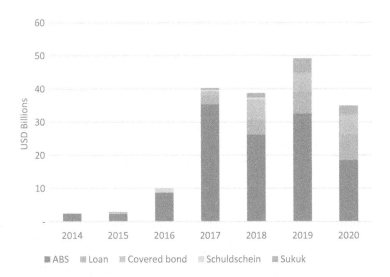

Figure 14.3 Non-bond Green Labelled Debt.
Source: CBI, 2021.

CBI market data indicates that at least $72 billion worth of green loans have been signed to date, with prominent borrowers including Spanish energy company Iberdrola, South Korean chemicals giant LG Chem, and Singaporean property developer M+S. Green loans are likely to benefit further from the growing market shift towards transition. According to some estimates, this market segment, which spans a more diverse borrower base than its green counterpart, comprises nearly $130 billion of annual lending (Nordea, 2020b).

The Climate-Aligned Universe

To understand the untapped potential for climate financing, it is important to also capture non-labelled climate-aligned bonds. These are instruments that are not explicitly labelled as green by an issuer, but can make a substantial contribution to financing climate solutions by funding issuers who undertake largely green activities. These issuers are identified based on their revenues, and the resulting alignment percentage serves as a proxy across their outstanding debt curve.

Many renewable energy companies offer straightforward examples of fully climate-aligned issuers. Denmark's Ørsted is such an issuer, owing to its shift from a fossil fuel energy producer (Dong Energy) to a 100% renewable energy company over the course of a multi-year business transition.

Identifying non-labelled climate-aligned debt is crucial to isolate capital flows financing green assets, which may not be as visible and transparent as labelled bonds. It is also key for discovering opportunities to scale up the labelled green bond market, and for investors to buy into new diversification and yield opportunities. CBI (2021) suggests that the size of the non-labelled climate-aligned debt market is just under $1 trillion of bonds outstanding.

Market Characteristics

This section describes the composition of the green bond market. Based on market data primarily from Climate Bonds Initiative and other sources where explicitly specified, the section examines key characteristics and use of proceeds objectives. All figures are dated to the end of 2020.

Market Size

Despite being a fraction of the overall debt universe, green bonds have witnessed impressive expansion. The market has grown at an average annual rate of 108% between 2007 and 2020. The largest increase by volume came in 2019 when annual issuance reached $266 billion – adding $95 billion to the 2018 total (see Figure 14.4).

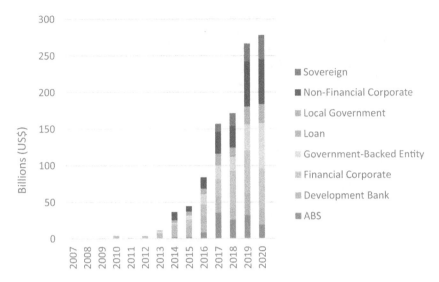

Figure 14.4 Annual Green Bond Issuance by Issuer Type.
Source: CBI, 2021.

Major Issuers

The first green bonds came from multi-lateral development banks: the European Investment Bank in 2007, followed by the World Bank in 2008. Since then, a further 41 development banks from across the world, including the likes of the Asian and African Development Banks, the International Finance Corporation, and the Nordic Investment Bank, have introduced impact bonds and become repeat issuers. The cumulative value from development banks now amounts to $159 billion or 15% of outstanding bonds. The largest deal from this segment is a July 2020 senior unsecured green bond worth €3 billion ($3.5 billion) from Germany's KfW, which notably increased its issuance programme in 2019 (Khadbai, 2019).

Most green bond issuance originates from corporates: non-financial and financial corporate issuers have each contributed around 20% of outstanding bonds. South African commercial bank Nedbank launched the first financial green bond in August 2012 (R4 billion/$481 million). Crédit Agricole and Bank of America joined in 2013. To date, $214 billion of bonds outstanding are issued by 259 financial institutions. Their share grew between 2017 and 2018 (from 15% to 29%), although 2019 saw the most debut issuers in this segment (51). The largest deal (¥30 billion/$4.4 billion) was issued by China's Bank of Communications in November 2016 (Figure 14.5).

Non-financial corporate bonds were pioneered by Vasakronan, a Swedish real estate company, which brought the first non-financial corporate green bond to market in 2013 (SEK 1.3 billion/$153 million). The pool of issuers

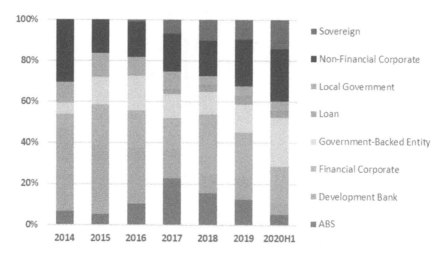

Figure 14.5 Relative Shares of Green Bond Issuer Types over Time.

has since grown to 350. The largest issuance was French energy utility Engie's €2.5 billion ($3.4 billion) green bond from May 2014. There is clear latent demand for this type of deal: nearly all (93%) of the buy-side green bond experts interviewed for the 2019 Climate Bonds Investor Survey highlighted corporate green bonds as their first preference in expanding their portfolios, and ranked (in order of importance) industrials, energy and utilities, consumer discretionary, and materials as the top industry sectors where they would like to see additional issuance (CBI, 2019c).

Government issuers are crucial to bring scale to the green bond market. Local governments, especially from France, were early adopters of the green format, mainly financing low-carbon infrastructure: the first deals came from Ile de France (€120 million/$146 million) and Provence-Alpes-Côte d'Azur (€375 million/$500 million) in March and July of 2012, respectively. When not accounting for the US muni market, most local government issuance comes from Europe (36%), Asia-Pacific (30%), and North America (30%, Canada only). The largest deal is a A$1.8 billion ($1.3 billion) green bond from Australia's Treasury Corp New South Wales from November 2018.

The US municipal bond market provides an interesting green finance avenue for local governments. The first green US muni bond was issued in 2013 by the Commonwealth of Massachusetts, and a further 181 local government issuers have since completed such deals. Additionally, 70 government-backed entities have issued green muni bonds. The total green muni bond issuance figure now stands at $50.7 billion, with the largest deal from the New York Metropolitan Transport Authority ($2 billion, December 2017).

Government-backed entities drive issuance in many markets, focusing on decarbonising underlying infrastructure, such as housing and public transport networks. Examples include the Japan Housing Finance Agency and Japan Railway Construction, Transport and Technology Agency, and France's public transport entities SNCF and Société du Grand Paris. The latter also claims the title of the largest government-backed entity green bond issued to date with a €3 billion ($3.3 billion) deal from October 2020.

The diversified local government green funding space is dominated by the Nordic local government funding agencies Kommuninvest, KommuneKredit, MuniFin and KBN. In February 2020, MuniFin became the first Nordic financial institution to publish a social bond framework. The first issuance against the framework was completed some six months later.

Sovereign green bonds have special value through their ability to meet latent investor demand, set reference benchmarks, catalyse local green bond markets, and contribute to a more diverse set of use of proceeds categories. These bonds often signal national commitments to build low-carbon economies and more than 15 countries have issued green debt. The Republic of Poland was the first in 2016, and was joined by Fiji, France, and Nigeria in 2017. Belgium, Ireland, Indonesia, Lithuania, and the Seychelles followed in 2018. Entrants from 2019 include Chile, Hong Kong Special Administrative Region, and the Netherlands, the latter of which issued the largest sovereign bond to date (€6 billion/$6.7 billion). In 2020, a further four sovereign issuers made their market debut as Egypt, Germany, Hungary, and Sweden issued their inaugural green bonds. Italy, the UK, and Denmark announced their intention to issue bonds in 2021 and beyond.

Total sovereign green bond volume stands at $86.5 billion. Several other governments have opted for social and sustainability labels, with Ecuador and Guatemala in the first category – the former as a global pioneer in January 2020 and the latter in a direct response to the Covid-19 pandemic in May of the same year. The states opting for sustainability labels include Luxembourg, Mexico, South Korea, and Thailand – all entering the market in 2020.

Bond Sizes, Tenors, and Currencies

Sixty percent of green bonds are of benchmark size or larger, with the remainder split between the $100–$500 million size bucket (24%) and under $100 million (16%) (Figure 14.6). Smaller deals are generally much more common in emerging markets – another potential barrier to scaling up green investment in markets that require adaptation. The average deal size for emerging markets is $289 and $120 million for developed markets. The latter is skewed by several small issuances from Fannie Mae; when these are excluded the comparative figure rises to $271 million. In contrast, the average deal size in the Bloomberg Barclays Aggregate Bond Index (Agg) is $1.9 billion, which is heavily influenced by large US Treasury bonds. The average sovereign green bonds value is $1.6 billion; this helps to further highlight the crucial role of sovereign issuers in building scale and mainstreaming the green bond market.

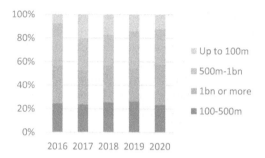

Figure 14.6 Green Bond Sizes.
Source: CBI, 2021.

Figure 14.7 Green Bond Currencies.
Source: CBI, 2021.

Almost three-quarters (74%) of green bond volume is denominated in USD or EUR. A further 21% is issued in CNY, SEK, CAD, AUD, GBP, JPY, CHF, and NOK. Hard currency denominations total 82% of all green issuance (Figure 14.7).

Green bonds have an average tenor of 13.2 years compared to a mean tenor of 8.9 years in conventional bond benchmarks. However, when grouping to tenor buckets, the emphasis shifts to shorter-dated paper: 29% have a term of under five years, and 37% are dated between five and ten years (Figure 14.8). This is in part due to corporates being the lead issuer type; the shorter-dated format generally corresponds better to their funding and liquidity needs. Long-dated paper (10+ years) makes up approximately a third of volume, and only 1% of green debt is perpetual.

The Changing Composition of the Market

The maturity, currency, and size profiles of the market may undergo a significant shift in the coming years due to the market entry of key entities. Perhaps most notably, the European Union has indicated that it may issue up

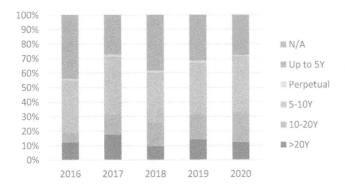

Figure 14.8 Green Bond Tenors.
Source: CBI, 2021.

to €225 billion (approximately $270 billion) in green bonds over the course of 2021 and the next couple of years thereafter. Further, when considering social and sustainability labels, large volume deals will potentially contribute to the investable GSS universe. An example is the EU's SURE social bond issuance programme, whose inaugural €17 billion ($20 billion) bond from October 2020 comprised 10- and 20-year tranches and the subsequent €14 billion deal 5- and 29-year tranches. Almost two-thirds of bond proceeds were allocated to ESG mandated investors. With an issuance ceiling of €100 billion, the liquidity and size of the SURE programme may encourage more investors to introduce product solutions knowing favourable demand, supply, and pricing dynamics are possible.

Geographical Spread

Developed markets constitute 72% of green bond issuance volume. Emerging markets currently make up only 19%, highlighting another area of latent demand and potential for added scale. The remaining 8% is from supranational issuers.

Europe tops the regional issuance ranking with 42% of all outstanding bonds (Figure 14.9). The European share has grown steadily over the years, with 2019 annual issuance peaking at 46%. North America and Asia-Pacific (APAC) are close in second and third place with 24% and 22%, respectively. It is worth noting, though, that without Fannie Mae's green MBS programme, the North American proportion drops to 17% and APAC's is boosted up to 25%. Further growth from the APAC and especially the ASEAN (Association of Southeast Asian Nations) region is expected as green finance centres emerge across the region and countries develop their own green and sustainable bond guidelines (see, for example, CBI (2019a)).

However, the top countries list reflects this only in part (Figure 14.10). The world's largest green bond market in terms of cumulative volume is the US.

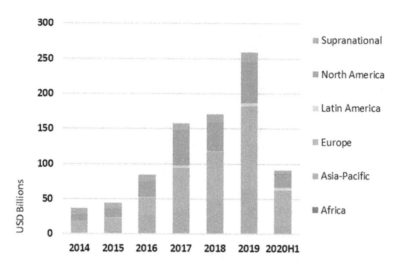

Figure 14.9 Regional Impact Bond Issuance.
Source: CBI, 2021.

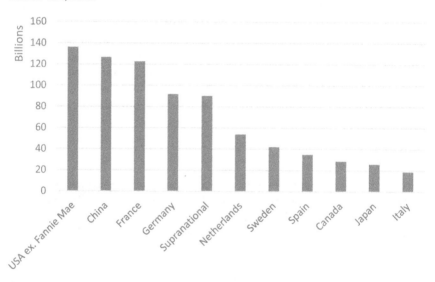

Figure 14.10 Top 10 Green Bond Issuer Countries: Cumulative Volume.
Source: CBI, 2021.

The country has contributed a total of $223.6 billion ($136.1 billion when excluding Fannie Mae). China, which has played a key role in catalysing local green bond markets, follows as a close second, having brought a total of $126.5 billion equivalent to market since the first Chinese green bond from GCN Wind Energy in 2012.

There are six European countries among the top 10 issuers. The larger economies like France and Germany are less surprising than perhaps Sweden, which continues to lead the Nordic region, helped by sovereign green issuance. Canada and Japan, respectively, fill the 8th and 9th places. Issuance from the former is likely to grow further as the Canadian government follows through on its intent to issue green bonds. Probable growth avenues for Japan also include sovereign bonds, as well as climate adaptation and resilience themed debt, and further labelled green bond issuance from climate-aligned issuers (Schumacher et al., 2020).

Market Analysis

Since the first green labelled bond in 2007, many market institutions have contributed to creating a credible green investment ecosystem. The earliest contributions were made by individual issuers, such as the European Investment Bank and the World Bank, which focused their green bonds to finance straightforward green categories, such as renewable energy production.

A comprehensive green classification system for assets and projects began with the Climate Bonds Initiative's Climate Bonds Taxonomy in 2013. The taxonomy led to a certification scheme based on a set of specific technical criteria spanning several industry sectors, which included stringent performance thresholds and disclosure requirements. Prominent examples of certified bonds include sovereign green bonds from the Netherlands and Chilean governments, government-backed entities in France and Japan, the New York Metropolitan Transport Authority, and German automaker Porsche.

The model of a green taxonomy has been supported by the European Commission's Action Plan on Financing Sustainable Growth, which recommended a classification system for sustainable activities to underpin a common framework for the green bonds market and broader sustainable finance. Further proposals for social and governance taxonomies could help to bring more rigour and fill a residual gap in the GSS bond market, providing investors with a tool to assess and compare bonds more accurately while supporting consistent investor reporting. However, it will likely be more challenging to create taxonomy thresholds in the social dimension given the often more qualitative aspects of social outcomes, and the lack of an overarching common sustainability target.

Regional Differences: The Case of China

Green finance has brought regional and local green bond definitions. A notable example is China – currently the world's largest green bond market – where key financial regulators introduced domestic guidelines in 2014. The three key players include the People's Bank of China, the National Development and Reform Commission (NDRC), the China Securities Regulatory

Commission, and the National Association of Financial Market Institutional Investors (NAFMII).

China's domestic green bond guidelines share common ground with international ones in promoting green and sustainable development, but certain differences exist. There are diverging areas of emphasis: whereas international guidelines stress climate change mitigation and adaptation, China's focus is on minimising environmental impacts through pollutant reduction, resource conservation, and ecological protection (CBI, 2019b). These priorities are an attempt to tackle the massive pollution that resulted from China's industrial policy over the past few decades. For several years China's Green Projects Catalogue recognised so-called 'clean utilisation' of coal projects, which were aimed at reducing gaseous air pollutants through washing and processing or coal gasification technologies. This was revised in 2020.

China's green bond guidelines offer some leeway to finance corporate general operating expenditures. For example, the NDRC allows for up to 50% of bond proceeds to be allocated to general working capital. In contrast, the internationally accepted norm is that a vast majority (e.g. at least 90% or even 95% to 100%) of proceeds should be allocated to green assets or projects. As China's market grows and matures, the country is likely to continue its active engagement with international market players to bring convergence between domestic and foreign green standards.

Other markets with dedicated green bond guidelines include the ASEAN region, Chile, India, Mexico, Morocco, and Peru.

Market Data

Despite more data now being available on green bonds from many organisations, deciphering the differences between different bonds from various issuers can be challenging. To help preserve the integrity of green labelling, the Climate Bonds Green Bond Database covers all green bonds and other green-labelled debt instruments issued globally. It tracks those that meet the database requirements set out in the dedicated database methodology separately from those instruments that do not, employing a binary classification system of aligned and non-aligned bonds aimed at helping investors and other market participants in spotting potential shortcomings in ambition or even outright greenwashing.

There are two requirements for issuer inclusion in the green bond database. First, the green debt instrument must be clearly and publicly labelled. Second, the issuer (or other parties including underwriters, external review providers or consultants) must make sufficient disclosure available to determine if the financed assets, projects, and activities are 'green'. Basic information, most notably an issue value and issue date, must also be available. For mapping green bonds the database methodology primarily relies on the Climate Bonds Taxonomy, sector guidance, and Paris Agreement-aligned metrics and indicators. The list of sectors, assets, projects, and activities evolves continually in tandem with market changes.

Bonds that fall short on any of the above requirements – i.e. non-aligned bonds – are added to an 'excluded bonds list'. Bonds may be excluded for three primary reasons. First, misalignment with the taxonomy. Examples include Chinese issuers' financing of thermal coal utilisation. Bonds with ineligible proceeds add up to approximately $68 billion of issuance volume to the end of 2020 (CBI, 2021).

Second, the types of expenditures financed. For example, operating expenditures (opex) have generally been considered as beyond the scope of green bonds unless the issuer can be classified as a pure-play, such as a dedicated renewables company. Bonds funding non-green opex add a further $39 billion of issuance.

Third, exclusion can result where there is insufficient disclosure. Transparency of allocation is key to investor confidence. The Climate Bonds European Green Bond Investor Survey (CBI, 2019c) found that satisfactory green credentials at issuance is the most important factor behind green bond investment decisions; 79% of investors would not buy a green bond if there was a lack of clarity. Climate Bonds data indicates that some $6.9 billion of green bond volume fails this transparency test.

What Is Being Financed?

The Climate Bonds Taxonomy sets out eight broad use of proceeds (UoP) categories eligible for green bond funding. Eighty percent of investors consider energy, buildings, and transport investment categories the most relevant thematic areas for investment (CBI, 2021). This aligns with the general allocation of UoP committed to by issuers (Figure 14.11).

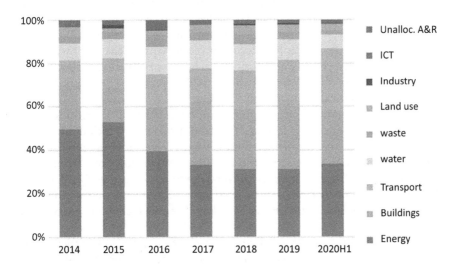

Figure 14.11 Green Bond Use of Proceeds Categories.
Source: CBI, 2021.

Early issuers focused their proceeds on funding renewable energy and low-carbon buildings, along with some transport assets and projects. For example, the EIB initially only financed renewables and building energy efficiency. Issuances from other development banks including the World Bank, the Nordic Investment Bank (NIB), and the African Development Bank (AfDB) had a wider mix of UoP, but the most significant allocations went to the top three categories, energy, buildings, and transport. These themes continue to be the most popular for green bond funding, with 35%, 27%, and 19% of cumulative allocations going to each category, respectively.

Proceed diversification has only been visible in the last couple of years. Energy is a good example: whereas utilities have issued green bonds since 2013 (France-based EDF was the first), grid operators have been relatively scarce with early exceptions from Netherlands-based TenneT (2015) and Finland's Fingrid (2016). Multiple entrants have started to emerge from across the U.S. and Europe, including the UK's National Grid and Spain's Red Eléctrica. In the mobility sector, public transport operators have been joined by less likely issuers, including automobile manufacturers Daimler, Porsche, Volkswagen, and Volvo. The moves by the car giants indicate growing investor and consumer pressure to electrify products and compete with dedicated manufacturers like Tesla.

In the transport category, green bonds fund low-carbon shipping with Japan's Nippon Yusen Kaisha, Mitsui O.S.K Lines, and Nissen Kaiun issuing a total of four bonds in 2018 and 2019 (total $0.2 billion equivalent). A further controversial example came from Teekay Shuttles, which raised $125 million in late 2019 to fund LNG-powered oil tankers. The deal, which was awarded a 'light green' classification by CICERO in their second opinion, was not considered aligned with green definitions due to the continued use of fossil fuels, referred to as the lock-in effect (Nauman, 2019).

Out of the smaller UoP categories, information and communication technology (ICT) has grown in popularity in recent years. Telia and Swisscom, which debuted in February and May 2020, became the fifth and sixth issuer allocating most of their proceeds to the ICT category. They joined peers Millicom, Telefónica, Verizon, and Vodafone.

Land use and industry are the most underfunded UoP categories when considering their emissions impact. The land use category includes forestry, agriculture, and other similar activities, which have great potential in sequestering emissions and contributing to other sustainability objectives, such as food security and biodiversity. Several forestry companies based in the Nordic and Latin American regions have leveraged green bond funding. Examples include Klabin, Stora Enso, Sveaskog, Svenska Cellulosa, and Suzano Papel e Celulose.

Agriculture and food, especially meat production, are also key themes for Latin America given the sector's importance in the region, the history of deforestation to facilitate food production, and attempts to preserve the Amazon rainforest. The topic continues to be widely discussed, especially since

Brazilian protein producers BRF and Marfrig came to market with green and transition bonds, respectively.

The COVID-19 pandemic appears to have generated appreciation for biodiversity issues amongst investors. Available solutions are currently limited but some sovereign green bonds already include relevant allocations: Fiji, Poland, and the Seychelles directed funds to forestry projects, national parks, and marine protected environments, respectively. Biodiversity is also one of the six environmental objectives within the EU Taxonomy.

Climate adaptation and resilience themes have grown. As industry guidelines develop and classify appropriate projects the market has also seen allocations increase. They also originate from a multitude of sectors, such as resilient water infrastructure and flood protection (the Netherlands), to food security and drought management (Indonesia), and adaptation to reduce damages from landslides (Kommunalbanken, Norway). The first bond to include an explicit resilience label was issued by the European Bank for Reconstruction and Development in September 2019. The bonds – aligned with the CBI Climate Resilience Principles – typically fund one of three broad categories of climate resilient projects and assets: infrastructure (water, energy, transport, urban communications); business and commercial operations; and/or agriculture and ecological systems.

Market Reflections

While the impact bond market has grown quickly, the market's breadth and depth are still insufficient to address many challenges ahead. Across the environment spectrum, climate change-related adaptation and resilience activities remain underfunded. Yet paradoxically, issuers lament the scarcity of projects to develop and finance and investors complain about the lack of impact bond supply (CBI, 2020b).

To encourage further development, more guidance is necessary. Issuers prefer more standardised definitions to support their ongoing impact bond issuance programmes and buy-side investors prefer stricter definitions to scale up the market (CBI, 2019b). The EU Taxonomy and similar initiatives are helping to establish the concepts and thresholds needed for investments in sectors that must transition and decarbonise. This includes criteria for high-emitting sectors.

Guidance is for the most part voluntary, which can create confusion with market participants. Bond underwriters report that key prospective issuers from high-emitting sectors were studying the green and sustainable bond market with great interest – but were held back by perceived reputational risk associated with their industry and (legacy) climate or sustainability performance.

A new 'transition' label for those issuers who feel that they cannot (credibly) market conventional green bonds is attractive to a growing number of corporate issuers. A distinction should be made, though, between activities that do not have a long-term role in a low-carbon economy (due to their high emissions and existence of substitutes) and those that do (despite their high emissions or that have an uncertain zero emissions path). In the absence of a market-adopted or binding standard, concerns about gaps or inconsistencies across labels continue and generate accusations of greenwashing. We believe the green label should only be used for eligible investments in activities or entities that have a long-term role to play *and* are either already at or near zero emissions or are following decarbonisation pathways in line with halving global emissions by 2030 and reaching net zero levels by 2050 (i.e. Paris Agreement compliance). Bonds that enable business-as-usual by extending the life of unsustainable business practices are not compatible with the purpose of the impact bond market.

The buy-side market now appears to assess green bonds in the context of issuers' overall sustainability performance, reducing opportunities for greenwashing. This may include using Environmental, Social and Governance (ESG) ratings and/or a proprietary methodology to assess issuer alignment with sustainability definitions and criteria. As a result, significant ESG controversy may result in an issuer's impact bond being rejected. Post-issuance controversy is also possible, as seen with the State Bank of India's green bond and concerns over its coal lending programme (Raqshan, 2020).

Debate amongst market participants also focuses on whether impact bond re-financing or only new financing should be permitted – also referred to as 'additionality'. The concern is that refinancing allows issuers to market their green credentials without further work towards new low-carbon, sustainable operations. Market guidelines are relatively uniform in their view: The Green Bond Principles and the Climate Bonds Taxonomy both posit that refinancing as well as new financing are eligible, as long as the shares of each is disclosed and a maximum refinancing look-back period (commonly three years) be respected and disclosed.

Refinancing projects can give investors confidence that issuers are continuously investing into low-carbon assets and projects. Some 89% of active green debt instruments come from repeat issuers (CBI, 2021). This implies that a large or growing pool of green assets and projects to (re)finance exists. Repeat issuance also establishes collaboration between market participants and within issuer organisations. This organisational learning is often perceived by issuers as even more important than lower funding costs (CBI, 2020c). Although only a small share of issuers commit to dedicating the capital freed up from refinancing to green investment, many provide further information about their wider climate and sustainability strategy as part of their green bond framework. This suggests that green bond issuance and a wider transition (or enhanced sustainability strategy) are complementary and happen in parallel – crucial for an issuer's transition to low-carbon operations.

Also, the additionality debate often downplays the fact that refinancing is the main role of bonds in the capital structure. Conventional bond issuers routinely rely on issuance to refinance rather than provide initial capital for assets and projects. Therefore, refinancing is natural and necessary for green bonds and there have been no noteworthy indications of lower demand for green bonds for refinancing proceeds versus new financing.

Conclusions

To prevent catastrophic changes to our life support systems we must invest $2.4tn annually in energy systems changes alone (IPCC, 2019). The investment required for developing countries to meet the UN Sustainable Development Goals is around $2.5tn per year (UNCTAD, 2019). Green and other sustainable debt issuance contributes to providing such finance.

As the most prominent impact instrument with more than $1 trillion of issuance, green bonds are a legitimate part of many investors' portfolios. They are in many ways identical to non-green bonds, serving a key function in the capital structure: refinancing existing assets to free up capital and facilitate new investment. Some key differences include selecting, managing, and reporting on use of proceeds, which is a new process for many issuers.

Market moves to better define green and impact bonds has improved much-needed diversification opportunities for investors and issuers alike. In tandem with green bonds, broader thematic bonds that seek positive environmental and/or social outcomes have accelerated, supported by post COVID-19 sustainability recovery goals. More recently, sustainability-linked bonds create financial penalties and incentives for issuers by focusing on broader sustainability goals, which, if well calibrated, can open up the possibility of more accountability for issuers and investors.

The number and quality of market participants makes impact bonds a transparent evolving asset class. Expertise is drawn from many segments and the market collaborates on ensuring structures and guidelines – ahead of regulatory efforts to define the market with its dedicated classification systems. Yet, regional differences qualifying green investment continue to challenge issuers and investors.

Green bond issuance is dominated by select sectors and use of proceeds focuses on green buildings, renewable energy, and (public) transport. Deal sizes are behind those of international benchmarks. The market is now established but needs to scale up faster and more purposefully. Voluntary and regulatory mechanisms are necessary to support issuers with verifiable strategies, targets, and performance, including in hard-to-abate sectors. This will require entities with some of the highest emissions levels to reorient themselves, planning and implementing new pathways in a world that has renewed priorities for sustainability and climate action.

Note

1 We would like to thank Miguel Almeida who reviewed and commented on an earlier draft of this chapter.

References

Climate Bonds Initiative (2019a), *ASEAN Green Finance State of the Market.* [online]. Available at: https://www.climatebonds.net/resources/reports/asean-green-finance-state-market-2019 (Accessed 26 April 2021).

Climate Bonds Initiative (2019b), *China Green Bond Market 2019 Research Report.* [online]. Available at: https://www.climatebonds.net/system/tdf/reports/2019_cbi_china_report_en.pdf?file=1&type=node&id=47441&force=0 (Accessed 26 April 2021).

Climate Bonds Initiative (2019c), *European Green Bond Investor Survey.* [online]. Available at: https://www.climatebonds.net/system/tdf/reports/gb_investor_survey-final.pdf?file=1&type=node&id=40171&force=0 (Accessed 26 April 2021).

Climate Bonds Initiative (2020a), *Climate Bonds Taxonomy.* [online]. Available at: https://www.climatebonds.net/files/files/CBI_Taxonomy_Tables_January_20.pdf (Accessed 26 April 2021).

Climate Bonds Initiative (2020b), *Financing Credible Transitions.* [online]. Available at: https://www.climatebonds.net/resources/reports/financing-credible-transitions-white-paper (Accessed 26 April 2021).

Climate Bonds Initiative (2020c), *Green Bond Treasury Survey.* [online]. Available at: https://www.climatebonds.net/system/tdf/reports/climate-bonds-gb-treasurer-survey-2020-14042020final.pdf?file=1&type=node&id=47035&force=0 (Accessed 26 April 2021).

Climate Bonds Initiative (2021), *Market Data.* [online]. Available at: https://www.climatebonds.net/market/data/ (Accessed 26 April 2021).

Climate Transition Finance and ICMA (2020), *Climate Transition Finance Handbook: Guidance for Issuers. December 2020.* [online]. Available at: https://www.icmagroup.org/assets/documents/Regulatory/Green-Bonds/Climate-Transition-Finance-Handbook-December-2020-091220.pdf (Accessed 26 April 2021).

Franklin, A., Davies, P., Domínguez, I. and Wyatt, K. (2020), 'Sustainability-linked Bonds Complement and Bolster the Sustainable Finance Market', *Environmental Finance.* [online]. Available at: https://www.environmental-finance.com/content/analysis/sustainability-linked-bonds-complement-and-bolster-the-sustainable-finance-market.html (Accessed 26 April 2021).

Green Bond Principles (GBP) and International Capital Market Association (ICMA) (2018), *Green Bond Principles: Voluntary Process Guidelines for Issuing Green Bonds.* [online]. Available at: https://www.icmagroup.org/assets/documents/Regulatory/Green-Bonds/Green-Bonds-Principles-June-2018-270520.pdf (Accessed 2 April 2021).

International Capital Market Association (ICMA) (2020), *Sustainability-linked Bond Principles.* [online]. Available at: https://www.icmagroup.org/assets/documents/Regulatory/Green-Bonds/June-2020/Sustainability-Linked-Bond-PrinciplesJune-2020-100620.pdf (Accessed 25 August 2020).

Intergovernmental Panel on Climate Change (IPCC) (2019), *Summary for Policymakers.* [online]. Available at: https://www.ipcc.ch/site/assets/uploads/sites/2/2019/05/SR15_SPM_version_report_LR.pdf.

Khadbai, B. (2019), *KfW to Ramp Up Green Bond Supply.* [online]. Available at: https://www.globalcapital.com/article/b1fd30y1jpy27x/kfw-to-ramp-up-green-bond-supply (Accessed 26 April 2021).

Loan Market Association (LMA) (2018), *Green Loan Principles.* [online]. Available at: https://www.lma.eu.com/application/files/9115/4452/5458/741_LM_Green_Loan_Principles_Booklet_V8.pdf (Accessed 26 April 2021).

National Aeronautics and Space Administration (NASA) (2020), *NASA, NOAA Analyses Reveal 2019 Second Warmest Year on Record.* [online]. Available at: https://www.nasa.gov/press-release/nasa-noaa-analyses-reveal-2019-second-warmest-year-on-record (Accessed 26 April 2021).

Nauman, B. (2019), 'Investors Balk at Green Bond from Group Specialising in Oil Tankers', *Financial Times.* [online]. Available at: https://www.ft.com/content/b1d4201c-f142-11e9-bfa4-b25f11f42901 (Accessed 26 April 2021).

Nordea (2020a), *Lessons from the Infant Sustainability-linked Bond Market.* [online]. Available at: https://insights.nordea.com/en/sustainability/sustainability-linked-bonds/ (Accessed 26 April 2021).

Nordea (2020b), *The Sustainable Loan Market: A Snapshot of Recent Developments.* [online]. Available at: https://insights.nordea.com/en/sustainability/sustainable-loan-market/ (Accessed 26 April 2021).

Porat, R. (2020), *Alphabet Issues Sustainability Bonds to Support Environmental and Social Initiatives.* [online]. Available at: https://blog.google/alphabet/alphabet-issues-sustainability-bonds-support-environmental-and-social-initiatives/ (Accessed 26 April 2021).

Raqshan, T. (2020), *Asset News, After AXA, Amundi Dumps Indian Bank SBI's Green Bonds over Coal Financing.* [online]. Available at: https://www.assetnews.com/asset-managers/after-axa-amundi-dumps-indian-bank-sbis-green-bonds-over-coal-financing (Accessed 26 April 2021).

Schumacher, K., Chenet, H. and Volz, U. (2020), 'Sustainable Finance in Japan', *Journal of Sustainable Finance & Investment*, 10(2), pp. 213–246.

United Nations Conference on Trade and Development (UNCTAD) (2019), *SDG Investment Trends Monitor.* [online]. Available at: https://unctad.org/system/files/official-document/diaemisc2019d4_en.pdf (Accessed 26 April 2021).

15 Using Bond Markets to Achieve Issuer Sustainability Outcomes[1]

Peter Munro

In the first two decades of the 21st century climate risk and opportunity has sharpened the attention of fixed income investors. Growing political commitment towards climate action has the potential to change the long-term credit rating outlooks of certain industries. Investors also face huge demand to support the transition to a low-carbon economy through green bonds, a specific bond structure first developed by the European Investment Bank (EIB) to fund projects with positive environmental impacts. Over the long term it is hoped green bond proceeds will support issuers' response to environmental transition and adaptation risks, delivering financial and sustainability outcomes.

Drawing upon the experience of EIB, the chapter identifies the key forces supporting the green bond market's growth since 2007 and its future development. The chapter starts by describing the EIB's unique position in capital markets. It then describes the key features EIB identifies in bringing a green, impact-oriented bond to market, and reflects on the factors that have driven the green bond market, the financial market impact of green bonds, and the catalysing force of regulation.

About the EIB

Owned by the 27 Member States of the European Union (EU), the EIB is the long-term financing institution of European Union and one of the main vehicles of common economic policy in the union. It is the largest multilateral lending institution in the world, with assets of EUR 554billion as of 31 December 2019.

The EIB's main priorities have traditionally been to provide long-term financing for large-scale infrastructure projects and to provide loans to banks to support their lending to small and medium-sized enterprises (SMEs). In general, EIB's activities aim to address market failure, to cushion the impact of economic downturns by acting counter-cyclically, and to provide sustainable and enduring investments, in the broadest sense.

DOI: 10.4324/9781003055341-19

The EIB is one of the world's largest and most frequent bond issuers, and the largest supranational issuer. It started issuing green bonds in 2007 and was the largest supranational issuer of this product over the subsequent decade.

EIB's lending/financing activities focus on the following areas:

- As the EU's Climate Bank, a priority focus is on climate and environmental sustainability: taking action to address the climate and environment emergency, notably in the critical decade 2021–2030.
- Innovation and skills: promoting skills and innovation at every level.
- Infrastructure: connecting Europe's citizens, internal markets, and economies.
- SMEs: supporting the backbone of the EU's economy.
- Cohesion: pushing for a balanced territorial development that will leave no one behind.
- Development: promoting sustainable growth, reducing poverty and inequality, and improving lives around the world, not just within the EU.

The EIB also invests in initiatives that create links between people, businesses, and economies. These include investments in:

- Economic resilience (e.g. the Economic Resilience Initiative, which is building economic resilience for the EU's Southern Neighbourhood and the Western Balkans).
- Circular economy to support a sustainable, competitive economy.
- Gender equality, to ensure the projects the EIB finances protect all parts of our communities.
- Sustainable oceans, to support a sustainable blue economy and initiatives to protect our oceans.
- Youth, to improve the younger generation's performance on the labour market.

In 2019, the EIB Board of Directors approved a new set of ambitious targets for climate action and environmental sustainability. These included aligning new financing activities with the principles and goals of the Paris Agreement from the start of 2021. This alignment commits EIB to making its financing activities consistent with a pathway towards EU commitments to net zero emissions in 2050 and with climate-resilient development. The commitment to net zero emissions means that new investment should not undermine efforts to achieve the 1.5°C warming threshold. Climate-resilient development requires, for example, that infrastructure built today be resilient to the risks posed over the course of its operating life by a rapidly changing climate.

As part of its new climate goals, the EIB will support €1 trillion of investments in climate action and environmental sustainability in the critical decade from 2021 to 2030, and will gradually increase the share of its financing dedicated to climate action and environmental sustainability to reach 50% of its operations in 2025. The EIB also announced that it would end financing unabated fossil fuel energy generation resulting in GHG emissions above 250 gCO$_2$/kWh and thus large-scale energy production based on unabated fossil fuels.

In November 2020, the EIB launched its Climate Bank Roadmap,[2] a business plan that sets out in detail how the EIB Group aims to support the objectives of the European Green Deal and support sustainable development outside the European Union, while accelerating the transition to a carbon neutral and climate resilient economy by 2050. The Roadmap revolves around four main workstreams: (1) accelerating the transition through green finance; (2) ensuring a just transition for all; (3) supporting Paris-aligned operations; and (4) building strategic coherence and accountability. This structure will help shape EIB Group business development, including with respect to financial and advisory product innovation.

In reviewing each of these focus areas, four general messages emerge as to the role of the EIB Group. The first is the need to substantially increase adaptation efforts, in line with the EU Adaptation Strategy. The second is the need to increase investment in innovative green technologies – from early-stage research through to pilot demonstration of technologies, complemented with support for new business models (such as battery storage, demand response, low-carbon hydrogen, e-charging). The third is the importance of driving down the long-term cost of capital for capital-intensive green infrastructure such as urban public transport, rail and energy networks, waste and water networks. The fourth is the importance of aggregation, scalability, and replicability in ensuring investment at scale; this is particularly relevant for adaptation, energy efficiency, and sustainable agriculture. The EIB is active across such areas today, in the EU and in developing countries.

EIB's lending activities are generally funded via bond issuance in the international capital markets. Its borrowing authorisation for 2021 is up to EUR 70 billion. EIB bonds are of the highest credit quality. The EIB is rated triple-A by Moody's, Standard and Poor's, and Fitch. Major factors backing the EIB's credit standing and triple-A rating include joint European sovereign ownership and support, outstanding asset quality, and conservative risk management.

EIB issues a very wide range of debt products, in terms of size, currencies, maturities, and structures. Its bonds are bought by institutional and retail investors around the world. Benchmark/reference bonds are characterised by large and liquid issuance sizes, using benchmark maturities, and with a regularity of issuance. The bulk of EIB's bonds are issued in benchmark size: in euro in the EARN format, in the global format in US dollars, and in sterling under the GBP benchmark programme. EIB's benchmark bond issues have historically offered a yield pick-up more than the sovereign benchmark. In addition to the benchmark issues in the core currencies, EIB also provides benchmark size issues in several other currencies.

In 2007, the EIB issued the world's first green bond, then labelled a Climate Awareness Bond (CAB). As of 2020, EIB remains among the world's leading issuers of green bonds, with over EUR 33.7billion raised across 17 currencies, including €6.8 billion in 2020. The EIB provides the market with benchmark CAB issuances in EUR, USD, and GBP, but has also issued CABs in AUD, BRL, CAD, CHF, DKK, HKD, INR, JPY, MXN, NOK, PLN, SEK, TRY, and ZAR. EIB is increasing the liquidity, size, and scale of green bond issuance, in addition to gradually building green reference yield curves.

Green Bond Issuance

The Drive for Transparency

In 2007, EU leaders set targets for climate action, including quantified objectives for greenhouse gas reduction. At the time, green finance and environmental, social, and governance (ESG) considerations by investors and issuers were not widespread and driving awareness across capital markets was extremely important. The EIB saw an opportunity to introduce a new instrument that would drive the attention of capital markets towards ESG goals, including science-based climate imperatives.

Demand for sustainable assets was not a mainstream allocation for investors when the EIB started issuing green bonds (see Table 15.1). This made green bond issuance a developmental challenge; there were few debt investors with a systematic approach to ESG, and there was a lack of established market precedents or practices on the sell-side. The EIB's inaugural CAB in 2007 was the world's first bond focusing on climate protection with a core new feature: the EIB pioneered the ring-fencing of proceeds for allocation to future EIB lending investments, with a focus on renewable energy and energy efficiency. In addition, the EIB committed to reporting on the management and allocation of bond proceeds. To support structural innovation further, the bond offered a return in the form of a single payment at maturity linked to a new ESG equity index, the FTSE4Good Environmental Leaders Europe 40 Index. Investors were also offered the option to use a part of their return to buy and cancel EU CO_2 allowances, issued under the EU Emission Trading System. The inaugural CAB bond issuance was in response to policy developments and tested niche demand from investors concerned about climate change.

In subsequent years, green bond issuance has become a strategic objective: contributing to the growth of the green bond market by supplying liquid, benchmark-size transactions while also meeting more targeted investor needs. The EIB's initiatives proved a public good by offering a template for green bonds that could be widely adopted. For example, impact reporting

Table 15.1 EIB Impact Bond Issuance (EUR m).

Year	Total	AUD	BRL	CAD	CH	DKK	EUR	GBP	HKD	INR	JPY	MXN	NOK	PLN	SEK	TRY	USD	ZAR
EIB CAB & SAB ISSUANCE (EUR million)																		
2021	2,937.32	787		651			1,500											
2020	10,522.90	302	7	345		201	5,050	682	33	17		2	175		674		3,035	
2019	4,099.60	342				402	1,150	874						232	187		913	
2018	4,520.31	1,082		468			1,500								259		1,211	
2017	4,289.41	220					2,200								498	26	1,346	
2016	3,846.95			343			1,250	655							258	23	1,319	
2015	3,959.65			342			2,400	1,119							27	36		36
2014	4,268.28				283		2,200	601			36				230		794	126
2013	1,377.90						1,150								191			36
2012	349.81														350			
2010	543.69	172	138													86		148
2009	214.29														214			
2007	600.00						600											
Total	41,530.10	2,905	145	2,148	283	603	19,000	3,930	33	17	36	2	175	232	2,887	170	8,618	347

was initially a key market differentiator but also supported greater transparency across the market. To support even greater progress, the EIB played a key role in the development of global market governance and standards, initially via the Green Bond Principles (GBPs),[3] and later by advocating for the establishment of a single EU taxonomy for sustainable activities.

The EIB's and the market's early green bonds brought a high level of clarity to impact investment in fixed income. The CABs set the pace with transparent use of proceeds for demonstrably environmental projects and activities, evidenced with reporting focusing on an eligible list of project categories, set out in the legal documentation. This legal commitment was a watershed moment, offering investors a formal statement of environmental intent that can improve accountability in spending investor capital. As noted by Aldo Romani, now Head of Sustainability Funding at EIB:

> Green bonds have been adding to the capacity of the market to assess with a high degree of confidence what is happening in underlying green activities. They are the opposite of greenwashing because they have created the possibility to ask questions regarding the underlying activities.
>
> (Cripps, 2018)

By introducing green bond transparency and disclosure standards, the EIB has set a high bar for other issuers. Compatible with the best practice standards the EIB helped define, all CAB issued bonds meet the four core components of the Green Bond Principles (GBP and ICMA, 2018): a use-of-proceeds framework; a process for project evaluation and selection; management or governance of proceeds; and reporting. These are elaborated on in the following sections.

Use-of-Proceeds Framework

From the start, to build market understanding and confidence, the EIB committed to allocate proceeds to clearly identified environmental project categories, with readily verifiable climate action credentials. The use of proceeds framework provides a description of proceeds that should be included in the legal documentation of green bonds.

The bond prospectus for each CAB issued after April 2019 states that proceeds will be allocated to activities that contribute to this purpose by avoiding or reducing greenhouse gas emissions or enhancing greenhouse gas removals through means, including through process or product innovation, in line with evolving EU sustainable finance legislation and the related technical expert group conclusions. Additional conditions and exclusions for eligibility include (EIB, 2020a):

- Investments in hydropower with 'greenfield' water storage capacity are eligible only if the net or relative greenhouse gas (GHG) emissions of the project are negative (i.e. the project results in GHG emission savings compared to the project baseline).

- Investments in nuclear energy are not eligible.
- Investments involving heat production, heat supply, and combined heat and power production are not eligible if coal is used.
- Investments involving the co-firing of fossil fuels and renewable fuels may be partially eligible, only if the overall GHG emissions of the project are below the threshold for the Bank's Emissions Performance Standard as applicable at the time of appraisal.

Project Evaluation and Selection Criteria

The GBPs state that green bond issuers should clearly communicate to investors the environmental sustainability objectives and the process by which the issuer determines how the projects fit within the eligible Green Projects categories and the related eligibility criteria. The EIB has adopted objectives consistent with the following articles of the Treaty on the Functioning of the European Union, and in the 2030 EU Climate and Energy Policy Framework, approved by the EU Council in 2014 (EIB, 2020a):

- Preserving, protecting, and improving the quality of the environment, protecting human health, prudent and rational utilisation of natural resources, promoting measures at international level to deal with regional or worldwide environmental problems, and in particular combating climate change.
- In the context of the establishment and functioning of the internal energy market with regard to the need to preserve and improve the environment, shall aim, in a spirit of solidarity between EU member states to promote energy efficiency and energy saving, and the development of new and renewable forms of energy.
- Minimum 40% (in 2021 updated to 55%) domestic reduction in EU GHG emissions by 2030 compared to 1990; minimum 32% share of renewable energy consumed in the EU by 2030; and minimum 32.5% improvement in energy efficiency by 2030.

CAB proceeds are allocated to lending activities that, in the new EU parlance, substantially contribute to 'climate change mitigation'. These investments include the following, and the eligibility has progressively been enlarged:

- Electricity and heat production from renewable energy sources such as wind, solar, aerothermal, geothermal, hydrothermal and ocean energy, hydropower, biomass, landfill gas, the organic portion of municipal waste incineration, sewage treatment plant gas and biogases; related renewable component manufacturing facilities; infrastructure associated with the supply of renewable energy such as electricity or heat storage, substations, and transmission lines; and investments in distribution systems to enable the penetration of small scale renewable energy generation.

- Energy efficiency projects such as high efficiency combined heat and power (CHP) plants (excluding coal), refurbishment and extension of district heating and cooling systems, substantial energy savings in commercial and industrial facilities, and public lighting; SME involved in energy efficiency component manufacturing, sale, or installation; building refurbishments achieving cost-optimal refurbishment levels; and the construction of near-zero energy buildings (from 2016 to 2020).

For renewable energy investments, markets intuitively recognise their importance. For energy efficiency, markets expect more detail on project selection criteria. A credible benchmark was adopted, in the form of the EU targets for emission reductions, which the EIB adhered to in energy efficiency projects. In short, the EIB was offering confidence that these investments were clearly associated with climate action.

Upon adoption of the EU Sustainability Taxonomy, CABs will highlight the sustainability of the relevant features of EIB's lending portfolio, in line with criteria established by the EU for capital market participants. The EIB is implementing a taxonomy transition plan and CAB development plans for this purpose. These are intended to ensure that CABs finance economic activities that substantially contribute to climate mitigation objectives and 'do no significant harm' to other environmental objectives. In 2020, the EIB announced a first extension of CAB-eligibilities from Renewable Energy and Energy Efficiency to two further areas: (1) electric rail infrastructure and vehicles and other electric public land transport vehicles, and (2) research, development, and deployment of innovative low carbon technologies.

Management of Proceeds

In line with subsequent GBP recommendations, the net proceeds of each green bond issue are allocated within EIB's treasury to an operational money market sub-portfolio. To address one of the lingering investor concerns regarding the delivery of environmental investments, the EIB promised regular reporting on use of proceeds, to assure investors of the progress of their investments. This entails communication and collaboration among different parts of the organisation, from bond originators to environmental sector experts, the latter responsible for project evaluation and selection, which requires a near real-time track record and allocation of all eligible net proceeds. A dedicated IT tool has been designed for the automated tracking of CAB-data, including the retrieval/processing/matching of eligible loans, eligibility percentages, disbursement and new issue flows, and unallocated balance of the CAB-proceeds. This results in reliable and standardised reporting of information on the use of proceeds.

Accountability is essential in communicating the expected bond out-comes. Specifically, the EIB promised that the allocation of proceeds would be tracked and reported transparently, in its formal audited reporting (EIB, 2020b). In addition, the EIB offered regular reporting via its website and newsletters. This would demonstrate the allocation of future disbursements to environmental projects, offsetting the volume of treasury holdings gener-ated by green bond issuance. This offered markets a new level of transparency and accountability. The EIB green bond approach, including reporting, is underpinned by a green bond framework. Reporting is subject to annual external audit.

Impact Reporting

Investors have a growing interest in credible and comparable reporting of impact. This involves rigorous metrics for quantitative and qualitative assess-ment of environmental performance.

The genesis of impact reporting for green bonds owes a significant amount to multilateral development banks (MDBs). The EIB had been working with other development banks on tracking and measuring climate finance to firm up a harmonised approach on impact reporting. In September 2014, during the United Nations (UN) Summit on Climate Change, the EIB – jointly with the African Development Bank (AfDB), the Asian Development Bank (ADB), the European Bank for Reconstruction and Development (EBRD), the International Bank for Reconstruction and Development (IBRD), and the Inter-American Development Bank (IDB) – published a statement to reinforce climate finance. The statement recognised the role of MDBs in cat-alysing the green bonds market and stressed that 'going forward, [the MDBs] aim to maintain [their] developmental role, in order to spur further sustaina-ble growth of the green bond market' (EIB, 2014).

The following year the EIB worked with other MDBs on a proposal for green bond impact reporting harmonisation, coordinating the work and drafting of the framework. The proposal was launched during COP 21 in December 2015 (EIB, 2015). This lent a dose of realism to bond issuers and investors, showing which metrics were most relevant. Also, it resulted in clearer views on which data could reasonably be sourced. For example, ex-ante estimates of impact were deemed a more realistic set of data for re-porting impact at scale. The alternative, ex-post impact evaluations could be technically or economically challenging, and would occur after investors had already allocated their capital. The coalition of expert development bank engineers, scientists, and economists behind such views offered a convincing thesis and helped investors to frame realistic demands for issuers. Over time a range of sectoral guidance was developed by the GBP Working Group on Impact Reporting, focusing on sectors in highest demand among GBP Mem-bers and Observers.

The EIB Climate Awareness Bond Impact Report indicates the EIB's share in the total project cost and provides quantitative information on ten impact indicators (pro rata as applicable):

1 Renewable electricity capacity added (megawatt (electrical) or MW-e)
2 Renewable electricity capacity rehabilitated (MW-e)
3 Renewable heat capacity added (megawatt (thermal), or MW-th)
4 Renewable electricity produced (gigawatt-hours (electrical) per year, or GWh-e/y)
5 Renewable heat produced (gigawatt-hours (thermal) per year, or GWh-th/y)
6 Primary energy savings (gigawatt-hours per year, or GWh/y)
7 Total transmission lines (kilometres, or km)
8 Smart energy meters installed
9 Absolute GHG emissions (kilotonnes of carbon dioxide (equivalent), or $ktCO_2e$)
10 Relative GHG emissions $(ktCO_2e)$[4]

The CAB impact report relies on information collected, verified, and validated independently by the Projects Directorate. The approach to GHG emissions calculations is transparent, addressing a recurring investor hope for clarity on methodology, to help validate credibility and assess comparability. The EIB's emissions methodologies are defined publicly, and updated regularly.

A detailed methodological process and operational management enables EIB to deliver consistent and regular reporting on green bond allocations. Transparency helps investors compare the impact of EIB's green bond activity both against other EIB bonds and against bonds issued by others. The EIB provides a project-by-project evaluation that can be aggregated to determine overall performance (see Table 15.2).

Table 15.2 Consolidated Impact Metric Indicators for 2019 Green Bonds Issued by EIB.

Metric	Sum
Renewable electricity capacity added (MWe)	7,266.145
Renewable electricity capacity rehabilitated (MWe)	1,127.8
Renewable electricity produced (GWh-e/y)	21,044.46
Renewable heat capacity added (MW-th)	585.14
Renewable heat produced (GWh-th/y)	2,895.73
Primary energy savings (GWh/y)	2,835.386
Total transmission lines (km)	5,208.5
Absolute GHG emissions (kt CO_2e)	2,849.1
Smart energy meters installed	43,962
Relative GHG emissions (kt CO_2e)	−11548.5

External Reviews

Third-party validation of an issuer's green bond framework and reporting builds credibility. Accountability through external reviews responds to investor requests for a layer of independent due diligence. Investors increasingly prioritise obtaining third-party assurance on the environmental character of investments to address the need for scalable analysis and their own sustainability portfolio investment mandates.

The vast majority of issuers employ external reviewers or verifiers from the outset. Reviews now typically begin by verifying the green bond framework, including expected environmental features of the use of proceeds, and post issuance verification may include assurance that funds were used as promised – first utilised by the EIB. The World Bank, by having its green bond framework reviewed by a scientific committee, had launched another now familiar feature of these independent opinions, commonly known as second party opinions (SPOs), and focused on establishing environmental credibility. The emergence of SPOs, typically evaluating a green bond framework and potentially other features such as allocations or reporting, has been a key development supporting the establishment of green bonds as an asset class. The EIB looked for ways to further underscore the quality of an SPO, and appointed an external auditor to validate its green bond approach via 'reasonable assurance', setting a new high watermark for an SPO.

The Success Factors Behind Global Standards

The green bond market has grown at an impressive rate. Global annual issuance has increased from less than USD 50billion in 2014 to USD 270billion in 2020 (Environmental Finance, 2021). The success of the GBPs and the subsequent surge in issuance are largely due to the broad support from high-quality market participants, who collaborated to build market standards, confidence, and acceptance. This broad support was facilitated by a global governance platform that oversees the green, social, and sustainability bond principles.

This platform, with a secretariat overseen by the International Capital Market Association (ICMA), developed the GBPs. It aimed to create more transparency for investors and develop standards for issuers. It is led by an executive committee combining issuers, investors, and underwriters in equal numbers, who oversee matters related to the Principles and guide the overall development of the market employing the Principles. In addition, in order to streamline and expedite management, a Steering Group was formed, where the EIB later provided its first chairperson.

Moreover, to ensure progress and assemble views efficiently, a series of working groups were created, many of which involved the EIB. These working groups were a fundamental driver of market development, covering critical areas and challenges, including: (a) green project eligibility (i.e. GBP use-of-proceed definitions); (b) impact reporting; and (c) frameworks, such as sustainability-linked bonds.

There was also valuable involvement from ICMA members and observers, who became increasingly involved in working groups. By 2020 there were 206 GBP Member firms and 174 GBP Observer firms globally. To further improve the balance of global and stakeholder representation, an Advisory Council was formed in 2019 to generate a broader range of recommendations, which EIB co-chaired. This balanced approach to governance is considered by EIB a cornerstone of the market's success. It ensured that a credible market could be built, based on consensus around what was both feasible for markets and credible from an environmental perspective (and social, in the case of social bonds).

To avoid stifling the early green bond market much of the proposed language in the Principles was tilted towards recommendations, rather than requirements. Other frameworks were more ambitious, with the Climate Bond Initiative's taxonomy ahead of its time as it responded to widespread market interest by setting firmer and more granular green definitions. By comparison the GBPs attempted to consolidate market consensus on issuance best practice.

A further important driver was the evolving political and market context. A fundamental vector for market growth was the Paris Agreement on climate action sealed in 2015, as were the UN Sustainable Development Goals (SDGs) established in 2014. These agreements confirmed and detailed a growing global consensus on sustainable development, and reaffirmed the scientific consensus that global emissions must drop dramatically for the world to avoid catastrophic consequences of climate change. However, despite clear emission reduction objectives, global greenhouse emissions continued to climb until the 2020 COVID-19 pandemic.

The EU Action Plan on Financing Sustainable Growth recognised the scale of the challenge across financial markets in Europe by setting transformative improvements. This includes a multi-year plan to set standards for issuers and investors on environmental and social standards (a taxonomy), reporting requirements at a product and entity level. Based on the recommendations of the EU Technical Expert Group, the EU has also been considering establishment of its own green bond standard for issuers.

Financial Market Impact

The first green bond from EIB in 2007 (a benchmark size €600 million issuance) was a landmark issue, establishing a product structure that was later largely translated into the essence of the Green Bond Principles. The EIB quickly but gradually built a green bond reference curve, starting in the euro bond market, with maturities up to 2047. Setting hard targets for climate action and environmental sustainability lending supported the EIB in developing its bond programme, both in terms of the financial proposition and the environmental objectives served.

By 2013, the US dollar green bond market reached a turning point, as the International Finance Corporation (IFC) tested the market with the first US\$1 billion sized green bond; the positive reception ended the debate on whether a benchmark sized dollar issue could be placed. Investor demand for green bonds has been the ultimate measurement of success; investors in EIB's impact bonds have seen them as an attractive investment.

Over time, evidence has emerged suggesting that investing in green bonds need not entail a downside, and could offer a performance upside. A market review offers evidence of potential benefits for issuers of green bonds, ranging across pricing advantages, reputational benefits, investor diversification, and employee and customer satisfaction. For example, in the first half of 2020, certain green bonds in both EUR and USD attracted larger demand, and exhibited greater spread compressions, than vanilla equivalents (CBI, 2020). A growing number of opinions highlight signs of a 'greenium', meaning that certain green bonds have priced inside the yield curve of comparable conventional bonds. While excess demand may have been one of the drivers, there is also market interest in the benefits of environmental risk mitigation (or opportunity gain) through such products, which could contribute to attractive risk adjusted returns.

Investors in EIB's impact bonds may benefit through the strong environmental credentials enabled by use of bond proceeds and through the attractive (as measured in terms of risk-adjusted financial performance) secondary market performance of green bonds. Although the EIB prices its CABs in line with regular bonds, secondary market performance has shown some signs of a green premium to the conventional yield curve (Figure 15.1).

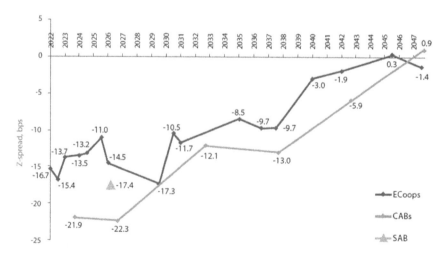

Figure 15.1 Outstanding EUR CABs Secondary Performance.
Source: Bank of America Merrill Lynch, as of 30 September 2019.

Credit rating agencies who have integrated environmental and social considerations into their published opinions have issued a growing number of rating actions linked to sustainability factors. S&P's rating assessment called the EIB an 'environmental standard-setter among multilateral lending institutions (MLIs) and, more broadly, among all debt issuers', referencing the EIB's climate ambitions and the New Energy Policy, launched in late 2019, as positive influences in its rating assessment (S&P, 2021). In its evaluation Moody's considers only Governance as a material ESG credit factor for the EIB, referring to its robust and conservative risk management practices and positively comments on the EIB's action on climate change and green bond issuance (Moody's, 2020).

Many investors and banks are seeking to reduce environmental risk exposure by increasing their investment in decarbonisation opportunities. The EIB is among the leading financial firms decarbonising its portfolios, having committed to 'Paris-align' all new business lending (from 2021), while also increasing the dedicated climate action share of proceeds to 50% by 2025. The EIB is also preparing a broad climate risk strategy, with a taskforce to value risks from climate change. This taskforce aims to enhance the Bank's consideration of all climate-related risks, including transition risk or stranded assets. This builds on existing environmental and social policies, which already include integrating carbon prices into economic evaluations. With such strategic progress and future orientations, green and sustainable bonds have the potential to grow as a source of funding and investment for the EIB.

External Market Catalysts: Regulation

Certain markets developed strongly following the publication of official guidance. China, Japan, the Association of Southeast Asian Nations (ASEAN), and certain Latin American markets introduced standards closely aligned to the GBPs to accelerate market issuance (Table 15.3).

The regional standards show clear differences, mostly focusing on the eligible criteria, as well as similarities, such as applying the four pillars of the GBPs. Standards are expected to become stricter over time as regulators seek to achieve climate or other environmental targets. This may emerge first in Europe with green bond standards linked to a common taxonomy, which are both elaborated on below.

Defining Green

The GBPs continue to adopt a market-led approach to optimising green categories, but the principles intentionally remained high level. This led experts and practitioners to develop more granular definitions, and external reviewers to use proprietary methodologies. Especially early on in the market's life, external review opinions left a degree of uncertainty over the bar for adequate green performance, an issue compounded by the absence at the

Table 15.3 Comparison of Official Green Bond Characteristics.

	ASEAN	China	India	Japan	EU
Scope	Guidelines	Regulation	Regulation (listing requirements)	Guidelines	Voluntary green bond standard
Uses four core components of the GBPs	Yes	Yes	Yes	Yes	Yes
Taxonomy	High level categories Exclusion – fossil fuels excluded	Taxonomy	High level categories	Detailed project categories	EU draft taxonomy
Incentives and support	Selected markets (e.g. Singapore)	Yes (also in HK) Green incentives proliferate	No	Yes Platform to publicise and inform	No
Verification	Recommended	Strongly recommended	Recommended	Recommended	Obligatory with verifier scheme
Impact reporting	No	No	No	Required	Required

time of granular official views. Markets were therefore keen to see more comprehensive green definitions, to resolve uncertainty about environmental merits. The Climate Bonds Initiative was arguably the first to offer a partial taxonomy in 2013, and the People's Republic of China created a Green Bond Catalogue in 2015.

The EU was the first authority to develop greater depth and to offer clear tools for achieving a uniform environmental standard. It convened a High-Level Expert Group and later Technical Expert Group on Sustainable Finance, where the EIB was a leading contributor. The objective was to create an EU Taxonomy or classification of sustainable activities that can provide clear screening criteria for adequate environmental performance.

The EU Sustainability Taxonomy, passed into law in 2020, is already being closely watched internationally, with other jurisdictions starting to publish similar taxonomies. The Taxonomy is also integral to the proposed EU Green Bond Standard. The EU Taxonomy is designed to be clear on environmental ambition, aiming to deliver on the carbon reduction commitments behind the Paris Agreement, and to be adaptable for use across borders. Apart from gradually developing screening criteria for substantial contributions towards six environmental objectives (climate as the first to be defined), the Taxonomy introduced minimum safeguards, including social and governance considerations, and filters out activities considered to cause significant harm to other environmental objectives.

The EU Taxonomy is an enabling framework designed to reduce uncertainty for issuers and enhance comparability for investors. It applies to the whole investment value chain, directly linking sustainable finance with the real economy. The EIB's response has been to align its green finance tracking with the Taxonomy and the EIB has been the first issuer to adopt new legal documentation for its green and sustainable bonds that allocates proceeds aligned with the Taxonomy. While internally tracking and updating lending criteria with the Taxonomy presents challenges, in particular collecting and verifying appropriate information for each economic activity, this exercise enables greater comparability, and broadens the range of factors that require review, strengthening the clarity of data regarding the impact of lending programmes.

The application of the Taxonomy therefore has impact across the balance, with both EIB's lending and capital markets teams in the process of applying the framework. For investors in EIB green bonds it is anticipated that the benefits of applying Taxonomy will include improved disclosure of environmental indicators. Across the financial industry, the international harmonisation of taxonomies has the potential to guide investors towards projects, bonds, or loans that have a more demonstrable impact.

EU Green Bond Standard – TEG Proposals

EU Technical Expert Group (TEG) proposals for an EU Green Bond Standard (GBS) offer a key market innovation, notably in linking to the EU Taxonomy. The proposals provide a more definitive and detailed view on product design, recognising a green bond framework as mandatory and offering a detailed template. The proposals also suggested that green bonds routinely include impact reporting and external review.

The TEG ideas for an EU GBS were designed to create a strong foundation to accelerate the flow of capital towards the EU's environmental objectives. The TEG saw the potential of the EU Taxonomy and of stricter requirements to improve the overall quality and impact of green bonds in the market. Alone, the rigour on Taxonomy marked a clear differentiator from existing standards. Nonetheless the TEG also advocated a degree of flexibility in the use of Taxonomy, as a transitional measure, recognising the challenges of implementing the emerging Taxonomy.

Responding to the TEG's GBS concept, and anticipating a potential future implementation enacted by regulation, the EIB was the first issuer to align its green bond documentation with the emerging GBS. This was positively received by the investor community, which is facing stricter disclosure rules around reporting against taxonomy in the EU.

The EIB aims to gradually align its internal CAB criteria with the potential EU GBS, if adopted. EIB has explicitly tuned CAB documentation to evolving EU legislation and is developing plans for CAB product development, including extending CAB eligibility criteria. The EIB's Climate Roadmap includes CAB product development and alignment with the potential GBS as an objective.

Conclusion

The EIB has always applied sustainability to its activities, aligning the integration of environmental, climate, and social considerations into operations and its role tackling climate change. As such, when the Bank issued the world's first green bonds in 2007, it was true to its overall strategy. Through the development of the green bond market the EIB has seen the hugely positive impact of wider engagement across financial markets.

Green bonds have created a new way to connect investors with green assets and put the issue of green investment at the heart of the climate change agenda globally. The combination of market consensus, good governance, transparency, accountability, and impact evaluation has become the bedrock for the growth of the market, as well as awareness of the role green bonds can play as part of an economic solution to climate change. The EIB's approach, with strictly green use of proceeds, transparent reporting on the use of proceeds and impact, along with third-party opinions adding accountability, has helped shape the basic template for green bonds.

Notes

1 The opinions in this article are solely the personal views of the author, and are not an official communication from the EIB.
2 https://www.eib.org/attachments/thematic/eib_group_climate_bank_roadmap_en.pdf.
3 For the most recent iteration of the GBPs, see GBP and ICMA (2018).
4 Both absolute and relative GHG emissions are only reported for projects whose estimated emissions are above one or both thresholds of significance adopted by the EIB: greater than 20,000 tonnes CO_2e per year for absolute emissions and greater than 20,000 tonnes CO_2e per year for relative emissions (positive or negative).

References

Climate Bonds Initiative (2020), *Green Bond Pricing in the Primary Market.* [online]. Available at: https://www.climatebonds.net/system/tdf/reports/cbi-pricing-h1-2020-21092020.pdf?file=1&type=node&id=54353&force=0 (Accessed 30 April 2021).

Cripps, P. (2018), 'Aldo Romani named Personality of the Year in Environmental Finance's Green Bond Awards', *Environmental Finance* (29 March 2018). [online]. Available at: https://www.environmental-finance.com/content/news/aldo-romani-named-personality-of-the-year-in-environmental-finances-green-bond-awards.html (Accessed 30 April 2021).

EIB (2014), *Multilateral Development Banks Agree to Reinforce Climate Finance.* [online]. Available at: https://www.eib.org/attachments/press/joint-mdb-statement-on-climate-finance.pdf (Accessed 30 April 2021).

EIB (2015), *Joint IFI Communication on a Revised Proposal for Green Bond Impact Reporting Harmonization.* [online]. Available at: https://www.eib.org/en/press/all/2015-283-joint-communication-on-a-revised-proposal-for-green-bond-impact-reporting-harmonization (Accessed 30 April 2021).

EIB (2020a), *Climate Awareness Bonds Framework.* [online]. Available at: https://www.eib.org/attachments/fi/eib-cab-framework-2019.pdf (Accessed 30 April 2021).

EIB (2020b), *European Investment Bank Group Sustainability Report 2019.* [online]. Available at: https://www.eib.org/attachments/general/reports/sustainability_report_2019_en.pdf (Accessed 30 April 2021).

Environmental Finance (2021), *Sustainable Bonds Insight 2021.* [online]. Available at: https://www.environmental-finance.com/assets/files/research/sustainable-bonds-insight-2021.pdf (Accessed 30 April 2021).

Green Bond Principles (GBP) and International Capital Market Association (ICMA) (2018), *Green Bond Principles: Voluntary Process Guidelines for Issuing Green Bonds.* [online]. Available at: https://www.icmagroup.org/assets/documents/Regulatory/Green-Bonds/Green-Bonds-Principles-June-2018-270520.pdf (Accessed 2 April 2021).

Moody's (2020), *European Investment Bank – Aaa Stable.* [online]. Available at: https://www.eib.org/attachments/fi/2020-08-moodys-eib-ca.pdf (Accessed 30 April 2021).

Standard and Poor's (S&P) (2021), *European Investment Bank.* [online]. Available at: https://www.eib.org/attachments/fi/external/sp_rating_report.pdf (Accessed 30 April 2021).

16 Impact Bonds: Issuers and Investors[1]

Radek Ján, Thomas Girard and Thibaut Cuillière

The Natixis Green and Sustainable Hub (hereafter 'the Hub') supports issuers of all types (including corporates, sovereigns, agencies, and supranationals) entering the impact bond market or enhancing their future offering. We guide our clients through their entire bond issuance programme, from the design and marketing of their framework impact strategies through to the syndication and distribution of bonds, as well as supporting with impact reporting. With involvement in many innovative transactions since 2014, the Hub has developed significant knowledge of investors' impact bond requirements and of how to deliver successful impact bond programmes.

Natixis CIB Research has been following the development in the bond impact market since its inception. In particular, we looked into the integration of ESG criteria and Green Bonds into fixed income portfolios as early as 2017, and in 2018 we started to publish an exhaustive review of Green Bonds performance. Since 2020, Natixis Research has been expanding its Green Bond Review, from corporate bonds to financial (senior preferred and non-preferred debt) bonds, covered bonds, agencies, supranationals as well as government bonds. We publish this analysis in a quarterly document, analysing the appetite for and performance of those impact bonds both on the primary and secondary markets.

This chapter starts by providing insights into the impact bond lifecycle. This is relevant because the process is more extensive than for ordinary bonds and responsible investors have certain expectations when impact bonds come to market. We present case studies of three impact bonds that show the impact opportunities seized by issuers in different sectors. We then examine a sample of the investors who regularly subscribe to or purchase such bonds to show their characteristics and focus. Lastly, we present a financial evaluation of impact bonds in both the primary and secondary markets. Our analysis of empirical data reveals differences in terms of subscription rates, spreads, issuance premia between impact bonds, and conventional bonds, and suggests that many of these differences are persistent over time. These differences also allow us to explore whether investors have stronger appetite for impact bonds, whether this influences bond pricing and whether, in secondary markets, there is a premium (or a 'greenium') for green bonds.

DOI: 10.4324/9781003055341-20

The Impact Bond Lifecycle

This chapter considers impact bonds as either green, social, sustainability, or sustainability-linked bonds since all these financial instruments are formally defined and governed by principles and guidelines developed by the International Capital Market Association (ICMA). However, it is worth highlighting that there is no standard or universally agreed methodology for assessing how 'impactful' a bond is. Some investors have developed their own in-house tools for this purpose while others rely on market labelling. Therefore, the term 'impact bond' can be used by some market participants in a different sense than in this chapter. Moreover, a financial instrument can provide positive environmental and/or social impacts without bearing any official label. Green bonds are a 'use of proceeds' type of impact bonds because they earmark (or ringfence) proceeds exclusively for the financing (or refinancing) of specific eligible green projects/activities as defined by the Green Bond Principles (GBP) (GBP and ICMA, 2018). Social bonds, defined by the Social Bond Principles (SBP), are also 'use of proceeds' type of impact bonds intended to raise funds for 'new and existing projects that address or mitigate a specific social issue and/or seek to achieve positive social outcomes' (SBP and ICMA, 2020). Sustainability bonds are 'use of proceeds' impact bonds financing (or re-financing) a combination of both 'green' projects (as defined by GBP) and 'social' projects (as defined by SBP). In contrast, sustainability-linked bonds are of an entirely different nature. The key feature of sustainability-linked bonds is that the financial and/or structural characteristics (e.g. coupon adjustment, premium at maturity) of the instrument can vary over time based on the achievement (or non-achievement) of predefined sustainability/ ESG objectives (The Sustainability-Linked Bond Principles and ICMA, 2020). It is relevant to note that the structuring features of both 'use of proceeds' bonds and sustainability-linked bonds can be combined in one single financial instrument, even though such transactions remain rare in the market as of 2021.[2]

Introducing a new impact bond begins with origination work which, if successful, results in a mandate for advisory and/or structuring roles. At Natixis, origination tasks on impact bonds span across all asset classes and sectors. These tasks are led by our internal specialists, based on our convictions that sustainability-related issues require expertise, are asset-class agnostic and that the integrity of our product offering is crucial to the longevity, scalability, and mainstreaming of green and sustainable finance. In practical terms, this means that the profiles and claims of issuers are assessed in terms of their ambitiousness, consistency, and materiality before entering the phase of structuring sustainable financing products to ensure the robustness and credibility of the final product.

There are several specific requirements for impact bonds that are absent from the origination and structuring process for conventional bonds, namely writing of the Green/Social/Sustainability/Sustainability-linked bond frame-works and assistance with external reviews and reporting. These require good knowledge of business challenges and opportunities related to climate, and other environmental, social and governance (ESG) topics, as well as under-standing the main sustainable finance trends (e.g. innovative deals, market data, evolution of the regulatory landscape, working knowledge of applica-ble standards and methodologies, as well the ability to use technical screen-ing criteria as provided, for instance, in the EU Taxonomy of Sustainable Activities[3]).

There are ten general steps for issuers to issue impact bonds (Figure 16.1). Eight of these steps are done systematically for every impact bond issuance as they are necessary to fulfil investors' expectations regarding integrity and trustworthiness while another two steps (the very first and very last) are op-tional, proposed by Natixis as an additional service for interested issuers. The time required for each phase depends on the type of issuer and on issuer's familiarity with impact bonds (inaugural or repeated issuance and the de-gree of knowledge about sustainability related topics in general). The process is usually longer for sovereign, supranational, and agency (SSA) issuers at around six months (up to eight months for sovereign issuers) due to the gen-erally greater variety of financed projects relative to corporate issuers, which in turn requires more work to determine eligible categories and criteria se-lection. In exceptional cases, the whole process can take much longer, even a year or more.

Step 1: Experience-sharing

Experience-sharing is optional for potential issuers. For issuers that are inter-ested, we organise meetings with other issuers so that a potential issuer can hear about the proposed services directly from clients who have already used Natixis' services in the past.

While this experience-sharing exercise is optional and an issuance of an impact bond can succeed without it, the following steps described below are done systematically. The first two mandatory steps, the creation of a Green/Social/Sustainability/Sustainability-linked Bond Framework and the elabo-ration of Second Party Opinion (SPO), are the essential part of the structuring process since these two steps are done only for impact bonds, hereby setting these financial instruments apart from conventional bonds. Most of the time spent in these two steps revolves around the definition of eligible Use of Pro-ceeds categories (to determine eligibility for financing from use of proceeds impact bonds) or around the selection of credible Sustainability/ESG Targets and of indicators for their tracking (in the case of sustainability-linked bonds) and choices related to Reporting (choosing relevant and meaningful indica-tors, which is important for all types of impact bonds). These steps are out-lined in more detail below.

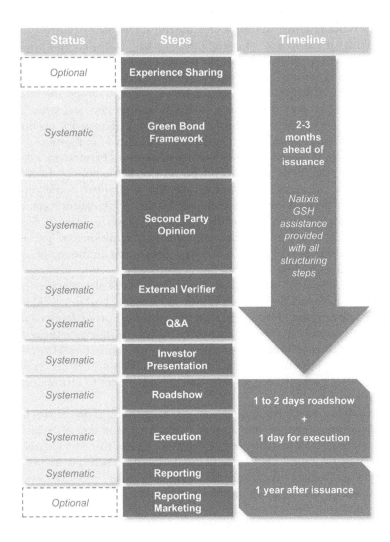

Figure 16.1 Green Bond Issuance Timeline and Key Steps.
Source: Natixis Green and Sustainable Hub.

Step 2: Green/Social/Sustainability/Sustainability-linked Bond Framework

Natixis coordinates development of all sections of frameworks. The degree of issuer involvement depends on how familiar the issuer is with the impact bond market. We promote discussions with all relevant internal stakeholders and teams to set-up bond governance and monitoring processes and to ensure alignment with market best practices. Many issuers will also look to link their bond programmes to the UN Sustainable Development Goals (SDGs) but this step is not required to issue a credible impact bond.

Eligibility refers to a set of criteria that has to be satisfied by a project, an asset, or an activity in order to benefit from financing from the proceeds of an impact bond. Typically, the proceeds raised through the issuance of a green/ social/sustainability bond are earmarked or ring-fenced for specific categories of activities or projects (explaining where the money goes and what is being financed). The Green/Social/Sustainability Bond Framework encompasses the issuer's commitment into what the proceeds raised are meant to be allocated. As such, the Green/Social/Sustainability Bond Framework references 'The Green Bond Principles' or The 'Social Bond Principles', which specify what criteria and conditions must be met for eligibility.[4] Some economic activities and projects are deemed eligible by their very nature (typically renewable energy or recycling) while others use quantified key performance indicators (e.g. absolute and relative quantities of emissions) to 'prove' their eligibility. Eligibility criteria can also vary depending on the socioeconomic or geographical context.

The Green/Social/Sustainability/Bond Framework also specifies how issuers ought to report on their allocation and impact. This can include more granular and tangible information than in traditional corporate social responsibility reports and can provide a way for investors to anticipate the outcomes of their investments through assets, processes, or technologies. However, being general-purpose instruments, impact bonds do not carry the credit risk of the specific project(s) nor do they link the repayment to future cash flows of the project(s).

Sustainability-linked bonds do not require earmarking of proceeds as they are general-purpose corporate instruments. However, the notion of 'eligibility' is present in the form of 'sustainability performance targets' that have to be achieved over time by the issuer. The choice of sustainability performance and of appropriate key performance indicators (KPIs) tracking issuer's progress towards the achievement of these targets is justified and detailed in the Sustainability-linked Bond Framework. For sustainability-linked bonds, investors expect that the KPIs chosen should be relevant for the sector and that the targets are ambitious and set in good faith. To ensure trust and reduce information asymmetry between the issuer and investors, structuring work on the sustainability-linked bond must provide transparent and understandable documentation regarding the methodological robustness, ambitiousness, and credibility of the targets. To this end, Natixis has developed a methodology to provide support for clients considering this new bond format choosing KPIs, justification of targets, and coordination of tenders for second party opinions (SPOs).

The market expectations relative to bond documentation, communication and, to a certain extent, reporting are similar for sustainability-linked bonds and for use of proceeds bonds. Expectations of sound mechanism and transparent documentations are reflected in the bond framework while expectations related to issuers communication and reporting are addressed, respectively, in roadshows and in reporting templates.

Step 3: The Second Party Opinion

The purpose of SPO is to provide an independent assessment of the alignment of an impact with the relevant market principles (Green, Social, Sustainability-linked Bond Principles) or guidelines (Sustainability Bond Guidelines). The exact scope of an SPO will vary on a case-by-case basis. Prepared by independent external specialists, the SPO process usually starts two or three weeks after the start of the writing of the Green/Social/Sustainability/Sustainability-linked Bond Framework (the two processes can go on simultaneously) and generally takes at least four to six weeks. We can play several roles in this process:

1   We provide assistance with the review and analysis of all potential SPO business pitches. Several SPO providers usually submit responses to a request for proposals offers to issuers. Natixis evaluates the proposals and the client decides which SPO provider to work with.
2   Throughout the life of the project, we support SPO providers with their methodology development and assist in discussions with the issuer. We will challenge SPOs if we disagree with their approach.
3   We proofread and comment on documents.

Writing of the Green/Social/Sustainability/Sustainability-linked Bond Framework and the elaboration of the SPO are the essential parts of the structuring process. Once both are successfully finished, the following steps are relatively straightforward and less time consuming.

Step 4: External Verification

External verification serves as another independent check on the framework and proceeds. We work with the issuer to define the scope of work and the type of analysis expected. Several types of external reviewers can undertake this task, depending on the nature of the impact bond. A list of external reviewers who voluntarily aligned with ICMA's Guidelines for External Reviewers is available on ICMA's website.[5]

Step 5: Q&A process

We assist the issuer with drafting question and answer (Q&A) sections dedicated to sustainability related aspects of the transaction (e.g. relevant market practice, the credentials of bond proceeds). To this end, the issuer benefits from a dedicated session with experts from Natixis to prepare answers.

This process helps to formulate the messaging during roadshows and reporting. While every issuance is unique, investors tend to ask similar kinds of questions. Based on our experience, we have prepared a list of questions that an issuer should expect for a green bond roadshow. Most fall into one of the six following general categories:

- Overall environmental strategy
- Green bond issuance strategy
- Use of proceeds & projects selection
- Management of proceeds and governance
- Execution considerations
- Impact reporting

Step 6: Investor Presentations

After the preceding steps are complete, Natixis aids with drafting or updating the sustainability strategy and/or corporate social responsibility (CSR) profile sections of investor presentations and assists with preparing the dedicated green/social/sustainability/sustainability-linked bond section of the investor presentation.

Natixis also provides issuers with the ESG profiles of the investors they will be meeting to give them a better understanding of how advanced these investors are in terms of responsible investment and climate/ESG strategy in their analysis and investment decision processes. These profiles also explain how these investors invest, whether they manage dedicated flagship vehicles (e.g. green, social, and/or sustainable/impact bond funds) or mandates, and what they look for (notably in terms of impact reporting) and, therefore, what kind of information they are likely to ask for during a roadshow. We often set up rehearsals with issuer representatives to prepare them for these meetings with ESG specialists or subject experts.

Step 7: Roadshow

The communication and marketing processes are crucial for the success of a new issuance, especially for the release of an inaugural transaction. This entails several components: a physical roadshow (or e-roadshow), conference calls, and global investor call. It is standard for banks to provide issuers with a list of relevant investors to target for a deal-related roadshow to ensure that the most committed investors are contacted for every type of sustainable bond issuance.

A physical roadshow, which may be a one-to-one or a one-to-few meeting, involves dialogue with credit analysts and portfolio managers that prioritise ESG and sustainable investment mandates. Most roadshows are in-person under normal circumstances, but Covid-19 has created opportunities to communicate with a greater number of investors in diverse markets thanks to e-roadshows.

Roadshows for impact bonds include dedicated communication to investors on elements not necessarily required for a conventional bond. For example, presentation of the issuer's CSR strategy and a review of its ESG performance (governance topics, discussion of possible controversies, climate or transition strategy, etc.) are a starting point for any credible narrative surrounding a new impact issuance format.

Roadshows require a detailed demonstration of the compliance of the Green/Social/Sustainability/Bond Framework with the ICMA bond principles' eligibility criteria, project selection, proceeds allocation, proceeds tracking, and reporting commitments. For Sustainability-linked bonds, requirements in terms of proceeds allocation are not relevant as this type of impact bond is not 'Use of Proceeds' format. Instead, the choice of KPIs and their trajectory over time is of utmost importance. The roadshow should also include the external independent experts' assessment, confirming that the bond is in line with market expectations and industry best practices when it comes to the ambitiousness of sustainability performance targets and the selection of KPIs. Moreover, an issuer could also provide a description on the various stages of the projects to be financed or refinanced to ensure transparency.

Step 8: Execution

Syndication banks increasingly focus on their impact bond distribution capabilities. This entails building a market intelligence on ESG investors, developing an understanding of how investors incorporate sustainability considerations in their actively managed fixed income investments and what are the main drivers for their investment decisions.

As a differentiating factor, Natixis proposes an investor ESG scoring methodology and ESG book analysis. Our ESG scoring methodology has been designed to help issuers better target key investors for the transaction and to favour the most committed sustainable investors through an allocation bonus given to those managing dedicated green, social, and/or impact bond funds and/or mandates.

Natixis also offers a comprehensive ESG book analysis to provide issuers with the breakdown of investors based on their ESG profile and determine the ESG share of the book. The book of each individual bond issuance can be assessed to ascertain how much of the issued amount has been allocated to different types of investors, from conventional fixed income strategies/portfolios to the various responsible investment strategies in use. This analysis can then be useful to identify investors who might be keen to tap an existing issue, to secure lead orders for next issuances, or when it comes to issue a private placement.

Steps 9 and 10: Reporting and Reporting Marketing

Reporting is a mandatory task required for every impact bond issuance. From a bank's standpoint, it involves supporting clients with assistance and comments on draft reporting for the first post issuance publication as well as for ongoing reporting updates. The Hub assists in identifying sound impact indicators, clarifying underlying methodologies and assumptions, and in presenting the information in a way that can be easily processed by investors for their own impact reporting.

The very last step, the reporting marketing, is optional but is of increasing commercial interest to companies to communicate with green investors about the projects' net positive environmental impacts and sustainability strategy.

While the main features and structuring procedures are always similar for each bond format within the impact bond family, some bonds stand out in the market for their distinctive features related to their size, nature of the issuer, or methodological innovations used in the structuring process. Some illustrations are provided in the following section.

Case Studies

Sovereign: United States of Mexico

Natixis acted as Structuring Advisor assisting the Mexican Ministry of Finance in the design of its inaugural SDG Sustainable Bond Framework.[6] The Mexican Government wished to establish a broad framework that would leverage its substantial work over the past few years implementing and working towards mapping the Federal Budget to the SDGs. This issuance marked the first time SDGs had been used as entry point eligibility criteria in a framework and not just as an afterthought (e.g. in *ex post* mapping).

The innovative features of this framework included applying geospatial eligibility criteria to ensure that only budgetary items targeting municipalities with the highest SDG gaps were selected. Geospatial or territorial eligibility enabled the prioritisation of vulnerable populations living in landlocked and disadvantaged areas. The geospatial eligibility uses granular open data collected through the Census of Population and Housing, which is then analysed by the National Council for Evaluation of Social Development. To account for regional disparities, a list of 1,345 municipalities (totalling roughly 22 million inhabitants out of a national population of circa 120 million people) has been defined. The Proceeds raised through future Mexico's SDG Bonds issuances will finance projects located in these 1,345 cities, which have been selected because of their illiteracy and school attendance rates, level of health services deprivation, lack of toilets, drainage, or piped water in houses, and absence of electricity access or basic equipment such as fridges. SDG localised financing guarantees that only budgetary programmes targeting the most disadvantaged areas and vulnerable populations are eligible (e.g. indigenous, elderly, and children).

Another innovative feature relates to the data being used to determine the locations where bond's proceeds are to be spent. Social or sustainability bonds frameworks often use national averages of socioeconomic data. In contrast, this framework specifically targets the bottom range of territories and populations in Mexico, particularly those living in the South of the country. A 2018 report published by Natixis focused on how issuers can go beyond merely relating to the SDGs and actively demonstrate their contribution. The methodology proposed in that report combined with the deep institutional commitment allowed Mexico to develop a Framework that actively demonstrates its SDG contributions.[7] The methodology used strong governance overlays, with a methodology and mapping of bond proceeds that are public. The framework is also the first in the world to receive an opinion from the United Nations Development Program on the framework's alignment to the SDGs.

In addition to the unique two-step eligibility criteria, Mexico made strong commitments to impact reporting, going beyond standard market practices. This will create feedback loops, which will further improve the data available to the government in addressing SDG gaps in the future. The impact reporting will benefit from data provided by the individual Ministries along with National Institute of Statistics and Geography (INEGI in Spanish), and the National Council for Evaluation of Social Development Policy (CONVAL in Spanish). The UNDP will also act as an official observer on the impact reporting, ensuring the most relevant metrics are monitored.

Agencies: Unédic

Unedic's mission is to implement unemployment benefits in France. In May 2020 during the Covid-19 pandemic, Unédic issued its inaugural €4 billion social bond which, at the time, represented the largest social bond ever issued worldwide. A second social bond followed in June, raising another €4 billion. Natixis was the sole structuring agent for the social bond framework and bookrunner for the social bond issues.

The framework, fully aligned with ICMA's social bond principles, covers major programs funded by Unédic. The social bond framework formally sets out Unédic's contribution to the French state's roadmap to tackle poverty, to provide the technical and professional skills required for decent work, and to narrow inequalities.

The proceeds fund covid-19 crisis measures: extending standard unemployment insurance programmes and implementing an exceptional job retention scheme involving subsidised part-time working covering 12 million private sector employees at the apex of the lockdown. These measures are naturally eligible in Unédic's Social Bond Framework in the category 'protecting jobs'. Therefore, the social bond framework emphasises the unemployment insurance's role as an automatic shock buffer, which played its full role in the economic context caused by lock-down measures and economic recession.

Unédic commits to greater transparency with the investor community on its methodology to evaluate workers' needs, including targeted allowances and benefits. Impact reporting will help investors assessing the outcomes of Unédic's financed schemes, particularly in terms of social justice and redistribution. Evaluation is at the heart of Unédic's missions and impact reports will be supported by a data analysis to assess and improve the efficiency of programs.

Bank: BPCE Green Covered Bond

Groupe BPCE published its Sustainable Bond Framework in August 2018 and updated the document in April 2020, based on external research and evolving generally accepted principles. Groupe BPCE's programme targets three broad areas:

1   Green bonds. Assets and activities financed deliver a positive contribution to climate change mitigation efforts (e.g. carbon dioxide (CO_2) emissions reductions) or other environmental challenges (e.g. biodiversity protection, waste management, water conservation, etc.).
2   Social bonds: Human development. This area addresses social sustainability challenges through contributions to economic systems (education, healthcare, social development, social housing, and relevant activities of local authorities) and that could potentially seek to benefit people who live and/or work in economically and/or socially disadvantaged areas or communities.
3   Social bonds: Local economic development. This area supports regional and community development and resilience through financing of small businesses, small and medium-sized enterprises (SMEs), local authorities, and non-profit organisations that seek to benefit people who live and/or work in economically and/or socially disadvantaged areas or communities.

The BPCE framework is noteworthy due to the level of granularity across each eligible loan category, associated eligibility criteria, and environmental and/or social objectives, as well as the contribution to specific SDGs' targets. Specific methodology notes for each criterion ensure high levels of transparency. For the €1.25 billion ten-year green covered bond issued on the 19 May 2020, the eligibility criteria for green bonds is the first methodology to use the Natixis Green Weighting Factor (an internal mechanism that allocates capital to financing deals based on their climate impact which, by adjusting the expected rate of return of each financing deal based on its environmental and climate impact, provides incentives for the bank to align with the goals of the Paris Agreement on Climate Change). The bond contributes to France National Low Carbon Strategy's objectives of reducing energy consumption in all sectors, including the building sector, and of reinforcing energy efficiency and support commitments to fund the energy transition and improve French building stock energy efficiency.

Understanding Impact Bond Investors

We can divide impact bond buyers into four generic categories:

1   Institutional investors with sustainable or ESG integration methodologies, but who also buy conventional bonds from issuers with strong ESG credentials/ratings.
2   Institutional investors with top-down green investment mandates, specifying green bonds appetite.
3   Investors with green bond funds (a small but growing niche: at the end of 2020, we identified 58 funds globally with a combined approximately US$17 billion in assets under management (AUM)). This category includes wider impact bond funds or strategies with dedicated impact sleeves.
4   Conventional (non-ESG driven) investors who consider green bonds like any other bond and buy such bonds due to their financial characteristics while paying little or no attention to the sustainable component.

The first three categories of investors can be considered as 'sustainable'. They tend to be 'buy and hold' investors following either an integration approach or thematic approach to ESG investing. However, it should be highlighted that the notion 'sustainable investor' remains multifaceted.

Furthermore, there is no such thing as a textbook definition of a 'green investor' and it is very challenging to obtain a clear view on the weight given to the green component of an investment decision-making process. Indeed, a single institution could place an order for many bond securities, some of which may be green and some others not. As a result, claims about the green or ESG share of a book should be taken with caution.

Nevertheless, there are several ways to form a view on the 'greenness' of an investor. For example, one could look at the investor's responsible investment strategy and policy, the investor's range of green and sustainable bond funds, the investor's membership of specific collective initiatives (e.g. the Principles for Responsible Investment (PRI), Institutional Investors Group on Climate Change, Climate Bonds Initiative, Climate Action 100+, Net Zero Asset Owner Alliance), and the investor's adherence to the Green Bonds Principles.

Interestingly, our experience shows a general tendency for an over-allocation to sustainable investors both because they are 'real money' investors and because issuers want to justify the sustainable features of the bond issue and the human and financial means devoted to it.

When considering investors' appetite for sustainable bonds, it is also note-worthy to look at the dynamics of new market players. Since its inception, the sustainable bond market has received particular support from asset owners with public service remits (or equivalent); these asset owners include sovereign wealth funds, pension funds, and insurance companies.

The Rationale for Fixed Income Investors to Invest in Impact Bonds

Investors' motivations for adding bonds to portfolios varies depending on their ESG investment style (integration, screening, and thematic). For buyers of impact bonds, we identify four key reasons:

1   To comply with increasing regulatory pressure on climate-related dis-closure: Impact bonds are unique in providing proceeds' transparency since eligibility criteria give a clear view of what is being financed. This helps investors meet regulatory scrutiny that requires investors to measure their exposure to climate risks and report on their contribu-tion to fight against climate change (such as Article 173 of the French Energy Transition Law and Article 29 of the French law on Energy and Climate).

2   To redirect investments as part of a decarbonisation strategy: Green bonds are a natural candidate for asset reorientation considering ongoing decarbonation and fossil fuel divestment strategies. This could also be true for sustainability-linked bonds, especially if they are framed around the energy transition. Investment is these securities could be considered as a good hedge when confronting changing public policy related to cli-mate change, energy transition, and broader sustainability issues.

3   To deliver positive environmental and/or social impacts: Due to their use-of-proceeds format, green, social, and sustainability bonds can serve as a powerful communication tool for institutional investors and asset managers to build project-based products without taking project credit risks. Indeed, these bonds bring transparency on the projects financed and the related reporting obligations push issuers to formalise monitoring

any environmental and/or social benefits brought by the projects. As such, they meet the growing expectations of responsible investors who want to demonstrate positive impacts of their investments, beyond ESG integration, and how they contribute to the SDGs.

4 To influence corporates' sustainable performance: While engagement related to ESG issues has historically been the domain of equity investors, sustainability-linked bonds could serve as a new tool for investors' responsible stewardship. Indeed, thanks to their financial characteristics (e.g. coupon step up or down) linked to meaningful sustainable KPIs for a given sector (such as CO_2 reduction, or renewables sourcing for high emitting industries), fixed income investors can influence corporate practices.

Geographic Dynamics

Globally, Europe represents the most mature market as shown by Figure 16.2, which provides a breakdown of annual impact bond issuance by region. This market for impact bonds is investor driven, with the momentum driven by institutional asset owners (in particular pension funds and insurers). France and the Netherlands are home to some of the main buyers of green bonds. Impact bonds are very often considered as an additional investment segment to SRI, as illustrated by the launch of several green bond funds and integration of green bond investing within decarbonisation or greening asset base strategies. European (many of them being French, but also British) underwriters are very active on the impact bond market. The European market has strong expectations when it comes to standardization as illustrated by the very wide endorsement of ICMA's Green Bond Principles and Social Bond Principles.

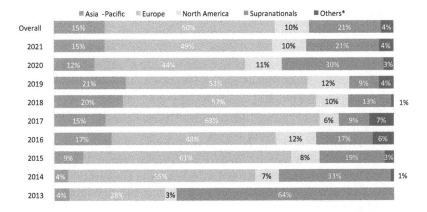

Figure 16.2 Impact Bonds Issuance Relative Weight by Region per year (%).

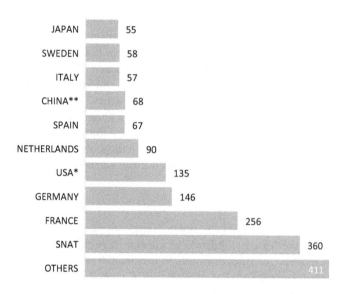

Figure 16.3 Top Ranking Countries by Issuance Volumes ($ billion).
Note: *Excluding municipal green bonds; **excluding local green bonds.

While Northern America has some very active players in the sustainable bond market, they remain relatively few for now (Figure 16.3). Some American underwriters have a strong presence in the Sustainable market, which can be seen in league tables for different sustainable bond formats. It is worth highlighting that the US Green Muni bond market has experienced a very strong development. Just like their European peers, Northern American players in the sustainable bond market also have strong expectations when it comes to standardisation as illustrated by the very wide endorsement of green bond principles.

The appetite of investors in the Asia-Pacific (APAC) region for impact bonds remains in its infancy and the market dynamics are driven by regulators rather than investors. Local subsidiaries of Western institutional investors are deploying their green strategy globally and are likely to be first movers in Asia. An ecosystem of signals can be identified for a very rapid ramp up of the Asian investor base: as of 2020, it remains to be seen whether the dynamics will come from SRI/broader ESG approaches, or from Green/energy transition financing needs.

Japan is an exception. The Japanese life insurance companies are active buyers with established appetite for green and social bonds. The Ministry of the Environment of Japan established its green bond guidelines in 2017 with the aims of catalysing the issuance of green bonds and developing the local market infrastructure.

Financial Evaluation of Impact Bonds

In this section, we analyse how impact bonds perform in primary and secondary markets relative to their conventional peers. We do not analyse every single existing bond in every currency. Instead, we have designed our review to focus on the largest and most liquid part of the impact bond market: Euro-denominated corporate A-rated and BBB-rated bonds as well as Euro-denominated senior preferred and senior non-preferred financial debt with a minimum issue size of €500 million, issued from 2018 onwards.

Differences between impact and conventional bonds in terms of pricing and performance can be observed in both primary and secondary markets. Primary market refers to the financial market where new securities, not previously traded on any exchange, are issued. Once issued, securities become available for trading by institutions and individuals. The secondary market is the financial market where such trading occurs. A security can be sold just once on the primary market but numerous times on the secondary market. On the primary market, securities are issued by the issuer to investors, meaning that proceeds from selling the security go to the issuer. Conversely, the issuer does not receive anything from a trade of its security on the secondary market: money goes from the buyer to the seller when a security is traded on the secondary market.

Every bond starts in the primary market where an investor can buy it directly from the issuer. Bond pricing in the primary market is influenced by many factors. Comparison of oversubscription rates between impact and conventional bonds within the same asset class and with comparable size reveals whether investor demand is stronger for one bond type over the another. Investors' appetite influences the pricing dynamics of newly issued bonds. These are visible in spreads tightening at reoffer vs initial pricing talk (IPT) as well as in the magnitude of new issuance premium (NIP). To make sense, these comparisons must be made for bonds issued by the same issuer type and in the same period in a market that is deep and liquid enough. We discuss these technical aspects in relation to our impact bond focus group below.

Oversubscription Rates

Oversubscription rates indicate the magnitude of investor appetite for bonds at the moment of their issuance. Oversubscription refers to a situation when demand for a security exceeds the offer. This is generally the case for bond issuance regardless of whether the bond is conventional or part of the impact bonds family. The comparison of oversubscription rates between bonds can reveal whether there is a difference in investor demand between these bond formats. Table 16.1 presents some general observations regarding oversubscription rates for various euro-denominated bond categories.

Our analysis shows that, on average, Euro-denominated impact bonds achieve larger oversubscription than their conventional peers. This is clearly

Table 16.1 Main Observations Regarding Oversubscription Rates for Various Euro-Denominated Bond Categories.

Category	Main Observations
BBB–rated corporate	Oversubscription rates for impact bonds are on average exceeding oversubscription rates for conventional bonds issued around a similar time. This trend has become particularly visible throughout 2020 and 2021.
A-rated corporate	Average oversubscription rates for impact bonds are exceeding oversubscription rates for conventional bonds, but the differences between the two are less pronounced in terms of magnitude and more heterogeneous over time: reaching similar average levels in some quarters, being higher for impact format in other quarters and higher for conventional format in other quarters still. Particularly high average oversubscription rates for impact bonds in this category occurred in Q2-20, due to strong investor appetite for impact bond issuance from Schiphol (nine-year, green), Swisscom (eight-year, green) and Prologis (12-year, green).
Senior preferred financial debt	Oversubscription rates for impact bonds strongly and consistently exceeded oversubscription rate for conventional format in every quarter throughout 2019 and 2020 and the trend continues through 2021, albeit with a less pronounced difference in oversubscriptions between the two formats
Senior non-preferred financial debt	Oversubscription rates for both impact and conventional bond formats were at similar levels until the end of Q2-20, in favour of the former in some quarters, in favour of the latter in others. However, since Q3-20, the oversubscription rates for impact bonds consistently exceed those of their conventional peers. Whilst the difference was particularly noticeable in Q3-20 (notably thanks to strong investor's appetite for six-year green Commerzbank and eight-year green Société Générale), the trend continues through 2021, although with less magnitude.

exhibited by the quarterly comparison of oversubscription rates between impact and conventional BBB-rated corporate bonds (Figure 16.4). While both conventional and Euro-denominated impact BBB-rated corporate debt have been oversubscribed in every observed quarter since the beginning of our observations in 2018, impact bonds achieved, on average, a higher oversubscription rate in all but three quarters.

This trend became particularly visible in 2020. For example with BBB-rated securities, a five-year €0.5 billion sustainability bond from healthcare specialist Philips received €6.5 billion in orders; and five-year green bonds from utilities E.ON and Iberdrola received orders of €6 and €8.75 billion, respectively. Longer-dated bonds saw similar oversubscription, with auto

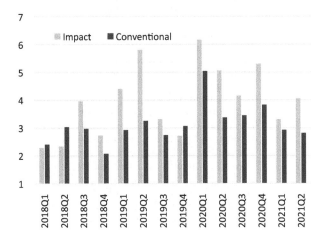

Figure 16.4 Average Oversubscription Rate for BBB-Rated Corporate Bonds.
Source: Natixis CIB Research.

manufacturers Daimler (ten-year: €1.0 billion priced and €5.6 billion in orders) and Volkswagen (12-year: €0.75 billion priced and €3.8 billion in orders) issuing their inaugural impact bonds.

This empirical finding shows that the supply of impact bonds is not sufficient to meet investor demand, despite the rapidly growing impact market. This in turn implies pricing differences between impact and conventional bonds, to which we now turn.

Spread Tightening

Closely related to oversubscription rates is the spread compression between the time of the IPT and the time of pricing. As part of the pricing process, bonds experience spread tightening. Stronger investor demand for a bond (reflected in higher oversubscription rates) results in a higher spread compression between the time of the IPT and the time of pricing. Table 16.2 presents some general observations regarding spread compression between the time of the IPT and the time of pricing for various euro-denominated bond categories.

Due to the stronger investor demand, euro-denominated impact BBB-rated corporate bonds experience higher spread compression (achieve a larger spread tightening) versus the IPT of their conventional peers (Figure 16.5).

The trend observed for Euro-denominated senior preferred financial debt is very similar to the trend exhibited by Euro-denominated BBB-rated corporate bonds. Since Q3 2018, impact bond issuers of senior preferred financial debt have been able to compress spreads further at reoffer vs. IPT more than for conventional bonds.

Table 16.2 Main Observations Regarding Spread Compression between the Time of the IPT and the Time of Pricing for Various Euro-Denominated Bond Categories.

Category	Main Observations
BBB-rated corporate	Tightening has been consistently stronger for impact bonds throughout the observed period.
A-rated corporate	More nuanced picture as the tightening levels were higher for impact format in some quarters and conventional format in other quarters, with no clear trend emerging. However, Q2-20 constituted a notable exception: tightening has been stronger for impact bonds as investors' appetite far exceeded the demand for similar conventional bonds. After this period corresponding to the first lockdown wave in Europe, the reoffer spread tightening versus IPT came back to similar levels as observed in Q4 2019, with slightly lower tightening exhibited by the impact format in the following quarters.
Senior preferred financial debt	Similar trends as for BBB-rated corporate debt, consistently in favour of the impact bond format
Senior non-preferred financial debt	Impact bonds' reoffer spreads tightened, on average, less versus IPT than conventional peers between Q1-20 and Q3-20 but the trend reversed in favour of the impact bond format in Q4-20 and continues through 2021.

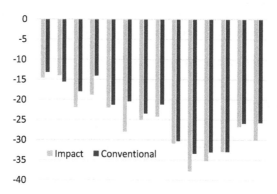

Figure 16.5 Spread – Initial Pricing Talk (IPT) for BBB-Rated Corporate Bonds.
Source: Natixis CIB Research.

New Issuance Premium

Closely related to both oversubscription rates and spread compression is the new issuance premium (NIP), another indicator that can be used to gauge pricing differences between comparable impact and conventional bonds. NIP refer to the extra yield received by the buyer (paid for by the seller) for a newly issued bond relative to how other bonds from the same issuer trade in the secondary market at the time a new bond is priced. To calculate NIP, we built yield curves for each issuer in our sample and interpolated the secondary curve on the maturity of the newly issued bond. NIP is influenced by broader macroeconomic factors at the time of the issuance. In general, a higher period of volatility will require a higher NIP. Our analysis took this into account: we compared NIP trends over time between impact and conventional bond formats in the same category of issuers, issued in a similar time.

Our analysis showed that impact bonds displayed a lower NIP than conventional bonds issued by similar issuers and at a similar time (Figure 16.6). This trend was consistent across periods and exhibited by all euro-denominated asset classes. Interestingly, the trend of lower impact NIP also held for senior non-preferred financial debt, which exhibits different behaviour in terms of oversubscription rates and spread tightening vs IPT.

Negative NIP has become a regular feature of impact bonds. For instance, an Enel eight-year green bond displayed a NIP of −3 basis points (bps) in 2018, and a Ferrovie green bond seven-year had −6 bps. 2020 saw a significant increase in the number of these bonds with negative NIPs, with examples including the Orange nine-year sustainability bond (−6 bps) and Icade Sante ten-year social bond (−14 bps). In September 2020 more than €7 billion of euro-denominated corporate issuance came in an impact format with spreads 36 bps tighter than their IPTs on average, meaning the tightening post IPT was twice as much as for conventional bonds (for similar average spread at launch, and without any big bias of beta). The impact bond oversubscription rate was almost five times, significantly higher than conventional bonds issued during the same period, despite some impact bonds displaying negative NIPs (which was not the case for conventional bonds). Although we had noticed higher appetite for impact bonds relative to conventional bonds since 2019, this was the first time that primary market indicators showed a divergence.

The empirical finding that impact Euro-denominated corporate bonds (A-rated and BBB-rated) and financial bonds (senior preferred & senior non-preferred) all display lower NIP than their conventional peers has practical importance for both issuers and investors. When an impact bond exhibits lower NIP than its conventional peers (same sector, same rating/asset class) issued at similar time, it means the issuer (seller) has to pay a smaller extra yield to the buyer compared with a conventional bond. This is, of course, positive for the issuer and a direct consequence of the stronger investor appetite for impact bonds relative to comparable conventional bonds.

Secondary Markets

This section evaluates the 'greenium' of impact bonds. Greenium is a measure of impact bond attractivity in the secondary market. It refers to a premium, either positive or negative, for impact (or sometimes specifically green) bonds relative to conventional bonds from the same issuer with similar characteristics. Calculating the greenium reveals which bonds are 'cheap', which are

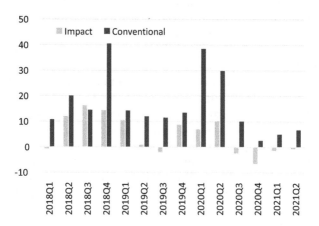

Figure 16.6 New Issue Premium for BBB-Rated Corporate Bonds.
Source: Natixis CIB Research.

'expensive', and whether investors can include impact bonds into their portfolio without sacrificing performance.

Similar to our methodology for primary markets, we analysed the parts of the market that are as deep and liquid as possible. We restricted the analysed bonds to those with an issue size of at least €500 million. Figure 16.7 illustrates the greenium map for euro-denominated corporate bonds. The X-axis shows interpolated z-spread on the conventional € curve for each issuer, the Y-axis shows observed z-spread for impact bonds. We define greenium as the difference between z-spread of green bonds and the interpolated z-spread for similar conventional issues from the same issuer.[8] As such, a greenium equal to zero would appear on the 45-degrees line; impact bonds situated on the 45-degree line are neither 'cheap' nor 'expensive' relative to similar bonds from the same issuer. Green bonds with negative greenium are situated below the 45-degree line, to the lower right corner of the chart. A negative greenium marks an 'expensive' impact bond from an investor point of view, a bond which is therefore *attractive* for issuers rather than investors. Conversely, a positive greenium marks a 'cheap' impact bond from an investor point of view. Bonds with positive greenium are situated above the 45-degree line, to the upper left corner of the chart.

The first conclusion of our analysis is that greenium is far from being a homogeneous phenomenon, as both positive and negative greenium can be observed in the secondary market.

Figure 16.7 is a snapshot at one point in time (in this case, March 2021), but greenium keeps evolving given its definition as a difference between observed and interpolated z-spreads. For this reason, we have constructed a panel with comparable green and conventional euro-denominated bonds to measure the trend in the greenium over time. By comparable, we refer to bonds from the same issuer and with 'similar' maturities. The greenium for euro-denominated corporate bonds, calculated as the difference between the average z-spread of

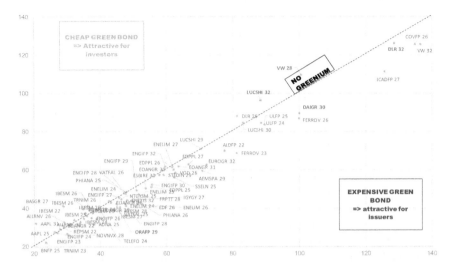

Figure 16.7 Greenium for Euro-Denominated Corporate Issuers (Analysis at Early June 2021).

Sources: Bloomberg, Natixis.

Note: X-axis: Interpolated z-spread on the conventional € curve for each issuer, Y-axis: observed z-spread for impact bonds.

our green euro corporate debt panel and the equivalent conventional bond sample, became positive after the announcements of the various lockdowns in Europe in March 2020. However, when the market started to recover in April 2020, impact bonds outperformed their conventional equivalents (Figure 16.8).

Since Summer 2020, the greenium has spread from the euro-denominated corporate market (where it started to become significant at the end of the year 2017, see chart 8 below), to other markets, such as dollar-denominated corporate bonds, and euro-denominated senior preferred and non-senior preferred bank debts. This phenomenon is shown in Figure 16.9 which measures the greenium as a percentage of the average z-spread of a conventional bond

Figure 16.8 Trend in Greenium for Euro-denominated Corporate Issuers (Analysis at early June 2021).

Source: Natixis CIB Research.

or index. Figure 16.9 shows that, at early June 2021, the negative greenium had become the rule rather than the exception.

Another observation relates to the greenium dependency on the maturity of the bond; generally, the longer the maturity, the higher the negative greenium. Figure 16.10 shows that the greenium was between −4 and −5 basis points (bps) for euro -denominated corporate debts of maturities between five and ten years, whereas the greenium was much more limited for short-dated bonds. This market observation is aligned with greater demand for impact bonds from insurance and pension funds, and with these investors tending to look for longer-dated bonds.

In some cases, however, the greenium becomes more difficult to calculate and can become technically biased. Some issuers have started to issue green bonds at the expense of conventional bonds, which makes greenium technically disappear over time. This is the case for some utilities such as Tennet or Iberdrola, where conventional spreads tend to tighten towards green bond levels. Since 2016, Iberdrola has issued only one conventional senior bond (IBESM 29 for €735 million) compared to 7 green bonds amounting in total to €5.7 billion. Similarly, Tennet issued its last conventional bond in 2011 for €500 million, followed by 19 issues of green senior bonds amounting to €11.6 billion.

It is also worth noticing that Gecina transformed all its outstanding bond issues of €5.6 billion into green bonds on the 26th May 2021, following a massive approval from its bondholders (92%). Further, the French real estate company also committed to apply for the green format for all of its future issues. Therefore, no Greenium can be calculated for that real estate company after the end of May.

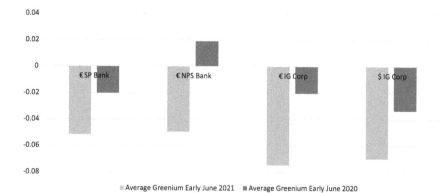

Figure 16.9 Trend in Greenium by Asset Class (Analysis at Early June 2021), as a % of average Z-spreads.
Source: Natixis CIB Research.

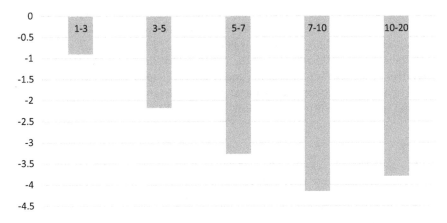

Figure 16.10 Trend in Greenium for Euro-Denominated Corporate by Maturity (Analysis at Early June 2021).
Source: Natixis CIB Research.

Conclusion

The success of the impact bond market is due in part to its credibility with investors and issuers alike. For investors, impact bonds provide new levels of scrutiny and transparency on themes that are critical to issuers' financial performance in the short and long term. Impact bonds are a commercial opportunity to build solutions for clients but also a way to respond to emerging regulatory and client scrutiny. For issuers, it has enabled new relationships to form with a broader investor base and for a common purpose, which is to enable a stronger response to shared environmental and social challenges.

Despite rapid growth, the impact bond market remains small. The process to issue an impact bond remains more meticulous and potentially costly than for conventional securities. There can be hurdles producing frameworks, independent verification or opinions, and annual reporting requirements. This limits its appeal to some issuers. But we believe the additional work producing impact bonds supports to issuers' understanding, control, and improvement of sustainability issues. This accounts for more proactive involvement from issuers across countries and issuance types that may not have strong sustainability legacies or a history of industry-leading performance.

Despite rising issuance, the market remains at a phase where demand exceeds supply. As a result, impact euro-denominated corporate bonds (A-rated and BBB-rated) and financial bonds (senior preferred & senior non-preferred) all exhibit pricing differences in the primary market compared to conventional bonds.

Our analysis of the secondary bond market shows the existence of a greenium spreading from the corporate debt market to all fixed income markets: to financial senior preferred, non-preferred and even covered bonds, as well as to agencies and supranationals. This greenium is persistent over time and tends to increase with the maturity of the bond and the credit risk of the issuer. As of early June 2021, this Greenium was between 5 and 8% of the z-spread of a similar conventional bond (for corporate and financial debts), between 2 and 3 times more (as a % of the spread) than our estimate back in June 2020.

Notes

1 We would like to acknowledge and thank, Cédric Merle and Laurie Chesné for their contributions to this chapter.
2 Verbund issued a world's first bond combining Use-of-Proceeds earmarking and KPI-linking mechanism in March 2021.
3 The EU Taxonomy of Sustainable Activities is publicly available at https://ec.europa. eu/info/business-economy-euro/banking-and-finance/sustainable-finance/ eu-taxonomy-sustainable-activities_en.
4 Sustainability bonds are currently understood in the market as a 'mixture' of green and social bonds in one instrument in the sense that proceeds of these bonds are allocated to eligible categories defined by The Green Bond Principles (GBP) and The Social Bond Principles (SBP). For this reason, there are no 'Sustainability Bond Principles', merely Sustainability Bond Guidelines which refer to GBP and SBP for definition of eligible categories for allocation of proceeds from a sustainability bond.
5 See https://www.icmagroup.org/sustainable-finance/external-reviews/.
6 Available at https://www.finanzaspublicas.hacienda.gob.mx/work/models/ Finanzas_Publicas/docs/ori/Espanol/SDG/UMS-SDG_Sustainable_Bond_ Framework.pdf.
7 Available at https://gsh.cib.natixis.com/our-center-of-expertise/articles/solving-the-sustainable-development-goals-rubik-s-cube.
8 The Z-spread (the zero-volatility spread) is the constant spread over the zero-coupon yield curve required to discounting a pre-determined cash flow schedule to arrive at its present market price.

References

Green Bond Principles (GBP) and International Capital Market Association (ICMA) (2018), *Green Bond Principles: Voluntary Process Guidelines for Issuing Green Bonds.* [online]. Available at: https://www.icmagroup.org/assets/documents/Regulatory/Green-Bonds/Green-Bonds-Principles-June-2018-270520.pdf (Accessed 2 April 2021).

Social Bonds Principles and (ICMA) (2020), *Social Bond Principles: Voluntary Process Guidelines for Issuing Social Bonds.* [online]. Available at: https://www.icmagroup. org/assets/documents/Regulatory/Green-Bonds/June-2020/Social-Bond-PrinciplesJune-2020-090620.pdf (Accessed 2 April 2021).

Sustainability-Linked Bond Principles and ICMA (2020), *Sustainability-Linked Bond Principles. Voluntary Process Guidelines. June 2020.* [online]. Available at: https:// www.icmagroup.org/assets/documents/Regulatory/Green-Bonds/June-2020/ Sustainability-Linked-Bond-Principles-June-2020-171120.pdf (Accessed 4 June 2021).

Part 5

Market Influencers

17 The Role of Sustainable Treasury Teams[1]

Arthur Krebbers and Jaspreet Singh

Corporate treasury teams are responsible for implementing policies that manage the financial position of their firms. Their day-to-day responsibilities range from managing bank deposits, supplier payments, and foreign exchange transactions to interest rate hedging and working capital management. Furthermore, they are also tasked with the issuance of new public debt.

NatWest helps corporate treasury and wider finance teams develop holistic sustainable treasury strategies, which encompasses many or all of these activities. Such strategies involve the adoption of sustainability or environmental, social, and governance (ESG) considerations (we will use the terms interchangeably in this chapter) within the relevant treasury workstream. Amongst other elements, this could include embedding sustainability features into a company's disclosure (e.g. when communicating with investors), into the key performance indicators of a financial instrument, or into the selection process of suppliers and counterparties. We define treasury functions that adopt this type of holistic sustainability approach as 'sustainable treasury teams'.[2]

This chapter discusses some of the key sustainability workstreams for these divisions as well as areas where NatWest assists corporates. Where feasible, we use specific case-studies to provide examples of current best practice – noting that ESG is a rapidly evolving field. The next sections are structured as follows. First, we introduce reasons for recent changes in treasury teams' approach to sustainability. Then we look at specific treasury workstreams in more detail: corporate sustainability reporting; ESG ratings management; financing and liquidity products; investor relations and engagement; cash management and bookrunner selection. We have excluded risk management as hedging instrument structures are still being determined and standardised. We also do not reference carbon markets which are a distinct commodity, which more treasuries are including in their operations and strategy. The structures being suggested are similar to those set out in the financing and liquidity product section, while ESG selection criteria of hedging counterparties follow those of bookrunners.

DOI: 10.4324/9781003055341-22

The Post-2015 Rise of ESG and its Impact on Treasury Teams

Until 2015, ESG investing matters were seen as non-core by most corporate treasury teams. Treasurers often had a natural conservatism around this topic, considering it as not directly relevant to their duty of prudently managing a company's financial position. Moreover, sustainability conversations at the time were often one-dimensional: 'Should I consider issuing a green bond?', to which the answer for many firms was negative.

The 2015 Paris Agreement created substantial and unprecedented global momentum around the critical ESG theme of climate change – as countries around the world agreed to limit global temperature to well below 2°C, preferably to 1.5°C, compared to pre-industrial levels. Finance was identified as a key enabler to support countries in implementing their national climate plans and increase their climate ambition over time.

Since 2015, climate change (and sustainability topics more broadly) has started to feature in many chief financial officer (CFO) and treasury conversations: in questions from investors, credit rating agencies, relationship banks, in questions from their boards, and in their own team meetings, often raised by employees. Such stakeholder pressure has led to a broadening of the role of treasury teams in relation to sustainability aspects. We have outlined some of the key areas of focus in Table 17.1.

Table 17.1 Areas of Focus for Treasury Teams.

Key Areas of Focus	Considerations
Funding strategy	• Green/ social / sustainable/sustainability-linked debt (bonds, term loans) • Private placements for specific projects • Allocation to ESG investors • Use of proceeds instruments • KPI-linked instruments
Institutional developments	• Regulation • Political initiatives • Industry-led
Sustainability strategy and key performance indicators (KPIs)	• Non-financial KPIs • Adherence to reporting standards e.g. Task Force on Climate-related Financial Related Disclosures (TCFD) • Peer best practices • Quantitative/qualitative balance
ESG rating management	• Close dialogue with major agencies (Sustainalytics, ISS, MSCI, etc.) • Target rating/ranking (publicly communicated)
Investor relations	• Disclosure on sustainability strategy and metrics • ESG investor engagement • Extracts from ESG agency report

Key Areas of Focus	Considerations
Lending instruments	• Liquidity: ESG pricing-based revolving credit facilities (RCFs) • Commercial paper
Cash investment strategy	• Sustainability criteria (exclusionary/impact focus) • UN-backed Principles for Responsible Investment (PRI) • Green/ESG deposits
Hedging strategy/ hedging	• Sustainability/ESG metric-based hedging • Hedging counterparties
Counterparty selection	• ESG/Sustainability questionnaires
Carbon markets	• Carbon offsets/credits • Monitor carbon regulations and pricing • Strategy for reducing net emissions

As sustainability becomes a focus of major institutional investors, it is also starting to have a direct impact on a treasurer's 'day job' of managing the company's financial position. Recent research is pointing towards various financial benefits of an improved ESG standing. Multiple studies have identified a link between a corporate ESG/sustainability focus and lower cost of corporate financing (see, for example, Eliwa et al., 2019). Companies with the weakest ESG credentials tend to trade with the widest CDS spreads, indicating that a corporate focus on ESG reduces a firm's risk and therefore its cost of debt capital (Hermes, 2017). Moreover, the growing issuance of impact labelled securities is creating a 'halo' effect, with green bond issuance positively correlating to improving equity prices (Krebbers, 2019).

Corporate Sustainability Reporting

From our experience with customers, being an effective sustainable treasury team often starts with embedding credible sustainability reporting.

Such reporting is increasingly becoming a commercial imperative: ESG investors, in fulfilling their duty of care towards their own stakeholders, expect corporates to be more transparent regarding their material sustainability risks and opportunities. This is highlighted by the investor survey result we show in Figure 17.1.

Additionally, regulators and other market participants, including rating agencies, are aligning their expectations on sustainability disclosures; calling for more authentic, measurable, credible, and standardised information to fully understand a company's current and future preparedness.

As a result, company disclosures on new topics such as climate change action plans, ESG risks and opportunities, and sustainability targets are forming a part of mainstream filings, investor communications, and announcements – and mark the first step we take with our customers in preparation for a sustainable debt issuance.

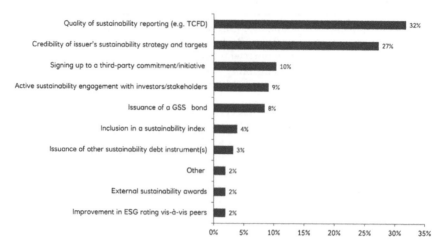

Figure 17.1 Investor Responses to Question: 'Which two actions best underscore an issuer's commitment to sustainability?'.
Source: NatWest, 2021.

Whether preparing for a sustainability-linked financing or communicating responsible corporate citizenship behaviours on a continuous basis, we have seen in our work with customers that companies face several common reporting challenges which include (1) identifying key stakeholders and their specific information needs; (2) aligning sustainability disclosures with broader corporate business strategy; and (3) moving towards consistent, measurable, and impact-focussed reporting.

Identifying Key Stakeholders and their Specific Information Needs

Companies typically start their sustainability reporting journey outward-looking, focussing on the impact of their business activities on the environment and society. However, corporate stakeholders are also increasingly interested in inward-looking reporting, which demonstrates how prepared a company is to address external sustainability-related factors and how this may impact performance.

To address this, many companies use established sustainability reporting standards for guidance. However, the sustainability reporting landscape has evolved rapidly with new and competing reporting frameworks being developed. The range of standards and frameworks – including the Global Reporting Initiative (GRI), the International Integrated Reporting Council (IIRC), the Climate Disclosure Standards Board (CDSB), the Sustainability Accounting Standards Board (SASB), TCFD, CDP, UN Global Compact (UNGC), and the Sustainable Development Goals (SDGs) – have created some confusion among publishers and users of the reports. As a result, we often get asked by our customers on how to identify the most suitable reporting standard for their specific business.

Each standard and framework has different objectives and focus areas, and companies need to think about which framework best suits the information needs of their diverse stakeholders. Recent consolidation of reporting standards should improve the consistency and comparability of sustainability information. Most notably, is the creation of the International Sustainability Standards Board (ISSB) which was announced at COP26 in November 2021 by the IFRS Foundation to consolidate IIRC, SASB and CDSB to deliver a comprehensive global baseline of sustainability-related disclosure standards. This is particularly relevant for investors who report ESG information in different ways and when benchmarking companies' ESG strategies.

While mandatory climate reporting in many markets is a sign of progress, such as in the UK and EU, companies can and are going beyond standardised industry reporting guidelines. We advise our customers to tell their full story, which goes beyond pure financials and includes a holistic view of the non-financial value they are creating. We have experienced that this is often easier said than done: at the start of their sustainability journey companies tend to have only limited or imprecise information about their non-financial performance such as their environmental and social impact. To close this gap, we have found that stakeholder panels, where companies invite customers and community representatives to jointly assess the most material issues facing the business and discuss possible solutions, can be an excellent tool to receive meaningful input for developing a sustainability strategy.

Aligning Sustainability Disclosures with Broader Corporate Business Strategy

Sustainability disclosures need to reflect a company's size, the key issues in its sector and geography of operation, and its product or service offering. This may require a broad sustainability approach and narrative, and hence presents a challenge for global companies operating in multiple lines of business.

A strong sustainability disclosure should demonstrate that a company fully understands its material issues and actively develops responsible business strategies aligned with its overall ambition and business strategy. As best practice evolves this is set to include a clear articulation of the firm's broader societal purpose, beyond the traditional focus of maximising financial returns for shareholders.

Case-Study: Enhancing ESG Disclosures

A Dutch utility was looking to further develop its sustainability reporting. A key driver was understanding how the company's disclosures performed against ESG rating agency methodologies and compared against peers.

NatWest assisted by analysing the company's ESG disclosures and conducting a gap analysis. This involved assessing the difference between the company's performance against various ESG ratings and the company's current sustainability reporting. This helped the company to identify areas where more information was required by the ESG rating agencies. By prioritising the reporting requirements that could make the largest improvement to the company's ESG ratings, these were identified as the key material issues. NatWest then conducted a benchmarking review to identify best-in-class disclosures by sector peers to see how others were making these disclosures.

This process helped the utility firm to focus on impactful changes to its disclosures, adding greater information around the environmental and societal impacts of operations as well as how the company interacts with its stakeholders.

Companies also need to examine the challenges they face delivering their business strategy and be transparent about; for example, future resource constraints potentially affecting their growth and expansion, and the positive and negative impacts on financial performance. We have begun to see companies addressing this by publishing clear position statements around specific sustainability topics and reporting extensively on specific risks and mitigating factors or actions.

Moving Towards Consistent, Measurable, and Impact-focussed Reporting

Nascent sustainability reporting is often characterised by commitments and selective sustainability measures. Companies need to review their internal approach to reporting as information users start to demand robust, reliable, comprehensive, and comparable data.

Challenges remain in how sustainability information is delivered internally within an organisation. Any investor relations, finance, marketing, or sustainability team requiring input and agreement on corporate messaging will appreciate the difficulty achieving consensus across multiple diverse functions. Similarly, sustainability metrics, which by their nature can be more aspirational, stretching, and sometimes less tangible than traditional financial metrics, do not always align with traditional financial targets and reporting. Some firms are choosing to produce a sustainability supplement as part of their annual report, with cross references between the two. Nonetheless, the direction of travel is merging both financial and sustainability reporting, with finance teams taking greater ownership over sustainability reporting. From our work with customers, we find the most effective approach is to understand sustainability as a company-wide project, requiring a dedicated programme management team alongside project teams with representatives from all corporate functions.

Higher-quality sustainability reporting will provide companies with the ability to differentiate themselves in the market, allowing them to access broader capital pools at more favourable pricing and align to the most relevant regulations. Many companies also acknowledge that this reporting will not only improve staff satisfaction and retention, but also help attract the growing number of customers who are seeking to do business more responsibly.

ESG Ratings Management

ESG ratings and scoring providers are becoming a topic of growing NatWest engagement with corporate customers.[3] It is partly for this reason that in 2019 we set up an ESG Advisory team, linked with our wider Rating Advisory business.

Our engagement with customers on this topic typically begins with a discussion on the nature of ESG rating operating models and their methodologies. Only then can treasury teams consider ways to best manage and, where appropriate, seek to improve, their ESG ratings.

In this regard, ESG rating agencies arrive at the overall rating of a company's ESG performance by calculating a composite score of individual ESG indicators. Initially, a set of material indicators are determined that affect a company. These are primarily derived from its sector of operation and can be tailored further depending on the company's business model, geographic operations, and its exposure to local factors, such as legislation and stakeholder expectations. Each indicator is then assigned a weighting and score that helps to compute an overall ESG score.

There are many differences in approach, in methodology, and in nomenclature between ESG rating agencies, which make ratings impractical to compare. We believe it is crucial for treasury and sustainability teams to understand the meaning of each rating. For example, Sustainalytics' ESG rating is an 'absolute' numerical score (0–100, higher worse) measuring unmanageable and manageable ESG risks. As an absolute score, the rating can be compared across companies and industries. In comparison, ISS ESG provides an absolute score but expressed as a letter range (A+ (best) to D- (worst)) and does not deconstruct manageable risks. And, in another contrast, MSCI reflects ESG performance relative to an industry/peer set, with the rating expressed as a different letter range: AAA (leader) to CCC (laggard). This is the immediately noticeable difference between the selected agencies, but there are many more.

Contrary to credit ratings, most of which are solicited and allow rating agencies to collect credit relevant information (including private information) through regular discussions with the treasury teams of the rated entity, ESG ratings are currently in most cases unsolicited. ESG rating agencies typically make their evaluations based on publicly available information or on commercial data such as corporate sustainability reports and information from corporate websites.

Therefore, treasury teams need to recognise their ESG ratings will be mainly driven by public information. This means that the rating is not influenced only by company performance, but whether that progress is communicated externally. Those not sharing their ESG ambitions, measures, and impacts will be penalised with a lower ESG rating (which may result in less favourable pricing for any debt issuances).

Figure 17.2 highlights how, based on our experience with customers, treasury teams tend to manage their ESG ratings. Many acknowledge that they

	None	Medium/selective	Extensive
Strategic importance	• No use of ESG ratings • No strategic interest or potential upside perceived in engaging with agencies	• Incorporation of ESG rating(s) in investor presentations, annual report, customer pitches etc. • Limited use case of ESG rating agencies	• Targeting of ESG rating metrics/positioning • Issuance sustainability metrics based financial products (e.g. loans) • Staff/management contracts linked to ESG rating metrics • Extended ESG rating agency license for benchmarking
Communication	• No response to surveys/requests for information • No bandwidth allocation • No feedback loop with comments	• Response to surveys/ requests for information from selection of ESG agencies • Focused feedback loop: address major inaccuracies/mistakes	• Panel of ESG agencies • Annual/more frequent calls to provide business updates • Proactively inform of key sustainability policy developments
Policy changes	• No impact on sustainability policies and targets • Risk management not informed by ESG assessments	• 'Quick wins': focus on areas that are most material to sustainability profile • Limited business alignment and resource focus on Sustainability	• 'Best in class' goal: working group across Sustainability, Treasury and management that assess policy changes needed to be best-in-class

Degree of engagement

Figure 17.2 NatWest Customers' Typical Approaches to ESG Ratings Management.

need to engage proactively and continually with rating agencies to understand and ensure ratings are accurate.

Critics point out that discrepancies in ESG ratings mean they are not easily comparable. Krosinsky (2018) highlights the correlation between the two major rating agencies, Sustainalytics and MSCI ESG Ratings, is 0.3. In comparison we usually see a correlation of c. 0.9 in credit ratings. Additionally, many investors use multiple ESG ratings or produce their own. Therefore, it is important for corporate treasury teams to assess which ESG ratings and data matter most to their investors.

This is especially important for private companies that may not have third-party ratings. Private issuers should expect to engage directly with ratings providers to get onto their coverage list.

We have identified the following best practice: First, a focus on two or three major ESG rating agencies. Second, identifying material information or rating drivers and a quick win strategy. Third, engaging proactively with agencies in information provision.

Case-Study: Obtaining a Solicited ESG Rating

A UK utility recognised the growing emphasis investors place on ESG ratings and asked NatWest to support them with obtaining a debut solicited ESG rating.

NatWest assisted the company by running an ESG rating Request for Proposal (RFP) process to help select an appropriate ESG ratings agency. This was an important step in order to choose the ESG agency that best understood the company's business model and would be collaborative through the ESG rating process. NatWest used its experience to help select which highly credible ESG rating agencies to reach out to for the RFP. Following the responses received and interviews held, the company chose ISS ESG to provide an ESG rating.

NatWest supported the company to optimally position its sustainability reporting with ISS ESG and helped them achieve an overall rating of B (two notches above the sector average of C+).

Following the successful ESG rating, the company issued a public bond highlighting its strong ESG credentials and rating, which was well received by investors.

Financing Products

Our customers typically find that issuing a GSSS (Green, Social, Sustainable or Sustainability-linked) labelled instrument – such as a bond for long-term financing and/or a bank loan for immediate funding – is a very tangible action a treasury team can undertake to show their wider commitment to sustainability. And in the case of a public market instrument, such issuance often gets substantial press and stakeholder attention.

In this section we describe the three main stages where we tend to assist in bringing this type of instrument to market: (i) selecting the instrument type, (ii) determining the appropriate label, and (iii) executing the transaction. These stages can take anywhere from four weeks to over a year to complete.

Case-Study: Debut Green Bond

Northern Powergrid is responsible for the electricity network that powers everyday life for 8 million people across the UK. Northern Powergrid distributes power to 3.9 million homes and businesses through its network of more than 64,000 substations, over 96,000 km of overhead lines and underground cables, spanning almost 25,000 square km. Its dedicated team of around 2,700 employees ensures this service operates 24 hours a day, 365 days a year – no matter what the circumstances – to maintain a safe, reliable, and efficient electricity supply.

Decarbonisation of electricity is essential if the UK is to meet its own zero carbon target by 2050, as well as the global targets of the Paris Agreement. Electricity networks like Northern Powergrid's play a central role in enabling this transformation, providing the infrastructure to link generator and consumer in new and flexible ways to drive change.

Northern Powergrid wanted to issue a Green Bond under a Green Finance Framework in order to demonstrate the link between the investment the company makes and the long-term environmental benefits for its customers. NatWest played a lead role in Northern Powergrid's debut Green bond issuance, assisting with their new Green Finance Framework in our role of Sole Structuring Adviser.

Northern Powergrid is the first UK electricity distribution network operator (DNO) to fund its investment plans by issuing a bond under a Green Finance Framework. The transaction marked an important step in the critical role that DNOs play in reaching the UK government's 'Net Zero by 2050' ambition. The 42-year £300 million proceeds invest in projects that support the take-up of low-carbon energy and lower the environmental impact in local communities across its network.

Instrument Structure

Determining the sustainability structure means clarity on three factors (see Table 17.2):

1   Sustainability disclosure: Finance teams reluctant to make any binding sustainability commitments could accentuate their sustainability strategy in transaction marketing materials (e.g. through incorporating an ESG rating in the terms and conditions, right below the credit ratings). The treasury team of a transportation company customer considered this approach the most fitting with their profile as an 'intrinsically green' firm, making all their (green and non-green) debt issues impactful.

2   Sustainability-linked: This requires that a bond attribute, typically the coupon, is linked to the company meeting a predetermined sustainability key performance indicator (KPI). Such a route is compelling for firms who don't want to face restrictions around identifying and maintaining a specific green and/or social pool of assets, or indeed companies who lack tangible assets for such a pool.

3   Sustainability use of proceeds: This involves a (not legally binding) pledge whereby the bond issuer commits to investing an equivalent amount of proceeds in projects and/or assets with demonstrable environmental and/or social benefits. It is the most suitable route for companies that have identified projects to raise a benchmark bond in the region of £250 million or €500 million, for example.[4]

Table 17.2 Structural Categories of Major Sustainability Debt.

Sustainability Disclosure	Sustainability-Linked	Sustainability Use of Proceeds
• Enhanced disclosure on borrower's sustainability profile • Internally sourced information • Externally sourced – e.g. solicited ESG rating	• Pricing/coupon linked to meeting a sustainability target	• Commitment to invest an equivalent notional in projects/assets with sustainability benefits

Instrument Label

There are many sustainability use-of-proceeds labels. Determining which is the most suitable requires careful assessment of the borrower's sustainability priorities, target investors, and wider stakeholders.

Corporate treasury teams can identify impactful and credible environmental expenditure, making the green bond route the most frequently considered. An increasing number opt for sustainability as their format of choice to also include socially focused expenditure, and thereby communicate a holistic strategy to the market. New labels are being used to promote specific sustainability propositions. Examples include gender equality, transition, circular economy, water/blue, and UN Sustainable Development Goals (SDGs). These instruments are more likely to be issued by experienced impact bond issuers.

Execution of Sustainable Finance Products

Besides selecting a suitable label, a sustainable financing instrument also affects other fundraising stages:

- Documentation: Sustainable debt instruments are typically issued under a dedicated framework. This typically requires at least four weeks of preparation time to produce. In addition, the legal prospectus incorporates the sustainability features and associated risk factors (often referencing this framework).
- Bank selection: For new or infrequent sustainable debt issuers, it is beneficial to appoint one or two banks as Sustainability Structuring Advisors to help with the project management. In addition, requests for proposals (RFPs) for regular bookrunner roles often incorporate questions around a bank's overall sustainability strategy and expertise (beyond the traditional debt capital markets questions).
- Investor engagement: When marketing a sustainable financing instrument, it is important for the issuer to present a credible sustainability

narrative that is informed by relevant market standards (e.g. showing how the sustainability strategy aligns with well-recognised market standards, as well as the structural features of the instrument).

- Allocation: When distributing bond instruments, companies often look to identify and then prioritise sustainability-focused investors. This can be done through assessing an investor's overall ESG commitments (e.g. signatories of the UN-backed Principles for Responsible Investment (PRI)) as well as the sustainability objectives of the specific investment funds that bonds are allocated to.

Liquidity Products

Sustainability-linked loans are similar in structure to sustainability-linked bonds (see Table 17.2). While most issuers use environmental KPIs, many now also use social or governance targets.

Market growth has been driven both by borrowers looking to show their commitment to sustainability, and lenders (banks) bound by the UN Principles for Responsible Banking to organise and support sustainable economic activity. Consequently, the Loan Market Association (LMA), an industry group for syndicated loans, developed the Sustainability-Linked Loan Principles (SLLP) to promote sustainable loans and ensure their integrity; they are comprised of five key areas: (1) Selection of Key Performance Indicators (KPIs); (2) Calibration of Sustainability Performance Targets (SPTs); (3) Loan Characteristics; (4) Reporting; and (5) Verification (LMA, 2022).

Elaborating on the more practical elements from these principles, borrowers and lenders need to discuss the choice of KPIs, pricing and costs, and reporting and transparency.

Choice of KPIs

The loan's underlying KPIs need to align with the borrowers' overall sustainability objectives and agenda. Typically, borrowers and lenders choose between one to five KPIs. While borrowers want to use quantifiable and comfortably achievable KPIs, it is important to formulate ambitious, 'stretching' KPIs, in line with the SLLP. Sustainability KPIs will need to be annualised to allow regular performance reviews throughout the duration of the loan. Some borrowers are using ESG scores provided by experts, such as rating agencies, instead of KPIs.

Pricing and Costs

Typically, lenders and borrowers agree on a 'two-way' pricing mechanism: If targets are met, the borrower may receive a margin discount. If targets are not met, then an equivalent margin premium will be added.

Borrowers can incur additional costs for such loans including fees for independent parties, which audit or assess KPI performance and annual reporting. Obtaining or using an ESG score from a rating agency for the loan can also come at a cost.

Reporting and Transparency

Documentation of the sustainability-linked loan typically includes:

- Definitions of agreed upon KPIs and performance targets.
- Agreed margin adjustment mechanic if targets are met/not met.
- A sustainability certificate, requiring the borrower to provide its verified sustainability performance to the lenders, usually on an annual basis.

While the preparations for a sustainability-linked loan can be completed in between two and four weeks, borrowers can opt for a lender taking on the role of a sustainability coordinator who can develop an execution plan and help select the KPIs for the loan as well as advise on the terms and conditions of the proposed documentation. Sustainability coordinators also act as a conduit between the lenders to achieve consensus on the loan facility and the underlying sustainability targets. As discussed in the Cash Management section below, we are also starting to see ESG features in other corporate liquidity products – most notably commercial paper.

Investor Relations and Engagement

Fixed income investors have enhanced their ESG focus and capabilities in recent years. While for many years it was a peripheral topic, ESG is now a core part of the investment decision-making process. This is apparent in the rise of proprietary ESG scoring techniques, frequent launches of sustainability fixed income portfolios, and frequent discussion of ESG topics at investor roadshows. Even for conventional bond issuances, we have found it is not unusual for 30–50% of investor questions to centre around ESG topics.

Against this backdrop, it can sometimes be tempting for corporate sustainability teams to hide behind ESG agencies and reporting standards to fulfil the growing information needs of their investors. However, it is essential to engage directly with the bondholders to understand their preferences among the varying sustainability accreditations and ratings.

Moreover, several of our largest customers use direct investor engagement to determine their panel of ESG agencies and focus areas in their sustainability reporting. Direct engagement reduces the inevitable miscommunication that occurs when information intermediaries set out their ESG narrative. Like a firm's credit story, their ESG story is too important to be left solely to external stakeholders.

Informal Channels

We regularly organise ESG speed dating sessions, either in the form of a single-company roadshow or as part of a conference for larger groups of companies and investors. These sessions offer privacy to tackle the more sensitive topics. They also deliver some soft factors to investors, including the body language of the management that provides a relevant insight into how enthusiastic and knowledgeable senior echelons are about their firm's sustainability objectives and activities.

Sustainability webinars are useful for outlining aspects of a company's sustainability strategy to the long tail of smaller, ESG-focused investors. While more time efficient, to full benefit issuers they require careful discussion with individual attendees to obtain feedback.

Formal Channels

More advanced ESG investors use in-house questionnaires to ask portfolio companies about their approach to ESG. This allows investors, at least partly, to remove ESG information specialists. These questionnaires link directly to the investment requirements of the investor, or a specific portfolio.

On the other hand, some companies conduct their own investor and stakeholder ESG surveys. These tend to centre on the sustainability topics most relevant to their company and that should be in focus for external reporting. If conducted regularly (at least once a year), they are a useful tool for companies to measure progress and to identify the ESG issues they need to emphasise.

Key Content to Consider

Whether in face-to-face meetings or via written means, when considering the key points to convey to their investor base, we advise corporate issuers to follow the 'four As':

- Ambition: showcase the areas you are leading your sector/peer group.
- Analysis: where possible, add quantitative information to back your ESG commitments.
- Alignment: focus on projects/initiatives that align with your overall strategy.
- Additive: discuss the marginal impact you are having, highlighting what is new or differentiating.

Cash Management

Investors' responsible investing activities predominantly focus on market instruments such as impact bonds and medium- or long-term conventional bond securities. This aligns with responsible investment trends that have emphasised taking a long-term investment perspective rather than taking short-term quarterly approaches to investing.

The COVID-19 pandemic has shown that the provision of short-term relief is also aligned with sustainable principles for companies and investors. Short-term cash investing should manage ESG risks and involve stewardship like other fixed income securities. Moreover, sustainability-minded corporate treasurers with large cash positions – which they hold not only to fulfil daily transactions of their business, but also to meet uncertainties and emergencies – consider themselves accountable to manage cash responsibly.

Most companies adopt a relatively prudent and conservative cash investment policy, restricting them from buying longer dated, tradeable instruments, such as bonds. Their universe of investable products typically includes deposits and money market funds, and in some cases commercial paper. Fortunately, ESG solutions are available across all three of these.

Deposits

Case-Study: ESG Deposits

Dutch local government-owned PZEM N.V. supplies and trades in energy products and services for business customers in the Netherlands and internationally. With sustainability at the heart of PZEM's strategy, its finance function was keen to further incorporate this into their cash investment policies.

NatWest worked with PZEM to structure a deposit product within its ESG Product framework that that matched their tenor and tranching requirements.

Frank Verhagen CEO of PZEM commented:

> At PZEM we always need to balance the interests of all our stakeholders, this also counts for how we invest our cash. Taking into account the current low interest rate environment and the prudent investment policy of PZEM, it is difficult to realise a return, let alone to expand our ESG policy to the finance function. We have valued the open dialogue with NatWest Markets on cash investment solutions for some time, but with the new ESG deposit they have managed to tailor a solution for us without compromising on any of our prudent investment policy ambitions.

ESG deposits make both ethical and business sense. Besides growing ESG-aligned assets, it has attracted 'stickier' deposits from a broader range of deposit counterparties. Several retail and commercial banks have also started introducing sustainability deposits. These are typically green in nature, with the associated pledge focused on investments in their renewable energy lending book.

Money Market Funds

ESG investments have spread from equity to credit funds and, in recent years, to money market funds. Various fixed income investors have announced holistic approaches where they incorporate responsible investment parameters into all their debt portfolios – including at the short end of the investment opportunity curve.

ESG-labelled money market funds tend to consider several investment approaches:

1   Excluding issuers active in environmentally or socially harmful industries.
2   Overweighting positions in companies with stronger ESG ratings.
3   Allocate holdings in ESG-labelled commercial paper.

The strategies maintain a very conservative approach to risk, ensuring they continue to be eligible for AAA credit ratings.

Commercial Paper

Recent years have seen a steady rise in sustainability-labelled commercial paper issuances. These fall within three categories:

1   Use of proceeds: Use-of-proceeds commercial paper effectively represents an impact bond with a short tenor. The issuer pledges to invest the raised proceeds in, for example, environmentally positive projects set out in a green finance framework. The framework is effectively an expanded green bond framework that explicitly allows the company to issue all forms of green-labelled liabilities, not just bonds.
2   Sustainability target: Sustainability target commercial paper associates the issuance with attaining a corporate sustainability goal. The company promises to provide a verified report once this goal has been reached. The trailblazing example in this space comes from Italian utility Enel in 2019.[5]
3   ESG rating: ESG-rated commercial paper promotes the strong ESG rating of an issuer. Should an issuer not meet a predefined ESG score and sector-relative ranking, they are required to inform noteholders. In September 2020, NatWest helped LafargeHolcim, a Swiss multinational company that manufactures building materials, launch its ESG European Commercial Paper programme to enable the company to issue ESG Notes if its Sustainalytics ESG Rating remained within the top 25% of its industry group. Failing to meet this condition, the firm could continue to issue notes under the programme, but they would not be designated as ESG Notes. The inclusion of an ESG Rating commitment helped to link LafargeHolcim's liquidity programme with its broader ESG targets. Given the short-dated nature of the commercial paper market, the public release obligation of falling below the ESG commitment was seen as the most appropriate penalty.

Bookrunner Selection

Sustainability-focused treasury teams are also becoming more focused on working with suppliers that share their values. Relationship banks seeking to win ancillary business therefore need to do more than solely demonstrate expertise in the relevant financial product, such as debt capital markets intermediation. Now, they also must demonstrate leadership in the ESG areas their corporate customers consider important.

Companies that want to take a systematic approach to embedding ESG selection criteria into their requests for proposals tend to focus on three aspects: (i) selecting ESG information sources for selection criteria, (ii) considering appropriate supplier assessment strategies, and (iii) drafting suitable supplier ESG questions.

ESG Information Sources for Selection Criteria

Most sustainable treasury teams prefer selecting their own list of ESG eligibility criteria for banks and other financial suppliers. It allows them to find the right mix between the sustainability themes they care about as well as quantitative and qualitative information.

A few firms also rely on third-party ESG sources, such as ESG ratings of their banking group. As these solutions develop and grow in market acceptance, this has the potential to become an embedded part of treasury counterparty requirements. We can expect to see firms expanding current hard credit rating standards for counterparties (e.g. 'A' or better) into credit and ESG rating standards.

Assessment Types

We have seen sustainable treasury teams embed their ESG criteria in various ways. Examples of our experience with customers include:

1   Onboarding, where the bank must provide a clear description of its sustainability strategy to satisfy the firm's onboarding process for new financial counterparties.
2   Deal-specific requests for proposals, where the set of questions for a project, such as a green bond issuance, includes a subset focused on the bank's sustainability goals.
3   Annual surveys, where a set of sustainability questions are sent to each relationship bank on an annual basis to ascertain a continued sustainability fit of the banking group.
4   Face-to-face meetings, where annual sustainability strategy-focused meetings are held with each relationship bank.

Type of Supplier/Bank Questions

The questions that NatWest customers have asked in order to gauge our ESG commitment and actions have included:

1   What is your bank doing on sustainability?
2   Who in the bank is ultimately responsible for sustainability?
3   What does your societal purpose mean in practice?
4   Which sustainable products and services do you offer?
5   Have you signed up to the UN Principles for Responsible Banking?
6   How do you intend to align with the Paris agreement and the UN Sustainable Development Goals?
7   What is the gender and ethnicity split of your staff and your senior management?
8   How do you support financial literacy in the communities where you are active?

Case-Study: Counterparty Selection

Region Stockholm ('Stockholm') is the regional authority/government responsible for public transportation, healthcare systems, and regional development for the capital area of Sweden.

Stockholm has been a pioneer in ESG financing, having launched its first green revolving credit facility (RCF) in 2015, issuing 11 green bonds since 2014 and recently issuing its first preventive healthcare bond (a bond with the aim of improving health by allocating funds and resources to individuals at risk of developing diabetes).

As a part of Stockholm's wider sustainability work, it started to evaluate its banking partners' own ESG work, to ensure that the institutions supporting Stockholm's green bond work took environmental and socials matter seriously, and to reduce the associated reputational risks. Stockholm started to host annual meetings with its banks to follow up on how each individual bank aligned to a selection of UN's sustainability goals.

The review is completed in two stages. First of all, a questionnaire is sent to each relevant bank with ESG-related questions. Once answers have been collected a follow-up meeting is held with questions/clarifications on the information received. After the meeting, Stockholm assesses whether the bank qualifies as acceptable or not acceptable under its ESG-related supplier criteria. Questions received so far have related to UN Sustainable Development Goals (SDGs) 5, 7, 13, 14, and 15.

Conclusions

Through the interactions NatWest has with treasury teams, we have seen how sustainability is becoming a top priority, having shifted within a few years from a 'nice to have' to a 'must have' consideration. While there is still some way to go, more treasurers are starting to evolve and wanting to lead truly sustainable treasury teams.

In our view, the increasing attention on this topic creates major opportunities. Treasury teams can find themselves having a 'multiplier effect' by influencing the investors, banks, suppliers, and other stakeholders they engage with. They can also take a holistic view as they know each part of the business and are uniquely positioned to help more areas of their firm adapt a sustainable business conduct.

For this reason, NatWest is actively supporting its customers in embedding sustainability across their treasury operations – be that through improved reporting, ESG rating management, investor relations, supplier selection, or the issuance of suitable ESG financing and liquidity instruments.

Every customer interaction reinforces that there is no 'one size fits all'. Different treasury teams will embed the sustainability best practices we have shared in ways that are most suitable to their company, strategy, and culture. It is also clear that ESG best practice is not a static concept; ESG is a rapidly developing space, necessitating an agile and iterative approach.

Money talks. Treasurers, as custodians of a company's money, should not underestimate the positive impact they can have on their company and the financial markets as a whole.

Notes

1 We would like to thank our colleagues, Varun Sarda (former colleague), Dr. Daniela Schwartz, Paul Dyer and Josh Hunt for their assistance in preparing this chapter.
2 Of course, treasury teams cannot implement many of these measures in isolation. In many cases, they require cross-functional working groups that involve other internal stakeholders such as: corporate social responsibility (CSR) or sustainability teams, legal, compliance, investor relations and management.
3 The most recognised specialist ESG rating agencies include MSCI, Sustainalytics, ISS ESG, VigeoEIRIS and Refinitiv, alongside benchmark and market data providers Bloomberg and Thomson Reuters. In addition, there are new entrants differentiating themselves by using big data, artificial intelligence, and machine learning to evaluate companies' ESG performance.
4 GBP 250 million is the benchmark size for the UK market and EUR 500 million is the benchmark size for the Euro market.
5 https://www.enel.com/investors/investing/sustainable-finance/ sustainability-linked-finance/sustainability-linked-bonds.

References

Eliwa, Y., Aboud, A. and Saleh, A. (2019), 'ESG Practices and the Cost of Debt: Evidence from EU Countries', *Critical Perspectives on Accounting*. [online]. Available at: https://doi.org/10.1016/j.cpa.2019.102097 (Accessed 8 May 2021).

Hermes (2017), *Pricing ESG risk in Credit Markets. Hermes Credit and Hermes EOS Research Paper*. [online]. Available at: https://www.hermes-investment.com/ukw/ wp-content/uploads/sites/80/2017/04/Credit-ESG-Paper-April-2017.pdf (Accessed 9 May 2021).

International Capital Market Association (ICMA) (2020), *Sustainability-linked Bond Principles.* [online]. Available at: https://www.icmagroup.org/assets/documents/Regulatory/Green-Bonds/June-2020/Sustainability-Linked-Bond-PrinciplesJune-2020-100620.pdf (Accessed 25 August 2020).

Krebbers, A. (2019), *Greeniums and "Halo" Effect – Green Bonds Make Financial Sense.* [online]. Available at: https://natwest.us/media/4072/sf-financial-benefits-of-green-economics_onpoint.pdf (Accessed 9 May 2021).

Krosinsky, C. (2018), *The Failure of Fund Sustainability Ratings.* [online]. Available at: https://medium.com/@cary_krosinsky/the-failure-of-fund-sustainability-ratings-bea95c0b370f (Accessed 9 May 2021).

Loan Market Association (LMA) (2022), *Sustainability Linked Loan Principles.* [online]. Available at: https://www.lsta.org/content/sustainability-linked-loan-principles-sllp/# (Accessed 5 June 2022).

18 ESG Data, Ratings, and Indexes

Kevin Kwok

Introduction

The fixed income market has lagged the equities market in adopting ESG analysis, but that has changed. According to Eurosif, a trade body, more fixed income assets are managed against ESG principles than equities in Europe (Eurosif, 2016). What makes integrating ESG in fixed income more relevant is investors' search for yield, which has resulted in many investors increasing their exposure to emerging market debt, alternative fixed income, and high yield. These are all asset classes with weaker sustainability characteristics.

ESG information is at the centre of efforts to develop suitable products and research processes across fixed income asset classes. MSCI ESG Research's (MSCI) ESG fixed income solutions are designed to help investors integrate ESG factors into their investment process, to help identify ESG-driven investment risks that may not be captured by conventional analysis, and to screen companies to align with an investor's values or specific mandate requirements.[1] MSCI's coverage includes 14,000 issuers including subsidiaries and more than 680,000 equity and fixed income securities globally.

This chapter explores how ESG information is used by fixed income investors. We start by outlining the MSCI methodology for corporate and sovereign ESG ratings, and analysing these ESG ratings, focusing on investment grade, high yield, and emerging market debt asset classes. With passive ESG investing increasing, we then discuss how index investment strategies are shaped with ESG criteria. Our final section explores the link between ESG ratings and performance.

MSCI'S ESG Ratings Methodology: Corporate

The MSCI corporate ESG ratings model – see Figure 18.1 seeks to answer four key questions:

I. What are the most significant ESG risks and opportunities facing a company and its industry?
II. How exposed is the company to those key risks and/or opportunities?

DOI: 10.4324/9781003055341-23

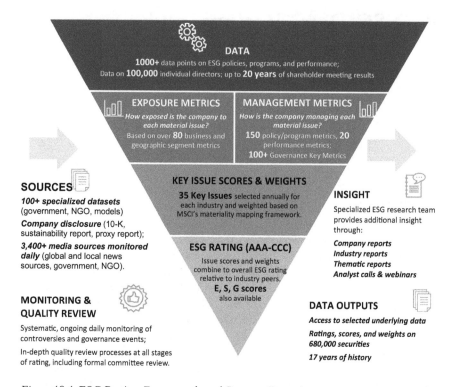

Figure 18.1 ESG Rating Framework and Process Overview.
Source: MSCI ESG Ratings.

III. How well is the company managing key risks and opportunities?
IV. What is the overall picture for the company and how does it compare to its global industry peers?

Data

MSCI aims to measure a company's resilience to long-term, financially relevant ESG risks. We leverage artificial intelligence and alternative data to produce investment-relevant insights to support investment decisions. We use a rules-based methodology to identify industry leaders and laggards in 158 Global Industry Classification Standard (GICS®)[2] sub-industries and assessed across 37 key issues.

In our view, an objective signal of a company's ESG risks cannot primarily be driven by an issuer's own corporate narrative. In MSCI's methodology, 35% of any given company's ESG rating, on average, is composed of scores that rely on what a company has disclosed through voluntary sources, while the other 65% is composed of scores using data from mandatory disclosures, enforcement and media sources, as well as specialised data sources

(Lee and Moscardi, 2018). Mandatory disclosures include the financial filings and proxy statements, which are typically required of publicly listed companies, or at minimum a bond prospectus from a private company. In addition, many large private companies with public bond issuances do provide annual reports.

It is important to acknowledge the significant differences between investment grade (IG) and high yield (HY) issuers. About 22% of issuers of IG bonds and about 47% of HY bonds had minimum to no disclosures as of 2017. HY also has a larger proportion of private companies, whose prospectus may be one of few documents that is publicly available to investors. Thirteen percent of unique HY issuers were private companies, compared with only 8% of the unique IG issuers. Of the 13% in HY that were private companies, 61% had minimal to no disclosures. To manage these information gaps, additional information sources are crucial to balance self-disclosed information. In the era of big data, the opportunity exists to extract more data from a wider variety of publicly available sources that can provide a more accurate and complete picture of companies' ESG risks and opportunities.

Material Industry ESG Risks and Opportunities

ESG risks and opportunities are posed by large-scale trends (e.g. climate change, resource scarcity, demographic shifts) and by the nature of a company's operations. Companies in the same industry generally face the same major risks and opportunities, though individual exposure can vary.

A risk is material when it is likely that companies will incur substantial costs (e.g. a regulatory ban on a key chemical input requiring reformulation). An opportunity is material when it is likely that companies could capitalise on it for profit, such as opportunities in clean technology for the LED lighting industry. MSCI's ESG ratings model focuses only on issues that are determined as material for each industry.

We identify relevant risks and opportunities for each industry through a quantitative model that looks at ranges and average values for each industry for several externalised impacts, including carbon intensity, water intensity, and injury rates. Companies with unusual business models for their industry may face fewer or additional key risks and opportunities. Once identified, Key Issues are assigned to each industry and company (Figure 18.2).

To understand whether a company is adequately managing a key ESG risk, it is essential to understand both what management strategies it has employed and how exposed it is to the risk. The ESG ratings model measures both risk exposure and risk management. To score well on what we call a 'Key Issue', management needs to be commensurate with the level of exposure: a company with high exposure must also have very strong management, whereas a company with limited exposure can have a more modest approach. Conversely, a highly exposed company with poor management will score worse than a company with the same management practices but lower exposure

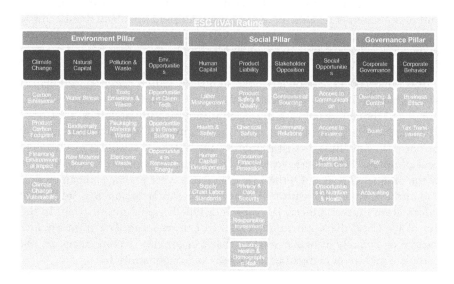

Figure 18.2 Corporate ESG Ratings Key Issue Hierarchy.
Source: MSCI ESG ratings methodology. Effective since November 2020.

to the risk. For instance, a utility focused on conventional power generation is required to have stronger measures for mitigating its carbon and toxic
emissions compared to a utility largely focused on electricity transmission
and distribution, which is generally less polluting than conventional power
generation. Our Key Issue scores are assessed on a 0–10 scale, where 0 is very
poor and 10 is very good.

A controversies assessment complements the ESG framework. A controversy case is defined by MSCI as an instance or ongoing situation in which
company operations and/or products allegedly have a negative ESG impact.
A case is typically a single event such as a spill, accident, regulatory action,
or a set of closely linked events or allegations such as health and safety fines
at the same facility, multiple allegations of anti-competitive behavior related
to the same product line, multiple community protests at the same company
location, or multiple individual lawsuits alleging the same type of discrimination. Each controversy case is assessed for the severity of its impact on society
or the environment and consequently rated Very Severe (reserved for 'worst
of the worst' cases), Severe, Moderate, or Minor. These results influence the
relevant Key Issue analysis.

Ratings Construction

Each Key Issue typically comprises 5–30% of the total ESG rating. The
weightings consider the negative or positive environment or society impact,

and the timeline we expect that risk or opportunity to materialise. A Key Issue defined as 'High Impact' and 'Short-Term' would be weighted three times higher than a Key Issue defined as 'Low Impact' and 'Long-Term'. Corporate Governance is always material and therefore always weighted and analysed. Where there are company-specific exceptions, weights depart from the industry standard weights but remain in proportion. The ESG ratings model is industry relative and uses a weighted average approach. Key Issues and weights undergo a formal review and feedback process at the end of each calendar year.

To arrive at a final letter rating, the weighted averages of the Key Issue scores are aggregated and companies' scores are normalised by their industries. After any overrides are factored in, each company's Final Industry-Adjusted Score corresponds to a rating between best (AAA) and worst (CCC). These assessments of company performance are not absolute but are explicitly intended to be relative to the standards and performance of a company's industry peers.

Formal quality review processes take place at each stage of analysis, including automated and manual quality checks of data and rating publication; industry and market lead oversight of ratings and reports; a methodology committee to approve of any exceptions, truncations, 'AAA' upgrades and 'CCC' downgrades, or major (2+) rating changes; and a Ratings Review Committee to review contentious cases. All matters pertaining to the mapping and classification of corporate entity relationships are handled by a dedicated ESG Fixed Income Methodology Committee.

Many ESG factors have traditionally featured in credit rating methodologies, but the role they play is often not well communicated (Goodman et al., 2020). Furthermore, ESG ratings are industry-relative, while credit ratings are more absolute, comparable across multiple sectors and asset-classes, and focus on borrowers' ability to repay their debt. We find that the MSCI ESG pillars and ESG Key Issues that underpin MSCI ESG ratings relate differently to companies' financial performance. For instance, depending on the time horizon, industry, and weighting scheme used, the relationship between simulated portfolios and performance varied (Giese et al., 2020).

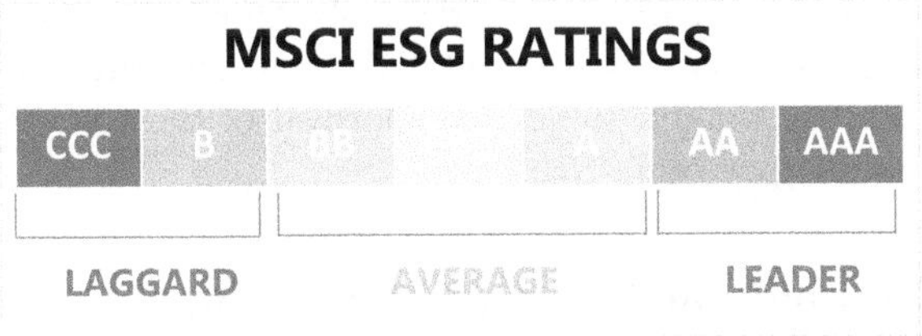

Figure 18.3 MSCI ESG Ratings Scale.
Source: MSCI ESG ratings methodology as of November 2020.

Corporate Entity Mapping

We believe issuers that lack standalone operations and/or exist solely to finance a related company's operations should inherit the ESG assessment of the related entity being financed, while subsidiaries with materially different operations from their parents warrant a standalone ESG assessment. Corporate entities (includes subsidiaries) within the MSCI ESG Research coverage universe are either:

- Assessed on a standalone basis;
- Assessed on environmental and social risks, but inherit corporate governance data from a parent entity;
- Not directly assessed but rather inherit the assessment from another entity, based on a set of mapping rules; or
- Not assessed due to there being insufficient information.

We categorise corporate issuers into several sub-types that seek to identify the primary purpose of each relevant entity within the corporate tree: (1) Group Holding Company, (2) Investment Holding Company, (3) Operating Company, (4) Management Company, or (5) Financing Company. Where a corporate issuer is directly controlled by a sovereign, the corporate will not inherit the sovereign's assessment and the determination of which entity to assess within the corporate family will be undertaken on the same basis as any other corporate issuer.

The key questions that corporate entity mapping rules aim to address for ESG ratings are (1) how to most accurately assess ownership-related risks; (2) how to identify the board with responsibility for strategic and capital allocation decisions; and (3) how to assess the operations of the group that are financed in whole or in part by the bondholders (including its supply chain and products and services). MSCI does not assess ESG ratings at the level of the individual security or bond. Instead, it asssesses ESG ratings at the issuer level and then applies this to all of the bonds issued by that issuer.

Answering these questions requires an evaluation of the entity's issuer type, the identification of the appropriate operational and governance reference entities (where applicable), and an assessment of business and geographic exposure. If environmental, social, or operational data is available but governance data is not (e.g. if the structure and membership of the board of directors is not disclosed), an issuer may be rated with the Corporate Governance Key Issue assigned a 0% weight, subject to approval of the ESG Ratings Fixed Income Methodology Committee.

MSCI ESG Ratings Methodology: Sovereigns

MSCI ESG Government Ratings assess 198 country's performance on ESG risk factors. The methodology and indicators used in these ratings are different from the Key Issue-based model used in MSCI's ESG Ratings for corporations. In this model, the ESG pillars are broken down into 6 risk-factor scores, and further dissected into 27 sub-factors derived from 99 data points. The Government Ratings are provided on a global spectrum, meaning that an 'AAA' assessment constitutes a best-in-class rating compared to the entire global sovereign universe.

Our assessment of the value creation process of a country has three components: (1) Resources, (2) Enablers, and (3) Performance (see Figure 18.4).

We consider resources a prerequisite for a country's development and performance. Because countries have varying amounts of natural, financial, and human resources, they have inherent advantages or disadvantages in converting these assets into productive goods and services. However, these are not the sole determinants of a country's ESG performance. Factors such as an effective government and judiciary, low vulnerability to environmental events and externalities, and a supportive economic environment can enable these resources.

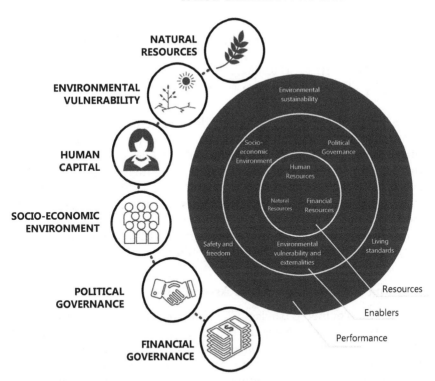

Figure 18.4 Value Creation Process of a Country.
Source: MSCI ESG Ratings.

ESG Pillar	Risk Factor	Risk Exposure Sub-factor	Risk Management Sub-factor
Environment	Natural Resource	Energy Security Risk	Energy Resource Management
		Water Resources	Water Resource Management
		Productive Land and Mineral Resources	Resource Conservation
	Environmental Externalities and Vulnerability	Vulnerability to Environmental Events	Environmental Performance
		Environmental Externalities	Management of Environmental Externalities
Social	Human Capital	Basic Human Capital	Basic Needs
		Higher Education and Technological Readiness	Human Capital Performance
			Human Capital Infrastructure
		Knowledge Capital	Knowledge Capital Management
	Economic Environment	Economic Environment	Wellness
Governance	Financial Governance	Financial Capital	Financial Management
	Political Governance	Institutions	Stability and Peace
		Judicial and Penal System	Corruption Control
		Governance Effectiveness	Political Rights and Civil Liberties

Figure 18.5 Government ESG Ratings Key Issues.
Source: MSCI ESG Government Ratings methodology.

Managing risks effectively supports the long-term competitiveness and sustainability of a country's economy and, in turn, the attractiveness of the country as an investment destination. In MSCI's Government Ratings, risk management and performance factors such as environmental sustainability, standard of living, and safety and freedom (Figure 18.5) define the parameters for calculating Risk Management scores (similar to the corporate ESG model). A country's relative ESG risk exposure is measured against its applied ESG risk management practices and demonstrated ESG performance to form the basis of our final ESG Government Ratings.

Analysing ESG Ratings across Asset Classes

Issuers in the Bloomberg Barclays Global Aggregate Index[3] tend to lean toward developed market companies that are larger and with more established ESG management processes. Conversely, issuers in the Bloomberg Barclays Global High Yield have a larger proportion of emerging markets and private companies with limited ESG resources. This is shown in the ESG ratings distribution: 26.2% of Global Aggregate issuers receive the highest ESG ratings (AAA-AA) whereas for high yield and emerging markets it is 8% and 5.7%,

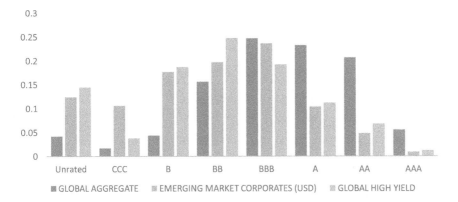

Figure 18.6 Fixed Income ESG Ratings Distributions.
Source: MSCI ESG Research as of December 31, 2020.

respectively (Figure 18.6). Global Aggregate issuers are also likely to have the lowest percent in the bottom rating category (1.7%) compared with 10.6% for emerging markets and 3.8% for high yield.

We now explore this in more detail with a look at investment grade and high yield issuers, and emerging market corporate and sovereign ESG ratings.

Investment Grade and High Yield

Weak ESG risk management practices are widespread across investment grade and high yield issuers. There are several ESG investment grade laggards, although fewer than in HY, as shown in Figure 18.7. Investors might assume that in the high yield space, with its higher leverage and increased likelihood of defaults, they would face major exposure to ESG risks, and this may be partially true. But ESG Leaders do exist, and sectors with more ESG Leaders do not necessarily imply an inverse relationship with ESG Laggards across both universes.

In high yield we identified some unexpected ESG leaders, such as Kosmos Energy ('AA' rating), an offshore oil and gas production company with operations primarily in Africa with minor operations in South America. Kosmos is a signatory to the UN Global Compact, a member of the Extractive Industries Transparency Initiative, and maintains strong anti-corruption policies and programmes with regular audits. It does face risks of operational disruption, as its business lines are prone to disturbing the marine ecosystem and causing oil spills. However, there were no reportable oil spills for over four years in the period analysed, indicating strong programs to address these risks. The ESG leaders also include Nokia ('AA' rating), a global technology front-runner that has one of the most rigorous responsible sourcing initiatives; its initiative extends to cobalt, which is not currently considered a

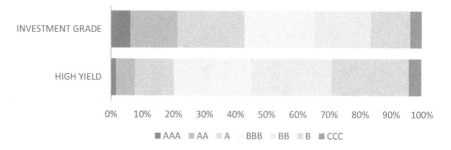

Figure 18.7 ESG Leaders vs ESG Laggards by GICS Sector.

Source: MSCI ESG Research; Based on Analysis of the Bloomberg Barclays Global Aggregate Index and Bloomberg Barclays Global High Yield Index as of December 31, 2017.

conflict mineral. As of 2017, about 83% of smelters and refiners in Nokia's supply chain were validated conflict-free by Responsible Minerals Assurance Process (RMAP) or mutually recognised programs. Nokia has a goal of reaching 100% conflict-free smelter and refiner status by 2020.

On the other hand, in the investment grade universe, Qualcomm Inc. (MSCI 'B' rating), a multinational semiconductor and telecommunications equipment company, has been cited as a frequent violator of antitrust laws around the world, and has received multiple penalties for anticompetitive practices over the last few years. Qualcomm also faces heightened challenges in retaining and motivating talent due to its ongoing restructuring activities that have resulted in substantial workforce reductions, as well as its recent major acquisitions, including the recently terminated NXP Semiconductors transaction. Upheavals of this magnitude can negatively affect employee morale and exacerbate risks of voluntary attrition, which is evident in Qualcomm's rising employee turnover over the last three years.

Wells Fargo, the third-largest bank in the US by total assets, was downgraded by MSCI to ESG Laggard ('B' MSCI ESG Rating) status in 2015 due to governance concerns. In 2016, Wells Fargo was downgraded again to 'CCC' on consumer protection and data security concerns. The context was a scandal at Wells Fargo involving the creation of millions of fraudulent savings and checking accounts without client consent. Wells Fargo received an historically harsh penalty from the US Federal Reserve, capping the firm's assets for an indefinite period. This type of penalty could become a new reality in the American banking industry, considering that 83% of American banks on the MSCI ACWI Index face elevated consumer protection risk, much greater exposure than that faced by global banks.

Limited ESG disclosure has been a consistent problem for HY investors in particular. Figure 18.8 illustrates the breakdown of levels of ESG disclosures by unique issuers in two comparable IG and HY indexes, as well as the percentage of ESG Leader, ESG Average, and ESG Laggard issuers in each disclosure

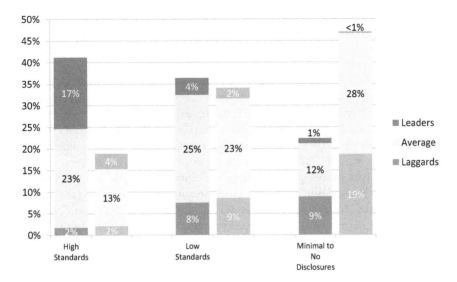

Figure 18.8 Level of ESG Disclosures by Index.
Source: MSCI ESG Research.

category. About 22% of issuers of IG bonds and about 47% of HY bonds had minimum to no disclosures as of 2017. HY also has a larger proportion of private companies, whose bond prospectuses may be one of the few documents available publicly to investors. Thirteen percent of unique HY issuers were private companies, compared with only 8% of the unique IG issuers. Of the 13% in HY that were private companies, 61% had minimal to no disclosures.

There is evidence of companies responding. For example, we have seen industry leaders in the US utilities sector collaborate to standardise ESG/sustainability reporting to better satisfy investor demand and build public trust; we expect other industries to follow. Despite these challenges, ESG ratings coverage for HY issuers has been increasing every year, and has improved more than 20% in terms of market value since 2012 (Kwok, 2018).

Although some HY issuers may be less able to weather challenging economic circumstances, increasing the risk of default, advances in ESG data, and analysis allow for greater differentiation. Similarly, in equities, the scarcity of company information in emerging markets, when compared with developed markets, potentially allows for a greater payoff from the application of local expertise and knowledge.

Emerging Market and Sovereign Ratings

Picking good companies is challenging, and doubly so when they are based in markets that can be complex and opaque to global investors. Twenty-four countries are covered in the MSCI Emerging Markets Index today, up from just ten when the index launched 30 years ago. To help navigate the evolving Emerging Markets investment universe, investors will rely on ESG signals to sift for quality in management – to help identify those companies that rise above their country's challenging environment.

Relative to their developed market peers, companies domiciled in emerging and frontier markets often start with weaker home country governance, human capital productivity, and natural resource management. Of the 24 markets that MSCI classifies as emerging markets, only 16% have ESG sovereign ratings above BBB, compared to 83% for developed market countries as of November 30, 2017 (Lee and Moscardi, 2018).

From a corporate perspective, there is a 'lottery of birth' where companies may have impediments to performance and investors may face a lack of transparency. In fact, investors appear to anticipate a premium precisely because they expect that country performance act as an extension of risks facing companies. The same is true for ESG ratings, where we assess the key ESG risks facing individual companies, such as labour or governance risks, relative to their global industry peers. Aggregated at the country level (on a capitalisation weighted basis), the gap is stark: companies domiciled in countries with strong ESG sovereign ratings, on average, were less exposed and better positioned to manage significant ESG risks than global peers. Furthermore, as the sovereign ESG ratings declined, ESG ratings of companies domiciled in these countries tended to fall below global industry peers, primarily due to their elevated risk profiles (Figure 18.9). This implies two things. First, the expectations for companies are partially set by their domicile country barriers. Second, companies that transcend those barriers could have ESG performance that rivals the most advanced developed market peers.

Historically, on-the-ground knowledge has been necessary to identify which companies are better positioned to transcend their country expectations. Active managers of emerging markets funds appear to have been more successful than developed markets fund counterparts in recent years, potentially because the scarcity of company information in these markets allows greater payoff to applying local expertise and knowledge. Advances in ESG data and analysis present an additional tool to filter companies at scale.

One approach to identifying emerging market companies that transcend their markets is to use assessments of companies' ESG performance. From a governance perspective, there can be vast differences in norms and practices, including the nuanced ownership and control characteristics that can be unique to each market. For instance, half of India-domiciled constituent companies assessed by MSCI are family firms, with a prevalence of family conglomerate structures that are complex and may disadvantage minority shareholders. Comparatively, more than half of the Chinese firms are state-owned where the possibility of misalignment between the strategic interests of the state and those of minority shareholders remains a key

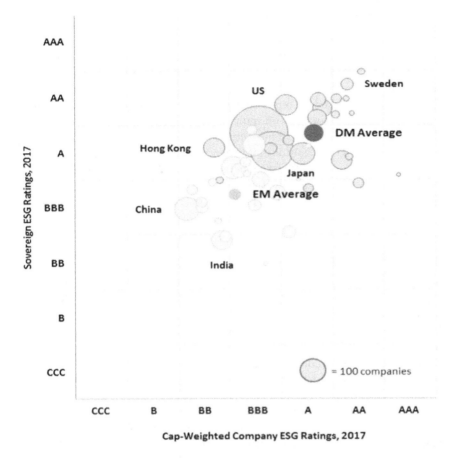

Figure 18.9 Average Sovereign and Corporate ESG Ratings.
Source: MSCI ESG Research.

governance risk. While understanding these market characteristics can help investors contextualise each company's governance practice, some global institutional investors may choose to apply a minimum, global governance standard. One way an investor could do this is by identifying country out-performers and then narrow the universe to the top half of companies that meet global governance standards or are above their domicile country's ESG sovereign rating.

Emerging markets economies are projected to continue fuelling global growth and demand over the next two decades. To capture some of that growth while controlling downside risks, especially given limited share-holder or bondholder rights in many cases, we anticipate that institutional in-vestors will increasingly turn to ESG analysis as a tool to help sort the wheat from the chaff in these complex and opaque markets.

Fixed Income Indexes

MSCI provides ESG indexes designed to help institutional investors effectively benchmark ESG investment performance and manage, measure and report on ESG mandates. In 2013, Bloomberg, a global leader in fixed income indexing, and MSCI developed a family of rules-based benchmark indexes that incorporate measures of ESG risk and exposures. The Bloomberg Barclays MSCI ESG Fixed Income Indexes include a range of investment grade, aggregate, corporate index, and multi-currency, high yield benchmarks addressing the evolving needs of institutional investors, who increasingly aim to incorporate ESG considerations into their strategic asset allocation.

Supporting more than 200 fixed income indices, MSCI uses the ESG methodology outlined in the first section to create benchmarks with specific ESG qualities and characteristics. The principal indexes fall into three categories: ESG integration, values-based, and impact. These are described below.

ESG Integration Indexes

MSCI ESG Leaders Indexes are market value-weighted indexes designed to represent the performance of fixed income securities from issuers that have high ESG ratings relative to their sector peers, to ensure the inclusion of the best-in-class companies from an ESG perspective. Companies are required to have an MSCI ESG rating of 'BB' or above to be eligible for inclusion in the MSCI ESG Leaders Indexes. The underlying principle in the construction of the indexes is to achieve cumulative sector coverage closest to 50%, while aiming to maintain index stability.

For each sector, the eligible companies are first ranked based on the company level ESG rating. If two companies have the same ESG rating, the company with the better ESG trend is given priority (i.e. a positive ESG trend is preferred to a neutral ESG trend, and a neutral ESG trend is preferred to a negative ESG trend). In the case of two companies with the same ESG rating and the same ESG trend, the existing ESG Leaders index constituent is given priority to maintain index stability. Figure 18.10 shows the Bloomberg Barclays Global Corporate ESG Weighted Indexes versus the non-ESG index; the ESG Index performance has similar total returns, but the credit risk is reduced by 5% and the average ESG score is at least 11% higher.

Values-Based Investing Indexes

Values indexes remove issuers that may be involved in business lines or activities that conflict with investment policies, values, or social norms. This includes a range of business activities including, adult entertainment, alcohol, gambling, tobacco, military weapons, civilian firearms, nuclear power, and genetically modified organisms. A combination of revenue % levels or absolute revenue amounts (in US$) are set for each activity. Controversial

Figure 18.10 ESG-Weighted Fixed Income Index Performance.
Source: Bloomberg Barclays Index and MSCI ESG Research, as of 18 December 2019.

behaviour screens exclude issuers involved in one or more 'very severe' controversies. Controversies assessments review ESG impacts of company operations, products, and services. The evaluation framework is designed to be consistent with international norms represented by the UN Declaration of Human Rights, the International Labour Organisation's Declaration on Fundamental Principles and Rights at Work, and the UN Global Compact. MSCI ESG Controversies Score falls on a 0–10 scale, with '0' being the most severe controversy and applied to most Values Indexes.

A controversy case can be one-off events or a series of multiple events that point to an underlying problem. Controversies include violations of existing laws and/or regulations or events that violate accepted international norms, including but not limited, to norms represented by global conventions. A single case is typically a spill, accident, regulatory action. Systemic cases may involve a set of closely linked events or allegations such as health and safety fines at the same facility, multiple allegations of anti-competitive behaviour related to the same product line, community protests at the same company location, and individual lawsuits alleging the same type of discrimination. Figure 18.11 shows performance for two versions of the Bloomberg Barclays MSCI Sustainability Indexes versus the non-sustainability version. The Bloomberg Barclays MSCI Global Corporate Sustainability BB+ includes an additional rating category

180.00
170.00
160.00
150.00
140.00
130.00
120.00
110.00
100.00
90.00
80.00

Dec-06 Jun-07 Dec-07 Jun-08 Dec-08 Jun-09 Dec-09 Jun-10 Dec-10 Jun-11 Dec-11 Jun-12 Dec-12 Jun-13 Dec-13 Jun-14 Dec-14 Jun-15 Dec-15 Jun-16 Dec-16 Jun-17 Dec-17 Jun-18 Dec-18 Jun-19 Dec-19

Bloomberg Barclays Global Aggregate - Corporate

Bloomberg Barclays MSCI Global Corporate Sustainability

Bloomberg Barclays MSCI Global Corporate Sustainability BB+

Figure 18.11 Sustainability Fixed Income Index Performance.
Source: Bloomberg Barclays Index and MSCI ESG Research, as of 18 December 2019.

tracking slightly under the return performance of the non-sustainability version, but similar to the ESG-weighted index, it has lower credit risk and a higher average ESG score. The regular Bloomberg Barclays MSCI Global Corporate Sustainability Index includes only ESG ratings BBB and higher, so it may exclude some bonds that add stronger returns, although they still reduce credit risk by at least 5%. However, the average ESG score may improve by as much as 19% in the sustainability index, excluding anything lower than a BBB ESG rating.

Impact Investing Indexes

Green bond indexes offer investors an objective and robust measure of the global market for fixed income securities issued to fund projects with direct environmental benefits. Securities are independently evaluated by MSCI along four dimensions to determine whether a fixed-income security should be classified as a green bond. These eligibility criteria reflect themes articulated in the Green Bond Principles and require clarity about a bond's: (1) Stated use of proceeds; (2) Process for green project evaluation and selection; (3) Process for management of proceeds; and (4) Commitment to ongoing reporting of the environmental performance of the use of proceeds. Both self-labelled green bonds and unlabelled bonds will be evaluated using these criteria for potential index inclusion. So long as projects fall within an eligible MSCI green bond category and there is sufficient transparency on the use of proceeds, a bond can be considered for the index even if it is not explicitly marketed as green.

Use of proceeds and project bonds are considered eligible if the use of proceeds falls within at least one of six eligible environmental categories: alternative energy, energy efficiency, pollution prevention and control, sustainable water, green building, and climate adaption (plus an Other category). Bonds are considered eligible if the issuer clearly delineates the specific criteria and process for determining eligible projects or investments in the bond prospectus or supporting documentation (e.g. green bond supplement, website, investor presentation, published second-party opinion).

A formal process to ring-fence net proceeds to the eligible use of proceeds must be disclosed in the bond prospectus or supporting documentation. Eligible mechanisms to ring-fence net proceeds include: direct recourse to eligible revenues or assets (e.g. a green securitised bond, green project bond, or green revenue bond); creation of a separate legal entity; creation of a sub-portfolio linked to the issuer's investment operations for eligible projects; or other auditable mechanisms whereby the balance of tracked proceeds is reduced periodically by amounts matching investments made in eligible projects during that period.

At issuance, the issuer must either report on eligible projects or state its commitment to report within one year of issuance. For reporting to be considered eligible, it must include one or more of the following: a list of specific projects/investments, including the amount disbursed to each individual project; aggregate project/investment categories, including amount disbursed to each project type; or quantitative or qualitative reporting on the environmental impact of the project pool (e.g. greenhouse gas emissions savings, reduction in water consumption, increased energy efficiency per unit of output, etc.). When an issuer fails to comply on an ongoing basis, the bond can be delisted from the green bond index (e.g. Engie and Brookfield Renewable Energy used the proceeds to fund a large-scale hydropower plants, which did not meet IFC Performance Standards).

ESG and Performance

In this final section we illustrate how ESG ratings relate to select credit performance measures. We focus on credit spreads for both corporate and sovereign issuers.

Corporates

Examining bonds over the three years from 2015 to 2017, the overall MSCI ESG rating highly correlates across all quartiles in both IG and HY markets (Table 18.1 and Table 18.2). The highest ESG rated companies (i.e. those in the top quartile) had the narrowest OAS spreads at 130 bps and 401 bps for

Table 18.1 Three-year Historical OAS Averages Based on Investment Grade Corporate Bonds, Equally Weighted.

	Quartile			
Score	1	2	3	4
1/31/2015–12/31/2017				
E	143.64	127.77	140.42	191.85
S	155.08	148.43	145.15	157.39
G	150.79	144.29	158.02	152.07
ESG	130.34	137.32	142.92	177.90

Source: MSCI ESG Research.

Table 18.2 Three-year Historical OAS Averages Based on High Yield Corporate Bonds, Equally Weighted.

	Quartile			
Score	1	2	3	4
1/31/2015–12/31/2017				
E	411.68	369.95	392.83	577.53
S	401.14	453.03	455.26	509.35
G	402.59	398.72	436.21	632.59
ESG	400.63	396.81	420.78	522.09

Source: MSCI ESG Research.

IG and HY, respectively; the lowest-rated ESG companies (i.e. those in the lowest quartile) had the widest spreads, at 178 bps and 522 bps.

The individual pillars' correlations were inconsistent, but with good reason: ESG ratings are weighted according to the importance of underlying industry key issues for all three ESG pillars, which provides a holistic view of a company. Each individual pillar represented in Table 18.1 and Table 18.2 is similarly calculated but based on the weighted average of issue scores underlying each pillar. Certain pillars are less relevant to certain industries. For example, a software company would be less susceptible to environmental risks like biodiversity and land usage, but those risks would be more important for an oil and gas company involved in exploration and drilling. The widest spread difference between any first and last quartile was over 230 bps, which occurred in the standalone HY governance pillar.

Another reason individual pillar spreads were less consistent than overall scores could be the low default risk inherent in investment grade bonds. Environmental and social factors may not immediately affect the overall creditworthiness of a company. Although investment grade quartiles showed less correlation, the spread difference between quartiles was quite minimal, evidencing little effect from ESG risks. However, using the balanced overall ESG scores produced a different result. High yield bonds showed better correlation, with wider differences between top and bottom quartiles. As fixed income investors increasingly look for evidence of companies' preparedness to tackle future regulations, contingent liabilities, and the governance of environmental and social risk management – these are all factors that are not necessarily well captured in traditional credit analysis – we expect the quartile spreads by pillar to correlate more clearly to spreads; for example, as investors embed environment goals within mandates.

Sovereigns

Bond investors have indicated more interest in the added value of ESG signals for sovereign credit precisely because of the continued deterioration in the credit worthiness of sovereigns over the past few years. For example, research from Allianz Global Investors found that while country credit ratings appear not to fully incorporate sovereign ESG risks factors, ESG risks are nonetheless at least partially priced into sovereign credit risk as evidenced by the correlation between sovereign ESG scores and credit default swaps (Hoerter, 2017). That is, ESG scores can be used, at least in part, as a proxy for the market assessment of credit risk for a particular sovereign.

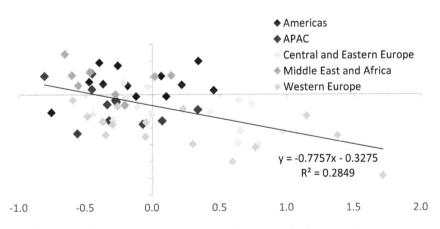

$$y = -0.7757x - 0.3275$$
$$R^2 = 0.2849$$

Figure 18.12 'Gaps' vs. Change in Log CDS Spread, by Region, in 2011.

Natural disasters, political upheaval, and corruption scandals are just a few of the shocks global investors have had to deal with in recent years. Analysis of ESG risk factors at the country level may help investors better understand the cause and consequences of these events, and how these fit into their sovereign credit risk assessment. This is important not just for global government bond investors, but for any investor that needs to consider country risk in its portfolio.

We find that countries with higher ESG Government Ratings on average saw their CDS spreads narrow by more, or widen by less, than lower-rated counterparts three years later for the rating period between 2011 and 2014 (Figure 18.12). The relationship between ESG ratings and changes in CDS spreads held within risk groups based on levels of CDS spreads in 2011.

We also find that the difference between actual CDS spreads and the expected CDS spread based on the ESG score in 2011 were also correlated with subsequent changes in CDS spreads between 2011 and 2017. The correlation between the 'gap' and changes in CDS spreads was strongest in Europe, while CDS spreads for countries in the Americas on average widened by more than suggested by their 'gap' and the opposite held true for countries in the APAC region.

Conclusions

Traditional credit analysis often overlooks sustainability factors that can impact operational and financial risks. ESG information complements the fundamental research process by aiding investors in the identification of issues that represent the greatest potential material risks across entire sectors, or for specific individual issuers. Bond investors have expressed their interest in the added value of ESG signals for both sovereign and corporate credit precisely because of deterioration in the credit worthiness of these issuers that can be attributed to such risks.

Some investors have raised concerns about the possibility of inherent biases in investment grade and high yield issuers. MSCI's methodology incorporates information beyond what issuers disclose, with the aim of creating ratings that avoid such potential disclosure and size biases. Under this methodology, issuers with high ESG ratings have tended to have tighter credit spreads, hence a lowered risk of default, while issuers with low ESG ratings were more susceptible to market fluctuations, across corporates and sovereigns, suggesting that the market is loosely pricing in such ESG characteristics.

Understanding the significance of different ESG issues is one of the most important aspects of achieving ESG factor integration into bond selection and portfolio construction, and we have identified two emerging phenomenon that are likely to impact how widespread and influential ESG in fixed income will eventually become. First, as investing on the basis of ESG principles continues to gain momentum, more and more investors are employing third-party ESG ratings in their own propriety models. But there are many ways to construct an ESG score, involving different combinations of financial and non-financial inputs, and a proliferation of ESG ratings and methodologies threatens to make comparability more difficult for end-investors. The framework outlined in this chapter is intended to address this growing concern through a unique combination of consistency, transparency, and rigour.

Second, ESG in fixed income is also beginning to spread into other sub-asset classes. Municipal bond issuers have been exposed to the demands of ESG investors for a shorter period, as reflected by a more limited disclosure of ESG indicators. Interactions between federal, state, and municipality-level factors add further to this complexity. Local government and sovereign ESG risks do not necessarily correlate, and may require further analysis. For structured debt, due to the additional difficulties involved in assessing asset pools, greater transparency would help investors to assess their risk exposure.

But the widespread adoption of ESG investing principles is not based solely on the readiness of fixed income investors to adopt ESG principles, but rather because ESG investing is finally becoming effective enough to reward their adoption. If ESG investing were to remain limited to values alignment and ethical investing, it might always remain niche. But as the increased emphasis on ESG materiality has demonstrated, ESG assessment tools have sharpened, and evaluation methods have grown, and there are fewer and fewer reasons for investors not to apply ESG research alongside traditional credit risk methods.

Notes

1 MSCI ESG Research LLC is a Registered Investment Adviser under the Investment Advisers Act of 1940, and is a subsidiary of MSCI, Inc.
2 GICS, the global industry classification standard jointly developed by MSCI and Standard & Poor's.
3 There are three principal bond universes evaluated in this section. The Global Aggregate index represents all corporate bonds of benchmark size, emerging markets represents all IG and HY bonds from corporate issuers in emerging markets, and high yield represents BB credit-rated and under bonds from all markets.

References

Eurosif (2016) *European SRI Study 2016*. [online]. Available at: http://www.eurosif.org/wp-content/uploads/2016/11/SRI-study-2016-HR.pdf (Accessed 15 April 2021).

Giese, G., Nagy, Z. and Lee, L. (2020), *Deconstructing ESG Ratings Performance* (MSCI ESG Research, London).

Goodman, J., Georgieva, A. and Nuzzo, C. (2020), *An Introduction to Responsible Investment: Fixed Income* (PRI, London).

Hoerter, S. (2017), *Financial Materiality of ESG Risk Factors for Sovereign Bond Portfolios* (Allianz Global Investors, Munich).

Kwok, K. (2018), *Does High Yield Receive the ESG Credit It Deserves?* (MSCI ESG Research, New York).

Lee, L. and Moscardi, M. (2018), *2018 ESG Trends to Watch* (MSCI ESG Research, New York).

19 Assessing the Responsible Investment Performance of Fixed Income Fund Managers

Tomi Nummela and Sarika Goel[1]

As an investment consultant, Mercer Wealth (Mercer) provides customised investment advice to help institutional investor clients make and implement better decisions for their investment strategies.[2] Mercer advises institutional investors on why and how to adopt sustainable investment approaches. This includes advice on integrating environmental, social, and governance (ESG) factors and broader systemic issues into investment research and decision-making, on implementing stewardship and ensuring that clients' approach to sustainable investment meets their fiduciary and other duties. In our advice we recognise the implications of ESG issues for long-term risk and return outcomes and the implications for client reputations of not meeting the expectations of their beneficiaries and other stakeholders.

This chapter looks at how investment consultants consider and provide advice on responsible investing factors. First, we visit the role of investment consultants in responsible investment. We chart Mercer's milestones and developments from almost two decades of advising clients on ESG, as well as from over a decade of assigning ESG ratings to investment strategies. We also discuss the history of fixed income ESG ratings and explore the trends in these ratings to gain a solid foundation to understand the industry today. Second, we describe in more detail how Mercer approaches ESG research and ratings, giving an overview of the process and pertinent issues we consider in our stand-alone ESG ratings. Third, we explore the use of ESG ratings and manager ESG assessments in practical investment consulting work.

The Role of Consultants in Fixed Income

Building Institutional Capacity

The role of investment consultants varies significantly in different geographical markets. While some markets, like the United Kingdom, have a regulatory requirement for certain asset owners to appoint actuarial consultants, most markets do not have such administrative obligation. Regardless of the roots of the relationship, a consultant is a trusted advisor providing insight on a wide variety of investment matters. A growing constant in the

DOI: 10.4324/9781003055341-24

consultant-client relationship is that financially material ESG considerations, in particular climate change, must be a meaningful part of an investment consultant's advice. Taking account of material ESG issues ensures that a consultant helps their clients to fulfil their fiduciary duty (the key aim of a consultant). While the asset owner types vary – pension, insurance, sovereign wealth, family office, endowments and foundations, outsourced chief investment officer platforms – and while ESG issues may present somewhat differently depending on circumstances, a consultant must bring responsible investing themes into all relationships in an integrated and material manner.

ESG integration challenges traditional ways of investment thinking and it is probably fair to say that, until recently, many of the more traditional investment consultants were sceptical about the value of focusing on ESG issues in investment decision-making. To address this scepticism (which remains in many quarters), a successful consultant must instil a high level of confidence and commitment among its employees to deliver on ESG advice. As an example, at Mercer, such confidence was built institutionally through early investment in responsible investment, in particular through strategic thought leadership. Mercer began the build-up of its ESG capabilities in 2004, establishing a dedicated investment advisory practice that expanded into manager research in 2006. Mercer was the original consultant to the UN-supported Principles for Responsible Investment (PRI), and was also a founding signatory to the PRI.

In 2008, Mercer began to provide forward-looking, standalone ESG ratings at the investment strategy level and in 2012, these ESG ratings were included in regular client reporting. Being the first mover was an advantage as it boosted Mercer's institutional confidence to integrate ESG capabilities across the firm as the rising tide of ESG focused investing gathered momentum going into the mid-2010s. In 2014, in a milestone commitment, where Mercer adopted a set of sustainable investment beliefs (see Figure 19.1).

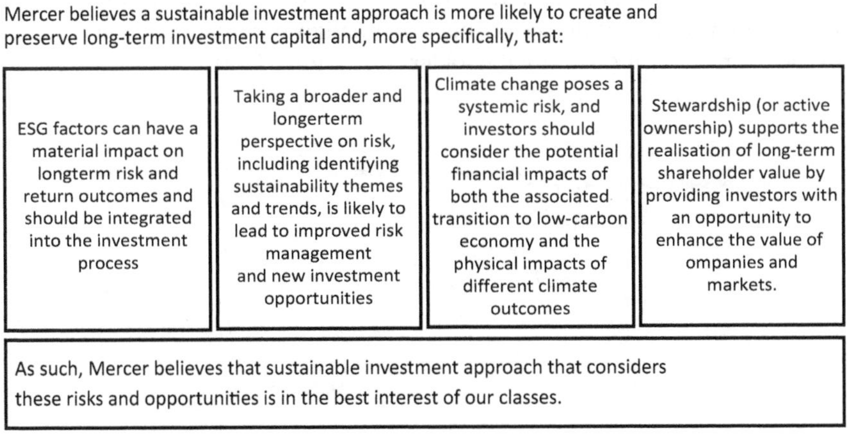

Mercer believes a sustainable investment approach is more likely to create and preserve long-term investment capital and, more specifically, that:

ESG factors can have a material impact on longterm risk and return outcomes and should be integrated into the investment process	Taking a broader and longerterm perspective on risk, including identifying sustainability themes and trends, is likely to lead to improved risk management and new investment opportunities	Climate change poses a systemic risk, and investors should consider the potential financial impacts of both the associated transition to low-carbon economy and the physical impacts of different climate outcomes	Stewardship (or active ownership) supports the realisation of long-term shareholder value by providing investors with an opportunity to enhance the value of ompanies and markets.

As such, Mercer believes that sustainable investment approach that considers these risks and opportunities is in the best interest of our classes.

Figure 19.1 Mercer Sustainable Investment Beliefs.

Mercer has also spent significant time understanding the impact of climate change across asset classes. In 2011, Mercer published its first report on climate change and its implication for strategic asset allocation. In 2015, prior to the Paris Agreement on Climate Change, Mercer brought to the market its seminal climate scenario analysis tool, which allowed asset owners to assess their strategic asset allocation under three different climate scenarios.

The critical lesson from Mercer's experience is that deeply meaningful responsible investment and ESG integration at a firm cannot be created overnight as complex factors such as cultural readiness and openness to adapting conventional investment thinking are required for success in the field.

What We Offer Our Clients

At Mercer, the processes of responsible investment advisory is a part of all investment services that consultants deliver to clients, including:

- Developing governance structures and skills
- Defining investment beliefs
- Undertaking investment strategy reviews
- Performing stress tests and risk modelling
- Monitoring investment performance and risk targets
- Selecting investment managers

A more specific "Responsible Investment Pathway" toolkit takes clients through various stages that allows them to fully incorporate sustainable investment approaches. The Pathway tool supports a clear strategy and implementation plan that enables asset owners to consider more nuanced, long-term thinking into their decision-making. This includes integrating ESG factors, broader systemic issues (e.g. climate change and sustainable development), as well as stewardship, into investment portfolios. The aim is not only to meet immediate investment objectives but also to align with the beliefs and values of members, customers and stakeholders (see Figure 19.2).

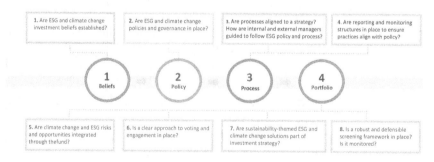

Figure 19.2 Overview of Mercer's Responsible Investment Pathway.

Mercer advises institutional investors on why and how to adopt sustainable investment approaches. We recognise the impact on long-term expected risk and return outcomes and client-specific considerations for stakeholder alignment as drivers for integration. How well a consultant undertakes the task of looking after its clients' objectives depends on the strength of the individual consultant's own investment beliefs and track record, as well as the consultant's access to research and the degree of ESG skillset across the organisation.

To support this work Mercer researches and assesses over 4,500 investment strategies on ESG integration approaches. Globally, Mercer has the largest investment strategy database of ESG ratings at the institutional investment strategy level. Among other initiatives, Mercer has expanded its climate tool offering to cover net zero portfolio decarbonisation methodologies and announced its Analytics for Climate Transition tool in late 2020. The climate tool was developed because institutional investors are seeking ways to assess the companies they invest in with respect to their commitment and ability to, transition to a net zero economy by 2050, with many setting an interim milestone of 45% emissions reduction by 2030. Increasingly, clients are looking for help setting portfolio investment baselines, assessing portfolio opportunities, establishing targets, and setting implementation plans that can be integrated with strategy and portfolio construction decisions.

Rating Investment Strategies

Mercer's Global Investment Research team provides research on the global asset management industry covering themes and opportunities, investment beliefs, and governance models of asset managers to give asset owners a well-researched base for asset allocation decisions. Mercer's Global Investment Manager Database (GIMD™) is the largest database of its kind globally. This proprietary, web-based database contains information on more than 7,000 investment managers and 35,000+ investment strategies globally across all main asset classes: equities, bonds, real estate, and alternatives. GIMD is fundamental to Mercer's investment manager research and underpins manager selection and investment monitoring for Mercer's asset owner clients. The database is used by all Mercer consultants.

Mercer's Manager Research team is focused on manager research and selection. The team's specialists undertake detailed due diligence globally on a range of investment managers and strategies in core and non-core areas to identify the best investment opportunities for client portfolios.

Investment Manager ESG Ratings

Mercer introduced its ESG ratings at the strategy level in 2008. These ratings are a qualitative assessment of the extent to which portfolio managers incorporate ESG factors and stewardship into their investment processes and decisions. The ESG integration framework is integrated into the overall manager research process, where the responsibility of assigning ESG ratings sits with the global manager research team. When Mercer researchers review an investment strategy, they determine both the investment rating as well as the ESG rating. Mercer has a robust governance structure in place for the review and ratification of these ratings, embedded within the structure and style of Mercer's overarching Four-Factor Manager Research Framework:

- Idea generation, which encompasses everything the portfolio manager does to determine the relative attractiveness of different investments.
- Portfolio construction, which refers to the manner in which the portfolio manager translates investment ideas into decisions on which investments to include in a portfolio and the weightings to give to these investments.
- Implementation, which refers to the capabilities surrounding activities that are required to achieve desired portfolio structure.
- Business management, which refers to the overall stability of the investment firm, the firm's resources, and its overall operations.

In line with these, the four-factor framework for ESG follows the Four-Factor framework across actively managed investment strategies. This is depicted in Figure 19.3.

ESG integration is about holistically understanding the risks and opportunities in a portfolio, including those are not necessarily readily apparent. The critical aspect is to understand what investment decision-makers, portfolio managers, and analysts are doing at the strategy level to address ESG issues given their relevance to the investment case. In particular, Mercer's ESG

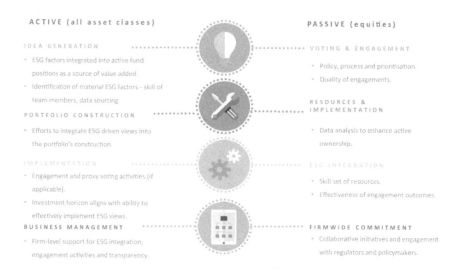

ACTIVE (all asset classes)

IDEA GENERATION
- ESG factors integrated into active fund positions as a source of value added.
- Identification of material ESG factors - skill of team members, data sourcing

PORTFOLIO CONSTRUCTION
- Efforts to integrate ESG driven views into the portfolio's construction.

IMPLEMENTATION
- Engagement and proxy voting activities (if applicable).
- Investment horizon aligns with ability to effectively implement ESG views.

BUSINESS MANAGEMENT
- Firm-level support for ESG integration, engagement activities and transparency.

PASSIVE (equities)

VOTING & ENGAGEMENT
- Policy, process and prioritisation.
- Quality of engagements.

RESOURCES & IMPLEMENTATION
- Data analysis to enhance active ownership.

ESG INTEGRATION
- Skill set of resources.
- Effectiveness of engagement outcomes.

FIRMWIDE COMMITMENT
- Collaborative initiatives and engagement with regulators and policymakers.

Figure 19.3 The Mercer Four-Factor Manager Research Framework.

ESG1	ESG2	ESG3	ESG4
ACTIVE			
Leader in the integration of ESG factors and active ownership into core processes.	Less advanced than ESG1 investors but with moderate integration of ESG factors and active ownership.	Limited progress with respect to ESG integration and active ownership, albeit with signs of potential improvement.	Little or no integration of ESG factors or active ownership into core processes and no indication of future change.

Ratings for passive equity strategies differentiate how well firms undertake their stewardship activities such as voting, engagement, industry collaboration and reporting.

ESGp1	ESGp2	ESGp3	ESGp4
PASSIVE			
Leaders in Voting & Engagement across ESG topics, with active ownership activities and ESG initiatives undertaken consistently at a global level	Strong approach to Voting & Engagement across ESG topics, and initiatives at a regional level, with progress made at a global level	Focus tends to be on Voting & Engagement on governance topics only, more regionally focused with less evidence of other internal ESG initiatives	Little or no initiatives taken on developing a Voting & Engagement capability, with little progress made on other ESG initiatives

Figure 19.4 Mercer ESG Rating Scale.

ratings qualitatively assess the consistency of ESG integration within the due diligence and decision-making process.

The ESG ratings range from ESG1 (the highest rating) down to ESG4 (the lowest rating). For a strategy to be assigned an ESG1, managers will tend to integrate ESG factors into the investment philosophy of the strategy and the investment process. A manager team/strategy awarded ESG4 undertakes little or no integration of ESG factors or active ownership into its core processes (Figure 19.4).

When Mercer's researchers review a strategy, they will determine an appropriate ESG rating. This rating sits alongside Mercer's traditional alpha ratings (A, B+, etc.) and is considered alongside all other relevant factors. Maintaining such 'parallel' ratings instils a disciplined process to embed ESG questions into Mercer's core research process and make the responses visible within that process. These ratings also allow Mercer to respond to the growing client demand for an independent assessment of current or prospective ESG integration and stewardship practices by managers.

Mercer's global manager research team has assessed over 4,500 investment strategies on ESG integration and stewardship. The provision of 'parallel' ESG and alpha ratings give Mercer's clients a robust multidimensional way to evaluate how managers approach ESG and stewardship; then assess how this contributes to their own investment risk and return profiles.

There are several advantages to separating ESG from alpha ratings. This separation allows us to:

- Identify managers who are genuinely integrating ESG factors and active ownership practices into their portfolio decision-making, with a range of different approaches, highlighting the innovative methods in which portfolio managers are approaching this.

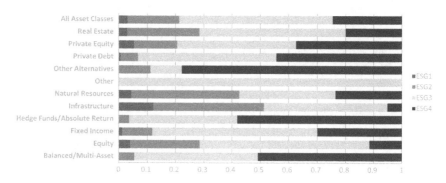

Figure 19.5 Distribution of Mercer ESG Ratings across Asset Classes at end December 2020.
Source: Mercer.

- Establish a disciplined process to embedding ESG questions into our core research process and to make the responses visible within that process.
- Meet client demand for the independent assessment of current or prospective ESG integration and stewardship practices by managers.
- Compare client portfolio comparisons with the Mercer GIMD universe at a point in time.
- Track ESG integration progress across the Mercer GIMD universe by asset classes over time and providers time series for further study.

As at June 2020, approximately 20% of ESG-rated strategies received the highest ratings of ESG1 and ESG2 (more information in Part 3). Figure 19.5 shows the performance range of ESG integration across the major asset classes.

Equities and example real-assets have historically led over fixed income and other asset classes in ESG integration, resulting in ratings distribution with a greater portion of highly rated strategies available to investors. In recent years, however, the fixed income asset class has made notable progress, particularly around industry initiatives and developments by asset owners, asset managers, and credit rating agencies. Further, increased client interest has led to asset managers placing a greater focus on ESG issues and launching sustainability-themed fixed income strategies.

Fixed Income ESG Ratings

Bond markets are no exception to the momentum in ESG moving from a niche area to the mainstream of investment practice. Furthermore, the quality of ESG integration in fixed income and the growing volume of investment strategies focus on sustainability themed fixed income is improving.

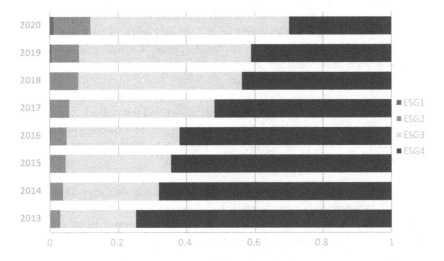

Figure 19.6 ESG Rating Trends in Fixed Income 2013–2020.
Source: Mercer.

The portion of the highest-rated two categories, ESG1 and ESG2, has increased from less than 3% in 2013 to over 10% in 2020 for the fixed income asset class. By way of comparison, in the same period, ESG1 and ESG2 rated equity strategies more than doubled from 11% to over 25% in 2020 (Figure 19.6).

While ESG investing is still most often considered as part of risk assessment in the due diligence process, and therefore at least theoretically fitting well into credit analysis, ESG-related factors are often considered to be more qualitative and less quantifiable in bonds. Key challenges for investors adopting ESG integration in fixed income include:

- The complexity of duration (e.g. what maturity of bonds of a fossil fuel producer is exposed to asset stranding? Is there a cut-off point?)
- Bond investors' lesser concern with capital repayments over a short horizon (e.g. are even shorter term ESG issues, perversely, too long term for bond markets to consider?)
- The less volatile nature of some fixed income investments (e.g. will ESG ever affect the spreads of large-cap blue-chip companies?)
- The high volume of sovereign debt in portfolios (e.g. can climate change genuinely have an impact on rates, inflation, and government ratings?)
- The difficulty of isolating ESG in the probability of default (e.g. will ratings agencies be able to analyse ESG issues sufficiently?)

Today, Mercer rates over 1,200 ESG fixed income investment strategies under nine different fixed income asset classes, which are further split into 24 sub-categories. Mercer's assessment of the quality of fund manager responsible investing techniques uses a consistent approach across asset classes that is aligned with the Manager Research Four-Factor Framework described above. The questions we ask include:

• How is ESG integrated into idea generation and portfolio construction?
• How do managers undertake stewardship at the investment strategy level?
• What firm-wide commitment is in place to support the overall growth of responsible investment across the business?

Within fixed income, ESG integration and stewardship can vary significantly according to the strategy type. Specific sub-asset classes have consistently shown more evidence of ESG integration in the investment process than others. In our experience, the degree to which asset managers have integrated ESG into their investment approaches tends to depend on several interlinked factors, including the sub-asset class focus and the investment style (see Figure 19.7).

For example, investment grade credit and buy and maintain credit strategies tend to display a more substantial degree of ESG integration (as shown by the higher ESG ratings in Figure 19.7) relative to other bond strategies. Most credit strategies tend to rely on a bottom-up fundamental assessment of an issuer's ability to service debt to drive excess return generation. Furthermore, stewardship has historically been more established for these two sub-asset classes (relative to governments), because of their generally better information disclosures and because of the generally longer-term investment horizon of investors in these sub-asset classes.

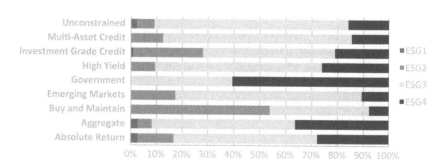

Figure 19.7 ESG Ratings across Fixed Income Sub-Asset Classes as at December 2020.

Source: Mercer.

Buy and Maintain Mandates Explained

Buy and Maintain is a style of credit portfolios that are constructed in a benchmark-agnostic manner to efficiently capture the credit premium. Mandates are often bespoke in nature with the investment objectives being tied to liability, duration, or cashflow matching rather than beating a benchmark. B&M mandates are designed to be low turnover in nature with long-term holding periods, often with the intention of holding securities to maturity.

As the name suggests, managers 'buy' a credit with the intention of 'maintaining' the position to maturity, collecting all payments along the journey. This longer time horizon makes it more likely for different ESG secular (e.g. climate change) and tail risks to play out, and by extension it forces the manager to consider how they might impact credit worthiness over the duration of the investment. These managers are focused with making sure they pick holdings that will pay them all the coupons and the principal by having a laser focus on downside risk as there is no additional upside beyond pull-to-par if you never intend to sell.

By their nature, buy & maintain portfolios rely on a bottom-up fundamental assessment of an issuer's ability to service debt to generate returns. Leading managers focus on integrating ESG into the credit evaluation process as seamlessly as possible and have developed proprietary approaches for assessing the most material sector and company-specific issues. The leading managers are generally not reliant on a single or a simple aggregate of third-party ESG rating provider for analysis, but instead take an informed and proactive approach to understanding the credit implications for the different sustainability issues most relevant to companies and sectors.

However, the approaches adopted differ and our research needs to acknowledge this. Some managers spend considerable time thinking about the riskiest holdings in their strategies. They periodically 'kick the tyres' on the companies with the biggest potential ESG risks to make sure they are sufficiently compensated for the exposure. Others assign ESG ratings to each holding on a scale, and some will not even consider investing in those with the worst scores. Leaders are also able to capture their activities in regular reporting for clients.

What We Look for When Assessing Managers

Mercer's approach to evaluating ESG integration discourages 'box-ticking' or prescribing a 'one size fits all' model. We look for consistency in the manager's effort to integrate ESG factors into their alpha generation and for beta enhancement via stewardship. Asset owners incorporating responsible investment beliefs within their fixed income portfolios will typically apply the following approaches:

1   The integration of ESG factors into fixed income investment processes as a risk management improvement tool.

2   Investment in sustainability themes or impact to achieve positive social or environmental outcomes.
3   Stewardship to enable financial system improvements.
4   Screening to align with values, reputation, or long-term expectations.

While practices vary, highly-rated strategies often have the following common features:

- ESG factors are embedded in the investment philosophy of the strategy with consistent integration across the four-factors we consider relevant for responsible investment implementation.
- Clear evidence that ESG factors feature in investment teams' decision-making process and corporate culture, with frequent and relevant examples.
- A long-term investment horizon and low portfolio turnover, which demonstrates the conviction of a fund manager's responsible investment strategy.
- A clear approach to reporting on a range of ESG metrics, demonstrating engagement with companies and the ability to improve company metrics.
- Stewardship policies and practices that include sufficient oversight, integration with investment decision-making and transparency.
- Collaboration with other institutional investors to improve company, sector, or market performance.

Government bond strategies might rely on top-down macroeconomic analysis informing directional duration or yield-curve positioning. This sort of top-down analysis can be harder to marry with an assessment of the externalities, or broader consequences, of individual company (or government) actions than a more fundamental approach. Furthermore, engagement at the regulatory level, especially for developed market countries, has historically been more challenging, both in terms of meeting milestones, as well as reflecting this in investment decisions. Collaborative engagements, or asset managers with larger AUM, may be more successful at engagement than individual or smaller asset managers. This is likely one reason that, to date, we have seen a smaller proportion of government bond strategies highly rated for ESG integration than credits strategies. In contrast, emerging market government strategies have tended to exhibit somewhat higher ESG ratings where anecdotally a number of fund managers have commented that they have greater ability to engage at the regulatory level.

One area where we see scope for improvement in ESG integration is in high yield credit. Given the extensive bottom-up credit analysis applied in a number of these strategies, we believe ESG factors can prove to be a fundamental part of this analysis. For example, governance structures are likely to play an influential role in determining the potential for default. One challenge often cited by asset managers in integrating ESG factors, particularly for high yield strategies, relates to the availability, consistency, and reliability of data. However, this could also be interpreted as an opportunity for thoughtful asset managers to differentiate themselves from their peers.

Investment styles such as active versus passive or fundamental versus quantitative can also influence the scope for ESG integration within fixed income. Buy and maintain credit strategies typically invest with a longer time horizon than other active credit strategies and tend to evaluate issues or issuers based on how they might perform until bond maturity. This longer time horizon increases the likelihood of ESG factors, such as environmental issues, materialising before the maturity of a bond. For example, a car manufacturing company's bond may be held within an active portfolio in the short term on relative-value considerations. However, if that company shows no sign of responding to regulatory changes and shifting toward electric car production, then investors are likely to consider bonds with 15-to 20-year tenors as far riskier than those with five years remaining. Similarly, other credit strategies with more focus on fundamental analysis tend to provide greater scope for higher ESG ratings relative to those with a more macro focus.

Fixed Income ESG Investing Acceleration

We view the increased attention to ESG-related issues in fixed income as positive for asset owners and investment managers. ESG factors are crucial within fixed income, especially when we consider how ESG factors relate to managing downside risk (e.g. the implications of the low climate transition for long-dated (20–50 year) new issues by fossil fuel companies that have not committed to the energy transition).

We also believe the upward trend of fixed income managers incorporating ESG will continue its momentum based on several factors, including overall increased regulatory focus, the pressure to expand stewardship activity into fixed income and growth in asset owner demand now that ESG governance is better understood and most resistance has subsided. Against the backdrop of rising manager ambitions and tightening global regulations (see Chapter 23), managers are exploring and refining best practice in terms of holding companies to account and using their influence as lenders of capital to manage all forms of credit risk. Managers have traditionally focused most attention on these issues before each new bond issuance, but given the duration of holding periods and the likelihood of relending to the same entity for new bonds or reissues, managers clearly also have an incentive to use their voice to ensure their place in the capital structure is respected. Activity might be through one-on-one engagement or collaboration between investors (e.g. to push the company to disclose a climate change strategy). Going forward we expect this to be an area of increasing focus with some managers already showing commitment to engaging meaningfully with companies across material sustainability topics.

In some geographies, in particular the UK and Europe, the de-risking trend of defined benefit pension funds and the increased climate scrutiny of insurance assets by the supervisory authorities is likely to have an impact. More emphasis on stress tests will drive asset owners through a cycle of ESG and climate-related governance and investment strategy decision-making across fixed income. This makes it clear that the options available to clients from fixed income will expand as new categories of fixed income are introduced to responsible investment themes and techniques. For example, we are currently seeing a strong focus on ESG in index and passive strategies.

Other investment styles, such as quantitative fixed income, may find it more difficult to incorporate ESG within the overall investment process. Quantitative fixed income strategies systematically base investment decisions on various market, accounting, or economic data and have often struggled to demonstrate how ESG risks are considered, often arguing that these risks tend to be more subjective. Although some progress has been made within quantitative equity strategies and ESG integration, we believe there may be greater scope for quantitative fixed income managers to introduce additional alternative data sources and non-financial metrics.

These wider changes in investment practice and in the investment markets all supports our expectation that changes will emerge in the fixed income ESG market with improved product supply, breadth of asset class exposure, and innovation.

Asset Owners and ESG Ratings

Investor Evaluation

Mercer's ESG ratings are used predominantly in the Process and Portfolio stages of the Pathway framework where they help to structure and monitor the incorporation of ESG factors into how clients manage ESG risks and opportunities. There is no standard practice for ESG integration, but we consider some common factors when assessing managers. First, we look at the structure and organisation around ESG integration. We look for a balance between providing analysts with the flexibility to incorporate the most relevant information and structure a robust and repeatable process. Second, we look at the internal and external resources available to support the investment process. Third, we look at how portfolio construction incorporates ESG factors and if this is commensurate with the philosophy of the strategy, such as performance maximisation.

In its simplest form, ESG ratings are an input into a manager selection exercise where all else being equal, clients will select from a shortlist of managers the investment strategy with the highest ESG rating.

Benchmarking managers on ESG ratings has increasingly become a vital component of a regular manager monitoring exercise. Clients can perform portfolio level ESG assessments, strategy by strategy, by using ESG ratings as reference points. Such assessments provide a high-level overview of a portfolio ESG rating relative to the respective asset class universes, allowing for like-for-like comparisons. A proprietary Mercer tool compares a client's aggregate portfolio and individual strategy ESG ratings – for example, comparing a client's growth fixed income strategy's rating against the growth fixed income universe in Mercer's Global Investment Manager Database. This, together with qualitative data and research reports, allows asset owners to monitor a manager's ESG practices to ensure alignment with its policy commitments and overall investment strategy.

Clients tend to monitor managers annually on their ESG integration performance, using this monitoring process to identify areas for improvement and requirements for manager engagement (see Boxes 19.1 and 19.2 for examples of what might be covered in this engagement). Low ESG ratings do not automatically lead to transferring investments to a new fund manager with a higher rated strategy. Instead, the manager's willingness and ability to enhance the process provides an opportunity for asset owners to engage with their managers to improve their approach to ESG integration.

BOX 19.1 Engaging Managers on ESG Integration

Leading asset owners are asking their managers to monitor and explain material ESG risks. They ask questions such as:

1   What are the most material ESG risks within my portfolio and how am I being compensated for them?
2   Are they predominantly idiosyncratic tail risks or systemic risks?
3   How are they split by company- or sector-level risks?

BOX 19.2 Engaging Managers on Stewardship

Leading asset are challenging their managers to demonstrate that not only are they identifying key risks but also holding companies to account and achieving positive outcomes. Two ways in which asset owners have improved stewardship monitoring have been to:

1   Request engagement reporting specific to the asset owner's portfolio.
2   Ask managers for evidence and case studies of positive outcomes (not just activity) across environmental, social, and governance issues.

By undertaking assessments, asset owners demonstrate that they are actively managing their sustainability practices, that they are meeting regulatory requirements and that they are engaged owners with their managers. The results of this monitoring can also be used to support reporting to and engagement with internal (e.g. asset owner boards, committees, executive management) and external stakeholders (e.g. beneficiaries, regulators, industry peers).

Concluding Comments

The role of investment consultants has developed as responsible investment approaches have grown. This reflects the growing sophistication and expectations of clients to move from the left of the Mercer's Responsible Investment Pathway to the right (see Figure 19.2). Over the past decade, consultants and investors predominantly focussed on education (in particular, addressing misconceptions about ESG as a purely ethical endeavour), on early strategic ESG signals (Beliefs), and on helping asset owners draft their initial approaches to ESG factors (Policy).

Today, the work is increasingly oriented towards processes and outcomes (Process & Portfolio). This is done through monitoring (ESG ratings, carbon footprint, engagement activity and outcomes), performing climate scenario analysis, manager selection exercises, maintaining regulatory compliance, and continuous development of the overarching process. In relation to policy development, broad commitments and explicit target setting at the portfolio level have come to fore. For example, discussions on climate targets (net-zero targets) and explicit portfolio carbon budgets (carbon intensity, potential emission, thematic investments). Generally public funds have been more active in making explicit climate commitments. We expect to see these commitments accelerate significantly as public pressure and policy initiatives proliferate.

While some consulting advice can be delivered with a high level of uniformity (such as regulatory compliance), the general nature and speed of innovation in sustainability does not lend itself to industry-wide automation. Mercer prides itself on thought leadership created in its global responsible investment specialist team. This team continuously develops new and more sophisticated approaches, often in cooperation with Mercer's clients. Mercer's "Future Makers Group" of asset owners has worked with Mercer to collaborate on integrating climate considerations into portfolios as well as considering the impact investment portfolios have from a climate perspective. The Group has been an invaluable sounding board in developing climate scenario tools and more recently, transition analytics and a portfolio-wide net-zero alignment framework.

While there is progress, challenges exist for clients adopting a responsible investment approach in fixed income. Many asset owners are still working on their strategic acceptance of fixed income ESG materiality, in particular for non-corporate asset classes such as sovereigns. Furthermore, the consultant's role in fixed income is still primarily policy-oriented. For example, asset owners do not regularly adopt policy requirements for annual monitoring of carbon risks within the fixed income asset class.

However, lessons from the more established asset classes (equities and real assets) and the wider acceptance of the financial materiality of ESG, the client take-up of ESG in fixed income is likely to be fast and shift to more process and portfolio development. While still facing some conceptual challenges from asset owners, fixed income stewardship is an area of particular relevance. High-quality and genuine engagement is a factor that has not yet been significantly explored by the industry, but will gain prominence.

It is important to recognise that, while ESG integration, climate change, and the Sustainable Development Goals are all receiving client attention, clients also have many other issues on their agendas, including funding, risk management regulation and governance. The practical consequence is that responsible investment is competing for board and management attention, and this may limit the rate of adoption or the resources that are available for this area of work. Investment consultants therefore have a critical role to play in ensuring that ESG issues receive the appropriate level of attention by asset owners, in supporting asset owners with the development and implementation of ESG and responsible investment strategies, and in ensuring that asset owners play their role in ensuring the sustainability and resilience of the investment system.

Notes

1 Until November 2021, Tomi Nummela was Principal, Responsible Investment Consultant at Mercer where he advised asset owners.

2 Mercer assists clients across the full continuum of institutional investing (corporate and public pensions, insurance, endowments, and foundation). Mercer's global advisory asset business advises on US$16 trillion of assets in total. Mercer has over 5,600 staff, including over 200 dedicated manager research analysts. Mercer also manages US$321 billion of delegated assets (as at December 2020). Mercer advises its clients on the formulation of investment strategies, on organisational structure, and on implementing asset allocation via third-party managers. Mercer DC and DB Master Trusts provide retirement solutions for employees and Mercer Fiduciary Management helps institutional clients to reach their investment goals and achieve better governance.

20 Delivering Sustainable Investment Objectives through the Capital Markets

Doris Kramer and Caroline Horbrügger

The need for investors to act on sustainable development-related issues has never been louder or more important. For American essayist Nathaniel Rich: 'Homo sapiens was the first species to alter the environment that sustained us – to the point that it might not sustain us anymore' (Rich, 2018). There is a clear need for timely action in the fight against humanities' global challenges, broadly represented by the UN Sustainable Development Goals (SDGs)[1] and the 2015 Paris Agreement on Climate Change.[2] This chapter focusses on financing sustainable development from the perspective of KfW, a promotional bank with a mission to improve economic, ecological, and social living conditions on a local, national, European, and global level.

We start with an introduction to KfW's mission and commitment to sustainability on a group-wide level. We then describe how KfW's liquidity portfolio applies responsible investing principles, and conclude by exploring how the bank embraces green finance activities in its green bond programme and in its market development role.

Sustainability at KFW

About KfW

KfW is Germany's flagship promotional bank. Founded in 1948 with funds from the Marshall Plan, KfW was initially tasked with financing the reconstruction of Germany after the Second World War. Since then, the development of KfW has been closely connected to the economic development of the Federal Republic of Germany, most recently demonstrated by KfW's support for Germany's economy during the COVID-19 crises.

KfW is an institution under public law, 80% of which is owned by the German Federal Government and the remaining 20% by the German federal states. As such, KfW has been supporting change, encouraging forward-looking ideas, and financing the sustainable development of the economy, society, and environment both in Germany and abroad. For this purpose, it has provided more than EUR 1.7 trillion in loans since inception. KfW's priority areas for financing are climate action and environmental protection;

DOI: 10.4324/9781003055341-25

innovation; small and medium-sized enterprises and start-ups; infrastructure investments by municipalities and communities; student and educational loans; export and project finance; international cooperation.

KfW's financing activities focus on the socially and economically important megatrends of climate change and the environment; social change; and digitisation and innovation. The protection of the environment and the fight against climate change are particularly important to the bank. KfW has set a green target ratio of more than 35% of its total annual commitment volume and is among the largest contributors to green finance worldwide. In 2020, KfW's green quota represented 33% out of a total of 135.3bn EUR in new loan commitments, an historical high given KfW's coronavirus aid programmes. If adjusted for those special coronavirus measures approximately 50% of new loan commitments were dedicated to finance environment and climate protection.

Policy Alignment

Several policy developments have directly impacted KfW's lending policy at a global, regional, and local level. At a global level, major political achievements like the Sustainable Development Goals (SDGs) and the Paris Agreement on Climate Change have demonstrated broad political support to tackle societies' greatest challenges. With the SDGs, countries have adopted a set of goals to end poverty, protect the planet, and ensure prosperity for all. Countries ratifying the Paris Agreement have pledged to keep the global temperature rise well below 2°C and disclose their efforts in nationally determined contributions (NDCs).

We have identified the transition to a carbon-neutral economy as one of the most significant and urgent challenges we face. Transitioning to a carbon-neutral society is not only about phasing out polluting sectors, but also about creating a more resilient and equal economy. The Paris Agreement emphasizes 'the intrinsic relationship that climate change actions, responses and impacts have with equitable access to sustainable development and eradication of poverty'.[3]

At a regional level, aiming for Europe to become the first carbon-neutral continent, the European Union has developed a roadmap to transform Europe into an 'economy where there are no net emissions of greenhouse gases by 2050, economic growth is decoupled from resource use [and] no person and no place is left behind' (European Commission, 2019). Investments needed to ensure a just transition into a climate-neutral economy and reach 2030 targets are estimated at EUR 260 billion per year in the EU alone (European Commission, 2020a).

In our home market of Germany, the national Climate Action Programme 2030, introduced by the Federal Government in 2019 together with a Climate Protection Law, introduced measures to reduce greenhouse gases. As part of this process, policymakers modified KfW's mandate to evolve the bank into a transformative promotional bank that supports the transformation of economic sectors and the financial market for a greenhouse-gas-neutral future. We now turn to what this means in practice.

KfW as a Transformative Promotional Bank

As a bank committed to responsibility at the highest level, KfW has the goal of integrating sustainability more deeply into the group. In mid-2018, the KfW Executive Board commissioned a new in-house project, the KfW Roadmap Sustainable Finance, with the aim of creating a stringent, multi-dimensional sustainability concept as an extended tool for managing KfW Group's business in line with sustainability-related aspects. The roadmap is intended to identify ways in which we can support the Federal Government in meeting its sustainability and climate targets even better.

Our roadmap was developed by a range of KfW's central units as well representatives from all of KfW's market areas. The roadmap focused on five sub-projects: (1) mission statement, (2) steering concept, (3) risk management, (4) communications, and (5) governance. A new sustainability mission statement was developed and published in 2019 (KfW, 2019).

The measurement of sustainability performance was identified as a priority. Since 2019, KfW has published an annual SDG mapping, outlining how KfW's activities for the respective year contribute to the 17 SDGs (see Table 20.1 which presents KfW's data for 2020).

Underpinning these headline figures are various practical actions that KfW has implemented in support of its commitment to responsibility. For example,

Table 20.1 KfW Group's Contribution to the SDGs in 2020.

UN SDG - *Sustainable Development Goals*	In EUR million
SDG 1 No poverty	10,057
SDG 2 Zero hunger	600
SDG 3 Good health and well-being	3,011
SDG 4 Quality education	5,074
SDG 5 Gender equality	4,894
SDG 6 Clean water and sanitation	1,833
SDG 7 Affordable and clean energy	40,465
SDG 8 Decent work and economic growth	71,922
SDG 9 Industry, innovation, and infrastructure	14,874
SDG 10 Reduced inequalities	8,587
SDG 11 Sustainable cities and communities	45,981
SDG 12 Responsible consumption and production	246
SDG 13 Climate action	43,166
SDG 14 Life below water	306
SDG 15 Life on land	797
SDG 16 Peace, justice, and strong institutions	6,842
SDG 17 Partnerships for the goals	12,635

Note: Financing Can Contribute to More than One SDG.

KfW analyses the greenhouse gas emissions from its financing portfolio, with the aim of delivering greenhouse gas reductions and achieving global greenhouse gas neutrality, while also focusing promotional work on projects that support climate change adaptation. Another focus was understanding how ESG and climate risks affect the bank's risk exposure; KfW became the first German bank and the first unilateral promotional bank to be an official supporter of the Task Force on Climate-related Financial Related Disclosures (TCFD) in October 2018 and began reporting climate-related risks and relating processes in its Sustainability Report 2019 (KfW, 2020). In the same year, 40% of KfW's commitments focused on the small and medium-sized enterprises (SME) sector. KfW supported 37,000 start-ups and SMEs and benefitted 83,000 people through academic studies or vocational training. KfW financings in developing countries and emerging economies led to a reduction of carbon savings of 8 million tonnes per year, and, 370,000 newly constructed or refurbished energy-efficient housing units were financed by KfW loans at favourable interest rates.

Going forward, the 'SDG contribution of KfW financings' and the 'Paris-compatibility of KfW financings' will be important parameters for KfW's central strategic steering. This will entail a group-wide expansion of KfW's impact management and measurement processes in order to capture more precisely what actual and sustained impacts – for example, jobs, greenhouse gas emission reductions, hospital beds – the projects co-financed by KfW generate. In addition, technology-oriented Paris-compatible sector guidelines will be identified for particularly emissions-intensive sectors. In a science-based approach, these sector guidelines will be derived from the Paris Climate targets and the resulting climate scenarios of the International Energy Agency with support from experts. They will be gradually implemented from 2021 onwards, with the first six sector guidelines implemented in Q3 2021. KfW's binding long-term goal in line with the German and EU climate policy is to have a greenhouse gas-neutral portfolio from the year 2050 at the latest.

As a further priority area of the 'tranSForm' project, KfW will further strengthen its organisational structure and procedures for ESG risk management. It is evident that the risks from changes in the environment and climate, social tensions, and weak governance can become increasingly stronger drivers for the financial assessment of our portfolios. We are gradually expanding the reporting on climate risks in our portfolio on the basis of the TCFD standard.

However, as a 'transformative promotional bank', we must go even further. It is our mission and aspiration to support our customers, the business community and the financial sector with our promotional offerings in the necessary profound structural transformation. The transition to a sustainable and climate-neutral economy can and should be a success story. It will require massive investment in modern technologies, while offering many new opportunities for the German industry.

Sustainable Investment at KFW

KfW considers sustainability not only in its core lending activities, but across its financial investments, too. KfW has applied a sustainable investment approach to its liquidity portfolio since 2008, having signed the Principles for Responsible Investment (PRI) in 2006. We believe companies that adopt strategic approaches to managing ESG issues will enjoy competitive advantages in global markets in the future and will outperform in the long term. By integrating the PRI principles into our asset management, we aim to drive forward sustainable business practices actively and transparency, while encouraging other market participants to follow.

KfW's €31 billion[4] liquidity portfolio is a pure fixed-income portfolio that is aimed at securing KfW's liquidity in times of distress. Largely pursuing a buy-and-hold strategy, the portfolio is risk managed through rating and term diversification rules as well as a bank-wide single borrower limit framework. The asset classes eligible for investment are government bonds and bonds issued by government-related issuers and agencies, covered bonds, financials, and asset-backed securities. In addition to requirements focussing on the credit worthiness of an issuer like minimum ratings and maximum terms, a sustainable investment approach is applied that consists of three elements: (1) integrating ESG criteria; (2) observing exclusion criteria, and; (3) engaging with bond issuers. Each of these elements is described below.

ESG Integration

KfW follows a best-in-class investment approach. This involves applying sustainability ratings as an overlay to the credit assessment. ESG scores are sourced and integrated into internal systems from an external sustainability ratings agency, currently ISS ESG, for the entire investment universe on a monthly basis. Only issuers with an ESG score among the best 50% of their sector are eligible for investment. For sovereign issuers, 'prime' status is the minimum rating standard expected. Sustainability ratings for ABS investments in the liquidity portfolio are based on the ABS originator, as sustainability ratings for ABS issuers (typically Special Purpose Vehicles) are not available and would not be meaningful.

We ensure that sustainability ratings incorporate a broad range of criteria relating to environmental, social and governance issues. For instance, a company's climate change strategy, carbon intensity, equal opportunities, and human rights as well as business ethics or executive compensation are factored into the business profile.

As part of the rating process, publicly available information provided by the company is evaluated. The sustainability rating agency also enters into a dialogue with issuers, to generate a rating score that is updated on a regular basis. Issuers are then ranked against their sector peer group. Based on ESG performance scores, KfW calculates the minimum value issuers must reach with their ESG score to reach the best 50% in their sector. If an issuer's ESG score does not meet the threshold, it is not eligible for investment. This information is distributed across KfW's investment management system and is obligatory for portfolio managers to consult before investing.

Exclusion Criteria

In addition, KfW applies exclusion criteria that are based on the 'IFC Exclusion List' and the exclusion list of KfW Group. This ensures that, as a matter of principle, no funds provided by KfW to issuers through the purchase of their bonds can flow into projects which, from our perspective, are likely to have unacceptable negative impacts on the environment, social conditions or governance. If issuers are financials, the exclusion criteria are applied to relevant equity participations given that loan books are not sufficiently transparent. In these cases, exclusion criteria are applied indirectly to participations held by banks of at least 50% or strategic participations in a company both of which generates at least 5% of its annual turnover on the basis of one or more of the products covered by the exclusion criteria, or which exhibits a controversy with regard to the exclusion criteria that is evaluated as 'severe' or 'very severe' by our research partner, ISS ESG (see Table 20.2).

Table 20.2 Exclusion Criteria for KfW's Liquidity Portfolio.

1	Production or activities involving harmful or exploitative forms of forced labour or child labour as defined in the ILO core labour standards.
2	Production, use of, or trade in pesticides/herbicides or other hazardous substances that are subject to international bans.
3	Trade in animals or animal products that are subject to the provisions of CITES (Convention on International Trade in Endangered Species of Wild Fauna and Flora).
4	Production of cosmetics, etc., involving testing on animals.
5	Commercial logging operations in primary tropical moist forests.
6	Investments which could be associated with the destruction (Note 1) or significant impairment of areas particularly worthy of protection (without adequate compensation in accordance with international standards).
7	Production or trade in controversial weapons or important components for the production of controversial weapons (anti-personnel mines, biological and chemical weapons, cluster bombs, radioactive ammunition, nuclear weapons).
8	Production or trade in radioactive material. This does not apply to the procurement of medical equipment, quality control equipment, or other application for which the radioactive source is insignificant and/or adequately shielded.
9	Nuclear power plants (apart from measures that reduce environmental hazards of existing assets) and mines with uranium as an essential source of extraction.

(Continued)

10   Prospection, exploration, and mining of coal; land-based means of transport and related infrastructure essentially used for coal; power plants, heating stations, and cogeneration facilities essentially fired with coal, as well as associated stub lines (Note 2).

11   Non-conventional prospection, exploration, and extraction of oil from bituminous shale, tar sands, or oil sands.

12   Production or trade in tobacco.

13   Controversial forms of gambling: operation of casinos, production of devices or other equipment for casinos or betting offices or companies that generate turnover via online betting (so-called 'short odds' are defined as 'controversial forms of gambling').

14   Any business activity involving pornography.

Notes:
1. 'Destruction' means (i) the destruction or severe deterioration of the integrity of an area caused by a major and prolonged change in the use of land or water, or (ii) the alteration of a habitat which leads to the inability of the affected area to perform its function.
2. Investments in power transmission grids with significant coal-based power feed-in will only be pursued in countries and regions with an ambitious national climate protection policy or strategy (NDC), or where the investments are targeted at reducing the share of coal-based power in the relevant grid. In developing countries, heating stations and cogeneration facilities essentially fired with coal can be co-financed in individual cases based on a rigid assessment, if there is a particularly high sustainability contribution, major environmental hazards are reduced, and if there demonstrably is no more climate-friendly alternative.

Engagement

Dialogue with bonds issuers forms an integral part of our sustainable investment approach. Since we exclusively invest in bonds, we do not – unlike equity investors – have a formal legal basis to engage with issuers and raise awareness of sustainability. However, we do have the ability to exert influence. With the aims of promoting a dialogue with bond issuers on sustainability and of raising awareness of sustainability, KfW has written an annual letter to the bond issuers in the liquidity portfolio since 2011. With the letter, issuers are informed about their current sustainability score and about KfW's investment approach. We also offer to enter in an open dialogue on sustainability topics. The responses to our letters tend to be very positive. We have anecdotal evidence that these letters have contributed to a more transparent disclosure of the sustainability activities of some issuers and have led to an intensification of the dialogue with the sustainability rating agency in several cases.

KfW also contributes to wider market transparency on sustainable investment through its annual disclosure under the PRI reporting framework. This information, on KfW's practices and approach with regard sustainable investment from the perspective of a pure fixed income investor, is assessed and published by the PRI. We see this reporting as crucial to raising awareness around sustainable investment practices in capital markets.

Going Green – KFW'S Support for the Green Bond Market

The investments needed to combat climate change and ensure a just and sustainable development globally far exceed available public funds. While green finance has traditionally been rooted in classical loan business, it has quickly become apparent that, given the enormous amounts required, capital markets are needed to finance the transition towards a sustainable economy and society. In explicitly articulating the use of bond proceeds, green bonds have raised the awareness of climate and environmental issues among capital market participants. By creating a new sense of responsibility, green bonds have also put focus on other sustainability dimensions, serving as a blueprint for social and sustainability bonds (See Box 20.1).

BOX 20.1 Sustainable versus Green Finance

- **Sustainable finance** is a broad approach embracing environmental, social, economic, and governance matters in financing
- **Green finance** corresponds to the financing of climate and environment protection projects
- The extended definition of green finance also includes **climate risks**

To promote capital market-based financing of environmental and climate protection and building on its experience in green finance and its standing in international capital markets, KfW decided to comprehensively support the development of the green bond market. Entering the market in 2014 as a green bond issuer and in 2015 as a dedicated green bond investor, KfW has been among the most active participants in the market segment.

Green Bonds Issued by KfW

Since its first successful bond issuance in 1958, KfW has established itself as a trusted and frequent borrower in international capital markets. Building on an explicit and direct guarantee from the Federal Republic of Germany, KfW bonds are considered a safe haven asset and are valued by a global investor base. Recognizing KfW's excellent credit standing, Moody's, Scope Ratings and Standard & Poor's have assigned triple-A ratings. KfW also benefits from being among the highest performers when it comes to its own ESG ratings, which confirm KfW's holistic sustainability approach. Aiming to act as a catalyst in driving this market forward and intensify the strategic dialogue about 'responsibility in capital markets', KfW has become a leading green bond borrower, issuing more than €31 billion to date[5] in various currencies and engaging in collaboration with investors across the globe during the process. This makes KfW one of the largest issuers of green bonds globally.

The proceeds of KfW's green bond issuance are linked to two promotional loan programmes, both aiming for climate change mitigation. KfW's loan programme 'Renewable Energy – Standard' offers financing at favourable rates to enterprises, private individuals, farmers and non-profit organisations to install renewable energy plants for electricity generation, combined electricity and heat generation and measures to integrate renewable energy into the energy system. In particular, photovoltaic panels, onshore and offshore windmills, hydropower (<20MW), and biogas and biomass plants are financed up to a project volume of EUR 50m. In addition to the green bond programme in 2019, KfW's loan programme 'Energy-efficient Construction' is aimed at the construction and acquisition of new energy-efficient residential buildings in Germany. The long-term financing option with an up to 30-year repayment term is eligible for buildings that use at least 25% less primary energy compared to the requirements of the current Germany energy saving ordinance for new buildings.

KfW regularly reports both on the allocation of green bond proceeds to the two loan programmes as well as on the impacts of these programmes. The impact is externally evaluated by one or more independent institutions. On a regular basis, KfW informs green bond investors what impact was achieved, especially in terms of greenhouse gas (GHG) savings (See Table 20.3).

Setting up the green bond programme, extending it in 2019, and maintenance has required a close collaboration between KfW's funding and loan departments, the development of internal expertise, and the establishment of internal processes for regular allocation and impact reporting. External expenses included the cost for a second-party opinion on KfW's green bond framework. While issuing green bonds is more costly than issuing traditional bonds, the benefits have included closer internal collaboration and the ability to attract new investors, Since 2014. KfW has been able to attract over 100 new investors. Dedicated green and socially responsible investors have been a particular target; in 2021, socially responsible investors bought more than 70% of KfW green bonds. Green bonds are also discussed by KfW in almost

Table 20.3 Estimated KfW Impact Data for Green Bonds Issued in 2020.

	2020
EUR net proceeds	8,350 million
Annual GHG emissions reduced/avoided	1.49 million tons
Annual renewable electricity generation	2.12 TWh
Annual renewable energy capacity added	1,085 MW_{el}
Annual energy savings	72,641 MWh
Number of jobs created/preserved	>100,000

every meeting with mainstream bond investors to further raise awareness for sustainability and green finance.

KfW's Green Bond Portfolio

On the investment side, KfW has been building a green bond portfolio since 2015. The initial target volume of the portfolio of €2 billion was reached in February 2020. Going forward, KfW will continue investing in green bonds and will maintain the portfolio volume at a level of €2–2.5 billion. Investing in green bonds not only advances KfW's sustainable investment strategy in global capital markets but also supports KfW's goal of contributing to the realisation of environmental and climate protection projects (e.g. in the areas of renewable energy, resource efficiency, environmentally friendly transportation, pollution prevention and control, sustainable water and wastewater management, or biodiversity). Backed by a promotional mandate from Germany's Federal Ministry for the Environment, Nature Conservation and Nuclear Safety, KfW's role as an investor is twofold. By investing in green bonds on a global scale, KfW aims to support market growth and to increase the use of green bonds as a capital market instrument for financing the transition to a low carbon economy.

In addition, KfW has a mandate to support the development of high-quality market standards and promote the qualitative development of the market segment. In its regular dialogue with green bond issuers, KfW transparently communicates its minimum requirements for green bond investment and gives feedback on green bond frameworks (see Box 20.2).

BOX 20.2 Minimum Eligibility Criteria for KfW's Green Bond Investments

- Clear description of the projects to be financed (including goals and projected impacts)
- Competent project selection as well as a fully transparent process of the management of proceeds
- A regular public reporting including project description, allocation of funds, and environmental impacts (quantified where feasible)
- A verification of the project selection and use of funds from an independent third party

---

Promoting Green Bond Market Harmonisation

KfW promotes market harmonisation through acting as a vocal advocate of the market in various international initiatives. KfW has been especially engaged in the Green Bond Principles, being a member of the Executive

Committee since 2015, and from 2018 until 2020 being part of the EU Technical Expert Group working on the proposals for EU Taxonomy and EU Green Bond Standard.

Green Bond Principles

Providing voluntary guidelines for green bond issuance, the Green Bond Principles have been a catalyst in evolving the green bond market. These Principles are frequently referred to in numerous frameworks of green bond issuers, in the investment criteria of green bond investors, in external green bond verifications, and in national green bond regulations. The backbone of the Principle's success has been their transparent, comprehensive, and cooperative process to address complex and global challenges and to provide solutions in an effective and practicable way. Providing a platform for the exchange of market participants involving issuers, investors, intermediaries, non-governmental organisations (NGOs), service providers as (sustainability) rating agencies, regulators, and other stakeholders in a continuous, interconnected, and equal process is a novelty in its extent and intensity of cooperation. In encouraging issuers to be as transparent as possible in a standardised way, the Green Bond Principles ensure that best practice spreads quickly and globally while allowing for specific approaches adapted to local conditions.

Active in various Green Bond Principles working groups, KfW has continued to emphasise the importance of impact reporting. Impact reporting has garnered increasing attention, as a means for the green bond market to underline its integrity and credibility, especially as issuers often provide information on future actions envisaged and will only achieve an environmental impact at a later stage when the allocation to green projects takes place. Thus, impact reporting serves to increase capital allocation to environmental sustainability projects, especially as a growing interest from investors for impact reporting appears to be driven by their own obligations to assess the relative merits of individual green bonds and report to their own investors and beneficiaries.

To enhance the transparency and integrity of the green bond market, a significant effort has been undertaken by the Green Bond Principles' Working Group on Impact Reporting, which KfW has been co-chairing since 2018, to further develop voluntary guidelines for assessing a project's environmental impact. This working group, which includes issuers, investors, underwriters, and environmental advocacy and advisory groups, focuses on the conveyance of key information reflecting the environmental benefits of the assets funded by green bonds that are aligned with the GBP. The goal is both to reduce the uncertainty for issuers and to ensure the timely availability of relevant information for investors and wider stakeholders by agreeing best practice for quantitative and qualitative disclosure of the 'impact' resulting from green bond investment.

The 'Harmonized Framework for Impact Reporting', published in December 2015 by 11 International Financing Institutions, including KfW, contains core principles and recommendations for reporting as well as impact metrics for Renewable Energy and Energy Efficiency projects. This served as a starting point for the Green Bond Principles Working Group on Impact Reporting, which continues to develop core impact metrics and guidelines for other GBP project categories (e.g. water and wastewater management, clean transportation, biodiversity, or waste management and resource-efficiency projects). This guidance was compiled in the *Handbook – Harmonized Framework for Impact Reporting* in June 2019 and has since been updated (Green Bond Principles and ICMA, 2021). The Handbook provides core indicators that capture the environmental impact of each project type and also provides reporting templates for issuers to report on a project-by-project or an aggregated portfolio basis.

The Green Bond Principles have also underpinned the development of solutions that can be applied to other areas of the transformation towards sustainability; examples include the Social Bond Principles (ICMA and the Social Bond Principles, 2021), the Sustainability-linked Bond Principles (ICMA and the Sustainability-linked Bond Principles, 2020) and the *Climate Transition Finance Handbook* (ICMA and Climate Transition Finance, 2020). The innovation of sustainability-linked bonds brought the sustainability profile and transition strategy on a corporate level into even more focus. Not necessarily following a use-of-proceeds concept, the defining characteristic of sustainability-linked bonds is that issuers set sustainability targets to be reached in a predefined time period. Depending on whether the issuer reaches such targets in time, the structural and/or financial characteristics of the bond change. For example, the coupon may rise as a penalty if the issuer misses the target. Sustainability-linked Bond Principles (SLBP) have been recently developed in a working group, which KfW has been contributing. Aiming to be a catalyst for further market development, the SLBP give best-practice recommendations on the selection of key performance indicators (KPIs), the calibration of Sustainability Performance Targets, bond characteristics, reporting, and external verification (ICMA, 2020).

EU Technical Expert Group

Looking to spur financial markets towards sustainable development and transition to a low-carbon economy, the EU commission set ten concrete measures in its action plan 'Financing Sustainable Growth' published in March 2018 (European Commission, 2018). A Technical Expert Group (TEG) was established to propose an EU taxonomy for sustainable activities, corporate disclosure of climate-related information, EU climate benchmarks and benchmarks' ESG disclosure, as well as an EU Green Bond Standard.

As a classification system to identify green and social economic activities the EU Taxonomy is set to create a common language for the definition of sustainability for the financial sector. Environmentally sustainable activities should significantly contribute to at least one of the six environmental targets of the EU, are not to harm any other environmental target ('do no significant harm'), fulfil minimum safeguards and technical screening criteria. The proposal for an EU Green Bond Standards recommends the introduction of a voluntary standard and is largely based on existent market practice. New and challenging is the fact that projects financed by an EU Green Bond must fulfil the requirements of the EU Taxonomy. Issuers must also formulate and publish a Green Bond Framework and report on the allocation of funds as well as on impacts achieved. Both framework and allocation reporting require external verification.

KfW was appointed to the TEG and contributed to the work streams for the EU Taxonomy and EU Green Bond Standard. Final TEG reports and recommendations were published in 2019 and 2020 respectively (European Commission, 2020b).

In 2021, the EU Commission published several (draft) delegated acts, on setting technical screening criteria under the EU Taxonomy for Climate Change Mitigation and Climate Change Adaptation as well as a (draft) delegated act for an EU Green Bond Regulation. These (draft) delegated acts follow the proposals developed by TEG to a substantial degree. In accordance with legislative procedures, it is likely that these (draft) delegated acts will enter into force after 2022.

Conclusion

A frequent question we receive asks if green bonds create real additionality. With many green bonds refinancing existing green assets the question appears merited. Are green bonds really initiating new green projects? While it is difficult to find a definite answer for all instruments, green bonds have created additionality in the sense that they have created a greater awareness of climate and environmental protection and have served as a blueprint for complementary social and sustainability bonds issuance. We see greater change on the horizon as corporate leaders have begun to focus more on green and social business activities, and there are wider debates occurring on what carbon-neutral economy means for business sectors and how capital markets can facilitate the transition.

KfW's commitment to promote sustainability in a capital markets context focuses on three areas where we can exert most influence. First, our investment operations integrate key sustainability themes and processes across our liquidity portfolio. Second, our green bond issuance programme integrates sustainability as a key objective and delivers the transparency to market participants underscoring this impact. Third, we act as an investor in green bonds and support wider capital market development by sharing our expertise and experience to drive market awareness and guidance. These efforts have made sustainability a driving force of our identity and will influence our work in future years.

From our perspective, green and social bonds are only one component of implementing sustainability in financial markets. Going forward, the sustainability profile and transition strategy at a corporate level must be a primary focus. Sustainable leadership is required that actively challenges current corporate strategies and business models – internally and externally. At the same time, reliable and clear political frameworks are beginning to steer the real economy towards climate neutrality, and this will require appropriate planning and investment management. This will push more investors to embed sustainability into their financial market activities and into their organisational governance and strategy.

Notes

1 https://sdgs.un.org/2030agenda.
2 https://unfccc.int/process-and-meetings/the-paris-agreement/the-paris-agreement.
3 https://www.un.org/ga/search/view_doc.asp?symbol=FCCC/CP/2015/L.9/Rev.1&Lang=E.
4 As of 31/12/2020.
5 As of 31/12/2020.

References

European Commission (2018), *Action Plan: Financing Sustainable Growth.* [online]. Available at: https://eur-lex.europa.eu/legal-content/EN/TXT/?uri=CELEX:52018DC0097 (Accessed 11 January 2021).

European Commission (2019), *A European Green Deal.* [online]. Available at: https://ec.europa.eu/info/strategy/priorities-2019-2024/european-green-deal_en (Accessed 21 July 2020).

European Commission (2020a), *Financing the Green Transition: The European Green Deal Investment Plan and Just Transition Mechanism.* [online]. Available at: https://ec.europa.eu/commission/presscorner/detail/en/ip_20_17 (Accessed 21 July 2020).

European Commission (2020b), *Technical Expert Group on Sustainable Finance (TEG).* [online]. Available at: https://ec.europa.eu/info/publications/sustainable-finance-technical-expert-group_en (Accessed 11 January 2021).

Green Bond Principles and ICMA (2021),

Handbook Harmonized Framework for Impact Reporting. [online]. Available at: https://www.icmagroup.org/assets/documents/Sustainable-finance/2021-updates/Handbook-Harmonised-Framework-for-Impact-Reporting-June-2021-100620.pdf (Accessed 27 October 2021).

ICMA and Climate Transition Finance (2020), *Climate Transition Finance Handbook.* [online]. Available at: https://www.icmagroup.org/assets/documents/Regulatory/Green-Bonds/Climate-Transition-Finance-Handbook-December-2020-091220.pdf (Accessed 2 April 2021).

ICMA and the Social Bonds Principles (2021), *Social Bond Principles* [online]. Available at: https://www.icmagroup.org/assets/documents/Sustainable-finance/2021-updates/Social-Bond-Principles-June-2021-140620.pdf (Accessed 27 October 2021).

ICMA and the Sustainability-linked Bond Principles (2020), *Sustainability-linked Bond Principles.* [online]. Available at: https://www.icmagroup.org/assets/documents/Regulatory/Green-Bonds/June-2020/Sustainability-Linked-Bond-PrinciplesJune-2020-100620.pdf (Accessed 25 August 2020).

KfW (2019), *KfW Group Sustainability Mission.* [online]. Available at: https://www.kfw.de/nachhaltigkeit/Dokumente/Nachhaltigkeit/Nachhaltigkeitsleitbild-en.pdf (Accessed 7 October 2020).

KfW (2020), *2019 Sustainability Report.* [online]. Available at: https://www.kfw.de/microsites/Microsite/nachhaltigkeitsbericht.kfw.de/pdf/200522_KFW_GRI-Bericht-EN.pdf (Accessed 2 October 2020).

Rich, N. (2018), *Climate Change and the Savage Human Future.* [online]. Available at: https://www.nytimes.com/interactive/2018/11/16/magazine/tech-design-nature.html (Accessed 20 July 2020).

Part 6

Investment Products

21 Investment Product Design and Development

Michael Ridley

The developing world needs high levels of expenditures to achieve sustainable development and simultaneously reduce its carbon emissions (United Nations, 2019). At the same time, quality emerging market green bonds potentially can deliver strong financial returns and a positive environmental impact: the combination of good financial returns alongside positive environmental and developmental impact has great potential for investors.

In 2018, HSBC Global Asset Management (GAM) set out to design, develop, and create an emerging market corporate green bond fund.[1] Twenty-four months later, the Real Economy Green Impact Opportunities green bond fund (REGIO) was launched.

The chapter begins by providing our perspective on green bonds, which we regard as an 'impact' financial instrument. We then outline our process for developing a fixed income impact fund (using REGIO as a case-study), which we divide into five steps: (1) identifying the impact target, (2) setting a stewardship process, (3) establishing impact investment guidelines, (4) creating a governance process, and (5) setting reporting expectations. We conclude by reflecting on the factors that need to be considered when developing such funds, including measuring green performance and reporting.

An Investment Perspective on Green Bonds

Most green bonds (as well as social and sustainability bonds) are issued in the 'use of proceed' format, which declare how the bond's proceeds will be put to work. This is something that does not happen with conventional 'general purpose' bonds. This use of proceeds format means that a green bond investor knows that the bond proceeds will fund environmental projects and, in many cases, what outcomes might be expected. At same time, the use of proceeds bond benefits from the whole credit quality of the issuing entity, rather than solely from the credit strength of the projects funded by the green bond.

Green bond investing is a reliable way to support expenditure in areas such as pollution emission reduction, technical innovation, and climate change resilience. Moreover, green bond issuance can have a positive catalytic effect across a company's sustainability efforts. When a firm issues a green bond,

DOI: 10.4324/9781003055341-27

this triggers conversations within the firm between the CEO's office, the Treasury department, and the operational departments, about what projects the green bond should fund. These conversations – as discussed in Chapter 17 – often help issuers consider which environmental investments to undertake and prioritise and broadens their understanding of sustainability risks and opportunities.

We divide the approaches to sustainable investment into three broad categories as follows: (i) 'socially responsible investment' (SRI), which is ethically motivated and focusses on exclusions; 'ESG integration' which adds ESG analysis as a risk mitigant on top of traditional credit analysis; and 'impact investing', which attempts to achieve strong economic returns in addition to positive environmental impacts. SRI investment may lead to financial under-performance, depending on the level and depth of exclusion criteria applied, making it unsuitable for many institutional investors. Fund managers running 'ESG integration' funds can buy green bonds, but often only as one element of their 'ESG integration' methodology. In contrast many impact bond funds aim over time exclusively to build up holdings of green and social bonds to achieve financial and non-financial outcomes.

Green bonds are likely to achieve positive environmental impact. But can they outperform financially? There are, as discussed in Chapter 16, strong reasons to think that green bonds may perform better than non-green bonds. One reason is the demand-supply imbalances for green bonds. Another is that the issuers of green bonds may simply be better prepared to respond to the rapid rise in environmental standards, consumer expectations, environmental laws, and carbon taxes; and better able to adapt to the physical impacts of climate change.

Emerging Market Green Bonds

Emerging market green bonds can play an important role for investors and policymakers. Massive expenditure is required in the developing world to lift poverty and increase responsiveness to universal sustainability challenges, which have only increased during the COVID-19 pandemic. The proceeds from green, social, and sustainability bonds, and the transparency and governing characteristics of these bonds, can enable more countries and companies respond to issues like climate change.

The United Nations Conference on Trade and Development has estimated that global annual investment of between \$5 trillion and \$7 trillion in required to meet the SDGs between 2015 and 2030. Based on investment levels measured pre-pandemic, it is estimated that the investment gap in developing countries is in the region of \$.5 trillion per annum (Niculescu, 2017).

Developing world green bonds can often deliver more significant environmental gains than developed world green bonds. For example, a green bond funding a wind farm in a dirty grid country like China or India is likely to have a greater carbon reduction impact. Such wind energy generation can replace traditional carbon intensive sources of power such as coal-fired power generation and help to meet demand for energy that is growing much faster than in developed markets. By comparison, funding a wind farm in Denmark is likely to replace gas-fired power generation or other renewables, meaning the carbon reduction additionality is lower.

The Fund Development Process

With the investment rationale firmly in favour of 'use of proceed' bonds, creating investment solutions for clients is a critical way to deliver sustainability opportunities where they are greatest. Developing our emerging market corporate green bond fund involved five key steps:

- Identifying the fund's purpose and objectives
- Building green markets
- Establishing impact investment guidelines
- Creating a governance process
- Setting reporting expectations

Identifying the Fund's Purpose and Objectives

Investors require clear and specific objectives when selecting investment products. In fixed income, the opportunities available are relatively limited; broadly there are developed markets and emerging markets, and within each of these investment grade or high yield securities, or a combination of these.

Given REGIO's objective of achieving positive environmental and social impacts in the developing world, we decided to focus our investments on the OECD Development Assistance Committee's list of official development assistance recipients; essentially these are low- and middle-income countries based on World Bank data on gross national income per capita, but excluding G8 members, EU members, and countries with a firm date for entry into the EU.

We decided to focus on emerging market corporate bonds rather than sovereigns or financials, although we agreed to initially invest 30% of the Fund's initial holdings in financial issuers but with the target of reducing this to a maximum of 25% within seven years. The decision to invest in corporates rather than financials was driven by the fact there is a shortage of corporate green bond issuance in the developing world, but less of a shortage of financial issuers. We therefore concluded that the REGIO fund could have more of a catalytic impact if it focussed on corporate issuers.

Another important reason for investing in corporates is that corporate green bond issuers provide more information than financial green bond issuers. This is because investors have more certainty about how a corporate spends the money it raises in a green bond than a bank that issues a green bond. A corporation can inform investors, for example, about which specific projects it wants to fund, the locations of the projects and the tangible benefits. Our experience with bank issuers is that they can generally can only say what type of projects they would like to invest in. There are notable exceptions; an example is refinancing projects that have already been funded, in which case banks can provide details about the specific projects being funded.

Our decision to set asset class restrictions, specifically that we would focus on corporate issuers, means that the fund can be styled as a 'Real Economy' fund because it buys mostly corporate emerging market bond, as opposed to financial or sovereign bonds. This approach gives investors a more direct exposure than if they were simply to buy AAA bonds issued by multilateral agencies operating in emerging markets. It also means that investors can benefit from a higher investment yield (one of the key attractions of emerging market investing).

Building Green Markets

The REGIO Fund aims to invest in high quality emerging market corporate green bonds. However, there is currently a shortage of high-quality emerging market green bonds to buy. Of those green bonds outstanding, many are not issued by corporates and many are not of sufficiently high quality for institutional investors. As a result, our strategy incorporates three elements.

First, we decided that we would build up the green bond allocation over time, with the fund holding a minimum of 20% of green bonds on inception but with a requirement that this must grow to 100% by the seventh years of the fund's existence.

Second, in recognising the need to grow the supply of emerging market corporate green bonds an extensive stewardship programme was designed with input from our responsible investment team. The programme involves explicitly targeting specific companies that do not yet issue green bonds, but have the potential to. This is done directly (e.g. through roadshows or outreach to companies) and through intermediaries (e.g. banks that underwrite new bonds and organise roadshows). By sharing our desire for more 'use of proceed' bond issuance, we hope that these banks may advocate for these instruments with more of their clients.

Third, we signed a Services Agreement with the private sector arm of a multilateral development bank. Under the Services Agreement, this entity will provide services designed to facilitate and accelerate the supply of green bonds issued by emerging market real sector borrowers. We identified a lack of skills and knowledge on green bonds as a potential obstacle to new issuance. Many emerging market companies, for example, lack clear sustainability strategies or proper resources to manage green bond proceeds. Developing focused education and consulting to potential green bond issuers can remove or reduce the challenges facing emerging market issuers.

Establishing Impact Investment Guidelines

Impact investment guidelines provide investors with transparency on how the fund will deliver on its impact objectives. Not only do they shape and determine what can be bought, but crucially for a fund with inherent allocation challenges, they explain what cannot be bought.

Early in the design of the REGIO emerging market green bond fund, a great deal of time and effort was taken up creating our Green Impact Investment Guidelines. This work was undertaken by HSBC Asset Management and a multi-lateral development bank that became the cornerstone investor.

Because the fund will allocate towards non-green bonds in the short-term, the investment guidelines consider both green and non-green bonds. Non-green bonds are general corporate purposes bonds. Given these bonds do not declare how proceeds will be spent, they cannot be asked to meet any specific security level restrictions; instead, they must only meet security level requirements.

The Green Impact Investment Guidelines prevent the fund from buying just any labelled green bond. The Guidelines demand that at least 90% of the green bond's proceeds fund eligible green projects – taken from the ICMA Green Bond Principles (GBP and ICMA, 2018) – and that the remaining 10% should not involve activities found on the excluded activities list. The permitted list of green expenditures includes:

- Renewable energy
- Energy efficiency
- Clean transportation
- Green buildings
- Sustainable water and wastewater management
- Climate change adaptation
- Pollution prevention and control
- Environmentally sustainable management of living natural resources and land use
- Terrestrial and aquatic biodiversity conservation
- Eco-efficient and/or circular economy adapted products, production technologies, and processes

The activities excluded from the list include 'power generation from fossil fuels'. This means that the fund, in theory, can buy a green bond issued by a fossil fuel firm (e.g. to build wind farms). However, if any of the bond's proceeds were spent on fossil fuel power generation that bond could not be purchased. In making this distinction, the fund expects to align with the Green Bond Principles, which state that firms do not have to be green to issue green bonds.

The Green Impact Investment Guidelines also state which of the 17 SDGs are supported when each of the green forms of expenditure are supported by a green bond. For example, a green bond funding 'renewable energy' supports SDG 7, 'affordable and clean energy'; a green bond funding 'pollution prevention and control' advances SDG 11 'sustainable cities and communities' and SDG-12 'responsible consumption and production'. By making the link between specific green expenditures and specific SDGs, the fund shows how bond allocations can provide broader benefits to society.

Creating a Governance Process

To ensure the fund has effective impact investment controls a Green Bond Oversight Committee was established. Every bond held by the fund receives approval from an investment-focused committee, plus the Oversight Committee on a unanimous basis.

The two committees have different objectives. The investment committee considers bonds for their credit quality, while the Green Bond Oversight Committee considers bonds for their ESG quality, including assessing whether the bonds meet the criteria outlined in the Green Impact Investment Guidelines. As a result, it checks whether bonds have suitable sustainability credentials, have material reputation risks, or are involved in activities antithetical to the ethos of the fund. This review process may involve reviewing the ESG assessment reports from two independent research firms, Reprisk and MSCI ESG Ratings, to add further insight on sustainability performance. The Green Bond Oversight Committee also considers the ESG criteria or credentials of each bond; with rising concerns over greenwashing this helps to provide a check against weaker impact bonds that may be eligible for inclusion.

To empower investors in the fund, an Advisory Committee of investors meet annually. This Committee's role is to approve, recommend, or change the Green Impact Investment Guidelines or investment restrictions.

Setting Reporting Expectations

Industry-wide efforts to improve ESG fund reporting are gaining attention with regulators in Europe prioritising standardisation. Transparency can take many forms, in the form of ESG ratings, third-party accreditation, or reporting against specific KPIs. There are advantages to all three methods and investors need to consider the merits of all approaches.

For investors looking for a demonstrable impact, reporting is a prerequisite. However, it is also important to acknowledge that such reporting It may be more challenging for emerging market issuers more than for developed market issuers due to the longer experience of developed market issuers in tracking, monitoring, and disclosing sustainability information.

Investors have a responsibility to report, especially for impact funds. At a minimum, this reporting should detail the proportion of a green bond's proceeds invested into each eligible activity, and the aggregated amount flowing to each eligible activity.

Figure 21.2 Methodology for Identifying the Best Location for Bond Proceeds.
Source: HSBC GAM.

We identified a key list of impact metrics that we believe investors would find most useful and relevant when assessing the impact of the fund (Figure 21.1). We anticipate adding to this list as the impact bond market evolves and reporting metrics change.

Performance

With green bonds key to this strategy, and an important part of many fixed income portfolios more generally, questions arise what the financial impact may be. We see a double benefit from green bonds: not only can they maximise environmental impact, but they can also financially outperform non-green bonds. We see three reasons why.

First, investing in green bonds, while using an ESG analytical overlay, gives an informational edge over non-green bonds; essentially more data is provided by green bond issuers. This does not mean that all green bonds are attractive. Rather, this information advantage is likely to be the greatest when green bond analysis is combined with ESG analysis (HSBC GAM, 2020a). Green bond and ESG research processes approach the world from slightly different angles. The traditional focus of the green bond market is on the bond being issued, its use of proceeds, where this is going to be put to work and the likely impact. By contrast ESG analysis focusses on the issuer of the security, not so much the security being issued.

Second, green bond issuers are often better positioned in relation to new market trends, environmental legislation, and large-scale consumer boycotts. One example is how Iberdrola's credit rating has fared much better than RWE's over the past decade as they responded differently to emerging challenges of energy transition in Europe from coal to renewables. Investors understand that firms could invest too heavily or too early in environmental technology, resulting in products that are too expensive or too far ahead of the market in terms of customer demand. We think it is better to be positioned in anticipation of regulatory or consumer environmental moves, than not to be.

Third, the process of issuing a green bond can be beneficial, allowing issuers to sharpen their focus and achieve operational efficiencies. Discussions about which projects should be financed or refinanced can help define and finesse a firm's overall sustainability strategy. A company with a strong environmental focus and a management team that is sensitive to ESG investors' concerns, may outperform its peers. We think this is particularly true of the emerging markets, where credit, regulatory, and market risks may be higher, and where good analysis and understanding of the ESG risks they face can serve as an effective risk mitigant. Impact today, outperformance tomorrow? By investing in green bonds investors may not only achieve green impact today, but also outperform non-green bonds in credit terms over time.

Maximising Environmental Impact

One way to measure environmental impact is via a metric that estimates the likely reduction in tonnes of carbon dioxide (CO_2) emissions achieved per dollar of bond outstanding. While some bond issuers, like Hannon Armstrong, do supply such a metric, most do not. Another approach is to use a green bond labelling system that does not just say whether a bond is green or not. CICERO, for example, labels the bonds either dark green, medium green or light green.[2]

An alternative method that we favour, is to consider what type of project a green bond is going to fund and in which country. We use the methodology presented in Figure 21.2, which effectively acts as a 'short cut' to informing us which types of green bonds we should buy; it helps inform decisions such as whether we should we buy green bonds funding renewable energy or energy efficiency, or whether we should buy green bonds funding projects in the developing world or the developed world.

Given that population and wealth are likely to rise the only viable – at this point in time – ways to cut CO_2 emissions are either to:

1 Cut a country's carbon intensity of energy, essentially by fuels switching – moving power generation to renewables from oil, coal, and gas; or
2 Cut a country's energy intensity of gross domestic product (GDP), by energy efficiency measures.

ICMA GBP Green Project Category	Indicative Reporting Criteria	Sustainable Development Goal
Sustainable water and waste water management	Cubic metres water saved or treated	SDG 6 Clean water and sanitation
Renewable energy	KWhr of renewable energy generated or KWh of power installed	SDG 7 Affordable and clean energy
	Tonnes of CO_2 avoided	
	Number of households or people with clean energy access	
Energy efficiency or KWhr saved	Tonnes of CO_2 avoided or KWhr saved	SDG 7 Affordable and clean energy
Clean transportation	Tonnes of CO_2 avoided or KWhr saved (compared to existing transportation)	
	Number of passengers per year per km (for type of transport)	SDG 11 Sustainable cities and communities
Pollution prevention and control	Tones waste recycled/reduced	SDG 12 Responsible consumption and production
	Number of projects where pollution prevention and control measures exceeded regulatory requirements and achieve 20% or more pollution/wast reduction compared to baseline (where available)	

Figure 21.1 Indicative List of Impact Reporting Metrics.
Source: HSBC GAM, 2020b.

Perhaps the most impactful way to cut the carbon intensity per unit of GDP is to undertake fuel switching: introducing renewable energy in dirty grid countries where new renewable energy plants replace coal fired power plants. Building a renewable energy plant in South Africa or China is likely to have more impact than installing renewable energy in France, given that France is already a 'clean grid' country.

That does not mean green bonds have less relevance in clean grid countries. In these countries we recommend that green bonds are used to fund public transport, metro, or rail systems. Where metros and railways are powered by low carbon electricity, such as in France, one can achieve positive environmental impact by getting people to travel by metro or rail, rather than by car or by plane.

We expect the trend of decarbonisation in the power generation to spread from Europe to around the globe. At the same time, decarbonisation may spread within economies on a sector-by-sector basis. Once a country has decarbonised power generation it may decarbonise transport, buildings, cooking and heating. This may involve getting cars, buses, and motorbikes to be powered by electricity, instead of oil, and running heating and cooking on electricity rather than gas.

Impact investors looking to achieve the greatest environmental gain, should understand how decarbonisation is likely to evolve, and choose to locate their investments for the most positive environmental impact. Emerging market corporate bonds, therefore, will often have greater environmental benefits, although the level of benefit will differ according to each country's context.

Conclusion

The emerging market fund run by HSBC GAM incorporates a carefully designed governance process and framework to hit specific targets. The objectives set by the fund are aspirational but with important environment and SDG goals, they are necessary for investors committed to confronting humanities' biggest challenges. Unique for the fund is a recognition that our responsibilities as a fund manager extend beyond allocating capital and include creating market awareness and supply of green bonds.

While impact investors face many practical challenges, including an inadequate supply of impact bonds and significant uncertainties in the outcomes that will be achieved, there are solutions to these problems. This means that investors do have the flexibility to decide what they want to achieve from their responsible investment strategy. For some, monitoring and measuring risk (through scenarios) will be practical. For others, it is taking bold action such as with an impact strategy or exclusion policy. Either way, the opportunities exist for investors to take control.

Notes

1 HSBC Global Asset Management (GAM) has USD580 billion assets under management in fixed income, equity and multi-asset funds. HSBC GAM launched its first Socially Responsible Investment Fund and joined the UK Sustainable and Finance Association in 2001, signed the Principles for Responsible Investments in 2006 and applies ESG analysis to 90% of its AUM.
2 https://cicero.green/our-approach.

References

Green Bond Principles (GBP) and International Capital Market Association (ICMA) (2018), *Green Bond Principles: Voluntary Process Guidelines for Issuing Green Bonds.* [online]. Available at https://www.icmagroup.org/assets/documents/Regulatory/Green-Bonds/Green-Bonds-Principles-June-2018-270520.pdf (Accessed 2 April 2021).

HSBC GAM (2020a), *Green Bonds – A User's Guide.* [online]. Available at https://www.assetmanagement.hsbc.co.uk/-/media/files/attachments/common/news-and-articles/articles/interest-with-principle.pdf (Accessed 21 May 2021).

HSBC GAM (2020b), *Green Impact Investment Guidelines.* [online]. Available at https://www.global.assetmanagement.hsbc.com/-/media/files/attachments/common/resource-documents/green-impact-framework.pdf (Accessed 21 May 2021).

Niculescu, M. (2017), *Impact Investment to Close the SDG Funding Gap.* [online]. Available at https://www.undp.org/content/undp/en/home/blog/2017/7/13/What-kind-of-blender-do-we-need-to-finance-the-SDGs-.html (Accessed 21 May 2021).

United Nations (2019), *Unprecedented Impacts of Climate Change Disproportionately Burdening Developing Countries, Delegate Stresses, as Second Committee Concludes General Debate.* [online]. Available at https://www.un.org/press/en/2019/gaef3516.doc.htm (Accessed 21 May 2021).

22 Understanding Trends and Drivers in Fixed Income Investment Products

Hortense Bioy and Benjamin Joseph

Sustainable investing, which includes any investment process incorporating environmental, social, and governance (ESG) factors, is not as prevalent in fixed income as it is in equities. But this is changing. To meet investor demand, asset managers have been actively building their capabilities and developing new strategies.

Morningstar[1] calculates that as of 31 March 2021 there were close to 900 ESG fixed income funds globally, with collective assets under management of $350 billion, representing less than a fifth of total assets in the ESG fund universe.[2] This does not include the growing number of funds that formally integrate ESG factors in a nondeterminative way in their investment processes to complement standard credit analysis.

This chapter analyses existing ESG fixed income funds available to investors, globally. The first section proposes a taxonomy that investors can use to navigate fund evaluation in fixed income. Second, we assess the global landscape of sustainable or ESG fixed income funds to show how the market has developed.[3] We focus on the two regions with the greatest adoption, Europe and the United States. Third, we outline the areas of fixed income where there are growing ESG investment opportunities. Fourth, we outline how we assess the ESG characteristics of funds, and what this assessment tells us about the fixed income product market.

A Taxonomy to Classify ESG Fixed Income Funds

Sustainable fixed income funds use various approaches to address sustainability preferences and investment objectives, including negative ESG screening, impact-oriented strategies, and best-in-class approach, where ESG scores are used to build portfolios that allocate to sustainability leaders. Approaches are usually used in combination and are by no means mutually exclusive. The three main sustainability approaches are discussed below.

Negative Screening

Negative screening – also referred to as ESG-related exclusions – focuses mostly on avoiding securities, issuers, or industries based on certain activities

DOI: 10.4324/9781003055341-28

and business practices. Exclusions are typically based on values, norms, or opinions. Common screens target companies in breach of the UN Global Compact principles and companies associated with controversial and nuclear weapons, tobacco, and gambling. More recently, amid a heightened public awareness of environmental issues and rising concerns about climate risks, the list of common exclusions has expanded to include thermal coal, tar sands, artic oil, oil sands, and traditional oil and gas producers and distributors.

Historically dominant, exclusions-only strategies have lost ground in recent years in favour of more elaborated strategies, which, in addition to values-based screens, invest in or tilt towards securities with better sustainability characteristics (positive screening) approach embedded in the early version of socially responsible investing to a more integrated approach. Actively managed sustainability strategies now typically consider material ESG factors into their investment decisions and engage with companies to improve their ESG practices. Many avoid ESG laggards.

While negative screening for corporate bonds is comparatively straightforward to implement, it is more challenging to apply to sovereigns, especially developed countries. It is reasonable to say that no government is beyond reproach but excluding key countries like the US based on its defence spending or environmental record would lead to undesirable outcomes for investors. Negative screening is easier to apply to emerging market countries where there is greater disparity in ESG profiles and where excluding countries, for example, based on their human rights records or corruption levels would not have a significant negative impact on portfolio composition.

Positive Screening

The positive screening approach – also often referred to as best-in-class – is the fastest growing ESG strategy, although how it is described in fund documentation varies. In broad terms, positive screening aims to invest in or tilt towards securities with strong or improving ESG characteristics. Typically, these strategies focus on issuers that fund managers, analysts, or third-party ESG data providers believe are addressing sustainability challenges that will make better investments. Many, including some that target themes such as climate change, focus on selecting or overweighting the best performers in the investment universe.

Research shows that investing in companies with high ESG scores or simply avoiding issuers with the lowest ESG scores tend to result in a quality tilt. This may mean that ESG-screened bond strategies lag the broad universe during risk-on phases but, equally, should provide a cushion in market downturns.

Impact

Impact bond strategies, which invest primarily in green bonds, microfinance, municipal bonds, and/or social bonds, are dominated by active funds and the assets undermanagement (AUM) are growing quickly. Impact bond funds pursue specific ESG or Sustainable Development Goal (SDG) themes and aim to contribute to measurable positive societal impact outcomes, alongside financial returns.

Fixed income investing is well suited to deliver impact as bond proceeds can be used for specific projects and causes. While it is possible to seek impact by buying conventional bonds and having a deep engagement strategy, directly funding sustainable projects through impact bond purchases has become the preferred path for fixed income impact strategies (Figure 22.1). Impact fixed income funds invest directly in bonds financing various themes, including affordable housing, community development, green energy priorities, green infrastructure, and water efficiency.

Green bond funds are by far the most popular investment vehicles to achieve impact, with around $25 billion of total AUM, followed by microfinance funds. While active management prevails amongst the green bond funds, the largest is an ETF with $3.3 billion of assets. The fund tracks the returns of the Bloomberg Barclays MSCI Green Bond Index. Products focused on municipal and social bonds remain small.

Impact funds can be found in multiple sector categories including diversified bonds, investment grade corporate bonds, government bonds, or municipals, matching the overall impact bond market. Within the diversified bond category, investors have the choice of 53 impact products, including six passive strategies.

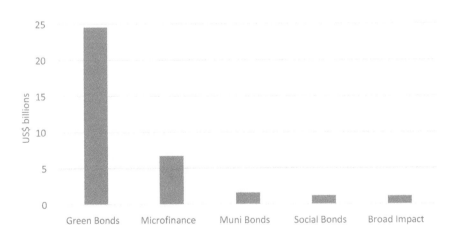

Figure 22.1 Impact Fund Assets by Underlying Security Focus.
Source: Morningstar Direct, Morningstar Research. Data as of March 2021.

Fixed Income ESG Investment Landscape: Measuring the Size of the Market

Flows and Assets Growth

Across all asset classes, ESG-focused funds now reach $2 trillion globally, as of March 2021. Yet, fixed income strategies account for only 18% of this universe (roughly $350 billion), whereas equity strategies represent 66% of total ESG assets under management (AUM). This is despite the wider fixed income asset class being larger than equities (Figure 22.2).

The complexity of bond markets, with their wide spectrum of different debt instruments, issuer types, and maturities, has held back ESG integration in fixed income and, in turn, sustainable fixed income products. This has been compounded by concerns over data availability, quality, and comparability, especially for sovereign debt.

While corporate bonds can now be assessed using robust ESG scoring frameworks, there are still questions how to best evaluate government debt. Materiality of ESG risks can be harder to determine as macroeconomic factors such as interest rates and inflation heavily influence sovereign bond prices. ESG assessments of governments appear to focus predominantly on governance information, although individual countries are starting to show greater risk exposure to environmental and social factors. Moreover, in the case of developed sovereigns, applying ESG filters can lead to out-comes that are difficult to implement. For example, ethically conscious

Figure 22.2 Proportion of Sustainable Fund Assets by Broad Asset Class (%).
Source: Morningstar Direct, Morningstar Research. Data as of March 2021.

investors may consider some US policies – such as capital punishment – to go against their most values. From an investment perspective, however, one must seriously consider, though, the implications of excluding the largest developed government bond market in the world from a government bond fund.

Meanwhile, for securitised debt, analysis is required on underlying collateral, not just the issuer. This may mean assessing thousands of assets, which can be very time-consuming for fund managers. Across all areas of fixed income, we identify lower awareness and the challenges of applying stewardship principles as slowing responsible investment adoption.

Product Launches

Growing interest in sustainable and impact investing has encouraged more fund managers to launch suitable products. Since 2016 product development has accelerated, reaching an all-time high in 2020 with 122 new fund launches (Figure 22.3), and a quarterly record of 44 new offerings in the three months of 2021. The growth has been seen across all sectors, including diversified, investment grade, high yield, emerging markets, and impact bond funds.

As of March 2021, there were 900 ESG fixed income funds globally. This universe is likely to expand further as demand rises and better-quality data becomes available, allowing asset managers to create more suitable and targeted products.

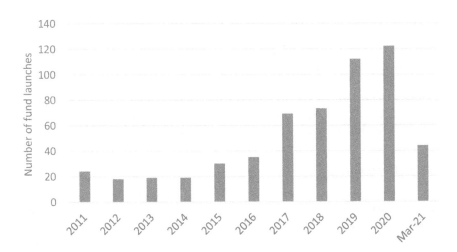

Figure 22.3 Growth in Sustainable Fixed Income Fund Launches.
Source: Morningstar Direct, Morningstar Research. Data as of March 2021.

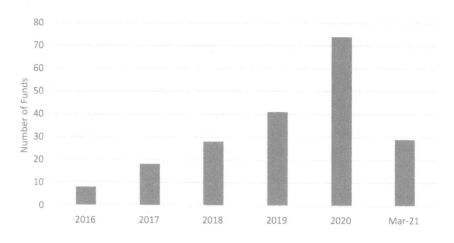

Figure 22.4 Growth in Repurposed and Rebranded ESG Fixed Income Funds.
Source: Morningstar Direct, Morningstar Research. Data as of March 2021.

Repurposing Mainstream Offerings

Launching new funds is not the only way that asset managers offer more investor choices. Converting existing funds into sustainable funds is rising. Investment managers change their funds' mandate by adding specific ESG criteria to their investment objectives and/or policies. In many cases, they have also changed the fund names to reflect their new mandates.

Repurposing and rebranding sustainable fixed income funds is increasingly common (Figure 22.4). Converting funds into a sustainable offering is a way for asset managers to leverage existing assets to build their sustainable funds business, thereby avoiding having to create funds from scratch and, in some cases, accelerate the time frame required to reach scale. This may also be a way for fund companies to reinvigorate funds that are struggling to attract inflows.

When repurposing their funds, most asset managers add terms such as 'sustainable', 'ESG', and 'SRI' to fund names to reflect the new mandate and increase visibility among investors looking to invest more sustainably.

Europe Dominates

ESG fixed income fund assets are predominantly located in Europe, comprising nearly 90% of all assets. European money managers pioneered ESG integration in fixed income management, with many firms building ESG research teams and launching socially responsible fixed income funds beginning in the early 2000s. Europe's advantage in sustainable investing appears

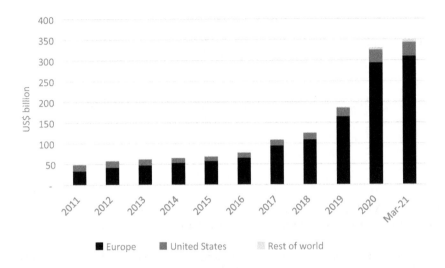

Figure 22.5 Growth in Sustainable Fixed Income Fund Assets Split by Domicile.
Source: Morningstar Direct, Morningstar Research. Data as of March 2021.

to be driven at least in part by local investor preferences. Since the 1970s, for example, Norway's sovereign wealth fund has developed sustainability criteria within its investment objectives, setting a standard for other large domestic asset owners to follow.

In more recent years, the 2015 Paris Climate Accord, greater sustainability-related disclosure requirements in several countries such as France and the Netherlands, and the release of the EU Action Plan on Sustainable Finance in 2018 have accelerated the adoption of ESG strategies by institutional investors across Europe. Institutional money has flown into sustainable fixed income funds at an accelerated pace (Figure 22.5). Retail investors have also contributed to the growth, though to a lesser extent. They still hold a smaller portion of European assets (between 10 and 25%, depending on classifications). This is in contrast with the US where the retail/institutional asset split is closer to 50/50.

Despite rapid growth, the US sustainable fund market continues to lag Europe, largely due to the political and regulatory environment. US regulation has fluctuated between a neutral stance to open discouragement by the previous Trump administration. Another factor explaining the slower adoption of sustainability products is greater scepticism about the correlation between ESG factors and performance. This is despite a growing body of research showing that integrating material ESG factors into an investment process can lead to lower spreads and better credit ratings for corporate bonds, and better performance and lower credit risk for sovereigns.

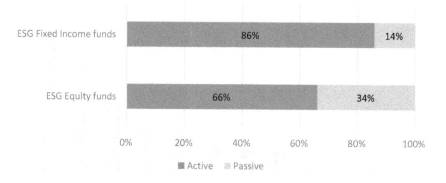

Figure 22.6 Market Share Comparison of Passive ESG Funds.
Source: Morningstar Direct, Morningstar Research. Data as of March 2021.

Outside of Europe and the US, assets in sustainable fixed income funds are also increasing but from a very low base. As of March 2021, we identified just 80 such products, half of which were domiciled in Canada and Australia.

The Late Rise of Passive ESG Investing

For all the growth in global sustainable fund assets, the passive ESG fixed income space remains at an embryonic stage, particularly outside Europe (Figure 22.6). As of the end of March 2021, there were only 101 such funds available globally, including 79 domiciled in Europe and just 15 in the US. These funds typically employ exclusions, best-in-class, tilting, optimization, and/or thematic approaches. Assets totalled $49 billion, representing 14% of the total assets held in ESG bond funds. In contrast, assets in passive ESG equity funds surpassed $431 billion at the end of March 2021 and accounted for 34% of total money invested in ESG equity funds globally.

Growth prospects for passive ESG bond strategies look very positive. Inflows into passive ESG bond funds hit a record $14 billion in 2020, with three funds gathering more than $1 billion in net inflows each (Figure 22.7), followed by the first quarter of 2021 which matched the entire performance of 2020.

Fixed Income ESG Funds by Asset Class

A sub-asset class breakdown reflects what one can see in the non-ESG space. The majority of ESG bond funds sit in investment grade corporate bonds and diversified bonds. These two categories house three quarters of all AUM (Figure 22.8).

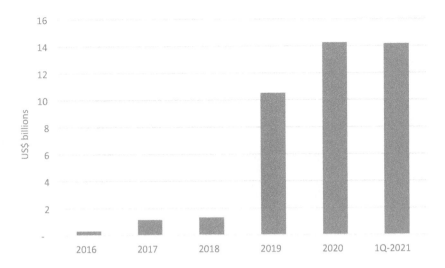

Figure 22.7 Net Flows into Passive ESG Bond Funds.
Source: Morningstar Direct, Morningstar Research. Data as of March 2021.

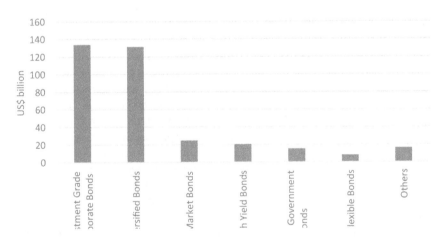

Figure 22.8 Fixed Income ESG Strategies by Sub-Asset Class.
Source: Morningstar Direct, Morningstar Research. Data as of March 2021.

Investment Grade Corporate Bond Funds

With $135 billion of assets, investment grade corporate bond funds represent
the largest ESG bond category. As has been seen for equities, integrating ESG
factors into investment grade corporate bond analysis has been aided by the
growing depth and breadth of ESG data disclosed by large companies.

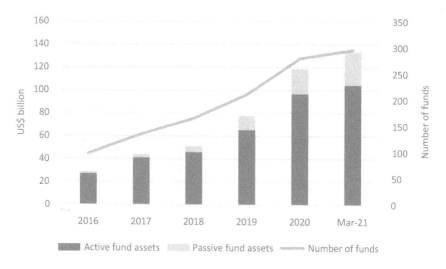

Figure 22.9 Sustainability Focused Investment Grade Corporate Bond Funds.
Source: Morningstar Direct, Morningstar Research. Data as of March 2021.

The wide choice of strategies in this sector has made it easier for investors to switch from their conventional investment-grade fund to a sustainable alternative. In terms of assets, active funds represent around 78% of invested strategies (Figure 22.9). Product availability is diversified. Investors have access to every segment of the maturity spectrum as well as impact-type of strategies.

On the passive side, the number of products remains limited (48 versus 289 active funds), although it is still relatively diversified, with ultra-short, short, intermediate, blend, and even green bond strategies now available. Two of the best-selling strategies are 'light green' offerings insofar as they only apply light exclusionary screens to their investment universe (e.g. excluding investment grade issuers involved in alcohol, tobacco, gambling, military weapons, nuclear power, adult entertainment, civilian firearms, and genetically modified organisms).

Others employ a best-in-class approach. For example, a recently launched Europe-based passive strategy invests in investment grade corporate issuers operating in the financial, industrial, and utility sectors with MSCI ESG Ratings of BBB or higher, and excludes issuers involved in business activities that are restricted according to predefined categories and issuers with a 'Red' MSCI ESG Controversy score.

Diversified Bond Funds

Diversified bond funds represent the second largest category of ESG bond funds. Their growth is shown in Figure 22.10. The diversified bond bucket is made up of Euro, US, and Global Aggregate bond strategies as well as benchmarked multi-sector offerings like core and core-plus strategies, which

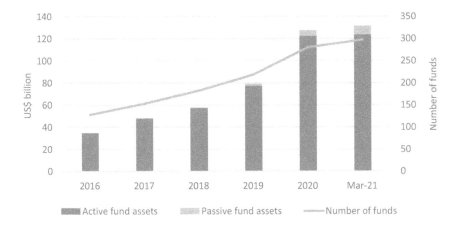

Figure 22.10 Sustainability Focused Diversified Bond Funds Growth.
Source: Morningstar Direct, Morningstar Research. Data as of March 2021.

typically invest in a mix of government, investment grade corporate, high yield, securitised, and emerging markets debt.

The largest fund in the category is German domiciled, with $3.1 billion of assets. The fund selects the most sustainable issuers (best-in-class approach) and invests mainly in euro-denominated corporate bonds, government bonds, and Pfandbriefe (a type of covered bonds issued by German mortgage banks that is collateralised by long-term assets), as well as other bonds issued by global issuers. The top US funds offer intermediate core-plus bond exposure, including one fund converted to an ESG strategy in 2017 and that has seen its allocation to impact bonds rise to 34%, two thirds of which is in corporate debt.

While the lack of ESG data in some underlying sectors like sovereigns, securitised assets, and emerging markets did not prevent active managers from offering multi-sector and global sustainable offerings, it has delayed developing index and passive diversified bond offerings. There are only 24 passive funds in the category, with an average track record of less than two years. The largest fund tracks the Bloomberg Barclays MSCI US Aggregate ESG Focus Index, which is composed of investment-grade treasury, government-related, corporate, and securitised bonds from issuers with stronger ESG practices. The overall portfolio is optimised to have a higher ESG rating than the base conventional index. Since its launch in October 2018, the fund had gathered $1.2 billion in assets, as of the end of March 2021.

Emerging Markets Bond Funds

The lack of available, reliable, and comparable emerging markets ESG data has challenged investors' integration of ESG factors. Consequently, the available sustainable emerging market funds and the pool of assets they manage

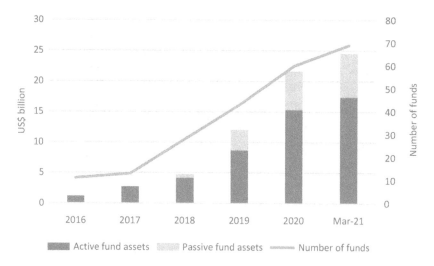

Figure 22.11 Sustainability Focused Emerging Market Bond Funds.
Source: Morningstar Direct, Morningstar Research. Data as of March 2021.

remain small but growing, with 69 distinct strategies globally representing just shy of $25 billion of assets (see Figure 22.11).

As of March 2021, the majority of these funds had less than two years' track record and were focused on sovereign debt. This is due to the lack of ESG disclosure from emerging markets corporate issuers.

With $3.2 billion of assets, the largest and one of the oldest funds invests in bonds issued or guaranteed by emerging countries or by international public bodies (such as the World Bank and the European Bank for Reconstruction and Development) selected on the basis of criteria related to sustainable development, such as social equity, respect for the environment, and equitable political and economic governance.

Meanwhile, there are only 12 passive options available, although these already represent nearly 30% of the category's assets. The largest, a Europe-based fund with $2.2 billion of assets, invests in debt instruments issued by sovereign and quasi-sovereign entities and applies an ESG scoring and screening methodology to tilt toward green bond issues or issuers ranked higher on ESG criteria, and to underweight or remove issuers that rank lower.

Developed Government Bond Funds

As of the end of March, there were 49 ESG developed government bond funds available globally, with just over $15 billion of assets (Figure 22.12). The low number reflects investors' challenges in incorporating ESG information to develop suitable funds.

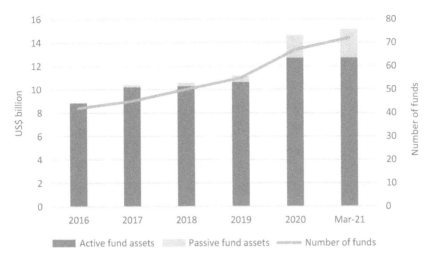

Figure 22.12 Sustainability Focused Developed Government Bond Funds.
Source: Morningstar Direct, Morningstar Research. Data as of March 2021.

Most funds in the category adopt a best-in-class or tilting approach, favouring countries with the highest ESG scores. One France-based manager primarily invests in bonds issued or guaranteed by eurozone states selected based on a normative and best-in-class approach. Furthermore, the fund excludes states that systematically and wilfully violate human rights and commit war crimes and crimes against humanity. This last criterion is unlikely to affect the investment universe as no Eurozone country currently fails on these criteria.

Another example, from the passive side, is a fund that overweights countries ranked higher on ESG criteria and underweights or removes those that rank lower. In the fund's framework, a country's ESG score reflects a mix of qualitative and quantitative analysis including values-based screening as well as positive screening, which rewards countries with robust ESG business practices. The fund's largest country exposures are the US at 40%, followed by Japan (19%), France (7), the UK (6%), and Germany (5%).

The developed government bond fund category also consists of funds that target impact. One example with $2.9 billion of assets under management is a US-domiciled fund invests in debt instruments that meet targeted impact themes such as affordable healthcare; affordable housing; arts and culture; disaster recovery; economic inclusion; education and childcare; enterprise development and jobs; and environmental sustainability.

High Yield Bond Funds

As for emerging markets, a paucity of good data for sub-investment grade-rated corporates has delayed wider ESG integration into high yield bonds.

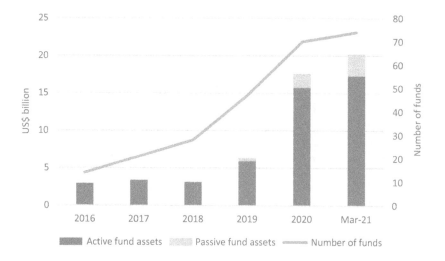

Figure 22.13 Sustainability Focused High Yield Bond Funds.
Source: Morningstar Direct, Morningstar Research. Data as of March 2021.

But 2020 and the first quarter of 2021 saw a raft of new and repurposed ESG high yield products come to market, bringing the total of such strategies to 74 with over $20 billion of assets, as of March 2021 (Figure 22.13).

While Europe-domiciled offerings outnumber US offerings, the two oldest funds in this category are US-based, launched in 1999 and 2001, respectively. One European fund seeks to invest in companies with strong fundamentals that also demonstrate the potential, through engagement, to create positive change. The SDGs are used as a framework for this engagement.

Meanwhile, all 13 passive high yield bond funds available to European and US investors at end-March 2021 had less than two-year track records. The most widely used benchmark avoids issuers with substantial revenue derived from controversial military weapons, civilian firearms, tobacco, gambling, adult entertainment, alcohol, nuclear power, and genetically modified organisms.

Flexible Bond Funds

This category is mostly composed of un-benchmarked, total return, multi-sector funds. Due to the variety of underlying securities and the widespread use of derivatives, applying ESG criteria to these strategies has been slow and recent. The oldest fund was launched in the US in 2014, but it was only in 2019 that this segment of the market really started to develop (see Figure 22.14).

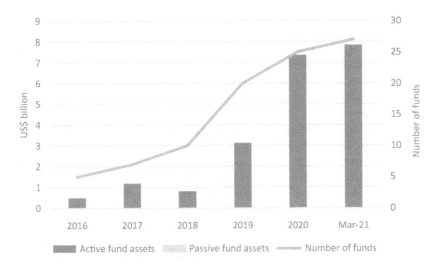

Figure 22.14 Sustainability Focused Flexible Bond Fund.
Source: Morningstar Direct, Morningstar Research. Data as of March 2021.

The category seems to be gaining traction. Launched in April 2020, the largest strategy reached $1.2 billion in just six months. The managers invest free of benchmark constraints across the entire global fixed income universe. The strategy relies on screens and ESG tilts to guide portfolio asset allocation alongside yield and risk considerations. ESG criteria are integrated into company credit valuations and certain industries like tobacco, weapons, thermal coal, and tar sands are screened out while the portfolio maintains a structural allocation to green, social, and sustainable bonds deemed eligible for investment.

The very nature of flexible bond strategies makes the development of passive strategies virtually irrelevant: all 27 distinct funds in this category, representing nearly $8 billion, are actively managed.

Others: Microfinance, Leveraged Loans, and Muni

The balance of sustainable fixed income strategies is made up mostly of funds focusing on microfinance, leveraged loans, or municipals.

Originally limited to the provision of micro loans to low-income individuals, entrepreneurs, and small businesses in developing countries who otherwise would have no access to financial services, microfinance has grown to become a much broader offering of financial services including savings and checking accounts, micro-insurance, and payment systems. Despite the capacity-constrained nature of microfinance funds, the fund menu has expanded to over 24 distinct strategies and a total of over $6.7 billion. One strategy, launched in 1998 as the first private and fully commercial microfinance investment fund in the world, has reached nearly $2.4 billion in assets as of March 2021 and is currently closed to new investors. The fund has attracted investors because it is a good example of a relatively diversified strategy. It spreads its investment to target no fewer than 11 of the 17 SDGs including no poverty, zero hunger, affordable and clean energy, or clean water and sanitation.

The ESG municipal category counts 10 US domiciled strategies for a total of $1.6 billion. This includes the third oldest of all sustainable fixed income strategies. Despite a track record since 1983, the fund remains a small, yet growing, offering less than $400 million AUM.

Only seven funds – four from one asset manager – account for less than 3 billion dollars in combined assets in the leveraged loans category. Integrating ESG criteria into loan analysis has proven challenging given the multi-layer analysis that is required and the real lack of ESG data on the underlying pool of debt. While an allocation to loans within a diversified fixed-income portfolio has not prevented strategies from claiming ESG credentials, running a dedicated strategy with a strong and demonstrated commitment to ESG principles is not straightforward.

The Sustainability Characteristics of ESG Fixed Income Funds

In 2016, Morningstar released the Morningstar Sustainability Rating (MSR) – also known as the Globe rating – to help investors use ESG information to evaluate their portfolios. Using ESG ratings from Sustainalytics, the MSR provides a reliable, objective way to evaluate how well funds are meeting ESG challenges, based on the ESG performance of their underlying holdings.

Methodology[4]

The Morningstar Portfolio Sustainability Score is an asset-weighted average of Sustainalytics' company level ESG Risk Rating. The Sustainalytics' company-level ESG Risk Rating measures how a company's economic value may be at risk from ESG issues. To be considered material to the risk rating, an ESG issue must have a potentially substantial impact on the economic value of a company and therefore on the risk/return profile of an investment in the company. The ESG issues that are material vary across industry groups and companies.

ESG Risk Ratings are aggregated to a Portfolio Sustainability Score using an asset-weighted average of all covered securities. Most major benchmark fixed income securities will have ESG Risk Ratings. Securities issued by companies that do not have ESG Risk Ratings, as well as short positions, options, and derivatives typically issued by third-party financial firms, are excluded from the methodology. To receive a Portfolio Sustainability Score, at least 67% of a portfolio's assets under management must have a company ESG Risk Rating. The percentage of assets under management of the covered securities is rescaled to 100% before calculating the Portfolio Sustainability Score.

Morningstar Sustainability Rating

Based on their Morningstar Historical Portfolio Sustainability Score, portfolios are assigned absolute category ranks and percent ranks within their Morningstar Global Categories, provided that a category has at least 30 portfolios with Historical Portfolio Sustainability Scores. A portfolio's Morningstar Sustainability Rating is its normally distributed ordinal score and descriptive rank relative to the portfolio's global category. Funds with the best 10% of scores within their peer group receive five globes (a 'High' rating, and those ranking in the next 22.5% receive four globes (an 'Above Average' rating). In other words, funds ranking in the top third of their peer group receive four or five globes. (Figure 22.15).

Using our sustainability methodology, we found that sustainable funds have significantly lower levels of ESG risk embedded in their portfolios. Four in five (80%) of sustainable funds in the Europe fixed income category receive the top ratings, 'High' or 'Above Average', compared with only one third of funds overall (Figure 22.16). At the other end of the scale, only 6% of sustainable funds receive the lowest rating, 'Low' or 'Below Average' globes, compared with one third of funds overall.

A higher number of US fixed income bond strategies achieve Morningstar's highest sustainability ratings. Over 97% are split between High and Above Average (Figure 22.17). Many US portfolios are passive ETFs that track best-in-class corporate bond indices.

Distribution	Score	Descriptive Rank	Rating Icon
Highest 10%	5	High	⊕⊕⊕⊕⊕
Next 22.5%	4	Above Average	⊕⊕⊕⊕
Next 35%	3	Average	⊕⊕⊕
Next 22.5%	2	Below Average	⊕⊕
Lowest 10%	1	Low	⊕

Figure 22.15 Morningstar Sustainability Rating Classification.

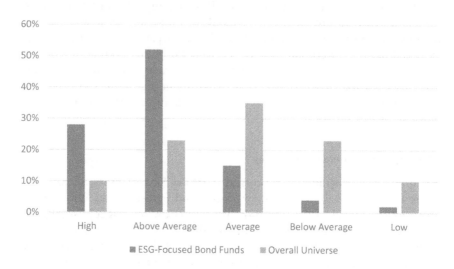

Figure 22.16 Morningstar Sustainability Rating for Europe Fixed Income Bond Strategies.
Source: Morningstar Direct. Data as of March 2021.

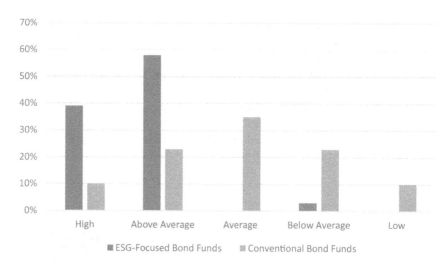

Figure 22.17 Morningstar Sustainability Rating for U.S. Fixed Income Bond Strategies.
Source: Morningstar Direct. Data as of March 2021.

Conclusion

The sustainable fixed income fund market has grown rapidly: the number of products and AUM has more than doubled in three years. Compared with equity strategies, investors still have fewer choices. But that will change as asset managers step up their sustainability investing capabilities and more reliable data becomes available. We see evidence of this with new active and passive strategies, repurposing of funds, and mirroring ESG versions of existing offerings to meet emerging investor demand.

For a new generation of investors, making a positive impact is a desirable objective. Fixed income can deliver impact with direct financing of specific projects with positive environmental and social outcomes. With the rise and democratisation of securities like green, climate, and social bonds, the impact fixed income fund space is promising, and places the asset class in a unique position versus equities.

Scrutiny of funds is likely to grow as our assessment suggests a varied application of ESG rules to construct fixed income strategies. It is essential that investors in ESG-focused strategies investigate how they align with the sustainability approaches they expect. In addition to understanding the ESG objective and policies, investors should also make sure they are comfortable with the outcome. While many sustainable bond funds exhibit significantly lower levels of ESG risk, some do carry higher ESG risk. Impact levels vary too.

Notes

1 Morningstar is a leading global provider of investment research. It offers a wide array of products and services, including ESG data, ratings, and analytics, to both retail and institutional investors. All of the data provided in this chapter is from Morningstar. Morningstar publishes ESG-specific market, which is available at https://www.morningstar.com/esg.
2 Morningstar's classification of sustainable funds is based on prospectuses, fact sheets, KIIDs, and other available resources. The Morningstar universe includes open-end funds and exchange-traded funds (ETFs) that claim to have a sustainability objective and/or use binding ESG criteria for their investment selection and portfolio construction.
3 This chapter uses 'sustainable' and 'ESG' interchangeably.
4 A full description of the methodology can be found at: 744156_Morningstar_Sustainability_Rating_for_Funds_Methodology.pdf.

Part 7

Looking Forward

23 Regulation, Policy, and Fixed Income

Will Martindale

In October 2017, the then European Commission Vice President for Financial Stability, Financial Services and Capital Markets Union, Valdis Dombrovskis, said 'we need to increase the private capital flow to sustainable finance' (Dombrovskis, 2017). Shortly thereafter, the highest echelons of European politics proposed reforms to ensure that 'The financial sector will have to throw its full weight behind the fight against climate change' (Juncker, 2018).

Global sustainable finance policy matters because it is already influencing investors and corporates. The Principles for Responsible Investment (PRI) identifies 'over 730 hard and soft law policy revisions, across some 500 policy instruments, which support, encourage or require investors to consider long-term value drivers, including ESG factors' (PRI, 2019a). Most of these policy revisions are asset class agnostic, impacting regulated investors across different markets, and that the growth in responsible investment-related regulation is recent and exponential (PRI, 2019a).

The policy reforms subsequently introduced in the European Union (and described later in this chapter) affect our understanding of modern investment, and require fixed income investors, like all investors, to integrate ESG issues into their investment decisions. Most policy initiatives relate to either financial products or institutional oversight, rather than specific to any asset class; however, policymakers have turned their attention to green bond issuance to accelerate investment. European policymakers, while recognised as leading responsible investment in the domestic market, are not outliers. Similar responsible investment policy reforms are underway in the UK, with industry or government-led taskforces underway across the world, such as Canada's Expert Panel and Australia's Sustainable Finance Initiative.

This chapter explores several of these policy reforms through a fixed income lens. It starts by explaining the drivers for regulatory action and how policymakers (and investors) are responding. It then proposes a responsible investment-related regulatory framework for fixed income investors, considering ESG integration, stewardship, and corporate disclosure requirements, with a specific focus on the role of credit ratings agencies and disclosure requirements for ESG-related ratings methodologies. It concludes with a discussion of the green bond issuance market.

DOI: 10.4324/9781003055341-30

Regulators and Responsible Investment

Drivers for Responsible Investment Regulation

There are several reasons why policymakers are turning their attention to responsible investment.

The first, and for securities regulators, the most important, is evidence demonstrating that ESG factors can affect investment value. Taking a fiduciary perspective, 'neglecting analysis of ESG factors may cause the mispricing of risk and poor asset allocation decisions' (PRI, 2016b). While fiduciary responsibility and ESG integration are further ahead in Europe than other markets, even within the US, where there is less consensus on responsible investing, there is growing acceptance that it provides 'attractive investment opportunities [that] can be capitalized on in US companies through the use of ESG integration, with the degree of financial materiality varying across individual sustainability factors, fundamental profiles and industry groups' (PRI, 2018). This perspective is increasingly supported by academic literature: a meta-study by Deutsche Asset Management and the University of Hamburg found that 62.6% of studies found a positive correlation between ESG factors and financial performance (Friede et al., 2015).

The second is to introduce minimum ESG expectations that can create a level playing field among investors, and to clarify terminology through the intermediation chain. Responsible investment has grown rapidly and organically. However, investors' interpretation of what qualifies as a sustainable investment continue to differ. This can lead to inefficiencies, with multiple interpretations by investors of both their responsibilities and of how they communicate their activities. It can also dissuade investment firms from developing in-house ESG expertise, given that the pace of market development can quickly make in-house processes redundant.

The third is to close the sustainability gap, responding to the widespread view that capital markets are unsustainable because they enable and support negative behavioural business practices. As just one example, analysis by Aviva using Carbon Delta's warming potential metric found that the FTSE 100 index was consistent with 3.9 degrees of warming (Aviva, 2019). With the UK committing into law a net-zero carbon emissions target by 2050, this gap represents a market failure that requires a regulatory response. European policymakers recognise the dichotomy; a reorientation of private capital towards sustainability goals is seen as a prerequisite to achieve the continent's overall sustainability strategy.

When considering ESG issues, regulators have tended not to focus on a specific asset class, but rather the entities the regulators are tasked to regulate. There are three exceptions identified in different markets, which will be explored later in this chapter. The first is green bonds, to raise capital for a specific set of economics activities. The second is credit ratings agencies, focusing on the methodologies used to determine a rating. And the third is stewardship, broadening their expectations beyond listed equity investors.

Characteristics of Modern Responsible Investment Regulation

Policy Is Holistic and All-encompassing

Rather than sporadic and responsive regulatory action, policymakers have created more holistic and encompassing strategies to advance sustainable investment. An example is Europe's High-Level Expert Group (HLEG) on sustainable finance, with similar initiatives underway in Canada and Australia. A stakeholder-involved, multi-year project is

> significant because they contain substantive policy reforms. But they also require policymakers to set out, often for the first time, how they understand the relationship between sustainability and finance, and the role finance is expected to play in addressing critical sustainability issues. This can help to break down the misconception that sustainability is a niche issue and give clear signals to investors on policy direction.
>
> (PRI, 2019a)

The European Commission appointed the HLEG's members towards the end of 2016. The group was 'given a mandate to prepare a comprehensive blueprint for reforms along the entire investment chain, on which to build a sustainable finance strategy for the EU' (European Commission, 2018). The group's recommendations led to the European Commission action plan for financing sustainable growth, which committed to ten interventions (European Commission, 2018):

1 Establishing a clear and detailed EU taxonomy, a classification system for sustainable activities.
2 Creating an EU Green Bond Standard and labels for green financial products.
3 Fostering investment in sustainable projects.
4 Incorporating sustainability in financial advice.
5 Developing sustainability benchmarks.
6 Better integrating sustainability in ratings and market research.
7 Clarifying asset managers' and institutional investors' duties regarding sustainability.
8 Introducing a 'green supporting factor' in the EU prudential rules for banks and insurance companies.
9 Strengthening sustainability disclosure and accounting rule-making.
10 Fostering sustainable corporate governance and attenuating short-termism in capital markets.

Investors Are Central to the Policy Process

Investors are increasingly involved in public policy development and implementation on sustainable finance. This reflects that sustainable finance is fast-evolving, with investment practice often running ahead of formal regulatory requirements; a good example relates to fiduciary duty where investors have integrated ESG considerations into their investment practices and processes ahead of being required to do so by legislation (see, for example, Sullivan et al. 2015, 2019). As such, in designing legislation, policymakers have generally sought to formalise industry good practice where it exists.

Investors are also involved because it is in their interests to do so. 'Public policy critically affects the ability of long-term investors to generate sustainable returns and create value' and 'Policy engagement by long-term investors is therefore a natural and necessary extension of an investor's responsibilities and fiduciary duties to the interests of beneficiaries' (Sullivan et al., 2014). More recent shifts in fiduciary concepts have created a shift amongst investors looking to 'support the stability and resilience of the financial system' (Sullivan et al., 2019).

Analysis of the PRI's annual investor reporting framework finds that in the years 2016 to 2019, a growing proportion of the investor signatory base engaged in responsible investment policy engagement activities, either on their own or in collaboration with other investors. Investors are likely to focus more on policy initiatives given the increasing attention of trade bodies towards ESG themes and the rising importance of sustainability to financial markets.

But while there is more investor focus on policy, there is often insufficient implementation, which may impede policy effectiveness. The PRI identified seven areas (see Box 23.1) that investors setting out to influence regulators on ESG themes should focus, arguing that this will improve the successful implementation of sustainable finance regulations.

BOX 23.1 Key to Effective Investor Engagement on Public Policy (PRI, 2020a)

1   Undertake policy engagement, aligning your engagement and investment objectives.
2   Work to policymakers' timetables, not your own.
3   Leverage arguments based on technical expertise.
4   Engage at all levels of the policy process, as well as through the media.
5   As far as possible, work together and speak with a coherent voice, especially where there is consensus.
6   Better understand the relevant dynamics of policy decision-making across committees and groups.
7   Be clear about who you represent and how policies impact your investor base.

The Focus Is Shifting from Generic Regulation to More Rigorous, More Specific, and More Technical Regulations

Earlier iterations of responsible investment-related policy tended to rely on principle-based implementation rules. For example, the 2016 revision of the Ontario Pension Benefits Act states that 'a plan's statement of investment policies and procedures is required to include information as to whether ESG factors are incorporated into the plan's investment policies and procedures and, if so, how those factors are incorporated' (FSCO, 2016).

In other words, ESG incorporation tended to be optional, and for pension plans that did incorporate ESG factors, the pension plan was required to disclose their policies and procedures to the regulator, potentially limiting further adoption. While at the time this was considered an important intervention, policymakers in other markets have since provided more precise regulatory requirements to accelerate further market acceptance.

In 2018, the UK revised its Occupational Pension Scheme Regulations. The revised regulation states that 'Funds must disclose their policies in relation to financially material considerations. This is defined as including ESG issues and climate change' (Department for Work & Pensions, 2018). In other words, disclosure is no longer optional, and ESG issues, including climate change, are considered financially material considerations for pension schemes.

In parallel, a series of market-led and regulatory initiatives have further intensified policymaker efforts to regulate responsible investment activities, most notably, the Financial Stability Board's (FSB's) Taskforce for Climate-related Financial Disclosures (TCFD), and the central banks' Network for Greening the Financial System (NGFS).

The TCFD initiative is a voluntary climate framework targeting companies, investors, lenders, insurers, and other stakeholders. The TCFD consider the physical, liability, and transition risks associated with climate change, supports firms' understanding of financially material climate change risks, and encourage firms to align their disclosures with investors' needs.

The NGFS's purpose is to strengthen the global central bank response required to meet the goals of the 2015 Paris Agreement and to enhance the role of the financial system to manage risks and to mobilise capital to support environmentally sustainable development. To this end, the NGFS defines and promotes best practices within and outside of the NGFS and conducts or commissions analytical work on green finance.

In 2019, policymakers started to introduce policy tools to align investment activities with sustainability objectives. The EU taxonomy, for example, is a tool to covering six environmental themes to help investors understand whether an economic activity is environmentally sustainable, and to navigate the transition to a low-carbon economy (European Union Technical Expert Group on Sustainable Finance, 2020a). Setting a common language between investors, issuers, project promoters and policy makers, the EU taxonomy helps investors to assess whether investments are meeting robust environmental standards and are consistent with high-level policy commitments such as the Paris Agreement. A platform for sustainable finance will develop further performance thresholds and, subject to regulation, taxonomies across other themes.

Taxonomies are under consideration in several other countries including South Africa, Canada, Australia, Malaysia, and India. The National Treasury in South Africa sought public comment on calls to 'create a taxonomy and a benchmark climate risk scenario for South Africa', arguing for greater consistency in refining both the problems and solutions to climate change, as well as international harmonisation (National Treasury, 2020).

There is Increased Focus on Sustainability Outcomes

Real economy outcomes are linked to attempts at closing the sustainability gap. Increased public attention to sustainability issues, as demonstrated through extreme weather events or the growing attention to climate change at a political level, have driven regulatory action in two ways: (a) from generic, or principle-based regulation to specific and technical requirements (as discussed above), and (b) from process-based regulation to outcome focused regulation. China is a good example of the latter, with policymakers prioritising environmental disclosures that will, first and foremost, improve air quality and the health and well-being of Chinese citizens, as well as contribute to global environmental goals.

Another example of the shift to outcomes is the UK Stewardship Code, revised in 2020. The Code introduces the terms 'society' and 'outcomes', stating that: 'Stewardship is the responsible allocation, management and oversight of capital to create long-term value for clients and beneficiaries leading to sustainable benefits for the economy, the environment and society' (Financial Reporting Council, 2020). Principle 6 of the revised Code states that 'Signatories take account of client and beneficiary needs and communicate the activities and outcomes of their stewardship and investment to them', adding that 'signatories should disclose the length of the investment time horizon' (Financial Reporting Council, 2020).

In the EU, the Sustainable Finance Disclosure Regulation requires investors, including investment managers, pension providers and insurers, to disclose a description of their policies to assess and their actions to address principal adverse sustainability impacts. Growing accountability for fund managers will drive improvements in portfolio exposure to sustainability themes.

A Responsible Investment–Related Regulatory Framework for Fixed Income Investors

This section proposes a framework for responsible investment-related regulatory intervention, developing on work prepared by the PRI in 2016.

Almost all existing regulations can be grouped into three broad categories that relate to different parts of the investment chain: (1) pension fund regulations; (2) stewardship codes; and (3) corporate disclosure requirements. These are not mutually exclusive; some responsible investment regulation, such as France's Energy Transition Law, traverse several categories (PRI, 2016a).

Pension Fund Regulations

Asset owners sit at the top of the investment chain. Their commitment to sustainability considerations is reflected in the services they are offered by their fund managers and service providers. Regulators' requirements have changed gradually, from ESG guidance, to comply or explain, and, more recently, prescriptive ESG integration rules such as those set out by the EU Sustainable Finance Disclosures Regulation and the UK Investment Regulations.

Common changes to these investment regulations have required trustees to publish annual implementation statements setting out how trustees' ESG and stewardship policies have been followed during the year (Sackers, 2020). In the UK, for example, trustees must update their Statement of Investment Principles to set out policies in relation to:

- 'Financially material considerations' (including ESG considerations and climate change)
- The extent to which 'non-financial matters' are considered
- Undertaking engagement activities in respect of investments (stewardship)

Pension rules now increasingly make sustainable investment considerations compulsory, rather than voluntary. Regulatory action focusing on asset owners' responsibility will lead to more scrutiny on the ESG practices of fund managers, whom typically are the agents employed by asset owners to run scheme investment strategies. Transparency will ensure that accountability will rise and improvements over time will need to be documented, embedding sustainability into pension scheme design and asset allocations.

Stewardship Codes

Historically considered by regulators as primarily relevant for equity investors, stewardship rules have extended to bondholders in recent years. This change is most clearly seen with the UK Stewardship Code, which introduced the first Code in 2010, subsequently adopted by many are other markets, and more recently extended its stewardship rules to become asset class neutral.

The Code, which ensures investors hold issuers accountable for their actions, takes a holistic focus on investors' entire investment enterprise.

There has been significant growth in investment in assets other than listed equity, such as fixed-income bonds and infrastructure equity. Signatories should use the resources, rights and influence available to them to exercise stewardship, no matter how capital is invested.

(Financial Reporting Council, 2019)

Specifically, the Code expects investors to exercise their rights and responsibilities as investors. The Code identifies four ways bondholders can do this; seeking amendments to terms and conditions in indentures or contracts; seeking access to information provided in trust deeds; impairment rights; and reviewing prospectus and transaction documents (Financial Reporting Council, 2020).

This broadening of focus away from equities and towards fixed income is being seen in other jurisdictions. Japan, which has recently accelerated its focus on corporate governance and responsible investment, refers to the responsibilities of institutional investors to enhance the medium- to long-term investment return for clients and beneficiaries by 'improving and fostering investee companies' corporate value and sustainable growth through constructive engagement, or purposeful dialogue, based on in-depth knowledge of the companies and their business environment' (Financial Services Agency, 2020).

In its 2017 revision, the Council of Experts on the Stewardship Code added: 'Important ESG (environmental, social, and governance) factors may affect medium- to long-term corporate value under each investee company's specific circumstances, both in terms of business risks and opportunities.'

Fixed income investors have demonstrated why and how stewardship is compatible with bond investing. Regulators have responded to approach stewardship with an asset class agnostic perspective, seeing that stewardship extends beyond corporate issuers, to also focus on sovereigns/agencies, originators, and counterparties. This is a clear sign of how far fixed income investors are embracing their role to create a sustainable financial system.

Corporate Disclosure Requirements

Most major securities regulators and exchanges now require ESG disclosures for corporates. In its 2014 revision of the Non-Financial Reporting Directive (NFRD), the EU stated that large companies must publish reports on the policies they implement in relation to a range of sustainability themes, including environmental protection; treatment of employees; respect for human rights; anti-corruption and bribery; and diversity on company boards (in terms of age, gender, educational and professional background (European Union, 2014). Enhancing and consolidating corporate disclosure requirements is a now a major focus of policymakers. For example, the period late 2020 and early 2021 saw proposals for increased collaboration among the voluntary disclosure networks such as SASB and GRI, a consultation on standardised disclosures led by IFRS, the introduction of formal TCFD

disclosure requirements in the UK, and renewed focus on corporate disclosures by European policymakers.

Inconsistent and incomplete disclosure has created more support for taxonomies that can introduce harmonisation and comparability. The EU taxonomy is one such attempt, which sets performance thresholds that will help
companies, project promoters, and issuers access green financing to improve
their environmental performance, as well as helping to identify the activities
considered environmentally friendly. This will help to grow low-carbon sectors and decarbonise high-carbon ones.

The EU Taxonomy is one of the most significant developments in sustainable finance and will have wide ranging implications for investors and issuers
working in the EU, and beyond. The Taxonomy sets performance thresholds (referred to as 'technical screening criteria') for economic activities that
make a substantive contribution to one of six environmental objectives (Box
23.2); do no significant harm (DNSH) to the other five environmental objectives, where relevant; and meet minimum safeguards, such as the OECD
Guidelines on Multinational Enterprises and the UN Guiding Principles on
Business and Human Rights (European Union Technical Expert Group on
Sustainable Finance, 2020a).

BOX 23.2 The Six EU Taxonomy Environmental Objectives

1   Climate change mitigation
2   Climate change adaptation
3   Sustainable use and protection of water and marine resources
4   Transition to a circular economy, waste prevention, and recycling
5   Pollution prevention and control
6   Protection of healthy ecosystems

These frameworks are being used by bondholders to evaluate the alignment
of individual portfolios. For example, BlueBay evaluated how its high yield
global ESG bond fund aligns with the EU taxonomy, undertaking a five-
part approach. First, BlueBay compared green bond holdings with the activities listed in the Taxonomy, making use of Bloomberg financial software's
taxonomy tool. At this stage, BlueBay did not consider the environmental performance of the activity; rather whether the activity was covered by
the Taxonomy. Second, BlueBay undertook in-house analysis to determine
whether the economic activity met the Taxonomy performance threshold.
Third, BlueBay screened against the DNSH criteria for each environmental
objective, as well as a controversy screen. Fourth, BlueBay screened against
the minimum safeguards, making use of Sustainalytics' taxonomy tool. Finally, BlueBay aggregated the alignment for each bond to determine the
portfolio alignment. (PRI, 2020b).

With taxonomies and frameworks more common, such as the UN Sustainable Development Goals and 'net-zero' goals, fixed income investors will be expected to disclose how their portfolios align. The EU has created the first regulatory requirements for investors that market their funds as sustainable, or as having an environmental objective, to disclose how, using the EU Taxonomy framework. This is not limited to pure-play green bond portfolios but potentially all bond portfolios with sustainability characteristics. While this will create implementation challenges for fund managers end-investors will benefit from improving comparability across sustainable investment solutions.

Developing the Green Bond Market

What constitutes a green or sustainable bond has been the subject of substantial industry discussion and development since 2009. The fixed income industry and supporting groups have independently created many of the frameworks, tools, and best practice standards used by participants. These collaborative efforts have helped to grow the green bond market to more than $1 trillion and create market diversification, including from both corporate and sovereign issuers.

Policymakers have been slower to focus on this burgeoning asset class. But to accelerate wider adoption the Climate Bonds Initiative identifies ten recommendations for regulators to use policy instruments that will ensure the market moves from the periphery of the fixed income universe to a more prominent role supporting wider sustainable finance objectives and promote the transition to a low-carbon economy (Climate Bonds Initiative, 2015):

1 Strategic issuance from public entities
2 Strengthening planning and pipeline transparency of green projects
3 Improving the risk-return profile of green bonds: credit enhancement
4 Tax incentives
5 Boosting demand: domestic fund mandates
6 Boosting demand and convening power: central banks
7 Market integrity: supporting standards development
8 Market creation and development: aggregation of small-scale green assets
9 Financial regulatory measures are important
10 International financial cooperation

In Europe, a voluntary scheme with rising importance was insufficient to meet the emerging sustainability gap. The HLEG's final report recommended policymakers 'Develop and implement official European sustainability standards and labels, starting with green bonds' (European Union Technical Expert Group on Sustainable Finance, 2020b). If the green bond market was become accessible to more investors and issuers, including through liability matching investment strategies, a regulatory standard and framework will support market changes more effectively. More intervention would provide a deeper degree of certainty, and potentially, lowers due diligence costs.

The Canada Expert Panel on Sustainable Finance shared a similar sentiment, recommending to expand Canada's green fixed income market and set a global standard for transition-oriented financing.

> Fixed income instruments represent the largest, and generally deepest, pool of capital in international markets. Leveraging this asset class to help achieve the goals of the Paris Agreement - and for Canada, the proposed Mid-Century Transition Path - will be key to delivering the scale of financing required to implement essential plans for resilient infrastructure, deep building retrofits, clean electricity generation and transmission and cleaner energy and resource production.
>
> (Government of Canada, 2019)

In March 2020 the EU Green Bond Standard was introduced with four key components: (1) aligning green bonds with the EU Taxonomy, DNSH safeguards, and technical screening criteria; (2) The content of a green bond framework produced by an issuer, such as the issuer's strategy and processes; (3) The allocation and impact reporting, to enable transparency on quantitative metrics, particularly environmental impacts; and (4) Requirements for external verification by an approved verifier, with accreditation agencies subject to regulatory oversight (European Union Technical Expert Group on Sustainable Finance, 2020b).

Additionally, to create demand and supply measures levers the HLEG recommended creating financial incentives and encouraging public and private sector bodies to issue green instruments. Several jurisdictions support incentives to reduce the up-front cost of bond verifications, although the impact is unknown and may be unnecessary in the short-term given the premium that exists for new bond issuance (European Union Technical Expert Group on Sustainable Finance, 2020b). Tax incentives are an option but would prove controversial from an investor and political perspective.

While China has developed its own green bond framework and market, it is looking to converge with the best practice standards elsewhere and drive better performance of domestic issuers. The People's Bank of China, the National Development and Reform Commission, and the China Securities Regulatory Commission issued a consultation on a revised Green Bonds Catalogue. The 2020 Catalogue was updated to unify domestic standards and ranges for green projects and address emerging issues, including improving the quality of the environment, climate change, and resource efficiency. This includes removing 'clean coal' and 'clean fossil fuels' projects as eligible green bond use of proceeds (China Dialogue, 2020).

Policymakers' focus on green bonds is expected to create higher quality green bond issuance. But with the recent evolution addition of sustainability and social bonds, regulators need to recognise that standards and financial solutions are moving at a faster rate than their policy tools. It will be important regulators introduce changes that support the market's overall growth rather than create new obstacles for investors and issuers; a more regulated market will potentially limit many existing and new issuers concerned about legal and reputation impacts.

Credit Rating Agencies and ESG Rating Agencies

Policymakers have spent more time scrutinising how credit ratings agencies consider sustainability issues within their credit assessments. While credit ratings provide a view on the probability of default, a longer-term investment horizon will have a more uncertain credit outcome. This is particularly the case for sustainability issues such as climate change, which are perceived to present long-term credit risks. A company may have negative externalities, such as high unregulated methane emissions, but also strong sound financial characteristics. The disconnect between sustainability and credit assessments has created a role for ESG rating agency that is distinct but complementary to traditional credit ratings.

Fixed income investors have increased their engagement with credit ratings agencies. More than 160 investors have encouraged systematic change of how issuers are evaluated against sustainability issues. Twenty-three credit ratings agencies have signed a global investor statement committing to:

- Evaluate the extent to which ESG factors are credit-relevant for different issuers;
- Publish their views transparently on the ways in which ESG factors are considered in credit ratings;
- Review the ways ESG factors are integrated into credit analysis as our understanding of these factors evolves;
- Maintain organisational governance and resourcing to deliver quality ratings, including ESG analysis where relevant;
- Participate in industry-wide efforts to develop consistent public disclosure by issuers on ESG factors that could impact their creditworthiness;
- Participate in dialogue with investors to identify and understand ESG risks to creditworthiness (PRI, 2020c).

The statement has been examined by European policymakers and, like green bonds, have identified this as an area where voluntary initiatives may not be enough. The HLEG recommended that credit rating agencies 'should systematically integrate relevant ESG factors and factors related to longer-term sustainability into their credit risk analysis and credit ratings' (European Commission, 2018). Subsequently, the European Securities and Markets Authority (ESMA) published guidelines on methodology disclosure requirements by credit ratings agencies, stating that the guidelines:

- Provide detailed disclosure guidance when credit ratings are issued. This will ensure a better level of consistency of the critical information included in press releases when making credit announcements; and
- Require greater transparency on whether ESG factors were a key driver of the credit rating action. This will allow investors to better assess where ESG factors are affecting credit rating actions (ESMA, 2019).

ESMA avoided making consideration of sustainability characteristics rating assessments mandatory. But with policy consultations re-examining the role and responsibilities of market participants, more enforcement is a possibility. Indeed, policymakers across different markets now routinely evaluate the role of investors in achieving sustainability objectives. This shift from passive, voluntary action to more assertive enforcement shows how policymakers see the purpose of investment managers evolving.

Conclusions

In the short history of responsible investment, policy initiatives have tended to lag industry practice. However, this is changing quickly. This chapter has shown the scope of reforms already underway and the specific areas expected to impact fixed income investors. Transparency is commonplace and active application of ESG issues into decision-making is the minimum requirement.

The policy activities covered in this chapter are only the start. Further policymaking is inevitable, for the simple reason that capital markets support unsustainable economic activity. The realities of climate change have become apparent, and it is inevitable that governments will be forced to act more decisively than they have so far (PRI, 2019b). Fixed income investors can expect greater scrutiny of sustainability integration activities across more asset classes and disclosure requirements, even in hard to evaluate areas like securitised finance.

In 2020, politically endorsed climate targets including from Japan and China committing to net zero carbon emissions by 2050 and 2060 respectively, cannot be ignored. A new Biden administration has also committed to taking a tougher line on climate and broader sustainability-related issues, which investors will need to pay close attention to (Insight Investment, 2020). Together with the UK and EU incorporating ambitious short-term climate targets further policy reforms are likely to directly and indirectly influence capital markets, and the long-foreshadowed strong policy response to climate change looks more and more certain (PRI, 2018).

References

Aviva (2019), *Why We're Stepping Up the Climate Fight.* [online]. Available from: https://www.aviva.co.uk/aviva-edit/in-the-news-articles/stepping-up-the-climate-fight/ (Accessed 13 February 2020).

China Dialogue (2020), *China's New Green Bond Catalogue Could Be Greener.* [online]. Available from: https://chinadialogue.net/en/business/chinas-new-green-bond-catalogue-could-be-greener/ (Accessed 4 November 2020).

Climate Bonds Initiative (2015), *So What's Next? How to Grow Green Bond Markets Around the World.* [online]. Available from: https://www.climatebonds.net/files/files/10%20point%20policy%20guide.pdf (Accessed 14 November 2020).

Department for Work and Pensions (2018), *Clarifying and Strengthening Trustees' Investment Duties.* [online]. Available from: https://assets.publishing.service.gov.uk/government/uploads/system/uploads/attachment_data/file/739331/response-clarifying-and-strengthening-trustees-investment-duties.pdf (Accessed 2 November 2020).

Dombrovskis, V. (2017), *Remarks by Vice-President Dombrovskis at the ECOFIN Press Conference in Luxembourg.* 10 October 2017. [online]. Available from: https://www.eumonitor.eu/9353000/1/j9vvik7m1c3gyxp/vkicj1n00wxa?ctx=vhyzmvnvbbzs&v=1&tab=1&start_tab1=110 (Accessed 19 October 2020).

European Commission (2018), *Frequently Asked Questions: Action Plan on Financing Sustainable Growth.* [online]. Available from: https://ec.europa.eu/commission/presscorner/detail/en/MEMO_18_1424 (Accessed 19 October 2020).

European Securities and Markets Authority (ESMA) (2019), *Guidelines on Disclosure Requirements Applicable to Credit Ratings.* [online]. Available from: https://www.esma.europa.eu/sites/default/files/library/esma33-9-320_final_report_guidelines_on_disclosure_requirements_applicable_to_credit_rating_agencies.pdf (Accessed 14 November 2020).

European Union (2014), *Directive 2014/95/EU of the European Parliament and of the Council.* [online]. Available from: https://eur-lex.europa.eu/legal-content/EN/TXT/?uri=CELEX%3A32014L0095 (Accessed 12 November 2020).

European Union Technical Expert Group on Sustainable Finance (2020a), *Technical Report.* [online]. Available from: https://ec.europa.eu/info/sites/info/files/business_economy_euro/banking_and_finance/documents/200309-sustainable-finance-teg-final-report-taxonomy_en.pdf (Accessed 3 November 2020).

European Union Technical Expert Group on Sustainable Finance (2020b), *Technical Expert Group: Green Bond Standard.* [online]. Available from: https://images.politico.eu/wp-content/uploads/2019/06/EU-GREEN-BOND-STANDARD.pdf (Accessed 24 November 2020).

Financial Reporting Council (2019), *Proposed Revision to the UK Stewardship Code.* [online]. Available from: https://www.frc.org.uk/getattachment/dff25bf9-998e-44f6-a699-a697d932da60/-;.aspx (Accessed 14 November 2020).

Financial Reporting Council (2020), *The UK Stewardship Code 2020.* [online]. Available from: https://www.frc.org.uk/getattachment/5aae591d-d9d3-4cf4-814a-d14e156a1d87/Stewardship-Code_Final2.pdf (Accessed 8 November 2020).

Financial Services Agency (2020), *Principles for Responsible Institutional Investors.* [online]. Available from: https://www.fsa.go.jp/en/refer/councils/stewardship/20200324/01.pdf (Accessed 22 November 2020).

Financial Services Commission of Ontario (FSCO) (2016), *Rules Concerning the Statement of Investment Policies and Procedures (SIPP).* [online]. Available from: https://www.fsco.gov.on.ca/en/pensions/legislative/Pages/rules-concerning-sipp.aspx (Accessed 19 October 2020).

Friede, G., Busch, T. and Bassen, A. (2015), 'ESG and Financial Performance: Aggregated Evidence from More Than 2000 Empirical Studies', *Journal of Sustainable Finance and Investment,* 5(4), pp. 210–233.

Government of Canada (2019), *Expert Panel on Sustainable Finance.* [online]. Available from: https://www.canada.ca/en/environment-climate-change/services/climate-change/expert-panel-sustainable-finance.html (Accessed 13 February 2021).

Insight Investment (2020), *Sustainable Investment Under the Biden Administration.* [online]. Available from: https://www.insightinvestment.com/globalassets/documents/recent-thinking/sustainable-investment-and-the-biden-administration.pdf (Accessed 05 November 2020).

Juncker, J.-C. (2018), *Sustainable Finance: High-Level Conference Kicks EU's Strategy for Greener and Cleaner Economy into High Gear.* [online]. Available from: https://ec.europa.eu/commission/presscorner/detail/en/IP_18_2381 (Accessed 23 October 2020).

National Treasury (2020), *Working Groups.* [online]. Available from: http://sustainablefinanceinitiative.org.za/working-groups/ (Accessed 4 November 2020).

Principles for Responsible Investment (2016a), *Global Guide to Responsible Investment Regulation.* [online]. Available from: https://www.unpri.org/download?ac=325 (Accessed 8 November 2020).

Principles for Responsible Investment (2016b), *US Roadmap.* [online]. Available from: https://www.unpri.org/download?ac=4353 (Accessed 13 February 2021).

Principles for Responsible Investment (2018), *Financial Performance of ESG Integration in US Investing.* [online]. Available from: https://www.unpri.org/download?ac=4218 (Accessed 12 October 2020).

Principles for Responsible Investment (2019a), *Taking Stock: Sustainable Finance Policy Engagement and Policy Influence.* [online]. Available from: https://www.unpri.org/Uploads/c/j/u/pripolicywhitepapertakingstockfinal_335442.pdf. (Accessed 12 October 2020).

Principles for Responsible Investment (2019b), *Inevitable Policy Response.* [online]. Available from: https://www.unpri.org/download?ac=9833 (Accessed 14 October 2020).

Principles for Responsible Investment (2020a), *Sustainable and Inclusive Covid-19 Recovery and Reform.* [online]. Available from: https://www.unpri.org/download?ac=10839 (Accessed 29 October 2020).

Principles for Responsible Investment (2020b), *EU Taxonomy Alignment Case Study: BlueBay.* [online]. Available from: https://www.unpri.org/eu-taxonomy-alignment-case-studies/eu-taxonomy-alignment-case-study-bluebay/6306.article (Accessed 12 November 2020).

Principles for Responsible Investment (2020c), *Statement on ESG in Credit Risk and Ratings.* [online]. Available from: https://www.unpri.org/credit-ratings/statement-on-esg-in-credit-risk-and-ratings-available-in-different-languages/77.article (Accessed 20 November 2020).

Sackers (2020), *ESG and Climate Change for Pension Funds.* [online]. Available from: https://www.sackers.com/app/uploads/2020/03/ESG-and-climate-change-for-pension-funds.pdf (Accessed 12 November 2020).Sullivan, R., Martindale, W., Feller, E. and Bordon, A. (2015), *Fiduciary Duty in the 21st Century* (UN Global Compact, UNEPFI, Principles for Responsible Investment and UNEP Inquiry into the Design of a Sustainable Financial System, London). [online]. Available from: https://www.unpri.org/download?ac=1378 (Accessed 26 April 2021).

Sullivan, R., Martindale, W., Feller, E., Pirovska, M. and Elliott, R. (2019), *Fiduciary Duty in the 21st Century: Final Report* (The Generation Foundation, PRI and UNEP FI, London). [online]. Available from: https://www.unpri.org/download?ac=9792 (Accessed 26 April 2021).

Sullivan, R., Martindale, W., Robins, N. and Winch, H. (2014), *Policy Frameworks for Long-Term Responsible Investment: The Case for Investor Engagement in Public Policy* (PRI and The UNEP Inquiry into the Design of a Sustainable Financial System, London). [online]. Available from: https://www.unpri.org/download?ac=1420 (Accessed 26 April 2021).

24 Measuring the Impacts of Climate Change[1]

James Edwards, Tamara Straus and
Natalie Ambrosio Preudhomme

Introduction

Climate change poses a major future risk to the stability of the financial system and the world economy. Our planet has already warmed by 1.1°C *above pre-industrial levels, and this warming* has already affected nearly every facet of the global economy, from infrastructure, agriculture, and commercial and residential property to human health and labor productivity (IPCC, 2018). In 2020 alone, the world experienced $268 billion in economic damage from the climate-influenced weather disasters, of which 64% were uninsured (AON, 2021). And although many governments have pledged to achieve net zero greenhouse gas emissions by 2050, global temperature rise is expected to significantly exceed 2°C *above pre-industrial levels, resulting in* radically changed microclimates, sea level rise, drought-induced famines, and other tipping point events (UN Environment Programme, 2019).

The uncertainties regarding the effects of climate change have created significant demand for methods that quantify and forecast climate change's financial impacts. Developing robust quantitative models, however, is a highly complex exercise. Climate risk analysis requires new tools, metrics, and analytics typically out of reach to most investors. Without these, integrating climate-related factors into financial decision making remains limited (Network for Greening the Financial System (NGFS), 2020a). Bridging this gap is becoming an ever more pressing issue, given that the risks of global warming, if left unmanaged, have the potential to cause damages beyond 10% of world GDP by 2050 (NGFS, 2020a).

In this chapter, we present a model to quantify the financial risks, and ultimately corporate credit risk, resulting from specific climate scenarios. The approach builds upon the Moody's Analytics' Public Firm Expected Default Frequency (EDF)™ model to understand the financial and credit implications of these possible climate futures. As a structural credit model that has accurately predicted default events for over 30 years in multiple global economic environments, the EDF model provides an attractive framework on which to quantify and understand the risks firms face from both physical and transition risk drivers.

DOI: 10.4324/9781003055341-31

This chapter is divided into four main sections. We first summarise the basic methodology behind the EDF climate risk model. Second, we provide an overview of our assessment for physical risk. Third, we focus on our appraisal of transition risk. Fourth, we conclude by discussing the implications of climate risk for credit investors.

Scenario Methodology Overview

The Moody's Analytics Climate-Adjusted EDF Model analyzes the financial and credit effects of many possible climate futures. The framework draws upon a number of climate data and modelling resources to define these scenarios and to calibrate ultimate impacts. In keeping with the taxonomy of risk commonly used in climate science, the methodology delineates climate effects into two broad categories – physical risk and transition risk – as follows:

- **Physical risk** encompasses the costs and other impacts arising from the physical effects of climate change on businesses' operations, workforce, markets, infrastructure, raw materials, and assets. Physical risks are further delineated as 'acute' (e.g. extreme weather-driven events such as wildfires, tropical cyclones, or floods) or 'chronic' (e.g. longer term shifts that may cause higher average temperatures or sea level rise).
- **Transition risk** encompasses the costs and other impacts associated with the transition to a lower carbon economy. It and can include policy changes, such as carbon taxes or cap and trade, new regulations on goods and services, reputational impacts, and shifts in market preferences, norms, and technologies.

Levels of physical and transition risk can vary dramatically between firms. Firms with facilities in Southeast Asia, the Middle East, and the Caribbean – areas with high exposures to climate hazards such as heat stress and tropical cyclones – will have relatively high physical risk. Firms in industrial sectors such as Coal, Oil & Gas, and Electricity Generation – which are affected by carbon transition policies – will have relatively high transition risk.

Although physical risk and transition risk methodologies are integrated in the EDF framework, we generate separate models because the inputs and drivers of physical and transition risk models differ. Transition risk requires analysis of a company's carbon footprint and fossil fuel reliance, as well as the complex economic impacts from government regulation, technological innovation, and global socioeconomic trends. Physical risk assessments rely largely on understanding the location of a company's physical assets and their exposure to climate hazards, which is largely informed by climate science modelling tools.

The first step to incorporating climate risk into any risk model is identifying plausible assumptions about the possible socioeconomic, policy, and technological paths that will result for the economic futures of different geographies and sectors. These economic futures will, in turn, result in different carbon emission paths, and ultimately, different contributions to increasing global temperatures.

Current best practice, influenced by both stress-testing conventions and climate science methods, is to isolate the continuous distribution of possible economic and climate futures into several representative climate scenarios. Each scenario represents a joint path of economic growth, emissions, and warming over a long period (typically, to the year 2100). By analysing the effects of climate under these scenarios, we can gain an understanding of the plausible impacts that global warming may have on individual risk profiles.

In this chapter, we present results using the representative scenarios from the Network for Greening the Financial System (NGFS) (NGFS 2020b); these are the default scenarios in the Climate-Adjusted EDF toolkit. The NGFS, a group of global central banks and financial regulators, has created these scenarios to serve as a basis for worldwide stress-testing regulation and financial oversight. The scenarios are the emerging standard for climate stress-testing and disclosure applications.

Figure 24.1 shows the NGFS's three standard climate scenarios – Orderly, Disorderly, Hot House – alongside the underlying carbon policy, inclusion of carbon removal technology, and Shared Socioeconomic Pathway (SSP). Shared Socioeconomic Pathways are used by climate scientists to describe plausible global developments, including sustainable development, regional rivalry, inequality, fossil-fueled development, and middle-of-the-road development. NGFS scenarios are based on SSP2, the so-called 'middle-of-the-road' scenario in which the world follows social, economic, and technogical paths not significantly different from historical patterns.

NGFS scenarios are built using several integrated assessment models (IAMs), which jointly estimate economic and climate consequences of the underlying carbon policy, technology growth, and socioeconomic trends exogenously assumed for each scenario. In the 'Orderly' scenario, a global carbon policy is implemented immediately, with a single global carbon price path employed to reach a 1.5°C end-of-century warming level. Carbon prices climb in a linear fashion

NGFS Representative Scenario	Carbon Policy	Carbon Removal Technology	Shared Socioeconomic Pathway
Orderly	Single global carbon policy path beginning in 2021, with goal to limit warming to **1.5°C** by 2100	Yes	SSP2
Disorderly	Single global carbon policy path beginning in 2030, with goal to limit warming to **2°C** by 2100	Limited	SSP2
Hot House	Current policy as of today	No	SSP2

Figure 24.1 NGFS Scenarios vis-à-vis Carbon Policy, Carbon Removal Technology, and Share Socioeconomic Pathways.

(this being estimated within the model as the least costly path), with a similarly orderly reduction in both emissions and temperature change. In the 'Disorderly' scenario, or late policy action, global carbon policy is not enacted until 2030. The neccesarily more aggressive increase in carbon prices to reach the desired end-of-century temperature target causes more extreme transition effects. Lastly, in the 'Hot House' scenario, no additional policy action is taken to reduce carbon emissions. This causes carbon prices to remain low, but emissions and temperature skyrocket with disastrous environmental and economic consequences. For the Hot House scenario, we also provide results based on a 95% upper-tail damage estimate ('Hot House 95P'), to understand worst-case scenario physical risk.

Figure 24.2 shows both the assumptions underlying the NGFS's three standard climate scenarios as well as the scenario-conditional forecasted paths of carbon prices, carbon dioxide-equivalent (CO_2-equivalent) emission rates, temperature change, and global physical damages.

For each climate scenario we select for analysis, we carry out several modelling steps to understand the financial and credit effects of the climate future

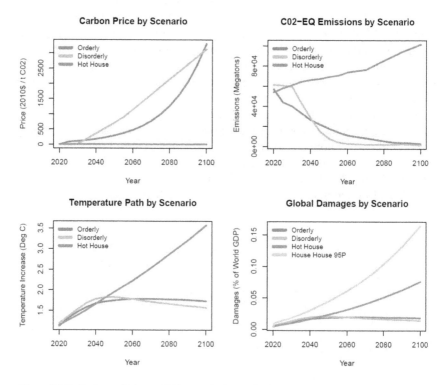

Figure 24.2 Carbon Prices, CO_2-equivalent Emissions, Temperature Paths, and Global Damage Estimates for NGFS Scenarios.
Source: Moody's Analytics.

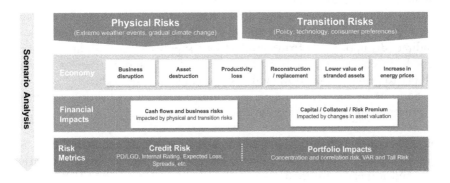

Figure 24.3 Process Diagram of Moody's Analytics' Climate-Adjusted Credit Impact
Analysis.
Source: Moody's Analytics.

in question (see Figure 24.3). First, we take the output from the NGFS scenarios, as well as additional climate data from Moody's ESG Solutions, to measure the magnitude of different 'raw' drivers of physical and transition risk. Next, we model the relationship between raw climate risk drivers and the economic environment at any point of time within a given climate scenario path. Third, we analyse how modelled economic environments affect the financial position and health of each firm operating therein. Finally, we identify the effect of climate change on a firm's finances and risk metrics over different time horizons.

The final step uses the Moody's Analytics Public Firm EDF model to quantify credit risk.[2] The model is a Merton-type structural model of credit risk.[3] Structural credit risk models are defined by explicit modelling of the total firm asset value (enterprise value) over time and by estimating the likelihood of a firm's asset value falling below a lower bound (the default point) within a certain time horizon. If the firm's predicted asset value does in fact fall below this default point, the firm is considered insolvent, and goes into default. Therefore, the likelihood of the firm asset value falling below the default point is also the probability of default.

In the next section, we look at the modelling features, inputs, and drivers for quantifying physical climate effects on corporate credit risk.

Modelling Physical Risk Credit Impact

To forecast the physical risks of climate change climate scientists have spent several decades building and refining sophisticated projections of greenhouse gas levels and associated rising temperatures under different emissions scenarios through 2100 and their influence on extreme weather events.

Moody's Analytics' climate-adjusted EDF methodology builds upon that research to forecast the effect of climate change on firms' financial health arising from climate-induced negative shocks on firms' asset values. Negative shocks can either occur through direct damage to a firm's physical assets (say, through an extreme weather event like a storm or flood), or through a more indirect disruption to a firm's productivity, supply chains or ability to sell its goods. In either case, the negative effect of climate and weather on a firm's ability to generate cash flows will reduce its market asset value.

Some of the characteristics of these climate-induced asset shocks which are captured in the methodology include:

- There is uncertainty about when damaging climate events and their associated asset shocks will occur, even within specific climate scenarios and at specific future dates.
- Different locations will have different exposure to damaging climate events, even for the same global temperature increase.
- The same damaging climate event has the potential to cause a different magnitude of asset depreciation to different firms, depending both on randomness and the firm's characteristics.

Figure 24.4 shows an example of climate change asset shocks within the EDF model. As stated above, the Public EDF framework estimates the firm's market asset value today (in this example, starting on 1 January) and the default point of asset value that triggers a firm's insolvency (a function of the firm's debt obligations). It shows possible paths that asset value might take over the relevant time horizon (in this example, a year). The firm's one-year probability of default (or EDF) can be considered the percentage of possible paths that fall below the default point in the year time frame.

To see how additional climate-induced asset shocks affect credit risk, consider an acute weather event that occurs with low probability but that causes a large depreciation of a firm's asset value. The weather event shown in the left chart occurs in late April during a potential future asset path (from the perspective of January 1), where there was little asset value change during the previous four months.

If the negative shock is big enough to reduce asset value below the default point (it is not in this example), the shock can directly cause firm insolvency. Even if the weather event does not immediately precipitate insolvency, however, the shock reduces the buffer between asset value and the default point. This reduction means that the normal asset volatility the firm experiences over the remainder of the year is more likely to push the firm into default. From the perspective of the start date (in this case, 1 January), the effect of the additional risk of marginal climate events is to increase the asset volatility of the firm within the year, increasing the probability of default. To the extent that the frequency of these negative shocks is predictable from the perspective of 1 January, they should be reflected in investor's valuation of the company. In this way, changing expectations of long-term shocks can cause shifts in short-term valuations of the company, leading to a second 'equity' pathway

a

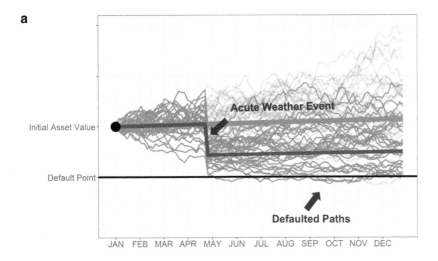

b

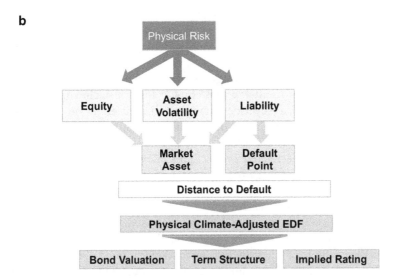

Figure 24.4 Effect of Physical Risk on EDF Value Drivers.
Source: Moody's Analytics.

between physical risk and market asset value. The third pathway, not shown directly in the example, comprises changes in the firm's liabilities (or capital structure) in response to or as a result of climate change.

By treating the effects of physical climate-related events as a series of negative shocks to the firm's asset valuation, the financial forecasting problem can be reduced to modelling the frequency and magnitude of these shocks. We achieve this process by leveraging several data and modelling sources:

- **Forecasts of global economic damage paths**: For a given scenario, an estimate of the global damages associated with physical climate risk (as a percentage of global GDP) can be derived from a combination of an IAM (which models the carbon emissions path associated with the scenario), a Global Circulation Model (which models the global temperature path resulting from the emissions path), and an Aggregated Damage Function (which forecasts global economic damages as a function of the temperature increase at any given time). Although we can run these models independently, the NGFS scenarios provide global damage estimates from an identical framework. We therefore use the NGFS estimates as a starting point.

- **Economic damage path forecasts associated with a firm's location**: Given a global damage forecast, different locations will have highly differential exposures to physical damage. To forecast these differences, we employ company risk scores from Moody's ESG Solutions which rank a firm's relative physical climate risk from 0 to 100 based on climate models, environmental datasets, and detailed data on the location of a firm's facilities and operations. The scores capture the firms' exposure to physical climate risk including floods, heat stress, hurricanes and typhoons, sea level rise, water stress, and wildfires. We calibrate these scores to forecast a firm's economic damage level for a given global damage level.

- **Converting economic damages to frequency and magnitude of asset shocks**: As a final step, we employ historical climate events to understand the typical severity of events and their effect on asset value. Because the Public Firm EDF model has been estimated for more than 30 years, we already have asset return measurements for firms affected by historical climate-related events. This allows us to convert between the predicted economic damages from a particular hazard type with a particular probability of occurrence and severity into a distribution of possible asset returns for each firm.

Figure 24.5 provides a summary of these modelling steps.

We use the example of Chevron Corporation, a leading American oil firm, to illustrate the output of the modelling framework. The most important output of the analysis from a credit risk perspective is the conditional probability of default (PD) term structures associated with each of the NGFS scenarios for a firm. In Figure 24.6, we show conditional annualised PD term structures on the left, compared to an unconditional baseline (not accounting for climate risk) term structure, and break out the increase from baseline in forward PD on the right panel. We additionally assume investors are not currently pricing in future physical damages, but then immediately begin to do so in the conditional scenarios.

For Chevron, a firm that has high physical damage exposure due to its facility locations in the Mexican Gulf and South America (which is

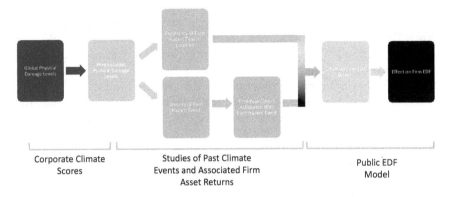

| Corporate Climate Scores | Studies of Past Climate Events and Associated Firm Asset Returns | Public EDF Model |

Figure 24.5 Physical Modelling from Global Damage Paths to EDF Metrics.
Source: Moody's Analytics.

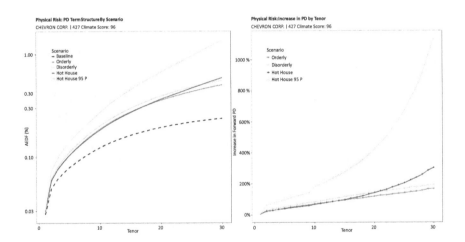

Figure 24.6 Example of Climate-Adjusted EDF Term Structures.
Source: Moody's Analytics.

reflected in a Moody's ESG Solutions physical climate risk score of 96), we see an immediate increase in risk as investors begin to price in future damage functions. Risk then further increases as more imminent physical damage causes additional volatility and further devaluation of the firm (Figure 24.5). The increases in PD in the conditional scenarios reflect highly material increases in risk for Chevron: the analysis suggests a one PD-implied rating notch increase at a one-year horizon, a two-to-three rating notch increase at a five-year horizon, and a two-to-four rating notch increase at a ten-year horizon.

Modelling the Credit Impact of Transition Risk

Modelling the mechanics of an economy in energy transition, particularly when that transition is occurring concurrently with a warming world, is a complex exercise. While the headline assumption of any transition scenario is a forecast of government policy (or lack thereof) over time, we must also make other key assumptions about population growth, productivity growth, and technology growth. Once we define a transition scenario, we model the effect of these assumptions on a cascade of linked economic drivers. These economic outcomes will affect the growth, competitiveness, and financial health of firms as they adapt to new risks and opportunities.

As with our physical risk methodology, our approach to measuring transition risk is to calculate its effects on the financial drivers of the Public Firm EDF model: equity paths, asset volatility, and liability/capital structure. Due to the complexity of the effects of transition risk on firms, however, it is necessary to go a step further and explicitly model the fundamentals driving the asset value process of the firm over time. The fundamentals that give a firm value are the discounted cash flows expected to be accrued by the firm over time. By modelling transition-adjusted cash flows, we can use properly discounted future earnings expectations to model transition-adjusted asset value processes. These asset value processes, in turn, dictate the expected paths of the Public Firm EDF drivers.

Figure 24.7 shows an example of the credit implications of such a shift in firm earnings expectations, once properly valued. From a current date of January 1, this example models a scenario where a new transition policy is announced mid-year. As is typical in climate change scenarios, the policy path is explicitly assumed, so the specific policy announcement happens with certainty on June 1. The certainty of the policy in our analysed (conditional) scenario does not mean, however, that investors within the scenario must at every point expect such a conditional path to occur. In this simplified example, investors do not anticipate the policy announcement, and on 1 June they account for the new information in their expected earnings forecasts and subsequent firm valuations.[4]

Since the policy announcement is certain, its effect on firm asset value affects all possible paths of asset volatility up to 1 June. In this example, the shock is proportional to the original asset values at that date). Note that for some paths where asset value has already depreciated due to normal business risk, this shock causes the firm to become insolvent (and thus default) immediately. Even in paths where the policy announcement does not immediately precipitate insolvency, the shock reduces the buffer between asset value and the default point, and the normal asset volatility the firm experiences over the remainder of the year is more likely to push the firm into default.[5]

The bold horizontal line in Figure 24.7 represents the unconditional path of expected firm asset value over the year, and the bold blue line represents the conditional path of firm asset value associated with the conditional

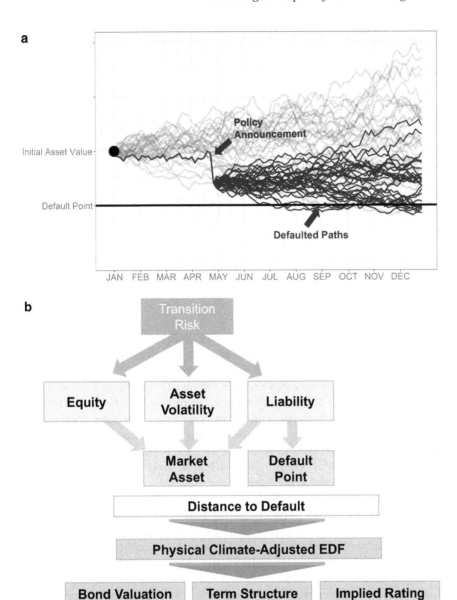

Figure 24.7 Effect of Transition Risk on EDF Driver.
Source: Moody's Analytics.

climate policy scenario. Note that although volatility surrounds this expected asset value path in both the conditional and unconditional paths, the firm's higher default risk in the policy scenario is driven by changes in expected

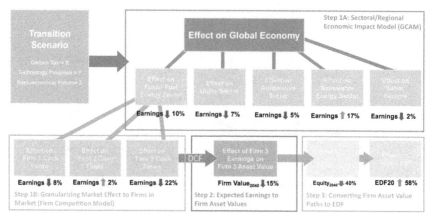

Note: All Values are Expository Only

Figure 24.8 Structure for Quantifying Effect of Transition Scenarios on Credit
    Metrics.
Source: Moody's Analytics.

asset value, not any change in asset volatility around this path. This outcome
occurs because the policy announcement is certain within the scenario, and
thus drives the firm's *expected* asset value path over time.

To understand how earnings are affected by the transition, it is necessary
to model a scenario's effect on competitive equilibria both between the production of different good types and on firms producing the same good within
each market. Figure 24.8 shows a more detailed look at how we move from a
transition scenario to earnings paths, the asset value process, and finally transition risk-adjusted EDF metrics (see, further, Watson et al., 2021).

The main steps in the process are:

- **Step 1A**: **Earnings projections on sectoral/regional level**: To understand the effect of the scenario on earnings in each sector/region combination, we leverage the General Change Assessment Model (GCAM).
  GCAM is distinctive among IAMs used by the NGFS to generate scenario pathways due to its highly detailed modelling of regions and industrial sectors, providing prices, production quantities, and itemised costs
  for over a thousand interlinked production technologies. These data enable us to calculate sectoral level earnings that account for technological growth and scenario-conditioned supply and demand shocks arising
  from each transition future.[6]
- **Step 1B**: **Earnings projections on a firm level**: To forecast earnings on a firm level, we augment the GCAM framework with a model
  of firm competition within each market. In the model, firms with
  potential differences in costs and non-price consumer preference set

profit-maximising output prices, leading to Nash Equilibrium market shares and earnings for each firm in the market. In addition to calibration on current market shares, the main driver of heterogeneity between firms are the emissions-intensity and energy-intensity of production. These different intensities, derived through a firm's Scope 1 and Scope 2 emissions that we sourced from Moody's ESG Solutions, cause relative costs to change over time as emissions and energy costs (typically) rise within a transition scenario. The result is a forecast of how a firm's market share and earnings will change over time because of its new level of economic competitiveness.

- **Step 2**: **Converting earnings projections to asset value projections**: We employ standard discounted cash flow techniques, while allowing flexibility to vary discount factors, if required.
- **Step 3**: **Measuring the effect of the scenario-conditional asset value process on EDF metrics**: The new asset value process links directly to the drivers of EDF, in turn giving a full-term structure of scenario-conditional expected default frequency metrics.

Figure 24.9 displays the climate scenario-conditional expected earnings paths, expected asset value paths, and EDF term structures for Chevron. The panel on the left shows the effect that the orderly and disorderly policies have on Chevron's expected earnings: the strong contraction in the oil and gas sector caused by the imposition of a carbon tax greater lowers Chevron's cash flows.

In the middle panel, we show the expected asset value path of Chevron within each scenario. As discussed above, these asset values are calculated by properly discounting the expected earnings paths of the firm, given earnings paths in each scenario, and investor expectations on the future probability of each scenario at each time horizon. For this example, we have assumed that the announcement (or non-announcement) of early policy in 2021 makes it certain to investors that the world is (or is not) on the Orderly scenario path. If early policy is not announced in 2021, it is still uncertain to investors whether the world is on the Disorderly or Hot House path until late policy is (or is not) announced in 2030. Note the effect of these paths on asset value: in the Orderly conditional scenario, asset values for Chevron drop off immediately upon announcement of the policy, even though largely differentiated expected earnings don't occur for for around 15 years. Since there is no delineation of the Disorderly and Hot House scenarios until the announcement (or non-annoucement) of late policy in 2030, the asset value of Chevron looks the same in those scenarios until that date, with a huge differentiation in Chevron's asset value occuring upon this announcement.

The effect of these large shifts in expected asset value of Chevron over time on Chevron's PD is shown in the right panel. As expected, these large differentiations in the expected efficacy of Chevron in these scenarios lead to large PD differences. The increase in risk is equivalent to a one-to-two notch deterioration in PD-implied rating in Orderly versus baseline in the first ten

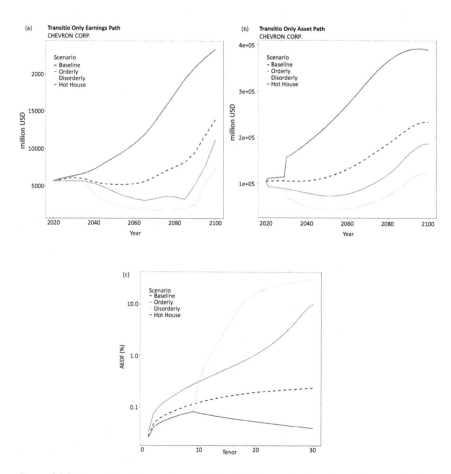

Figure 24.9 Transition Scenario-conditional Expected Earnings, Expected Asset
Value, and EDF Measures for Chevron Corporation.
Source: Moody's Analytics.

years, and to a five-notch higher risk in Disorderly following the announcement of late policy in 2031.

Implications of Climate Risk for Credit Investors

Using the methodology described above, we have analysed the effect of the
NGFS scenarios on credit risk for the over 40,000 global firms in the Public
EDF universe (representing nearly all publicly traded firms worldwide). This
exercise allows for examination of the magnitude and distribution of physical and transition credit risk across firms in different regions and industrial
sectors.

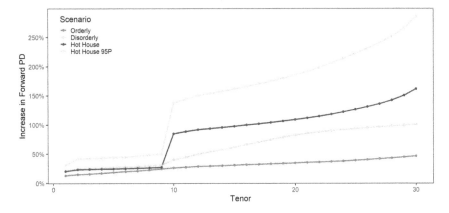

Figure 24.10 Increase in Physical Climate-Adjusted PD by Tenor and Scenario. Source: Moody's Analytics.

Figure 24.10 shows the average probability of default increase worldwide for firms when accounting for physical risk. Average risk increases gradually over time within each scenario, with increases initially modest but growing more material over time. The most extreme increases are for the most extreme physical damage scenarios: that is, both mean and tail outcomes in the 'no policy' Hot House scenario.

One of the key drivers of relative risk within each scenario and time horizon is the physical climate risk score, which represents relative exposure of firms to physical risk based on the location of their facilities and operations. Figure 24.11 shows the tight relationship between these physical climate risk scores and the increase in physical risk-adjusted PDs. An important takeaway from this graph is the non-linear relationship between the climate scores and the increase in PD. Since the Moody's ESG Solutions physical climate risk scores are roughly uniformly distributed, the majority of physical risk is concentrated in the highest quartile of exposed firms. This shows that practitioners must identify these most highly affected names and enhance their risk management practices to mitigate credit risk from this group of publicly traded firms.

Figure 24.12 shows physical climate risk exposure by country including floods, heat stress, hurricanes and typhoons, sea level rise, water stress, and wildfires, based on Moody's ESG Solutions data. One takeaway is that risk can be quite idiosyncratic to individual countries within a given region, based on factors such as vegetation, elevation, and distribution of population and economic activity. Even within countries, there is a a great deal of risk variation, which means that it is important to understand firms' risk based on the precise location of their facilities.

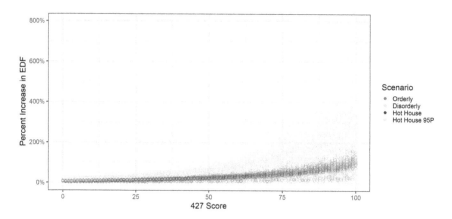

Figure 24.11 Relationship between PD Increase and Relative Physical Climate Risk Score.
Source: Moody's Analytics.

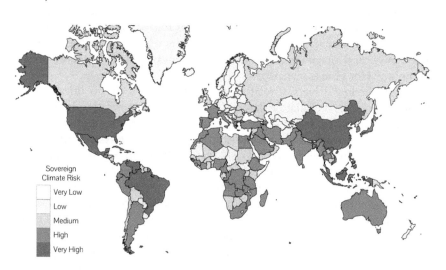

Figure 24.12 Physical Climate Risk Score by Country.
Source: Moody's ESG Solutions.

Figure 24.13 shows examples of facility locations, colored based on their heat stress scores by location. Clearly, it is not enough to categorize firm physical risk only by country: the specific location of firm facilities must be taken into account to understand the magnitude of credit exposure to physical climate change.

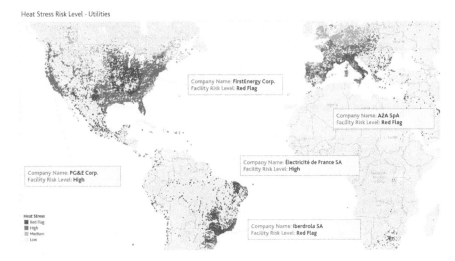

Figure 24.13 Physical Climate Risk Scores by Facility Location and Hazard.
Source: Moody's ESG Solutions.

The effects of transition-adjusted credit risk are even more concentrated than those of physical risk for a subset of firms. The NGFS scenarios model credit taxation policies redistributed back to taxpayers: this is a reasonable and generally assumed mechanism of carbon taxation in climate literature. As such, the general economywide costs of transition are relatively small compared to the redistributive effects of the growth and contraction of specific high-emission and -energy intensive industries.

Due to these economic dynamics, transition-adjusted credit risk is concentrated in carbon-exposed industries. Figure 24.14 shows average expected default frequency increases over different scenarios and time horizons for several highly exposed sectors. Note there are sectoral winners and losers in this redistribution of revenues and earnings. Fossil fuel industries, such as coal, natural gas, and oil production, are hit most heavily in carbon policy scenarios. This results from the presence of clear energy alternatives that become more economically competitive due to carbon taxation policy. Alternatively, transportation sectors remain largely resilient to the effects of carbon taxation despite being high emitting. This is a result of the presence of low-emitting technologies within these sectors, and the relative price inelastic demand for transportation due to the lack of a clear substitute product.

On the other hand, sectors such as electricity production benefit in terms of lower credit risk from the early and late policy scenarios, reflecting the substitution of energy demand to electricity. In general, a firm that benefits from a carbon policy scenario will be hurt by a no policy scenario: this is because the firm's current value is based on the expectation of some likelihood of each of these possible futures occurring. If, from the perspective of

	Sector Name	Mean of 1 Year PD Increase			Mean of 10 Year PD Increase		
		Early Policy	Late Policy	No Policy	Early Policy	Late Policy	No Policy
Strongly Energy-related Sectors	Coal to Liquid Refining	194.6%	-21.6%	-21.6%	2154.7%	2473.8%	-61.9%
	Gas Processing	194.6%	-21.6%	-21.6%	2154.7%	2473.8%	-61.9%
	Coal Extraction	353.5%	-36.5%	-36.5%	410.3%	882.0%	-76.0%
	Delivered Coal	131.9%	-16.7%	-16.7%	164.5%	161.9%	-40.7%
	Delivered Gas	449.4%	-4.1%	-4.1%	114.3%	434.4%	-50.2%
	Oil and Natural Gas Extraction	68.2%	-9.4%	-9.4%	55.4%	211.6%	-49.8%
	Oil Refining	16.6%	-5.6%	-5.6%	22.0%	120.3%	-39.0%
	Delivered Refined Liquids	14.2%	-4.2%	-4.2%	10.7%	44.4%	-20.2%
	Bicycle/Motorcycle Manufacturing	8.3%	-3.2%	-3.2%	6.8%	-2.8%	0.3%
	Automotive Manufacturing	7.4%	-3.3%	-3.3%	5.5%	2.4%	-6.3%
	Shipping	19.6%	-2.7%	-2.7%	4.3%	-0.1%	33.3%
	Rail Freight	3.6%	0.9%	0.9%	3.2%	-10.2%	37.8%
	Mass Passenger Transport	1.6%	0.6%	0.6%	1.1%	-4.0%	16.2%
	Aviation	0.1%	0.8%	0.8%	-2.1%	0.2%	8.8%
	Road Freight	-2.9%	1.6%	1.6%	-2.5%	-2.2%	9.0%
	Nuclear Fuel Generation	-6.9%	4.1%	4.1%	-6.9%	-39.5%	495.9%
	Fertilizer Production	-9.0%	11.6%	11.6%	-7.9%	-21.1%	149.7%
	Concrete Production	-17.0%	12.3%	12.3%	-11.8%	-55.1%	565.0%
	Electricity Production	-23.9%	18.5%	18.5%	-19.3%	-56.2%	1784.6%
	Delivered Electiricity (Industrial)	-23.9%	18.5%	18.5%	-19.3%	-56.2%	1784.6%
	Delivered Electiricity (Building)	-21.8%	19.2%	19.2%	-20.5%	-48.8%	1184.8%
	Delivered Electiricity (Transportation)	-25.5%	23.7%	23.7%	-25.2%	-58.7%	1690.3%

Figure 24.14 Mean Increase in Transition-Adjusted PD for Highly Exposed Sectors. Source: Moody's Analytics.

the firm, the less advantageous scenario occurs, the firm's valuation will be reduced to reflect this new reality.

Figure 24.15 shows mean PD increase and notching changes for a representative portfolio of large firms from these high transition exposed sectors. The average PD increase becomes very large for a portfolio with this construction; many firms have PD-implied rating deteriorations of three notches or more. Understanding the relationship between transition risk and credit risk for firms in these sectors can help investors identify which types of firms to pay close attention to when developing risk mitigation strategies. The different relationship between physical and transition risk on firms and sectors creates a complicated risk management landscape for investors, but also provides opportunities for balancing risk.

Conclusions

Across the finance system there is now widespread recognition that the world needs to limit greenhouse gas emissions or face severe impacts from climate change. Although government action will dictate the timeline for emission reductions by applying policy tools, financial institutions can proactively mitigate climate-related physical and transition risks within their holdings by applying quantitative and qualitative methods.

The effects of physical climate change and carbon transition on credit risk varies widely between different scenarios and different time horizons. To

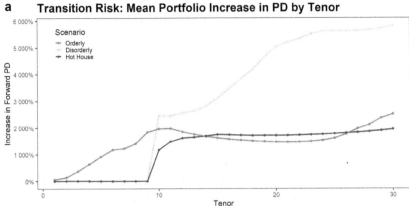

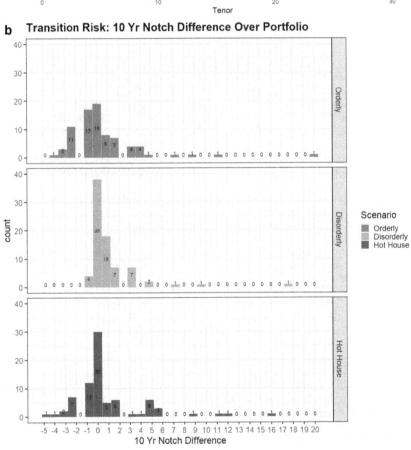

Figure 24.15 PD and Rating Notch Increase for Representative Global Portfolio in High Transition Exposed Sectors.

Source: Moody's Analytics.

complement this high variance, the majority of the increase in credit risks are concentrated in a relatively small subset of global firms. For financial institutions, this unven distribution of risk results in potential peril but also myriad opportunities.

Understanding the pattern of risks via scenario analysis and internal methodologies will enable financial institutions to realign their investments, identify potential opportunities such as mispriced risks or bonds, and anticipate the needs from issuers for more support as part of their own adaptation and transition away from fossil fuels. The heightened focus of investors, lenders, and regulators on the risks and opportunities from a warning world and a potential shift to a low-carbon economy mean that asset prices are likely to become increasingly more responsive to climate risks in the near future. This adds to the relevance of a systematic process that integrates climate and broader environment risks into financial risk management.

Notes

1 The views expressed in this chapter are those of the authors and are not necessarily the views of Moody's Analytics or Moody's ESG Solutions. It is also relevant to note that Moody's Analytics and Moody's ESG Solutions are separate groups from Moody's Investors Service (commonly referred to as Moody's).

2 The Public EDF model is a commercialised version of the KMV credit risk model. CreditEdge^{TM} is the product name for the Public Firm EDF model.

3 The Merton model is a widely used credit risk model deployed by analysts and investors to understand how capable a company is of meeting financial obligations, such as debt, and weighing the general possibility that credit default will occur.

4 Both current and future investor expectations on the relative likelihood of future climate outcomes have important implications on the firm's asset valuations and, ultimately, credit risk. Because of this, we explicitly model scenario-conditional investor expectation paths at different timesteps within each scenario. We provide default expectations at all time horizons for each conditional scenario, and we allow users to customize this themselves to understand the sensitivity of these expectation assumptions on outcomes.

5 In practice, a firm may be able to respond to a shock in asset value by de-leveraging, effectively lowering its default point in relation to its asset value (this is the 'liability' pathway discussed above). Because the relative ability or inclination of firms to achieve this is unclear, we typically assume that default point changes are uncorrelated with asset shocks. This assumption is conservative in that it results in the largest credit risk increases.

6 Clearly, calculating the expected economic and financial outcomes of climate drivers until the end of the century is a more speculative process than traditional stress-testing applications, which typically forecast far shorter time frames and economic environments with direct historical analogues. As such, it is important for practitioners to understand the assumptions underlying the modelling of these forecasts and to the test the sensitivity of the results obtained to these assumptions.

References

AON (2021), *Weather, Climate & Catastrophe Insight: 2020 Annual Report.* [online]. Available at: https://www.aon.com/global-weather-catastrophe-natural-disasters-costs-climate-change-2020-annual-report/index.html?utm_source=prnewswire&utm_medium=mediarelease&utm_campaign=natcat21 (Accessed 25 May 2021).

Watson, D., Edwards, J. and Cui, R. (2021), *Connecting ESG Assessments into the Credit Portfolio* (Moody's Analytics). [online]. Available at: https://ma.moodys.com/rs/961-KCJ-308/images/Moody%27s%20Analytics%20Webinar%20-%20Connecting%20ESG%20Assessments%20into%20the%C2%A0Credit%20Portfolio%20Chapter%201.pdf (Accessed 25 June 2021).

Intergovernmental Panel on Climate Change (IPCC) (2018), *Global Warming of 1.5°C. An IPCC Special Report on the Impacts of Global Warming of 1.5°C Above Pre-industrial Levels and Related Global Greenhouse Gas Emission Pathways, in the Context of Strengthening the Global Response to the Threat of Climate Change, Sustainable Development, and Efforts to Eradicate Poverty.* [online]. Available at: https://www.ipcc.ch/site/assets/uploads/sites/2/2019/06/SR15_Full_Report_High_Res.pdf (Accessed 25 May 2021).

Network for Greening the Financial System (NGFS) (2020a), *Overview of Environmental Risk Anaysis by Financial Institutions.* [online]. Available at: https://www.ngfs.net/sites/default/files/medias/documents/overview_of_environmental_risk_analysis_by_financial_institutions.pdf (Accessed 25 May 2021).

Network for Greening the Financial System (NGFS) (2020b), *NGFS Climate Scenarios for Central Banks and Supervisors.* [online]. Available at: https://www.ngfs.net/sites/default/files/medias/documents/820184_ngfs_scenarios_final_version_v6.pdf (Accessed 25 May 2021).

UN Environment Programme (2019), *Emissions Gap Report 2019.* [online]. Available at: https://wedocs.unep.org/bitstream/handle/20.500.11822/30797/EGR2019.pdf?sequence=1&isAllowed=y (Accessed 25 May 2021).

25 Fixed Income Markets and Responsible Investment

The Past, the Present and the Future

Rory Sullivan and Joshua Kendall

The investment management industry is facing rapid and potentially disruptive change. Sustainability (or environmental, social, and governance, or ESG, in industry jargon) issues have risen to the forefront of investment thinking, driven by regulation, by societal expectations, and by the need to support a socially and environmentally resilient economy. Investors have responded by making commitments to responsible investment, by taking explicit account of ESG issues in their investment processes, by encouraging the companies and other entities in which they invest to have high standards of social and environmental performance, and by supporting public policy action on issues such as climate change.

As we discussed in the introduction to this book, fixed income, despite its scale and importance, has often been overlooked in discussions around responsible investment or around the role that the capital markets might play in financing the low carbon transition or the UN Sustainable Development Goals (SDGs). In part this is because of the misguided perception that responsible investment is not relevant to fixed income, and in part because of the lack of a clear view on how the fixed income markets might be scaled to meaningfully support the delivery of global action on climate change and sustainability-related goals.

Addressing the Myths about Responsible Investment and Fixed Income

When we started discussing this book back in 2017, we observed that practitioners' views on responsible investment in fixed income were quite different to their views on responsible investment in other asset classes. In listed equities and property, to provide just two examples, responsible investment had shaken off its traditional association with ethical investment, and was widely recognised as an important and legitimate part of mainstream investment practice. Yet, in fixed income, responsible investment was still seen as an anomaly. Most investment managers addressed demands to act responsibly or to take account of ESG issues by pointing to their organisation's responsible investment policy, and by offering investment products that held green bonds

DOI: 10.4324/9781003055341-32

or that excluded controversial activities such as mining or coal-fired electricity generation. When we asked whether more could be done, we generally encountered the same arguments: the investment case was unclear, fixed income investors did not have the same formal rights as equity investors, and the business case for action was not obvious.

The evidence presented in this book – from major investors, from credit ratings agencies, and from investment consultants – suggests that many bond investors now routinely integrate ESG issues into their fixed income investment research and decision-making, engage with fixed income issuers, and collaborate with their industry peers to drive awareness and action on sustainability and fixed income.

Despite recent progress, four arguments – or, more accurately, myths – around why fixed income investors cannot act on ESG issues, persist: (a) bondholders cannot influence the practice and behaviour of issuers, (b) ESG issues are not financially material in bond markets, (c) focusing on ESG issues is incompatible with fiduciary duty, and (d) there is no business case for responsible investment in fixed income. We discuss each of these in more detail below.

Myth 1: Bondholders Cannot Influence the Practice and Behaviour of Issuers

Responsible investment really started in equity markets. Equity investors have formal rights as shareholders (for example, to vote shares and to attend annual general meetings). These rights have meant that stewardship (engagement and voting) has long been recognised as an important investment tool, allowing investors to appoint (and to remove) board directors, confirm remuneration policies, and approve strategic business changes. The fact that fixed income investors do not have similar formal rights has often been used to argue that bondholders lack influence. This argument has then been extended to argue that stewardship is much less relevant to fixed income investors.

The evidence in this book comprehensively refutes that argument. Fixed income investors can exert significant influence over companies and over other entities that look to raise capital through the debt markets. The reality is that many issuers have no choice but to come to the debt markets for capital, and this gives bondholders the opportunity to engage and influence. Company and issuer roadshows are increasingly used by bondholders as an opportunity to engage with senior management to interrogate their performance and to make calls for additional information or for changes in practice and performance. Bondholder influence is not confined to investment grade corporates, but is also being seen across the universe of fixed income markets, including in high yield, sovereigns, and asset-backed securities, to name but a few.

The mechanisms of influence are not confined to direct investor-issuer engagement. Two are particularly noteworthy. The first is that issuers recognise that measures to reduce risk (e.g. through improved social or environmental performance) may help to reduce their cost of capital. The second is that many fixed income investors are now active participants in collaborative networks that bring investors together to influence companies directly and indirectly. These investors are also often involved in setting market standards, such as better transparency in credit ratings, to help drive market standards that also influence wider market actors.

While the myth that fixed income investors cannot exert influence has been dispelled, there are still important barriers. These include: the weaknesses in the ESG-related disclosures provided by many issuers, the infrequency of engagement opportunities (in particular for issuers who only occasionally look to access the capital markets), and the lack of insight into who the other holders of an issuer's debt might be (which limits the potential for collaboration). There is also the practical reality that, in many fixed income sub-asset classes (sovereigns or mortgage-backed securities, for example), stewardship is still relatively nascent and further work is needed for the quality and scale of stewardship to reach the level now routinely seen in investment grade corporate markets.

Myth 2: ESG Issues Are Not Financially Material

Answering the question of whether ESG issues are financially material in fixed income can be addressed in several ways. The first is whether ESG issues are of sufficient scale to, at least occasionally, hamper an issuer's ability to repay a bond or to pay coupons when they are due. The answer to this is clearly that, at least in some cases, ESG issues may be financially material. However, this answer has often been qualified by reference to the likelihood of such an event occurring and the timeframe over which such an event might occur. Events that might happen at some distant point in the future (for bond investors, this has often been treated as beyond the lifetime of the bond issue in question) have tended to be ignored or significantly downplayed. Such an approach might be justified for a single, relatively short duration bond. However, in practice, many bonds are refinanced and many issuers need to return to the bond markets, which means that the time horizon of fixed income investors is significantly extended. Of course, investors may choose to trade or sell bonds that are exposed to ESG risks, but the increase in buy and hold strategies (allowing investors to capture the liquidity premium) and the fact that more investors are thinking about future risks mean that investors cannot simply ignore ESG risks or assume that other investors will ignore these risks.

For many of the investors profiled in this book, ESG integration is seen as a strategy that can create value at the portfolio level, allowing clear outperformance over a range of timeframes. Depending on how sustainability issues are analysed, ESG integration can allow investors to avoid or reduce their exposure to companies or issuers that do not manage ESG issues effectively or their exposure to assets that are exposed to systemic risks (e.g. to the physical impacts of climate change).

Investors' ability to benefit from analysis of ESG issues has been facilitated by the improving depth and breadth of ESG ratings and assessments, and the much-reduced costs of accessing ESG data and analysis. As with active ownership, there are challenges, in particular with the ability to access high quality data. While investment grade issuers and publicly listed high yield issuers often provide robust, investment-useful information on ESG-related risks and opportunities, there are still significant data gaps in high yield and emerging markets, although these gaps are starting to be addressed through investor pressure and policy action (e.g. mandatory disclosure requirements). There are also corners of the fixed income market – asset-based securities, and municipal markets are two examples – where much more needs to be done.

Myth 3: Focusing on ESG Issues Is Incompatible with Fiduciary Duty

There is a long-standing debate about whether a focus on ESG issues (investment integration, active ownership, public policy engagement) might represent a breach of the fiduciary and other duties owed by investors to their clients and beneficiaries. While the debate is less polarised than it was, the belief that focusing on ESG issues harms investment returns remains widespread (in particular in North America). This belief is often reinforced by the belief that portfolio diversification is an effective risk mitigation strategy (although the systemic risks presented by climate change challenge that view).

This book points to three compelling arguments why fiduciary duty requires investors to incorporate ESG issues into their investment analysis and decision-making processes, to encourage high standards of ESG performance in the companies or other entities in which they invest; to understand and incorporate beneficiaries' and savers' sustainability-related preferences; and to support the stability and resilience of the financial system. These reasons are that (Sullivan et. al, 2019):

1   ESG incorporation is an investment norm: As the examples and data presented in this book show, ESG integration and stewardship are now common practice. Furthermore, any conception of due skill, care, and diligence requires investors both to consider all relevant factors (including sustainability-related factors) and to manage them. Turning to client preferences, understanding, and taking account of client sustainability preferences is central to aligning with a client's interest. The interests of beneficiaries frequently extend decades into the future, requiring a focus on broad sustainability issues within investment processes.

2   ESG issues are financially material: This is not just about the avoidance of downside risk, which is the traditional focus of fixed income investors. This book also presents multiple examples of investors benefitting from the opportunities presented by sustainability themes through, for example, the demand for capital to support sustainability objectives and the potential 'greenium' from green and sustainability-related investments.

3   Policy and regulatory frameworks are changing to require ESG incorporation: There are now over 700 hard and soft-law policy revisions, across some 500 policy instruments, that support, encourage, or require investors to consider long-term value drivers, including ESG issues. Many of these policies explicitly state that ESG incorporation and active ownership are part of the duties that investors owe to their clients and their beneficiaries. The converse is that investors that fail to incorporate ESG issues may be failing in their fiduciary duties and are at risk of facing legal challenge in some jurisdictions. These general pressures for action are reinforced by specific expectations in relation to fixed income, as measures such as reporting on fixed income stewardship activities and green bond issuance programmes become more common.

Myth 4: There Is No Business Case for Responsible Investment in Fixed Income

Many market commentators have dismissed the market for responsible investment in fixed income, describing it as specialist niche (to be met with products such as green bonds) or as a soft mainstream market with limited longevity. Yet, the evidence is that the opposite is the case; market and client demand for responsible investment is strong, dependable, and growing. For example, as many of the contributors to this book attest, large asset owners routinely apply a responsible investment lens to their investing processes and in their monitoring of third-party managers. These asset owners are pressing investment managers to take account of ESG factors in their investment decision-making, to engage with the companies and other entities in which they invest and to demonstrate the investment and social and environmental benefits that result from these activities. These expectations are being integrated into manager selection, appointment, and monitoring processes. This pressure is reinforced by the emphasis being placed by investment consultants – who effectively act as gatekeepers to many institutional assets – on responsible investment. The large investment consultants now routinely evaluate the competence of fixed income managers in appraising sustainability information and incorporate this evaluation into their recommendations to clients. Investment managers recognise that their ability to achieve and retain 'buy' recommendations, means that ESG and responsible investment need to be integral parts of their investment practices and processes.

Building a Fixed Income Investment Market that Is Fit for the Future

Despite the progress that has been made, we are a very long way from having a financial system that can be considered sustainable. To take just one example, annual climate finance flows into adaptation and mitigation activities are around US$500–600 billion dollars per annum. While this is a large number, it is estimated that the investment required to achieve a low-carbon economy and keep global temperature rise to 1.5°C above pre-industrial levels is between US$1.6 and 3.8 trillion annually between now and 2050 (Climate Policy Initiative, 2020). This gap in investment is compounded by the huge amounts of capital being invested in fossil fuel-related activities (coal mining, oil and gas production and distribution, fossil fuel power generation); the Climate Policy Initiative estimates that, in the period 2015 to 2018, annual global investment in these areas was consistently three to four times higher than investments in renewable energy (Climate Policy Initiative, 2020). A similar picture emerges when we look at areas such as water and waste management and biodiversity conservation; the level of investment is not only significantly less than what is needed, but capital is often flowing into areas and activities that are likely to be damaging to society and to the natural environment.

Addressing this disconnect between where capital is invested and where it needs to be invested is the great policy – and investment – question of our time. If policymakers and investors cannot reorient capital flows, we are likely to cause irreparable harm to our society and to the planet.

We do not pretend to have all, or even a fraction, of the answers. However, the data, evidence and case studies presented in this book do provide many insights into how fixed income investors and the wider investment system might catalyse and accelerate change to deliver a more sustainable economy. We synthesise these insights into four recommendations.

Recommendation 1: Recognise that the Role of Investors is to Invest

This sounds obvious but it goes to the heart of discussions around responsible investment. The case for fixed income investors to take account of sustainability-related information is clear and, as we have discussed, this requires them to consider the implications of ESG factors over all time periods. However, the point we want to emphasie here is that the core job of fixed income investors is to deliver the returns sought by their clients. These investors will tend not to invest in situations where they cannot make reasonable risk-adjusted returns. It is striking how often this is forgotten in discussions around sustainability, or how often policymakers expect investors to invest in ways that deliver sustainability outcomes even when the fundamental economics of the investment do not work.

There is an important corollary to this point which is that if fixed income investors are expected to scale up their investments in sustainable activities, they need to be appropriately incentivised. The bond markets are structured to price sustainability information and amending this primary objective to force other outcomes will impact the fundamental purpose and practices of the fixed income investor to efficiently allocate capital. Bondholders are aware of the need to shift capital at scale to deliver sustainability outcomes, and are well placed to do so. However, in far too many cases (as we see with the example of climate change) the available incentives are simply not sufficient to catalyse this change.

Recommendation 2: Address the Market Failures in Fixed Income Markets

The fixed income markets do not function effectively when it comes to sustainability-related factors. Many of the reasons are classic market failures, including:

- Principal-agent problems, where asset managers do not act in the long-term interests of their asset owner clients, often because they focus on short-term rather than long-term drivers of business value. Principal-agent misalignments are also prevalent in fixed income markets where issuers make decisions which are not in the long-term interests of the entities that they are responsible for.
- Bounded rationality, where investors fail to consider the full range of factors that are relevant to their decisions. A particular issue in sustainability is the emphasis on short-term performance, and a corresponding lack of attention to longer-term drivers of business or investment value. In bond markets, time horizons tend to be short, often reflecting the credit rating agencies' methodologies.
- Information asymmetries, where investors do not have the information that they need. In fixed income, much of this relates to the lack of information about the performance of issuers (e.g. in emerging markets, in structured finance), and the lack of information about how investment managers are taking account of these issues in their investment decision-making and in the composition of their portfolios.

As this book shows, while they remain prevalent, many of these market failures are being corrected. For example, the significant improvements in the quality and quantity of sustainability-related data have enabled investors to integrate sustainability-related considerations into their research and decision-making processes. These improvements have been driven by a range of factors, including investor demand, formal disclosure regulations, and voluntary sustainability disclosures.

Another area of progress has been the general strengthening of oversight through the investment chain. A recurring theme through many of the chapters is the growth in asset owner interest in responsible investment, and how this is cascading through the investment system through to investment managers, to companies and other issuers, and to service providers (e.g. credit rating agencies explicitly accounting for sustainability-related issues in their issuer ratings, and investment consultants explicitly analysing how effectively fixed income investment managers account for sustainability-related issues in their investment practices and processes). These changes will reinforce the pressures for investors to strengthen their focus on ESG issues.

Recommendation 3: Support Innovation

One of the most striking findings from this book is how quickly new sustainability-related practices and ideas have been adopted by the wider investment market. Examples include the growth in green, social and sustainability bonds, the development of innovative approaches to engagement, and the use of a wide range of sustainability-related metrics in investment decision-making. This is well illustrated by the rise of the impact bond market which has helped some investors to, at least in part, move away from a traditional risk management approach towards a more outcome-led sustainability approach. Impact bond markets also provide important new pools of capital that can support the transition to a low-carbon, sustainable economy, and offer routes for bond issuers to embed sustainability outcomes more explicitly. The breadth of issuance – corporates, sovereigns, municipals, and structured debt – shows the opportunity available to issuers to align their financing and sustainability programmes.

Recommendation 4: Encourage New and Different Actors to Get Involved

A sustainable financial system will not be delivered through a single transformative initiative. Rather, multiple actors have important roles to play, and many of these actors already play a role. To provide just one example in fixed income markets: multilateral development banks have been hugely influential in catalysing and supporting the development of innovative segments such as green bonds. Other actors – credit rating agencies, investment consultants, treasury departments as well as regulators, asset owners, and asset managers – have also played important roles in driving changes such as improved disclosures, new standards and innovative products.

Closing Reflections

We are at the point where there is a critical mass of sustainability expertise within investment firms, credit rating agencies, investment consultants, and the banking sector. There is a body of experience on how to integrate sustainability-related considerations into investment processes, on how to invest in line with sustainability goals, and on how investors might – individually and collectively – positively influence other actors in the investment system.

We are no longer dealing with the question of how we build awareness and knowledge, but of how investors and their agents scale up and accelerate action. It is clear that bond markets can respond to demands to scale up their responsible investment-related efforts and, subject to the right incentives being in place, to increase the flow of capital to sustainability-related areas. The challenge now is to convert this into real and sustained action, which delivers the sustainable economy of the future.

References

Climate Policy Initiative (2020), *Global Landscape of Climate Finance 2019.* [online]. Available at: https://www.climatepolicyinitiative.org/publication/global-landscape-of-climate-finance-2019/ (Accessed 12 July 2021).

Sullivan, R., Martindale, W., Feller, E., Pirovska, M. & Elliott, R. (2019), *Fiduciary Duty in the 21st Century: Final Report* (The Generation Foundation, PRI and UNEP FI, London).

Index

Note: **Bold** page numbers refer to tables; *italic* page numbers refer to figures and page numbers followed by "n" denote endnotes.

ADB *see* Asian Development Bank (ADB)
AfDB *see* African Development Bank (AfDB)
African Development Bank (AfDB) 292, 306; green bonds 283
Agenda for Sustainable Development (2030) 70
Allianz 80
Apple Inc. 224; bonds 10, *10*; credit default swaps *29*, 30; credit quality 29; credit rating 40–42; credit spreads 26, 27
ASEAN (Association of Southeast Asian Nations) 287, 311, **312**
Asian Development Bank (ADB) 306; green bonds 283
Australia: Sustainable Finance Initiative 449
Aviva 450

Bank of America: credit structural shifts 188; green bond 283
Bank of Communications, green bond 283
Bank of England, interest rates 19
Bloomberg Barclays Aggregate Bond Index 285
Bloomberg Barclays Global Aggregate Index 222, 370
Bloomberg Barclays MSCI Global Corporate Sustainability Index 377–378
Bloomberg Barclays MSCI Green Bond Index 429
Bloomberg Barclays MSCI Sustainability Indexes 377
Bloomberg Barclays MSCI US Aggregate ESG Focus Index 437

BlueBay Asset Management 96, 98, 112; sovereign issuer ESG output metrics 110, **111**
BPCE Green Covered Bond 326–327
BRAVO Residential Funding Trust 2019–2022 183–184
Brazil: ESG factors in sovereign debt investing 102, 104, *104*; inflation-linked bond markets 18; Liberum Ratings 80
Breckinridge Capital Advisors (Breckinridge) 233–238, 246, 247
BRF 293

CA100+ *see* Climate Action 100+ (CA100+)
Calvert Investment Management 158
Canada Expert Panel on Sustainable Finance 459
Capital Asset Pricing Model (CAPM) 63
Carbon Delta 450
Carbon Disclosure Project (CDP) 89, 193
CBI *see* Climate Bonds Initiative (CBI)
CBOE Volatility Index (VIX) 109, 110, 113n5, 114n8
CCOO 80
CDP *see* Carbon Disclosure Project (CDP)
CDSB *see* Climate Disclosure Standards Board (CDSB)
Ceres 237
CFA Institute Research Foundation 223
Chevron 472–473
Chile: credit relevance of social issues 192
China: China Securities Regulatory Commission 289–290, 459; Green Bond Catalogue 312; green

finance 289–290; growth of 134;
National Association of Financial
Market Institutional Investors 290;
National Development and Reform
Commission 289, 290, 459; People's
Bank of China 289, 459
China Chengxin International Credit
Rating 80
Church of Sweden 80
CICERO 276, 277, 292
Citi 224
Climate Action 100+ (CA100+) 87, 328
Climate Bonds European Green Bond
Investor Survey 291
Climate Bonds Green Bond Database 290
Climate Bonds Initiative (CBI) 4, 266,
277, 279, 282, 312, 328; climate-
aligned debt market, size of 282;
Climate Bonds Taxonomy 289–291;
Climate Resilience Principles 293;
Financing Credible Transitions 280;
Green Bond Principles 76, 78, 255,
266, 276, 279, 303; Climate Bonds
Investor Survey 284
Climate Bond Standard 76, 78, 277
Climate Disclosure Standards Board
(CDSB) 347
Climate Policy Initiative 1
Climate Transition Finance Handbook
280, 411
Commonwealth of Massachusetts 284
COP 21 306
CoreCivic 189
Credit Agricole, green bond 283

Daimler 292
Deutsche Asset Management 450
Do No Significant Harm
(DNSH) 457, 459

EBRD *see* European Bank for
Reconstruction and Development
(EBRD)
EIB *see* European Investment Bank (EIB)
ENEL 32, 90
Environmental Defense Fund 162
Environmental Protection Agency 248
E.ON 332
Equifax 228; bond spreads movement
228–230, *229, 230*
ESMA *see* European Securities and
Markets Authority (ESMA)
Etihad 281

EU *see* European Union (EU)
European Bank for Reconstruction and
Development (EBRD) 306
European Central Bank: bond-buying
programme 211; net asset purchases 21;
refinancing operations rate 19
European Commission 191, 451; Climate
Bond Standard 76, 78, 277
European Green Deal 121, 300
European Investment Bank (EIB) 4,
298–314; benchmark bond 300–301;
Board of Directors 299; Climate
Awareness Bond Impact Report 307;
Climate Bank Roadmap 300, 313;
external reviews 308; financial market
impact 309–311, *310*; green bond
issuance 301–303, **302, 307**; green
bonds 283; impact reporting 306–307,
307; lending/financing activities 299;
management of proceeds 305–306;
project evaluation and selection criteria
304–305; regulation 311–313; use-of-
proceeds framework 303–304, 309
European Securities and Markets
Authority (ESMA) 116, 460–461
European Union (EU) 71, 121, 286–287,
401; Action Plan on Financing
Sustainable Growth 289, 309;
Adaptation Strategy 300; Commission
412; Council 304; covered bonds
53; Emissions Trading Scheme 198,
199, 301; ESG regulation 191–192;
Green Bond Regulation 412; Green
Bond Standard 313, 411, 412, 459;
Guidelines for Establishing a Green
Financial System 191; High-Level
Expert Group 312; Low Carbon
Markets Regulation 191; Non-
Financial Reporting Directive 89,
191, 456; SURE social bond issuance
programme 287; Sustainability
Taxonomy 305; Sustainable Finance
Disclosure Regulation 454; Sustainable
Finance Disclosures Regulation 455;
taxonomy environmental objectives
457; Taxonomy for Climate Change
Mitigation and Climate Change
Adaptation 412; Taxonomy of
Sustainable Activities 293, 312–313,
318, 412, 453–454, 457; Technical
Expert Group on Sustainable Finance
309, 312, 313, 342n3, 411–412
Eurosif 162

Eurozone, interest rates 21
Extractive Industries Transparency
Initiative 198

Federal Home Loan Mortgage
Corporation (Freddie Mac) 245
Federal National Mortgage Association
(Fannie Mae) 245, 288; 285; Green
Rewards programme 281
Federal Reserve 19, 21, 113; climate
mitigation policies 121; federal funds
rates 110, 113n5; quantity of assets,
reduction of 21; target rate for Federal
Funds 19
Financial Stability Board (FSB) 453
Fingrid 292
Fitch Ratings (Fitch) 4, 80, 177, 194;
climate policies 190–191; ESG Bank
survey 189; ESG general issue risk
categories **179**; ESG Relevance Scores
187–189, **189**, 192
France: Article 29 of the French law
on Energy and Climate 328; Article
173 of the French Energy Transition
Law 328; inflation-linked bond
markets 18; National Low Carbon
Strategy 327; social harmony and
labour 125–126
FSB *see* Financial Stability Board (FSB)
FTSE4Good Environmental Leaders
Europe 40, 301

GBP *see* Green Bond Principles (GBP)
GBS *see* Green Bond Standard (GBS)
GCN Wind Energy 288
Germany: Climate Protection Law 401;
Federal Ministry for the Environment,
Nature Conservation and Nuclear
Safety 409
Global Impact Investing Network
(GIIN): impact investing 254, 256, 265;
Investor council 262; IRIS metrics 255
Global Industry Classification Standard
(GICS®) 364
Global Investment Manager Database
(GIMD™) 387, 397
Global Reporting Initiative (GRI) 89,
193, 456
Global Sustainable Investment Alliance
(GSIA) 161
Goldman Sachs Asset Management 80
Governance and Accountability
Institute 237

Government National Mortgage
Association (Ginnie Mae) 245
Green Bond Oversight Committee 422
Green Bond Principles (GBP) 76, 78,
255, 266, 276, 279, 303, 304, 309,
317, 328, 329, 342n4, 378, 410, 421;
Working Group on Impact Reporting
306, 410
Green Bonds Catalogue 459
Green Bond Standard (GBS) 313
Green Loan Principles 76, 276
GRI *see* Global Reporting Initiative (GRI)
GSIA *see* Global Sustainable Investment
Alliance (GSIA)

'Harmonized Framework for Impact
Reporting' 411
HCM *see* human capital management
(HCM)
High-Level Expert Group
(HLEG) 451, 460
HIPSO framework 255
HLEG *see* High-Level Expert Group
(HLEG)
HSBC 425; Global Asset Management 5,
417, 421, 426n1; Socially Responsible
Investment Fund 426n1

Iberdrola 282, 332, 423
IBRD *see* International Bank for
Reconstruction and Development
(IBRD)
ICMA *see* International Capital Market
Association (ICMA)
IDB *see* Inter-American Development
Bank (IDB)
IFC *see* International Finance
Corporation (IFC)
IFRS Foundation 347, 456
IIRC *see* International Integrated
Reporting Council (IIRC)
IMF *see* International Monetary
Fund (IMF)
Indonesia: capital city, relocating 119–121
Insight Investment 197–198; Landmine
Checklist 198–199, **199**; *Putting
Principles into Practice* 198; qualitative
and quantitative process methods
201–207; stewardship 200–201
Institutional Investors Group on Climate
Change 198, 328
Inter-American Development Bank
(IDB) 306

International Bank for Reconstruction
and Development (IBRD) 306
International Capital Market Association
(ICMA) 277, 308, 309, 317; Climate
Transition Finance Handbook 280;
Green Bonds Principles 77–78, 276,
279, 329, 421; Guidelines for External
Reviewers 321; Social Bond Guidance
278–279; Social Bond Principles 278,
279, 325, 329; Sustainability Bond
Guidelines 279
International Finance Corporation (IFC)
283, 310
International Integrated Reporting
Council (IIRC) 193
International Labour Organisation:
Declaration on Fundamental
Principles and Rights at Work 377
International Monetary Fund (IMF) 84
International Sustainability Standards
Board (ISSB) 347
ISAE3000 277
Islamic Development Bank 281
ISSB *see* International Sustainability
Standards Board (ISSB)
Italy, inflation-linked bond markets 18
iTraxx Europe Investment Grade
index 30

Japan: ageing population dynamics
124–125; green bond guidelines
and taxonomy 76; interest rates 21;
Japan Credit Rating Agency 277;
Japan Housing Finance Agency 285;
Japan Railway Construction 285; life
insurance companies 330; Ministry
of the Environment of Japan 330;
Transport and Technology Agency 285
Jensen's alpha 63
John Deere 224
J.P. Morgan EMBI Global (EMBIG)
Index 113n5, 114n5

KBN 285
KBRA *see* Kroll Bond Rating Agency
(KBRA)
Kemble Water Finance Limited (Kemble):
Rating Watch 182–183
KfW 4, 283; about 400–401; contribution
to SDGs in 2020 **402**; engagement 406;
ESG integration 404–405; exclusion
criteria 405–406, **405–406**; green
bond investments, minimum eligibility
criteria for 409; green bond market,

support for 407–412; green bond
market harmonisation, promoting
409–410; green bond portfolio 409;
green bond principles 410–411; green
bonds issued by 407–409, **408**; policy
alignment 401–402; sustainability
at 400–403; sustainable investment
at 404–406; as transformative
promotional bank 402–403;
'tranSForm' project 403
Klabin 292
KommuneKredit 285
Kommuninvest 285
Kraft Heinz 40
Kroll Bond Rating Agency (KBRA) 4,
116–117, 116–117; credit risk 117–119;
ESG risk management, evaluation of
121; governance indicators in public
finance analysis 130; sovereign and public
finance credit analysis 124
Kyoto Protocol (1997): Clean
Development Mechanism of 258

Latin America, pulp and paper companies
189–190
Legal & General Investment
Management 80
LG Chem 282
Liberum Ratings 80
LIBOR rates 36n1
LMA *see* Loan Market Association
(LMA)
Loan Market Association (LMA): Green
Loan Principles 276; Sustainability-
Linked Loan Principles 279
London Stock Exchange 11
Los Angeles (LA) 123; Green New Deal
Sustainable City pLAn 122
Low Carbon Markets Regulation 191
Lower Manhattan Climate Resilience
Study 122–123

Macaulay duration 22
Macroeconomic Outlooks, ESG risk
assessment in 134–135
Marfrig 293
Marks & Spencer 40
McKinsey 7-S framework 47
Mercer Wealth (Mercer) 384; Analytics
for Climate Transition tool 387;
consultants in fixed income, role of
384–386; ESG Rating Scale *389*;
Four-Factor Manager Research
Framework 388, *388*, 392; Global

Investment Manager Database
(GIMD™)387; Investments 4; rating
investment strategies 387–396;
Responsible Investment Pathway 386,
386; sustainable investment beliefs *385*
Millicom 292
Mitsui O.S.K Lines 292
Moody's Investor Services 10, 41–42,
46, 80; alphanumeric scale for the
preliminary issuer rating 49; Analytics'
Public Firm Expected Default
Frequency (EDF)™ model 465, 466,
469; Climate-Adjusted Credit Impact
Analysis *469;* climate risk for credit
investors, implications of 478–482,
479–483; credit impact of transition
risk, modelling 474–478, *475, 476,
478;* physical risk credit impact,
modelling 469–473, *471, 473;* scenario
methodology overview 466–469,
467–469
Morningstar 427, 445n1; Morningstar
Historical Portfolio Sustainability Score
443; Morningstar Portfolio Sustainability
Score 442; Morningstar Sustainability
Rating 443–444, *443, 444*
MSCI Emerging Markets Index 374
MSCI ESG Ratings 422; across asset
classes 370–375, *371;* construction
366–367; corporate credit spreads
379–381, **380;** corporate entity
mapping 368; data 364–365; emerging
market and sovereign ratings 373–375,
375; ESG Controversies Score 377;
ESG integration indexes 376; ESG
Leaders Indexes 376; fixed income
indexes 376–379; Government
Ratings 370, *370;* investment grade
and high yield 371–373, *372, 373;*
impact investing indexes 378–379;
methodology 363–370, *364;* risks and
opportunities 365–366, *366;* sovereign
issuers credit spreads 381–382, *381;*
sovereigns 368–370; values-based
investing indexes 376–378, *377, 378*
MSCI ESG Research 4, 46; ESG ratings
219, 350; Fixed Income Factor Model
64; Human Capital Theme Scores
231n2
MuniFin 285

National Grid 292
Nationally Recognized Statistical Rating
Organization (NRSRO) 116

Natixis 4, 324, 325; CIB Research 316;
Natixis Green 316
NatWest Markets 4
Nedbank, green bond 283
Network for Greening the Financial
System (NGFS) 79, 135, 453, *467,*
467–469
Net Zero Asset Owner Alliance 328
New York City (NYC) 123; OneNYC
2050 122
New York Metropolitan Transport
Authority 284, 289
New York State: Erie County Fiscal
Stability Authority 129; Fiscal
Stability Authority 129; Fiscal Stress
Monitoring System 129; State
Comptroller 129
NFRD *see* Non-Financial Reporting
Directive (NFRD)
NGFS *see* Network for Greening the
Financial System (NGFS)
Nippon Yusen Kaisha 292
Nissen Kaiun 292
Non-Financial Reporting Directive
(NFRD) 191, 456, **467**
Nordic Credit Rating 80; sovereign
wealth fund 433
Nordic Investment Bank (NIB) 292:
green bond 283
Norway: Council on Ethics 127, 128;
Government Pension Fund Global
(GPFG) 127, 128; Norges Bank 127,
128; sovereign wealth fund 127–128
NRSRO *see* Nationally Recognized
Statistical Rating Organization
(NRSRO)
NYC *see* New York City (NYC)

OECD 126; Development Assistance
Committee 419; Guidelines on
Multinational Enterprises 457; on
prime working age 131n2
Ontario Pension Benefits Act (2016) 453
Operating Principles for Impact
Management (OPIM) 253, 255,
256, 262
Ørsted 282

Pacific Gas & Electric 225–226
Paris Agreement on Climate Change
(2015) 70, 87, 122, 135, 299, 309, 327,
351, 400, 401
Pfandbriefe 437
Pictet Asset Management 4

PIMCO 3, 80, 152n1; engaging with sovereigns 141–143; environmental scoring for sovereigns 140–141, *140*; ESG in sovereign investing 144–148, *145*; ESG risk factors in credit research, evaluation of 136; municipality ESG score, SDG factors in 147, **148**; sovereign debt performance 148–151, *149*; sovereign ESG framework 133–134, **137**, *138*, 152n2, 152n3, 152n4; sovereign issuers, evaluation ESG risks in 136–138
Porsche 289, 292
Porter's Five Forces 47
Principles for Responsible Investment (PRI) 2, 3, 5, 68–70, **69**, 88, 96, 163, 172, 190, 191, 198, 253, 255, 328, 385, 404, 406, 477; active ownership 161; annual investor reporting framework 452; effective investor engagement on public policy 452; Emerging Markets Investor Alliance 142; ESG in Credit Risk and Ratings Initiative 79–83, *83*; integration 78–79, *79*; screening 76–77; signatory base *70*; signatory practices 76–79; Sovereign Working Group 142; Statement on ESG in Credit Ratings 117; thematic investing 77–78, *78*; Timeliness 171
Prussia, German Pfandbrief system 53

Qualcomm Inc. 372

Real Economy Green Impact Opportunities (REGIO)419–421; green bond fund 417
Red Electrica 292
Refinitiv 46
REGIO *see* Real Economy Green Impact Opportunities (REGIO)
Reprisk 422
Royal Bank of Canada 96

Samsung Electronics Co., Ltd.: credit quality 30
SASB *see* Sustainability Accounting Standards Board (SASB)
Saudi Arabia: credit relevance of social issues 193
SBP *see* Social Bond Principles (SBP)
SDGs *see* Sustainable Development Goals (SDGs)
Second Party Opinion (SPO) 276, 277, 318, 321

Secular Forum (2020) 134
Sequoia Mortgage Trust 2020–2023 184–185
ShareAction 163
SLBs *see* Sustainability-Linked Bonds (SLBs)
SLLs *see* Sustainability-Linked Loans (SLLs)
SNCF 285
Social Bond Principles (SBP) 255, 266, 278, 279, 317, 342n4
Societe du Grand Paris 285
SOFR *see* USD Secured Overnight Financing Rate (SOFR)
SONIA 36n1
South Africa: ESG in sovereign investing 146
South American Sovereign Nation 144
S&P Global Ratings 80
SPO *see* Second Party Opinion (SPO)
State of North Carolina (NC): Local Government Commission (LGC) 129
Stora Enso 292
Sustainability Accounting Standards Board (SASB) 89, 193, 234, 456
Sustainability Bond Guidelines 266, 279
Sustainability-Linked Bonds (SLBs) 280, 317, 411
Sustainability-Linked Loans (SLLs) 279, 280
Sustainable Development Goals (SDGs) 87, 90, 112, 141, 143, 278, 309, 320, 324, 329, 353, 360, 400, 418, 421–422, 429, 458, 486
Sustainable Finance Disclosure Regulation 454, 455
Sustainable Hub 316, 324
Sustainalytics 46, 350
Suzano Papel e Celulose 292
Sveaskog 292
Svenska Cellulosa 292
Swedbank 226–227
Swisscom 292

Task Force on Climate-related Financial Related Disclosures (TCFD) 87, 89, 190, 193, 403, 453, 456–457
Telefónica 292
Telia 292
TenneT 292
Tesco 281
Tesla 292
Treaty on the Functioning of the European Union 304

UK: Council of Experts on the Stewardship Code 456; fixed income ESG investing acceleration 396; inflation-linked bond markets 18; Investment Regulations 455; 'Net Zero by 2050' 352; Occupational Pension Scheme Regulations 453; Stewardship Code 200, 201, 454–456; TCFD disclosure requirements 456–457

UNDP *see* United Nations Development Program (UNDP)

Unédic 325–326; Social Bond Framework 326

Union of Concerned Scientists 131n1

United Nations (UN): Declaration of Human Rights 377; Global Compact 371, 377; Guiding Principles on Business and Human Rights 457; Summit on Climate Change 306; Sustainable Development Goals 87, 90, 112, 141, 143, 278, 309, 320, 329, 353, 360, 400, 418, 421–422, 429, 458, 486; 2030 Agenda for Sustainable Development 70

United Nations Conference on Trade and Development 418

United Nations Development Program (UNDP) 325

United States (US): climate risks 242–244, **244**; Federal Reserve (*see* Federal Reserve); governance indicators in public finance analysis 128–130; inflation-linked bonds 18; local climate leadership in 121–123; municipal bond market 284; municipal bonds 152n5; National Weather Service 122; Securities and Exchange Commission 116; state and local governments 240–244, *241*, **244**; Treasury 18, 26, 113n5, 233, 285

United States of Mexico 324–327; BPCE Green Covered Bond 326–327, 326–327; Unédic 325–326; National Council for Evaluation of Social Development Policy (CONVAL in Spanish) 324, 325; National Institute of Statistics and Geography (INEGI in Spanish) 325

University of Hamburg 450

University of North Carolina, School of Government 129

UN *see* United Nations (UN)

UoP *see* use-of-proceeds (UoP) bonds

USD Secured Overnight Financing Rate (SOFR) 24, 36n1

use-of-proceeds (UoP) bonds 266, 291, *291*, 292, 303–304, 318, 323, 411

US *see* United States (US)

Vancity Investment Management 80

Vasakronan 283–284

Verisk Maplecroft 95–96, 98, 112

Verizon 292

VIX *see* CBOE Volatility Index (VIX)

Vodafone 292

Volkswagen 224, 292

Volvo 292

Walmart 221, 222

Womenomics initiative 124

World Bank 84, 292, 419; green bonds 283

World Economic Forum (WEF) 1, 84

Zurich Insurance Group (Zurich) 4, 253; bond evaluation process, for impact assets 266–267; bond quality 267–268; core investment approach 259–261; footprinting **264**, 264–265; Green Bond Principles 266, 267; Guidelines for Sustainability Bonds 266; impact investing in 259–272, *260*, **264**; impact metrics 269; responsible investment KPIs *260*; Social Bond Principles 266; use-of-proceeds bonds 266

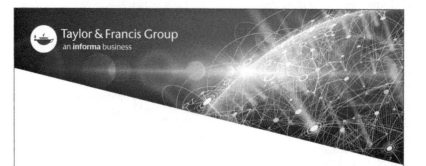